The New Naturalist Library
A SURVEY OF BRITISH NATURAL HISTORY

LAKELAND
THE WILDLIFE OF CUMBRIA

Editors
Sarah A. Corbet ScD
S.M.Walters, ScD, VMH
Prof. Richard West, ScD, FRS, FGS
David Streeter, FIBiol
Derek A. Ratcliffe

To all those who have found inspiration and delight in the wild animals and plants of Lakeland

The aim of this series is to interest the general reader in the wildlife of Britain by recapturing the enquiring spirit of the old naturalists. The editors believe that the natural pride of the British public in the native flora and fauna, to which must be added concern for their conservation, is best fostered by maintaining a high standard of accuracy combined with clarity of exposition in presenting the results of modern scientific research.

The New Naturalist

LAKELAND
THE WILDLIFE OF CUMBRIA

Derek Ratcliffe

7 October 2002

With 43 colour plates and over 130 black
and white photographs and line drawings

HarperCollins*Publishers*

HarperCollins*Publishers*
77–85 Fulham Palace Road
Hammersmith
London W6 8JB

The HarperCollins website address is:
www.**fire**and**water**.com

Collins is a registered trademark of HarperCollins*Publishers* Ltd.

First published 2002

© D.A. Ratcliffe 2002

Pictures © as in credit. All uncredited pictures © D.A. Ratcliffe

The author asserts his moral rights to be identified as the author of this work

ISBN 000 711303 X (Hardback)
ISBN 000 711304 8 (Paperback)

Printed and bound in Great Britain by the Bath Press
Colour reproduction by Saxon Photolitho, Norwich

Contents

Editors' Preface	7
Author's Foreword and Acknowledgements	8

1 Lakeland in Outline — 12
  Geographical limits — 12
  Main features — 12
  Climate and weather — 14
  Geology — 19
  Land management and natural productivity — 31

2 The Lakeland Naturalists — 34
  Botanists — 34
  Zoologists — 42
  Organised data collection — 57

3 The Estuaries: Sands and Salt Marshes — 59
  Salt-marsh vegetation — 61
  Sediment invertebrate communities — 65
  Birds — 66
  Wildfowling — 76
  Other animals — 78

4 The Coast — 79
  The subtidal zone — 79
  Marine mammals — 80
  Fish and fisheries — 80
  The intertidal zone — 81
  Shingle beaches — 83
  Sand dunes — 84
  Sea cliffs — 91
  Semi-coastal habitats — 95

5 The Lowlands: Farmlands, Heathlands and Woodlands — 100
  Farmlands — 100
  Heathlands — 109
  Woodlands — 111

6 The Lowlands: Peatlands, Tarns and Rivers — 125
  Peat mosses — 125
  Fens — 136
  Tarns and ponds — 140
  Rivers — 142

7 The Limestone Foothills	**145**
General features	145
Roudsea, Humphrey Head, Arnside and Hutton Roof	147
Lyth and Winster	152
Shap Fells	155
The northern limestone	159
Animals	162
8 The Lake Dales, Woodlands, Lakes and Streams	**165**
Farmlands	165
Woodlands	167
Lakes and streams	191
9 The Lake Fells	**207**
Vegetation	207
The alpine flora	212
Animals	226
10 The Pennines	**249**
Vegetation and flora	250
Animals	268
Moor House research	280
11 The Borders	**282**
Vegetation and flora	282
Animals	287
Afforestation and defence	296
12 The Future: Conservation Problems and Approaches	**303**
The problems and impacts	303
The geographical picture	310
Available measures for conservation	312
Pervasive environmental change	321
The future	323
Appendices	**325**
1. Cryptogams	325
2. Arachnids	331
3. Protected areas in Cumbria	334
4. Organisations concerned with Lakeland nature and its conservation	343
References and Further Reading	**344**
Gazeteer	**354**
General Index	**358**
Species Index	**367**

Editors' Preface

The lakes and fells of the Lake District possess a range of exceptional habitats and scenery, valued alike by distinguished local and visiting naturalists and by the many who appreciate the landscapes. This interest was recognised by the publication of the New Naturalist *The Lake District – a Landscape History* in 1973, reprinted in 1977 and 1989. The principal authors, W. H. Pearsall and W. Pennington, had a long acquaintance with and very active interest in the Lake District, and they were both very much pioneers of the ecology of the lakes and of the historical interpretation of the landscapes. In particular, they wrote of how the landscape and natural history had been affected by human occupation from prehistoric times to the present day. One of the contributors to that volume was Derek Ratcliffe, a naturalist in the widest sense of the word, who has an intimate knowledge of the area, stretching over many decades. Now he has written his own natural history of Lakeland, the extended area around the Lake District which includes the coast, the Solway Plain and adjacent parts of the Pennines and the Borders, encompassing the county of Cumbria. The book therefore greatly extends the variety of habitats described and discussed, now including habitats of the coast and estuaries, the mosses and blanket bog, and the associated agriculture. The nature and interest of the fauna and flora of each of the natural regions of the area are discussed. This approach, complementary to the previous volume, thus enlarges the area described, placing the natural history of the Lake District within the wider context of the natural history of Cumbria and indeed of Britain. The reader will very soon appreciate, as did the Editors, that Derek Ratcliffe's knowledge of the natural history of Lakeland is phenomenal and surely unique, accumulated at first hand over a long period which has seen many changes, and covering with the same authority, for example, the birds and the higher and lower plants. He speaks with particular experience about the changes he has seen in his lifetime, an experience much enhanced by his own researches and by his long professional association with the Nature Conservancy and Nature Conservancy Council, latterly as Chief Scientist. With his long-term knowledge of the Lakeland fauna and flora, he is able to bring into focus the relation of present conditions to those of the recent past and to give an account of the outstanding interests of Lakeland natural history. Moreover, his knowledge of agriculture, forestry, conservation history and measures, and management policies, enlightens his views and adds weight to his opinions on the changes he has seen and on problems of the future. Here lies the outstanding interest of the book: a personal account by a remarkable natural historian, which will give many new insights to those who visit or reside in Lakeland, and who are concerned with the present and future fauna, flora and landscapes.

Author's Foreword and Acknowledgements

There is already an excellent New Naturalist on *The Lake District* (1973), but it is long out of print. The authors, William Pearsall and Winifred Pennington, emphasised human history and its influence on the landscape and land-use ecology of the Lakes. After an interval of nearly 30 years, the Editorial Board thought it timely to consider a new volume on the area, with a somewhat different emphasis. I persuaded them that it should also be expanded beyond the National Park boundaries that circumscribed the previous book, to encompass the old faunal area of Lakeland that coincidentally equates so closely with the new county of Cumbria defined in 1974, thereby appreciably extending the variety of terrain, habitats and wildlife that has to be considered.

From my schooldays in Carlisle I came to know the wonderfully diverse range of country that was within reach in what was then Cumberland. There were the farmlands, woods and peat mosses of the immediately adjoining lowlands, while the great salt marshes and sand flats of the inner Solway, and the sand dunes, shingle beaches and mussel scars of its outer shores were easily accessible too. Southwards was the Skiddaw massif, northernmost of the wonderful Lake fell groups, while to the east the long Pennine range rolled away from Cold Fell to Cross Fell and beyond into the old Westmorland. In the north-east were the desolate moorlands of the Borders behind Bewcastle and Gilsland, forming the south-western end of the Cheviots. Later, I came to know the more distant parts of the region, though my knowledge of the south is necessarily rather limited and patchy.

This is a book largely about the wildlife of Lakeland – its flora and fauna – and deals with some of the changes that have occurred, both in my lifetime and before. As it is based especially on my own experiences, it deals particularly with the northern half of the region, which I know best. In this respect, too, it complements the Pearsall and Pennington volume, which gives greater emphasis to the southern part, though it necessarily deals more briefly than their work with the National Park area. It is also a natural history rather than a human history and, as I am neither a meteorologist nor geologist, the treatment of climate, rocks and land-form processes is limited to their relevance to the wildlife scene. More detailed accounts of these subjects were given by Pearsall and Pennington. As some tribute to the memory of bygone generations of local naturalists, I have devoted a chapter to a brief account of the history and contribution of these dedicated amateurs.

I decided to structure the book according to the main geographical and ecological subdivisions of Lakeland that its geological history has come to suggest: the estuaries and open coast, lowlands, limestone foothills, central

Lake District, Pennines and Borders. The alternative approach, of chapters based on the main taxonomic groupings of wildlife, has certain advantages and was adopted by the first modern book on the subject, the multi-authored *Natural History of the Lake District* (Hervey & Barnes, 1970).

A book covering so large a region is bound to be selective in its treatment, and biased towards its author's interests. I am aware that it may seem to be mainly about the vegetation, vascular plants and birds that particularly figure in each chapter, but these are the best-known groups. I have tried, within the limits of my knowledge and the literature, to deal with mammals, reptiles, amphibians, fish, butterflies and dragonflies, besides making selective mention of mosses, liverworts, lichens, moths, beetles, molluscs and other invertebrates. This risks leaving specialists in these groups unsatisfied, but there is simply not space to do them justice by invited contributions in a broadly aimed work of this kind. A few less popular groups are dealt with in the Appendices: bryophytes, fungi and arachnids.

The National Vegetation Classification presented in *British Plant Communities* (Rodwell, 1991–2000) now gives a framework for dealing with the range of variation in Lakeland vegetation. I have given the code for the relevant communities, though without enlarging on formal features. Interested readers will also find a summary of its application to the region in *A Flora of Cumbria* (Halliday, 1997).

Lakeland was my youthful stamping ground, which I explored by bus, train, bicycle and on foot, in search of birds above all, but also butterflies, moths and dragonflies. Later I became a botanist as well and plant-hunting gave me additional reason to seek out the wide range of habitats on offer, from the seashore to the highest tops. I went where the wild creatures and plants drew me, and delighted especially in exploring the untrodden corners of Lakeland that featured least in the guidebooks and travel writings. Not that I was ever constrained by boundaries drawn on maps, and I made forays into the adjoining counties of Northumberland and Yorkshire, and even more into the quiet hills of the Southern Uplands in Scotland.

My parents encouraged my early interests in natural history and were always supportive of my enthusiasm for field work in Lakeland, regardless of the anxieties caused by my often solitary roamings and late returns home. They also made the wonderful decision to move from London to Carlisle when I was nine years old, and so paved the way for the eventual appearance of this book.

When I was about 12 I began attending meetings of the Carlisle Natural History Society, which remained active during the War then raging in Europe through the commitment of a stalwart group of members, and produced one of its most notable achievements, *The Birds of Lakeland* (Blezard et al., 1943), during this time. I came then under the influence of a remarkable quartet of self-taught naturalists, Ritson Graham, Tom Johnston, Frank Day snr and, above all, Ernest Blezard, who encouraged and inspired me. Ernest became my informal tutor in natural history, and I owe more than I can ever say to his example, in the pursuit of knowledge in the field, and the need for standards in the way one proceeds and behaves.

Besides the immeasurable debt to these early mentors, this book owes much to a large number of people. From earlier generations and now passed away, I should mention Edward and Edith Steward, Jim and Ruth Birkett, Ralph and Dorothy Stokoe, Walter and Lilian Thompson, Marjory Garnett and Winsome Muirhead. Among the youthful companions with whom I began to explore the region, I thank Peter Coates and Kenneth Slater, in particular. Of the Lakeland naturalists now active, I am grateful especially to Geoff Horne for his invaluable bird information and field companionship over many years. Roderick Corner has helped me with plant records and joined in numerous botanical forays. David Clarke and Stephen Hewitt at Tullie House Museum have given me generous and unstinted help in the preparation of this book and I am much in their debt. Both read the chapter on Lakeland Naturalists and David commented on the dragonfly sections. Other friends who have read and criticised chapters or sections are Donald Pigott (lake woods), Katherine Hearn (conservation), Phil Taylor (conservation), Geoffrey Fryer (fresh waters), Geoffrey Halliday (limestone foothills) and John and Hilary Birks (lowland peat mosses), and I am grateful for their comments. I thank the specialists who have contributed accounts for the Appendix: John R. Parker (Arachnids) and Peter Marren (Fungi). Ian Slater, Karen Slater, Paul Glading, Des O'Halloran, Chris McCarty and Frank Mawby of English Nature's Cumbria Team have been most helpful in supplying information on SSSIs and answering queries.

Geoffrey Halliday has most generously allowed me to reproduce three coloured figures and 12 dot distribution maps from *A Flora of Cumbria* (1997). For the geology map I acknowledge also the consent of the Yorkshire Geological Society. Brian Young commented helpfully on my attempt to give Lakeland minerals a mention. Ron Baines, Ingram Cleasby, John Callion, Roy Clapham, Peter James, Francis Rose, Geoff Naylor, Paul Stott, Terry Pickford, G. D. Rankin, David Sutcliffe, Helen Bennion and M. Kernan have helped me with information of various kinds. Unadorned name references indicate personal communications.

While much of my field work in Lakeland was during my holidays and other spare time, I acknowledge the debt to my former employers, the Nature Conservancy and Nature Conservancy Council, for the additional opportunities and scope that my work allowed in the region. And I much appreciate the help received over the years from former colleagues in the NC and NCC, especially within the Lakeland region – Ian Prestt, Des Thompson, Ron Elliott, Helga Frankland, Ian Bonner, Ken Park, John Mitchell, Terry Wells and Paul Burnham, while Dick Seamons, Malcolm Rush and Robin Fenton have helped me over references and photographs.

The literature has been an important source of information, with the Revd H. A. Macpherson's *Vertebrate Fauna of Lakeland* (1892) especially valuable for early data. *The Transactions of the Carlisle Natural History Society*, and particularly volume VII *The Birds of Lakeland*, have provided much detailed knowledge of local wildlife. Geoffrey Halliday's *A Flora of Cumbria* has been an invaluable work of reference in dealing with the vascular plants. From its data, I have made some mention of the critical groups of hawkweeds, eyebrights and lady's mantles, but have drawn the line at the 43 'species' of brambles and 123 of dandelions.

The *Solway Firth Review* (1996) produced by the Solway Firth Partnership, and the *Morecambe Bay Strategy* (1996) by the Morecambe Bay Partnership are valuable works dealing with all aspects of coastal ecology, and contain extremely useful lists of references. The annual county natural history report *Birds and Wildlife in Cumbria* produced by the Cumbria Naturalists Union is a mine of information on all groups in recent years, and the twice yearly *The Carlisle Naturalist* is also a most informative record, especially for invertebrates.

I am grateful to Ronald Mitchell, David Clarke, Bobby Smith, Keith Temple, Rob Petley-Jones, Geoff Horne, Dave Walker, Richard Speirs, Bob Wright, Bill Davidson, Daphne Graham, the late J. P. Harding, Tullie House Museum and the Cambridge University Collection of Aerial Photography for supplying photographs: where no name is appended, I took the photograph.

I thank Richard West for his editorial comments on the work, and the HarperCollins team of Isobel Smales, Debra Sellman, Katie Piper and Myles Archibald for their efforts in its production.

My wife Jeannette has been a frequent field companion, and I owe much to her help and encouragement in writing this book.

Derek Ratcliffe

1

Lakeland in Outline

Geographical limits

To most people, Lakeland and the Lake District are probably just alternative names for the same area of north-west England – the country of Wordsworth and his fellow Lake poets and, more recently, the area of dale, lake and fell encompassed by the National Park. To local naturalists, Lakeland has for long signified a much larger faunal region, first defined by the Revd H. A. Macpherson in his scholarly treatise *A Vertebrate Fauna of Lakeland* (1892) as covering the old counties of Cumberland, Westmorland and Lancashire North of the Sands. It corresponds also to the diocese of Carlisle plus the parish of Alston, whilst more recently it has become the new county of Cumbria, though adding the former north-west corner of Yorkshire covering the Howgill, Garsdale and Dentdale fells (Plate 1).

Given this wider geographical identity, Lakeland is a much more diverse region than the more narrowly understood Lake District. Besides the radiating dales with their series of lakes and intervening ridges and massifs of high fells, there are the farmlands of the surrounding plains with their main river valleys, remnant woodlands and peat mosses. These are bounded by the varied coastline, with the great estuaries of the Solway and Morecambe Bay to north and south, and in between the systems of sand dune and shingle beach that give way to high cliffs at St Bees Head in the middle. Eastwards the land rises steeply to the main watershed of the northern Pennines and the boundary takes in the headwaters of Tees and South Tyne draining broad and high moorland catchments. In the far north-east there is a more gentle rise in elevation to the moorlands of the Borders at the south-western extremity of the Cheviot range (Plate 2).

In all Britain, there is only one other region of similar size that can show a comparable range of physical and ecological variation to delight the visitor with a passion for scenic beauty and natural history – Snowdonia, if the wider boundary of its National Park be taken, together with Anglesey.

Main features

The climatic, geological and physiographic influences that have moulded the Lakeland scene also determined the possibilities for human occupation and the subsequent pattern of land management and development. Agriculture has always been limited in the uplands by the constraints of high altitude, with its unfavourable climate, and of adverse topography, with steep and rocky terrain, and unproductive soils. This is a region mainly of pastoral farming, especially of sheep in the uplands, and arable is mostly restricted to the drier lowlands. The late twentieth-century farming revolution has nevertheless ridden roughshod over the region and left its wildlife much the poorer. The natural endowment of mineral resources, of coal, iron and other metallic ores, gave rise to industries that have lately faded away, but the quarrying of stone and working of gypsum and barytes continues in places as the tail end of the 'sunset' industrial age in Lakeland. Yet Cumbria has also seen the entry of the new and more controversial nuclear industry on a part of its coast that had remained unspoiled. No amount of playing with names – whether Windscale or Sellafield or whatever else – will remove the sinister shadow that those gaunt buildings cast over their environs through the outfall of radionuclides to land and sea. And, in the far north-east, the lonely moorlands of the Borders have been transformed by a blanket of conifers and forest tracks, and their peace destroyed by the thunder of warplanes.

Wordsworth described the Lake District as 'a sort of national property', and its importance to the natural heritage was recognised formally when it became the first National Park in Britain, in 1951. The lakes themselves, each one different from the rest, gave the area an especially magical beauty. And while at first seen as awesome and intimidating, its mountains have become some of the best-loved in the world. The Lake fells became popular with walkers during Victorian times and, with Snowdonia, were the birthplace of rock climbing as a recreation in this country. The intimate topography and varied scene, with numerous routes that can be satisfyingly followed during a single day, make fell-walking here an especially diverse and pleasurable experience. Although of only modest proportions overall, no two massifs are alike, and there are varying grades of difficulty, from simple tramping of easy tracks to more serious scrambling over rocky obstacles that requires some care and skill. Few areas of the globe have been written about so much, or have so many passionate devotees.

Within this central part of the region, tourism has steadily taken over as the main economic activity, and the district has become one of Britain's major recreational areas. There are no quiet times and few quiet places any more, for the tourist season now lasts virtually the whole year round, and untrodden corners or unclimbed crags have become fewer with each passing year. In the summer, road traffic grinds to a halt at times in the most congested places, and the more popular fells carry an endless procession of walkers throughout fine days. Increasingly the beaten tracks make their conspicuous way over the slopes and summits, worn feet deep in places and canalising water which erodes them still deeper. Stone pavements and staircases are the only answer to footpath erosion, and the price one has to pay for the freedom of the fells.

The Lakeland of today is thus not the same as that of my youth, and I feel bound to look at some of the major changes of the past half-century or so that I have witnessed. The wildlife has to share the region with a considerable and still extending human presence. Yet we have to make the most of what remains, and to celebrate the richness of the wild flora and fauna that still draws naturalists to the region, and enthuses those fortunate enough to live there. I shall look first at some of the main features of the physical environment that determine wildlife habitat.

Climate and weather

Precipitation

The meteorological feature that most strikes visitors to Lakeland – if they have not heard of it in advance – is that it is an especially wet area. The heavy rainfall of the central Lake District is legendary, and many who came to enjoy the scenery return home to tell of repeated wettings and washed-out holidays. In particularly wet years the hay cannot be gathered in until summer is well advanced and, before the introduction of fast-maturing strains of oats and barley, cereal crops could sometimes not be harvested at all. Yet there are wide variations from place to place (Plate 3), and some areas are relatively dry. The Solway Plain and Eden Valley are the driest part of Lakeland, with annual precipitation of only 800–1,200 millimetres, and around Burgh-by-Sands it falls as low as 762 millimetres. The southern fringe of the region is slightly wetter, and only at Barrow-in-Furness and Walney does rainfall drop below 1,200 millimetres.

It is the high mountains that bring down the rain, and there is a rapid increase as they are approached, though even here quite large differences occur within a short space. There is an especially steep gradient between Keswick with 1,475 millimetres to 3,300 millimetres at 'Rainy Seathwaite' at the head of Borrowdale only 12 kilometres away and 50 metres higher above the sea. The extreme is consistently recorded at the gauge by Sprinking Tarn, with a mean of 4,700 millimetres. Elsewhere in Britain, only the Snowdon range and the mountains around the head of Glengarry and Loch Hourn in the western Highlands have a rainfall as great as this. The central group of fells with the Scafells, Bow Fell and Great Gable is the wettest, and the northern Skiddaw group and eastern High Street range have less extreme rainfall. The Pennines experience a rain-shadow effect from the Lake fells to westward, and even on Cross Fell the annual fall is only 2,065 millimetres, while Alston at 300-metre elevation has a mere 1,200 millimetres. The lower uplands of the Borders are even drier with a maximum of 1,400 millimetres.

The frequency of rainfall is, however, more important than the total amount, in its effects on soils and vegetation, and thus on general productivity of the land. The amount of moisture in the air, when no rain is falling, is also important. Cloud cover and lack of sunshine help to maintain a general dampness of atmosphere, and limit evaporation and transpiration. Frequent low mist on the mountains helps to explain the abundance of moisture-loving plants. Carlisle has an annual rainfall of only 825 millimetres, but wet roofs and drizzle in the air are familiar features of the place. The meteorological category of the 'wet-day' (a period of 24 hours with one millimetre or more of rain) is the best measure of precipitation in explaining many ecological patterns associated with variations in wetness of climate, both within Lakeland and across Britain. Only the Solway Plain and the edge of Morecambe Bay have fewer than 140 wet-days, but even the wettest central fell area has only just over 200.

This shows that, despite its tremendously heavy rainfall, the central Lake District does not have quite the same unrelieved wetness of climate as the mountain ranges of the western Highlands and Islands and western Ireland, where annual wet-days are often well over 220, though total rainfall may be below 2,540 millimetres. In Lakeland, the rain often falls in great deluges, producing torrent streams with scoured courses and flooding in some of the dales, and the hillsides ooze with water for days afterwards. Yet drought periods, of up to 30 days, are quite common during anticyclonic spells, and everywhere then dries out. The thunder of Lodore Falls can be heard in Keswick after a couple of days of continuous rain, but they dry to a trickle after prolonged drought. And so, although bog mosses luxuriate almost everywhere, even on steep ground, there is not quite the same ubiquitous tendency to peat formation nor the same profusion everywhere of moisture-loving mosses and liverworts as in the far west of Scotland and Ireland.

Temperature

The oceanic climate that gives Lakeland its wetness also brings equable temperatures, especially in the west. Summers are never very hot nor winters especially cold. Meteorological maps of temperature are adjusted to sea level to remove the effect of altitude (Meteorological Office, 1952) and show a fall in annual means from 9.5°C around Morecambe Bay to under 9.0°C north-east of the Eden Valley. The south-western coastal fringe from Ulverston to Maryport is the mildest in winter, with average January minimum temperatures of 2.0–2.8°C. These fall with distance north-eastwards, until along the Pennine and Borders limits of Lakeland they are only 0.5–1.0°C. Conversely, there is a rise in July maxima from 18.4–19.0°C along the south-west coast to 20.0–20.6°C to the east of Shap. Overall, the figures show a slight increase from Atlantic conditions in the coastal west to a more continental climate in the farthest inland parts of the east.

On the ground, the actual temperatures are related to altitude, according to the fall of 1°C for every rise of 150 metres above sea level. Even without allowing for the increased wind-chill factor, the highest tops at 900 metres thus have temperatures 5°C lower on average than the valley bottoms below. Maximum day temperatures fall even more rapidly, and fell-walkers have the common experience of ascending from the warmth of the sheltered dale foot into arctic conditions on the exposed summits. The Pennines are a cooler region in both summer and winter than the isotherm maps suggest, for there is very little low ground. Some annual monthly mean temperatures for widely scattered places across the region are Millom (9 metres) 9.4°C, Keswick (76 metres) 9.1°C, Appleby (134 metres) 7.8°C, Moor House (560 metres) 5.6°C and Great Dun Fell (847 metres) 3.4°C.

The south-west coastal strip from St Bees to Barrow has the lowest frequency of frost and the mildest winter temperatures, though it is far from frost-free. The average number of days a year with air frost increases with both distance from the sea and rise in altitude, for example, from 42 at Sellafield to 84 at Appleby and 160 on Great Dun Fell. Night temperature inversions during still winter weather can produce severe frosts in certain

Fig. 1.1 Caldbeck Fells of Carrock Fell and High Pike from Caldbeck Common, showing morning mist from temperature inversion.

valley bottoms and basins well inland ('frost hollows'). Yet it is only in the very hardest winters that the bigger lakes freeze over, and they often appear to moderate low temperatures locally by the warming effect of their water bodies. Windermere froze solid in 1878–79, 1894–95, 1928–29, 1946–47 and 1962–63, to the great enjoyment of skaters. Festivities held on the ice drew large numbers of people in these years – up to 50,000 in 1929. The temperature regime explains why Lakeland has only a modest presence of plants – both native and introduced – which have low frost tolerance; but a fair number of those adapted to the cold conditions of the mountains.

Snow

There is an obvious general tendency for snowfall to increase with altitude and falling temperature. It is a common experience in winter to find the higher fells all white above a certain sharp cut-off line, below which precipitation has simply fallen as rain (Plate 33). To discount this altitude effect, the Meteorological Office uses the average number of days with snow falling on low ground (below 200 feet – 61 metres) as a measure of snow frequency. The maps based on this parameter show a gradient from ten days on the west Cumbrian coast to 20 days in the central Lake District and 25 days in the Pennines along the eastern border. Since there is no ground at so low an elevation in the Pennines, the records here were reduced by one day for every 50 feet (15 metres) above the 200 foot altitude. Detailed records from Ben Nevis and Fort William (at its base) showed that at an altitude of 3,000 feet (914 metres), there were an average additional 70 days with snow falling, compared with ground at 0–200 feet.

The second measure of snow, which takes account of the altitude effect, is the number of days with snow lying over more than half the ground representative of the observation station at a standard morning hour. The duration of snow cover depends on temperature, frequency and amount of snowfall, as well as elevation and proximity to higher ground. The maps (Meteorological Office, 1952) show that from December to March, the Pennines consistently have a higher number of mornings with snow lying than the Lake fells; and the whole northern Cross Fell massif averages 50 days or more a year, whereas only the highest parts of the Helvellyn and High Street ranges reach this figure. Manley (1973) recorded an annual average of 70 days with snow lying at Moor House, while the higher levels of Cross Fell had 105 days. He noted that most heavy snowfalls come from the east and north-east, causing the Pennines to be noticeably more snowy than the Lake District.

The first snow usually falls on the fells before the end of October, but both frequency and amount vary greatly between years. In a typical winter, snow cover on low ground is thin (up to 15 centimetres), short-lived and mainly in January and February. On the hills it is usually intermittent, and warm fronts with rain from the Atlantic can quickly reduce a complete cover to a patchwork or strip it altogether. There are often late blizzards in March or occasionally April or even May, which blanket the uplands again, but the later falls tend to be shorter-lived than those in midwinter. Snow patches linger variably on the highest mountains until late in the spring, and the longest-lasting ones are in the same sheltered places each year: the eastern hollows of the Helvellyn range from Brown Cove to Great Dodd, the high gullies of the north-facing cliffs of Great End and Scafell, and both the northern and south-western slopes under the broad summit cap of Cross Fell (Plate 36). In some years these will last until early June before finally melting out. Only exceptionally does snow persist into July on the Lakeland fells. Probably, on average, Cross Fell has the longest lasting snow in the region – it lies in the snowiest area and its extensive summit plateau makes a large gathering ground for snow, which then blows off and accumulates on the upper slopes below.

The Lakeland mountains thus fall far short of the Scottish Highlands in the amount, continuity and duration of snow cover. In the central Grampians and Cairngorms, especially, there are typically huge amounts of snow at the higher levels in April, and many hills have extensive snow beds in June. On Ben Nevis and in the Cairngorms a few of these late snow beds last the whole year round, except in the hottest summers. The differences point to the more oceanic and less arctic character of the Lake fells and their much lesser amount of vegetation influenced by prolonged snow cover.

There have in my lifetime been two exceptionally severe winters. February and March of 1947 were memorable for the amount of snow. Blizzard followed blizzard to pile up monumental drifts, in the fell country especially. Many hill farms and dwellings were cut off for weeks, and parts of the uplands became almost inaccessible. Huge numbers of sheep died on the fells, and the populations of many birds were greatly reduced, though the carrion-feeders had a surfeit of food. When the final thaw eventually came, in late March, it did so rapidly and with heavy rain caused flooding on low-lying ground. This was the occasion of the last great floods in the East Anglian Fenland. Early 1963 had less snow, but once it had fallen, severe and prolonged frost set in, to lock much of the land in a mantle of white for several weeks. Sheep mortality was again tremendous, and some of the birds suffered terribly, the stonechat, wren, lapwing, dipper, kingfisher and heron being major victims. The lakes froze over during both these winters. Recent winters have been relatively benign, with a few exceptions, and snowfall has often been slight.

Wind

Windiness is an integral part of the oceanic climate. Western seaboards are inevitably windy and, to make the point, the exposed section of Cumbrian coast between Silloth and Millom shows a good deal of wind-shaping of trees, with growth leaning away from the prevailing onshore winds from the south-west. Windspeed also increases with altitude, and this causes the high tops of the westernmost fells to receive a furious wind-blasting during the severe westerly gales that can rage at any time of year, but especially in autumn and winter. Manley (1973) recorded windspeeds on the high Pennines, and found an average of about force 5 (19–24 mph) on Great Dun Fell, with extremes of an hourly wind of 99 mph and a gust of 134 mph. No records have been made on the higher Lake fells, but on the Scafell range in particular windspeeds must reach still greater extremes.

The Cross Fell range also experiences a peculiarly local phenomenon, the Helm Wind (see Uttley, 1998). When the wind sets from east to north-northeast, cold air from the long dip slope spills over the Eden Valley scarp and rolls down it in a relentless blast to blight the fell-foot country over a five mile zone beyond. It can blow for days on end, and is accompanied by characteristic cloud formations. The Helm itself is a heavy roll of murk that settles along the fell shoulders to obscure all the higher ground, but opens above the fell-foot to a strip of clear blue sky parallel to the scarp and flanked westwards by another great cloud bank, the Bar. Depending on the variable conditions, the wind can blow along a lengthy stretch of the fell-foot, from Castle Carrock in the north to Brough in the south, but Cross Fell is the storm centre. Manley (1973) says that similar downhill winds can occur among the Lake fells under suitable pressure systems, but are less well defined under the more irregular topography. The Cumbrian lowlands are otherwise subject to rather low average windspeeds.

Sunshine and cloud cover

While these are clearly related to topography and rainfall, Manley (1973) points out that, in duration of bright sunshine, the Cumbrian lowlands compare quite favourably with other English localities at similar latitudes. The higher fells are often mist-shrouded when the lowlands are sunlit, and the cloud base has a tendency to fall westwards within Lakeland, being lowest on the fells of Wasdale, Eskdale and Duddon. Average annual duration of sunshine is only 840 hours on Great Dun Fell summit, against 1,150 at Moor House, 305 metres lower. But Ambleside under the high central Lake fells has only 1,140 hours and Keswick 1,270, compared with 1,396 at Carlisle, 1,425 at Silloth and 1,515 at Sellafield. At Keswick, sunshine is at a maximum in May, but reaches only 39 per cent of the theoretically possible figure.

Among the steep high fells there are significant aspect effects, especially during the short winter days when the trajectory of the sun remains low, and many north to east-facing slopes stay in shadow. Even in summer, shaded aspects often receive too little sun to dry out, and their greater dampness is reflected in the nature of their vegetation.

Geology

The scenic character of the region has been moulded down the ages by periods of rock formation, both as marine sediments and through volcanic activity, ancient earth movements and denudation by the elements and, finally, by the sculpting processes of glaciation. Complex folding of old Ordovician and Silurian rocks was succeeded by the deposition of successive layers of younger Carboniferous strata and then New Red Sandstones. During the Tertiary there was then a great uplift of this central mass into a slightly elongated dome, followed by development of a radial drainage pattern centred on the Scafell area. Valleys cut through the younger overlying strata were then superimposed on the older rocks below, giving the characteristic wheel-spoke structure to the evolving Lake District. More general denudation of the younger Triassic, Permian and Carboniferous deposits eventually gave the mountain systems that remain today. The later folding and faulting of the Carboniferous Pennine uplift was also followed by erosion of its uppermost strata. Younger sedimentary rocks of Permian and Triassic age came to occupy most of the northern lowlands (Plate 4).

The end of the Tertiary period, a million years ago, saw the basic structure of the region well established, and the successive glaciations of the Quaternary then progressively deepened the valleys and carved out the high rocky hollows and crags, and gouged the trenches that became lakes. At the higher levels, frost-shattering, snow and ice action tore at the bedrock and piled masses of loose material over summits and slopes. Glacial action also spread great layers of drift over the lower ground, obscuring the underlying rocks with fluvio-glacial sands, gravel and boulder clay, heaped in places into moraines, drumlins and eskers. Coastal processes built up new marine sediments, especially in the larger estuaries, formed shingle beaches and sand dunes, and cut sea cliffs. Land movements in relation to sea level lifted these soft deposits and produced raised beaches locally. And wherever ground remained waterlogged, from the coastal plains to the high watersheds, deep layers of peat developed.

Geology has thus determined the range of physical features that have become plant and animal habitats and made scenery. It has formed topography, from high mountains and vertical cliffs to level plains; mountain corries, gorges, lakes and watercourses; fissured limestone pavements, moraine features of diverse kinds, and peat bogs; and the overlying substrates varying from boulder fields and screes to mineral and organic soils. It has also produced local variations in climate, by virtue of the mountains that rise up to 900 metres above the lowland plains and create an altitudinal gradient of increasing severity in meteorological conditions.

The Lake District

The unique system of fells, dales, lakes, tarns and streams comprising this celebrated area has evolved from the four oldest geological formations of the Lakeland region, spanning the Ordovician to the Carboniferous. The oldest rocks of all are the Ordovician Skiddaw Slates, which form the northern block of fells with Skiddaw (931 metres) itself and Blencathra (868 metres), the Buttermere group with Grasmoor (851 metres) and Robinson (737 metres), and the lower north-western arc of hills from Thornthwaite through Loweswater to Kinniside Common. A southern outlier forms the whaleback of Black Combe (600 metres) behind Millom. These sedimentary rocks are relatively soft, and their characteristic topography is of soaring slopes, steep but smooth; deeply incised gills with cascading streams; and graceful rounded or conical summits. Erosion has been by water as much as ice action, though there are glacial features in the narrow ridges and truncated spurs of Blencathra front, and the deep corries of Bannerdale, Scales Tarn and Bowscale Tarn. The cliffs tend to be rather broken and sloping, but there are lofty sheer faces at Force Crag and Dove Crags on Grasmoor. Many steep fellsides are covered with loose, slaty screes that are still extending in places.

The Eycott Hill lavas date from late in the Skiddaw Slate period and outcrop in a broad northern band from the outlying hill of Binsey through Roughtengill to High Pike, and then in separate blocks from Eycott Hill itself, Matterdale Common, and around Ullswater and Bampton, with another outlier behind Millom. They do not contribute in any distinctive way to scenic variety, unlike the later Borrowdale Volcanic Series, which are the most extensive of the Ordovician formations. This mass of igneous rocks forms all the most rugged ranges of the central Lake fells from Scafell Pike (977 metres) and the Pillar to the Langdale Pikes, Coniston Old Man, Helvellyn and Fairfield, and High Street. It has the highest and steepest cliffs, the most elevated summits, the rockiest slopes, the deepest corries and the biggest waterfalls. The Borrowdale Volcanic rocks are extremely variable, from hard, fine-grained, flinty ashes (tuffs) – which founded a Stone Age axe-head industry – and lavas (rhyolite and andesite) to more friable breccias and faulted materials.

The variable hardness of these Borrowdale Volcanic rocks has given the uneven and rugged topography of the central fells, with irregular knobbly slopes and rocky summits. Under ice action they have formed the highest inland cliffs in England, with the great climbing walls of the Pillar Rock (200 metres), Scafell Crag and the East Buttress, Dow Crags, Pavey Ark, Esk Buttress, Gimmer Crag, the Napes Ridges, Dove Crag at Hartsop, Eagle Crag in Birkness Combe, Eagle Crag in Greenup Gill, Gate Crag in Borrowdale, Raven Crag above Thirlmere, and the Castle Rock of

Fig. 1.2 A classic corrie and ice-gouged lake, Blea Water, High Street Fells, Mardale. The tarn is 63.1 metres deep. (Ronald Mitchell.)

Triermain, as the most notable. The ice has also carved many deep corries in these rocks, of which Blea Water in the High Street range is perhaps the most classic in form (Fig. 1.2). Many of these elevated hollows have tarns in rock basins or dammed by moraines. The over-steepened U-shaped valleys have numerous hanging valleys with waterfall ravines below, and in Borrowdale itself the Watendlath valley and Lodore Falls are a particularly fine example. Wasdale Screes with its great crumbling escarpment, immense chasms and gullies, and vast talus slopes, is a spectacular geological feature (Plate 25). Numerous angular boulder fields occupy the high summits and shoulders, and block screes cover many slopes below. In places, fine-grained ashes have been altered secondarily by compression to give slaty cleavage, and quarried as the durable Lakeland greenslate at Honister, Borrowdale and Langdale. The Borrowdale Volcanic scenery is seen to perfection on the Scafell range from upper Eskdale or Wasdale (Plate 31). Running along the southern edge of the Borrowdale Volcanics is a thin band of the Coniston limestone, but this has no impact on the scenery and little more on soils or vegetation.

Proceeding along the geological timescale, the next formation is the Silurian sandstones and shales that form the lower and gentler southern part of the Lake District, and also the outlying Howgill, Middleton and Barbon Fells where Lakeland borders the Yorkshire Pennines in the southeast. The sequence of sedimentary Stockdale Shales, Brathay Flags, Coniston Grits, Bannisdale Slates and Scout Hill Flags contains rocks of variable hardness that have formed low, irregular and sometimes rocky hills and ridges, with intervening valleys. This undulating country of hills

Fig. 1.3 The mountain crags and tarns: Pavey Ark above Stickle Tarn, Langdale.

and hollows extends from the Duddon mouth to the southern Shap Fells, and contains the large lakes of Windermere and Coniston Water. The Howgill–Barbon Fells more closely resemble the Skiddaw Slate hills in their rounded form, steep but smooth sides, and deep water-worn gills, with waterfalls and crags at Black Force (Fig. 9.3) and Cautley Spout, but are lower, reaching 676 metres on the Calf. Quarries to work the slaty beds of the Silurian rocks have been excavated, especially on Kirkby Moor.

The ensuing Devonian period saw extensive mountain building, with much folding and faulting of rocks, and formation of synclines and anticlines across the Lake District, accompanied by several massive igneous intrusions. The last included a local intrusion of granite at Shap and a much larger mass from the foot of Wasdale across lower Eskdale to just north of Black Combe. Granophyre was intruded over a large block centred on lower Ennerdale. In the Skiddaw fells, a complex of gabbro, granophyre, diorite and felsite was intruded at Carrock Fell. While Carrock Fell stands out as an angular, rugged mass against its rounded slate neighbours, the hills formed by the other igneous intrusions mostly blend in scenically with their neighbours on the Borrowdale Volcanic.

The Carboniferous foothills

The whole Lake District was once overlain by Carboniferous rocks, but extensive erosion has pared them down to a discontinuous peripheral ring up to 20 kilometres wide. Limestone is conspicuous along this band as large outcrops, with the bare, gleaming white rock exposed as tabular, fissured pavements, vertical scars and screes. From the south, and anticlockwise, beginning at the small outcrop of Hodbarrow Point at Millom, the limestone extends across the Furness peninsula and then Cartmel, where it forms the promontory of Humphrey Head. Across the Kent estuary low limestone hills begin at Arnside Knott and extend through Silverdale at Middlebarrow and Underlaid, though this area is shared with Lancashire. Farther inland are Hutton Roof Crags and Farleton Knott, rather higher hills with extensive pavements. West of Kendal other hills have scarp crags and screes as their main features, at Scout, Cunswick and Whitbarrow Scars, but pavements occur in places. After a northwards break in the limestone ring, this outcrops again as massive pavements on the eastern Shap Fells around Orton and Asby. The limestone belt then curls round south of Penrith, through Caldbeck to Cockermouth, narrowing all the time, and finally peters out at Egremont in west Cumbria. There are low scars at Knipe near Bampton and in Greystoke Park, and small pavements at the last and near Blindcrake, but much of the limestone north of Shap is overlain by drift and not directly visible, except in the many places where it has been quarried.

The Pennines
Along the eastern side of Lakeland are the massive uplifts of Carboniferous strata that form the Pennines. At the south end the Silurian Howgill–Barbon Fells are separated by the Dent Fault from the Carboniferous fells of Crag Hill, Whernside (736 metres), Rise Hill, Baugh Fell, Swarth Fell and Wild Boar Fell. This last group drains mostly westwards to the Lune, but Wild Boar Fell forms the western flank of the Mallerstang valley in the Eden catchment. The River Eden rises on High Seat (709 metres) where the extensive moorlands of Swaledale in Yorkshire march with the steeper fells of Mallerstang and Kirkby Stephen. The whole of this part of the Pennines forms the northern end of the Askrigg Block, which ends at the A66 Stainmore road. Most of these hills are composed of thick beds of gritstone and shale, which outcrop as crags on both sides of Mallerstang. Limestone is rather limited in occurrence, with potholes on Ease Gill above Leck, pavement at Fell End Clouds on the west side of Wild Boar Fell, more potholes and fragmentary pavement on Tailbridge Hill, a horseshoe of crag in Dukedale (Rigg Beck) and deep ravines along some of the tributary streams of the upper Eden, such as Ais Gill and Hell Gill.

North of the A66 road is the Alston Block of the Pennines, stretching to the northern extremity of the range overlooking the Tyne Gap. This contains the most extensive continuous area of ground above 600 metres in the whole of England, with the highest summit in the Pennine Chain on Cross Fell (893 metres) and four other tops above 750 metres. On the Eden Valley side there is a long and continuous scarp slope extending north-westwards from Brough to Castle Carrock, due east of Carlisle, a distance of 50 kilometres. This contrasts with gentle moorlands on the eastern dip slopes, which form the headwaters of the Rivers Tees and South Tyne (Plate 36). In the south, thick beds of limestone alternate with the grits and shales and are extensively exposed as pale grey scars and screes along the scarp slope. Tiers of these outcrops rise along the fell front between Helbeck and Long Fell, and other limestone bands appear at higher intervals, finally girdling the entire summit plateaux of Little Fell (764 metres) and Mickle Fell (776 metres), though most of the last hill lies in Durham.

The length of the Eden scarp is penetrated at right angles by a succession of deeply cut and steep-sided valleys, in some of which limestone crags and screes are again extensive, as in Scordale and Knock Ore Gill. Here also, the Great Whin Sill, a huge igneous intrusive sheet of quartz dolerite, is exposed as dark, vertical and sub-columnar bands of cliff, feeding screes below. The most spectacular of these exposures in Cumbria is the horseshoe of crag, completely even in height, at the head of the deeply cut High Cup Dale (Fig. 1.4), but there are lesser outcrops in Ardale under Cross Fell, at Cash Force on the Tynehead moors, and in the picturesque gorge of the Black Burn under Cold Fell. Along the foot of the Pennine scarp in its middle reach, a line of low, conical hills, exemplified by Knock and Dufton Pikes, marks the presence of the Cross Fell Inlier, an upthrust of the same Ordovician Skiddaw Slates and Eycott Hill lavas that form the northernmost Lake fells.

The greater part of the Cross Fell range is built of gritstones and shales, and with distance north the limestone exposures become steadily thinner and lower in elevation. There are still good scars and screes on Cross Fell itself, but north of the Hartside road, the limestone outcrops are only minor and on the Tindale Fells fronting the Tyne Gap they have virtually disappeared. The Coal Measures reappear here and have been worked on

Fig. 1.4 Horseshoe of basaltic whin sill cliffs and screes at High Cup Dale, near Appleby.

Fig. 1.5 Summit cap of Cross Fell girdled by gritstone block screes, from fell-fields on Skirwith Fell.

a small scale around Midgeholme. The large summit plateau of Cross Fell is a mesa formed from a capping of hard gritstones that have shed a rim of block scree around the steep slopes immediately below (Fig. 1.5). It contrasts with the slightly lower and rounded twin peaks of Little and Great Dun Fells in line to the south-east. Much of the main Pennine watershed within the Alston Block is broad, and both here and on the gently contoured dip slopes, impeded drainage has given rise to extensive blanket bogs with deep peat. In places the bogs are still actively growing, with a high *Sphagnum* cover, but they are also quite widely gullied into dry peat haggs, and in places sheet erosion has denuded the surface down to the underlying till or bedrock.

The Borders

The remaining upland area of Lakeland is the Border moorlands north of Bewcastle and Gilsland, which is also composed of Carboniferous rocks, predominantly sandstones and shales with thin or impure beds of limestone. The terrain is mostly gently undulating or even flat, with broad watersheds and plateaux, and the elevation rather low, reaching a maximum of only 518 metres on Sighty Crag. The ground is mostly drift-covered and the bedrock little exposed, with the only significant crags in the deep Irthing gorge which extends for four kilometres above Gilsland, though there is a lesser gorge at Sunday Burn Linns higher up the river. The summit of Christianbury Crags is crowned with a distinctive gritstone tor (Fig. 11.1), and there are a few other minor outcrops and block screes on the Bewcastle side.

The gentle contouring of the moorland area has given extensive waterlogging and a general tendency to blanket bog formation, especially on the Gilsland side. The huge and featureless catchment of the Irthing and King Water known as Spadeadam Waste formerly had numerous areas of level bog with a spongy, *Sphagnum*-dominated surface. The best of these, Butterburn Flow, lies on a terrace above a loop of the upper Irthing, which here follows a deep and canal-like course cut in glacial drift up to seven metres deep. Lower down the river again courses rapidly over a stony bed and cascades over the waterfalls of Moss Catherine and Cramel Linn (Plate 43). The headwaters of the Liddel and Lyne drain rather steeper valleys on the western, Bewcastle, side of this massif, but even here wet and peaty soils predominate and there is rather little dry heather moor. The once wild and desolate character of this moorland district is best conveyed by its old name, The Waste of Cumberland.

The northern and western lowlands

The Permian and Triassic rocks that together comprise the New Red Sandstone underlie the whole Solway Plain north of Maryport, except for an area west of Carlisle with Lower Lias strata belonging to the Jurassic period. The New Red Sandstone then extends along the broad reach of the Eden Valley, following the Pennine fell-foot as far as Kirkby Stephen. After the Carboniferous rocks between Maryport and Whitehaven, the New Red forms a belt along the coast and its low hinterland from St Bees Head to near Millom, and then on to Walney Island and the mainland tip of the Furness peninsula. Most of the Permo–Triassic area is low-lying, but it rises to a conspicuous ridge of low hills along the Eden Valley from King Harry to Whinfell. The hard Permian flags of this ridge have been quarried for paving stones at Lazonby Fell and elsewhere, but the Triassic beds hewn from Shawk Quarry south of Dalston and used to build Carlisle Castle and Cathedral were of softer material.

Much of the low ground is overlain by glacial boulder clay and sands or, along the edges of the estuaries, by marine alluvium raised above sea level by tilting of the land. On waterlogged level ground here, large lowland peat mosses have developed over the mineral substrate. In places, especially to the east of Carlisle and along the south-west coastal strip, the glacial sands form a drumlin country of dry hillocks and wet hollows in which numerous small peat bogs have formed. The bedrock is little exposed, except along the valleys draining to the Carlisle basin, where the rivers have cut down to form rocky sections, seen at their finest along the Eden gorge between Lazonby and Armathwaite with crags up to 30 metres high (Plate 12). On the coast at St Bees Head is a fine range of vertical sandstone sea cliff (Fig. 4.6), but the Cumbrian shores are otherwise mostly low and flat, fringed by shingle beaches with variable amounts of sand. Sand dunes have formed in several places, while around the main estuaries, extensive systems of salt marsh have developed on marine warp. The sediment tends to be of fine sand rather than silt and is mostly deficient in lime.

The southern lowlands

The belt of low country between the southern fringe of the Lake fells and the coast from Morecambe Bay to the Duddon is much narrower and more dissected than that in the north. The development of raised bogs on former marine alluvium is repeated on either side of the Duddon estuary, on the eastern side of the Leven and on the western side of the Kent estuary. Except for an area of Triassic rocks at Walney Island and the tip of the Barrow peninsula, much of these southern lowlands lies on Carboniferous strata. The valleys of the Kent, Lyth and Winster have fertile pastures and meadows that reflect the frequent influence of limestone in the formation of their soils. The rivers that flow into Morecambe Bay are faster-running than those that enter the Solway.

Minerals and mining

Cumbria is famous for its wealth of minerals, many of which have been mined commercially. Young (1987) stated that, of around 600 minerals 'species' estimated as present in Britain, about half occur in Lakeland. Flinty volcanic ashes were first worked for axe-heads as long as 5,000 years ago, and the Romans extracted lead and silver in the Pennines. Serious mining development began in Elizabethan times, and reached its peak during the eighteenth and nineteenth centuries. Mining was always dependent on world markets in metals, and characterised by closures and reopenings according to major price fluctuations. Increasingly over the last 50 years once-famous mines closed permanently, until hardly any remain active.

North-west of the National Park, the Carboniferous belt changes seawards from limestone to Coal Measures: the West Cumberland Coalfield which was extensively mined. Large ore bodies in the limestone deep beneath the surface here contained high grade deposits of haematite (ferric oxide) which, with the local coal and limestone, gave rise to the industrial belts from Maryport to Whitehaven and at Millom and Barrow-in-Furness. Jenkinson (1885) listed no less than 86 blast furnaces in these districts, of which 60 were producing pig iron in 1883. Smelting has ceased in the region and although there is still an active steelworks at Workington, the evidence of this former industry is more to be seen in the many signs of dereliction – old quarries and mines, spoil heaps and slag banks. The haematite deposits are mostly worked out and only the Florence Mine near Egremont is still in operation. The huge excavation left by the Hodbarrow iron mine at Millom was subject to subsidence and has been flooded to form an artificial lake, now an RSPB reserve. Coal mining is also virtually at an end. Coal Measures, mainly as sandstones and shales, also extend from the north end of the West Cumberland coalfield past Aspatria to the Caldew valley below Sebergham. Coal seams at the northern end of the Pennines were also worked for a time.

The Caldbeck Fells are especially celebrated for their rich variety of minerals associated with the igneous intrusions at Carrock Fell, High Pike and Roughtengill. Many are colourful compounds of lead, zinc and copper, which were the chief metals sought, but tungsten ores were worked at the Brandygill Mine. These deposits are world famous for the many rare and unusual minerals that accompany the main ores. The Ordovician rocks of Lakeland elsewhere are quite widely mineralised, and the Skiddaw Slate fells had important mines at Blencathra, Force Crag, Thornthwaite (all lead and zinc) and Goldscope (lead and copper), while the Borrowdale Volcanics had Greenside at Glenridding (lead) and the several copper mines of the Coniston Fells. Lead smelting gave a high yield of silver at some mines but, although widespread in the Lakes, gold is in too small quantity for mining to be commercially workable. The famous Seathwaite graphite mine supplied large amounts of this substance and founded the Keswick pencil industry, but was worked out long ago. The Carboniferous rocks of the Pennines are extensively mineralised, and lead has been mined widely, especially around Alston and Nenthead. While the lead mines are now all abandoned, barytes is still worked at the Silverband Mine on Great Dun Fell. Gypsum mines in the Eden Valley near Carlisle are now in disuse, but this substance and anhydrite are still mined at Kirkby Thore.

The commercially important ores included galena (lead sulphide), cerussite (lead carbonate), sphalerite (zinc sulphide), chalcopyrite (copper iron sulphide), wolframite (iron manganese tungstate), scheelite (calcium tungstate), barytes (barium sulphate), gypsum (hydrated calcium sulphate) and anhydrite (anhydrous calcium sulphate). In the course of mining, finds of many spectacular crystals and also uncommon minerals, both metallic and non-metallic, were put aside for mineral collectors who would pay well for fine or rare specimens. Many went to museums and, within the region, Tullie House and the Keswick Museum have particularly fine collections. Crystals of calcite, aragonite (Fig. 1.6), dolomite, barytes, galena, fluorite and quartz are especially beautiful in form and colour. Typical fluorite (calcium fluoride) is mauve or pale purple, but local varieties are pale blue, green and yellow. Size is often impressive: a single quartz crystal from Brandygill is 36 centimetres long and weighs nine kilograms (Day, 1928). The prize was the rare linarite (copper lead sulphate) with deep azure blue crystals, known only from the Caldbeck Fells, but the sky-blue hemimorphite (zinc silicate), blue-lavender plumbogummite (lead aluminium phosphate), yellow-green pyromorphite (lead phosphate chloride), orange-yellow-green mimetite (lead arsenate chloride) and deep green malachite (copper carbonate) from the same fells are beautiful also (Cooper & Stanley, 1990). Combinations of two or more different minerals can be especially striking.

On a different note, the Keswick Museum houses the Musical Stones or Rock Band, a gigantic xylophone of slabs of metamorphic Skiddaw Slate tuned into musical sequence by the inventor, Peter Crosthwaite, in 1785.

Patterned ground

On the higher fells are distinctive surface features attributable to processes of frost-sorting of soils and debris (solifluction) that characterise high arctic regions. Under the alternate freezing and thawing of moisture in the ground, particles of different sizes become sorted, forming stone networks

Fig. 1.6 Aragonite (calcium carbonate) crystals from west Cumberland, 26 centimetres long: one of many beautiful Lakeland minerals. (Tullie House Museum.)

with soil hummocks of finer material on level ground, while on gentle slopes they elongate into stone stripes with intervening soil ridges. In places there is also a downwards slumping of the surface material to produce a regular terracing or staircase effect, and formation of lobed screes. All these features occur in Lakeland, though they are mostly less dramatic than the real arctic forms. They were investigated by Hollingworth (1934) among the Lake fells, where they tend to be better developed on the Skiddaw Slate than the Borrowdale Series – soils derived from the Slate have a higher silt content and, hence, a greater water-retaining capacity. These features mostly occur above 600 metres, and are best developed on high plateaux and spurs where the ground is level or only gently sloping, and a bare, stony fell-field terrain prevails. Good examples of soil hummocks and ridges were on Broad End of Skiddaw and Stybarrow Dodd, while striped screes are more widespread, as on Helvellyn and Skiddaw. Terraces are well developed on Skiddaw, Raise (Helvellyn range) and Robinson, which also shows interesting frost shattering of bare slate debris.

The best examples of such phenomena are, however, in the Pennines. The plateau of Tailbridge Hill above Kirkby Stephen has a short limestone turf over brown soil thrown into innumerable regular hummocks averaging somewhat less than a metre across. These are best appreciated in evening sunlight when the shadows pick out the system in fine detail over the whole area (Fig. 10.5). Altitude here is only 455–535 metres. The best solifluction features of all are on the summit cap of Cross Fell at 855–900 metres, the largest high plateau in Lakeland. On the flat there is an obvious system of soil hummocks about a metre across, elongating into low ridges where the ground slopes (Fig. 10.4). In places there is also a network of large, bare blocks with much larger dimension, of several metres across, not completely regular, but with mainly vegetated and slightly raised ground between (Fig. 10.17). Aerial photographs also show a still larger-scale network, evidently of grassy depressions, that is not obvious on the ground (Fig. 1.7).

Large-scale stone nets and terraces are understood to be periglacial features, which formed under ice age conditions, or shortly after, when the ground was free of ice but the climate much more severe than at present. Sorting movements of the scale involved are hardly conceivable under existing climate. The age of the smaller-scale features is more uncertain: they may have formed long ago and persisted or been maintained up to the present day. Some geomorphologists nevertheless believe that they can

Fig. 1.7 Aerial photograph of patterned ground on Cross Fell summit plateau, showing small-scale hummocks and ridges and large-scale network. 1979. The tracks of the Pennine Way are beginning to appear around the summit cairn bottom right. (Cambridge University Collection of Aerial Photographs: copyright reserved.)

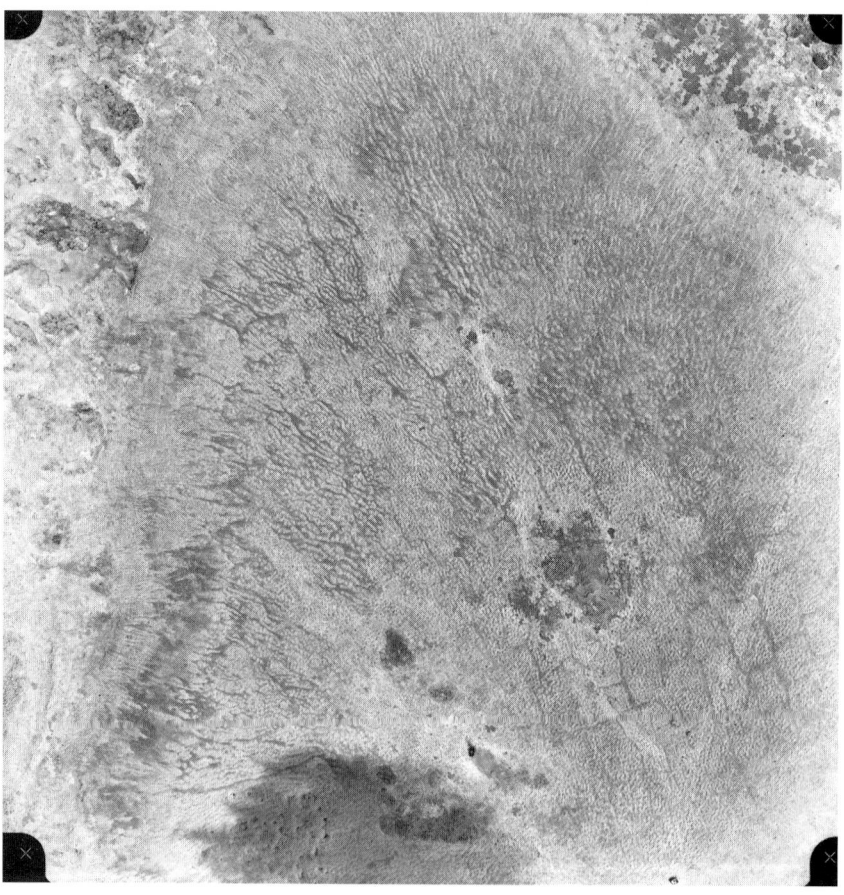

form quite rapidly even under present conditions, and I have seen sorting into partial nets and stripes on old mine debris of no great age, which supports this view.

Land management and natural productivity

The history of human occupation of the Lake District and its impact on the land and fresh waters have been admirably dealt with by Pearsall & Pennington (1973). In general terms, much of what they describe and interpret is relevant to the wider region of Lakeland as defined on p. 12. The story of forest clearance and wetland draining to create land for raising domestic stock and growing crops is now a familiar one. The systems of walled fields of the hill farms, occupying the base of the hills up to the limits of cultivation, and the predominantly treeless hillsides, with only patchy woodland cover, have become an essential part of the Lakeland scene. Yet they are almost wholly artificial, and contrast strangely with the more natural mountain landscapes of Scandinavia, where the situation is reversed and upland farms – if they exist at all – form mostly small enclaves within a vast spread of forest land that reaches far up the fells to the climatic limits of tree growth, and is often topped by a zone of scrub with mountain willows, dwarf birch and juniper.

The influence of geology

The chance that endowed the region with a particular complex of rock types also prescribed much of the biological character that we see today. The amount of available lime, mostly in the form of calcium carbonate, in the parent rocks that have given rise to the soils, is crucially important in determining which kinds of plants will occupy an area of land or inland water in Britain. It also has a large effect on the level of biological activity and fertility of the soils, and this in turn influences the 'carrying capacity' of land for many animals. Hardness of the rock also affects the rates of weathering and erosion that shape the landscape and control the rate at which the essential nutrients bound in the solid material are released to the soil.

As almost pure calcium carbonate, the Carboniferous limestone is the most influential of the parent rocks in this respect. It gives rise to calcareous soils with pH 7.0–8.0, often containing free lime as solid particles, and with a high clay content that has substantial base-exchange capacity, so that these soils are well buffered and not easily leached. On steep or unstable sites, these substrates are black rendzinas or red-brown loams, while in moist situations they are wet clays with rich 'mull' humus. In places, the limestone bedrock is buried under a deep layer of glacial drift, but where this contains abundant lime the clayey soils are similarly base-rich. The limestone-derived soils mostly support vegetation with a naturally varied flora, but their productivity is often limited by insufficient nitrogen and phosphorus. When the deficient nutrients are added through either manures or artificial inorganic fertilisers, they become extremely productive with a high carrying capacity for grazing animals. The farms on limestone soils thus tend to be the most bountiful in the region. In the hill country, these rich substrates allow farming, and especially arable crops, to extend to higher altitudes than on poorer soils; and in the eastern Pennines, around Alston, where they combine with continental conditions and warm summers, cultivation reaches its highest levels at around 550 metres.

Within the Carboniferous series, some of the shale beds are moderately calcareous, but the gritstones are mostly acidic and deficient in lime. The Permo–Triassic rocks that occupy so much of the lowlands are not only poor in lime but they also yield sandy loams that are more porous, with a lower base-exchange capacity than the clays. In situations where enclosure and cultivation have not occurred, their soils are often leached and podsolic, with base-deficient upper horizons and a surface layer of acidic 'mor' humus. On waterlogged ground, some degree of gleying, showing symptoms of anaerobic, reducing conditions with grey ferrous (instead of red ferric) iron, tends to occur. Varying depths of acid surface peat are found, and where drainage is most strongly impeded and stagnant, blanket bog has formed a smothering mantle. On these acidic substrates, pH values range from 3.5 to 5.5. Except for the intractable deeper peats, they can be improved by appropriate fertiliser additions, including lime, and their productivity raised to a reasonable level, as has been done over much of the lowlands. Their inherent low fertility is, however, a factor that continues to place higher demands on farming practice.

The geological descriptions of the wide range of variation in the volcanic rocks of the Lake District (for example, Marr, 1916; Shackleton, 1966; Moseley, 1978) convey little of their significance to soils and vegetation. These rocks are very variable in soil-forming properties, but are predominantly hard and non-calcareous, giving base-deficient and infertile soils, especially on the flinty ashes and rhyolites. Here and there are more basic materials, such as dolerite and some andesites, which release more calcium to the derived soils, though their hardness limits the rate at which weathering can make it available. Sometimes the calcium is in a combined form not easily broken down, and under the extremely high rainfall, leaching may remove soluble nutrients faster than they can be replaced. Under these conditions, the process that Pearsall (1950) called flushing is important in maintaining locally enriched soils. This involves the transport of soluble nutrients washed out of soils at higher levels to lower ground in the surface drainage water. Faulted areas are often charged with veins and nodules of calcite, from which lime is more readily available to soils and plants.

The Silurian grits and shales of southern Lakeland are softer than the Borrowdale rocks and generally give soils of moderate fertility. They are again variable in chemical composition and, although often acidic, they have relatively calcareous beds in places. The large igneous intrusions of Eskdale granite and Ennerdale granophyre give soils that are almost wholly acidic, and the Skiddaw Slates, though softer and more easily weathered, are similarly lacking in available lime.

The development of agriculture

Apart from the generally unfavourable soils, the mountainous terrain and adverse climate of the Lake District have severely limited agricultural development, and the enclosed land is mainly sheep and cattle pasture or hay meadow. The unenclosed fell country both here and in the Pennines has become a vast sheepwalk.

The original vegetation of the region within the forest zone on basic soils evidently consisted of woods with a varied tree and tall shrub composition – ash, wych elm, pedunculate oak, silver and downy birch, hazel, bird cherry, blackthorn, hawthorn, sallow, yew and, in the south, small-leaved lime. On the acid soils there was less variety and sessile oak, birch, rowan and holly were the main species. Juniper was common in both types. The field layer under the woody canopy was mainly of mixed medium to tall herbs on the rich soils, and bilberry, great woodrush, bluebell, grasses, bracken and other ferns on the more acidic substrates. Above the tree line on calcareous soils were natural mountain meadows with a wide variety of herbaceous plants, becoming smaller in stature with altitude, and there were probably areas of high-level willow scrub in places. The poorer soils of former woodland had extensive heaths of ling heather with bilberry, cowberry, crowberry and other dwarf shrubs.

Under the influence of heavy grazing and fire, the dwarf shrub heaths gradually became replaced by a range of acidic grasslands and bracken. This has given much of the hill country its prevailing greenness, or the contrasting russet tones of bracken in autumn and winter that are valued as a scenic asset, but deplored by farmers. It was the nineteenth-century fashion for grouse shooting that led to the management of some moorland areas for their heather (the staple diet of the red grouse), and so preserved a decent extent of this important habitat. In the Lake District itself, this interest has passed, and surviving heather ground is in retreat, but the gentler areas of Pennine moorland are still extensively managed for grouse. Earlier landowner enthusiasm for forestry maintained and even extended the native woods, especially of oak, but when the modern, state-sponsored programmes of reforestation emerged, they were almost entirely of conifers alien to the region, and increasingly managed by methods best described as tree-farming.

The upshot is that the Lakeland of the last 200 years has been a region with a flora and fauna severely modified from its original, pre-human state. Woodland and wetland kinds have declined greatly in abundance and with some loss of species, but there has been a gain in those of derived semi-natural habitats and the farmlands. The treatment of animals regarded as competitors with man, especially over game, has altered the natural balance between predators and prey, but some species have also had advantage from human activities that have boosted their food supply. The industrial age has left a legacy of pollution with more subtle effects, especially on flora, and this extends into the indefinite future under the threat of global warming and sea level rise. Perhaps the most immediate concern, however, is the inexorable deterioration of wildlife habitat across the whole farmland scene during the last 60 years, and the continuing losses that result.

2

The Lakeland Naturalists

As the botanical and zoological strands of Lakeland natural history evolved along rather different tracks, I have decided that separate treatment is neater and more appropriate than switching back and forth in trying to maintain chronological order in an integrated account. In preparing this chapter, I have drawn upon the excellent account of the history of botanical recording in Cumbria by Geoffrey Halliday (1997), and the earlier memoirs by William Hodgson (1898) for Cumberland, and Albert Wilson (1938) for Westmorland. For animals, Macpherson's (1892) account of the early zoologists, the *Transactions of the Carlisle Natural History Society* from 1909 to 1996, and the centenary account of the Society itself by Stephen Hewitt (1996), have been invaluable sources of information.

This account deals especially with the relatively few earlier figures. Lakeland has, as elsewhere, experienced the great growth in interest in natural history, and it becomes more difficult to mention all those active on the present scene. I have tried to name a few of those whom I know, or know about, though selection is invidious, and I apologise to anyone whose contribution may appear neglected, and make collective acknowledgement of all those whose work is keeping the long tradition of Lakeland natural history alive and flourishing.

Botanists

Botanical exploration is regarded as beginning with three visits by the learned John Ray (1628–1705) in 1661, 1668 and 1671, in which he recorded several distinctive northern plants of Lakeland, including roseroot, bird's-eye primrose, yellow balsam, yellow saxifrage, alpine bartsia, northern bedstraw, spignel, alpine lady's mantle and water lobelia. The first local botanist was Thomas Lawson (1630–91), originally from Low Furness, who became a Quaker schoolteacher at Great Strickland, south of Penrith. He botanised widely in both areas and in 1688 sent Ray a list of 150 plants, with localities, which Ray used in a second edition of his *Synopsis methodica stirpium Britannicum* (1696). The list was published by the Ray Society in 1848 and includes oyster-plant, foxglove, alpine clubmoss, mountain sorrel and mossy saxifrage.

William Nicholson (1655–1726) was another cleric, who became rector of Great Salkeld and later Bishop of Carlisle. He listed many new plant records in a manuscript handwritten in Latin and dated 1690. William Hodgson examined this manuscript and extracted records that he published in his *Flora of Cumberland* (1898). They included horseshoe vetch at Shap, wood bitter-vetch at Great Salkeld and Blencarn, wood vetch near Workington, perennial flax at Great Salkeld, spring gentian on Alston

Moor, Jacob's ladder near Dalemain, and deadly nightshade at Carlisle.

Kendal produced two eighteenth-century botanists. John Wilson, shoemaker, baker and later teacher of botany at Newcastle-upon-Tyne recorded Westmorland plants and published a book *A Synopsis of British Plants in Mr John Ray's Method* in 1744. William Hudson (1730–93), who later became an apothecary in London, recorded a number of flowering plants and bryophytes for Westmorland, and also wrote a general work *Flora Anglica*, first published in 1762, with two later editions. This was the first English flora to adopt the Linnaean binomial system of nomenclature. James Jenkinson, schoolmaster of Yealand, listed plants in that area of south Westmorland, and he too wrote a general treatise *A Generic and Specific Description of British Plants ... with Notes of their Localities*, published at Kendal in 1775.

It was not until the early nineteenth century that more substantial lists of plants began to appear. Dawson Turner and L. W. Dillwyn's *The Botanists' Guide through England and Wales* (1805) has a long catalogue of both flowering plants and cryptogams for Cumberland, based especially on records by Turner himself, the Revd John Dodd of Aspatria, the Revd W. Wood of Whitehaven and the Revd John Harriman of Egglestone in Co. Durham. Nathaniel J. Winch of Newcastle-upon-Tyne published a list of Cumberland plants in the *Newcastle Magazine* in 1824, but criticised some of the Turner & Dillwyn records for the Keswick area as extremely doubtful, and based on the authority of the nature guide Hutton 'whose incapacity is undoubted' (Hodgson, 1898). These dubious records were taken from an earlier list in Hutchinson's *History of Cumberland* (1794).

Although he was a geologist, some mention of Jonathan Otley (1766–1856) is appropriate at this point, since his work paved the way for an understanding of one of the major influences on the botany of Lakeland. Living in Keswick, Otley was a humble clockmaker who explored the district in his spare time and interpreted its structure. He described the three great rock groups of the Lake District and helped his fellow Cumbrian Adam Sedgwick, Professor of Geology at Cambridge, to make the first exposition of the region's major geological features. Otley published various papers on his findings and included an essay on geology in his celebrated guide to the Lakes, which also drew together topography, meteorology and natural history (Smith, 2000). John Bolton of Ulverston, who also assisted Sedgwick, published a classic in 1869: *Geological Fragments collected principally from rambles among the Rocks of Furness and Cartmel*.

The father of plant geography, Hewett C. Watson (1804–81), came to the Lake District in 1833 and added many records, which were incorporated in his update of Turner & Dillwyn, *The New Botanists' Guide to the Localities of the rarer plants of Britain*, Vol. I (1835), Vol. II and Supplement (1837). After him, the Victorian botanists visited in increasing numbers and some published records of their finds: Joseph Woods (1835), Edward Newman (1844), J. Sidebotham (1845) and William Borrer (1845).

A group of Quaker botanists consisted of George Gibson, J. Tatham and the two James Backhouse, father and son. The Backhouses were the discoverers of some of the Upper Teesdale rarities, and were notable plant-hunters. Among their best finds in the Lakeland Pennines were alpine forget-me-not on Little Fell, alpine saxifrage at High Cup Scars, yellow marsh saxifrage at several sites on the Westmorland Pennines, rock violet on Warcop Fell, shady horsetail in Swindale, and a mysterious form of field fleawort on Helbeck Fell that has baffled taxonomists, because it cannot be re-found. In the Lakes they found alpine hawkweed on the Scafell range. The younger Backhouse continued to work the Lake District fells after his aged father gave up hill botanising, and discovered black sedge, glaucous meadow-grass and alpine pearlwort on Helvellyn in 1865, though the last record has escaped notice. In 1869 he found mountain avens and shrubby cinquefoil on Helvellyn, and alpine saxifrage, black sedge, bog bilberry and pyramidal bugle on the High Street range. Downy willow was added on Helvellyn in 1872. The younger Backhouse also took a great interest in the hawkweeds, even then regarded as a difficult group. He grew many collected from Lakeland and elsewhere, to observe which characters remained constant in cultivation, and in 1856 published a monograph of the British *Hieracia*.

A group of local fern enthusiasts included a medical practitioner Dr F. Clowes, a gardener Isaac Hudhart, and J. Coward, who all worked from Windermere, and found most of the nine recorded localities for oblong woodsia, six for holly fern, and several for hay-scented fern. The greatest find was a colony of the Killarney fern discovered by W. Crouch in 1863. In the Borrowdale area Charles Wright and his daughter were the finders of forked spleenwort and its rare hybrid with maidenhair spleenwort. Wright also found northern buckler fern near Keswick. Many other fern-hunters came to the region and the depletion of the less common species through the Victorian fern-mania was well advanced even by 1865, as the little book on *The Ferns of the English Lake Counties* by W. J. Linton made clear. In Keswick, J. Flintoft hit on the idea of selling sets of pressed ferns and mosses in book form, and these became widely distributed: they occasionally appear in the secondhand-book catalogues.

Another eminent Quaker botanist from Yorkshire, J. G. Baker, then a professional at the Royal Herbarium, Kew, came to the Lakes and later wrote the first *Flora of the English Lake District* (1885). This included many of his own records, as well as those of Watson, the Backhouses and others up to that time, and contained the first records for Furness, many contributed by Miss E. Hodgson of Ulverston. During the late nineteenth century, the 'lower' plants were increasingly recorded. G. Stabler paid attention to the mosses and liverworts, especially in Westmorland, while J. A. Martindale attended to the lichens and in Langdale discovered a remarkable abundance of *Umbilicaria crustulosa*, a conspicuous species still unknown outside Lakeland in Britain. C. H. Binstead added many bryophyte records, and other contributions came from visiting bryologists such as W. H. Pearson and B. Carrington. The Lakes' writer Beatrix Potter (1866–1943) was an enthusiastic mycologist who made a beautiful series of some 300 watercolour drawings of the larger fungi, which are mostly in the

Armitt Library, Ambleside. W. P. K. Findlay used 59 of them to illustrate his *Wayside and Woodland Fungi* (1967). Her interests in the group were quite scientific, and a paper on *The Germination of the Spores of the Agaricineae* was read to the Linnean Society in 1897, though she withdrew it from publication, evidently with the intention of doing further research first.

Towards the end of the nineteenth century, William Hodgson (1824–1901) compiled plant records for his native county, and in 1898 published the *Flora of Cumberland*. A teacher for many years at Watermillock above Ullswater, he botanised widely in that area, Inglewood Forest and the Solway. Hodgson acknowledged using Baker's Flora records and also lists by Baker from the Alston and Gilsland districts. He paid tribute to help from several west Cumberland botanists: the Revd H. Friend in Cockermouth, Miss E. J. Glaister at Skinburness, the Revd Robert Wood of Westward near Wigton, Joseph Adair and Gardner Chambers of Egremont, David Tweddle of Workington and especially William Dickinson of Workington, who made a large herbarium. There was also Joseph Robson of Gosforth, who contributed some interesting records, but also a few which seemed highly improbable; the Revd F. A. Malleson of Broughton-in-Furness; and Dr John Leitch of Silloth, who listed the numerous alien plants on the ballast hills, which originated from ships bringing overseas grain to Carr's flour mills beside the Silloth docks. Since it was an age in which collections of pressed plants were understood to be the stock-in-trade of every self-respecting botanist, later workers puzzled over the apparent disappearance of Hodgson's herbarium, but there is no evidence that he ever made one.

The dawn of the twentieth century saw the launch of plant ecology as a new branch of botanical science. One of the first concerns was the description and mapping of vegetation, and the earliest local contribution was by Francis J. Lewis, lecturer in geographical botany at the University of Liverpool, who spent three years recording the plant communities over 560 square miles of the Eden, Tees, Wear and Tyne catchments. His maps were published at the scale of 1:63360 in the Geographical Journal for 1904, and are still a valuable basis for determining vegetation change in the northern Pennines since that time. Lewis was also interested in vegetation history and was one of the first to investigate peat deposits for the evidence they contained. Some of his claims were later questioned, and the 'arctic' (implying Late-glacial) plant beds that he described on Cross Fell were shown to be no more than Boreal in age (Godwin & Clapham, 1951). He also listed Rannoch rush from the blanket bogs of Stainmore, where no one else has ever seen it.

In 1911, A. G. Tansley organised a British meeting of the International Phytogeographical Excursion, and a visit to Cross Fell summit was made. The next ecological studies were of the lakes themselves by William H. Pearsall. His father, also W. H. Pearsall, of Dalton-in-Furness, was a taxonomic botanist, and the two discovered a waterweed and slender naiad both new to Britain in Esthwaite Water in 1914. Pearsall junior went on to study the hydroseral development of vegetation around this lake, and published an account in 1918. He also made a wider study of vegetation development around all the main lakes and published this in 1921. Pearsall, who later became Professor of Botany at University College, London, was the driving force in the setting up of the Freshwater Biological Association on Lake Windermere in 1931, and became honorary director. The FBA became the leading centre for limnology in Britain, and its field and experimental laboratory studies have contributed greatly to advancement in the fundamental science of freshwater physics, chemistry and biology.

The terrestrial ecology of Lakeland failed to attract similar attention. In 1925 W. Leach wrote a paper on the two high-level oak woods at Keskadale and Birkrigg in the Grasmoor fells, and in 1930 followed this with an account of plant succession on screes. When Arthur Tansley published his monumental *The British Islands and their Vegetation* in 1939, it contained few other references to Lakeland vegetation besides the work by Lewis, Pearsall and Leach. There was a species list for Naddle Forest, Haweswater, but other woodlands were neglected, and there was nothing on the montane vegetation.

Meantime, the traditional botanists had been steadily extending knowledge of plant distribution. *The Victoria County History of Cumberland* (1902) (the companion volume on Westmorland was never published) included an updated plant list by William Hodgson, while C. H. Binstead covered mosses and liverworts. R. E. Leach, A. Ley, W. R. Linton and W. M. Rogers contributed lists of plants between 1902 and 1907. In Cumberland, T. Scott Johnstone recorded in the Carlisle area, Harry Britten in the Eden valley around Great Salkeld and Langwathby, and W. Wright Mason around Melmerby under Cross Fell. Britten made the remarkable find of a large population of the Breckland plant smooth rupturewort on gravelly ground near Great Salkeld in 1905. From 1913 to 1934 George Bolam botanised in upper South Tynedale around his retirement home in Alston and contributed many interesting records, including several of the spring gentian from Alston Moor. W. G. Collingwood's book *The Lake Counties* (second edition, 1933) contained a list of rarer plants by S. L. Petty revised by Mary Thompson, Agnes Drury and A. G. Hayes. James Murray paid close attention to mosses and liverworts in Cumberland and published lists in *The North Western Naturalist* during 1926–37. He also contributed a memoir of William Hodgson in 1928.

The botanical landmark of the inter-war years was the publication of Albert Wilson's *The Flora of Westmorland* (1938). It was outstanding for its time and is still a work that can be consulted with much pleasure. His descriptions and well-chosen photographs admirably convey the varying physical and botanical character of the different parts of the county. Wilson (1862–1949) (Fig. 2.1) had botanised extensively in Westmorland, especially in the more neglected areas – the Morecambe Bay, Kendal and Shap limestone, the Eden valley and the Pennines – and had a wide circle of helpers. He acknowledges especially the assistance of Dr A. Sprott and his son W. A. P. Sprott of Appleby, J. F. Pickard of Leeds, Gertrude Bell of Ambleside, C. H. Binstead of Hereford, H. Britten junior of Whitby, C. W.

Fig. 2.1 Albert Wilson. (H. Wilson.)

Coward of Grasmere, Mrs Dent of Maulds Meaburn, Mrs T. J. Foggitt of Thirsk, J. B. Foggitt of Kirkby Lonsdale, J. N. Frankland of Nelson, Miss Mason of Kirkby Stephen, W. A. Sledge of Leeds, A. Thompson of Sheffield and H. Walker of Bowness. Wilson himself added much to knowledge of the bryophytes and lichens of the county. His *Flora* not only reveals the striking botanical richness of Westmorland, but gives the sense that he explored the county in its floral heyday, when the colourful meadows, pastures and roadsides were everywhere, and the farming improvers had yet to wreak their havoc.

While World War II dampened down activity for a few years, it was during this sombre episode that moves were made to promote the conservation of nature and National Parks as part of post-war reconstruction in Britain. Professor Pearsall was again a prime mover on the biological side and as one of the founding fathers of the official Nature Conservancy, set up by Royal Charter in 1949, he became Chairman of its Scientific Policy Committee. His classic New Naturalist book *Mountains and Moorlands* was published in 1950, and contained a distillation of his lifetime's experience of upland ecology, much of it drawn from the Lakeland fells and dales. Pearsall was instrumental in the setting up of the Merlewood Research Station of the Nature Conservancy, near Grange-over-Sands, and in the purchase of the Moor House National Nature Reserve as an experimental study area for moorland ecology in the high Pennines. Another valuable work of this period was J. A. Steers' *The Coastline of England and Wales* (1946), which had physiographic descriptions, with botanical information, of the Cumbrian coast.

In Cumberland, Dorothy and Ernest Blezard had recorded plants widely since the 1920s and set down their finds on a card index. Dorothy published a paper on the local speciality around Carlisle, the pine-wood orchid creeping lady's tresses (Blezard, 1946). C. Winsome Muirhead, living near Abbeytown, had begun botanising in the 1930s and, after the War, joined the staff of the Carlisle Museum in charge of the herbarium. She began collecting records towards a new Flora of Cumberland, and compiled a substantial card index to this end, but moved to Edinburgh around 1955. The Revd (later Canon) G. A. K. Hervey held the living of Buttermere, then Gilsland and finally Great Salkeld, from the early 1920s to 1967. In all these areas he botanised widely and left many records of the local flora. He also wrote the account of plants in the *Natural History of the Lake District*, which he jointly compiled with J. A. G. Barnes. In Borrowdale, quarryman botanist Fred Jackson was a fern enthusiast who found rare hybrids of forked and other spleenworts, and an outlying station for the rigid buckler fern at Honister Crag.

I collected Cumberland plant records for some years from 1953, and visited habitats and places all over the county. My interest was especially in the uplands, and I worked the more productive high fells of Westmorland as well, publishing a paper on *The Mountain Flora of Lakeland* in 1960. I was able to confirm the existence of several long-lost species, but not mountain bladder fern or alpine timothy grass (I re-found this in the Pennines). The northern crowberry was a new find for the region. For the mosses and liverworts I concentrated on the old county of Cumberland, and made a number of new Lakeland records.

Soon after the Nature Conservancy was set up, in 1949, it contacted local naturalists for advice and help in identifying and surveying potential Sites of Special Scientific Interest (SSSIs), which it had a duty to notify to planning authorities. Ernest Blezard was approached for the Carlisle area, and reported on a number of sites such as peat mosses and fens. One of the tasks that arose from my job with the Nature Conservancy in 1956 was the survey and recommendation of important examples of major habitats as SSSIs. This was based mainly on descriptions and assessments of vegetation and flora, though with any known faunal interest included also. I made a good many recommendations for new SSSIs in Cumbria, including some large upland areas, such as the Skiddaw Fells, Wasdale Screes, Armboth Fells, Cross Fell, Appleby Fells, Tailbridge Hill–Lodge Edge and Geltsdale, and most of these were duly acted upon by designation.

During the late 1940s and 1950s field meetings of the Botanical Society of the British Isles and the British Bryological Society were held in the Lakeland area. While adding to knowledge of plant distribution, they also contributed to the depletion of this flora, since virtually all members were collecting for their personal herbaria. In 1954 the BSBI launched its scheme to map the British vascular flora on the scale of the 10 x 10 kilometre squares of the national grid, focusing the attention of botanical field work and recording on a countrywide objective. The project stimulated a systematic search of each county to give a full picture of species' distribution, with checking of old records as well as making new ones. I acted as referee of the records for Cumberland (VC 70) and Geoffrey Wilson did likewise for Westmorland and Furness (VC 69). The resulting *Atlas of the British Flora* (Perring & Walters, 1962) was a milestone in British botany.

In 1966 the Nature Conservancy decided to review its National Nature Reserve acquisition programme, first by identifying all sites of national importance to biological conservation in Britain. I was appointed Scientific Assessor to the review, but it was a team effort involving groups sifting the best sites for each major habitat: coastland; woodland; lowland grassland, heath and scrub; open water; peatland; upland grassland and heath; and artificial habitats. The work was completed and a report submitted by 1970, but the work was not published until 1977, as *A Nature Conservation Review* (Ratcliffe (ed.), 1977). Cumbria had one of the main concentrations of these key sites in Britain, representing all the main habitats, and they are listed in the Appendix.

At Ferry House, Windermere, Winifred Pennington continued Pearsall's studies of lake development and ecological history of the district based on the biological evidence, especially from analysis of the pollen and diatom record in sediments. She published extensively on this in technical papers, and in 1973 produced the New Naturalist volume on *The Lake District*, following the plan and notes that Pearsall had left at his death for a work he had intended to write.

Local botanists were active in Lakeland during the 1960s and 1970s. Ralph Stokoe of Cockermouth made a special study of aquatic plants, and surveyed most of the important lakes and tarns (Stokoe, 1983). He discovered spring quillwort new to northern England in three places, six-stamened waterwort in numerous places, and pillwort in several sites. Jim Birkett in Little Langdale rediscovered lanceolate spleenwort near Millom, glaucous meadow-grass on Helvellyn, black sedge on High Street, marsh clubmoss in Little Langdale and hay-scented fern beside Windermere. Tony Warburton made interesting finds on the Eskmeals dunes, in coralroot, round-leaved wintergreen and tree mallow. Lakeland seemed to lose popularity with visiting botanists around this time, however; more distant regions such as the Highlands were now more accessible, and overseas holidays were beginning to boom. The BSBI annual listings of Plant Records gave few for the area, but perhaps also because it was by now well covered.

In 1991, John Rodwell of Lancaster University published the first of his five volumes of *British Plant Communities*, a national classification of vegetation types commissioned by the Nature Conservancy Council in 1974 to provide a tool for the survey, mapping and other study of vegetation. The sample plot data used to define the different communities included many lists from the Lakeland area, and the vegetation of the region can now be dealt with according to Rodwell's classification, since the fifth and final volume of the series was published in 2000. Donald Pigott, Professor of Botany at Lancaster University, planned and supervised the work on the National Vegetation Classification, and conducted his own ecological studies of Lake woodlands, the small-leaved lime, fen succession at Esthwaite Water and limestone vegetation.

Geoffrey Halliday at Lancaster University embarked in 1974 on the compilation of a flora for the whole of the new county of Cumbria. He established a network of enthusiastic field botanists scattered around the region to make as full as possible a survey of vascular plant distribution on a tetrad basis (2 x 2 kilometre grid squares). I was pleased to give him my own records for the district, together with the card indexes compiled by Winsome Muirhead, and Ernest and Dorothy Blezard, which had come into my keeping. Nearly all of this information was collected before 1970. Halliday's aim was to map the flora according to records made during the survey, i.e. from 1974 onwards. This involved also checking as many as possible of the older records, to verify their continued existence or to suggest their deletion as extinct. The recorder network worked assiduously for over 20 years, and Halliday made every effort to deal with critical groups such as hawkweeds, dandelions, eyebrights, brambles and lady's mantles.

A *Flora of Cumbria* by Geoffrey Halliday was published in 1997, and was well worth waiting for. It is a magnificent achievement, second to none among recent county Floras, with tetrad dot distributions of all but the very rarest species on a pleasing background of a coloured relief map of Cumbria, and informative text. This is the pinnacle of botanical progress in the region, and a credit to all concerned. The work is dedicated to eight of the recorders who did not live to see its completion, and Halliday makes acknowledgement to a long list of contributors. It is a work that every serious Lakeland naturalist should own. In 1996 the BSBI embarked on a repeat botanical mapping survey to update the 1962 *Botanical Atlas*. Recording closed in 1999 and the new publication is forecast for 2002.

Botanical work in the region continues, with Roderick Corner, Jeremy Roberts and Mike Porter – among others – adding further good records. The remarkable find of dwarf birch on the Border moors of Spadeadam in 1999 was made by a forester, Bill Burleton, in company with Simon Webb of English Nature. Keith Raistrick and a team of recorders are compiling records towards a bryophyte flora of Westmorland and Furness (VC 69). My own card index of Cumberland mosses and liverworts, begun in the 1950s, is also intended to provide the basis for a similar account. Lichens have been given special attention by Ivan Day, while records of fungi are reported in *The Carlisle Naturalist*, especially by Geoff Naylor.

This is an appropriate point at which to end my review of botanists and look next at the zoologists.

Zoologists

In zoology the first figure of note was Dr John Heysham (1753–1834), a Lancastrian who settled in Carlisle as a medical practitioner in 1778 and later performed also the role of magistrate. He showed early enthusiasm as a bird collector and among his own exploits were the shooting of a female peregrine at the nest near Gilsland in 1781, trapping merlins on Rockcliffe Moss in 1783, and shooting and trapping hen harriers on Newtown Common in 1783–85. His published writings were few, but in 1785 he contributed an article on the nesting of three pairs of hen harriers that regularly bred in young plantations on Newtown Common, then just west of Carlisle, but long since swallowed up by the westward expansion of the city. He was in touch with other leading ornithologists and helped Latham over the plumage of the hen harrier in his *History of British Birds*. Heysham continued to enlarge his collection of stuffed birds and skins and other animals, and in 1796–97 published a *Catalogue of Cumberland Animals*, based on his collections. His manuscript notes contained the first breeding record of the dotterel in Britain in 1784, with an accurate description of eggs sent to him from Skiddaw, and authenticated by the shooting of the bird at the nest.

A still more substantial figure in natural history was his son Thomas Coulthard Heysham (1791–1857), who appears to have assisted his father in his two roles and was left with a patrimony sufficient to pursue his all-round interests as a somewhat reclusive gentleman of leisure. T. C. Heysham was also a collector of various groups, especially birds and their eggs, but appears to have relied a great deal on local agents to supply him with material. He was also in regular correspondence with the major ornithologists of the day, such as Yarrell, Gould, Hewitson, Doubleday, Hancock and Gurney. The younger Heysham took a special interest in the dotterel and in 1831 began exhorting his contacts to obtain birds and eggs. Adult dotterel were easily obtained but eggs were more elusive and he had no success until 1835 when, presumably acting on a tip-off, he sent James Cooper to Whiteside in the Lakes. Cooper walked the 35 miles to the mountain top, and came on a pair of birds. Having no success, he slept on the summit, found the nest with three eggs the next morning, and walked back to Carlisle with his prize. Macpherson has detailed the rest of Heysham's dotterel pursuits, which led to his publishing a celebrated paper on the bird in the *Magazine of Natural History* for 1838.

Heysham's collection extended to birds overseas and he made numerous observations on bird migration. He collected insects and provided much information on the entomology of the Carlisle area to various authors of national treatises. His wide zoological interests included the parasites of birds and cetaceans. He was also a botanist, who first discovered the whorled caraway on Kingmoor on the northern outskirts of Carlisle, and noted Wilson's filmy fern on Skiddaw. His influence in Lakeland ornithology can be gauged by the frequency with which his name appears in *The Birds of Cumberland* and *The Fauna of Lakeland*.

Another early Victorian zoologist of note was Thomas Gough, medical doctor of Kendal (1804–80), whom H.A. Macpherson held in high esteem. While birds were his first love, he was an all-rounder interested in fish, insects, plants, fossils and geology. He was also a microscopist, studying diatoms and other minute organisms. Gough's only ornithological records were in the notes for numerous lectures that he gave in Kendal, but show him to have been an acute observer of the habits of birds, with ring ouzels, waxwings, merlins and red kites especially mentioned. He helped to establish the Kendal Literary and Scientific Institute, and put much effort into enlarging the collections of the Kendal Museum.

By the mid-1800s, several local naturalists emerged in the records. Some of them were enthused by the dotterel in particular and annually hunted the high tops for their nests, among them William Greenip of Keswick, who is credited with finding at least 11 nests with eggs between 1852 and 1874.

Francis Nicholson came frequently from Manchester to follow the foot packs of hounds, indulge in the then legal sport of cock-fighting, and referee Cumberland and Westmorland wrestling contests. But another of his pastimes was dotterel searching and he supplied Macpherson with an essay on its breeding habits which is quoted in *The Birds of Cumberland*. A little-known figure was William Watson of Kendal who contributed an interesting paper on Lakeland birds to *The Naturalist* for 1888. He too was a dotterel enthusiast and clearly knew a good deal about them. He also had important observations on the twite in the Lake fells, a bird that largely escaped the notice of others here.

Among earlier insect hunters, Thomas Bold of Newcastle was a coleopterist who published species lists for the Gilsland area of Cumbria and the river Irthing at Lanercost in the 1850s and 1860s. Jane Donald (later Longstaff) of Carlisle published accounts of the terrestrial molluscs of the district in the 1880s and 1890s.

The most remarkable Lakeland natural historian of the nineteenth century was the Revd Hugh Alexander Macpherson (1858–1901) (Fig. 2.2). Born in India, he came to Carlisle as a curate in 1882 and, after an absence in London from 1885–88, lived in Cumberland at Carlisle and Allonby until 1899. Having inherited estates on the Isle of Skye, he was a frequent visitor there and he also made various trips to mainland Europe. Macpherson was a man of enormous enthusiasm and energy for his chosen interest in zoology, who accomplished a great deal in his short life. His writings were backed by the large personal acquaintance with his subject that he sought in the Lakeland countryside. Never particularly robust in health, his passion sometimes exceeded his endurance in the field, and more than once he had to be carried off in exhaustion from a peat moss excursion on the back of his henchman James Smith.

Once in Carlisle, Macpherson soon set about assembling bird records for the area, and joined with local ornithologist William Duckworth in writing *The Birds of Cumberland* (1886). In 1888 he was greatly excited by the large invasion of Pallas's sandgrouse to Britain, and quickly wrote a paper on its occurrence in the region. He collected birds in the fashion of the

Fig. 2.2 Hugh Alexander Macpherson. (CNHS.)

time, but concentrated on promoting the Carlisle Museum and building up its collections instead of amassing a private hoard. He laboured mightily in compiling local records, and in 1892 published his magnum opus *A Vertebrate Fauna of Lakeland*, covering the area of Cumberland, Westmorland and Lancashire north of the Sands. This fine work stood for long as the major information source on the animals of the region, and is still a fascinating and scholarly account of their earlier history. Some species, such as the dotterel, golden eagle, sea eagle, pied flycatcher, pine marten, polecat, badger and salmon, are treated at considerable length. No less than 262 species of bird are listed. In common with other contemporary works, the number of records based on creatures shot or trapped jars somewhat today, but that was the way of his time.

Another of Macpherson's interests was the range of devices and stratagems used across the world for catching birds, for whatever purposes. He travelled abroad in search of relevant information, and in 1897 published his second great compilation *A History of Fowling*. He was disappointed that this work did not command the interest he had anticipated. A frequent contributor to the zoological journals of the day, one of his last writings was the account of vertebrates for the *Victoria County History of Cumberland* (1902). Macpherson left numerous notes on the animals of Skye which J A Harvie-Brown used after his death in joint authorship of *A Fauna of the North-west Highlands and Skye* (1904). His other notable contribution was to provide leadership to the embryonic and struggling Carlisle Entomological Society set up by four youthful enthusiasts. At a meeting in his house, it was decided to widen the scope of the group, and the outcome was the founding in 1894 of the Carlisle Entomological and Natural History Society with Macpherson as its first President. The first volume of an ongoing series of *Transactions* was published in 1909.

Having campaigned for collections and displays of local natural history in the new museum at Tullie House proposed by Carlisle Corporation, Macpherson was appointed Honorary Director when it opened in 1893. Through this connection, he was able to secure the use of a meeting room for the new Society in the Museum, an arrangement that has happily continued ever since. Interested readers will find a fuller account of this remarkable man's life and influence in the memoir by Linnaeus Hope (1912) and the centenary account of the Carlisle Natural History Society by Stephen Hewitt (1996). He belonged to a line of clergymen natural historians whose ministrations to their flocks had severe competition from their real life's passion.

Cumberland was well supplied with entomologists at the end of the nineteenth century. George B. Routledge (1864–1934) was a Lepidoptera enthusiast who became a leading figure in the Carlisle Natural History Society, serving as its President more than once. He published papers on butterflies and moths of the county in the *Transactions* for 1909, 1912, 1923, 1928 and 1933; Orthoptera in 1928; Neuroptera, Trichoptera and Aculeate Hymenoptera in 1933. Routledge was a gentleman of leisure and magistrate who lived at Tarn Lodge near Castle Carrock. He was an avid collector, and the lower trunks of the trees around his house were said to be black from years of 'sugaring' for moths. His extensive cabinet collections were given to Tullie House Museum.

The leader of the four teenage founder members of the Society was Frank Henry Day (1875–1963), who developed an amazing all-round and largely self-taught knowledge of the chief orders of insects, but especially beetles. Even by 1902 he was sufficiently knowledgeable to write the account of insects for the *Victoria County History of Cumberland*. Later secretary to a timber merchants by profession, he contributed papers on Cumberland Coleoptera to the *Transactions* in 1909, 1912, 1923, 1928 and 1933; and Hemiptera–Homoptera and Odonata in 1928. In 1943 he updated the status of Cumberland butterflies in the *North Western Naturalist*. F. H., as he became known, was a pillar of the Carlisle Society and its Secretary and then Treasurer for many years. He was still going strong when I first joined the Society as a schoolboy, around 1941, and one of the regular features of the meetings in those days was his contributions to the exhibits sessions – carefully set specimens of some choice items handed round for examination, to the accompaniment of learned commentary by F. H. He encouraged my youthful efforts as a bug-hunter, and I learned a good deal from him. His large collection of Coleoptera, in store boxes finely made by himself, was presented to Tullie House Museum.

Harry Britten (1870–1954) was slightly older than Day, but did not appear in the Carlisle Society until 1902. He began work as a railway signalman at Salkeld station, but soon became gamekeeper on the nearby Nunwick estate, which gave him great scope for exercising his natural history interests. Britten was an amazing self-taught all-rounder. He left annotated copies of the *Flora of Cumberland* and the *London Catalogue of British Plants*, which showed his familiarity with the local botany, and he made many interesting finds (see p. 38). In 1909 he contributed a paper on Mammals of the Eden Valley to the first volume of the *Transactions*, and followed this with one on the Arachnids (spiders, harvestmen and false scorpions) of Cumberland in 1912. But Britten's keenest interest was in some of the more obscure groups of insects. He gravitated as a professional taxonomist to the Hope Department of Entomology of Oxford University in 1913 and from there to the Manchester Museum in 1918, becoming a national authority on the Hemiptera–Homoptera. An obituary described Britten as 'the greatest British entomologist since the days of Curtis and Stephens'.

James Murray was another remarkable all-rounder, who early on specialised on molluscs and wrote on the land and freshwater shells of Cumberland in 1909. He contributed many insect records to the compilations of Day and Routledge, and published records also in the national entomological journals. In his later years he concentrated on the parasitic Hymenoptera and also on mosses and liverworts (p. 38). His collections were given to Tullie House Museum by his widow. He lived at Abbeytown and latterly at Gretna. In the south of the region, A. E. Wright at Grange-over-Sands studied Lepidoptera, Diptera and Hymenoptera during the

1920s to the 1940s and published records in the *North Western Naturalist.* Also in Grange, J. Davis Ward recorded Lepidoptera and Diptera too.

These were the leading figures among a whole group of Cumbrian entomologists active during those times. Other names were J. B. Hodgkinson, H. A. Beadle, G. Dawson and M. Dixon. Most of these were working men naturalists of the kind whose enthusiasms were the main inspiration for the countrywide wave of Victorian and Edwardian natural history societies. Leisure time was short and mobility limited, especially in the days before the bicycle, but anywhere within a walking distance of 15 kilometres or so was workable. The nearby Orton Woods, but also the more distant Baron Wood above Armathwaite, became great stamping grounds for the Carlisle entomologists. The bug-hunters would set off on Saturday afternoon after their work places closed (no five-day week then!) and get down to business on arrival. In fine weather they would sleep out, enjoy a whole day's collecting on Sunday, and finally walk back home that night. Some would stay up into the small hours setting their captures, before turning up for work sharp on Monday morning.

During the same period 1890–1910 there were others who were active in the region in pursuit of birds. First was the little group of Solway fisherman–wildfowlers who, in the course of their daily round, saw and shot many uncommon birds. William Nichol of Skinburness (1854–1934) and James Storey of Anthorn (1865–1946) were the leading figures, both punt gunners of fame who spent their lives by the great estuary. Thomas Peal of Burgh-by-Sands was another veteran wildfowler, while Robert Raine ran a gunsmith and fishing tackle business in Carlisle and had a large circle of contacts amongst the field sports devotees. They acted as informal tutors to a new generation of budding ornithologists who absorbed their fieldcraft and received their more interesting records. When the next ornithological work on the region was produced, *The Birds of Lakeland* in 1943, their observations appear frequently as a statement of their contribution to knowledge.

The second group was of egg collectors who mostly came from outside the region, intent on finding nests and taking clutches of raven, peregrine, buzzard and dotterel in particular. One of them was Edward S. Steward (1873–1954), a wealthy ear, nose and throat surgeon from Harrogate who later retired to Windermere. There was also W. Dodd of Barrow-in-Furness, J. J. Baldwin-Young from Sheffield, J. F. Peters, H. Massey and G. H. Lings, all from Manchester. They belonged to a time when nearly every serious ornithologist collected eggs, and should be judged according to the ethos of their day. Steward and his wife Edith compiled a list of raven and peregrine breeding places and their occupation with considerable historical importance, and Peters was a great dotterel hunter whose records give an invaluable picture of the bird's breeding status during 1905–24.

Not all the raven and peregrine enthusiasts were eggers, even in those days. The Revd Percy W. Parminter, who latterly lived at Waberthwaite near Muncaster, took a special interest in these birds, and his records add to the earlier picture of distribution. He enthused George D. Abraham, the elder of the two Keswick brothers famous as pioneer rock climbers, who in 1919 wrote an interesting chapter on the birds of the Lakeland crags in one of his mountaineering books. In this he fulminated against 'A certain well-known collector who visits the Ullswater district each year and has almost completed his hundred clutches of ravens' eggs'. Whether apocryphal or not, the tale suggests that these birds had a hard time even before 1920.

Lakeland produced one outstanding ornithologist to follow Macpherson's lead around this period. Eric B. Dunlop was the son of the squire in Westmorland Troutbeck, and did not have to worry too much about earning his daily bread. Another raven and peregrine man, he was in touch with other locals and also built up a valuable list of breeding haunts and records for 1900–14. Dunlop found the Carlisle Museum a useful source of study material and contacts and was often there, usually walking from Troutbeck and back. He published papers on Westmorland birds and the peregrine in the *Transactions* for 1909 and 1912, and had begun to compile records towards a revision of the birds section of Macpherson's Fauna. He was also particularly interested in the incubation of birds' eggs. Dunlop was elected President of the Carlisle Society in 1913–14, but when War broke out he was in North America. He came home in 1916 and enlisted in the Border Regiment. After being commissioned as an infantry lieutenant he was posted to France, and was killed at the front on 19 May 1917. His manuscript paper Lakeland Ornithology 1892–1913 was published posthumously in the *Transactions* for 1923, with an appendix by Linnaeus Hope, in whose care it had been left. Eric Dunlop's diaries are now in the Alexander Library of the Edward Grey Institute in Oxford University. Thus did Lakeland lose the most promising young ornithologist of a generation.

Linnaeus E. Hope (1864–1944) was a taxidermist in Penrith during the 1880s and 1890s, and was commissioned by Macpherson to prepare many of the exhibits for the new displays in the Carlisle Museum. In 1901 he was appointed Curator at the Museum and was responsible for its development into the important institution that it became. He was helped in building up the bird collections by D. Losh Thorpe, a wealthy enthusiast who bought important specimens for the Museum. Linnaeus Hope was a museum rather than a field man, but he was a stimulus to the Natural History Society, becoming its President in 1902–03. He set up the first local biological records centre in the country in the Museum in 1902, and played a leading role in the establishment of the Kingmoor Nature Reserve by the Carlisle Corporation on the northern outskirts of the city in 1913. His paper on The Gulls and Diving Birds of the Solway in the *Transactions* for 1909 contained an early response to allegations of bird damage, in the analysis of the stomach contents of 100 black-headed gulls, which showed them to feed largely on invertebrates and not fish, as fishermen had claimed.

In 1913 the veteran Northumbrian naturalist George Bolam (1859–1934) retired to Alston and spent his last years there. He was a fine all-rounder, but birds were his primary interest and he wrote *The Birds of Northumberland and the Eastern Borders* (1912). An accurate and reliable observer, he contributed many records from this eastern nook of the Pennines. His manuscript journals are in the Hancock Museum, Newcastle-upon-Tyne. Bolam's great friend Abel Chapman ventured into Cumberland at times, and mentioned the county in his writings on the Borders. Another Northumbrian naturalist, Matthew Philipson, lived at Haltwhistle, and was an acute observer of birds, who contributed an interesting account of the curlew and black grouse going back to the 1910s.

During the 1920s, local eggers came to the fore and joined in the plunder of raven and peregrine eyries. Ronnie Porter and others covered the Keswick area, while Frank Pepper in Borrowdale worked that area. The next decade saw another wave, with Denis Cockbain, Eric Telford and Pearson Douglas in Keswick farming the local eyries; and Edward Wightman from Sedbergh and R. A. H. Coombes from Bolton-le-Sands scouring the eastern fells. Jim Birkett in Little Langdale was a brilliant rock climber who applied his talents to reaching especially difficult nest sites, and was never beaten by one. He was the only man ever to reach the peregrine eyrie in the middle of the fearsome 100 metres overhanging face of Dove Crag above Hartsop. To these daring young men it was a sport and the eggs were the trophies of the chase. Some later gave up and others turned over a new leaf. Pearson Douglas became a dedicated and able bird photographer, while Jim Birkett marked eggs to spoil them for collectors and monitored eyries for the RSPB, and also became an accomplished botanist who added many good records to knowledge of the Lakeland flora. Over many years, W. C. Lawrie of Workington photographed peregrines and ravens in the Buttermere valley. The records of all these people continued to build up the twentieth-century picture of raven and peregrine territory distribution and occupation, making it one of the best documented regions in Britain for these birds.

During the 1920s and 1930s another group of birders in the Carlisle Society had been working away steadily in different parts of the Lakeland region, recording their observations year by year. They decided to aim for the joint compilation of a Lakeland avifauna, and by 1939 had produced a manuscript version. Three of the authors lived in Carlisle: Ernest Blezard, Ritson Graham and Tom L. Johnston, while the fourth, Marjory Garnett, was in Windermere. Ernest Blezard (1902–70) (Fig. 2.3) was the prime mover and became Editor. He was a remarkable man, born at Greenodd in Furness, whose parents moved to Carlisle when he was seven. From his early promise as a field naturalist and taxidermist he became in 1926 assistant to the then director of the Tullie House Museum, Linnaeus Hope, and when Hope retired in 1929 he took charge of the natural history and 'byegones' work there. Styled as Keeper of Natural History and Post-Medieval Antiquities, he remained in the post until his retirement in 1966.

To do justice to Ernest Blezard's contribution to Lakeland natural history would require a separate book. He was appointed Librarian of the Carlisle Society in 1926, and became Secretary and Editor of the *Transactions*, and was finally elected President in 1968. His early papers on raven and buzzard for the *Transactions* in 1928 and 1933 have much origi-

Fig. 2.3 Ernest Blezard. (W. F. Davidson.)

nal field observation, but it was his editorship of *The Birds of Lakeland* that really made his mark. Produced under difficult wartime conditions and published in 1943, this was a model in skill and economy in the presentation of a massive body of information. It was singled out for praise as a regional avifauna by James Fisher in an essay *The Last Hundred Bird Books* in 1948. Ernest said later that, had he known beforehand of its success, he would have aimed at a more ambitious treatment. The work listed 290 species of bird for the region.

Ernest Blezard was among the last of the great all-rounders, but he was a specialist on birds, combining an unusual breadth of knowledge from the field and the museum. Through dissecting many birds in his museum work, he developed a great interest in their food, and later volumes of the *Transactions* contained papers by him on this subject, as well as supplements that updated *The Birds of Lakeland*. His room in Tullie House became a kind of clearing-house for Lakeland natural history information, with a stream of visitors bearing specimens or records, seeking enlightenment, or just exchanging the news. He was informal mentor to generations of budding naturalists, and his sense of public duty gave added effect to the role of the Carlisle Museum as a major educational institution in north-west England. The bird room as it then was showed taxidermy as a fine art in a display of mounted birds in their habitats unsurpassed in the whole country. From his teens, Ernest Blezard kept a detailed record of all his more significant field outings, and these are lodged in the County Archives. His last field trip, four days before his sudden death, was to see the recently returned golden eagles in their Lakeland nesting haunts.

Tom Johnston (1875–1948) (Fig. 2.4) was employed by a Carlisle firm making hats, and belonged to an era when leisure time was limited and mobility restricted to what walking or cycling could allow. He especially worked the Solway, with its salt marshes, peat mosses and woods, though Geltsdale was also a favourite haunt. Friendly and natural, he made rewarding friendships with wildfowlers, gamekeepers, farmers and other country people whose work brought them into daily contact with wildlife and who were able to add much to his knowledge. He contributed a paper on the nesting of the willow tit to *British Birds*, and several papers on birds of the Cumberland Solway to the Society's *Transactions*: on waders in 1909, on the barnacle and greylag geese in 1933 and 1946, and on the great black-backed gull in 1952, the last posthumously. Of the four authors, his contribution to *The Birds of Lakeland* went back farthest, for he was a contemporary of both Macpherson and Dunlop.

Fig. 2.4 Tom Johnston. (CNHS.)

Fig. 2.5 Ritson Graham. (M. Notman.)

Ritson Graham (1896–1983) (Fig. 2.5) was another elder statesman of the Carlisle Natural History Society. A railway engine driver on the Carlisle–Leeds line, he was active in local politics as a Labour City Councillor for many years, becoming Mayor of Carlisle in 1956–57. But Ritson's real passion was watching birds and mammals in the quiet places of Cumberland – the Solway, Inglewood Forest, the Pennines, the Skiddaw Fells and, above all, the Border uplands of Bewcastle, Spadeadam and Gilsland. He returned every year to the last area to spend part of his precious fortnight's holiday in solitary exploration of these lonely moorlands, staying at remote shepherds' cottages or even sleeping rough on the moor.

From 1927 to 1938 Graham contributed bird notes from Cumberland to the *North Western Naturalist*, and papers on Local Wildfowl (1928), the Roe Deer in Cumberland (1933) and the Badger in Cumberland (1946) to the Society's *Transactions*. From the 1940s until almost the end of his life he wrote a regular weekly nature column for the *Carlisle Journal* and then the *Cumberland News*. His most important work was, however, posthumous, in the publication in 1993 of a manuscript he had left on the wildlife of his beloved Border moorlands. Entitled *A Border Naturalist* by his friends, this book assumes greater value as a record of an area that became transformed even within his lifetime, as I shall relate in Chapter 11.

Marjory Garnett (1896–1977) came from a well-to-do family in Windermere and had plenty of leisure time in which to follow her interest in birds. Her information from south-eastern Lakeland was important in covering a then otherwise under-recorded area for *The Birds of Lakeland*. She made observations on breeding merlins and buzzards over many years, but was also a waterfowl enthusiast who visited the coast a good deal during autumn and winter. Perhaps her most important contribution was her observations of the winter birds on Lake Windermere, on which she gave a paper to the *Transactions* in 1946. Though a photographer and painter, Marjory identified with the age of collecting of birds and their eggs, and could make cabinet skins herself. In 1932 she went with Edward and Edith Steward to the Pasvik Valley and the Varanger Fjord in arctic Norway. The trip so impressed itself on her memory that in 1970, at the age of 74 and on her own, she returned to Vadsö to wander again among the northern birds on the lonely tundra of the Varanger fjells that had captured her imagination. Her diaries and records are in Tullie House Museum.

The early years of bird-ringing owed much to the efforts of Robert H. Brown (1901–80), who lived at Cumdivock south of Carlisle, and worked for the Milk Marketing Board. For a long time, Robbie was a loner who eschewed the company of fellow birders, and worked away diligently on his own. He detested egg collecting and his nest-hunting was entirely to find and ring the young of as many birds as possible, which he did with great commitment. Robbie eventually became a regular attender of the Carlisle Society's meetings and contributed to them himself, notably with a talk on ringing 10,000 birds. At some time in that era he was the country's top ringer. Finally he was elected President of the Society. With advancing age he came to rely on younger and more agile companions, especially Geoff Horne, to climb awkward trees and difficult crags to put the rings on for him, always showing great frustration if a nest proved inaccessible after a risky attempt! Towards the end of his life, he published privately his own book *Lakeland Birdlife 1920–1970*, which is a very personalised treatment, dealing largely with his own experiences and records.

Between the Wars, the active entomologists had included the Revd H. D. Ford, Vicar of Thursby, and his son E. B. Ford, both dedicated lepidopterists. Edmund Ford went on to become a distinguished Oxford University scientist and founder of ecological genetics, who wrote the celebrated first New Naturalist volume on *Butterflies* in 1945. They collected together in the Carlisle area, and *Butterflies* contains colour photographs of the variable marsh fritillary from Great Orton and large heath from the Solway mosses. In Penrith, W. F. Davidson was an all-round naturalist who founded the Penrith Natural History Society. He developed a great interest in minerals, and turned a hobby into a business by exporting fine specimens from the still active local mines to American museums and private collectors. Alan F. Airey, Arthur Astley and Oliver Wilson were local ornithologists who wrote about and recorded birds in Westmorland and Cumberland.

Ralph Stokoe (1921–81) was a chartered accountant in west Cumberland who had a great interest in birds, and compiled an summary update of the

1943 work entitled *Birds of the Lake Counties* in 1962. He realised the potential of Grune Point near Silloth for studying bird migration and developed a trapping and ringing station there. Later he turned to botany, first orchids, then ferns, and finally specialised in aquatic plants, adding much to knowledge of their distribution in Lakeland (p. 41). Ralph came home unscathed from the War, but Raymond Laidler (1918–94) was not so lucky. An enthusiast for the crag birds, he was invalided home from Libya with shell fragments embedded inoperably in his knees, but gamely resumed his walking of the fells and other wild places even when in some discomfort. Ray turned to insects and plants, and became an authority on the local moths and dragonflies. He believed in translocations of endangered species and tried to keep local populations of rare orchids and butterflies going in this way.

Walter Thompson (1897–1986) was the epitome of the local naturalist. A postman for most of his life, his early days involved a foot round of 14 miles from Kirkby Stephen to Barras under Stainmore, which gave him ample opportunity to observe the birds of that area. But it was the Mallerstang valley and its surrounding fells that drew Walter most strongly, and especially Tailbridge Hill and Lodge Edge where he was never happier than watching the lapwings, golden plover, dunlin and ring ouzels. Except for a few years in Penrith, when – with a van – he delivered mail to Patterdale, Shap and Keswick, he spent the whole of his life in Kirkby Stephen, and recorded the changes in birdlife observed over his long lifetime. In the same district, R. W. (Bill) Robson was a farmer at Warcop who became a keen bird-ringer, and observed the birds of the Westmorland Pennines over many years. From Arnside, J. A. G. Barnes was a diligent bird observer on the southern estuaries, and recorder for south Lakeland generally. He joined with botanist Canon Hervey in producing the valuable multi-authored *Natural History of the Lake District* (1970), the only across-the-board account of the plants and animals since Macpherson. In Carlisle, Stuart and Dorothy Illis followed the hill birds in particular. Gamekeeper David Imrie wrote interestingly on animals from his cabin in the woods near Braithwaite.

Now that Sedbergh has been placed in Cumbria, the oldest natural history institution in the region is the Sedbergh School Ornithological Society, which goes back to 1888. It has waxed and waned according to the chance of changing enthusiasm inevitable in a school turnover in time, but its records are a solid foundation of bird information for that part of the region. Ingram Cleasby, who himself helped to make the late 1930s a particularly productive period, has recently written a book *Birds and Boys at Sedbergh* (1999), which is a fascinating account of their achievements over many years, and summarises knowledge of birds in that district. This record is the more remarkable as the sphere of operations was largely limited to the radius from Sedbergh that the boys could walk or run, since special permission had to be given even for bicycles, and lifts in masters' cars were a still more occasional luxury.

Later generations took advantage of the mobility conferred by the motorcar age. In the 1920s and 1930s only the more affluent could run a decent car, though motorbikes were more popular. In 1938 Ray Laidler, Peter Day and Sandy Bannister had a £5 Austin Seven in which reverse gear was defunct, requiring that it be lifted bodily to turn around, while the clutch had to be manipulated with the assistance of the front passenger tugging on a cord. From the 1950s all parts of the region were within reach of any other part during the same day. Modern private transport has greatly eased the visiting of widely separated places over a short period. It has facilitated the annual checking of all the peregrine and most of the raven territories in the region, with the recording of breeding success and the ringing of young.

A group of enthusiasts has monitored the Lakeland peregrine population since the dark days of the mid-1960s, when the 'crash' had reduced numbers to a mere handful of pairs and most nesting places were deserted (see p. 232). Geoff Horne of Dalston (Fig. 2.6) has led this effort, regularly covering the whole northern part of the region. This has required increasing effort as the population recovered and then surged to new heights, and by the 1990s he was checking 50–55 territories a year, with help from John Davidson in Cockermouth. In the south, Paul Stott, Paul Marsden and Terry Pickford from Blackpool have covered another 18–20

Fig. 2.6 Geoff Horne.

territories annually. Geoff Horne has examined the contents of 1,058 eyries and ringed 1,072 young peregrines, which may well be a world record. The combined effort has ensured that the Lakeland peregrine population is one of the best known and documented in the world.

With the growing numbers of keen ornithologists, individuals have increasingly focused on particular species for intensive study: Geoffrey Fryer on buzzards, Dave Shackleton on merlins, Derek Hayward on ravens, John Callion on stonechats and whinchats, while John Strowger and John Callion have become the modern dotterel searchers-in-chief. The wealth of bird records in general allow the Cumbria Bird Club to produce a valuable annual report on the status and distribution of birds in the county, and the numbers of some colonial breeders are counted annually. The national wildfowl and wader counts organised by the Wildfowl and Wetlands Trust and the British Trust for Ornithology are well supported in the region, and the BTO schemes for Nest Records, Ringing and Migration studies, Common Birds Census (now Breeding Birds Survey) and species enquiries all receive Cumbrian contributions.

Study of other animal groups flourishes also. The now popular bats have two study groups, for Cumberland and for Westmorland and Furness, which monitor populations, put up roost boxes and give advice and assistance to the public. Mammals receive a good deal of attention, and John Webster has studied various species, including the dormouse, for many years. Neville Birkett has been studying the Lepidoptera and Diptera of Lakeland for well over 50 years. The Lepidoptera have also been studied by Bill Kydd, Keith Porter and the late Ted Hancock. Butterfly Conservation now has a Cumbrian branch that does much recording, monitoring and conservation work locally. T. T. Macan of the Freshwater Biological Association added greatly to knowledge of the aquatic insects, and has been followed more recently by David Bilton of Carlisle. Roger Key in English Nature has revised the lists of Cumbrian beetles, and the molluscs have been extensively studied by Barry Colville.

There has lately been an encouraging revival of interest in the invertebrates of Lakeland. Continuing the early enthusiasm for their study in the Carlisle Natural History Society, John R. Parker in Keswick has long been the authority on arachnids for the region, and has been largely responsible for boosting the Cumbrian total of species to 326, out of some 650 recorded for the whole of Britain. Now in his 90th year, he is probably the only survivor of the Carlisle Society from the pre-1940 years. Jennifer Newton is a more recent spider enthusiast who is adding interesting records to the regional list. David Clarke has a special interest in dragonflies; Geoff Naylor, Richard Little, Mike Clementson and Neville Birkett in butterflies and moths; Magnus Sinclair, David Atty and John Read in beetles; Stephen Hewitt in Heteroptera, Neuroptera, Diptera (with Neville Birkett and John B. Parker of Penrith) and Orthoptera (with Jennifer Newton); and Neil Robinson in bees, wasps and ants.

Freshwater biologist Geoffrey Fryer, formerly of the FBA, has written a fascinating account of the whole range of aquatic life in *A Natural History of the Lakes, Tarns and Streams of the English Lake District* (1991). This is a very readable and informative account of just about everything to do with these important habitats within the National Park.

Organised data collection

The long tradition of dedicated amateur natural historians has borne fruit in the many Floras and Faunas that have been compiled especially from their records, and that continue to appear, presenting new and updated purviews of Lakeland wildlife. This wealth of talent and energy is also harnessed to more recent schemes for the recording and monitoring of plant and animal distribution and abundance across Britain, as in the botanical mapping organised by the Botanical Society of the British Isles, and the mapping, ringing, counting and species enquiries of the British Trust for Ornithology. Interest and activity have also progressed beyond the straightforward study and enjoyment of nature to concern for its future, and the need for conservation measures. The national recording schemes themselves contribute to this end. Tullie House Museum maintains a computerised database of animal (mainly) and plant records sent in by naturalists around Cumbria, with entries now totalling nearly a quarter of a million, including a Cumbria Bird Club dataset of 60,000 breeding bird records. Tullie House has already produced several provisional atlases covering various taxonomic groups, and CBC will be publishing a Breeding Bird Atlas in 2002. The new Flora of Cumbria has a computerised database.

The Cumbria Wildlife Trust has evolved as one of a national network of bodies able to acquire and manage land for its wildlife value, and has established a network of nature reserves. CWT has various specialist wildlife groups, and many of its members, as also of the local societies, also support the national non-governmental organisations, such as the RSPB and Plantlife. They have also given assistance to the official nature conservation agency, formerly the Nature Conservancy, now English Nature. The Cumbria Naturalists' Union acts as an umbrella organisation to the separate societies. It publishes the valuable annual report on *Birds and Wildlife in Cumbria*. Malcolm Hutcheson acted as editor for these reports through the 1970s and 1980s, and Mike Carrier through most of the 1990s. Alastair Crowle edited the Bird Report during 1999–2001.

The Nature Conservancy itself, with a presence in Lakeland since the early 1950s, contributed to the development of wildlife studies in the region. Its regional staff, led by Ron Elliott and later Helga Frankland, formed close links with local societies and their members, in assessing conservation needs and developing their programmes. Reserve wardens and other resident staff were active participants in field work: Michael Rawes and Terry Wells at Moor House and Frank Mawby on the Solway have made notable contributions. The Conservancy also funded a good deal of biological survey in Cumbria through its 'in-house' programmes and contract research. The National Trust's biological survey teams and their local ecologist and wardens have added much information of the flora and fauna of the extensive Trust land-holdings in Lakeland.

While this book does not purport to cater for geology, other than as a major environmental factor, the extensive survey and mapping of the region conducted by the British Geological Survey since the nineteenth century should be acknowledged. The old sister counties of Cumberland and Westmorland still have separate Geological Societies. The especially rich variety of minerals in Lakeland has received much attention locally, notably by W. F. Davidson and F. H. Day junior.

Perhaps the more academic professional scientists, in the Institute for Terrestrial Ecology, Freshwater Biological Association (these two now combined as the Centre for Ecology and Hydrology) and the Universities, remain somewhat detached from this body of amateur enthusiasm, apart from individuals who are motivated to join in. They plough their own furrows in advancing basic science, and tend to talk a language and publish papers that create a communications gap with the rest. Some of their leaders, William Pearsall, Winifred Pennington and Geoffrey Fryer have ably shown how the more esoteric reaches of academic science can be told as a simpler and fascinating story to a wider audience eager for such knowledge. The tradition of the New Naturalist is to reach 'the informed layman' as well as the established naturalist and learned scientist, and this book leans towards the older style of natural history that was the beacon of my early years in Lakeland.

3

The Estuaries: Sands and Salt Marshes

Lakeland lays claim to two of the largest estuaries in Britain, the Solway Firth in the north and Morecambe Bay in the south, though only part of each belongs to the region. The Solway is shared with Scotland, where the saltings of Caerlaverock and Kirkconnell Merses on the Nith estuary are particularly notable, while the southern part of Morecambe Bay with the Lune and Wyre estuaries belongs to Lancashire. The Duddon is a third important estuary wholly within the region as is the lesser system of Irt, Mite and Esk converging at Ravenglass.

The Solway Firth begins only six kilometres below Carlisle, where the river Eden becomes tidal, between Beaumont and Rockcliffe. The Border Esk enters the estuary just south-east of Gretna, beyond which the whole north shore of the Solway lies in Scotland. Its outer limits are arbitrary, but the inner English Solway extends as far as Grune Point, commanding the southern entrance to Moricambe Bay: a district of salt marshes and, at low tide, vast sand flats with meandering river channels.

In the 60 years that I have known the Cumbrian Solway, not much has changed. The railway to Silloth behind the sea-wall embankment to Burgh Marsh has long gone, and the cooling towers of the Chapelcross nuclear power station sprouted across the estuary in 1958 to dominate the Solway scene. Yet it otherwise all looks the same. From the road, the great level expanse of Burgh Marsh still stretches unfenced and inviting far into the distance. It was always a free and open place where people could wander as they pleased. Out on the marsh, the large Greystone pool remains with its puzzling rounded granite boulder that humans must have dumped there long ago. The tall monument to King Edward I, who died here in sight of the Scotland he intended to invade, still stands prominently on the highest part of the marsh near its north-east end. Kestrels continue to perch and roost there as they always did.

From the still eroding brow edge you can watch the ceaseless ebb and flow of the tides across the great sand flats built up by sediment from the rivers Eden and Esk that enter the head of the Firth (Fig. 3.1). The river channels remain at low tide, flowing seawards, narrow and deep in places, but wide and shallow elsewhere. Their sinuous courses and branching arms across the flats, and the endlessly varying patterns of ripples and lines in the sands, are a thing of beauty in themselves. When the tide flows at the head of the Firth it often comes in with a rush. A big spring tide with a following gale can be a spectacular and awesome sight. Tearing in with a large frontal wave or bore, it races up the narrowing estuary and within minutes the whole vast expanse of flats is open, choppy sea. Having viewed the spectacle, the onlooker does well to retreat to higher ground beyond the

Fig. 3.1 Estuarine flats and channels between Drumburgh and Port Carlisle, Inner Solway.

marsh. So quickly, the creeks behind fill up and bar the way, and then the water spills over the brow edge and begins to flood the whole marsh. Burgh is the highest-lying of the Solway marshes, but during a really big tide the complete stretch from Dykesfield to Drumburgh is submerged and the road floods to a depth that stops traffic along it. Woe betide anyone caught far out at such times – they will be lucky to escape with a wetting.

Burgh is only one of the great salt marshes of the Cumbrian Solway. The biggest and most important for wildlife is Rockcliffe Marsh, lying opposite across the Eden estuary and bounded on its north side by that of the Esk. Unlike Burgh, where the owner Lord Leconfield long ago gave the public the right to roam at will, Rockcliffe Marsh has always been kept a strictly private place by its owners, the Mounsey-Heyshams of Castletown House. It is to this privacy that Rockcliffe no doubt owes much of its importance as a sanctuary for birds, for the winter wildfowl and wader populations would otherwise have suffered far too much shooting, and the springtime breeders much more nest-robbing and general disturbance. It is now a nature reserve of the Cumbria Wildlife Trust by agreement with the owners. On the north side of the Esk is a small section of marsh at Mossband. Campfield Marsh fringes the north side of the Cardurnock peninsula west of Bowness-on-Solway and is an RSPB reserve. The other important marshes are those of Moricambe Bay towards the outer Solway: Newton Marsh between the outflows of the Rivers Wampool and Waver, and Skinburness Marsh between that village and the Waver.

At the opposite, southern end of Lakeland, the salt marshes of Morecambe Bay are also extensive, but the largest areas belong to

Lancashire, and Cumbria claims only the smaller patches around the estuaries of the Kent, Gilpin, Winster and Leven, the Cartmel coast and South Walney. The Duddon estuary has good fringing salt marshes on both sides, especially the west, with an outlier at North Walney; and the Ravenglass estuary has small areas.

Salt-marsh vegetation

The Solway sediment is mainly fine sand, with lesser amounts of silt, for the lower courses of the rivers entering the Firth all flow over Permian Sandstone bedrock and superficial deposits derived largely from this parent material. It forms firm sandbanks and flats in the tidal reaches, and quicksands are seldom encountered, except in Moricambe Bay. Although eelgrasses colonise the intertidal sands on the Scottish side, these sediments are devoid of vascular plants on the Cumbrian Solway and have only a few algae such as *Enteromorpha*. Where the sand deposits rise high enough above tide levels for flowering plants to colonise, the main pioneer is the common saltmarsh-grass. Its stolons spread out radially to form expanding patches, which gradually coalesce into a continuous sward. Increasing amounts of sediment are trapped as the grass cover extends, and the sand level rises until other salt-marsh plants can establish (Fig. 3.2). The glassworts are local on the Solway, but become abundant on the muddier substrates of Moricambe Bay. These are salt-marsh communities SM 8 and 10 (Rodwell, 2000). The cordgrass is well established on the Scottish Solway, but on the Cumbrian side has been seen only in small quantity on Newton Marsh (Halliday, 1997).

Fig. 3.2 New salt marsh forming below Drumburgh, Inner Solway, 1987.

Other salt-tolerant plants that enter at an early stage in the salt-marsh succession and help to build up a closed sward are sea arrowgrass, sea plantain and seablite, followed by thrift, sea milkwort, saltmarsh rush, greater and lesser sea-spurrey, buck's-horn plantain, red fescue and creeping bent: communities SM 13, 16 and 27 (Rodwell, 2000).

With rising marsh level through sand accretion, drainage channels develop in places and become persistent features, in the branching creeks that resemble miniature river systems. The largest ones nearest the estuary are quite deep and form uncrossable barriers when full of water. Some marshes have also acquired systems of saltpans where residual hollows in the developing marsh have become deepened by water scour. They are best represented on Newton Marsh and around the Cardurnock peninsula, but Burgh and Rockcliffe Marshes have a smaller number of larger pools (Fig. 3.3). On Burgh these have changed little over the last 50 years.

Over the millennia following the retreat of the last ice sheets, the salt marshes of the district have been affected by land–sea level changes. The remains of an ancient drowned forest are visible at times on the Cardurnock flats, and must date from a time when the sea level was far lower than today. Since then, the slow tilting of Britain's land mass about a south-west to north-east axis has affected this region. The land to the north of this line has risen in relation to sea level, while that to the south has fallen. Steers (1946) has described the series of marine alluvial terraces, raised

Fig. 3.3 A large pool on mature salt marsh, Burgh Marsh, Inner Solway.

beaches and old cliffs cut in boulder clay along this part of the Solway that tell of successive elevations of the land above the sea.

The inner zones of the Lakeland estuarine marshes thus lie well above the level of normal tidal inundation, and are flooded only during the more extreme high spring tides. Their vegetation has become modified by the colonisation of plants not normally associated with saline conditions, and so has tended to take on the character of neutral grassland: MG 11 (Rodwell, 1992). Autumnal hawkbit, smooth hawk's-beard, meadow buttercup, white clover, bird's-foot trefoil, stag's-horn plantain, carnation sedge, glaucous sedge, common sedge and common bent are typical species. The highest and driest parts of some marshes, notably Burgh, had numerous dense clumps of common rush, though this has largely disappeared in recent years on this site. Their soils consist of brown, sandy loams from which the salt has mostly been leached.

More local plants of the salt marshes are sea rush, distant sedge, long-bracted sedge, saltmarsh flat-sedge and hard grass. In places, freshwater seepages produce brackish conditions with a distinctive flora, including sea club-rush, hemlock water dropwort, parsley water dropwort, brackish water-crowfoot, celery-leaved buttercup, wild celery, flat-sedge, brooklime, yellow flag, false fox sedge, common spike-rush and jointed rush. Examples of this community (S 21, Rodwell, 1995) may be seen along the inner edge of the strip of marsh west of the old Solway viaduct. Dry grassy banks along the marsh edge here have spiny rest-harrow, a rather uncommon Lakeland plant; and the still rarer lesser and seaside centaury belong to such ground.

The young salt marsh forms a palatable sward that supports quite large numbers of domestic animals, mainly sheep during the winter and cattle in the spring and summer. On these heavily grazed marshes, robust maritime plants such as common scurvy-grass and sea aster occur mainly on the sides of creeks and ditches, where they are more protected. The grazing and treading also help to consolidate the turf, which has long been cut and sold for use on sporting lawns, formerly at Wimbledon, but now mainly bowling greens. The top three centimetres of the soil with its sward rooting layer are removed rotationally, with cuts of up to a hectare at a time, and the bared surface regenerates again to closed grassland in about ten years.

All traces of the former natural transition from salt marsh to woodland on higher and drier ground beyond the influence of salt water have long since vanished from the Solway. The marshes pass immediately to farmland, and in most places the two have been sharply separated by the building of sea-wall embankments of earth and stone, to limit landward penetration of sea water. In places the banks and higher marsh edges become densely grown with gorse, and along the edge of Campfield Marsh this makes a spectacular display of luminous yellow during May (Plate 5). It is referable to community W 23.

After thousands of years of slow building up, the marshes often erode along their seaward edges, which retreat towards the land with an unstable brow edge. Some undercutting of the vertical sand face occurs during high tides, but it is mainly the weight of water absorbed along its perimeter that causes the marsh edge to collapse in large blocks onto the slope below as the tide recedes. The position of the river channels determines the course of events. Where a channel runs close in along the marsh edge and creates a steep gradient between the two at low water, erosion follows; but where the channel moves away and the change in level becomes very gradual, accretion usually occurs. Rockcliffe Marsh has consistently enlarged and over the last 75 years has gained 286 hectares, while Burgh Marsh across the Eden channel has tended to lose ground.

Comparison with the 1:10560 Ordnance Survey map of 1901 showed that by 1949 Burgh Marsh had lost an average width of 70 metres along virtually the whole of its length. Loss of the outer marsh continued, and a large creek near Dykesfield completely disappeared through erosion. Between 1949 and 1999 a further 200-metre strip of marsh along this sector had vanished. Yet around 1980 the Eden channel west of Boustead Hill moved away from Burgh Marsh, and a quite large area of new marsh soon developed below Drumburgh (Fig. 3.2). This has, in the 1990s, been completely lost again as the river channel moved once more towards the Drumburgh shore. On the whole, the Cumbrian Solway marshlands have increased in extent during the twentieth century (Table 1).

Table 1 The balance of accretion and erosion on Cumbrian Solway salt marshes.

	Year	
	1924	2000
Rockcliffe Marsh	689 ha	975 ha
Burgh Marsh	522 ha	568 ha (518 ha following later erosion)
Bowness–Cardurnock Marsh	119 ha	164 ha
Newton Marsh	556 ha	532 ha
Skinburness Marsh	527 ha	627 ha

Areas are calculated from Ordnance Survey 1:25000 maps for 1924 and 2000, but these dates only approximate to the precise years of field survey. Burgh Marsh has since lost at least 50 hectares of new marsh at the western end.

On Burgh Marsh, two sloping banks parallel to the seaward edge separate three terraces at different levels. Although the vertical difference in elevation at each bank is only about 30 centimetres, this affects frequency of submergence of the different terraces during high tides. Their presence is an interesting demonstration of the natural processes at work down the ages. The banks represent old erosion edges of the marsh, which were followed by re-advance of new marsh again beyond the retreating margin. The new marsh also built upwards again, but its failure to regain the original level is a measure of the upward tilting of the land during the intervening period. There is a third and larger bank below the highest and driest part of the marsh where the Edward I monument stands, but this ground represents a much earlier period of rise in land level in relation to the sea.

The plant communities of salt marshes on Morecambe Bay, the Duddon and Ravenglass closely resemble those described, but have certain species scarce or absent on the Solway, such as the sea-lavenders, sea purslane, sea wormwood, grass-leaved orache, strawberry clover and the aggressively invasive cordgrass, all typical of the early stages of salt marsh development farther south in England and Wales. Cordgrass is frequent in almost all the salt marshes of Morecambe Bay, and covers extensive areas especially off Rampside. It is also well established in the Ravenglass estuary (Halliday, 1997). Narrow-leaved eelgrass occurs in the Walney channel, but is too rare to be ecologically significant. Brackish ditches with fen communities on the southern estuaries are among the few extant Cumbrian localities for common meadow-rue. Salt marsh communities SM 6, 14, 15 & 17, and brackish reedswamp S 4 (Rodwell, 1995, 2000) are added on the southern estuaries.

On the inner side of Walney Island, salt marsh is more intimately mixed with sand dunes, shingle and boulder scars than on the Solway, showing an interesting relationship between these three types of coastal habitat. On the west side of Roudsea Wood, abutting the Leven estuary, there is a transition from salt marsh through alder wood to oak wood – one of the very few places in Britain where such a juxtaposition can be seen today. It is, however, a change produced by increase in ground level from the recent coastal sediment to a bluff of Silurian bedrock, and is not a true example of the final stage of salt marsh succession to woodland.

Sediment invertebrate communities

These are described by Connor et al. (1995), and vary according to coarseness of sediment, degree of shelter and dilution of salinity by freshwater inflows. On the sandy mud of mid and lower shores of the inner Solway, the ragworm is abundant, along with other smaller polychaetes and oligochaete worms. The burrowing sandhopper (amphipod) is locally plentiful and bivalves include the Baltic tellin and cockle, while the mudsnail is common in places. The mud surface is often covered with green algae such as *Enteromorpha* spp. and *Ulva lactuca*. On sandier shores this community grades into one with dense beds of lugworms, as well as ragworms and other polychaetes such as *Pygospio elegans* and *Nephtys hombergii*. Where the sand is less muddy on moderately exposed shores, the bivalve *Angulus tenuis* may be present in high densities along with a wider range of polychaete worms but fewer amphipods.

Muddy sand of the lower shores on the open and exposed coast has dense populations of the burrowing sea urchin and razor shells, along with a rich variety of polychaete worms and bivalves. This type occurs mainly on the Scottish outer Solway. On mid to upper shores with fine, muddy sands and a freshwater influence, over much of the inner Solway, the furrow shell is plentiful, with cockles or Baltic tellins. Sandy upper shores of the open coast are less hospitable habitat, with only a few species of burrowing amphipod, mainly *Bathyporeia* spp., the isopod *Eurydice pulchra* and the polychaete worm *Scolelepis squamata*. With increasing wave exposure and sand movement, this beach habitat becomes barren, whereas community diversity rises with reduction in wave action and increase in fine sediment. Finally, the upper edge of the intertidal zone, where decaying seaweed accumulates as a strand line, has a community of small sandhoppers, especially *Talitrus saltator*, and isopod crustaceans.

The intertidal flats of Morecambe Bay also range from fine sand to thick mud and have much the same community of invertebrates, with the Baltic tellin, mud-snail and sandhoppers especially abundant (Morecambe Bay Partnership, 1996).

These intertidal invertebrate communities are of tremendous importance as the food supply of estuarine birds, especially the family of waders. They are also vital feeding grounds to many fish that inhabit the shallower waters of the Cumbrian coast, and provide a nursery area for several species (see Chapter 4).

Birds

The birds of the estuaries are generally regarded as their most important wildlife feature, with the intertidal flats, sandbanks and saltings forming the feeding and resting habitat of large and diverse populations the year round, while the salt marshes are major spring and summer breeding places for some species. The international importance of the Solway and Morecambe Bay as ornithological sites is recognised in several conservation designations, especially for their numbers of waterfowl in autumn and winter. The breeding birds will be treated in this chapter but, because of the their wider movements between estuary and open coast, passage migrants and winter visitors to the Cumbrian shores will mostly be dealt with together in the next chapter.

Spring and summer

Even before the throngs of wintering wildfowl and waders thin out through emigration to their northern breeding haunts, the nesting birds return to claim their springtime territories. First are the lapwings, some of whose winter flocks may have chosen locations nearby or even on the marshes. They reappear in February in an open year and disperse into their separate pairs across the saltings, to wheel and tumble with creaking wings and plaintive voices as they engage in energetic display against their neighbours. The first eggs are laid in early April, but many are lost to predators and so have to be replaced by repeat layings – perhaps even twice or more – so that many pairs are sitting full clutches in May. The lapwings mostly lay in the closest grazed grassland, and their completely unconcealed nests are protected only by the aggressive behaviour of their owners, which swoop fearlessly at intruding rooks and crows. The 1940s and 1950s had dense breeding populations of lapwings on most of the marshes, though mainly on the middle reaches. Few people counted birds in those days, but an estimate of 50–100 pairs per square kilometre would seem a reasonable figure for the best ground on Burgh Marsh. I seldom sought peewit nests deliberately, but found them while searching for redshank and dunlin, and usually logged at least four or five during an afternoon's walk.

Lapwing numbers on Burgh collapsed after the terrible winter of January–March 1963, and stayed low for many years. Not until 1990 was there a recovery and in that year I was pleased to find the density of nesting birds approaching what I had remembered from my youth. Frank Mawby estimated up to 70 pairs that year. But it did not last and numbers faded away to low levels again: 12–15 pairs in 1997, but 24 in 1999. Rockcliffe Marsh has remained the best area, though the total of 100–150 pairs reported in 1975–78 (G. D. Rankin) had declined to 90 in 1998 and 42 in 2000.

The redshank was the next most abundant wader of the marshes. On Burgh they avoided the most densely rush-grown inner marsh, and began nesting where rush clumps were thinner and more scattered. Nests were hollowed out within these smaller tufts, or in the taller tussocks of fescue and bent left by the unevenness of cattle grazing. They are usually well hidden, with a tenting-over of the grass leaves around the scrape. The birds show little of the lapwing's aggressive nest defence, and rely on such concealment, though this afforded only partial protection from egg-hunting predators, and sucked eggs of both redshank and lapwing were scattered around with about equal frequency. Many trial nest scrapes were made by the birds before laying, which began around 20 April. On spotting an approaching intruder, the sitting birds usually fly straight from their nests and then stay quiet. The off-duty birds are feeding or resting elsewhere, and I often found more nests than there seemed to be birds about. It is different when the eggs have hatched, for both parents then fly around close by, scolding an intruder with anguished yelps.

The birds on Burgh Marsh also had to contend with human nest robbers. Birds'-nesting boys probably took only a modest toll, but during the 1950s some marshes were reputedly scoured by locals to feed the eggs of the larger birds to hungry trail hounds. The redshank population held up until 1963 when – as with the lapwing – it collapsed and has never really recovered. Redshank numbers in earlier years were high. Tom Johnston once found over 40 nests in a day on Rockcliffe Marsh, but Burgh had fewer and 12 in an afternoon was my best score, but probably 50–100 pairs bred there. Rockcliffe still has fair numbers, with 50 pairs in 1997, but only 40 in 2000, and well down from 120 pairs in 1975–78 (G. D. Rankin). The failure of redshank and lapwing to recover their former numbers on Burgh Marsh is puzzling. As the Castletown estate was keepered, predators may have been kept down and human robbers discouraged on Rockcliffe, but the large numbers of cattle on Burgh Marsh suggest that heavy grazing and trampling is a factor in its permanently reduced bird populations. Breeding pairs have increased at Campfield Marsh, managed for its birds by the RSPB. E. S. Steward knew high breeding densities of redshanks on some of the northern salt marshes of Morecambe Bay during the early twentieth century, but there is no recent information on numbers there.

My favourite salt-marsh wader was the dunlin. Although nesting mainly on the Pennine and Border moorlands, it had long been known as a breeder on the sea level saltings of the Solway and Morecambe Bay. Salt-marsh nesting dunlin were indeed known as far south as the estuaries of the Cheshire Dee and Teesmouth. On Burgh Marsh they occupied the same ground as the redshanks and also nested in small rush clumps or grass tussocks, though with daintier scrapes to hold their pale green or olive, brown-marked eggs. Laying in early May, they too suffered predation, and clutches could usually be found well into June. When their young were hatched, the parent dunlins became confiding, and followed human intruders closely, running and flitting around close by with their anxious purring calls.

Macpherson believed that these coastal dunlin were larger and less brightly coloured than those on the inland moors, but this view was later discounted. The more obvious difference was that the bird bred at far higher density on the coastal marshes than on the uplands, where pairs were mostly thinly scattered. Abel Chapman visited the Solway marshes with his brother Alfred in 1888 and remarked that they found more nests of this bird and redshank in one day than they would find in years of walking the Border moorlands. Tom Johnston once found seven nests in a day on Burgh Marsh, which was reckoned the best Solway haunt for nesting dunlin. Even though the bird probably never here approached the incredible breeding densities on the Hebridean machair marshes, it was evidently once in relatively high numbers on the Lakeland saltings. Yet even by 1943, Blezard et al. were reporting a serious decline here. Numbers remained modest through the 1950s, with perhaps up to a score of pairs on Burgh Marsh, but crashed in 1963. Odd pairs reappeared thereafter, but the last nest I knew on Burgh was in 1968 and I have heard nothing of others since then. Three to five pairs are reported to cling to their Rockcliffe haunts, but the species has otherwise vanished as a coastal breeder in the Lakeland region.

Oystercatchers nest widely over the salt marshes, though not in large numbers, and pairs are usually well spaced out. They occupy mainly the outer zone, laying their eggs in open scrapes among the short turf in early May, but repeating as necessary after the loss of first clutches. Even their large size and aggressive behaviour towards predators are not a complete defence against nest-robbing enemies. Their numbers were prone to fluctuation, year by year, and have been less subject to long-term decline than other waders. During 1975–78 a total of 80–150 pairs were counted on Rockcliffe Marsh, and there were still 147 pairs in 1998.

Common snipe are often flushed from the inner parts of Burgh Marsh, especially wet ground, and along ditches, and are often heard drumming. The monument end was their best area, but the numbers that nest are almost impossible to determine. Snipe nests are among the more difficult to find, and I have seen only three during all my days on the Marsh. They were all in thin rush clumps on the inner marsh, on dry ground, but with wet feeding places nearby. Sometimes, it seemed that birds present were not necessarily nesting. A few pairs of curlews nest on the inner, rushy parts of Burgh Marsh. They are wary birds and on these great plains can spot intruders from afar, so that they leave their nests in good time. The triple note of alarm from a distance tells that a nest with eggs is somewhere around, but it will not easily be found, for watching the bird back on such ground is difficult.

Ringed plovers breed on the marshes in small numbers, but their main habitat is the shingle beaches of the outer coast. They favour gravel areas and in recent years have been virtually confined to parts of Rockcliffe Marsh with such habitats, including gravel roads. In 1998, 15 pairs bred, but all the nests were washed away by a high tide. In recent years, more exotic waders have occasionally nested on the Solway. With the return of the black-tailed godwit to Britain from the 1950s, the species began to appear here, and a nest was found on Rockcliffe Marsh in 1970 (Brown, 1974). The New Atlas also recorded breeding in the Ravenglass area during 1988–91. Spring sightings of ruffs were followed by rumours of nesting on another marsh, but this was never proved. Both species continue to appear on the Solway and Morecambe Bay, but have not become established as breeders, so that present conditions may not suit either. Small trips of dotterel formerly appeared on the salt marshes in spring, en route to more northerly breeding haunts, but in recent years their passage has been over higher ground well inland.

The other important nesting birds of the Solway salt marshes are the gulls and terns. In Macpherson's day, lesser black-backed gulls bred mainly on the peat mosses, but in 1907 breeding began on Rockcliffe Marsh and in 1928 this site received a great influx from the ancient colony on Bowness Moss. Numbers grew to 350–400 pairs in 1943 (Blezard et al., 1943). The growing colony was joined by increasing numbers of herring gulls, with a ratio of 5:1 in a total 1978 population of 1,500 pairs (G. D. Rankin). By 1998, the combined population had reached around 9,000 pairs. Most of the gulls occupy the outer half of the marsh towards the Point, building their grass nests in the grazed sward and laying their eggs from mid-May. At current numbers their droppings and castings must appreciably enrich the marsh soil with nitrogen and phosphorus, while the numerous carapaces of small crabs and mollusc shells they leave will add calcium. A smaller lesser black-back colony with the odd pair of herring gulls bred on Newton Marsh in the 1940s and 1950s, but I have no recent information on it. Occasional pairs also tried to nest on Burgh, but did not persist.

A pair or two of great black-backs were established on Rockcliffe Marsh quite early on, and have also increased along with their smaller relatives, numbering 64 pairs in 1996 but only 39 in 2000. Black-headed gull colonies have also long been known on the marshes, but have fluctuated in size. That on Rockcliffe Marsh numbered some hundreds up to 1934, but then declined to a low ebb in the 1940s. It had increased to around 2,000 pairs in 1978 and still numbered 1,267 pairs in 1989, nesting separately from their bigger relatives, but by 2000 had dwindled to ten pairs. Modest numbers (at least 150 pairs in some years) bred on Newton Marsh up to at least 1950, but I have heard nothing of this colony lately. A few pairs occasionally bred on Burgh Marsh in the late 1940s. Tom Johnston found a nest of the common gull on Newton Marsh in 1914, but this species has bred only sporadically on the Lakeland coast, despite its well-established colonies along the Scottish Solway. Breeding was shown in three 10 kilometre squares of the inner Solway in the first Atlas 1968–72, but none in the New Atlas 1988–91.

Along with the gulls are colonies of common terns on Rockcliffe and Newton Marshes. That on the first site numbered around 150 pairs in 1934, but declined thereafter to less than 50 pairs in the late 1940s. They were mostly in a cluster on the Esk side of the marsh edge abutting the open sands. An increase to 200–250 pairs by 1975–78 was accompanied by a wider dispersion within the black-headed gull colony, but had declined to 47 pairs in 1997 and 30 in 2000. The Newton colony was always smaller, with 30 pairs in 1950. Both places sometimes had a few pairs of arctic terns with the commons. Burgh Marsh had nine pairs of common terns in 1949. In 1926, R. H. Brown found a single pair of sandwich terns with a chick among the common terns on Rockcliffe Marsh.

The salt marshes themselves are not important nesting places for ducks. Shelduck are conspicuous in May, flighting in couples to and from the sands to their nests, which may be some little way inland, wherever rabbit burrows or dense vegetation afford suitable sites. Some lay in gorse thickets and others on drier parts of the peat mosses with long heather. Small numbers of mallards breed, usually in rushy ground, and there are occasional pairs of teal and shoveler. Red-breasted mergansers were nesting around the edge of Rockcliffe Marsh by the mid-1970s. Moorhens breed along the bigger ditches with fresh or brackish water on the inner marshes.

Of the smaller birds, skylarks are by far the most numerous, and their rather open nests among grass tussocks or sparse rush growth are easy to spot. They have declined greatly from the 1950s, though 55 pairs were reported on Rockcliffe Marsh in 1997. Meadow pipits are rather sparse breeders and reed buntings only occasional. Little groups of sand martins tunnel their nest holes into the steep sand faces along the bigger creeks, and a few pairs of swallows build under the bridges of railway sleepers spanning the main creeks and channels. Groups of linnets and yellowhammers nest in the gorse thickets on the marsh edges. Occasional nesters include yellow wagtail and pied wagtail.

The breeding birds of the southern estuaries are much the same as those of the Solway, except that gulls and terns are mostly on the adjoining sand dune systems, leaving the waders pre-eminent. In the 1940s and 1950s the Solway gull colonies had to contend with a good deal of egg-taking for food, which put back their nesting season and saw many nests still with eggs in July. And besides predation, all the salt-marsh birds suffered the occasional flooding by exceptional tides between April and June, which could destroy every nest. So, summer was often far advanced before the nesting birds and their young left the marshes to gather in flocks on the flats or to move away to more distant parts. Before the last had gone, the first arrivals among the passage migrants were appearing in late July, to herald the change in bird season on the estuaries.

Autumn and winter

The major Lakeland estuaries have long been a celebrated haunt of passage and wintering populations of swans, geese, ducks, divers, gulls and waders. Macpherson (1892) detailed their importance, and later observers contributed pieces on the main groups, for example, Hope (1909, 1912), Johnston (1909, 1933, 1946, 1952) and Graham (1928). *The Birds of Lakeland* (Blezard et al., 1943) reviewed information to near mid-twentieth century, and this was updated in summary by Stokoe (1962). The ensuing decades produced much fuller data with the annual counts of wildfowl and waders organised by the Wildfowl Trust and British Trust for Ornithology. Prater (1981) summarised this up to 1980, while Pritchard et al.(1992) gave figures for 1985/86–1989/90 over the whole upper Solway, the whole of Morecambe Bay, and the Duddon estuary. Since then the annual reports of the Cumbria Naturalists Union are valuable sources for Cumbria (Table 2).

The breeding waders are already beginning to flock and move around by July. Successful nesters may do so even in June. Lapwing parties are perhaps the most noticeable, and their numbers are steadily augmented, first by birds from inland parts of the region and then in the autumn by large flocks arriving from abroad. Johnston (1909) estimated 10,000 on Burgh Marsh alone in 1902, with comparable flocks on other marshes. Numbers for the whole south Solway averaged 12,300 during 1969–75, but the maximum in 2000 was 5,614 birds. Redshanks, dunlins, ringed plovers, oystercatchers (Fig. 3.4) and curlews show the same tendency to end-of-summer increase in flocks by the addition of local birds and then of more numer-

Fig. 3.4 Oystercatcher flock on intertidal sands of the Solway. (Bob Wright.)

Table 2 Peak numbers of estuarine birds.
These are taken from the Cumbria Bird Report for 2000 (Crowle, 2001).
Bracketed figures are for the month of the count. Because of possible movements between estuaries, only peak figures for the same month can be added together.

Species	South Solway	Duddon	South Walney	Furness Coast	Leven estuary	Flookburgh Marsh	Kent estuary
Great-crested grebe	205(2)	36(7)	36(8)				
Cormorant	474(1)	114(8)		828(9)	116(8)	132(9)	60(9)
Pink-footed goose	6,200(3)	3,000(3)					
Barnacle goose	14,790(3)						
Shelduck	1,265(2)	554(11)	1,358(11)		1,588(9)	362(6)	3,343(9)
Wigeon	2,404(12)	579(12)	1,899(12)		853(11)	680(12)	281(12)
Teal	2,079(12)	870(1)	490(1)				221(9)
Mallard	782(9)	921(8)	339(9)		306(7)		1,069(9)
Pintail	454(12)	539(12)			269(10)		1,251(11)
Eider		415(4)	4,582(7)	2,600(10)	445(8)	127(7)	
Goldeneye	211(3)	119(1)	67(1)		46(3)		
Merganser	65(2)	240(2)	171(11)		47(11)		
Oyster-catcher	10,531(10)	5,448(9)	6,305(12)	12,960(10)	3,314(7)	10,480(8)	1,796(8)
Ringed plover	524(4)	232(11)	323(5)	156(10)	70(11&12)		
Golden plover	4069(11)	800(12)	2,000(1)	222(9)			
Grey plover	475(9)	468(1)	472(1)	325(10)		244(12)	
Lapwing	5,614(9)	920(12)	1,821(11)		702(9)		1,074(9)
Knot	4,700(11)		2,005(10)	2,204(1)			
Sanderling		606(11)	810(5)				
Dunlin	9,967(1)	7,500(1)	2,411(2)	4,246(11)		145,000 (11)	
Bar-tailed godwit	1,253(12)		80(1)		321(7)		
Curlew	2,687(9)	2,561(2)	1,819(8)	1,657(1)	591(9)	2,200(10)	1,787(1)
Redshank	1,572(8)	2,808(12)	2,175(10)	1,500(9)	1,003(9)		
Black-headed gull	no count	3,803(8)		1,331(1)	5,750(9)	1,576(10)	8,355(8)

ous visitors from farther afield, later in the autumn. Golden plover flocks appear during July, first evidently the local breeders, and then the birds from northern Europe. Moulted by the time they join up, the southern and northern birds become indistinguishable, and it is unclear whether they mix in their flocks or stay separate.

Many of the different waders that arrive from more distant lands at the end of summer and into autumn are a mixture of birds that stay only briefly and move on to other wintering grounds, and others that winter on the Lakeland estuaries. A few species once regarded mainly as passage migrants are now known to winter regularly in small numbers. Beginning in July, a few greenshanks and green sandpipers appear, and passing small parties of whimbrels and black-tailed godwits. Later, a few ruffs and spotted redshanks frequent the sands and saltings. Bar-tailed godwits are much more numerous arrivals, some of them in breeding plumage with the red-fronted males especially handsome.

Later come the large flocks of knots, with a total population approaching 10,000 birds, mainly in Morecambe Bay. Dunlins become the most numerous waders of the Lakeland estuaries: Flookburgh Marsh alone had a peak of 145,000 birds in 1997. Sanderlings and grey plovers number around a thousand each. Turnstones are most numerous in Morecambe Bay, and on the Solway prefer the outer coast with its pebble beaches and mussel scars. The less common passage migrants include little stint, curlew sandpiper and grey phalarope, while Temminck's stint, wood sandpiper, red-necked phalarope and avocet are rarities.

For many waders, the intertidal flats and sandbanks provide their main invertebrate food supply, and the salt marshes are mainly a refuge and roost at high tide when their foraging grounds are submerged. Yet the short-billed species, lapwing and golden plover in particular, favour the saltings on which to feed. Modest numbers of snipe and a few jack snipe are, however, long-billed waders that winter on the marshes, feeding in wet places there.

To many people, the geese are the most exciting birds to visit the estuaries in autumn. The grey geese have undergone changes during the last century or so. When Macpherson wrote in 1892, the bean goose was the common goose of the Solway, albeit in modest flocks of up to 100 birds or so; but by 1898 the pink-footed goose was displacing it as the most numerous species. Bean geese continued to visit the Solway marshes, mainly in Moricambe Bay, in decreasing numbers up to about 1940, but are hardly ever seen in the region nowadays. The Solway is now a noted haunt of pink-feet, with internationally important numbers, which arrive from mid- to late September. Rockcliffe Marsh soon became their headquarters on the Cumbrian Solway. From an early flock of 500 in 1904, numbers built up through the next few decades, and in 1941, RAF pilot R A Carr-Lewty estimated 15,000 pink-feet from an aerial survey of the Marsh on 20 October. Numbers vary from year to year and the Scottish sector has the larger population, but numbers build up on the south Solway towards the end of winter, and 12,109 birds in February 1998 represented 12 per cent of the world population. Pink-feet in Morecambe Bay are mainly in the Lancashire part, and the Duddon is more favoured, with 3,000 birds on Millom Marsh in late March 2000.

The greylag was regarded by Macpherson as the rarest of the grey geese in Lakeland, but had increased to outnumber the bean goose on the Solway by 1920, favouring especially the Moricambe Bay marshes, where flocks varied from 200–500 up to 1935, but then fell away almost to nothing by 1960. On the southern estuaries of Morecambe Bay and the Duddon, numbers also built up to some hundreds during the inter-war period, and remained at this level subsequently. Since the 1960s, the status

Fig. 3.5 Barnacle goose flock on Solway salt marsh. (Bobby Smith.)

of this goose has been altered by the breeding and release activities of wildfowlers, which have boosted greylag populations by the addition of feral birds, frequenting inland as well as coastal haunts. Both European and Greenland races of white-fronted geese winter fairly regularly in small numbers on the Solway, and less often on the southern estuaries.

The Solway has long been a celebrated haunt of the barnacle goose (Fig. 3.5). In Macpherson's time this was the commonest goose of Rockcliffe Marsh, though he noted a changed preference for Moricambe Bay by 1888, attributed to the greater amount of new marsh there. He observed a flock of 1,000 on Newton Marsh in 1890. After a similar number in 1929, barnacles declined seriously in the 1930s, but had begun to recover on Rockcliffe Marsh by 1942 (Blezard et al., 1943). From that time they increased until the whole inner Solway was holding in winter the total Svalbard population of the barnacle goose, numbering 11,220 birds during the period 1985/86–1989/90 (Pritchard et al., 1992). Caerlaverock Merse on the Scottish side is their preferred haunt during much of the winter, but there is usually a movement in early March, with most of the birds shifting to Rockcliffe Marsh and remaining there until they return north in late April. In 1998 there were 7,500 on Burgh Marsh on 18 January, and no less than 20,000 on Rockcliffe on 20 April, representing a large increase since 1990. Although John Ray noted this goose as frequent on the Lancashire coast, its appearances on Morecambe Bay have of late been only sporadic.

Only small numbers of brent geese winter on the Lakeland estuaries, their preferred haunts being the muddier east coast inlets with large amounts of eelgrass and algae. The Duddon was the most favoured place, but the brents have preferred the Foulney/Rampside area in recent years. Yet the largest flock for many years, of 50 birds, was seen on Rockcliffe Marsh in 1947 (Stokoe, 1962).

All the geese have traditionally used the estuarine sandbanks as refuges for resting and roosting, and moved to the salt marshes to feed on their nutritious grasses or when displaced by high tides. During the 1900s they took increasingly to flighting inland to feed on farmland, at one time especially on stubble, but latterly on both permanent grasslands and the young growth of autumn-sown cereals. This has created a local problem of damage to crops and claims for compensation, though the difficulty has been greatest over the concentrated attentions of the barnacle flock on farmland around Caerlaverock.

The swans do not form an important element of the winter wildfowl population, and they are as much inland as estuarine birds. Mute swans appear variably in both north and south, but the other two species occur mainly on the Solway. Bewick's swan was formerly regular here, but is now sparse and erratic, whereas the whooper swan has increased in both numbers and regularity of appearance – Pritchard et al. (1992) gave the total Solway population as 290 pairs (2 per cent of the world population) during 1985/86–1989/90.

Ducks are well represented on all the main estuaries, but Morecambe Bay has the greatest numbers of most species, though the proportions within the Lakeland sector cannot be identified. Among the dabbling ducks, this is true of shelduck, wigeon, mallard, teal and pintail. The Duddon has good numbers of these species also. The wigeon was formerly the most numerous duck in winter, but has declined on the south Solway since 1950. Shovelers are now mostly in small numbers everywhere on the Lakeland coast, while gadwall and garganey are scarce visitors.

Of the diving ducks, goldeneye and red-breasted mergansers are the most regular and numerous visitors to all the estuaries. Eiders appear in numbers only on Morecambe Bay, close to their breeding station on Walney Island, and common scoters have a similar, mainly southern presence. In contrast, scaup have been more abundant in recent years on the Solway, while pochard are mainly on the Duddon. Goosanders, tufted duck and long-tailed duck are everywhere few and irregular, and the velvet scoter and smew are rarities.

The main estuaries have large gatherings of gulls during the non-breeding period, many of which come at dusk from inland feeding grounds to roost in safety on the intertidal flats and sheltered waters. Some of the birds, especially black-headed gulls, feed on the sands during the day. Both the Solway and Morecambe Bay receive over 100,000 gulls at peak periods (Prater, 1981). Common gulls are mainly on the Solway, where they are the most numerous species, followed by the black-headed gull. On Morecambe Bay, lesser black-backed and herring gulls reach greater peaks than on the Solway, with 40,000 and 20,000 in 2000. Great black-backed gulls are in much more modest numbers on both estuaries. Together with the foxes that work the sands and saltings, especially at night, these big gulls make an end to birds crippled by gunshot. Although flocks appear in autumn, the terns leave the estuaries in winter for southern haunts.

Of the remaining waterfowl, the cormorant has important wintering populations, with some hundreds on both the Solway and Morecambe Bay. Small numbers of red-throated divers appear on both inlets, but black-throated and great northern divers are only occasional visitors. Of the grebes, the breeding little and great-crested appear regularly on the estuaries in winter, and the Slavonian, black-necked and red-necked are scarce visitors. Small numbers of herons follow the salt marshes and shores during autumn and winter. A few raptors are drawn by the abundance of prey. Peregrines are frequent after their recent super-recovery, and the appearance of one can cause great commotion among the waterfowl. Merlins sometimes hunt the marshes for small passerines, and kestrels search for voles. Short-eared owls are occasional visitors to the saltings, but hen harriers only rarely appear.

Dry lists and figures fail to convey the excitement of the scene on the big estuaries when their multitudinous bird visitors are in good strength, and especially when they are on the move. Both the flow and ebb of the tides cause bird movements, the one as they are driven from the lower flats to the higher banks and saltings, and the other as their feeding grounds are exposed again. Great flocks of the smaller waders, dunlin and knot, wheel and weave in unison as their leaders change course, the rest following with a fascinating precision. The geese signal their intentions with a babble of voices, and the lifting skeins presently enliven the skies as they head for feeding grounds inland. The barnacles are especially noisy and their shrill cackles mark the whereabouts of both flocks on the ground and those heading off elsewhere. Drakes whistle amidst the massed packs of wigeon on the sands, and the mallard ducks quack harshly. At quiet, windless times, the singing of a drake goldeneye's wings carries far as the bird travels the estuary, and the wails of the big gulls ring plaintively at some unseen source of alarm. The experience is enriched by the wonder of the skies at dawn and sunset, which the wildfowl painters have striven to capture in their endlessly varied moods. Yet the tranquillity of the scene at morning and evening flight is usually punctuated by gunshots, to remind the watcher that others are there for a different purpose, and that some birds of the estuaries will be reduced by human hand before the winter's end.

Wildfowling

The Lakeland estuaries had, as elsewhere in Britain, brought forth a hardy breed of men who made a living from fishing and, during autumn and winter, the shooting of wildfowl to sell for food, as well as for their own tables. Their history is better known on the Solway than on the southern Lakeland inlets, though they lacked a dedicated chronicler such as Arthur Patterson who movingly told the story of the Breydon Water wildfowlers in Norfolk. Some were punt gunners, but others relied mainly on shoulder guns. William Nichol of Skinburness, James Storey of Anthorn, James Bryson of Glasson, James Smith of Drumburgh and Thomas Peal of Burgh-by-Sands were the leading veterans. Despite the hardness of their lives all five passed their eightieth year and two lived on to more than ninety. Jim Storey lived until 1946, but probably the last of the old generation of fowlers to pass away, certainly among the punt gunners, was Billy Skelton of Glasson. I used to see him occasionally in the late 1940s, working his punt between Burgh and Rockcliffe Marshes, but a few years later – despite his familiarity with its dangers – he was drowned on the Solway.

So passed the age of professional fowlers who depended on the birds for a livelihood. They were succeeded by the amateurs in what became a growing following of wildfowling as a sport. The wealthy gentlemen shooters had been around for a long time, from the Victorian years of Ralph Payne-Gallwey and Abel Chapman, whose writings had done much to popularise shore-shooting and punt gunning. But numbers grew from the 1950s and wildfowling clubs came into existence, under the umbrella of the Wildfowling Association of Great Britain and Ireland (WAGBI), later renamed the British Association for Shooting and Conservation (BASC). Efforts were made to promote a code of good conduct and to instil a sense of responsibility in the wildfowling fraternity. The Solway Wildfowlers' Club began to acquire shooting rights on that estuary and to control the kind and amount of shooting, instead of the previous free-for-all on some marshes such as Burgh. Rockcliffe Marsh had long been managed as a private shooting preserve, though poaching was sometimes considerable, while on the Caerlaverock Merse National Nature Reserve a permit system was introduced to regulate wildfowling and a part was set aside as an unshot sanctuary. Growing mobility brought wildfowlers to the region from afar, and amateurs with gunning punts towed behind cars were also able to visit the estuaries with little restriction on their activities.

It is difficult to gauge the numbers of wildfowl killed over the years, and to estimate the effect these may have had on population trends of the species concerned. Few bag records appear to have survived to show the overall impact, though a few notable feats are in print to indicate the scale of destruction that both punt and shoulder guns could achieve. William Nichol once killed 40 barnacle geese in the Waver estuary with a single shot of his punt gun, and on a wild day and night on Newton Marsh, Thomas Peal bagged 22 of this species with his twelve bore. Tubbs (1996) studied the effects of shooting on some southern England estuaries, using a valuable series of wildfowl bag records together with data on recent trends in numbers after wildfowling became much reduced. He concluded that sustained heavy wildfowling pressure has had an appreciable effect in reducing goose, duck and wader populations and holding them at levels below the carrying capacity of their habitats.

Besides this, the success of the wildfowl sanctuary at Caerlaverock speaks for itself. Within a few years it had drawn most of the Solway barnacle geese to take refuge there, at least until the end of the shooting season made it safe for them to move to Rockcliffe. The pink-feet similarly learned that they were better off on the Nith and withdrew from the English side until late February. Wildfowlers have augmented greylag numbers, but in the eyes of some naturalists the numbers of feral birds have tainted the purity of the native population and taken management to the level of artificiality. Wildfowling is still popular, but bird-watching has become even more so, and there will continue to be an uneasy relationship between the two. All those concerned about the wildlife of the estuaries must, however, join forces in opposing their common enemy, the exponents of modern 'progress' (see Chapter 12).

Other animals

The other land animals of the estuaries are rather few. Foxes range the salt marshes widely, especially at night, and pick up any wildfowl injured by shooters, but their dens are mostly on higher ground. Otters increasingly frequent the tideway, and mink are well established (see Chapter 4), as additional predators with which the birds have to contend. On the higher and drier marshes such as Burgh, brown hares occur in some numbers, and colonies of rabbits tunnel into banks and sea walls. Natterjack toads breed here and there in brackish or fresh pools along the salt marsh edges, mainly in Moricambe Bay and around Ulverston. The great-crested newt occurs along the landward edges of salt marshes on the inner Solway. Birkett (1970) notes that sea asters are good for insects, and names the moths *Phalonia affinitana*, *Coleophora tripoliella* and *Bucculatrix maritima* as salt-marsh species.

4

The Coast

The open coastline of Lakeland beyond the main estuaries of the Solway and Morecambe Bay may be said to extend from Grune Point to Walney Island. It is a varied seaboard, much of it fringed by shingle beach and sand dune, but with high sea cliffs at St Bees Head along the middle section. The coast from Maryport to Whitehaven and at Barrow-in-Furness is heavily industrialised, while the nuclear complex at Sellafield near Seascale is a more modern intrusion. The only coastal lagoons are of man-made origin, but the flooded haematite mine at Hodbarrow, Millom, and the Cavendish Dock at Barrow-in-Furness have acquired some importance as bird haunts. Flooded gravel pits at South Walney also qualify under this habitat.

The *Solway Firth Review* (Solway Firth Partnership, 1996) and *Morecambe Bay Strategy* (Morecambe Bay Partnership, 1996) are important sources of information on which I have drawn in compiling brief accounts for this and the next sections.

The subtidal zone

This shows a gradient from sediment varying from mud and fine sand to coarse sand and gravel, to submerged rocky 'scars' that are areas of pebbles, cobbles and boulders remaining from the erosion of boulder clays and other glacial deposits, and finally to bedrock. The shallow seabed habitats of the Cumbrian coast are mainly sandflats and sediment banks, especially in the inner parts of the main estuaries. Where these are traversed by shallow river channels, mobile animals live on the sediment surface, but dwellers within the sand are absent. Towards the outer parts of the estuaries, with more varied sediments, the benthic (seabed) community becomes more diverse, and as channel depth increases the fauna within the sand develops markedly.

In the outer estuaries, fine sands on the edge of channels have the bivalves *Mactra corallina* and *Donax vittatus*, while coarse sands contain *Spisula solida*. Areas of silt and mud are colonised by the polychaete *Nephtys cirrosa* and the bivalves *Fabula tenuis*, *Abra alba* and *Nucula sulcata*, and have the sea mouse and starfish *Astropecten irregularis*. The brown shrimp and flounder live on the sediment surface, and when salinity increases in the summer, the hermit crab and cuttlefish penetrate well up the estuary. Faunal diversity also increases seawards, with spider crabs, swimming crabs, starfish *Solaster papposus* and brittlestars. Mobile invertebrates are the main food of many kinds of fish, though polychaete worms are more important to flatfish.

The subtidal scar grounds have a diverse fauna of sponges, soft corals, bryozoans including *Flustra foliacea*, tunicates such as red sea squirt, hydroids, horse mussels and the 'reef-building' honeycomb worm *Sabellaria alveolata*. This community is extensive between Maryport and Allonby Bay. Subtidal bedrock is very localised on the Cumbrian coast and mainly between St Bees Head and Harrington. It has kelp forest of *Laminaria hyperborea*, with abundant foliose red algae, some of them growing on the kelp stipes. These are colonised by the bryozoans *Electra pilosa* and *Alcyonidium hirsutum*. Algal growth beneath the kelp is often dense, but not species rich. The anemone *Actinothoe sphyrodeta* is common. As depth increases the kelp thins out but red algae remain abundant, but below the level that supports photosynthesis, sponges, hydroids and ascidians cover the rock surface. Richer communities occur on the more extensive subtidal bedrock areas of the Galloway coast.

Still deeper sea-water communities are recognised (Solway Firth Partnership, 1996), but are not considered here.

Marine mammals

Both common and grey seals frequent the sea off the Cumbrian coast, but in small numbers. Common seals haul out irregularly on rocks, shingle or sandbanks within the Solway, and in numbers usually below ten animals. Grey seals are more often seen on the Scottish Solway, where up to 150 animals may beach, but there are hauling out sites at intervals from Drumburgh to South Walney and Foulney. Of the cetaceans, only 12 species have been recorded since 1980 within 60 kilometres of the coast in the eastern Irish Sea (Solway Firth Partnership, 1996). Only three species are present throughout the year or recorded as annual visitors in the Solway Firth: harbour porpoise, bottlenose dolphin and common dolphin. The first is seen in small numbers off St Bees Head, mainly between July and September, while bottlenose dolphins are occasionally seen also in late summer. Common dolphins are observed now and then, especially in the vicinity of Maryport and sometimes with the other species.

Fish and fisheries

The marine fish of coastal Cumbrian waters have long been harvested commercially, both from the shore and at sea. On both the Solway and Morecambe Bay, haafnetting is the traditional way of taking salmon and sea trout in the river channels that course over the intertidal flats. The net is slung on an E-shaped wooden frame nearly five metres wide, with which the fisherman wades into the water on either flood or ebb tides, moving position as the level rises or falls. Standing in the tideway to a maximum depth of 1.4 metres, during the runs of fish, the fisherman faces the current and holds the frame firmly against the water, ready to twist it if a fish swims into the pockets of net trailing either side of him. On the southern estuaries and the Scottish Solway, stake nets strung out in a line between poles are another method of catching the same fish. Drift nets operated from small boats are also used on the Cumbrian Solway. Sea angling is a popular sport, whether from the shore, inshore or deep sea, and to support it there is a good deal of bait-digging on the intertidal flats, mainly of lugworms, ragworms and shore crabs.

In 1991 sea fishing produced landings into the ports of the whole Solway of just over 2 per cent of the UK commercial total. The main Cumbrian Solway fishing ports are Silloth, Maryport, Workington and Whitehaven. Shell fishing (molluscs and crustaceans) is important, with scallops and queen scallops (mostly from the Scottish side), mussels, cockles, whelks and periwinkles predominant, and taken mainly by dredging. Landings of cockles were by far the most important in tonnage up to 1992, after which stocks became depleted, and mechanical harvesting was banned to allow their recovery. Crustaceans of commercial value include lobster, edible crab and brown shrimp, caught in pots or beam nets. While 130 fish species are recorded from the Solway within a line from the Mull of Galloway to St Bees Head, some 30 form the core of the local fishery, taken mostly by trawlers. They are a mixture of pelagic (mid-water and migratory) species, notably herring and mackerel, and demersal (bottom-dwelling) kinds, such as cod, whiting, plaice, Dover sole, flounder, dab, turbot, grey mullet, monkfish, rays (mainly thornback) and dogfish.

In the south, Barrow and Flookburgh have the main fishing harbours. Shell fisheries are again important, with cockles especially on either side of the Kent estuary, and mussels generally abundant on the scars (skears) of Morecambe Bay. Mechanical harvesting of cockles is now forbidden, but mussels are taken by dredging as well as by hand. Oysters are farmed at South Walney and Bardsea Sands. Pink shrimps are another major item, taken by trawls behind boat or tractor, and lesser numbers of prawns, scampi prawns, crabs and lobsters are caught. Of the fish, the migratory salmon, sea trout and eel are important in catches, while marine and estuarine species of commercial value include bass, cod, herring, flounder, plaice, sole, whiting, rays and whitebait (juvenile herring and sprat).

Some of the smaller fish and shellfish are important as food for coastal birds. Species such as sprat and sandeel are not taken commercially, but with cockles and mussels there may be more definite competition between humans and birds. Rare fish of the Solway include five species that migrate up fresh water to spawn: twaite shad, allis shad, smelt or sparling, sea lamprey and river lamprey. All except the smelt are Annex II species in the European Union Habitats and Species Directive. The first three are known to inhabit the Cree estuary in Scotland, but their present status in Cumbria is unclear, though Macpherson had records of all three. The two lampreys are present in the Rivers Derwent and Eden, and the sea lamprey occurs off Walney Island. A long list of fish is recorded for Morecambe Bay, of which the common goby and butterfish are the commonest intertidal species (Morecambe Bay Strategy, 1996).

These are regularly occurring species, but there is a large number of others that may be regarded as vagrants or occasional visitors, with exotics such as swordfish, porbeagle shark and sturgeon. Basking sharks may also occur more regularly, though in small numbers.

The intertidal zone

Much of the open coast from Grune Point to Workington, and then from St Bees village to Morecambe Bay, has an intertidal zone of sandbanks thickly littered with boulder scars exposed at low water. These are an important habitat with a varied fauna, and are especially well represented between Silloth and Dubmill Point in the north, and around Walney and Foulney Islands in the south. The scars lie above the sand, but are variably subject to scouring or burial by sand under wave action. When exposed to colonisation, their pioneer animals include barnacles and algae, both green such as *Enteromorpha* and *Ulva*, and red, especially *Porphyra*. If the rock remains exposed, there is further colonisation by periwinkles and brown seaweeds (*Fucus* species).

Where the scars are not periodically submerged under sand, a more varied community develops, though the dominant species can change rapidly. Organisms of the rocky subtidal zone are able to extend upwards onto these scars. The breadcrumb sponge is widespread and conspicuous, and the reef-building honeycomb worm *Sabellaria alveolata*, which reaches its northern British limits on the Solway, locally forms extensive sand hummocks and reefs over the shore. In places there is heavy colonisation by mussels which take over the scars, smothering the worms and causing their reefs to collapse – hence the local name of 'mussel scars' (or scaurs, in Scotland). Ross reefs formed by *Sabellaria spinulosa* occur in Morecambe Bay, and pink shrimps are associated with these (Lumb, 2000). The *Sabellaria* reefs are regarded as nationally important marine features, while the scars are feeding places for fish and both breeding and wintering birds, especially oystercatchers.

Rocky shores with intertidal bedrock and boulders occur mainly between Workington and St Bees Head. They show a characteristic vertical zonation of communities in relation to degree of tidal immersion, as described by Connor et al. (1995). Within the uppermost splash zone above high tide level is a colourful lichen growth of *Verrucaria maura* (black), *Caloplaca marina* (orange), *Xanthoria parietina* (yellow) *and Lecanora atra* (grey). Below this at the top of the true intertidal zone *Verrucaria maura* persists, but with algal growth of channelled wrack, spiral wrack, and periwinkles. On exposed shores there is a band of barnacles *Chthamalus montagui*, but in sheltered places wracks are dominant, with the introduced Australasian barnacle *Elminius modestus* occasional. Next, the mid-shore level bedrock and boulders have wracks (especially bladder and knotted), barnacles (especially *Semibalanus balanoides* on exposed shores) and dogwhelks, with edible mussels. The lower-shore level has serrated wrack with coralline algal crusts covering much of the rock surface, and barnacles, dogwhelks and limpets. Overlying this is a dense turf of red algae with *Palmaria palmata, Mastocarpus stellatus, Corallina officinalis* and *Lomentaria articulata* extending up the shore below overhangs and in crevices.

Rockpools on these shores have a dense covering of encrusting coralline algae on which *Corallina officinalis* often forms a dense turf, with filamentous and foliose red algae such as *Chondrus crispus, Ceramium rubrum* and *Mastocarpus stellatus*. The associated animals include periwinkles, topshells and limpets, often abundantly. The beadlet anemone is often present in pits and crevices. Sub-tidal fringe communities are mostly restricted to the rocky coast around St Bees Head. They have a canopy of kelp over a coralline rock crust and some of the red algae mentioned above, with barnacles and the brown seaweed *Alaria esculenta* on the more exposed shores.

The account by Lumb (2000) of Cumbrian marine habitats and wildlife contains detailed descriptions of *Sabellaria* reefs and other important features. The author notes the interest of the saline lagoon of Cavendish Dock, with its large population of beaked tasselweed.

Shingle beaches

Shingle with variable amounts of sand covers much of the foreshore from Grune Point to Whitehaven and then from St Bees village to the south end of Walney Island and Foulney Island. The strand-line flora is much the same whether the beach is backed by sand dunes or by harder ground. Typical plants of unstable sand and shingle beach are sand couch-grass, lyme grass, sea sandwort, sea rocket, sea bindweed, sea campion, sea holly (Plate 9), yellow horned poppy, spear-leaved orache, Babington's orache, frosted orache and the Isle of Man cabbage. The last is nationally an extremely local coastal species for which Cumbria is the British headquarters. More locally are sea cabbage, saltwort, Ray's knotweed, sea beet, sea radish, henbane, English stonecrop and hoary mugwort, a handsome garden escape. Shingle communities SD 1, 2 & 3 and foredune types SD 4 & 5 (Rodwell, 2000) are represented here.

The oyster-plant had many localities on the Cumbrian shore between Maryport and Walney in the nineteenth century, but decline had set in by 1900. The known colonies gradually disappeared, and the last remaining plants were at South Walney and Foulney in the 1970s. It seemed likely that the species was extinct, but then small colonies were found – or re-found – near Workington and Bootle (Halliday, 1997). A single plant discovered at Mawbray in 1985 was buried by sand after a winter storm two years later, and the problem for oyster-plant is the redistribution of beach material during such events. But the same must happen to many other strand-line plants, so why do they manage to re-establish, whereas the oyster-plant finds it much more difficult? This is a northern plant, which flourishes on the strand lines of the Arctic Ocean, and so appears adapted to rather cold conditions. The loss of its southernmost British localities in Norfolk and North Wales may be connected with the warming of climate during the last hundred years, and perhaps in Cumbria it hangs on under conditions marginal for seed germination and establishment.

Another northern shingle plant, the sea pea, was reported long ago from the 'west Cumberland coast', according to an old herbarium sheet. A single patch was found in 1975 at Seascale but soon after destroyed by beach disturbance (Halliday, 1997). It is a distinctive plant and one to look out for on this coast. The rough cat's-ear is an extremely local plant of the sandy and stony shore from Drigg to Millom: it is an inland plant in eastern England, but strictly coastal in Lakeland. The rare slender club-rush also occurs on a coastal bank near Silecroft.

Fig. 4.1 Rest-harrow on fixed dunes, Mawbray, Outer Solway.

Sand dunes

Starting in the north, the first sand dunes extend southwards from Grune Point to Allonby, with interruption by the town of Silloth. The sand is non-calcareous and the flora somewhat limited. The seaward line of sandhills partly stabilised by thick tussocks of marram-grass (SD 6, Rodwell, 2000) is mostly rather narrow here. It passes into a zone of stable dune covered with a colourful community that includes sand sedge, rest-harrow (Fig. 4.1), thyme, lady's bedstraw, ragwort, biting stonecrop, bird's-foot trefoil, common storksbill, little mouse-ear, bird's-foot, wild pansy and harebell. Buck's-horn plantain is common and rates as one of the most widespread coastal plants (Fig. 4.2). The sand-binding moss *Tortula ruraliformis* is abundant in places. Dune communities SD 7, 8 & 12 (Rodwell, 2000) cover these types. Though patchily distributed, two lovely plants in particular make spectacular displays among the more stable dunes during the summer – the magenta-flowered bloody cranesbill (Plate 6) and the cream-flowered burnet rose (Plate 10). They grow in unusual abundance around Allonby. Spring vetch is rather rare and mainly towards Silloth.

Wet hollows or 'slacks' are not well developed among the northern dunes, and have a limited flora with plants such as marsh pennywort, silverweed, common sedge and common spikerush (slack community SD 17, Rodwell, 2000). On dry parts of the inner dunes, thickets of scrub have developed in places, with blackthorn, elder, gorse, broom, brambles and the large-flowered, spiny alien Japanese rose. The introduced tree lupin is also well established and spreading.

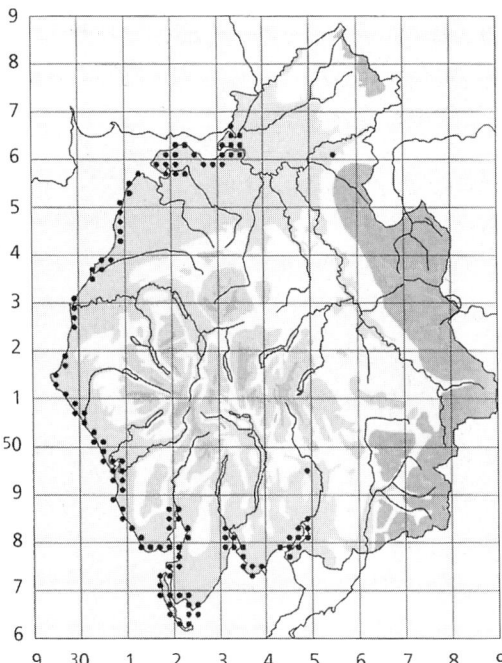

Fig. 4.2 Distribution of buck's-horn plantain, a widespread coastal plant. (Halliday (1997), Map 690.)

The dune systems at Drigg and Eskmeals around the estuary of the Esk and Irt are much more extensive, with large series of marram sandhills, and the sand has a slightly higher lime content in places. Sea spurge and Portland spurge are plentiful, along with field gentian, sticky storksbill, common centaury, carline thistle, sand cat's-tail, early forget-me-not and small cudweed. Areas of stable dune have abundant sea buckthorn, which forms thickets at Eskmeals (SD 18, Rodwell, 2000). It has been eradicated at Sandscale and North Walney because of its aggressively invasive ways and similar control is proposed at Eskmeals. Slacks are quite well developed, with creeping willow, bog pimpernel, and, at Eskmeals, coralroot orchid and round-leaved wintergreen, and there are dune heaths with heather and bracken.

It is only on the southern dune systems of the Duddon estuary at Haverigg, Sandscale Haws (Roanhead) and North Walney (Fig. 4.3) that lime-rich sand occurs and the flora becomes diversified accordingly. The Sandscale system has massive marram sandhills rising to 30 metres with large slacks in between that hold water during wet times (Fig. 4.4). The dry dunes have rarities such as bee orchid, pyramidal orchid, blue fleabane, ploughman's spikenard and the pale pink-flowered form of bloody cranesbill. Moist slacks have crimson marsh orchid, marsh helleborine, dune helleborine, green-flowered helleborine, large populations of coralroot and round-leaved wintergreen, yellow bird's-nest and grass of Parnassus (communities SD 15 & 16, Rodwell, 2000). Moonwort and adder's tongue

Fig. 4.3 Marram sandhills at Sandscale Haws, Duddon estuary.

are dune ferns on basic sand. While the Sandscale vascular flora is rich the bryophytes are disappointing, probably because much of the dune system appears to have become nitrogen and phosphorus enriched. The South Walney dunes are less basic, and their vegetation shows local modification by the large gull and rabbit colonies, as in the spectacular abundance of ragwort in some areas.

Plant rarities of the Lakeland dunes are yellow bartsia only known now at North Walney, but formerly at Silloth, an eyebright, lesser chickweed, hound's tongue, maiden pink, chaffweed, allseed, slender thistle and small adder's tongue. There is an old record for purple milk-vetch at Grune Point: a plant widespread on the Galloway sea cliff-tops opposite, but otherwise unknown on the Cumbrian coast. Yellow vetch was known at Sandscale up to 1968 (Halliday, 1997).

Breeding birds of shingle and sand dune

The beaches and coastal dunes are important breeding bird habitats. The ringed plover is the most widely distributed species occurring all along the low sandy and shingle coast, and is the most tolerant to human disturbance. Dubmill Point to Mawbray Bank had 13 pairs and Grune Point ten pairs in 2000, although these sections are greatly disturbed by recreation seekers, often with dogs. The Cumbrian breeding population is, however, said to have declined since 1984 (Crowle, 1999). Oystercatchers nest widely along the outer Cumbrian coast, though not in large numbers, the largest concentrations being in the south, with 100 pairs on South Walney

Fig. 4.4 Aerial view of dune systems and intertidal flats at North Walney and Sandscale Haws. (Ronald Mitchell.)

and 41 on Foulney in 2000. The shelduck is another fairly widespread species, nesting in the sand dunes and at varying distances inland, either in rabbit holes or thickets of gorse and long heather. Skylarks and meadow pipits breed widely along the grassy upper margins of beaches and on dunes, and wheatears are found where there are rabbit holes. Merlins formerly nested on the marram sandhills of the Cumbrian coast (Blezard et al., 1943), but there are no recent records.

The sand and shingle beaches of this coast were long known as a favoured haunt of the little tern (Fig. 4.5), though the colonies were noto-

Fig. 4.5 Little terns feeding young – a declining seabird. (Bobby Smith.)

riously fickle and inconstant in their occupation and numbers at any one locality. The main nesting places have been Grune Point, Mawbray-Dubmill Point, Siddick, Drigg, Haverigg, Hodbarrow, Borwick Rails, Roanhead, Walney Island and Foulney Island. The Grune colony increased from low numbers in 1900 to over 100 pairs in 1917, but then dwindled away almost to nothing by 1930. It had recovered to over 20 pairs by 1935, but then declined again (Blezard et al., 1943). I saw 15 pairs in 1946, but in 1948 only one pair remained here and the colony seemed to have moved to Mawbray, where I found about 15 pairs. In recent years, very few little terns have nested along the coast north of Maryport (though there were nine pairs in 1993), and the main breeding strength has been either side of the Duddon estuary. Hodbarrow has become the prime locality, with 29 pairs in 1998, though the total Cumbrian population was down from 65 pairs in 1993 to 44+ pairs in 2000.

The sand dunes at Drigg (Ravenglass) and Walney Island are time-honoured nesting places of the sandwich tern, though latterly as alternative sites. Colonies have waxed at one and waned at the other over a long period. Breeding was known at Walney from 1843 and the Ravenglass colony appeared some years later. Both groups flourished and increased slowly up to 1930, but in 1931 most of the birds left Walney while Ravenglass showed a great increase, reaching around 400 pairs by 1932 (Blezard et al., 1943). The number of nests at Ravenglass remained fairly steady at 400–450 during 1954–60, with the Walney colony reported as extinct in 1962 (Stokoe, 1962). Yet the position was again reversed, with Ravenglass deserted since 1988 and the birds all back at Walney, where 720 pairs were reported in 1992 (Pritchard et al., 1992). Another sandwich tern colony was established on the RSPB Hodbarrow reserve in 1991, and this has lately been the sole Cumbrian nesting place, though only 340 pairs were counted in 2000.

Ravenglass and Walney are also long-established nesting places of the common tern. There were no earlier counts of numbers, just vague mention of 'large colonies' at both sites, but a peak of 600 pairs at Ravenglass was recorded in 1955. Around this period, the Walney colony declined to low numbers, but a new colony was founded in 1955 at Foulney Island and rapidly grew to 460 pairs by 1958 (Stokoe, 1962). Numbers here later decreased through rat infestation, and by 2000 the south Lakeland population was reduced to 40 pairs at Hodbarrow. The common tern colonies have often had small numbers of arctic terns nesting on their fringes. Walney Island was for a long time the only haunt and numbers rose to a hundred pairs or more in 1913, but Ravenglass was colonised soon afterwards. In 1955 arctic terns began breeding with the new common tern group at Foulney and reached over 200 pairs by the following year. They were reduced to 55 pairs there in 1997 and 33 in 2000. The roseate tern, rarest of the British breeding species, has nested sporadically in the other tern colonies on the Cumbrian coast. Ravenglass, Walney and Foulney have all been breeding places, but usually with only a few pairs and a maximum of eight in 1961 (Stokoe, 1962). None was recorded during the New Atlas survey of 1988–91, or since.

Tern colonies in general are prone to quite sudden and striking fluctuations and movements. Those of the north Norfolk coast have a similar history of erratic switching between different places. The withdrawal of little terns from the northern beaches could be a human disturbance effect, and the protection afforded on its more southerly breeding stations has evidently been beneficial. Yet the breeding places of the other terns at Ravenglass and Walney have long been protected as reserves, and need other explanations for their movements. Some observers believe the huge increase of large gulls at Walney has caused the terns to desert. There is some evidence that sandwich terns actually seek the company of nesting black-headed gulls, which they more nearly equal in size, as an additional protection against predators. As the account of this last species below will show, the fortunes of terns generally may be linked to predation levels, especially by ground predators. Some movements may be related partly to high tide losses of nests, and storm changes to the sand, shingle-beach and dune nesting habitats. But perhaps the birds show a caprice that defies explanation.

The tern nesting place at Hodbarrow is an interesting development. The excavations of the old haematite mines behind Hodbarrow Point became flooded after mining ceased in 1968, forming a land-locked lagoon of some 80 hectares separated from the sea by embankments. It was acquired by the RSPB as a reserve, and under the RSPB's protection the tern colonies nest securely on an island in the lagoon.

The black-headed gull colony on the marram sandhills at Ravenglass had long been famous even when Macpherson wrote, and it continued to flourish under protection by the Muncaster estate, which had special dispensation to take the eggs, under the county bylaws protecting the bird elsewhere in Cumberland. There were never any reliable counts in earlier years, and Blezard et al. (1943) simply said 'many thousands'. It was widely believed that this was the biggest colony in Britain, with around 50,000 pairs. This was later regarded as an exaggeration, and a more modest total of some 13,000–16,000 pairs in 1958 became the authentic maximum, at least in later years. Both Macpherson and Blezard et al. remarked on the frequently high mortality of both adults and young, but despite many years of systematic farming of the eggs, the breeding population held up remarkably well. A decline to 6,000 pairs by 1951 may have reflected much increased egg-taking during the 1940s.

Simpson (2001) has given a valuable account of the more recent history of the Ravenglass gullery, which also became celebrated through the behavioural studies of Niko Tinbergen and his Oxford team between 1953–67. After decline to 6,000–8,000 pairs during the 1960s, numbers rose to around 10,000 during the early 1970s, but then began to drop away again and by 1981 were down to 2,500 pairs. After further decline the colony became extinct in 1985, and has remained so, apart from occasional attempts by a few pairs to re-establish. Serious breeding failure was noted during these later years, and was complete in 1980 and 1984. After considering all the possible factors, including radioactive pollution from nearby Sellafield, Simpson concluded that much increased predation by foxes on adults, eggs and chicks was the main cause of decline to extinction. This was linked to recurrent myxomatosis epidemics that periodically removed the rabbits that were previously preferred by the foxes and provided a dietary buffer for the gulls, as lemming peaks do for northern birds such as willow grouse and ptarmigan against their predators. In years when rabbit numbers recovered, the fortunes of both gulls and terns were maintained or improved. Ringed plovers and oystercatchers also suffered severely from fox predation, but shelducks, breeding deep in rabbit burrows on the dunes, were unaffected in either numbers or breeding success.

Walney Island was an earlier breeding station of black-headed gulls, but the colony never reached a large size and faded away as the numbers of the bigger gulls increased there. This bird also formed a colony at the Hodbarrow lagoon, some 400 pairs breeding with the terns in 2000. A large colony of black-headed gulls on Banks Marsh in the Ribble estuary to the south had increased to 20,000 pairs by 1989, and may have drawn off some of the Cumbrian coast population.

Lesser black-backed gulls began to colonise Walney Island in 1926 and by 1934 up to 250 pairs were established, with 35 pairs of herring gulls, mainly at South Walney (Blezard et al., 1943). The numbers of both species built up steadily and by the 1969 the lesser black-backs here, at 17,500 pairs, were around one third of the British and Irish total (Sharrock, 1976). After a decline to 10,000 pairs by 1985 (Gibbons et al., 1993), numbers were up to 22,000 pairs in 1997 and still at 18,400 pairs in 2000. The herring gull population reached a similar peak around 1970 and then declined to a present 10,000 pairs. This remains the largest mixed colony of these two species in Europe, and the lesser black-backs represent 20 per cent of the world population. Niko Tinbergen made further studies of gull behaviour here, besides his Ravenglass black-head work. Great black-backed gulls nest in smaller numbers with the other species, the South Walney maximum being 120 pairs, though this is a large colony by English standards. The population was down to 80 pairs in 2000. Common gulls have nested occasionally at Ravenglass and Walney, but have not become established here as they have in the north Pennines.

The eider is a northern and mainly Scottish sea duck, and the first English nest was found on South Walney Island in 1949 by A. V. Millard. The bird then steadily increased until in 1992 a total of 1,500 breeding females was recorded at South Walney, with another 300 at Foulney Island, one of the largest distinct populations in Britain. There was a rapid decline to 500 nests on South Walney and 89 on Foulney in 2000. Littlewood (2000) ascribes this decrease to a combination of decline in availability of small mussels (the staple food), increased fox predation, and an outbreak in 1992 of viral duck enteritis. He suggests that although the large gulls may take some eider eggs and chicks, the presence of the huge lesser black-back and herring gull colonies nearby has been beneficial in deterring other predators and disturbance, thereby allowing the eider population to flourish.

Sea cliffs

For well over a century, the Moss Bay steelworks at Workington tipped the molten slag from their furnaces onto the adjoining shore, where it solidified layer upon layer, reaching a depth of 30 metres or more. The sea has since attacked this new deposit relentlessly, cutting it back to form a new line of sea cliff as high as the slag is deep. It is a strange coast, the line of black crag rising from the wave-cut platform of a rock with superficial resemblance to a volcanic breccia, and almost completely sterile as a medium for plants. Farther south, beyond Harrington, scarps have formed in the Coal Measures on rising ground overlooking the railway. The rock is soft and shaly, and these are not cliffs so much as steep, unstable banks prone to slumping, with pockets of wet, clayey soil in gullies and on gentler ground. There are plants of interest, in tangles of everlasting pea, beds of giant horsetail, hemp agrimony and northern marsh orchid, while patches of the uncommon sand leek grow on the adjoining railway banks.

There are quarried cliff faces of sandstone at Redness Point south of Parton with a few birds, and between Bootle and Silecroft are crumbling boulder clay cliffs up to 30 metres or more in height, but with little wildlife interest. The real cliffs of the Cumbrian coast are south of Whitehaven, where the Permian sandstone rises into the fine precipices of St Bees Head extending over six kilometres and up to 100 metres high (Plate 7 and Fig. 4.6). The line of crag is broken only at the little inlet of Fleswick Bay, though in places, especially in the north, long heathery slopes run down to near the shore. These are dangerous cliffs, often vertical or overhanging, and with much loose rock and large blocks ready to topple over. There

Fig. 4.6 St Bees Head looking south: the main bird cliffs are the whitened faces. Sellafield nuclear complex farther along coast. (Ronald Mitchell.)

is an undercliff of wave-cut platform with variable amounts of fallen boulders and slabs, and it is possible to walk the whole way round below the escarpment at low water, though with a wary eye on the tide. The cliff top is abrupt for much of the way, and cultivated farmland runs close up to the edge, so that there is little of the maritime heath or grassland and scrub that is often a productive wildlife habitat. Only a narrow strip of red fescue–Yorkshire fog grassland (MC 9, Rodwell, 2000) and an earth-topped wall or fence separates the farmed land from the cliff edge.

The dull red sandstone is mostly acidic, though a few thin base-rich strata and wet seepages may be found. The flora, in consequence, is limited in variety and poor in lime-loving species. True maritime plants are in abundance, with thrift, sea campion, common scurvy-grass, red fescue, and sea plantain, while English stonecrop, sheep's bit and wild carrot become abundant around the cliff tops. Less common coastal plants are sea spleenwort, rock samphire, rock sea-lavender and rock sea-spurrey. The cliff-face communities MC 1 & 8 (Rodwell, 2000) are represented. Sheltered slopes have patches of scrub with elder and blackthorn, and a herb-fern community with woodland and damp meadow affiliations, containing rosebay willowherb, meadowsweet, hogweed, angelica, red campion, herb robert, hemp agrimony, pendulous sedge, giant horsetail, primrose, bush vetch, soft fog, early purple orchid, lady fern, broad buckler fern and hart's tongue. Two woodland species have here their largest Cumbrian populations by far – wood vetch and soft shield-fern. The hay-scented fern, a Lakeland rarity, grows sparingly among heather on shady slopes, and plentiful open ground plants include bloody cranesbill.

St Bees Head lacks several plants common on the more basic greywackes and shales of the Ordovician and Silurian sea cliffs on the Galloway coast opposite. There is no rock-rose, spring squill, purple milk-vetch, golden samphire or black bog-rush. And its flora contrasts even more sharply with that of the limestone promontory at Humphrey Head to the south, though this is so sheltered from maritime effects that its affinities are with the limestone habitats of Chapter 7.

A shallow valley behind the headland runs south from Whitehaven to near St Bees village, and contains sands with lake sediments, which are exposed in low scarps at the southern end. These proved to be of late glacial age, with an interesting flora.

Breeding birds of sea cliffs

St Bees Head is the only station of sea cliff nesting birds in north-west England, excluding the Isle of Man. It was known as such to Thomas Pennant in the eighteenth century, and its continuing importance caused the RSPB to acquire the headland as a reserve in 1977. Its colonies of several species greatly exceed those at any of the Galloway sea cliff haunts across the Solway, though there are no breeding gannets. In earlier days, before naturalists counted anything much beyond the contents of their collections, there were no figures for the numbers of birds, but in May 1956 Ralph Stokoe made the first census of the breeders (Stokoe, 1962). First are the guillemots, which occupy the horizontal shelves of the biggest faces, mainly on the North Head. Earlier vague estimates of 'hundreds' may have been wide of the mark. On the section south of the lighthouse an excellent vantage point overlooks a large, recessed ledge with a jostling crowd of birds (Plate 7), but most of the guillemot ledges can only be seen from the cliff foot or, still better, from the sea. The 1956 count was of 2,009 birds.

Macpherson (1892) noted that guillemots and razorbills were prone to heavy mortality after winter storms, with many bodies washed up on nearby shores, especially towards Seascale. In 1969 a catastrophic mortality of auks – the Irish Sea Disaster – came especially to public attention. While winter storms were again blamed by some, bodies of guillemots and other species proved to have high levels of PCBs, and others believed that these and perhaps other pollutants contributed to the large-scale deaths. There were also several oiling incidents around this period. The guillemot breeding population certainly seemed depressed for some years, and the viewable ledge on the North Head had a much reduced number of birds in 1977. After that, numbers steadily picked up again (Plate 7) and approached 6,000 in 1988. After a dip to 4,255 in 1992, the 2000 count gave a total of 7,340 birds on the ledges in May and June. Though still dwarfed by northern Scottish colonies such as Handa and Fowlsheugh, this is a respectable population for southern Britain.

As usual in most seabird stations, razorbills are far fewer than guillemots, for they mostly nest singly, in separate crannies often hidden from view.

For this reason, they may also be underestimated. Stokoe counted 60 breeders in May 1956, but said this was very much less than the total. Recent counts are of low hundreds – 318 in 1992 and 251 in 2000. Puffins were first proved to nest in 1937, and have never bred in more than small numbers. In 1940, 15 birds were counted, and from 1961 to 1991 hovered around 20, but in 2000 only ten were seen. Instead of the usual burrows in earthy banks, puffins lay their eggs under fallen blocks on ledges or in cracks in the sheer faces, especially horizontal fissures (Stokoe, 1962). Scattered pairs of black guillemots use similar sites, often well up from the cliff base: they declined from 15 pairs in 1987 to eight in 2000.

Fulmars colonised the Head quite early on in the great expansion of the species around the British coasts. The first breeding record was in 1940, when five pairs occupied ledges and at least one egg was laid. By 1956 at least 150 occupied sites were counted, and the colony continued to expand along the whole cliff range, leading to competition with other birds for nest sites. More recently numbers have crashed, with only 26 pairs in 1998, but 51 occupied nests were counted in 2000, and another 15–17 pairs on the lower cliffs north of Whitehaven. Kittiwakes were not known to nest on St Bees Head in earlier times, but in 1932 some 20 pairs were established and from this nucleus the colony steadily enlarged and spread along the more precipitous sections. In May 1956 a total of 1,650 pairs was counted at nests (Stokoe, 1962). This is the highest count, and numbers dropped to 923 pairs in 1989, climbed back to 1,630 in 1994, but were down to 1,341 in 2000. Herring gulls were numerous in Macpherson's time, but probably less so than in more recent decades. The full survey in 1956 gave a count of 1,670 occupied nests, using almost all the available sites on the cliffs. There was subsequently an overspill on to the cliff tops, with a few pairs often attempting to nest on fields there; but in 2000 only 544 sitting birds were counted. A single pair of great black-backs nests in most years.

Although cormorants had long roosted on the Head, even in 1943 breeding was unproven, and the first nest was not found until some years later. Stokoe (1962) said that a few pairs bred by then, and in 2000 there were 31 nests. Despite the scope for considerable expansion, the main nesting place of cormorants on the English Solway has been a disused bombing target in Moricambe Bay, where 54 nests were counted in 1999. Shags appear sporadically around St Bees, but nesting is unknown there, despite the existence of numerous breeding haunts along the Galloway and Isle of Man coasts.

Peregrines (Plate 8) have a traditional nesting haunt on St Bees Head and Macpherson, who watched a pair at their eyrie here in 1885, noted that they fed mainly on pigeons and stock doves from the cliffs. Nesting was probably regular up to around 1960, but peregrines went missing from the sea cliffs in the great population crash that hit the Lakeland birds by 1961, and it was not until 1977 that a pair was reported breeding again. By 1981 two pairs were found nesting, one on each Head. Since then two pairs have bred in some years, but in others only one pair. Their frequent associate, the raven, also has a long history of nesting, which continues up to the present day. In some years, two pairs have bred, with sometimes another pair on rocks north of Whitehaven.

St Bees Head was the only regular nesting place of the rock pipit in Lakeland, and in May to early June 1956, 28 pairs were counted, mostly feeding young (Stokoe, 1962). Since then, the species has taken to the slag-bank cliffs at Workington, where eight pairs were counted in 1998. Rock doves formerly bred in small numbers but, as in so many haunts, the native stock is now so diluted by crossing with feral domestic pigeons that the true wild race no longer exists. Stock doves also nest in crannies of the cliffs. Stonechats find nest sites in the heather and bracken slopes of the less precipitous sections, and along the places where the cliffs tail away to lower ground.

The chough has long vanished from Lakeland. Macpherson & Duckworth (1886) said two or three pairs bred at St Bees up to 1860, but disappeared soon after. Nesting was also thought to occur on the limestone cliffs at Whitbarrow Scar, a little way inland in south Lakeland, around this time. Apart from occasional sightings, the chough has not returned to St Bees, which might seem surprising, since the headland faces the Isle of Man where the species has a strong population. It is also not far from former haunts on the Galloway coast occupied at least until the early 1900s. The explanation probably lies in the disappearance of short cliff-top heaths and grazed pasture that are the feeding habitat of the bird; and the now heavily cultivated ground behind the escarpment does not satisfy its needs.

Semi-coastal habitats

In places, especially on the lower-lying coast, the strictly maritime habitats pass immediately inland to others difficult to categorise: though most owe their character to past human activity, many are also influenced by proximity to the sea. Some are waste ground left after industrial withdrawal, and some have soils modified by tipping, including ballast from ships around docks. There is a great assortment of 'weeds' on some of these sites, with numerous aliens and casuals that are listed by Halliday (1997) but not dealt with here. Here and there are communities that have attained the status of semi-natural grassland or heath, with native plants of note. An especially important example was found at Maryport only in 1983 when about 100 flowering spikes of purple broomrape were discovered along with common broomrape, the first being a very rare plant otherwise confined to southern England. Large colonies of pyramidal orchid have been found on industrial sites at Maryport and Workington, and coastal grassland between Flimby and Siddick. The banks of the old iron mine at the Hodbarrow lagoon are an important orchid site, with abundant marsh, spotted, pyramidal and bee orchids, the last with up to 2,000 spikes and the largest colony in Cumbria (RSPB).

Such ground is highly vulnerable to further development, especially for building sites, so that its wildlife interest tends to be fragile. The narrow strip immediately inland from the coast has certain features that owe their presence to the influence of the sea. First is the noticeable frequency of wind-shaped trees, with deformed growth leaning away from the prevailing onshore winds. Certain plants are especially plentiful on stone-faced earth dykes along roadsides and field edges near the sea, such as sheep's bit, English stonecrop and black spleenwort, while the rare lanceolate spleenwort had a northern outpost in this kind of habitat near Millom.

Autumn and winter coastal birds

The Solway coast is quite an important landfall for migrant birds. Grune Point north of Silloth had long been known as a 'hot-spot' from the records of wildfowler–fisherman William Nichol of Skinburness. In 1958 Ralph Stokoe set up a mist-netting and ringing station at Grune, which he ran until the late 1960s, though he increasingly handed over the work to Geoff Horne, Ray Laidler and Ronnie Irving. The earlier results were described by Stokoe (1962). Small fields along the centre of the ancient shingle spit were bounded by tall hedges of hawthorn, blackthorn and gorse, which gave good mist-net sites. Beyond these and inland from the fringing shingle, sand and salt marsh was a dense scrub of gorse, brambles, thorns, briars and elder. Together with the tall trees and shrubbery within the garden of Grune House, this was a great draw for birds during both spring and autumn migration. Horne and Laidler continued the trapping and ringing until 1986, but farming 'improvements' increasingly spoiled the good mist-netting sites and reduced the attractions of Grune for migrating birds, and the work was then abandoned.

Passerines and especially the thrushes predominated among the Grune migrants. Blackbirds were the most numerous, followed by willow warbler, dunnock, yellowhammer, linnet, robin, tree sparrow, whitethroat, reed bunting, chaffinch, blue tit, goldcrest and greenfinch, within a tally of 172 species (Stokoe, 1962). Visible migration could be striking when the wind was strong and steady, and large numbers were often seen flying directly against north-easters. Bob Spencer saw 7,000–8,000 thrushes moving thus on 21 October 1983. Autumn arrivals were mainly from Scotland northwest across the Solway, and spring departures in the reverse direction. The proportion of continental migrants was unknown apart from the obvious redwings and fieldfares. The spring passage tended to have rather fewer birds and species, but with a greater concentration than autumn. The passerine flocks were attended by various raptors and owls seeking easy pickings. Occasional vagrants recorded during 1958–86 included barred and yellow-browed warblers, while Nichol's earlier records added Greenland falcon and Richard's pipit, among others.

Among other land birds, large numbers of skylarks are sometimes to be seen on passage along the Cumbrian coast, with up to 1,000 at South Walney, and short-eared owls are fairly regular visitors to the coast in small numbers.

In addition to the coastal passage migrants and wintering birds noticed under the estuaries (Chapter 3), there are others that belong as much to the open coast of Lakeland, although Bowness-on-Solway on the inner

Firth is as good a place as any to see many of them. The numerous gulls are the common, black-headed, lesser black-backed, herring and kittiwake. Great black-backs are in smaller numbers, and the uncommon species include Mediterranean, little, Iceland and glaucous gulls. Of the skuas, the pomarine and arctic are regular passage migrants in moderate numbers, especially in spring, while the great skua appears more sparingly. The four breeding tern species are fairly common passage migrants, but the black tern is less numerous, though 210 were seen in May 1990.

Most of the cliff-breeding seabirds leave the cliffs in winter, and the truly maritime species take to the open sea. The auks may visit their ledges very early in the year, before taking up full residence in the spring, and numbers of herring gulls and fulmars are sometimes to be seen in the depths of winter. Most of the cliff-breeders are around the Cumbrian coast during the rest of the year, and of the species that do not nest in the region, the Manx shearwater and gannet are common offshore summer visitors and passage migrants, while the storm petrel, Leach's petrel and shag are uncommon visitors. A few winter bird visitors are more to be seen on the open coast than the estuaries, notably the purple sandpiper, which prefers rocky shores. It occurs mainly from St Bees to Workington, where the harbour is a favourite resort, with up to 50 birds, but Walney Island and Foulney are also regularly frequented.

Of the waterfowl, the common sea ducks, in decreasing order of abundance, are eider (6,000+ maximum), common scoter (1,000+), scaup (450), long-tailed duck (10–20) and velvet scoter (1–10). The grebes are well represented in coastal waters as passage migrants and winter visitors, with the great crested (580 at Bowness in January 1999) and little grebe (50 at Cavendish dock and Hodbarrow in December 1999) common, and the red-necked and black-necked grebes scarce. All three divers are regular winter visitors and passage migrants to the coast: the red-throated is the commonest, with 100+ at Bowness, while the black-throated and great northern are uncommon, with numbers usually in single figures.

Other animals of the open coast

The Cumbrian coast is important habitat for otters, although probably most of these animals are not wholly maritime, as they are in parts of Scotland, but move between inland waters and the sea (Solway Firth Partnership, 1996). Their home ranges are large and complex, with males covering 20–40 kilometres but females only 4–9 kilometres, and using five to ten resting sites (holts) on the coast. They hunt especially on rocky shores with a well-developed seaweed zone, notably kelp beds where their fish and crustacean prey is abundant, and do not usually range far out to sea. Salt marshes, shingle beaches and sea cliffs are much less preferred as hunting grounds, but otters feed along the freshwater margins fringing the coast, where they take eels, coarse fish, salmonids, amphibians and birds. Their holts on the coast maybe as close as 0.5–0.75 kilometres, in tree roots, rabbit holes, boulder or stick piles, breakwaters, or field and road drains. Some of these are used for breeding, though the number is not known. On the Cumbrian Solway, otters frequent the lower reaches of all the major and lesser streams from the Esk to Moricambe Bay, and have shown a 31 per cent increase in this area during 1985–95 (Strachan & Jefferies, 1996). The Scottish Solway population has evidently supplied a surplus that has helped to promote this recovery in northern Lakeland. On Morecambe Bay, otters are found sporadically on the Rivers Kent and Leven, where their numbers may be increasing, with a separate population on the River Bela near Milnthorpe (Morecambe Bay Partnership, 1996).

A far less welcome mammal predator is the mink, which has become widespread on the Cumbrian coast, following its escape from fur farms along the Scottish Solway shore. It is said to be continuously distributed along the English Solway coast as far south as Beckfoot near Silloth, and present from there to St Bees Head, but to be declining in 1995 (Solway Firth Partnership, 1996). Mink are also present between the Leven and Kent. They prefer undisturbed rocky shores with a wide littoral zone, and especially bouldery beaches or rocky shores with rock pools, backed by pasture, rough grazing and woodland with rabbits. They take a wider range of prey than otters, and on the coast this is mainly inshore fish, crustaceans and birds. Control by trapping has had little success except by concentrated local effort (Solway Firth Partnership, 1996).

Cumbria is the British stronghold of the natterjack toad (Fig. 4.7), with 23 of 39 known sites (Banks, 1997). Of the 23 sites, 15 are coastal, with sand dunes the preferred habitat in size of populations, though the inner edges of salt marshes are also important. It has at least four dune-slack colonies along the open coast from Silloth to Allonby, with those at Wolsty and

Fig. 4.7 The natterjack toad, a scarce amphibian with its British headquarters in Cumbria. (Rob Petley-Jones.)

Mawbray holding hundreds of adults. The Ravenglass (Drigg) dunes have another important population in slacks and pools dug for the species. The dunes at Haverigg and Sandscale Haws flanking the Duddon estuary, and pools at Hodbarrow, are other major sites. In the Ravenglass pools the natterjacks sometimes have severe competition from large numbers of frogs, but these are subject to marked fluctuations, so that the toads have periodic increases. The common toad also competes with the natterjack in places, and with both great crested and palmate newts, and predates the spawn of all three in some of the pools. The natterjack is regarded as endangered in both Britain and continental Europe, and the Cumbrian population has international importance.

The stable inner parts of the Drigg dunes are a noted place for adders, but this reptile is much less generally distributed along the Cumbrian coast than that of Galloway across the Solway. There are no recent records of the grass snake, but the slow worm and common lizard occur on some of the dune systems.

The sand dunes are good insect habitat, for a variety of groups. Of the butterflies, the dark-green fritillary has important colonies here, where the violets on which the larvae feed are plentiful, the grayling is widespread and common blues are often abundant. Towards its northern limits in west Cumbria, the gatekeeper becomes increasingly restricted to the mild coastal belt, and the small blue is presently known only between St Bees and Maryport, though it was formerly more widespread inland. Several local moths are especially associated with these coastal habitats – four species of dart (Archer's, sand, coast and white-line), the Portland moth, satin moth, dark tussock, pod lover, galium carpet and shore wainscot. Two fairly recent discoveries are the white colon and oblique-striped, the second at its northern limit here (Birkett, 1970). The thrift clearwing occurs at St Bees Head. The cinnabar is now found mainly on the coast, and especially on sand dunes where the larval foodplant, ragwort, is abundant. Six-spot burnets are also probably more often seen on coastal dunes than in inland habitats.

Dunes are important habitats for beetles, with those at Ravenglass best known (Key, 1996). The Red Data tiger beetle *Cicindela hybrida* of the intertidal sand is confined to dunes in Cumbria and Lancashire. The large weevil *Otiorhynchus atroapterus* and marram weevil *Philopedon plagiatus* are common among the fore-dunes. The cliff slopes at St Bees Head have two notable insects in the dark and speckled bush-crickets, and the headland is a productive site for beetles, with the metallic flower beetle *Oederema nobilis* reaching its northern limit here (Key, 1996).

5

The Lowlands: Farmlands, Heathlands and Woodlands

The Cumbrian Lowlands are the Solway Plain, the Carlisle Basin, Inglewood Forest and the Eden Valley as far south as Appleby, the narrowing coastal strip under the western fells from Cockermouth and Maryport to Millom and Barrow, and the southern valleys and coastal plains outside the National Park and the main limestone areas. The northern and western lowlands are almost wholly on non-calcareous drift soils derived from Permian or Triassic sandstones or Coal Measures, but in the south the parent materials vary from Triassic sandstone to Silurian grits and shales, and Carboniferous limestone. Though contrasting sharply with the central Lakeland scene, the Lowlands add much in diversity and interest to the region as a whole.

Farmlands

These are mainly enclosed and intensively managed agricultural areas, but they have in places retained important semi-natural habitats in woodlands, heaths, rough grasslands and peat mosses. Under modern farming trends, all these 'wastelands' have been under pressure from 'improvement' which usually spells death for their wildlife, or at least its more interesting elements. The familiar processes of reclamation have expanded the area of intensive pasture or arable, through destruction of the original habitat by ploughing, draining and under-draining, herbiciding, fertilising and sowing with crops, including commercial grass strains. Hedges have been removed wholesale to enlarge field sizes, and necessary barriers have increasingly been wire fences and, lately, electric fences. Old flowery meadows have been converted almost everywhere into high production rye-grass swards. On the limestone ground north-west of Penrith farmers could not resist attacking even the once delightfully floral roadside verges, and turning them into dull, featureless strips of grass. The black bags of big bale silage and the white bags of NPK fertiliser are stacked all over the place, and the plains and foothills increasingly take on the flush of bright emerald green in the spring that speaks of a huge deluging of the land with plant nutrients.

Plants

As is widely and frequently lamented, this onslaught on the countryside has caused serious declines in all manner of wildlife. Some once widespread and even common plants are reduced to scarcity and a few of the more local species have apparently gone. Among the species whose flowers

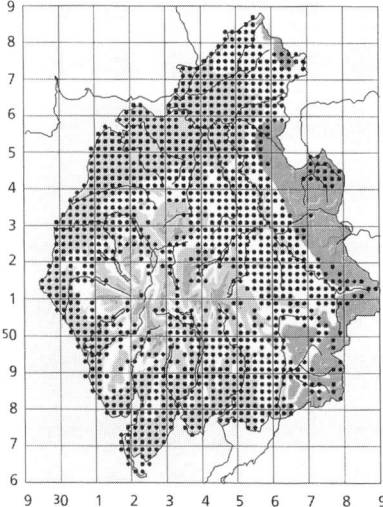 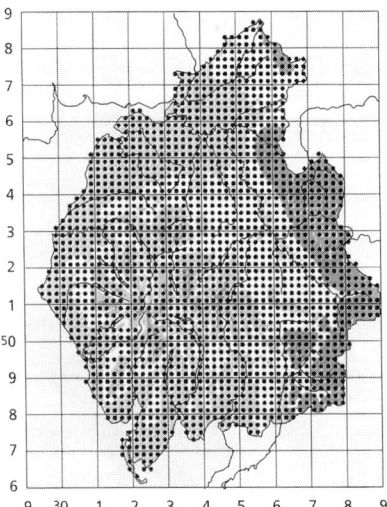

Fig. 5.1 Distribution of curled dock, a widespread plant over all the Cumbrian lowlands. (Halliday, 1997, Map 199.)

Fig. 5.2 Distribution of common sorrel, a widespread Cumbrian plant in both lowland and upland habitats. (Halliday, 1997, Map 196.)

once coloured the hay meadows, the globe flower, melancholy thistle, meadow and wood cranesbills, water avens, great burnet, betony, early purple orchid, common spotted orchid, greater and lesser butterfly orchids, fragrant orchid, twayblade, frog orchid, ox-eye daisy and lady's bedstraw have declined from local abundance to scattered occurrences. On the limestone many damp pastures were once coloured pink with bird's-eye primrose, but few plant-rich examples have survived and these mainly in the uplands. The little burnt orchid once had scattered colonies along the Eden Valley, sometimes on the actual river banks, but they have all disappeared (Halliday, 1997).

Many of these plants have survived, locally in some abundance, on roadside verges and banks, railway sides or undisturbed corners that have chanced to escape serious attention by farmers or developers. These are now the main habitats for some species, such as meadow cranesbill, bistort, crosswort, field scabious, greater knapweed, dewberry, musk mallow and orpine, and the hedge bedstraw is especially plentiful on verges and their hedge bottoms in the lowlands of the northern half of the region (Fig. 5.3). Since this last plant is a notable calcicole in southern England, perhaps a different physiological ecotype has evolved here. Tufted vetch, bush vetch, meadow vetchling, knapweed, foxglove, harebell, red campion, yarrow, bird's-foot trefoil, germander speedwell, cat's-ear, smooth hawk's-beard, sheep's bit, slender St John's wort, wood sage and common polypody flourish in places on the sandy soils of the Permian belt, but the more lime-demanding plants are absent. Yet, even where not deliberately

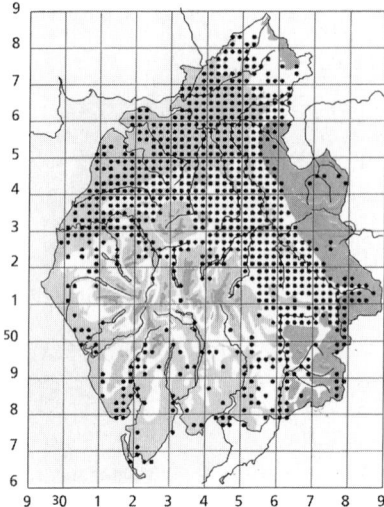
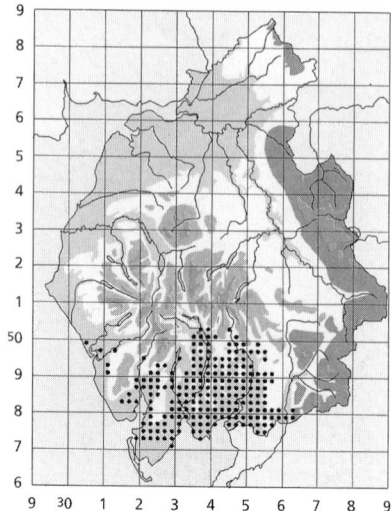

Fig. 5.3 Distribution of hedge bedstraw, a common lowland plant in the northern half of Cumbria. (Halliday, 1997, Map 766.)

Fig. 5.4 Distribution of black bryony, a frequent hedgerow plant in southern Cumbria. (Halliday, 1997, Map 1168.)

'improved', many roadside verges on the sandstone have deteriorated florally, probably through the pervasive effects of fertilisers and herbicides applied to the adjoining fields, which must spill over to affect these edges, leaving the grasses dominant.

Other habitats on the sandstone such as tracks, sandpits and quarries have some less common plants in birds'-foot, thyme-leaved sandwort, restharrow, sand-spurrey, annual knawel, cudweed, field cudweed and heath cudweed. Rarities of sandy soils include field mouse-ear, bugloss and viper's bugloss. The Eden Valley formerly had a remarkable outpost of smooth rupturewort, one of the special plants of the East Anglian Breckland. It was described as growing abundantly in a gravelly field near Great Salkeld, and was known from 1905 up to at least 1940, but seems to have disappeared. As elsewhere in Britain, the once familiar weeds of arable land are much reduced: corncockle almost gone, cornflower now rare, but corn marigold still frequent on the Solway Plain. Weeds of waste ground are nevertheless still well represented (see Halliday, 1997).

The hedges are predominantly of hawthorn on the more acid soils, though gorse, holly, elder and gooseberry are sometimes abundant, but red and black currant less so. On the limestone, especially around the head of Morecambe Bay, there is a greater variety of other shrubs, such as blackthorn, spindle, dogwood and privet. From the end of June, wild roses, mainly dog rose and soft-downy rose, make colourful displays in many hedges, shrubby places and woodland edges. Black bryony is often in hedges in the south of Cumbria, but it has a sharply defined northern limit (Fig. 5.4), while traveller's joy has an even more restricted southern distri-

Fig. 5.5 Black spleenwort growing on a mortared wall: a widespread lowland fern.

bution, mainly around Grange-over-Sands. White bryony is rare and not regarded as a native here.

Mammals

The mammals have been less affected by losses than the birds, though the brown hare is now far less numerous on the farmlands than 50 years ago. The rabbit has recovered strongly from the myxomatosis epidemic of 1954–55, and its subsequent recurrences, and its present abundance in many lowland areas partly explains the spread of the buzzard here. It probably also helps to sustain the fox as a widespread lowland animal. It is difficult to know whether the bats have suffered decline as in so many districts, because earlier knowledge of them was so scanty. Much increased interest in this essentially lowland group has given a fuller picture of their status (Webster, 1996). The pipistrelle and brown long-eared bat are the most widespread and numerous species, with exceptional roosts of the first containing up to 1,000 individuals. The whiskered bat is thought to be widely but thinly distributed, while the closely related Brandt's bat is scarcer, though identification problems make their separation difficult. Daubenton's bat is a local species, usually associated with rivers or lakes, and Natterer's bat is reported from a few widely scattered localities. The noctule has been seen in many parts of Cumbria, and several roosts have been located. T. C. Heysham had specimens of the barbastelle from near Carlisle, but this bat is unknown in Lakeland subsequently.

The short-tailed field vole, wood mouse, bank vole, common shrew and pygmy shrew remain common, and important food items for the still fairly numerous stoats and weasels, which are less persecuted than formerly, through the reduction in gamekeeping. The polecat had disappeared, but Webster (1996) says that animals from the native Welsh stock have been released regularly over the last 20 years, and that the species is becoming quite numerous and breeding well along parts of the Eden valley. He notes that recent road casualties are from the Eden valley, Wigton, Bassenthwaite and south Cumbria.

Birds

Many of the birds have taken a hammering under the agricultural onslaught. Corncrakes were never common in my time, but in the 1940s and early 1950s, a few were to be heard rasping away in hayfields around Carlisle in most years. Corn buntings were patchy, but had some favourite stretches of road, where the males jingled from hedges and telegraph wires and the females incubated in the hay crops. They began on the western outskirts of Carlisle, along the Burgh road to Kirkandrews, and the road between Finglandrigg and Fingland was always a good spot for them. The coast from Silloth to Allonby and beyond was another notable area, they were around Plumpton on the Penrith road, and there were eastern outposts along the Pennine fell-foot, from Langwathby to Kirkby Stephen. Tree sparrows were locally plentiful, the road with old trees from Hutton End to Hutton-in-the-Forest being a noted stretch. The grasslands had many tree pipits, making their song flights from hedgerow trees and bushes, and sometimes nesting in the roadside verges or railway banks.

Lapwings were all over the farmlands of the Cumberland lowlands and in 1909 Tom Johnston recorded finding 16 nests in the same field. Snipe drummed over many a marshy meadow and rough pasture, and Ernest Blezard found five nests in an afternoon on Wragmire Moss nine kilometres south-east of Carlisle. Curlews were reported as widespread breeders in the Solway Plain and elsewhere around Carlisle in 1909, and they steadily increased here up to the early 1950s, commonly nesting on arable cropland as well as meadows and rough pastures. Two pairs nested in the main Carlisle Cemetery in 1951, one of them successfully hatching out on a grave mound. In 1955, three pairs bred on farmland within the Carlisle racecourse, an area of some 30 hectares. Redshanks also increased on wet grasslands on low ground over the same period, and yellow wagtails were widespread though sparing breeders in these habitats too. Grey partridges were common birds of the farmland, and many of the numerous field ponds had moorhens nesting by their edges.

The populations of all these birds in the farmed Cumbrian lowlands are greatly reduced. Corncrakes have completely vanished and it is many years since one was even heard. Corn buntings have gone from around Carlisle and the Pennine fell-foot, but they hang on along the outer Solway coast, while tree sparrows are still widespread but thinner on the ground in the Solway Plain and Inglewood Forest. Tree pipits were decreasing by 1962 and they are now scarce away from the fell-foot country. Lapwings seem fewer with every passing year and it is possible to drive quite a distance through the farmlands before seeing even a single one, though occasionally a little group of a few pairs will be found. Wragmire Moss was drained out of existence, and it would be difficult to know where to look for a snipe's nest in the lowlands nowadays. The curlews have mostly retreated to the peat mosses, marginal land and lower moorlands, though widely scattered pairs still nest on the intensively farmed land. Redshanks and yellow wagtails are much reduced, partridges sparse, and moorhens more restricted than hitherto. Macpherson (1892) knew as breeders three species that have long gone from Lakeland – woodlark, wryneck and red-backed shrike – the last two being virtually extinct in Britain now.

The whole Solway area west of Carlisle and south of the River Eden was mercifully free of private estates and their gamekeepers, so that predators were less systematically controlled than in many parts of Britain. Carrion crows and magpies were always widespread there, and the desultory shooting by farmers and nest-robbing by boys had little effect on their numbers over a long period. Many crows nested in hedgerow trees as well as woods, and with an average distance between neighbouring pairs often of 400 metres or less, there was no difficulty in inspecting a dozen or so nests in a morning. While a lot of nests were robbed, the crows would carry on repeating, and their later nests were often successful, for when the leaves on deciduous trees expanded there was better concealment. Ernest Blezard noted that a pair were robbed of three successive clutches in one spring, yet succeeded in rearing young from a fourth. Magpies often nested in thick hawthorn hedges as well as taller trees, and many territories had a cluster of nests in varying stages of disrepair, besides that currently occupied. Both these birds are mainly invertebrate and vegetable feeders, and despite the outcry at their robbing of other birds' eggs and young, this seems to be a very secondary source of food. Whatever their depredations, they did not prevent the songbird populations in the same areas maintaining healthy levels all through the times, from 1940 to 1960, when I knew the Solway best.

Rooks were also well distributed through the lowlands, and their colonies were a familiar feature of villages and farms where suitable clumps of tall trees provided nest sites (Fig. 5.6). Some rookeries are of considerable antiquity, and the still-thriving one at Dykesfield existed at least back to the 1920s. Another that I knew first in 1943 at Moorhouse in the same area moved a kilometre or so south-west when its nesting wood was felled, and then shifted over three kilometres farther west after storms damaged its second wood. When the BTO conducted the last national rook census in 1975, Cumbria was found to have one of the highest breeding densities in the country. Even though many areas showed population decline since 1940, and this was attributed to the general intensification of farming,

Fig. 5.6 Rookery in field-edge trees, Thringill, near Kirkby Stephen.

McAlone et al. (1997) found a county total of 44,738 nests in 1996, compared with 32,755 in 1975, an increase of 37 per cent. My impression is of an increase in the Cumbrian lowlands over the last ten years, in both the number of rookeries and the sizes of some. They are one of the few birds to have done well from intensified management of pastureland, probably because the high nutrient levels boost numbers of earthworms and other invertebrates.

Jackdaws remain quite common though limited in the lowlands by nesting sites in the form of suitable buildings, tree holes and the monstrous growths of dense shoots made by planted lime trees. They were familiar on the chimneypots of Carlisle and other towns, having learned to nest in flues where fires were never lit. Stokoe (1962) relates the interesting tale of how three jackdaws were trapped inside the chimney of a Skinburness house when a domed wire guard was placed over the top one February. Free members of the colony were then seen feeding the captives through the wires. One bird fell dead into the bedroom grate below, a second descended of its own accord and was released, but the third was fed for two months before it too came down the chimney and was released, strong and plump. The jackdaws then all left. Starlings are numerous through the Cumbrian lowlands, competing with other tree-hole breeders for nest sites. Their winter roosts are perhaps smaller and fewer than hitherto, but a flock of 25,000 birds was reported from the Kirkbride/Wigton area in 2000. Roosts with ten times this number or more occur on the Scottish side of the Solway.

Kestrels are widespread across the lowlands, though not particularly common, and breed mostly in old crow nests in tall trees. Their favourite haunt is a clump of Scots pines rather than extensive woodland, and some nest in scattered hedgerow trees. Smaller numbers nest in old quarries and riverside rocks, and on buildings that provide lodgement. The barn owl is also well distributed over the lowlands, nesting in tree holes and buildings, but has declined in the region as elsewhere in Britain. Blezard et al. (1943) reported it as increasing around Carlisle, where several pairs then bred within the city boundary, but changes in farming practice later proved detrimental. Its population is reported as increasing again and is presently estimated at 140–170 pairs for Cumbria. Ian Armstrong has boosted the Solway population by providing nest boxes, which suggests that nesting sites, rather than food supply, may be the main limiting factor at present. The little owl is another species of open farmland country with scattered trees and woodland clumps. It was no more than a casual visitor to Lakeland in 1943 but, after the first known nest in 1944, it spread from the south and became thinly distributed over much of the region, extending north of Carlisle (Stokoe, 1962). Nest sites are in tree holes, rabbit burrows, old quarries, stone walls, buildings and natural rocks. Its present stronghold is in southern Cumbria and it is said to be declining in the north.

The farmland hedges, lane sides, road or railway verges and uncultivated rough ground (now mainly cut-over woodland) have a varied assortment of nesting birds, with a familiar list of common species: blackbird, song thrush, chaffinch, greenfinch, linnet, redpoll, yellowhammer, wren, willow warbler, whitethroat, dunnock, cuckoo, pied wagtail and long-tailed tit. Goldfinches are less constant in occurrence and mistle thrushes rather sparse. Skylarks are one of the few birds nesting on the farm fields, while swifts, swallows, house martins, house sparrows and starlings are especially associated with human habitations, both rural and urban. Swifts were seen in 1943 evidently nesting in crevices of the sandstone cliffs in Baron Wood, as an unusual departure from normal habits (E. Blezard). The sand martin nests especially where excavations have left bare sandbank faces. A familiar bird of town gardens and shrubberies, the collared dove is one lowland species that is flourishing.

Insects

Some of the rough, unimproved hay meadows and pastures in the Solway Plain and Inglewood Forest had abundant devil's bit scabious, and were famous for their colonies of the marsh fritillary butterfly (Fig. 5.7), whose larval foodplant this is. Orton Woods only three kilometres west of Carlisle had a noted haunt of the insect in rough meadows around the woodland edge. In good years at the end of May, the air was fairly dancing with these butterflies over the largest, Tyson's Meadow. Orton was well known for varieties, and among the earlier collectors were the Revd H. D. Ford, Vicar of nearby Thursby, and his son E. B. Ford, who wrote the first and classic New Naturalist *Butterflies* in 1945, which figures specimens from this locality. Nearly all the old meadows around Orton Woods were 'improved' and the foodplant eradicated in the 1960s. The surviving fragments of untreated

Fig. 5.7 Marsh fritillary: a famous Lakeland butterfly, now known at only three locations, two of them in Inglewood Forest. (David Clarke.)

grassland with the scabious became too small to hold a viable population of the butterfly, and it died out.

Another five kilometres west-north-west, Finglandrigg Woods also had good marsh fritillary meadows around their edges, but the best were also ruined similarly. The butterfly hung on in the last one but, despite efforts to manage it after the area became a National Nature Reserve, the insect fizzled out in 1991. The marsh fritillary survives in at least two localities in Inglewood Forest, where areas of rough grassland have chanced to remain unaltered, but suffers serious setbacks during wet summers.

Other notable butterflies of the old meadows from Orton to Greystoke are dingy skipper, dark green fritillary and small pearl-bordered fritillary. The lowlands more widely also have numerous ringlets, meadow browns, wall browns, common blues, small heaths, small coppers, large skippers and green-veined, small and large whites. Orange tips are a common springtime butterfly wherever their larval foodplants, lady's smock and jack-by-the-hedge, are abundant, and the summer flowers draw small tortoiseshells and peacocks. Immigrant red admirals and painted ladies vary in numbers from year to year, and clouded yellows are still more erratic: 1947 was a great summer for the last, but former numbers are probably a thing of the past, though it was widespread in 1992. Of the rare visitors, the Camberwell beauty turns up now and then.

The fritillaries have all become scarce, especially the pearl-bordered, but many of the other butterflies remain common along roadside verges, railway banks, field edges, green lanes and waste ground of all kinds. A noteworthy species of railway embankments and cuttings is the small blue, for its foodplant, the kidney vetch, has an important habitat there. This plant belongs to open and unstable or disturbed habitats, but is fairly soon crowded out by more vigorous plants. Colonies of the small blue thus tend to be ephemeral, fading out and re-appearing elsewhere as the fortunes of their foodplant dictate. A once-famous colony in a deep railway cutting at Cowran, on the Carlisle-Newcastle line, was extinct in 1950, for the place had become smothered by brambles and bracken.

The distinctive lowland moths include the large yellow underwing, dark arches, garden tiger, cabbage moth, angleshades, ghost swift, white ermine, burnished brass, silver Y, beautiful golden Y, magpie and vapourer, to name a selection. Less frequent nowadays on roadside verges are the drinker, whose grass-feeding caterpillars were once common there, and the chimney sweeper. The large elephant hawk (Plate 14) has become more frequent with the increase in its larval foodplant rosebay willow-herb, but the narrow-bordered bee hawk, which fed at lousewort flowers in the old meadows, is now seldom seen. Of the rare migrant hawk-moths, the death's head appeared occasionally in potato fields and the convolvulus at petunia and tobacco flowers, while larvae of bedstraw and striped hawks were found in different years on fuchsias in the grounds of Tullie House Museum.

Biting flies can make life tedious at times during summer, especially the numerous grey clegs and the persistent green-eyed *Chrysops caecutiens*, but large horseflies such as *Tabanus sudeticus* and *T. bisignatus* are less common. The grasshoppers include the widespread common green, common field, meadow and common groundhopper (Hewitt, 1993).

Heathlands

Cumberland had a good many outlying fragments of lowland heath similar to those of southern England, with heather, gorse and bracken, especially on the podsolised sandy soils of the Permian area. Possibly this was the vegetation of Newtown Common, where in 1785 Dr John Heysham found three nesting pairs of hen harriers within two kilometres of the western edge of Carlisle; but it was even then recently planted with young trees, and reclamation of such habitat proceeded apace during the nineteenth century. It has continued to lose ground in recent years as the improvers sought every bit of reclaimable land.

The largest areas of dry *Calluna* heath were on the ridge of low sandstone hills flanking the Eden Valley, mainly on the west side, from King Harry's Common and High Stand in the north to Whinfell south-east of Penrith. Around five square kilometres here have been lost to afforestation and reclamation to farmland even since 1960, especially on Lazonby Fell and Baronwood Park, and the biggest remaining expanse is on Wan Fell. The once open road across Baronwood Park now fences off the lush cattle and sheep pastures that have replaced the heather moor. The dry edges of the Solway peat mosses also have similar heath, recently derived from bog. Fragments of good heathland occur at intervals along the lowland coastal strip of west Cumbria, as at Salta Moss, Nethertown, Hallsenna Moor and Whitbeck Moss. There are few lowland heaths in south Lakeland, except behind the dunes at North Walney and Sandscale, and the last has a species-rich wet heath. Many remaining heaths show invasion by Scots pine and birch, and where unchecked by fire or deliberate management, this can lead to replacement by woodland or scrub.

Plants

Apart from the dominant ling heather, other dwarf shrubs are abundant, especially on the sandstone hills: bell heather and bilberry, with cowberry on Lazonby Fell illustrating the affinities with subalpine heath of the fells (heath community H 9, Rodwell, 1991b). Crowberry is rare and more often on the peat mosses, while petty-whin is a dwindling representative of both lowland and upland heaths. Some sites become invaded by common gorse, but this is often held back by deliberate burning. The heaths typically have a mossy underlayer with *Hypnum jutlandicum, Pleurozium schreberi* and *Dicranum scoparium*, but in places they are rich in lichens of the Cladonia 'reindeer moss' group, especially *C. portentosa*. *Hypogymnia physodes* is abundant on heather, and in bare places are other lichens such as *Cladonia coccifera, C. pyxidata, C. floerkiana, C. furcata, C. gracilis, C. macilenta, C. rangiformis, Cetraria aculeatum* and *Baeomyces roseus*.

In places, the dry heath grades into a moister type with cross-leaved heath, heath rush and round-leaved sundew (M 16), and then into real bog. The complete sequence may be seen at Walby Moor, just east of Carlisle, where the dry heath also has abundant western gorse (H 8). Finglandrigg Woods west of the city have an area of open shallow bog, grading into heath with scattered pines, and this has a remarkable abundance of the dwarf gorse (H 2). This plant of heathland in southern England has several isolated northern outposts around Carlisle, but the Finglandrigg population is by far the biggest. At Kingmoor on the northern outskirts of Carlisle, a strip of heath with an interesting flora, including dwarf gorse, petty-whin and whorled caraway, has deteriorated and lost these species in recent years. Damp ground on Wan Fell provided outposts for whorled caraway and marsh clubmoss: neither has been seen in the last few years. Marsh gentian is a plant of southern wet heath and valley mire; Halliday (1997) reports it as still on Walney Island, evidently in a heathy community, but its only other extant site, in Furness, is described as 'a marshy field'. The uncommon moss of damp heathland, *Hypnum imponens*, has several localities on Cumberland heaths.

Animals

Many farmland birds also occur on the heaths, but a few are especially characteristic. Nightjars once nested widely among the heather and bracken, and had a favourite haunt on Penrith Beacon until at least 1955. They may still occur sparingly, but are seldom reported. Stonechats were typical of good heather ground, and whinchats also bred on the heaths, especially where these had areas of rough grassland. Open growths of colonising pine have now and then drawn both crossbill and siskin to nest. Curlews breed on many heaths, while both meadow pipits and skylarks are common. Tree pipits bred where scattered trees and tall shrubs provided songposts. Redpolls sometimes nest in long heather, and both linnets and yellowhammers are associated with gorse.

The mammals also include many farmland species, but have no others that belong especially to heathland. Foxes, badgers, stoats, weasels, rabbits, hedgehogs and field voles are all widespread on lowland heaths, and roe deer range over some of them. Adders are widespread, though less often seen than on the peat mosses, and common lizards are usually present. Frogs and toads occur wherever there is wet ground. The grayling is a notable butterfly, and there is a group of day-flying moths virtually identical with that found on upland heaths and described on p. 247. Heather here, as in the uplands, occasionally suffers defoliation by heavy infestations of heather beetle. The mottled grasshopper is found especially on dry heathland.

Woodlands

Fragments of native woodland have survived widely across the lowlands, albeit in mostly modified form and with the addition of numerous artificial plantations of varying kind and size. Virtually all the oak woods are the replanted successors to earlier forest, but have probably retained the same flora. Some of the best oak woods have been felled and largely replaced by conifers during the last 50–60 years – Walton Wood near Brampton, Park Wood near Wigton, Flimby Wood near Maryport, Coombs Wood near Armathwaite, and Melkinthorpe Wood near Penrith, for example. On more basic soils are mixed broadleaved woods in which oak shares dominance with ash, birch, wych elm (formerly) and hazel as understorey. Birch wood springs up naturally on felled woods that are not replanted. Alders are widespread on damp alluvial soils, and in waterlogged ground often accompanied by willows. Aspen also occurs widely, often as clones evidently originating from a single tree.

Planted Scots pine, beech and sycamore spread around of their own accord, and there is a sprinkling of exotics. Field maple is widely scattered though probably native only on the southern limestone, and the frequent hornbeam is probably all planted, though it regenerates in places. Many of the most interesting lowland woods are a mixture of types, reflecting varying soil conditions and vagaries of past management. Some also combine with other habitats to give still greater diversity of flora and fauna within a single area (see p. 116).

The peat moss pine woods raise questions about the status of this tree. In many places where Scots pines have colonised the drier edges of raised bogs or the centres of smaller mosses, they have clearly come from adjoining older plantations, though the regenerating growth is self-sown and has a natural look. The colonising trees vary from vigorous normal specimens to contorted and dwarfed forms showing degrees of checked growth through waterlogging. In some localities, the appearance of the pine-grown bogs so resembles the taiga forest bogs in Fennoscandia that it is tempting to believe that these trees are truly native to the site (Plate 17).

The pollen record for several peat mosses of the Cumberland Lowland (Walker, 1966) shows Scots pine constantly present though at low frequency right through the postglacial period up to the latest horizons examined, dating to 2,800–3,300 years ago. Pearsall & Pennington (1973) and John Birks consider it possible that native pines did survive on lowland mosses and even became a source of seedling pines when it later became fashionable to plant this tree. Scots pine was clearly limited in ancient times by the availability of dry acidic substrates, but these would be continuously available around the drier edges of the peat mosses, even during the past 4,000-year episode of human forest clearance.

Birches colonise the drying bog edges readily and soon produce dense thickets of young growth that later open out through self-thinning. Birch woods are found around or on most of the lowland raised bogs and some of the older blocks contain quite large trees (Plate 16). They are mostly of downy birch, but silver birch occurs in a few places. Some peat moss woods have rowan and holly, and one on the north-east edge of Bowness Moss has an abundance of Swedish whitebeam, evidently from a planted source. The peat moss woods add to the diversity of habitat in these places.

Some of the most interesting lowland woods are along the rivers draining to the Carlisle basin, which have cut rocky glens and gorges along their lower courses. Mostly these are on acidic Permian Sandstone, but in a few places, Carboniferous rocks give more basic soils. The Eden gorge between Lazonby and Armathwaite is the most spectacular of these rocky glens, well known locally via the Nunnery Walks which, from the Staffield side, first follow the deep and dank waterfall ravine of the tributary Croglin Water (Fig. 5.8), and then the Eden banks along the much wider and more open main river valley. There is a fine view of the 30-metre vertical New Red Sandstone crag of the Chain Rock, which drops sheer into the river on the opposite side (Plate 12). Coombs Wood on the north bank was a victim of World War II felling and coniferisation, but blocks of broad-leaved woodland remain (Plate 15). The crags continue at intervals to near Armathwaite, and then there are lesser outcrops near Hornsby, Cotehill, Corby and, finally, Rockcliffe, while upstream more rocks occur at Eden Lacy, Udford and near Appleby.

To the south of Carlisle, the River Petteril has a sandstone glen at Wreay Woods, while the Caldew runs through a rocky limestone section above Sebergham and its tributary stream of Parkend Beck has cut a deep little limestone ravine at the Howk, almost in Caldbeck. Gelt Woods near Brampton are another local beauty spot along the narrow rocky glen of a tributary of the River Irthing. Here, some of the sandstone crags owe their presence to quarrying, said to go back to the Roman era. Patches of woodland extend along the Gelt north of Castle Carrock, and overlie limestone bedrock. Below Gilsland, the River Irthing has a fine section of steep, cliff-girt valley at Combe Crag below Low Row. The River Lyne has two secluded rocky sections between Kirklinton and Shankbridge End, and after branching into the Black and White Lyne below Roadhead, these twin streams each have another. The River Liddel, forming the Border between

THE LOWLANDS: FARMLANDS, HEATHLANDS AND WOODLANDS   113

Fig. 5.8 Waterfall of Croglin Water, on New Red Sandstone, Nunnery Walks, Kirkoswald.

Cumbria and Scotland, has a rocky glen cut through Carboniferous strata at Penton Linns.

Plants

The lowland woods are usually fenced against stock, so that they are mostly ungrazed and have a more luxuriant ground vegetation than typical hill woods. Those on the most acid and especially peaty soils often have a dominance of broad buckler fern that excludes most other plants (Fig. 5.9), while dry woods may have a comparable abundance of bracken. Other acidic podsolic soils have dense growths of great woodrush and bilberry. In some woods on mildly acidic brown earths there is great abundance of bluebells, with greater stitchwort, red campion, wood sorrel, wood anemone, wood sage, heath violet, three-nerved sandwort, hairy woodrush and soft fog. As soil base status and nitrogen content increase, growths of bramble become increasingly represented, and reduce the field layer diversity. Many of these lowland woods fall into the category W 10 of Rodwell (1991a), but the fern-rich ones belong to W 4 & W 11, while pine woods approximate to W 18.

Fig. 5.9 Dominant growth of broad buckler fern in peat moss birch wood, Finglandrigg Woods National Nature Reserve, near Kirkbride.

Many mixed broad-leaved woods on basic substrates have a varied herbaceous community with dog's mercury, wild garlic, herb robert, primrose, sanicle, water avens, herb bennet, enchanter's nightshade, celandine, self-heal, bugle, wild strawberry, barren strawberry, sweet woodruff, wood speedwell, ground ivy, common figwort, moschatel, wood sedge, false brome, hairy brome, wood meadow-grass, wood melick and giant fescue. Creeping buttercup, golden saxifrage and remote sedge are typical of wet, clayey seepages. More local plants of the basic woods are wood forget-me-not, goldilocks, wood stitchwort, large bitter-cress, herb paris, giant horsetail, hemp agrimony, cuckoo pint, broad-leaved helleborine, bird's-nest orchid, early purple orchid, pendulous sedge, smooth sedge, greater tussock-sedge and wood millet. These woods belong to W 9 and W 5–7 (Rodwell, 1991a). In most of the glen woodlands, geological differences in substrate produce examples of both acidic and base-rich woodland.

The rarer plants of the Eden gorge are especially within the enriched alluvial flood zone of the river, which receives water from limestone head-streams: they include the scarce and delicate yellow star-of-Bethlehem, which flowers in March; round-fruited rush; an outlying colony of bird's-foot sedge; northern bedstraw, sand leek and wild onion. Alternate-leaved golden saxifrage grows in rocky places and heath cudweed along the sides of sandy tracks. The upper Gelt has a locality for the very rare sword-leaved helleborine. Wood fescue grows only on the English side of Penton Linns, while variegated horsetail is confined to the Scottish bank.

All the river gorges have sections with dank, shady rocks and banks where ferns luxuriate and often stay green through winter: broad buckler fern, male fern, lady fern and hard fern are all in profusion, and on the more basic substrates are fine clumps of prickly shield-fern and hart's tongue. The soft shield-fern is local and more in the south, also on basic soils. Bracken is everywhere and the Eden gorge has especially tall growths. Bracken and bramble communities W 24 & 25 (Rodwell, 1991a) associated with woodland and scrub are widespread.

While exploring one of these glens in 1956 I made a startling find. A small cave in a shady rock face had a cluster of fern fronds hanging down from its roof, and when I peered closely at them it dawned on me that this was the famous Killarney fern. There were just seven fronds and the longest was only 11.5 centimetres, but it was the real thing. I hoped there would be more, but not another vestige of the fern ever turned up, either in this glen or any other. Sadly, after the winter of the great frost of early 1963, only the shrivelled dead fronds remained. In 1957 I came upon a tiny patch of its smaller relative, Tunbridge filmy fern, on shady rocks in another lowland glen, where it clung to existence. Many years later, I could find no trace of the fern, and concluded that it, too, was a victim of the great 1963 frost or the drought of summer 1976.

These warmth and moisture-loving filmy ferns had evidently hung on under marginal conditions after human actions had opened up their habitats and reduced once healthy and more abundant growths to last depleted remnants. A chance extreme of weather was the last straw in their struggle to survive. Even under a wet climate, many of these delicate, moisture-loving plants depend on continuous shade of leafy trees in summer. Remove this and they die. The rarer species also appear to have limited regenerative powers, at least under present conditions. Once gone, they do not re-establish of their own accord. In ancient times, say 5,000 years ago, the woods of this district would probably have had local abundance of the Tunbridge filmy fern and also hay-scented fern, another oceanic species now absent from north Cumbria and confined to the mild and humid south-west.

The lowland woods often have abundant growths of mosses and liverworts, though mostly of common species such as *Pleurozium schreberi, Hylocomium splendens, Hypnum cupressiforme, Thuidium tamariscinum, Plagiothecium undulatum, Dicranum majus, D. scoparium, Polytrichum formosum, Mnium hornum, Leucobryum glaucum, Lophocolea bidentata* and *Pellia epiphylla*. The wooded sandstone glens and their outcrops also provide habitats for some rarer species, which mostly have their main Cumbrian occurrences in the woods of the wetter Lake District (see Appendix list). Lichens are well represented, with *Bryoria fuscescens, Cetraria chlorophylla, Evernia prunastri, Parmelia caperata, P. saxatilis, P. sulcata, Peltigera praetextata, P. horizontalis, Platismatia glauca, Usnea subfloridana, Ramalina farinacea, Ochrolechia tartarea* and *Sphaerophorus globosus*. The lichen flora has, however, been depleted by atmospheric pollution and acidification, and species of the Lobarion community, even *Lobaria pulmonaria*, are now quite rare. Mosses of the genera *Ulota* and *Orthotrichum*, which grow on branches and twigs of trees and shrubs, have also declined through this effect.

Fig. 5.10 Horse's hoof fungus on birch, Baron Wood, Eden Valley.

The rich fungus flora of the woodlands is dealt with briefly in Appendix 1 (Fig. 5.10).

Other woodlands

Some woodlands are difficult to classify, because of their mixture of habitats, as at Orton Woods three kilometres west of Carlisle. The name Orton Moss still appears on the Ordnance Survey maps, and part of the woodland and carr occupies the site of former raised bog. In an old peat cutting was a surviving fragment of bog with hare's-tail and common cotton-grasses, bog rosemary and bog myrtle on a carpet of bog moss. It was kept open only by periodic cutting of the invading birch and willow, but this has lapsed and the bog community has almost disappeared. The poor fen associated with the willow–birch carr has abundant alder buckthorn, bottle sedge, narrow buckler fern and, until recently, wood small-reed. The carr community probably belongs to W 2 (Rodwell, 1991a).

Although pines and oaks have been cut for timber at intervals, Orton Woods are largely unmanaged and have an unkempt appearance well deserving the term 'wildwood'. Holly forms a dense understorey in places and many trees are festooned with trailing masses of honeysuckle. Luxuriant growths of broad buckler fern cover the woodland floor in many places, and there is still a good deal of tall bilberry. Damp ground has abundant bogmoss and hairmoss. Petty whin survived as a relic of open ground, but when last seen was becoming smothered by the encroaching trees. Royal fern, lesser wintergreen and bitter-vetch are other uncommon plants. Another five kilometres west-north-west of Orton are Finglandrigg

Woods, with a similar mixture of woodland types, including extensive willow carr, as well as dry and wet heath and acidic grassland (see p. 110).

Scattered around the lowlands are many small to medium-sized plantations of Scots pine. While mostly undistinguished botanically, some of those around Carlisle have long been famous as the habitat of the northern pine-wood orchid creeping lady's tresses. In several the plant attained an abundance seldom seen in its truly native localities in the ancient Highland pine woods (Plate 13). One by one, its pine-wood haunts were felled and the plant destroyed. The best of the more recent stations was Irongill Wood near Welton, but the orchid had already become much reduced through invading holly before this wood was levelled in 1997. It survives sparingly in a handful of places, including Whinfell Forest east of Penrith. Attempts have been made to keep it going by transplants, as by R. Laidler in Orton Woods, where its original pine compartment was felled in 1956, and in Thurstonfield Woods where it was unknown previously.

It has been supposed that these Cumbrian occurrences are introductions, through the planting of Scottish seedlings carrying the mycorrhizal stage of the orchid. The colony on Cumwhitton Moss nevertheless has a native appearance, growing under birch as well as pine, and through *Sphagnum* carpet; and it is in company with other northern pine-wood plants such as cowberry, crowberry, lesser twayblade, lesser wintergreen and the mosses *Ptilium crista-castrensis* and *Dicranum polysetum*. The association of all these plants with Scots pine also supports the view that this tree could be native to some of its peat moss sites. The pine-wood community here is referable to W 18 (Rodwell, 1991a) of the Highlands.

Mammals

In my youth, red squirrels were constantly present in the woods of the Solway Plain and Eden Valley, whether coniferous or broadleaved, or mixtures of both. Their dreys were numerous, usually high in the trees, but I once found one with young in a tall hawthorn hedge adjoining a wood just outside Carlisle. They remained widespread at least into the 1960s, but are reported to have become a declining and perhaps threatened species within more recent years (Webster, 1996). Orton and Finglandrigg Woods remain strongholds in the Solway district. Regrettably, the steady expansion northwards of the grey squirrel has reached Lakeland during the last 20 years. Webster (1996) says that it is widespread in the Arnside and Silverdale district and is appearing in southern parts of the Lake District. There are a few isolated records for the north of the region. The extensive new conifer forests of Cumbria, especially in the Borders district, may prove to be a red squirrel refuge if broadleaved woodlands become an insecure habitat (see p. 187).

Roe deer were not well known to Macpherson in 1892, but there is a suspicion that he was not fully informed on their status then. Vague references to small numbers around Naworth, Netherby and the Eden Valley imply that their Cumbrian refuge was the preserved estates of the major landowners. Britten (1909) regarded them as stragglers in the Eden Valley, possibly becoming more established near Armathwaite. Ritson Graham took a keen interest in the roe and traced its expansion in Cumberland, which he believed began in the War period 1914–18, when woodcutters invaded its well-established haunts and caused the animals to disperse to less disturbed places. The animal began to appear in woods at Orton and Thurstonfield west of Carlisle, and Sebergham and Rosley to the south. He found that they tended to follow the river valleys, of Caldew, Petteril, Gelt, Cairn and Irthing, exploring both up and down and settling in the most congenial wooded spots. Colonisation of Greystoke Park was stopped, because of alleged damage to young trees, and the animal was not a permanent inhabitant of the west Cumbrian industrial belt. When Graham summarised his findings in 1933, the roe was a widespread resident in woodlands through most of Inglewood Forest and north-east Cumberland up to Liddesdale on the Scottish Border, and in the eastern part of the Solway Plain.

Webster (1996) states that roe deer are now generally distributed in suitable habitat, but are especially numerous in the south of Cumbria, where they are often accused of damage by gardeners. Graham found that woods of mixed trees were preferred, but those with abundant oak seemed favoured above all. The availability of food, in the form of plentiful ground vegetation, especially herbs and shrubs such as bramble and raspberry, is important, and the tendency to winter wanderings appeared linked to search for the best fodder.

The badger provides perhaps the most remarkable story of any Lakeland mammal. Macpherson (1892) clearly believed that the animal was long extinct as a wild species in the Lakeland area and that the few killed within the previous 20 years or so were either escapes from captivity or deliberate releases. He catalogued the history of unremitting persecution, dating from churchwardens' records of bounty payments, and from the barbarous practice of badger-baiting, which led to its virtual elimination by the mid-nineteenth century. The first bounty record was in 1658, and in Kendal parish 73 badgers were paid for during an eight-year period. The entries in the parish registers became fewer before they finally ended. Macpherson also noted that the frequency of the word 'brock' in place names pointed to a former wide distribution of the creature in Lakeland.

Not long afterwards, Macpherson (1902) asserted that wild badgers existed in Westmorland and thought it possible that they had survived in sequestered parts of Cumberland. There was a dearth of information until after the 1914–18 War period, when Ritson Graham developed an interest in badgers, and had within two years or so logged a total of 52 setts that he had personally visited. He continued to add to the list in succeeding years, and in 1946 was able to show that the animal was generally distributed through the Cumberland lowlands, and even fairly common along the Eden Valley. It was also widespread in other parts of Inglewood Forest, the valleys draining from the Pennines and Border moorlands, the Solway hinterland and inland from the western industrial belt. Graham noted that there was in most of these districts a sprinkling of ancient, traditional setts, but that the majority were of fairly recent origin, resulting from a decided increase over the previous 25 years. Tree cover was preferred, and he found that the majority of earths were on wooded stream banks, from narrow ravines to broad river valleys, though tree, scrub or bracken-covered banks away from watercourses were also commonly used. There were also some setts in treeless localities, in disused quarries and sandpits, old coal drifts, thick hedgerows and bare hillsides. Mostly they were in quiet places, but quite often no more than a field's length from farmhouses.

Webster (1996) notes that the pattern of increase and range expansion has continued, to the point where the badger is now widespread and indeed numerous in most suitable habitats through Lakeland. Road casualties are frequent and low level persecution continues, but Cumbria now has regional badger protection groups and the county does not have a bovine TB problem to prompt official 'control'. The badger is thus one of the Lakeland wildlife success stories, attributable to declining persecution and the animal's own resilience in making a comeback.

Birds

The sparrowhawk was once present in many lowland woods, and markedly faithful to its nesting places, for occupied nests usually had a cluster of old ones within a radius of about 50 metres, representing use over a succession of years. Not all the small woods were regularly occupied, though, and some pairs switched between alternative copses. The favourite nest trees were pines and larches, often well grown and presenting a challenging climb, but in the peat moss woods they could be found nesting in birches and even willows quite low down. Breeding density could be fairly high, and in woods just west of Carlisle, Rattlingate had two pairs only about 100 metres apart within 20 hectares during 1943–45, Orton Woods three pairs in 60 hectares, and Sowerby Wood four pairs in 120 hectares. Since suitable nesting woods tended to be widely spaced, amidst large areas of farmland where the hawks mostly hunted, they probably bred closer together here than if woods had been more regularly distributed.

This was a bird I always loved to seek out, and searched for and climbed to nests each May, to see the beautiful white and rust-blotched eggs. In 1947 I found a freshly broken egg beneath a new but empty sparrowhawk nest in Orton Woods. It was puzzling at the time, since the tree was unclimbed, but in the 1950s I found eight other nests containing one or more broken eggs. This matched my finding of frequent egg breakage in peregrine eyries during these years, but an explanation was lacking for some time. In Chapter 9 I relate how this led to the discovery that the eggshells of both species had become markedly thinner from 1947. By the early 1960s, the headlong declines of both sparrowhawk and peregrine populations across Britain were in the news, with the blame pinned squarely on the organochlorine insecticides of agriculture. Egg breaking and breeding failure were an integral feature of these 'crashes', and clearly linked to the decrease in eggshell thickness.

When the role of the organochlorine pesticides in causing catastrophic deaths of farmland birds and declines of birds of prey was firmly established, they were increasingly withdrawn from use. Over the next two decades the affected species gradually recovered in numbers. Ian Prestt followed the decline and early stages of recovery by monitoring sparrowhawk numbers in several study areas, one of which was the Solway Plain. In 1964, only two out of 14 territories were occupied by nesting pairs, but by 1966 eight out of the 14 had successful pairs. Yet, in 1968 the position had not improved further, and even by the early 1970s sparrowhawks in the Solway area showed only partial recovery. Some territories where pairs had returned and bred successfully again showed breeding failure or complete desertion. Orton Woods and Sowerby Woods regained their former complement of three and four pairs, and in other parts of Lakeland there appeared to be a steady recovery, with numbers returning almost to normal by 1980. Within a few more years, the Solway sparrowhawks appeared to be flagging still further again, and Geoff Horne watched the species steadily disappear from Sowerby Wood and other woods across to Broadfield. Frank Mawby, warden of the Finglandrigg Reserve, has found a single pair nesting there in recent years (there used to be at least two), and several other once regular mossland sites have only the odd pair between them. The species is now only a sparse nester in this district. Geoff Horne believes dwindling food supply is now the problem, for the noticeable decline in small passerines on farmland on the Solway Plain has seriously reduced the availability of prey.

By contrast, there has been an important raptor gain in the lowlands over the last 20 years, through the spread of the buzzard (Fig. 5.11). When Macpherson wrote in 1892, buzzards were restricted to the fells and dales of the Lake District and the Lakeland Pennines, where probably the majority nested on rocks rather than trees. Blezard (1933) noted the potential for spread back to the adjoining lowlands, but reported that four birds wintering in 1922–23 in woods just south of Carlisle were killed. He recorded the first return to the Eden Valley with the successful nesting of a pair on Blaze Fell above High Hesket in 1926. Greystoke Park closer under the Lake fells had become a stronghold by this time. Blaze Fell remained occupied and by the 1950s there were pairs on Lazonby Fell, in Baron Wood and High Stand above Cotehill. Further increase was very slow, but during the last ten years, buzzards have been nesting in several woods close to Carlisle, and they have bred in those around the edges of peat mosses on the Solway Plain (G. Horne, F. Mawby). This increase matches the phenomenal spread of the buzzard across southern Scotland during the last 20 years, and suggests that farmers and keepers have finally got the message that this is a beneficial predator to have around. A recovery of rabbit populations has, however, been a major factor underlying the trend. Kestrels breed in some woods but hunt over open country. The goshawk has begun to nest in the lowland woods of both south and north Cumbria, and may be set to increase.

Fig. 5.11 Buzzard at nest with young, a raptor on the increase across the lowlands. (Keith Temple.)

The woodland owls are represented mainly by the tawny owl, which is widespread throughout the lowlands, breeding usually in disused nests of crow and magpie. Several pairs nest in some of the larger woods, but this species seems to be less numerous nowadays than it was 50 years ago. Long-eared owls were once frequent over the Solway area, especially around the edges of the peat mosses, where they used old crow nests in the scattered birch and pine copses. Their numbers collapsed around 1940, for reasons unknown, and they have never recovered in the Solway area, though they occur sparingly through Inglewood Forest. Jays are common in the wild woods of the Solway, for nobody bothers them there, while carrion crows and magpies have a safer refuge than along the field edges. Large flocks of wood pigeons roost during the winter, and Orton Woods drew mixed flocks of rooks, carrion crows and jackdaws to spend the night in the trees.

Woodcock breed widely through the lowland woods, and their numbers are boosted by autumn immigrants from northern Europe. Shy and secretive birds, their habits are hard to penetrate, but their apparent preference for earthworm food limits their numbers on acidic soils, and they were always few as breeders and difficult to find in the woods of the peat mosses. They were more numerous in Inglewood Forest, and woods on more basic soils from the southern outskirts of Carlisle to the limestone belt west of Penrith were dependable nesting haunts. Hirons (1980) found that the crepuscular 'roding' flight of the males is to find or attract females, rather than advertise territory, and that the males are probably serial polygamists. This, rather than double-broods, may explain why June and July nests are common, after the first wave in March–April.

Herons are dual habitat birds, but their habit of colonial nesting in trees makes it easier to consider them as woodland species. The district has always been well endowed with heronries since records began, though the permanence of any one colony has depended on woodland management, and there has been a good deal of movement as nesting woods were felled. The 1928–29 Census of Heronries gave 24 colonies in Lakeland, of which 18 were in Cumberland. Since then there has been a good deal of dispersal, with reduction in the average size of heronries. The longest known colony is at Dallam Tower in Westmorland, which dated back at least to the late eighteenth century. The total of 32 nests, in some unspecified Victorian year, appears to have been the largest of any Lakeland heronry known to Macpherson. In 1958, it was still the largest, with 47 nests, and though it was down to 38 in 1962, in 1998 it was flourishing with 61 nests. Most colonies did not exceed 10–20 nests, and in recent years they have tended to be mostly in single figures. The 1998 count gave 178 nests in 16 colonies. While estate woodlands were favourite haunts, some recent breeding places have been otherwise.

The site of felled woodland, large glades and open growths of colonising trees on heaths or peat moss edges formerly attracted breeding nightjars. The great spotted is the most widespread and numerous of the woodpeckers, breeding especially where old birches die off to leave dead stumps in which they can easily excavate their nest holes. Its smaller relative the lesser spotted woodpecker is only a scarce and perhaps sporadic breeder in the north, up to the Carlisle area, but more regular in south Cumbria. The green woodpecker spread through Cumbria in the early 1950s, during its northward British expansion, and became quite widespread, nesting in most of the larger woods. It later seemed to thin out markedly, while still remaining widespread, and its distinctive voice is less often heard. Wood pigeons nest in woods of all kinds, but perhaps favour coniferous plantations in particular: they are one of the commonest woodland birds, but stock doves are local while the turtle dove has declined over the past century and is no longer known to breed.

The warblers are well represented, first by the willow warbler, which is numerous in the peat moss birch woods, and in woodlands generally where the ground cover is rather open and short. Chiffchaffs are widespread but much less numerous, and wood warblers occur, but are more associated with the hanging fell oak woods. Blackcaps and garden warblers are mainly in the ungrazed lowland woods, which have a dense layer of brambles and other undergrowth in which they can nest. Whitethroats are widespread in the more open types of woodland and scrub, but are less numerous than formerly, while lesser whitethroats are also widely scattered in scrub and said to be increasing. Pied flycatchers and redstarts are other species found mainly in the fell country woods, but occur in small numbers in many lowland woods also. Spotted flycatchers are somewhat patchy in occurrence nowadays and may be another declining species.

Goldcrests are mainly birds of the conifer plantations or mixed woods, while bullfinches prefer scrub birch thickets, and willow tits are especially in damp woods where numerous rotting birch stumps allow them to dig nest holes. Marsh tits are more sparsely distributed through a variety of lowland woods. The common and widely distributed songbirds of lowland woods include chaffinch, robin, wren, blue tit, great tit, coal tit, long-tailed tit, tree creeper, blackbird and song thrush. Mistle thrushes are frequent but at rather low density in woodland. The rarities among breeders include the siskin, usually in conifers, and the hawfinch, which in Cumbria nests mainly in scrubby places, including within gardens, rather than in typical woodland. Wood pigeons are common everywhere.

Insects

Woodlands are an important habitat for several insect groups. Butterflies of the more open sites include the small pearl-bordered and dark green fritillaries, green hairstreaks and holly blue, while the purple hairstreak is widespread in oak stands. The southern limestone woods add several more extremely local species (see pp. 163–4). Many kinds of moths belong to woodland, and the larvae of a remarkable number feed on willows and/or poplars (including aspen), especially the quakers and sallows. The adults range outside their breeding places and many are taken at light traps and 'sugar' in more open places. As a selection of characteristic species, there are poplar and eyed hawks, goat moth, puss moth, old lady, buff tip, alder moth, sallow kitten, yellow horned, frosted green, peach blossom, Svensson's copper underwing, herald, December moth, lackey, orange underwing, large emerald, oak lutestring, poplar lutestring, pebble and scalloped hook-tips, and several prominents (iron, coxcomb, pebble and lesser swallow).

Certain localities became especially famous among local entomologists. Only fuller survey will show how much this reflected intrinsic richness or the amount of attention they received, though some gained through their complexes of different habitats. Orton Woods was one of the important sites, being conveniently placed close to the western outskirts of Carlisle. Part of their importance was in the fringing meadows described above, but the woods themselves had a rich insect fauna. This was one of the northernmost stations for the holly blue butterfly, and it was good for both purple and green hairstreaks. A long list of moths is recorded for the area. In 1896 and 1897, F. H. Day took the marsh moth, otherwise known only from the East Anglian Fenland. The malachite beetle is a distinctive insect still present. Still nearer Carlisle is Sowerby Wood (Newby Cross to the old entomologists), which used to have areas of open woodland, with pine and birch, grassland, heath and shallow bog. It had many of the notable insects of Orton, but was acquired by the Forestry Commission and converted to a large and uniform plantation of Scots pine, with the loss of most of its former interest.

Known then under the general name of Baron Wood, the main Eden gorge above Armathwaite was another great stamping ground of the original Carlisle entomologists, and figures in many of the earlier insect records. It was a noted butterfly locality, with all the above-mentioned species plus pearl-bordered fritillary, and older records of comma, wood white, brown hairstreak and Duke of Burgundy (Routledge, 1909). Notable moths included the narrow-bordered bee hawk, angle-striped sallow, slender brindle, green arches, scarce silver Y and light orange underwing (Routledge, 1912). There was a great variety of beetles, especially longhorns and weevils (Day, 1909).

6

The Lowlands: Peatlands, Tarns and Rivers

Peat mosses

The Cumbrian lowlands have numerous peat bogs forming important oases of near-natural vegetation in the agricultural plains. They appear as flat, wet moorlands, many almost at sea level, and represent refuges for a whole assemblage of plants and animals that contrast strangely with the surrounding farmland. Few other people ever visit them and they are patches of wilderness where the naturalist can roam and enjoy an ancient landscape that may have changed very little over thousands of years.

The lowland mosses are mostly of the kind known to peatland pundits as raised bogs, from their slightly domed shape in profile, with a deep central mass of peat, tapering off to a shallower layer at the drier edges. The classic raised bog structure, with a zone of fen and stream around the bog edges (lagg), has largely been lost through draining and peat cutting along the margins. The largest raised bogs are on the Solway hinterland, at Bowness Moss (Common) (840 hectares) and Wedholme Flow (760 hectares), with Glasson, Drumburgh and Oulton Mosses a good deal smaller. Solway Moss close to the Scottish Border at Gretna is quite large, but Todhills (Rockcliffe) Moss and Scaleby Moss farther inland much smaller. Still farther inland, the large peat mosses at Bolton Fell and Walton-Broomhill Mosses have many features of raised bogs, but occupy low plateaux on rising ground at 100 metres and so have some structural features of upland blanket bog: they are best regarded as intermediate types. Some rather small mosses in the undulating glacial sand country east of Carlisle have the typical vegetation of raised bogs, but occupy distinct basins and valleys, as at Moorthwaite, Cumwhitton, Faugh and Hayton Mosses, Unity Bog near Brampton, and Black Dub at Carlatton.

Ferguson (1892) declared that, 'Scaleby, Solway and Bowness Mosses, and Wedholme Flow, are but puny and degenerate survivals of vast morasses that once covered the alluvial flats bordering on the Solway, and stretched eastward from the vicinity of Rockcliffe along the north of Carlisle for many miles.' It is unclear on what historical evidence this statement was based. Milligan (2001) suggests that on the Cardurnock peninsula, reclamation was extensive, and notes that in 1845, 'several hundred acres of mossland known as Bowness Flow was begun to be drained ... and two years later was ready for cultivation making good farm land.' The hard and unnatural edges to all the peat mosses (Fig. 6.1) well convey the impression that farmland has gained at their expense; but by how much is

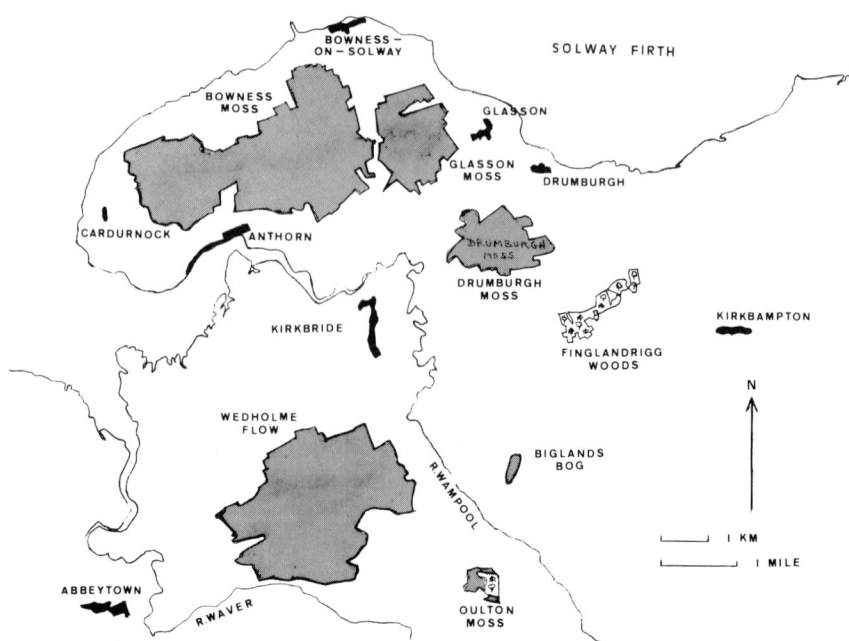

Fig. 6.1 The present extent of raised bogs on the South Solway: the artificial edges abutting farmland are apparent from the present configuration.

difficult to assess. I suspect that most of the farmland of the Solway hinterland was derived from woodland, drier heath or fen, and that the deep, wet and acid peat of the mosses largely escaped this conversion, so that these ancient bogs have survived over areas not greatly reduced from their original extent, though with some attrition at the shallow edges.

In southern Lakeland, raised bogs occupy part of the coastal plain behind Morecambe Bay, at Foulshaw, Meathop and Witherslack Mosses west of the Kent estuary and the Roudsea Mosses (Deer Dyke and Stribers) east of the Leven, with the smaller Rusland Moss farther inland. Wilson (1938) stated that these were the remnant of a more extensive tract of peatland, of which Witherslack Moss was a degraded example, but, again, no evidence is given. Raised bogs also occur on both sides of the Duddon estuary, at Shaw Moss, White Moss and Herd House Moss. Black Moss near Egremont, White Moss at Mungrisdale, and perhaps Shoulthwaite Moss in Naddle are other scattered small inland examples. Some of these raised bogs are, strictly, within the National Park, but all are essentially lowland in character.

Using pollen analysis and examination of peat stratigraphy and plant remains, Donald Walker (1966) studied the developmental history of the raised bogs of the Cumberland lowlands, while Smith (1959) investigated those of the Morecambe Bay area. Scaleby Moss was the site of a landmark development – the first application of radiocarbon dating to the chronology of postglacial changes in vegetation revealed by studies of British lake and peat deposits. The coastal raised bogs have formed mostly over estuarine alluvium (warp) raised above sea level by land uplift following deglaciation. This isostatic change continues still, with northern and western Britain rising, and the south-east sinking (see also p. 62). Outer raised beaches and inner ridges of boulder clay may have promoted waterlogging and allowed the development of peat-forming vegetation. After an initial phase, during which fen vegetation with reed and sedges formed over the mineral substrate, acidification took place, with extensive colonisation by bog mosses *Sphagnum* and the upward growth of the bog surface, forming an increasing depth of acid peat. The earliest deposits with plant material and pollen grains were dated to the transition from the Boreal to the Atlantic periods, some 7,500 radiocarbon years ago.

The more inland bogs such as Scaleby, Moorthwaite and Abbot Mosses, formed mostly within wet hollows in the general cover of boulder clay and sandy till, and in some cases within 'kettleholes' – deep water-filled hollows where masses of dead ice decayed *in situ* amidst glacial deposits. Their basal material is usually lake mud with remains of aquatic plants such as pondweeds and water lilies, changing above into fen and sometimes woody peat indicating alder, willow or birch carr woodland. There is again a later change to acidic bog peat with *Sphagnum* remains dominant. These bogs formed earlier than the others, with their underlying lake muds shown to be of late-glacial age, dating back to 11,000–12,000 radiocarbon years ago.

On all the peat mosses, the main period of acidic bog development began around 4,000–5,000 radiocarbon years ago, and has continued ever since, though not at a uniform rate: layers of more humified peat, sometimes with tree remains, indicate phases of drying (retardation layers), evidently in response to periods of lower rainfall. They were overlain by 'recurrence surfaces' with fresh, unhumified *Sphagnum* peat suggesting a return to wetter conditions. While similar in present surface features, the different raised bogs are far from uniform in their postglacial history. Milligan (2001) notes that average peat depth on Bowness Moss is four metres, compared with only two metres on Drumburgh Moss, indicating a much longer history of continuous peat formation on the former. Peat depth of nearly 14 metres has been measured in the middle of Bowness Moss.

Vegetation

All these bogs were once characterised by a living surface vegetation dominated by *Sphagnum* – from which the 'peat moss' name derives – with a lesser amount of vascular plants, chiefly cotton-grasses, heather, cross-leaved heath, deer sedge, bog asphodel, bog rosemary, cranberry, round-leaved sundew, great sundew and white beak-sedge. The bog mosses were mainly hummock builders which create rapid upward growth of the bog surface – *S. magellanicum*, *S. papillosum* and *S. rubellum*. Pools with open water were few, but the least disturbed bogs had typically undulating surfaces with numerous wet hollows containing other *Sphagna* – *S. cuspidatum* and *S. pulchrum*. Where the ground was naturally drier, towards the bog edges, vascular plant cover increased and the bog mosses declined, or were replaced by other species: *S. subnitens*, *S. compactum*, *S. tenellum* and *S. molle*.

Beneath colonising birch, *S. fimbriatum* soon becomes abundant, and older birch woods on the site of former peat mosses often have abundant large hummocks of *S. palustre*. The Rodwell (1991b) bog communities M 2, 3, 16 and 18 are all represented, and M 21 is in the valley mires.

Human activity has caused the peat mosses to dry out in varying degree. Digging of drains and cutting of peat, especially where this creates a steep face at the bog edge, tap the water table at the adjoining surface, but the most damaging cause of drying is fire. In my time, the best large area of actively growing surface on the Solway raised bogs was on the northern part of Glasson Moss, which in 1952 had a completely intact bog moss carpet. Besides the usual species, there were some hummocks of *Sphagnum imbricatum*, many of *S. fuscum*, and many of the very rare moss *Dicranum bergeri*, while *S. pulchrum* grew in nearly every hollow. Parts of Bowness Moss and Wedholme Flow were almost as good. All these areas were later burned. Ironically, although the best part of Glasson Moss was made a National Nature Reserve in 1967, it suffered three subsequent fires, and the last, in 1976, was catastrophic: the whole surface was burnt and in drier places reduced to a layer of peat ash, while much of the living *Sphagnum* surface was killed. The smell of peat smoke was strong in Carlisle 15 kilometres eastwards. Hardly any bogs escaped the local pyromaniacs. Scaleby Moss seemed to be on fire somewhere about every year. Added to this has been the effect of peat winning on many mosses, from a local and unimportant scale to extensive commercial extraction that has virtually destroyed the surface vegetation (see Fig. 12.4). Small wonder, then, that the peat mosses are not in as good a state as 50 years ago.

In years following fires, the ground can appear white as snow in summer, through vigorous flowering of cotton-grass responding to the stimulus of a fertiliser top-dressing effect (Fig. 6.2). The result of drying – from whatever cause – is to reduce *Sphagnum* cover and increase that of vascular plants, which in extreme cases dominate the bog surface over a desiccated skin of bare peat. Lichens increase in abundance on the bare, dry peat and may form a mosaic with plants such as heather: *Cladonia portentosa* and *C. uncialis* are common. Cut-over parts of Bowness, Glasson and Drumburgh Mosses now have dense growths of heather with few other plants. Old peat cuttings that hold water usually show regrowth of *Sphagnum* carpets, but the prevalent species is *S. recurvum*, so often a disturbance indicator.

The drier bog edges became colonised in many places by the little fringes and clumps of birch and pine wood described in Chapter 5, and patches sometimes developed out in the middle. The line of the old railway across Bowness Moss has a fringe of birch and willow scrub woodland. Some of these scrubs acquire luxuriant growths of witches' beard lichens *Usnea*, giving them a distinctly primeval appearance. On some smaller mosses, trees have encroached sufficiently to give wooded bogs, as at Moorthwaite, Cumwhitton, Meathop and Rusland Mosses. The fire of 1976 destroyed much of the fringing woodland to Glasson Moss, but it has recovered and has to be kept in check by cutting where it is too vigorously invading the main bog surface.

Plate 1. Roads, towns and selected villages in Cumbria

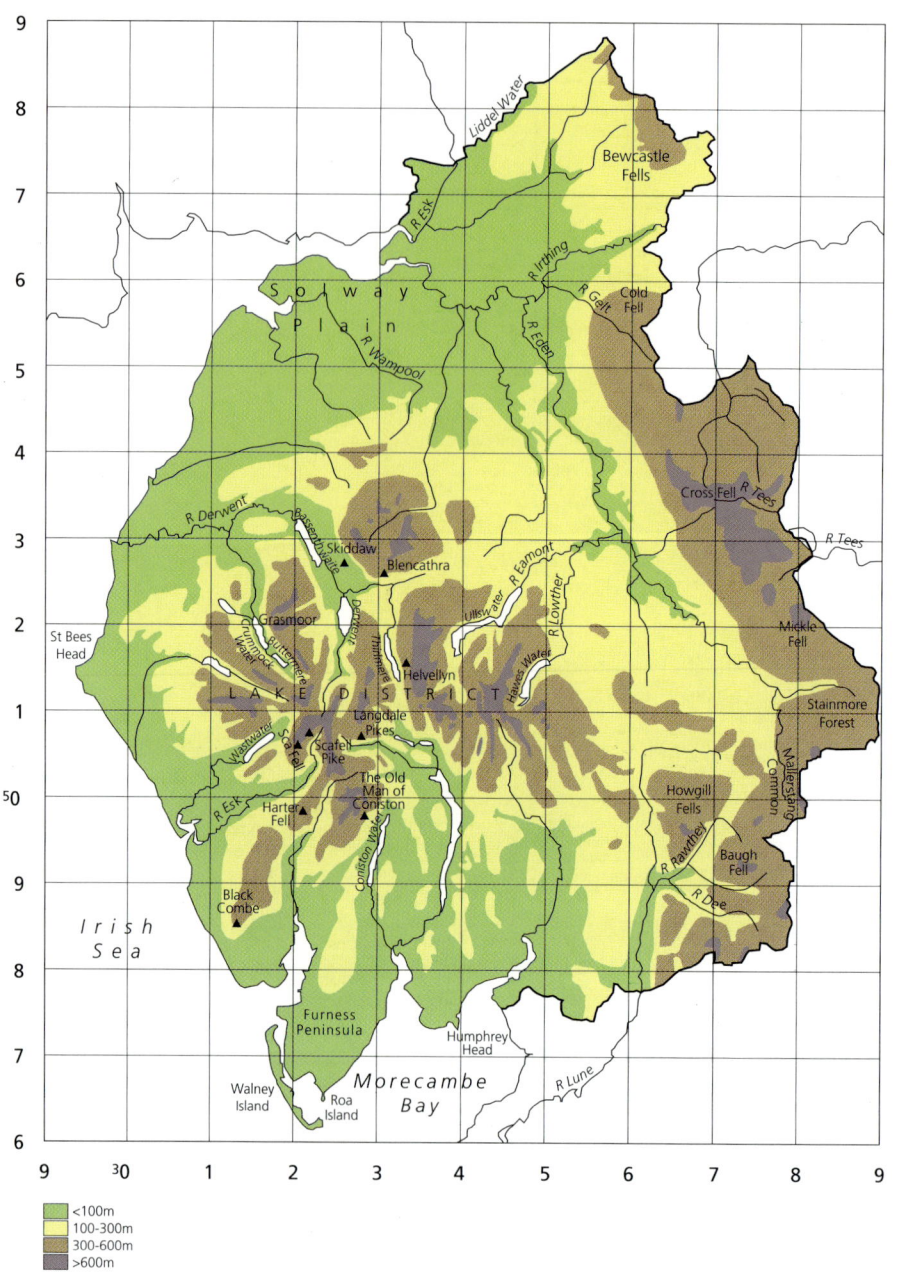

Plate 2. Physical features of Cumbria. (Halliday, 1997, Fig.1.)

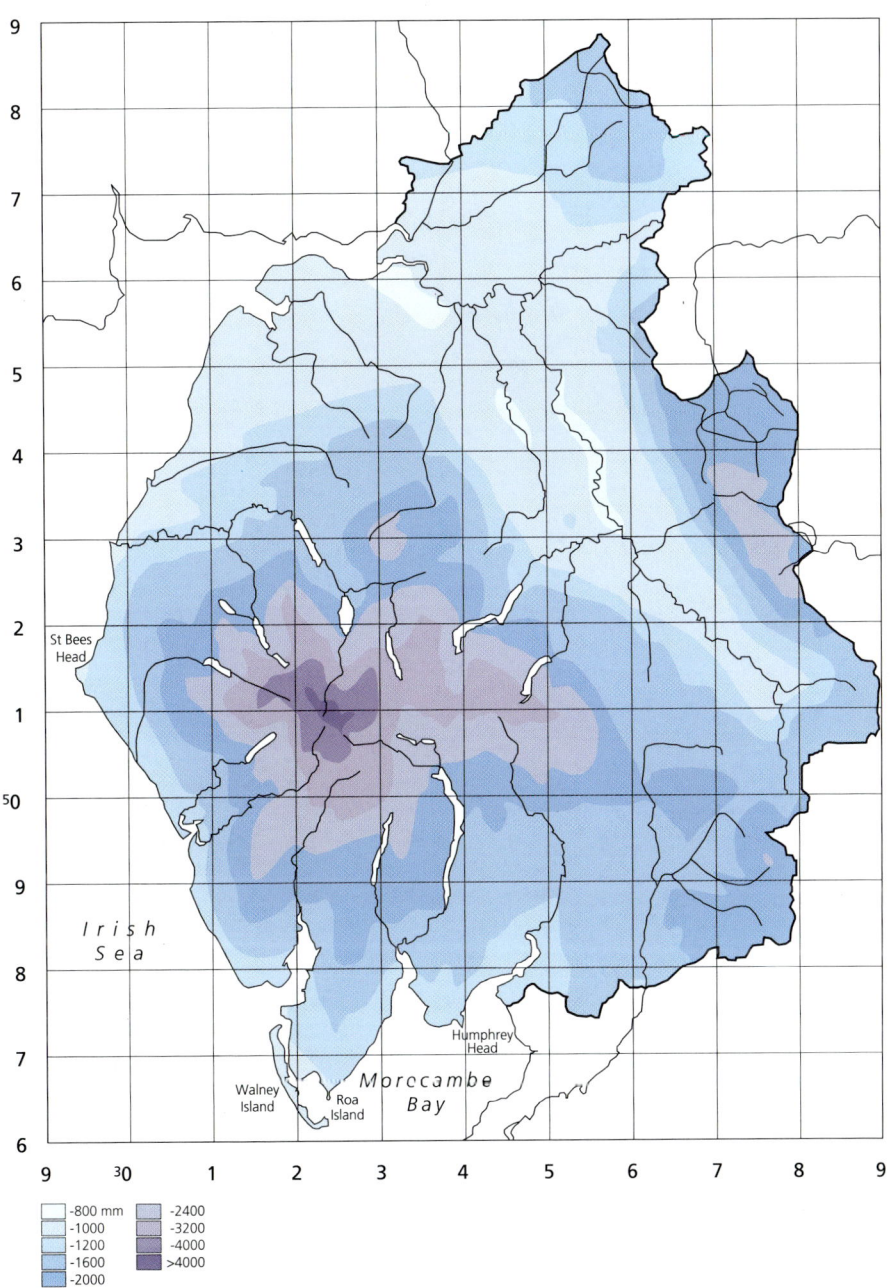

Plate 3. Average annual rainfall over Cumbria, 1941-70 (Halliday, 1997, Fig.3.)

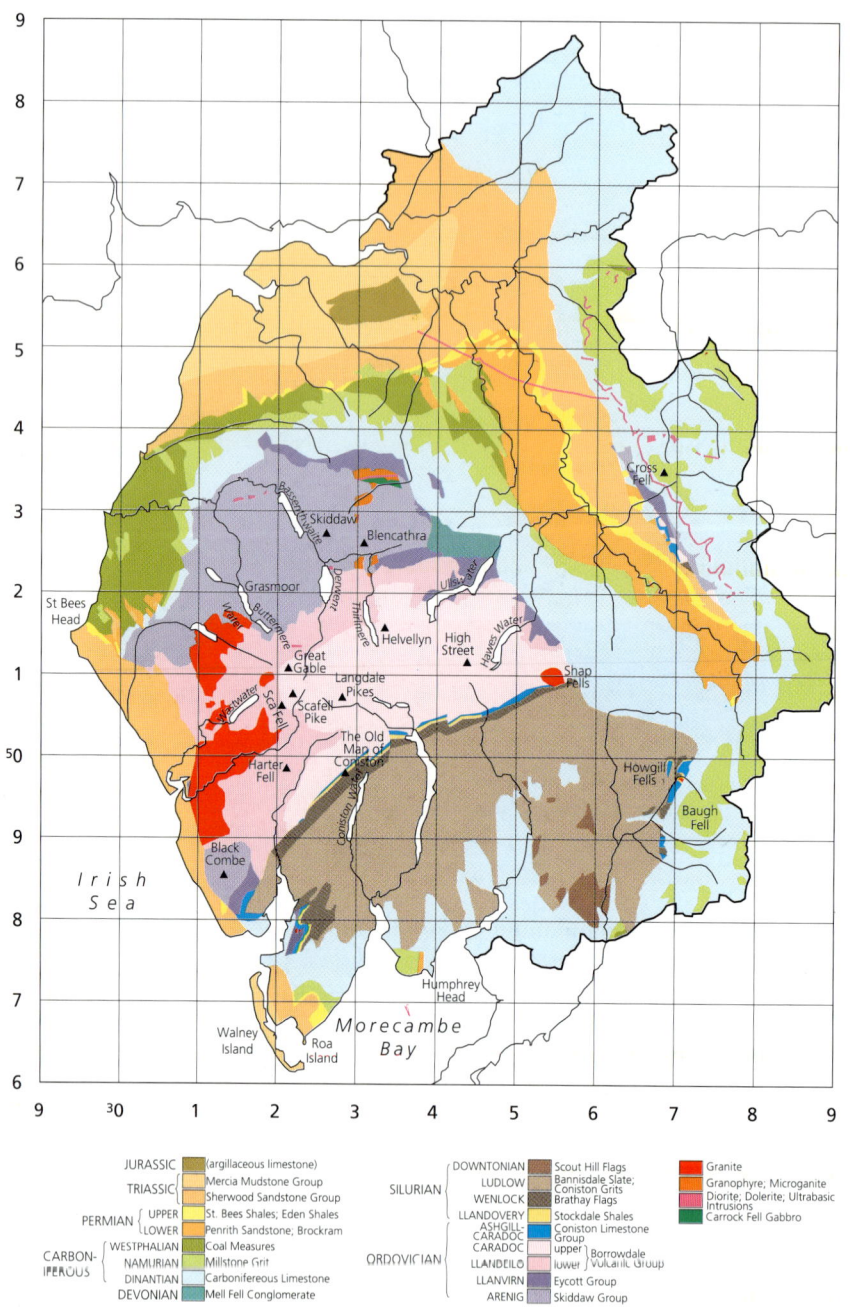

Plate 4. The geology of Cumbria (Halliday, 1997, Fig.2.) with permission of the Yorkshire Geological Society, from Moseley, F (ed.) 1978, supplemented by Dr Halliday to include north-east Cumbria.

Plate 5. Gorse and saltmarsh looking to Campfield Marsh, near Bowness-on-Solway, Inner Solway.

Plate 6. Seaward dunes with marram and bloody cranesbill near Allonby, Outer Solway.

Plate 7. Seacliffs of New Red Sandstone with guillemot and kittiwake ledges at St Bees Head in 1983. (Geoff Horne)

Plate 8. Peregrine, king of the crags. (Keith Temple)

Plate 9. Sea holly, a characteristic shore plant.

Plate 10. Burnet rose, a sand dune and shingle ornament.

Plate 11. Foxgloves, a colourful calcifuge.

Plate 12. Wooded gorge of the River Eden between Lazonby and Armathwaite, with Permian Sandstone crags.

Plate 13. Creeping lady's tresses under Scots pines in Irongill Wood near Welton.

Plate 14. Large elephant hawk-moth, widespread in the lowlands: its larva feeds on rosebay willow-herb.

Plate 15. Broadleaved lowland wood at the Nunnery Walks, Kirkoswald.

Plate 16. Edge of raised bog with bog myrtle, flying bent and birchwoods at Drumburgh Moss.

Plate 17. Bog hollows and hummocks with bogmoss, cotton-grass, heather and cranberry at Moorthwaite Moss in 1960.

Plate 18. Bog asphodel, a common peat moss plant.

Plate 19. Yellow saxifrage and golden moss *Cratoneuron commutatum*, widespread in calcareous mountain flushes.

Plate 20. Sunbiggin Tarn, an upland calcareous marl lake on the Carboniferous limestone of Shap Fells.

Plate 21. Rigid buckler fern in grike of limestone pavement.

Plate 22. Alpine catchfly at Hobcarton Crag, Lorton Fells.

Plate 23. Floral road verge on Shap limestone with wood cranesbill, meadow buttercup and burnet saxifrage.

Plate 24. Heathery grouse moor showing bracken invasion, Skiddaw Forest and River Caldew.

Plate 25. Gullied crags and screes of Borrowdale Volcanic rocks and nutrient-poor lake, Wasdale Screes and Wastwater.

Plate 26. Ungrazed crag ledges with shrubby cinquefoil, roseroot and meadowsweet, Wasdale Screes.

Plate 27. A fell valley with scattered ash trees: Langstrath and Eagle Crag.

Plate 28. Derwentwater and Lodore-Barrow Woods in 1958. The reed bed has since disappeared.

Plate 29. Wilson's filmy fern mixed with *Scapania gracilis*, *Dicranum scoparium* and *Isothecium myosuroides* in Naddle Forest.

Plate 30. Seatoller Woods at the head of Borrowdale: the richest wood for Atlantic mosses and liverworts south of the Highlands.

Plate 31. Rugged Borrowdale Volcanic fells: the Scafell range from upper Eskdale.

Plate 32. Skiddaw Slate fells under snow: Bannerdale and Blencathra from near Berrier.

Plate 33. Ullswater from Barton Fell, looking to the Helvellyn range.

Plate 35. High Brown Fritillary: a nationally scarce butterfly of the southern limestone. (Rob Petley-Jones)

Plate 34. Common hawkers pairing: the most widespread large dragonfly. (Richard Speirs)

Plate 36. Cross Fell from Hartside: extensive blanket bogs on the Pennine dip slope, rising to zone of high snow patches. Sheep grazing patch of limestone grassland.

Plate 37. Alpine forget-me-not on high limestone band of Little Fell.

Plate 38. Red grouse, bird of the heather moors.

Plate 39. Golden Plover incubating on burned heather moor. (Bobby Smith)

Plate 40. The moss *Orthothecium rufescens* in a Pennine gill.

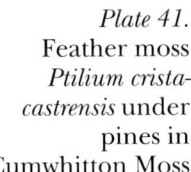

Plate 41. Feather moss *Ptilium crista-castrensis* under pines in Cumwhitton Moss

Plate 42. Mallerstang valley from Aisgill, with buttercup meadow and sycamores, and gritstone "edge" behind.

Plate 43. Waterfall of the R. Irthing in torrent, Cramel Linn, Gilsland. Young forests appearing on the moor behind.

Fig. 6.2 Copious flowering of hare's-tail cotton-grass after fire, Glasson Moss National Nature Reserve.

The flora of the peat mosses is rather limited in variety. They are a British stronghold of bog rosemary (Fig. 6.3), whose pink bells add to the rich colour mosaic of the varied bog moss carpet, with its shades of red, brown, yellow and green (Plate 17). Thickets of bog myrtle, usually towards the

Fig. 6.3 Bog rosemary, a local peatland plant with a stronghold on the Cumbrian peat mosses.

Fig. 6.4 Heath spotted orchid: the commonest Lakeland orchid, widespread on acidic heaths, grasslands and bogs.

bog edges, give a bright orange glow when their catkins open (Plate 16). Flying bent is often abundant here, giving community M 25 (Rodwell, 1991b). Here and there, heath spotted orchids (Fig. 6.4) are an attractive addition, with especially vigorous clumps probably of hybrid origin. Occasional plants of lesser butterfly orchid are surprising, from the species' usual need for base-rich soils. Oblong-leaved sundew grows sparingly in a few places round the edge of Glasson and Oulton Mosses and Wedholme Flow, but fir and stag's-horn clubmosses once known from the last seem to have gone. Several peat mosses east of Carlisle have unusual lowland occurrences of the bog bilberry, which in Scotland is a plant of higher mountains. Most of its Cumbrian localities have from one to a few patches, but on Unity Bog near Brampton this small shrub grows in extraordinary abundance and luxuriance, forming bushes up to a metre tall (Fig. 6.5). In some years it flowers and fruits well in this locality. Foulshaw Moss in the south formerly had a rarity in the marsh gentian, near the northern limits of its British distribution, but it was destroyed by afforestation.

Fig. 6.5 Bog whortleberry in unusual luxuriance at Unity Bog, near Brampton.

Towards the edge of Scaleby Moss is a long-established colony of the Labrador tea, which is the tall and large-leaved *Ledum groenlandicum* form and not the smaller Fennoscandian *L. palustre* (Fig. 6.6). Its presence here is a mystery: it is a shrub occasionally grown in gardens, and may have been a bird-sown introduction to this bog. Plants of the same species on

Fig. 6.6 Labrador tea naturalised at Scaleby Moss, near Carlisle.

Foulshaw Moss have disappeared. Wedholme Flow has a still more puzzling occurrence of the pitcher-plant of North American *Sphagnum* bogs, which is well established but was never recorded by the older botanists. Halliday (1997) believes it was planted here, as at three other sites in the southern Lake District. It was becoming so rampant that control measures were begun to keep it in check (Frank Mawby).

Animals

The peat mosses have no special mammals, possibly because their feeding value is pretty low. Ferguson (in Macpherson, 1892) refers to frequent finds in the peat and elsewhere of red deer antlers much larger than those of the living animals in central Lakeland, but they probably lived mainly in much more productive woodland habitats, and vanished as agriculture took over. Roe deer occur in small numbers on some mosses, but belong mainly to the wooded fringes. Foxes find a refuge here, in drier places, but range mainly over the farmland beyond in search of food. The polecat was a widespread Lakeland animal in the first half of the nineteenth century, but had been reduced to rarity when Macpherson wrote, in 1892. By that time, its last stronghold was among the peat mosses and wild woods of the coastal lowlands, both north and south. Even here, it had gone by the 1920s. Macpherson attributed its decline to the introduction of the steel gin trap, but it was also hunted relentlessly and the growing use of strychnine to poison predators was no doubt another adverse factor.

The birds of the peat mosses were first recorded by Macpherson. The red grouse here finds a suitable habitat down almost to sea level, and once occurred in sufficient numbers for shooting to be worthwhile. It has long been at a low ebb, but still hangs on sparingly on the larger bogs, where the 'becking' males can be heard challenging each other in spring. Up to 1900 a few pairs of golden plover and dunlin nested on the largest coastal mosses, but then faded away. The plover were still on the inland Hethersgill mosses in the mid-1950s, but have probably gone now. Among other birds of the northern moorlands, the merlin once bred on the hummocks of several mosses, but has not been recorded nesting for many years, while the twite was known especially from Glasson, and has bred on one or more of the Solway bogs in recent years. The hen harrier was an occasional nester, especially on Solway Moss, but known during the twentieth century only as an irregular winter visitor to the mosslands. Curlews are the most conspicuous of the nesting birds, with their evocative display flight and song as they stake out territories in April. The mosses have become their lowland refuge as they have lost ground over recent decades across the agricultural deserts. Small numbers of redshank, snipe and oystercatchers breed, especially towards the bog edges, but this is a minor habitat for them.

The meadow pipit is probably the commonest bird, though not abundant nowadays; there are a few skylarks and reed buntings, and stonechats occur on drier heathery ground. Some of the rough, densely rush-grown fields around some moss edges, possibly reclaimed from former peat ground, used to be a great nesting haunt of grasshopper warblers, but there is no information on present status. Nightjars also bred on the drier and more open bog margins, among heather, bracken and open woodland, and the older naturalists could remember when five or six males could be heard reeling at once in the dusk. They have long gone, and even in the 1940s and 1950s, the only place at which I ever found them nesting was Scaleby Moss, where a pair or two had hung on.

The rearing of various ducks from pinioned birds released onto artificially dug ponds around the edge of Solway Moss during 1890–1925 was described by Blezard et al. (1943). Mallard, teal, wigeon, shoveler, pintail, garganey, gadwall, tufted duck and pochard were all introduced in varying numbers to breed, in order to boost the stock of shootable wildfowl on the Netherby estate. During this period the occasional nesting of wigeon and pintail on other coastal mosses of the Solway could have been connected with this local farming of duck. Shelduck have long nested naturally in long vegetation around the drier moss edges in both north and south Lakeland.

The other bird interest was the nesting colonies of gulls. Macpherson & Duckworth (1886) record black-headed gulls as breeding numerously on Wedholme Flow, Bowness and Solway Mosses, Salta Moss near Allonby, and Bolton Fell. The colonies evidently numbered up to several hundred pairs, but they declined almost to extinction by the 1940s. The same writers also said that lesser black-backed gulls bred gregariously, with 'many pairs' on the first three mosses, but the largest colony was in the south at Foulshaw Moss where several hundred pairs had been known for at least 50 years. In 1943, this lesser black-back colony was still flourishing, though a second one on the Roudsea Mosses had declined. Herring gulls also nested on Foulshaw, though they were outnumbered by the lessers by about ten to one.

The finest of the gulls, the great black-back, bred on both Wedholme Flow and Bowness Moss in smaller numbers – about 15 pairs in 1885. Wedholme was occupied by two or three pairs up to 1920, and a pair or two were then known also on Drumburgh Moss and occasionally on Glasson Moss, up to 1934. Bowness became the main nesting haunt and numbers gradually increased to a peak of 20 pairs in 1925–26 (Johnston, 1954). There was then a slow decline and in 1948 I saw three pairs, with a dozen or so pairs of lessers, and a few black-headed, but they all abandoned Bowness Moss soon afterwards. The only great black-backs known to nest on the Cumbrian Solway since then have been amongst the now huge colony of lessers and herring gulls on Rockcliffe Marsh. Foulshaw Moss ceased to be gull habitat when it was afforested from 1955. All the mossland gull colonies suffered heavy egg-taking over a long period, and this was believed to play some part in their fluctuations and movements, and eventual demise. Around the grass nests and on favourite perching hummocks were numerous traces of their food from the shore – bivalve shells, crabs, shrimps and sea urchins which with their droppings must have added considerably to the limited nutrient budget of the bog. Yet there were no obvious vegetation changes of the kind described by Ritchie (1920) and Pullen (1942) for Scottish moorland with colonies of black-headed gulls.

Macpherson noted that a few pairs of common terns bred every year on Solway Moss, an unusual habitat in Britain, but one widely used by arctic terns in Fennoscandia. An even more intriguing record was the taking of a clutch of black tern eggs on Solway Moss in 1855. This bird normally makes its nest in real swamp, but Macpherson's later description of black-headed gull nesting habitat on a coastal moss – probably Solway Moss – spoke of pools with water lilies, which would seem to fit the bill. Such pools have long since disappeared and whether they were natural or had been dug out as duck ponds or for fuel peat is uncertain. A former pool near Rogersceugh on the edge of Bowness Moss was known as the 'lily pond', but it was evidently artificial.

The lowland mosses are a noted haunt of the adder, and few of them, even the smallest, are without this reptile. Their communal hibernation dens are in dry places around the mossland edges or off the peat ground altogether. Now and then a newly emerged group, all lying about close together, is seen and reported as a 'swarm' of adders, but they disperse later and are mostly found singly, including on wet ground, during the summer. Ernest Blezard once came upon a recently surfaced group at Finglandrigg and was struck by the range of colour – gold, yellow, red, brown, silver, even black. Many are killed by the larger conflagrations that periodically engulf so many of their peatland habitats, but enough usually escape to build up numbers again in a few years. In the heat of summer they sometimes take refuge in the mossland woods. Common lizards are also widespread on the bogs.

The insects include many of those from the moorlands of the Lakeland interior. One of the most distinctive is the large heath butterfly, which occurs on almost all of these lowland bogs, including some of the smallest. From mid-June its dun-coloured form is familiar on sunny days, flitting restlessly low over the bog surface, and seldom seeming to settle. The older books repetitively said that the eggs were laid on white beak-sedge, but the insect occurs in many places without this plant, so it clearly has other larval food-plants – evidently including cotton-grass, deer sedge and flying bent. The variable presence of eye-spots on the wings in this species has always fascinated entomologists, who distinguish three geographical races. Most of the larger populations inclined to variation, but individuals with the largest eye-spots characteristic of the southern race were found only on the Morecambe Bay mosses. Those of the Solway bogs were mostly the typical northern England form with intermediate eye-spots, but some approached the Scottish race in which the eye-spots are reduced to tiny dots or nil and the colour is darker (Routledge, 1909).

The southern peat mosses fringing Morecambe Bay at Witherslack were once famous for the silver-studded blue, and were the most northerly regular localities for the butterfly in Britain. They disappeared, evidently all at once in 1942. Some declare that severe late frost over the district at a critical time in the life cycle was the cause, but others believe extinction resulted from a disastrous fire. With no other colonies within a long distance, this sedentary insect could not recolonise the lost ground of its own accord, and so it has remained quite firmly extinct. Green hairstreaks occur on some mosses, especially near birch woods and gorse thickets, and the common browns and whites are around the grassy edges, while the vanessids often visit heather in flower. The large day-flying moths, emperor, fox and northern eggar, whose larvae feed on dwarf shrubs, are all common on the mosses, though varying in numbers from year to year. Other distinctive moths include the forester, clouded buff, marsh oblique-barred, Manchester treble-bar, purple-bordered gold, common heath, grass wave, Haworth's minor, light knot-grass and square-spot dart.

The dragonflies are represented widely by the common hawker (Plate 34), four-spotted chaser, black darter, emerald damselfly and large red damselfly, which breed in ditches and old flooded peat cuttings. The speciality of these habitats is the Boreal–alpine white-faced dragonfly, once known from three Solway bogs. It died out at Cumwhitton Moss through woodland encroachment and drying of its breeding hollows, and appears lost from Oulton Moss, but persists in water-filled peat cuttings on Scaleby Moss, where English Nature have dug deep new pools to extend its habitat. It is rare in Britain generally, but surprisingly so, for in Fennoscandia it seems to be in virtually every bog and swarms in many of them. The bog bush-cricket occurs on Wedholme Flow and the southern Lakeland mosses, while the common groundhopper, and common green and meadow grasshoppers, are more widespread.

Peatland exploitation

The mosslands are one of the most important habitats surviving from a bygone age before farming dominated the lowlands. Their wet and acidic bogs resisted cultivation and had little value as grazing land. Probably their chief value was in providing fuel peat before coal became the main source of heat and energy. Scaleby Moss was almost entirely cut away to supply the city of Carlisle (Walker, 1966), and the extensive cuttings at Moorthwaite, Cumwhitton and White Moss at Walby were probably for the same purpose. Half the peat dome of Black Snib, a small raised bog near Longtown, was removed long ago, most probably to supply fuel peat to that place or Carlisle. Around 1900 chemical works were set up beside Glasson and Drumburgh Mosses to produce ammonia fertiliser, paraffin wax and other substances. Extraneous materials such as animal bones and guano were used, but the operations were associated with extensive peat cutting in the vicinity. It is unclear now whether this peat contained substances involved in the chemical processes, or whether it was used simply as fuel. Still later, the utility of unhumified *Sphagnum* peat ('moss litter') as a growing and composting medium in horticulture was realised, and a more concerted attack on the lowland peat bogs began.

In 1948, the Cumberland Moss Litter Company began extracting peat from systems of trenches on the east side of Bowness Moss and the south side of Glasson Moss. Processing sheds were set up at Glasson Moss and light railways ran onto the bogs to carry the cut peat. Yet within a few years the company removed its plant and transferred operations to the north side of Wedholme Flow, apparently because borings indicated highly humified peat below the upper layer of good moss litter at Bowness and Glasson. Donald Walker, who made detailed pollen analytical studies of these bogs, reckoned they had merely hit a 'retardation layer' representing an ancient period of drying and slower bog growth (p. 127), overlying a considerable depth of fresh, unhumified moss peat. The company's departure saved most of Bowness and Glasson Mosses from further damage, though the surface of the cut areas shrank downwards and developed dense growths of heather and some invading birch wood.

The commercial peat cutters also moved in on Solway Moss and Bolton Fell, and ruined both as examples of lowland bog. The former is completely degraded to a bare peat surface over its whole extent (Fig. 12.4), and the latter appears to be heading the same way. Some two square kilometres on the east side of Wedholme Flow have also been reduced to a black wasteland, but a sizeable area in the west and south-west was in different ownership and survived until SSSI status was able to defend it against further encroachment. Solway Moss was, in 1771–72, the scene of a famous bog-burst, vividly described by Thomas Pennant. From a total area of 600 hectares, some 120 hectares discharged a 'Stygian tide' of semifluid black peat up to four metres thick that engulfed several farmhouses, though without human loss of life. It was said that the side of the bog that burst, evidently on the east since the peat flow reached the River Esk, had been weakened by extensive peat cutting along that edge. Most likely the event was also preceded by heavy rain, swelling the unstable peat body and increasing the pressure on its edges.

Fens

Few genuine fens remain among the lowland peatlands, and the best examples, such as Newton Reigny Moss, belong to the limestone areas (Chapter 7). They were once more widespread in the Solway district, and Cardew Mires, a famous swamp west of Dalston, was reputedly the former haunt of bitterns, but had largely been drained away by 1892. Others occupied the shallow valleys of Black Dub and Holme Dub between Allonby and Abbeytown, but are now pastureland, except for a small patch of rich fen at Thornhill Moss near Southerfield.

Many lowland bogs in small valleys and hollows among the glacial drift are subject to variable conditions of nutrients and aeration in the groundwater supply, and their vegetation varies from typical acidic peat moss kinds to a range of fen types, especially that known as 'poor fen', with bottle sedge, common sedge, bogbean, marsh marigold, marsh cinquefoil, red rattle, common cotton-grass and bogmosses associated with slight enrichment (*S. squarrosum*, *S. teres*, *S. subsecundum* and *S. contortum*) and also patches of willow carr, mostly of grey willow. Their communities are referable to M 4 & 5, and W 2 (Rodwell, 1991a and b).

Fig. 6.7 Enclave of raised bog within rich fen and carr at Biglands Bog.

An interesting remnant of such mixed peatland is Biglands Bog, occupying a few hundred-metre stretch of the Bampton Beck immediately east of Biglands village, south of Kirkbride. It is mostly fairly rich fen with abundant reed-grass, sedges and willow carr, containing slender, greater and lesser tussock- and brown sedges, alder buckthorn, and grey and bay willows, besides the plants just mentioned; but has a contrasting nucleus of acidic bog with *Sphagnum* carpet and typical plants such as bog rosemary, bog asphodel, cranberry, white beak-sedge and cotton-grass (Fig. 6.7). Along the outer edge of this bog, and within the *Sphagnum* carpet, there were in 1954 pools containing copious 'brown mosses' typical of calcareous fen such as *Drepanocladus revolvens*, *Campylium stellatum*, *Scorpidium scorpioides* and *Acrocladium giganteum*, pointing to an unusual water chemistry, with sudden changes from acidic to base-rich. Other plants around these pools were bog sedge, great sundew and butterwort. Seepage of polluted water later destroyed these interesting pools. While the site is too small to be an important bird locality, both garganey and spotted crake were suspected of nesting here in the 1950s. The sluggish Bampton Beck flowing through the centre was once a great haunt of water voles.

The Eden valley between Carlisle and Kirkby Stephen has many small peatlands in glacial hollows. Moorthwaite Moss near Cumwhitton is a cut-over peat moss with surrounding pine wood that has seeded onto the bog surface. The old peat cuttings have regenerated one of the best examples of active *Sphagnum* bog, with a hummock and hollow structure and great abundance of bog rosemary and cranberry; but the hollows are less distinct than when I first knew it in 1948 (Plate 17). The other typical acidic lowland bog plants were well represented, and bog asphodel attained great luxuriance under the freedom from grazing and partial shade of the pines (Plate 18). Only a small patch of poor fen occurs here, but the adjoining Cumwhitton Moss is a more varied peatland complex. Though mainly a mixture of open peat moss and pine–birch wood over acid peat, it contained a central area subject to more base-rich seepage. Old peat cuttings here have abundant tussocks of greater tussock-sedge and a patch of willow carr had broad-leaved cotton-grass, lesser tussock-sedge, red rattle and the rare moss *Tomentypnum nitens*. The marsh fern has been found recently – one of its very few Cumbrian occurrences.

Some of these small basin and valley mires have suffered deterioration or even total loss. Tarn Wadling at High Hesket was noted for cranberries, probably in poor fen, but also had open water with water lobelia. It was drained around 1850, but still held open water in wet years, and had a thriving black-headed gull colony in 1920, while pochards nested here in 1927 for the first time in Cumbria. Sandford Mire near Warcop had a notable rich fen flora, said to include alpine bartsia, up to 1938. Both sites were completely reclaimed to farmland later. Cliburn Moss under Whinfell, east of Penrith, is another cut-over and partially pine-grown acidic bog, rather like Cumwhitton Moss, where fen and bog communities have regenerated in the wet hollows. Many of the plants named for Biglands Bog were present, with again a mixture of species needing acidic and base-rich conditions. Although still good in 1956, the site has deteriorated markedly in recent years and some of these species are evidently lost. There is still open, spongy swamp in the north, but recent deep drains tap the bog and the south end is now a jungle of invading birch and willows. In 1957, the little hollow of Whitefaugh Moss near Brampton had a young pine plantation on a cut-over bog in which the old peat 'pots' had regenerated *Sphagnum* lawns with the densest carpets of cranberry I ever saw. In 1998, there was a mature pine wood and not a trace of bog vegetation remained, only the dried-out hollows of the former peat cuttings.

While the majority of these peatlands in wet basins and valleys have escaped reclamation or major physical damage, a few have been affected by the seepage of nutrients from surrounding farmlands. Increases of nitrogen and phosphate are shown especially by the mosses, with great increase in *Rhytidiadelphus squarrosus* and *Acrocladium cuspidatum* in fen and marsh, and in *Aulacomnium palustre* and *Sphagnum recurvum* in acidic bogs. *Tomentypnum nitens* has disappeared from Cumwhitton Moss and from two of its upland sites through such enrichment.

The Solway tarns of Thurstonfield and Monkhill Loughs had areas of fringing sedge swamp, fen and willow carr, and the small Moorthwaite Tarn near Wigton had by 1950 become completely filled in by colonising fen and abandoned by its once large colony of black-headed gulls. When I saw them in 1957, the abandoned Solway Moss duck ponds (p. 133) looked like natural patches of fen, with reed, bulrush and reed sweet-grass, though these plants had been introduced for cover. A fragment of rich fen carr with greater spearwort and lesser tussock-sedge has survived at Temple

Sowerby Moss, close to the A66 road. Udford Moss near the foot of the River Eamont had a few interesting plants, including bog sedge. Pockets of poor fen occur on or under the low sandstone hills flanking the Eden, as around Blackmoss Pool near Armathwaite; and a long hollow on Wan Fell north of Penrith has a more uniformly acidic poor fen with tall bog sedge and in 1934 held a large colony of black-headed gulls (E. Blezard).

The lowland fringe of west Cumberland also has a series of mainly mixed peatlands in hollows and valleys of the coastal glacial deposits. Salta Moss near Allonby is mostly a cut-over raised bog, but with areas of poor fen and willow carr. Silver Tarn near Nethertown is a poor fen, Low Church Moss at Beckermet a slightly richer fen and carr, and Hallsenna Moor near Drigg a mixture of poor fen and acidic heathland. Towards Millom, Whitbeck Moss, Baldmire, Kirksanton Moss and Spunham Moss are other examples of poor fen with carr woodland. Characteristic plants of these west coast peatlands are royal fern, marsh St John's wort (Fig. 6.8), bog pimpernel and lesser skullcap. In southern Lakeland, there are a few small examples of lowland poor fen in the Silurian foothills, such as the valley mire just east of Tarneybank Tarn, a site for tall bog sedge, and on the moors between Torver and Gawthwaite. Burns Beck Moss near Killington Reservoir is an interesting complex of raised bog and valley mire with no fewer than 19 species of bog moss, reflecting conditions from strongly acidic to mesotrophic.

Marshy fields with marginal ditches, perhaps the remnants of former fen, and sluggish lowland becks, produce an assortment of moisture-loving

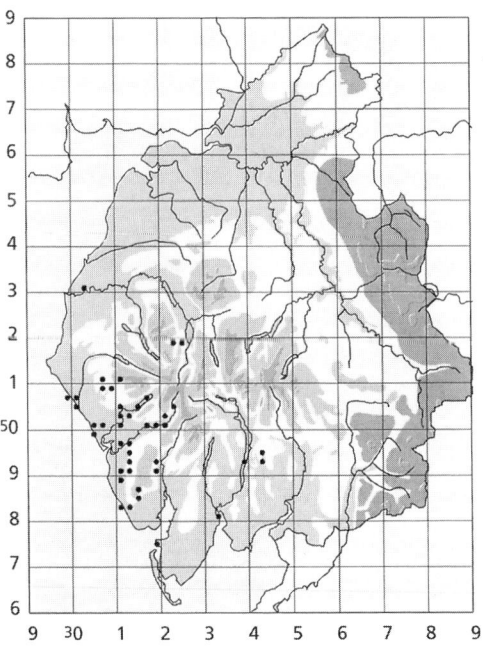

Fig. 6.8 The distribution of marsh St John's wort, a plant of south-western occurrence in Cumbria. (Halliday, 1997, Map 218.)

plants such as great hairy willowherb, water forget-me-not, amphibious bistort, water pepper, fool's water-cress, marsh ragwort, water-cress, marsh yellow-cress, brooklime, short-fruited willowherb, lesser pond sedge and floating sweet-grasses.

Tarns and ponds

The lowlands have a number of small lakes, some of artificial origin but adding habitat diversity to the agricultural scene, and with some value for waterfowl and dragonflies. In the Solway area, the two artificially dammed Loughs of Thurstonfield and Monkhill were once noted bird haunts, with fringing swamp and carr where mute swans, coots, dabchicks, water rails and sedge warblers bred. Monkhill, in particular, could be good for wildfowl in winter, especially in stormy weather, when up to 1,000 wigeon would take shelter there; and they were regular haunts of Bewick's swan. Monkhill Lough was drained in the 1960s when its dam was destroyed, and has become an expanding willow carr, in which almond willow is abundant. It was a former site for rigid hornwort, while Thurstonfield had needle spike-rush, floating club-rush and yellow sedge *Carex viridula* ssp. *viridula*. Though natural, Martin Tarn near Wigton and Talkin Tarn near Brampton are rather bleak sheets of water with mostly bare margins: the second holds modest numbers of winter wildfowl at times.

The line of sandstone hills along the Eden valley has a series of small tarns, at Carlatton, Blackmoss Pool, Blaze Fell and Lazonby Fell, where black-headed gulls bred, mostly in small numbers but reaching several hundred pairs at the first site in 1932. Whins Pond east of Penrith has some interest as a waterfowl haunt, especially in winter.

Along the coast, Siddick Pond north of Workington is an important bird locality observed over many years by Ralph Stokoe and others (Stokoe, 1952). Originating as a swampy depression in the old course of the River Derwent, it became flooded through industrial excavations and building of railway embankments, and has developed communities typical of Cumbrian mesotrophic standing waters. Quite large beds of common reed occur in the deeper water, along with a fair selection of aquatic plants such as amphibious bistort, pond water-crowfoot, common water starwort, water plantain and pondweeds; and species of the wet margins, including yellow flag, meadowsweet, rushes, spike-rush and water forget-me-not – communities A 19, S 4 & 10 (Rodwell, 1995).

Stokoe reported that among the Siddick passerine birds, 39 were regular and 15 occasional visitors, many species being attracted by the herbaceous and shrubby vegetation of the railway banks and other surrounds. In the other bird groups, 32 were regular and 35 occasional visitors, with the ducks (16 species) and waders (18 species) especially well represented. The Pond is a noted autumn and winter haunt of mallard, teal, wigeon, shoveler, pochard, tufted duck, cormorant, curlew and coot. The occasionals include osprey, ruff, black tern, black-necked grebe and black-tailed godwit. The reed beds were a favoured roost of starlings for over 50 years, with peak numbers of 20,000 in 1948. They were also one of the few breeding places of the reed warbler in Lakeland. The introduced ruddy duck bred here in 1997, and pochard do so regularly. Nesting species total 35.

South of St Bees, Braystones Tarn had some local aquatic and fen plants, such as lesser water-plantain, nodding and three-lobed bur marigolds, and royal fern, but is now within a caravan park. Sellafield Tarn appears to have dried out. Barfield Tarn at Bootle is a small, nutrient-poor lake. In the southern Silurian foothills east of Kendal and in the Ulverston peninsula, outside the National Park, are numerous mostly small tarns, such as Terrybank Tarn near Mansergh, which Wilson (1938) noted as having considerable botanical interest. Some are artificial reservoirs and Killington Reservoir between Kendal and Sedbergh is the largest, constructed in 1829 to service the Lancaster–Kendal canal. Killington, with its tree-covered island, and the adjoining Lily Mere, have assumed some importance as all-year-round bird haunts, as the Sedbergh School records show (Cleasby, 1999). Its breeding species include black-headed gull (3,800 pairs in 1999, having increased at the expense of Sunbiggin Tarn), Canada goose (333 birds in June 1999) and great-crested grebe, while the passage migrants and wintering visitors show a varied selection of waterfowl, with mallard, wigeon and goosander. Lily Mere is notable for the dense rafts of floating club-rush (Halliday, 1997).

Farm ponds of varying size can be quite important wildlife habitats, especially as breeding places for amphibians. One densely grown with rush clumps at North Scales farm, near Heads Nook, had a black-headed gullery that grew to over 1,000 pairs in 1955, but then faded away as colonies of

Fig. 6.9 Cumbria Wildlife Trust nature reserve at disused Bowness-on-Solway gravel pits.

this bird are prone to do. Other smaller ponds, especially along field edges, have either been filled in or have grown over naturally, causing considerable decline in moorhen numbers. The first nesting of tufted duck in Cumberland in 1922 was on rush-grown ponds at Cumwhitton and Thiefside beside the A6 road, but the second of these has gone, also. Sand and gravel extraction has, however, created many new tarns and ponds in more recent years, and some of these have developed bird and other interest. The sizeable tarns at Longtown, Oulton and Cardew Mires are examples, while the smaller Bowness ponds are a CWT reserve (Fig. 6.9). Some of the larger ponds remaining from mining of gypsum at Cocklakes near Cotehill were a regular haunt of little grebes. In the south, the brown hawker dragonfly appears on tarns and ponds from Barrow to Silverdale. The southern hawker is now quite widespread in lowland Cumbria and often seen at large garden ponds.

Rivers

Though less turbulent than in their upper courses among the uplands, the main rivers of the lowlands are mostly rather swift-flowing over stony beds. Only where they enter the sea are there slow and tidal sections with sandy beds. The Waver and Wampool flowing to Moricambe Bay are perhaps the exceptions. Rising at modest elevations on the limestone foothills, at 320 metres on Faulds Brow and 250 metres on Warnell Fell, they follow slow and meandering courses through the lowlands, and carry a higher content of clay and silt to the sea than most Lakeland rivers. The Eden is the largest and longest river at 105 kilometres, and collects as tributaries the lesser streams of Lyvennet, Lowther and Eamont from Westmorland, the Irthing from the Borders, the Caldew from Skiddaw Forest and the Petteril from Inglewood Forest. It is one of the least polluted rivers in northern England, and important also for the wide range of ecological conditions, including the entry of limestone streams in the upper catchment, and lower erodible sandstone giving extensive areas of gravel and silt, which provide good spawning and nursery areas for fish. The lowest section of the River Esk from Dumfriesshire belongs to Cumbria, and the Liddel, which joins it near Scotsdyke, forms the Border Line with Scotland. Flatter sections have deep alluvial banks, and after prolonged rain the Eden at Carlisle runs redbrown with a large volume of suspended sediment. On the west the main rivers are the Ellen from the Uldale Fells, the Derwent from Bassenthwaite which collects the Cocker, the Ehen from Ennerdale, the Irt from Wasdale and the Esk from Eskdale. In the south, the Duddon, Leven and Kent form important estuaries.

Vegetation

The slower waters of the main rivers and their banks have communities of aquatic and semi-aquatic plants of some distinctness. The Eden is notable for river water-crowfoot (Fig. 6.10 and community A 18, Rodwell, 1995), blue water speedwell, amphibious bistort, flowering rush, Canadian waterweed, horned pondweed and curled pondweed, while its banks have hemp agrimony, creeping yellow-cress, tansy, clustered bellflower, green figwort,

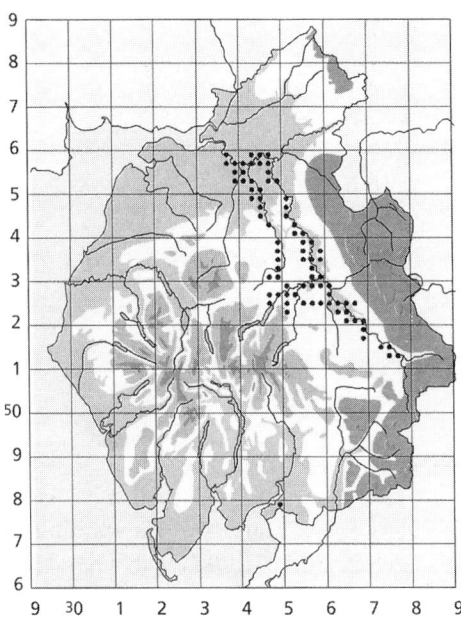

Fig. 6.10 The distribution of river water-crowfoot, a plant almost confined to the River Eden and River Petteril in Cumbria. (Halliday, 1997, Map 87.)

wood club-rush, sand leek, slender tufted sedge and the alien broad-leaved ragwort and Indian balsam.

Animals

The steep faces of alluvial sand forming the banks of some of these rivers in their lowland sections are breeding habitat for kingfisher and sand martin. The one is strictly territorial and pairs dig their breeding tunnels at fairly wide intervals. Blezard et al. (1943) describe the kingfisher as common on the Eden, Kent and Lune, and constant to its nesting haunts except when severe winters decimate its numbers, after which recovery may take several years. R. W. Robson noted a substantial long-term decline in numbers on north Westmorland rivers by 1962. The species seldom ranges to the headwaters of rivers, but occurs as far up the South Tyne as Alston. During the autumn and winter, kingfishers regularly move to the tidal reaches of the rivers and a few frequent the salt-marsh creeks. The colonial sand martins have groups of varying size along all the main rivers, the largest numbering 80 pairs or more. On seven miles of the River Eden above Appleby, with six colonies of 50–70 pairs some years before, only about 50 nests in total could be found in 1960 (R. W. Robson, in Stokoe, 1962). Unlike kingfishers, sand martins are not restricted to nesting places beside water, and many sand and gravel pits have flourishing colonies.

Goosanders and red-breasted mergansers now breed regularly on the bigger lowland rivers, having colonised them during the last 50 years. Cormorants have long had a roost on the red sandstone cliffs in Baron Wood, but are not known to nest there.

The Cumbrian stronghold of the otter is on the northern lowland rivers draining to the Solway, especially the Eden, Caldew, Petteril, Irthing, Gelt, Lyne, Liddel, Waver, Wampool and Ellen (Hewitt, 1999a). Otters occur along the Eden as far as Kirkby Stephen, on the tributaries of Lowther and Lyvennet and on bigger streams draining from the Pennines. The water vole was formerly widespread along the more sluggish lowland streams from north to south, and its demise on most of them is associated with the appearance of mink, which are now widespread on lowland watercourses.

The Eden is a famous Atlantic salmon river, with one of the largest populations of this fish in northern England. The records of ecclesiastical fishery disputes show it to have been celebrated thus as far back as the early thirteenth century. The salmon are able to run high into the headstreams in search of spawning sites. The Eden is proposed as a Special Area of Conservation for this and four other fish species listed as Annex II species under the European Union Habitats and Species Directive: sea lamprey, river lamprey, brook lamprey and bullhead, and also Atlantic stream crayfish. It also has major populations of eel, roach, chubb, dace, loach, three-spined stickleback and minnow.

Among the notable invertebrates, the banded demoiselle occurs mainly along the lower Eden from Rockcliffe to east of Carlisle, and on the lower Waver (Clarke, 1996), these being its northernmost British occurrences. The beautiful demoiselle was formerly on the Eden and Petteril near Carlisle, but has not been seen for many years. It is still in the south, but mainly on minor streams within the National Park. Beaumont Marsh by the Eden mouth produced a pair of the rare immigrant yellow-winged darter in the 1950s. The giant lacewing is especially along the Eden, and often found resting under bridges.

The River Ehen has probably the largest population of the freshwater pearl mussel in England, with high densities in places and an estimate of over 100,000 individuals for the entire river. Because of its increasing scarcity in mainland Europe, it is listed as an Annex II species under the European Union Habitats and Species Directive, and the River Ehen is accordingly proposed as a Special Area of Conservation. The conservation importance of the site is further enhanced by the presence of juveniles, indicating recruitment within the last four years, in contrast to many potentially moribund continental populations with only mature mussels (Brown et al., 1997).

7

The Limestone Foothills

The occurrence of the Carboniferous limestone is shown in Plate 4 and has been described in outline on pp. 22–5. The surface presence of limestone is less widespread than the geological map would suggest. In many places it is covered with deep layers of drift or loess: where this contains abundant material derived from limestone, the soil is calcareous, but where it is acidic or peat-covered, the limestone influence is negated, but may appear in drainage water. And although it is shown in Plate 4 as extensive in the Borders region north of the Tyne Gap, the rocks here belong to the Scottish Calciferous Sandstone Series, in which limestone occurs only as thin and impure bands.

General features
Many of the limestone hills have rock exposures as cliffs and screes. The cliffs – scars locally – are mostly low, but on the hills west of Kendal, notably Whitbarrow Scar, they reach heights of 30 metres or more and attract rock climbers. The special feature of these low limestone hills is, however, exposure of the bedrock as massive tabular 'pavements', either flat or gently inclined, with surfaces closely and deeply fissured by vertical crevices (grikes) that average from 30–40 centimetres wide and 90–180 centimetres deep. The intervening pavement surfaces (clints) may form fractured and loose layers of surface rock or consist of solid masses over many square metres. Geologists still argue over the precise manner of their formation, but the general process has involved the downwards percolation of water, especially along vertical joints in the limestone, gradually but variably dissolving away material to create the complex systems of grikes. Denudation has then exposed the bare rock surfaces, in some places over areas of two or three square kilometres. Many pavements have scattered erratics, either of limestone or other rock types, such as gritstone, showing that they were scraped bare by ice during glacial periods. In places, pavements obviously lie close to the surface, poking out just here and there, but are buried under a layer of soil and sometimes deep drift, carrying a closed vegetation.

The clint and grike formations are fascinating in their rock sculpture as well as their flora. Differential weathering produces an endlessly varied surface and vertical structure to the variably textured limestone. In places are massive blocks of pavement, flat and smooth as a table, with few grikes. More typically the clints are interrupted at every stride by fissures that vary from shallow scoops and pockets to deep clefts, their sides showing all manner of rugosities. Here and there, where the crevices are wider and more numerous, are piles of pancake rocks, of varying looseness, but often with the top layer rickety and ready to seesaw at an incautious footstep.

Shallower runnels typically drain radially into corner swallow holes, but in places (especially Hutton Roof Crags) these runnels form parallel series ('rakes') running down the slope of inclined pavement. Numerous pillars and columns have been carved out by weathering, and rock fragments of all sizes have collapsed into the grikes. Sometimes, broken chunks of rock have a jagged and many faceted form, but there is a progressive widening and rounding of grikes with time.

The grikes create conditions of shade and humidity akin to those of dense woodland, while their structure mostly prevents grazing by larger herbivores. They have accordingly become important for a distinctive flora, with a mixture of essentially woodland plants together with others that need open conditions and freedom from grazing. This is a rare habitat in Europe, and the Lakeland pavements are, together with those of adjoining parts of Yorkshire and Lancashire, the main occurrences of this important geological and ecological feature in Britain. Only the Burren of Co. Clare in western Ireland has a greater extent of limestone pavements.

For long the limestone pavements were left undisturbed, but the value of their loose rock as ornamental rockery stone was realised, and they rapidly came under attack by surface mining from the early 1960s. On the more fissured and fractured pavements, much of the surface rock is loose and can simply be lifted off, and crowbars can lever the less solid layers apart. Such activity proceeded apace and some of the more solid structures were assaulted with mechanical diggers and even explosives, in what became quarrying operations. Stone removal destroys the grikes and leaves a flat scree of mostly small, loose limestone fragments that is almost valueless as plant habitat. Many pavements were damaged and some were completely ruined before conservation action saved the best remaining examples, as nature reserves or Sites of Special Scientific Interest. Under the Wildlife and Countryside Act 1981, special Limestone Pavement Orders became available to local authorities, English Nature and the Countryside Agency to protect still further sites.

One understands the attractions of these weathered limestones as rockery stone, but it is shameful that so many of the pavements have been despoiled in some degree by this destructive activity. In their comprehensive survey, Ward & Evans (1976) found that only 3 per cent of 537 pavements, mainly in Cumbria and Yorkshire, showed no detectable damage – and that was a quarter of a century ago. They are quite irreplaceable features. Geoff Hamilton spoke out in his TV gardening programmes against the mining of limestone pavements and helpfully showed how passable imitations of their weathered stone could be made of concrete in moulds.

The soils of the limestone are thin, dark rendzinas, well-drained brown or red-brown loams, and moister clay-loams often formed on drift: all are highly calcareous and often contain free lime. In moister situations, humus is usually of the 'mull' type, grading into base-rich fen peat where waterlogging is permanent.

Besides the open communities of rock habitats, semi-natural vegetation remaining on the limestone soils is of woodland, herb-rich grassland,

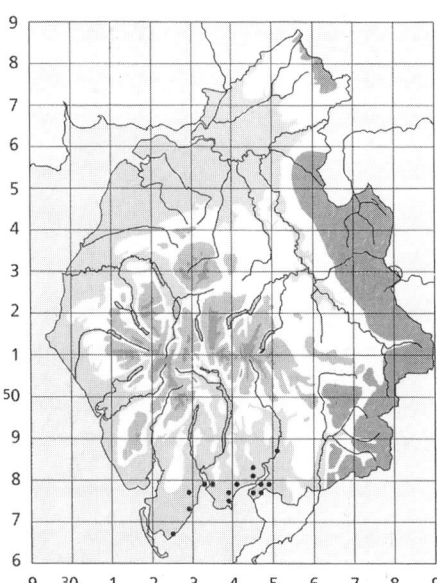

Fig. 7.1 The distribution of green-winged orchid, a plant confined to the Morecambe Bay limestone in Cumbria. (Halliday, 1997, Map 1188.)

marsh or fen. The grasslands are often heavily grazed, and have a short sward in which the grasses are intimately mixed with dicotyledon herbs: many speccies are depauperate and seldom able to flower in these situations. This complex of calcareous habitats gives an extremely rich flora, and the limestone foothills have been described as the northern equivalent of the southern England chalk downs. The two districts share a good many species in common, but the Cumbrian limestone has a distinctive northern element and its varied rock habitats support a plant assemblage that has no counterpart on the smooth downlands of the south. Some distinctive calcicoles are confined in Lakeland to the limestone fringing Morecambe Bay, and reach their northern British limits as native plants here (Fig. 7.1). The flora is mainly lowland and sub-montane, but there are a few montane species, notably holly fern growing at only 260 metres.

Roudsea, Humphrey Head, Arnside and Hutton Roof

This southernmost group of limestone outcrops forms scattered low hills to the south and south-west of Kendal. Woodland is one of its important habitats, beginning with Roudsea Wood east of the Leven estuary. The Wood covers two ridges of contrasting geology separated by a shallow valley containing a fen and small tarn. The western ridge is acidic Bannisdale Slate with sessile oak wood, but the eastern one is limestone with a more varied woodland, of mainly pedunculate oak, ash, small-leaved lime, gean and birch, with a little wild service tree and field maple, both apparently native, and some stands of yew. There are typical limestone shrubs such as buckthorn, spindle and the rare mezereon, as well as hazel, holly, hawthorn, guelder rose and blackthorn. The field layer has abundant false brome and dog's mercury, and lily-of-the-valley is locally plentiful. The rich woodland flora includes columbine, giant bellflower, toothwort, gromwell, tutsan and stone bramble. More open places have fly orchid, ploughman's spikenard, pale St John's wort, sand leek, star of Bethlehem, fingered sedge and blue moor-grass.

The rich valley fen between the two ridges has reed, several sedges – greater and lesser tussock, cyperus, elongated, bladder and brown – blunt-flowered rush, purple and wood small-reed, common meadow-rue and marsh fern, while the tarn has common and lesser water plantains. Along rides with a transition from dry limestone soils to peat there is the large yellow-sedge growing in one of its two known British localities. The whole Roudsea NNR, with its complex of habitats including adjoining peat mosses, is extremely rich botanically, and contains at least 340 species of vascular plant. West of the Leven estuary, the limestone is less notable botanically, though the strongly calcareous Urswick Tarn south of Ulverston has some interesting aquatic plants, such as water dock, greater spearwort, mare's tail, lesser bulrush and the two bur marigolds.

The rocky promontory of Humphrey Head, 53 metres high and flanked by cliffs in places, projects into the sheltered sandy head of Morecambe Bay west of the Kent estuary. Its base is lapped by gentle waves and only at high water, so that the saline influence is shown by some of the typical maritime plants, including rock samphire, mostly near the base of the headland, but the slopes have a scrubby woodland or rocky limestone grassland. Deadly nightshade grows amongst the scrub and a cave formerly had maidenhair fern, but this was probably collected out. The chief fame of Humphrey Head is as the refuge of a small group of rare southern lime-loving plants that grow only in a few widely separated places in Britain. The most abundant are the spiked speedwell, which is in fair quantity in the turf and on rock ledges, and hoary rock-rose along the cliff edge. Spotted cat's-ear survives with a total of some 30 plants on ungrazed ledges, while goldilocks is reduced to one or two patches on ledges of the sheer cliff. This is the most northerly British locality for three of these species (not hoary rockrose), and all are survivors from a once more widespread distribution on base-rich substrates in postglacial times and of grasslands prevalent in the ice age beyond the ice margins.

In the Arnside area, on the east side of the Kent estuary, one of the finest limestone pavements of all is at Gaitbarrows, just outside our boundary in Silverdale, and the best examples on the Cumbrian side are in Underlaid and Middlebarrow Woods. The modest eminence of Arnside Knott (159 metres) lies nearest the sea, and has rather little exposed rock other than a southern scarp slope with scree. It has a varied range of woodland and scrub, with oak, ash, birch, hazel, yew and juniper, but the presence of abundant introduced Scots pine, larch and sycamore detracts from the appearance of naturalness. Tall shrubs of calcareous soils include buckthorn and Lancastrian whitebeam, while the low-growing rock-rose is abundant. Woods in the adjoining Arnside Park are a locality for the rare saprophytic yellow bird's-nest, and there are at least two localities in the

Arnside area for the very rare baneberry. Deadly nightshade, gromwell, dropwort and wild basil are southerners of grassy places among scrub and woodland in the area. Green hellebore is evidently native here and in other scattered places on the Morecambe Bay limestone, and the rarest of the polypody ferns *Polypodium cambricum* has several localities in this area.

More open ground near the crest of the hill has limestone grassland and an interesting area of heath in which calcifuge shrubs such as ling and bell heather are mixed with species such as burnet rose, grasses and small herbs typical of limestone soils – a northern equivalent of the 'chalk heath' of the southern England downlands. The flora here is rich, with spring cinquefoil, squinancywort, dark red helleborine, rare spring sedge, fingered sedge and rock violet – the last in by far the lowest of its four British localities. There are old records for burnt orchid and maidenhair fern, and the latter still survives on limestone outcrops close to the sea in this district. Other limestone grassland near the edge of Morecambe Bay between the Ulverston peninsula and Silverdale supports colonies of autumn lady's tresses and green-winged orchid at or near their northern British limits, and two colonies of spiked speedwell. Hale Moss near Burton-in-Kendal is a remnant calcareous fen with a rich flora, including black bog-rush, bird's-eye primrose and northern marsh orchid.

Rising to 274 metres east of the M6 motorway is the broad ridge with Dalton Crags, Hutton Roof Crags, Clawthorpe Fell and Farleton Knott. Limestone pavement is extensive here, and probably the best of this feature in Lakeland, in the variety of its form and the associated plant communities. Farleton Knott has mainly bare pavements, with very deep grikes

Fig. 7.2 Limestone pavements with extensive scrub development at Hutton Roof Crags, near Milnthorpe.

Fig. 7.3 Aerial view of Hutton Roof Crags, with limestone pavements, scrub and woodland. Clawthorpe Quarry in distance. (Ronald Mitchell.)

in places, but the southern part has been somewhat spoiled by limestone removal. The other areas are little damaged and Hutton Roof Crags (Figs 7.2 and 7.3) have extensive development of patchy scrub with ash, hazel, rowan, guelder rose, yew, juniper, blackthorn, hawthorn, holly, Lancastrian whitebeam, wych elm and sycamore. Gorse forms dense patches in places. The grikes have an abundance of woodland plants, notably hart's tongue, dog's mercury, stone bramble and herb robert. Calcicole ferns are well represented, with prickly shield-fern, maidenhair spleenwort, wall-rue and brittle bladder fern, while the northern green spleenwort is occasional.

Two special grike ferns are the rigid buckler fern and limestone fern. The first is abundant, forming fairly dense clumps with distinctive grey-green – almost blue-green – fronds (Plate 21), and in Britain is almost confined to the Carboniferous limestone of northern England. The limestone fern is more patchy here; it bears a superficial resemblance to the oak fern, but has a different 'jizz' (Fig. 7.4) When I first encountered this fern, in the Craven limestone pavements, I was struck by its strongly aromatic smell, but have been puzzled on meeting with it subsequently to find this distinctive odour lacking.

The clints show all stages in colonisation of bare rock to form a closed grassland, dominated by blue moor-grass, and a more mixed type with ver-

Fig. 7.4 Limestone fern in deep grike of pavements at Little Asby Scar, Shap Fells.

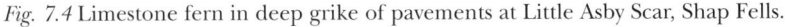

nal grass and bents. This in turn shows transitions to an acidic heath community with heather, bilberry, tormentil and wavy hair grass, developed on the quite extensive areas of wind-blown loess that overlie the pavements in places. Bracken becomes dominant on larger pockets of leached soil on broad terraces. There is also an intermediate community, again corresponding to southern 'chalk heath', with a mixture of the limestone and heathland species. In the more open places and short turf are noteworthy limestone plants in dark red helleborine, bloody cranesbill, rock-rose, horseshoe vetch, squinancywort, angular Solomon's seal, spring sandwort, spring cinquefoil, hairy violet, hairy rock-cress, burnet rose, dropwort, fly orchid, ploughman's spikenard, carline thistle, bird's-foot sedge, mountain melick and meadow oat-grass. Some herbs are more associated with patches of scrub, such as pale St John's wort and lily-of-the-valley. Scars at the north-west end of Farleton Knott have much lesser meadow-rue.

The woodlands and scrub of the southern limestone belong mostly to types W 7, 8, 9 & 21 (Rodwell, 1991a). Fen vegetation belongs to M 9, grasslands to CG1, 8–10, and pavement communities to OV 38 & 39 (Rodwell, 1991b, 1992, 2000).

Lyth and Winster

West of Kendal are two broad limestone ridges, the first from Brigsteer to Helsfell east of the Lyth valley and the second the mass of Whitbarrow between Lyth and Winster, north-east of Witherslack (Fig. 7.5). The smaller hill of Yewbarrow forms an outlying ridge immediately north of Witherslack (there is another Yewbarrow, eight kilometres to the west, on

Fig. 7.5 Woods and cliffs on Carboniferous limestone at Whitbarrow Scar, Winster Valley, near Kendal.

the Silurian). They are quite low, reaching only 229 and 215 metres, but show well-marked scarp and dip slope structure, with extensive scars and steep screes facing to the west at Scout Scar and Cunswick Scar on the first ridge, and still higher cliffs facing west and south-east at Whitbarrow Scar on the other. The Helsington ridge has a good deal of flat scree but rather little pavement, while Whitbarrow has long lines of low upper scarp and scree, and many somewhat fragmented pavements (Fig. 7.6). There are notable woods at Brigsteer, Underbarrow and around Witherslack, but extensive conifer plantations on the eastern, dip slope of Whitbarrow are a complete anomaly.

The woods vary from sessile oak–ash high forest with dense brambles near Witherslack Hall to lower stands of mixed ash, wych elm, oak, birch, small-leaved lime and hazel on more calcareous soils, and scrub with hazel, yew, juniper, guelder rose, buckthorn, privet and Lancastrian and rock white-beams where rock is near or at the surface. Wilson (1938) noted special abundance of whitebeam on Yewbarrow. On the plateau of Whitbarrow, blackthorn forms low patches on flat scree, while the western scarp slope has patches of pure yew wood (community W 13). At the south end of the Helsington ridge, Brigsteer Wood was an abandoned coppice-with-standards of the mixed ash type (above). The coppice was mainly of hazel with ash and sycamore frequent in both coppiced and standard form, oak and birch as standards, and alder along the alluvial base. The associated shrub and field layers are species-rich and similar to Roudsea Wood, with mezereon, locally abundant wild daffodil and lily-of-the-valley, and a good range of woodland orchids. Under National Trust ownership, about half the wood was felled after 1961 and replanted with conifer–broadleaved mixtures containing much larch and beech (not native in northern Britain). These changes were regarded as one of the worst examples of insensitive management for nature conservation, and the Trust has been under pressure to restore the semi-natural character of the wood by removing the non-native trees.

Besides the woodlands and scrub, these limestone hills have much the same variety of other habitats as the Hutton Roof ridge, with grassland and heath ranging from calcicolous to acidic, and rock features in which scar and scree are more extensive than pavement. There is the same profusion of common calcicoles such as blue moor-grass, false brome, yellow oat-grass, crested hair-grass, quaking grass, spring sedge, glaucous sedge, rock-rose, small scabious, limestone bedstraw, hairy violet, mullein, hoary plantain, fairy flax, salad burnet, harebell, wild thyme, maidenhair spleenwort, wall-rue and hart's tongue. The flora is equally rich in uncommon species, with nearly all those listed for Hutton Roof and Farleton Knott. The rigid buckler fern and limestone fern are again locally plentiful, and rustyback fern occurs in natural habitats. In addition there is a noteworthy abundance of the rare hoary rock-rose on top of the scars, hound's tongue and fingered sedge are on Whitbarrow, and the limestone shrubs mezereon, spurge laurel and mountain currant occur sparingly as evident natives. The bryophyte flora of these hills is extremely rich, with rarities such as

Fig. 7.6 Aerial view of Whitbarrow from north end, showing scars, screes, pavements, scrub and woodland. Part is a CWT reserve. (Ronald Mitchell.)

Rhytidium rugosum, Homomallium incurvatum, Tortella nitida, Campylium calcareum, Isothecium striatulum and *Pleurochaete squarrosa*. The small calcareous lake of Cunswick Tarn below Cunswick Scar is rich in aquatic and fen plants, including great fen-sedge.

Some important plants have evidently been lost from Whitbarrow, most notably the lady's slipper orchid, for which nineteenth-century records were claimed. The sword-leaved helleborine and yellow bird's-nest have not been seen for many years, and an apparently native colony of chives at Rus Mickle, last seen in 1937, could be a victim of afforestation. Marsh helleborine was last seen at Cunswick Tarn in 1952.

Shap Fells

The third area with massive exposures of limestone is the range of low hills mainly east of Shap village and the M6 motorway, forming a bridge between the Lake fells and the Pennines. Reaching only 412 metres above Orton, it contains an important series of pavements, woodland, grassland and wetland.

On the east side of Shap Fells, close to Kirkby Stephen, is the deep valley of Smardale, clothed in woods of ash, wych elm, oak, birch, hazel, aspen and hawthorn, and opening out above into limestone grassland (Fig. 7.7). It contains a rich limestone flora with over 100 vascular plant species. Part of the glen is ungrazed and the steep woodland slopes have a herb-dominated field layer. The line of the former Tebay to Darlington railway runs along the east side of the valley and crosses the top of the wooded section

Fig. 7.7 Wooded limestone glen from disused viaduct at Smardale, near Kirkby Stephen. Presence of old Norway spruce suggests this is secondary ash–birch wood, despite its botanical richness.

by a fine viaduct, while the still used Carlisle–Settle line crosses its foot on another viaduct. The disused rail trackway has an unusual abundance of lesser wintergreen, and the grassy banks have a fine colony of bloody cranesbill and abundant rock-rose, while the more open slopes have a profusion of blue moor-grass. Fly orchid occurs here, along with early purple, fragrant, common spotted, greater butterfly, bird's-nest and frog orchids, greater twayblade and broad-leaved helleborine. Other noteworthy plants are bird's-foot sedge, horseshoe vetch, stone bramble, melancholy thistle, carline thistle, saw-wort, wood cranesbill, marjoram, mountain melick and green spleenwort. The valley is now an important reserve of the Cumbria Wildlife Trust.

The limestone pavements of the Orton–Asby–Sunbiggin area are the most extensive of these habitats in Cumbria and lie at the higher elevation of 300–400 metres, but they are almost devoid of scrub, apart from very stunted hazel, ash, blackthorn, hawthorn and bird cherry rooted in the crevices (Fig. 7.8). The grike communities and species are well represented and the pavements are set in limestone grasslands with a wide range of calcicoles. Those immediately around Sunbiggin and towards Potts Valley have been somewhat despoiled by limestone removal, but the Great Asby pavements, now a National Nature Reserve, are little disturbed and have fine rigid buckler fern and limestone fern, as well as green spleenwort, brittle bladder fern, hart's tongue, male fern and prickly shield-fern: community OV 40 (Rodwell, 2000). More fragmentary pavements occur on Crosby Ravensworth Fell, but have little apart from abundant green spleenwort and bladder fern. The Orton limestone ridges have patches of pavement, but a

Fig. 7.8 Limestone pavements devoid of scrub but with a rich grike (crevice) flora, at Great Asby Scar, Shap Fells.

much larger extent of rocky grassland with a short, grazed turf in which the bird's-foot sedge is widespread. Rare plants of this ground are dwarf milkwort, hutchinsia, spring cinquefoil, rare spring sedge and baneberry.

Sunbiggin Tarn and its vicinity are important for the range of calcareous habitats, beginning with the Tarn itself and its marshy surrounds (Plate 20). The Tarn is a small upland marl lake, and the bottom of its shallow eastern half is covered with stoneworts, while deeper water has an abundance of curled pondweed. There is a thin fringing growth of reed, and a few clumps of great fen-sedge still persist in its highest British locality. The southern arm is covered with a fen that now encloses the smaller Cow Dub Tarn, and has sedge swamp with bottle, slender, tufted, yellow, and greater and lesser tussock-sedges and a carpet of brown mosses in which *Drepanocladus cossonii* is especially abundant. Bogbean, marsh cinquefoil, kingcup, water and marsh horsetails, and flat-sedge are also plentiful. The community belongs to M 9 (Rodwell, 1991b) and was described by Holdgate (1955b). This south-west sector has become nutrient-enriched by the long-established black-headed gull colony, and perhaps also by the addition of fertiliser on the surrounding land, so that its moss carpets are in less good condition than 50 years ago.

To the west is Tarn Moor, a shallow valley in the glacial drift drained by a meandering stream from Cow Dub. Here, an interesting complex of vegetation has developed, ranging from acid bog with *Sphagnum* to calcareous springs, flushes, marsh and wet pasture (Holdgate, 1955a). Some of the springs have tufa-forming mounds of the golden moss *Cratoneuron commutatum*, and there is short rush and sedge marsh with black bog-rush, jointed rush, broad-leaved cotton-grass, few-flowered spike-rush, dioecious, yellow, tawny and carnation sedges with brown moss carpets. Grass of Parnassus, red rattle, butterwort, marsh valerian, purple and crimson marsh orchids, and flat-sedge are plentiful, while the damp pastures in June are pink with a profusion of bird's-eye primrose. The montane hair sedge occurs sparingly, and calcareous flushes on the surrounding moor formerly had abundant yellow saxifrage, but this seems to have disappeared through grazing, for this is sheepwalk. Communities M 10, 11 & 37 (Rodwell, 1991b) are represented.

On the higher moor away from the calcareous seepages, the more leached and acidic drift has typical heather ground, formerly managed as grouse moor. In places, there is an intermediate community where the base-rich soil is still near the surface, and the limestone protrudes in places. This is another example of northern herb-rich *Calluna* 'limestone heath', with wood anemone, lady's bedstraw, northern bedstraw, salad burnet, bitter-vetch and bird's-foot trefoil. The heather moorland shows all stages in replacement by *Nardus* grassland, and is clearly continuing to lose ground. Tarn House Tarn at Ravenstonedale is also in a limestone catchment, but neither it nor its adjoining marshy ground can compare with the botanical interest of Sunbiggin.

Within enclosed pastures near Orton and Crosby Ravensworth, calcareous flushes similar to those on Tarn Moor are the habitat of alpine bartsia, one of the Upper Teesdale specialities, growing with hair sedge, viviparous bistort, flat-sedge and other plants of these habitats listed above. Some of the pre-war hay meadows of this district were fabulously rich in colourful and fragrant flowering herbs. Wilson (1938) described one on the limestone near Great Asby that had meadow and bloody cranesbills, clustered bellflower, ox-eye daisy, great and salad burnets, black and great knapweeds, small scabious, kidney vetch, rest-harrow, lady's bedstraw, saw-wort, marjoram, betony, rough hawkbit, hoary plantain, twayblade, fragrant orchid and the rare perennial flax. The herb-rich meadows with community MG 3 (Rodwell, 1992) have lost ground enormously, but a few survive and the best are notified as SSSIs. Some populations of these distinctive herbs are much reduced and perennial flax has lost two of its five known colonies in the area (Halliday, 1997). Some of the northern meadow communities with wood cranesbill, globeflower and melancholy thistle (Fig. 7.9) are now as well represented on roadside verges and railway banks as anywhere (Plate 23). It was while botanising in the hay meadows of this district in 1988 that Geoffrey Halliday found a plant completely new to the British flora – the leafless hawk's-beard, a tall yellow-flowered composite

Fig. 7.9 Melancholy thistle flowering vigorously on limestone roadside verge at Kelleth, near Tebay.

Fig. 7.10 Marsh helleborine, an orchid of rich fen, but here on old railway banks at Cumbria Wildlife Trust nature reserve Waitby Greenriggs, near Kirkby Stephen.

with only basal leaves. It grows on a bank amongst other limestone meadow plants and is to all appearances native.

The northern limestone

The band of Carboniferous limestone extending north-west from Shap Fells and forming an encircling belt of low foothills around the northern Lake fells, ending at Egremont, has very little exposed rock. There are low scars at Knipe near Bampton and in Greystoke Park, and rocky stream glens at the Howk, Caldbeck and the Caldew above Sebergham; but otherwise the only cliffs are in the numerous quarries – some active and others disused – between Shap and Egremont. Small areas of pavement occur in Greystoke Park and at the Clints near Blindcrake, but they have only common calcicoles such as rock-rose (Fig. 7.11) and small scabious, and none of the notable plants of the Westmorland pavements. Much of the limestone band is drift-covered, and while this is strongly calcareous between Lowther and Caldbeck, it is sufficiently acidic on Fauld's Brow for heather moorland to have developed.

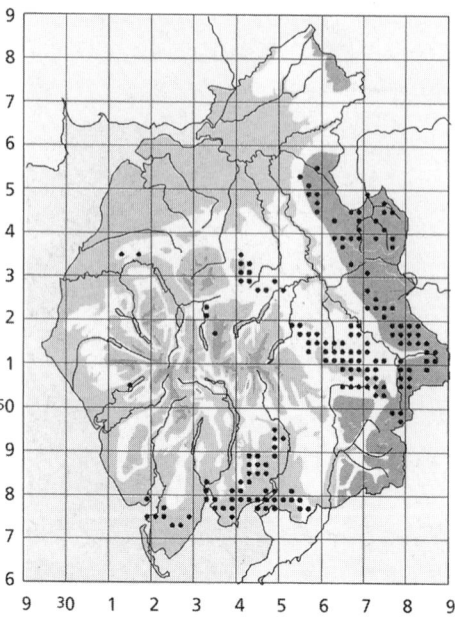

Fig. 7.11 Distribution of rock-rose, a plant almost confined to Carboniferous limestone in Cumbria. (Halliday, 1997, Map 226.)

There was once, nevertheless, a considerable botanical interest in places along this limestone band. There were good floral meadows and pastures in Greystoke Park and around Lamonby, with abundance of globeflower, bird's-eye primrose, purple marsh, crimson marsh and both butterfly orchids. On the south side of the road from Lamonby to Thanet Well was an area of rough, damp and lightly grazed pasture with these species, great burnet, devil's bit scabious, saw-wort, ox-eye daisy, water avens, zig-zag clover, bird's-foot trefoil, pepper saxifrage, hedge bedstraw, limestone bedstraw, marsh valerian, wood anemone, knapweed, tufted vetch, bush vetch, bitter-vetch, betony, yellow-rattle, red rattle, kingcup, glaucous sedge, twayblade, heath spotted, common spotted, fragrant, frog and early purple orchids. Burnt orchid was also recorded. The community was probably a rich variant of MG 5 (Rodwell, 1992).

Farther south, on Johnby Moor, this herb-rich grassland graded into an acidic heath with ling, bell heather, cross-leaved heath, flying bent, lesser wintergreen, lesser twayblade and petty whin. In places the calcifuges and calcicoles were intimately mixed, giving a highly unusual limestone heath in which, for instance, bird's-eye primrose and fragrant orchid grew amongst ling. Either the soils were of intermediate lime-richness or they were a mixture of calcareous and acidic components in the drift.

Sadly, nearly all these floral grasslands and heaths have gone. Pasture improvement, first with basic slag, ruined those around Lamonby and Thanet Well. Afforestation obliterated the best grasslands in Greystoke Park and the unique limestone heath on Johnby Moor. SSSIs covering a single grassland in a narrow field beside the Thanet Well–Johnby road, and a few verges in this area, represent the once large area of the habitat, and a tiny fragment of Johnby Moor has been left unplanted as an example of the grass-heath.

At one time it seemed that linear strips of similar rich grassland communities would at least survive on the broad roadside verges of the area, from Lamonby and Hutton Roof to Hewer Hill, Sebergham and Sowerby Row. These unusually wide verges (three or four metres across) could be explained in the same way as those of the southern chalk, namely, that in the days of cattle drives, clay soils derived from chalk (or limestone, farther north) rapidly became puddled, so that the route was widened to avoid both cattle and drovers becoming mired. The same effect occurs where popular walking tracks, such as the Pennine Way, cross peaty ground. These clay verges were colourful with fine displays of bird's-eye primrose, water avens, various orchids, pepper saxifrage, tufted vetch, clovers and bird's-foot trefoil, and contained most species of the good pastures. In places willow invasion reduced their botanical interest, but periodic cutting kept this encroachment at bay.

Then, around 1990, local farmers evidently decided that this was wasted land that could earn them more money, and set to work to 'improve' these verges. A layer of topsoil was dumped to bury the existing vegetation, and then seeded with commercial rye-grass in the same way as in the hay meadows. The verges were mown when the grass was tall and the cut presumably used to make yet more silage. The business was apparently quite legal, the verges along unclassified minor roads belonging to the owner of the immediately adjoining land. Quite long stretches of roadside around Hewer Hill and Sour Nook were treated thus, completely destroying their botanical interest. This novel kind of 'reclamation' is still continuing in the area, as along the B5305 road, which should be under County Council management. So, anyone who thought that roadside verges would remain, as last refuge fragments of semi-natural habitat in the rural wildlife deserts, should revise their ideas.

The Greystoke limestone outcrops produced a few plants of note, in spindle, lily-of-the-valley and blue moor-grass, while a more leached grassland here had abundant mountain pansy. The herb-rich grasslands of the railway banks between Blencow and Penruddock just south of Greystoke were also productive, with meadow cranesbill, field scabious, greater knapweed, clustered bellflower, kidney vetch, burnet saxifrage and wild carrot. Giant bellflower is a common hedgerow and woodland plant on the limestone, and a small wood in the area, since coniferised, had an abundance of the rare yellow star of Bethlehem.

The most important other habitat in this area was the rich fen at Newton Reigny Moss, between Greystoke and Penrith, in a hollow fed by calcareous springs. Up to the 1930s it had a swamp with open water, partly in old peat cuttings, where greater bladderwort grew and a colony of black-headed gulls nested. There were also brown moss carpets with bird's-eye primrose. During the early 1940s a deep ditch was dug through one side of the Moss, lowering the water table and causing a drying that has reduced its wildlife interest, especially for plants. The marginal zone of willow carr, which includes the local bay-leaved, tea-leaved and dark-leaved willows, has encroached widely into the open fen and is threatening to shade out the once abundant great fen-sedge. The black bog-rush has declined greatly, bog sedge just hangs on, and marsh helleborine has disappeared. Some fen species survive, such as greater spearwort, bogbean, marsh cinquefoil, slender, bottle, brown and lesser tussock-sedges. Fen communities are mainly M9 while the carr includes WI & 3 (Rodwell, 1991a and b).

There were formerly other areas of unimproved limestone grassland with interesting flora, farther to the west at Catlands Fell, Aughertree Fell, Blindcrake and Tallentire Hill, and the last site had two notable species in the pyramidal and burnt orchids. Their botanical interest has largely been destroyed by the usual processes of fertility enhancement. In his *Flora of Cumberland* (1898), William Hodgson said of the bird's-eye primrose that, 'On the hilly ground over the highway leading from Tallentire and Gilcrux to Bothel and Ireby, and extending for several miles, this pretty little favourite is abundant.' It has largely disappeared and Halliday (1997) gives a single tetrad record for this whole area. The area north from Warnell Fell is almost its western limit on the Cumberland limestone band. Old limestone quarries from Cockermouth to Egremont once held several colonies of the bee orchid, here at its northern limit on the west side of Britain, but only one is known to survive. This is at the Clints Quarry near Egremont, where pyramidal orchid also occurs in its only extant limestone site in Cumbria. Baneberry has been recorded from woods near Cockermouth but is unlikely to be native.

Animals

The vertebrates of the limestone foothills are largely species present in other areas and habitats, and there is no fauna to parallel the distinctive calcicole flora. Among the mammals, red, roe and muntjac deer are all well represented, and the group of red deer in the rich woodlands here produce large stags with antlers of up to 14 or even 16 points. Rabbits formerly swarmed on many of these productive soils. Roudsea Wood is a well-known locality for the dormouse, and among the small rodents, the field vole, bank vole and wood mouse are abundant.

Of the birds, the hawfinch occurs in the southern, well-wooded and scrub-grown areas around Kendal and the Morecambe Bay hinterland, and probably benefits from the variety of fruit and berry-bearing trees and shrubs. Now an uncommon and sporadic nester in the region, the twite has been recorded breeding on the Shap Fells in several recent years, albeit on the heather moorland. Sunbiggin Tarn continues to hold one of the longest-established black-headed gull colonies in Cumbria, though it has declined rapidly from peak numbers of about 8,000 pairs in 1989 to only 46 pairs in 2000. Uncommon waterfowl that nest around the Tarn include shoveler, tufted duck and gadwall, while wigeon occasionally breed and black-necked grebes did so in 1935. The limestone pastures of the Shap Fells held numerous lapwings (at least until the last few years), and damper ground had higher than usual densities of breeding snipe and redshanks. A few pairs of golden plover bred on Orton Scar, and curlews were widespread though probably no more numerous than on other geological formations.

During the recent dramatic increase in peregrine numbers, quarries along the limestone tract have become occupied as nesting places, in one case in still very active workings where the birds are subject to almost constant daytime disturbance. Ravens also breed in at least two disused limestone quarries. In Smardale, peregrines bred in a cavity in one of the buttresses of the disused viaduct from 1984–88, but lost their site when it was restored as an architectural masterpiece. Ravens have also nested on the structure. Lower down the valley, a detached wood has a long-standing heronry. The pool in Shap Blue Quarry drew black-headed gulls which built up to 500–700 pairs in 1999, but had fallen to only 70 odd pairs in 2001.

In the south, the limestone foothills provide habitats for grass snakes and slow worms, which are uncommon in the region, but adders are rare or absent. Flooded workings in the disused Clints quarry at Moota near Cockermouth are regarded as an important European site for the great-crested newt.

Among the animal groups, the limestone foothills are probably most important for their butterflies. They contain the only two extant English localities for the Scotch Argus at Arnside Knott and west of Kirkby Stephen, where it is plentiful during good years. In both places the larvae feed on the abundant blue moor-grass. In its only other former northern England localities at Grass Wood in Wharfedale and Castle Eden Dene, Co. Durham, this butterfly evidently depended on the same grass. In Galloway it is widespread and plentiful on the acid moorlands, with flying bent as its larval foodplant. The most important (because rarest) species, the high brown and pearl-bordered fritillaries, are restricted to the low-lying southern limestone areas, especially those near the coast. They benefit from the extent of open woodland, with abundant violets as larval foodplants, on the rocky terrain, where the pavements, screes and other bare habitats prevent the establishment of a dense tree cover. Although Gaitbarrows just over the border in Lancashire is its single best site, this is now about the most important area in Britain for the high-brown fritillary (Plate 35), which has declined enormously over the last half-century.

The silver-washed fritillary, another species dependent on violets, is now locally plentiful in the same Morecambe Bay open limestone woods, though whether it has always hung on, re-established naturally or been introduced is unclear. Away from the coastal sandhills, the dark-green fritillary is mainly a limestone butterfly, mostly in the south but also in the Greystoke area and farther west to Cockermouth. The marsh fritillary once had a group of colonies in the pastures and meadows with abundant devil's bit scabious around Lamonby and Sowerby Row, north-west of Penrith, and still survives in at least two of these.

The other notable species is the Duke of Burgundy, here in a cluster of Morecambe Bay locations far from their next nearest colonies on the

North York Moors. With primroses and cowslips as the larval foodplants, it too needs the open woods and scrub with shelter in warm sunshine. The northern brown argus has major colonies on the southern hills and around Kirkby Stephen, the larvae feeding on rock-rose. Brimstones breed where the buckthorns grow, but range widely over the district as adults. The speckled wood is a true woodland species and presently expanding its range northwards, though it is suggested that it was reintroduced to the area in fairly recent years. Recent records of the wood white and marbled white are also thought to be unauthorised introductions, and the reappearance of the grizzled skipper on the Morecambe Bay limestone in 1997 is similarly suspect (Asher et al., 2001; Fryer, 2001). Although none is confined to the limestone band, the dingy skipper occurs widely, and the large skipper and common blue are especially abundant along it, while the grayling is widespread in the south. The brown hairstreak and small skipper, once known on the Morecambe Bay limestone, have disappeared or at least not been recorded for many years.

Certain moths are recorded especially from the southern limestone area north of Morecambe Bay: the oak hook-tip, buff arches, satin lutestring, small elephant hawk-moth, great prominent, scarce prominent, marbled brown, pale tussock, least minor, white-marked, northern footman, common footman, four-spotted footman, clay triple-lines, square spot and short-cloaked moth. The Roudsea NNR is extremely rich, with well over 300 species recorded (Gibbons, 1997).

The limestone grasslands north of Morecambe Bay have a few species of beetle unknown elsewhere in the county (Key, 1996). Metallic green flower beetles such as *Psilothrix viridocaeruleus* and *Oedemera lurida* reach their northern limit here. The discovery of the waterpenny beetle in a small flush in Smardale represented a whole family of beetles new to northern England. The sulphur beetle has recently been found on Humphrey Head. Newton Reigny Moss appears to have been a hotspot for Arachnids, for Britten (1912) recorded at least 93 species there, although it was one of his favourite collecting grounds and other fens received less attention. The red wood ant is now confined to the Morecambe Bay limestone and has declined even there, though it remains abundant on Arnside Knott and has other colonies in the Arnside–Silverdale area (Robinson, 2000).

Molluscs naturally tend to follow the calcareous formations, and some species are especially widespread and abundant on the limestone foothills. The district provides two proposed Special Areas of Conservation for two tiny snails listed in Annex II of the European Union Habitats and Species Directive: the narrow-mouthed whorl snail on the Morecambe Bay pavements and Geyer's whorl snail in calcareous flush fens at Sunbiggin Tarn. The large chrysalis snail, the very rare crystal snail and the commoner milky crystal are noteworthy molluscs of the Orton limestone. On the coast, the apple snail reaches its northern British limit at Humphrey Head.

8

The Lake Dales, Woodlands, Lakes and Streams

The actual lakes occupy a considerable part of many valleys in the Lake District proper, but the dale bottoms are otherwise mainly farmed land, with their patterns of walled fields enclosing improved pastures and hay meadows, which ascend the lower slopes to around 300 metres. Remaining woods are irregularly scattered, and mainly of the 'hanging' type on steep slopes, but there are some local patches of valley floor woodland on wetter ground.

Farmlands

There is very little arable land, for the extremely wet climate does not favour cultivated crops. I can remember, as a boy, seeing forlorn fields of oats that failed to ripen during a wet summer. With the development of fast-maturing strains, a little barley and oats are grown now, and some root crops (mainly potatoes and swedes), but the bulk of cultivation is for hay. Up to World War II these hay fields were mainly of native grasses, cock's-foot, timothy, sweet vernal, red fescue, bents and meadow-grass, with a good mixture of dicotyledon herbs. The globeflower, wood cranesbill and melancholy thistle communities (MG 3 – Rodwell, 1992) of the limestone were well represented in the Lakes meadows. Even by the 1950s they had become scarce through improvement, but fringes of the herb-rich communities often remained around the field edges. Fred Jackson told me in 1955 that good patches of globeflower around Stonethwaite in Borrowdale had lately disappeared. I remember a fine great burnet meadow at Rosthwaite in Borrowdale at this time, and there was still abundance of melancholy thistle around field edges at Watendlath and in Kentmere, and of wood cranesbill with a little wood bitter-vetch at Boot in Eskdale.

As everywhere else, these hay meadows were mostly given the full treatment – ploughing, fertilising and re-seeding with commercial rye-grass. There were still good herb-rich meadows of the type with yellow-rattle, ox-eye daisy, betony, red clover, great burnet, harebell and eyebright at the foot of Deepdale, near Patterdale, in 1977, but I do not know if they have survived. Many once familiar hay meadow herbs are now quite local or scarce, and the best growths are either on cliff ledges where the sheep and cattle cannot reach them, or on banks beside rivers, roads or railways, which remain largely unmodified. The now familiar feature of the Lake hill farms, as in the lowlands, is the white bags of NPK fertiliser and the black bags of big bale silage that the hay crops go to produce. The fell sheep are increasingly wintered and lambed on the low ground, often in

Fig. 8.1 Stone barn, sycamores and intakes at Bretherdale Head, Shap Fells.

sheds, and the heavily grazed pastures of the enclosed fields and intakes have short grass swards almost devoid of botanical interest. Indeed, the general practice of carrying winter feed of hay and silage by tractor or 'quad' bike to the sheep in these places is steadily reducing them to a slough of mud and animal excrement.

The dales farms were never notable bird haunts, but they had some lapwings, and the yellow wagtail was a characteristic species. The one has almost vanished and the other is much scarcer. Rooks have increased on the farmlands and new colonies have appeared in many places, in small woods, clumps and isolated trees around the steadings. Over many years I have watched the rookery in Mungrisdale spread out and overspill into various extensions of the original colony. The fine spreading sycamores so typical around farms (Fig. 8.1) often have clusters of nests with their noisy, busy occupants. Carrion crows remain numerous though solitary nesters, and evidently have a non-breeding surplus that feeds a good deal on the hill pastures, in pairs or parties. Jackdaws, starlings, house sparrows, house martins and swallows follow the hill farms, and chaffinches are usually around, while scattered pairs of mistle thrushes build in windswept trees close by.

Bats are associated with the more open fell-bottom country with buildings and scattered hollow trees for roosting and breeding. The pipistrelle and long-eared are fairly common, but the noctule, whiskered, Natterer's and Brandt's bats are rather scarce.

The damper pastures of the fell bottoms are often rush-grown, and such ground around Troutbeck under Great Mell Fell has a few snipe and

Fig. 8.2 Sweet cicely, a culinary herb that flourishes along roadsides, usually near houses.

curlews, but is less productive for waders than the marginal land of the Pennines and Borders. Perhaps the best habitat of this kind in the Lakes is on the lacustrine delta of the Greta, separating Derwentwater and Bassenthwaite Lake, where an extensive marsh system varies from damp rushy meadows to fen with sedge and reed-grass. It floods in winter and is attractive to birds at all seasons. There were formerly good numbers of nesting snipe, redshanks and curlews, and black-headed gulls built up a fair colony. Though numbers of these birds are now less, it probably remains their best breeding site in the Lakes.

The roadside verges of the dales have botanical interest, though less so than those of the limestone areas. Roadsides bounded by walls often have abundance of Welsh poppy and sweet cicely (Fig. 8.2), neither of them native, and the second once cultivated as a source of aniseed. Foxgloves are frequently an attractive item. The ubiquitous stone walls are an important habitat for mosses and lichens. The drystone kind often have little else, but some support sparse growths of calcifuge ferns, including parsley fern. Navelwort is a notable plant but confined to the south-west sector, and its scarcity in Lakeland contrasts with its abundance in Snowdonia. Mortared walls are colonised by lime-loving ferns, notably maidenhair spleenwort, wall-rue and, more locally, rustyback and black spleenwort (Fig. 5.5).

Woodlands

Pollen analysis of lake sediments, organic muds and peat has given a picture of forest history throughout the postglacial period, summarised by Pennington (1997). Extensive scrub woodland of birch and juniper invaded the tundra grasslands and heaths formed on the land freed by the receding ice-sheets at the end of the Devensian glaciation, from about 15,000 years ago. Ice of the Loch Lomond re-advance returned to the mountains around 12,200 BP (Before Present) and restored tundra conditions more generally for another 1,400 years. The birch–juniper phase then recovered, but was followed by rapid spread of Scots pine to form a Boreal coniferous forest. Then, from 9,500 BP, came increasing amounts of oak, alder, elm and hazel, so that broadleaved forest came to predominate.

As climate became warmer, the tree line climbed the fellsides to reach its maximum upwards extension at the postglacial climatic optimum, around 7,500 BP. The upper limits of woodland varied according to exposure, but probably reached 600–700 metres in places. From 3,000 BP to the present, temperatures cooled, evidently by a mean annual 2°C, and the forest limit fell back by 100–200 metres. By this time, human settlers were increasingly clearing the forests to create open ground for grazing land and cultivation, a process that by AD 1000 had left the district heavily denuded of its former woodland cover. The once abundant elm declined markedly while forests were still extensive, probably reflecting an earlier attack by fungal disease akin to that which has scourged our elm populations in recent decades. Most probably, the original upper forest changed above into a zone of low scrub, composed of willows, juniper and stunted birch, merging in turn into the dwarf shrub heaths of the montane zone, but this scrub has entirely disappeared.

The unravelling of forest history in illuminating present distribution and character of the Lake woods is a fascinating story. The evidence is for a history of intensive use during the last 2,000 years, for timber, posts, poles, bobbins, firewood and charcoal for a local iron-smelting industry. As a result, hardly any woodland could be considered original, except along the rugged sides of gorges and on cliffs. The rest has nearly all regrown or been replanted on the site of earlier forest, and interest centres on whether such woods are primary (resulting from continuous presence) or secondary (restored after a non-wooded phase) (Peterken, 1996). Without detailed study, especially of documentary evidence, it is difficult to know to which category any particular site belongs, but there is clearly a good deal of secondary woodland on ground once kept as grazing range.

Today, these woods represent a much dissected remnant of the original forest cover, though they are among the richest and most attractive habitats in the Lakes. Borrowdale is the finest of the dales in terms of woodland of native trees, as regards both its extent and quality. The lower slopes are in places clothed with broadleaved woodland to the craggy skyline, giving the impression – however illusory – of a primeval forest-clad landscape as it must once have been (Plate 28). There are breaks in the tree cover, but a road journey from Great Wood to Seathwaite conveys this sense of almost continuous forest, with few alien conifers to spoil the effect. Yet mid-nineteenth-century paintings of the area around Castle Crag and the Bowder Stone show mainly bare hillsides, and woodland must have expanded since then. Moreover, the woodland is locally dominated by birch, evidently of secondary origin, after removal of oak; as in the beautiful little side valley of Troutdale which is almost completely wooded, save where bold crags break the cover. Some of the finer stands of 'maiden' oaks, in Great Wood, Lodore Woods and Johnny's Wood at Longthwaite, are conspicuously even-aged and uniform, suggesting a planted origin. The presence of old charcoal-burners' hearths is a reminder of past intensive use.

The low hillsides bounding Windermere and Coniston Water, and the Duddon Valley, also have a large extent of broadleaved woodland, but in the other dales it exists mainly as scattered blocks on otherwise bare hillsides. Naddle Forest on the rugged slopes south of the Haweswater dam, and an adjoining side valley, is perhaps the best other example of fell woodland. Good stands occur elsewhere at Hallin Fell, Glencoyne Wood and Low Wood at Hartsop, in the Ullswater valley; Scales Wood, Buttermere; the Side Woods, Ennerdale; around Nether Wasdale; Muncaster Fell, Eskdale; around Tilberthwaite and Elterwater; and lower Longsleddale.

There are also extensive plantations of exotic trees that have a different and largely artificial character. Pearsall & Pennington (1973) have given a good account of forestry in the Lakes, including the coming of the conifers in the nineteenth century, when private owners planted much larch, Scots pine, Douglas Fir and Norway spruce. This conifer preference solidified with the plantations of Manchester Corporation around Thirlmere (Fig. 8.3) in the early 1900s, but serious objection arose much later. Between the Wars, the newly created Forestry Commission considered this an appro-

Fig. 8.3 Coniferous afforestation around Raven Crag, Thirlmere.

priate region for planting new forests, and acquired land in Whinlatter, Thornthwaite, Bassenthwaite, Ennerdale, Eskdale, Dunnerdale and Grizedale for this purpose. The fine oak woods at Wythop on the west side of Bassenthwaite were felled and entirely replaced by conifers, in the extension of policy to coniferisation of existing woodland.

These State plantations soon drew serious criticism from guardians of Lakeland scenery, and in 1935 a large petition, led by the Revd H. H. Symonds, protested against further commercial planting in the centre of the district. In 1936, the Forestry Commission signed an agreement with the Council for the Preservation of Rural England, undertaking not to seek to afforest more land within a 300 square mile area of the central Lake District. In the same year, Symonds published *Afforestation in the Lake District*, an angry and impassioned onslaught on the disastrous visual impact of 'the serried ranks of conifers'. Symonds had launched the Friends of the Lake District in 1934 to give a weightier defence of the scenic beauty, and it grew to become one of the most effective regional conservation bodies in Britain.

The dull, dark uniformity and hard, unnatural edges of the plantations, especially in Whinlatter and Ennerdale (Fig. 8.4), have continued ever since to annoy everyone with an eye to scenic values, and to be quoted as examples of insensitive and inappropriate forestry. Their worst aspects are being alleviated at last by patchwork felling, but the silk purse–sow's ear analogy applies. Larch has been upheld as a benign influence, and Pearsall & Pennington quote a eulogy by Commission Conservator Jack Chard in

Fig. 8.4 The unloved conifer forests around Deep Gill and below Red Pike, Ennerdale.

defence of this tree, in particular. It is true that the deciduous larch can be a colourful addition to scenic beauty, in both spring and autumn, but the needle-covered floor of a solid larch plantation can be as sterile and devoid of vegetation as in any other dense block of conifers.

The National Trust was also for many years under the influence of the prevailing orthodoxy on forestry and upheld the same undeviating worship of non-native trees, especially conifers and beech. Following the Commission's lead, it proceeded to coniferise existing broadleaved woodland, such as the block of spruce and larch at Burtness (Birkness) Wood above Buttermere (but see also Brigsteer Wood, p. 153). Perhaps the biggest disaster for nature conservation was when war-time felling tore the heart out of Great Wood above Derwentwater, and conifers were planted in the resulting large gap. Private woodland owners were manoeuvred into the same practices by the conditions of State grant-aid available for planting. The Dalegarth Woods in Eskdale have substantial areas of conifers. Even in the 1960s and 1970s fine oak woods were being felled on the slopes above Lake Windermere and replanted with non-native species; and conifer under-planting of thinned oak woods is still continuing in this area. An estimated 9 per cent of broadleaved woodland in the National Park has been converted to conifers since 1945 (Phil Taylor).

While not objecting to non-native conifers in principle, I begrudge their replacing already scarce semi-natural woodland, or destroying habitats important in their treeless state. Where conifers blend in with an existing patchwork of broadleaves, they can create a pleasing mixture of woodland. The slopes above Thirlmere around Launchy Gill and Raven Crag (Fig. 8.3) illustrate the point, though the unrelieved conifers on the opposite slopes of Helvellyn are in contrast. The Forestry Commission has made strenuous efforts to develop and manage its Grizedale Forest in Furness as a showpiece to demonstrate what commercial afforestation can achieve, by creating a mixture of conifer blocks in mosaic with existing hardwoods, and the outcome is one of its more successful attempts to address criticisms of its scenic impact. This is a lower level site on better soils where opportunities for diversification are greater than on many upland areas. But hard-edged blocks of conifers will always jar scenically. Their shortcomings in wildlife interest are dealt with on p. 185 and, more especially, in the account of blanket afforestation in the Borders, pp. 296–302.

Practice in management of existing woodlands began to change with the Forestry Commission's Policy for Broadleaves in 1985, a change of heart urged by a House of Lords committee, having considered the conservationists' case. The National Trust has also adopted a more benign forestry policy, for example, by removing conifers that are particularly out of place, and promoting regeneration of native broadleaves, as in Great Wood. A shrewd observer of the woodland scene, Susan Johnson, read the small print of the Act of Parliament permitting construction of the reservoir, and found a statutory requirement to replant the Thirlmere woods with native species. Despite the embarrassment of this revelation, North West Water (now United Utilities) have yet to comply in full with their legal obligations: present action is mainly felling of non-native species and reliance on natural regeneration, mostly birch so far.

The trees and tall shrubs

The present woodlands of native trees are broadleaved, with predominance of sessile oak, often in almost pure stands, on the mainly acidic, podsolised soils, but in places with some birch (W 11 & 17, Rodwell, 1991a). Many are 'hanging' woods on steep and often rocky lower fell slopes (Plate 28), where high sheep numbers may maintain bare scree and eroding soil. There are also more local mixtures of oak with ash, wych elm, birch, hazel, blackthorn, hawthorn, bird cherry and, very locally, small-leaved lime, usually on more base-rich brown earths (W 9, Rodwell, 1991a). The trees in many of these woods have been coppiced, as the multiple stems on old stools reveal, and in some sites a variety of species have been treated thus: the Seatoller Woods (Plate 30) have no fewer than 12 coppiced kinds of tree or tall shrub. Most of the fellside woods are open to sheep and heavily grazed, but some of the lower-level areas are fenced against stock (though not deer), and show associated communities developed under lower grazing.

In stature, the oaks vary from fine 25-metre trees of good form, with shapely trunks and spreading limbs, as in the bottom part of Great Wood, to multiple stemmed (mostly coppiced) growth, and low, somewhat contorted trees on steep slopes with shallow soils, or on crag faces. They extend commonly up to 350 metres, and in the Newlands fells the two high-level woods at Birkrigg and Keskadale reach 430–460 metres (Fig. 8.5). This is probably not the true climatic tree line in the Lakes for, although oak goes little higher, scattered birches, rowans and hollies ascend the crags to at least 520 metres. Ash trees in deep sheltered gills also reach 25 metres, but wych elms of similar stature in Great Wood were, sadly, lost to the Dutch elm disease that ravaged this district in the 1980s, taking out wych and common elms alike. Wych elm was an important tree in some woods on basic soils, as in parts of the Seatoller Woods, where its loss has thinned the canopy. The birch is mainly the downy species, which grows to more modest size, but sometimes reaches 18 metres. Alder occurs widely around the edges of the lakes and on alluvial stream banks or wet hillsides with seeping water.

Donald Pigott (2001) has made a special study of small-leaved lime in the Lake District, where it is quite widespread, especially in the south, though mostly sparse. He has found that it has survived, with wych elm and ash, particularly along rocky gills that escaped the general clearance of woodland on the easily accessible ground elsewhere. The limes are often ancient descendants of the original trees that occurred more widely through these woodlands, after their first establishment nearly 6,000 years ago. Many have huge bases, up to several metres across and reckoned up to 1,200 years old, from which much younger (150–200 years) clusters of stems have grown. They may well indicate surviving fringes of original woodland. The adjoining oak and birch woods that have regenerated, either natural-

Fig. 8.5 High-level oak wood at Keskadale, in Newlands Vale.

ly or through planting, and often after an open grassland phase, contain much younger trees, mostly no more than 100–150 years old. Interestingly, the limes seldom now set fertile seed, and Pigott has shown that this reflects a temperature drop of about 2°C in mean annual temperature since the establishment of these southern, warmth-loving trees.

Rowan and holly occur as a patchy understorey in many oak woods on the more acidic sites, and probably originally formed a more continuous tall shrub layer. Hazel grows sparingly as an undershrub in some oak woods, but forms pure patches locally on the richest substrates, sometimes under ash but also on its own. Bird cherry, with its spikes of white, lilac-like flowers, is frequent on the basic soils, but prone to wind damage, with trees and branches falling over and then producing new growth, so that tangled patches often occur. Native yew is widespread but most abundant on the southern Silurian formation, where its dark evergreen form is conspicuous when the broadleaved trees are bare of leaves. It is scattered around

Fig. 8.6 Juniper scrub near Dob Gill, Wythburn, above Thirlmere.

Borrowdale, but Wordsworth's 'Fraternal Four' at Seathwaite became reduced to a single large tree, of considerable girth, but still looking healthy.

This is one of the best districts in Britain for juniper scrub, though fire has reduced its extent and sheep prevent regeneration. Dense thickets still clothe lower fellsides in many places, with forms from rounded and spreading to tall and columnar (Fig. 8.6). It belongs to community W 19 (Rodwell, 1991a). The most extensive juniper area is on Birk Fell above Ullswater, where it grades into birch wood below, but is in pure stands on the slopes above. Other good juniper scrubs are at Wythburn on Thirlmere, around Blea Tarn in Little Langdale, near Tarn Hows, Yewdale, above Torver, Glenridding on Ullswater, and Swineside on Carrock Fell.

Lack of tree and tall shrub regeneration is a general problem in the grazed Lake woods, for the sheep and deer crop any seedlings. Oak and ash produce abundant seedlings in many woods, but few survive. Sycamore is still more prolific, but – perhaps fortunately – most of its seedlings also come to nothing. Under high tree stocking rates with closed canopy, regeneration is neither to be expected nor necessary in the shorter term. Many of the taller oaks would see out every human living now, despite foresters' reservations about 'over-mature' trees. The real problems are where the existing woods have thinned out and taken on a distinctly moribund appearance, with only old trees, for these will die out if no young replacements grow up. Fencing to allow seedlings to grow up into decent-sized young trees is then necessary. The National Trust has done this, both in plots and over whole woods, but the process is not helped when farmers deliberately let their sheep in to crop the taller herbage that results.

Fig. 8.7 Massive oaks in park woodland at the eastern end of Glencoyne Park, Ullswater.

Here and there are park woodlands, with scattered trees or clumps of various species, but especially oak. Glencoyne Park above Ullswater is a good example. At its Aira Force end are some fine and massive oaks (Fig. 8.7), but there are also lines, strips and patches of ash, alder, hazel and bird cherry. Glencoyne Park also has another feature, in its open growth of tall, aged hawthorns. These open thorn scrubs occur in various parts of the Lakes and adjoining Pennines, and also in North Wales. Tony Bradshaw pointed out that they are even-aged, and so must date from a single flush of regeneration, which he suggested may have been during an agricultural recession, when sheep were removed (or much reduced) long enough for the bushes to establish. They could have been bird-sown, especially by itinerant flocks of fieldfares and redwings. It is difficult to see otherwise how such shrubs could have become established under relentless grazing that so effectively suppresses most woody seedlings.

Field layer

In grazed woods, the ground beneath the trees is mostly dominated by grasses, bracken or other ferns. In oak woods on acid soils, the grasses are sheep's fescue, wavy hair grass, creeping soft-grass and bents. There are also abundant small herbs, such as tormentil, heath bedstraw, wood sorrel and wood sage, and often depauperate shoots of bilberry. The oak woods where entry is closed to sheep are dominated by dense growths of tall bilberry or, more rarely, great woodrush, just as in lowland counterparts (p. 113). A convincing demonstration that bilberry is the more natural type and grassland derived from it may be seen in Glencoyne Wood, where a garden fence separates ungrazed and grazed sides. Only in a few places does heather grow inside woods, for it cannot tolerate the shade of a thick canopy. There is a little in the high-level Birkrigg–Keskadale oak woods, where the trees are more open and grazing is light on the rocky slopes.

The oak woods on slightly less acidic brown soils have a greater variety of herbs, and belong to W 10 rather than 11 (Rodwell, 1991a). Bluebells are usually present and often abundant, but only produce their glorious sheets of flowers in lightly grazed or ungrazed woods. In these western locations they flourish equally in adjoining open places from which the trees have been removed. Wood anemone, wood sorrel, greater stitchwort, red campion and heath violet are also plentiful where grazing is not too heavy. Polypody fern is almost the only vascular epiphyte on the trees, and even ivy is absent from many hill woods, for it is a grazing-sensitive plant.

The Lake woods are almost devoid of northern vascular plants typical of the Boreal forests. The only example, the serrated wintergreen, is rare and does not grow here on the woodland floor, but on dry, shady rocks within woods, or in tree-less ravines and on open crag faces. Ferns are conspicuous in the oceanic climate, especially bracken, which forms dense and dominant stands in the more open woods (Fig. 8.8). It is an important natural component of these hill woods, though probably not in its present smothering luxuriance. Some stands are more than head high and daunting to penetrate after rain, and many growths successfully suppress all other subsidiary flora. The climbing fumitory is one of the few herbs that can cope with bracken.

In rockier woods, with block screes and outcrops, male fern, scaly male fern, lady fern, broad buckler fern, hard fern and lemon-scented fern are

Fig. 8.8 Hill oak wood in autumn at Low Stile Wood, Seatoller, Borrowdale: a National Trust property.

Fig. 8.9 Luxuriant fern communities in rocky oak woods at Johnny's Wood, near Rosthwaite, Borrowdale.

all abundant and luxuriant (Fig. 8.9). In the less heavily grazed woods and on the sides of their shady ravines, oak and beech ferns grow finely. But the most distinctive plant of these western hill woods is the little Wilson's filmy fern, resembling a delicate dark green moss, and forming dense patches on the shady faces of blocks, outcrops and tree bases (Plate 29). In some north- to east-facing woods and on walls of damp waterfall ravines, it forms mats up to a metre square or more. It is an important member of the oceanic or Atlantic flora, depending on the constantly moist atmosphere maintained under this extremely wet climate by the shade of trees or of sun-less rock faces.

The related Tunbridge filmy fern is slightly paler green, with a more flattened frond, bearing toothed instead of smooth, flask-shaped indusia. It is much rarer in Lakeland than Wilson's fern, and apparently confined to the mild Eskdale area, where it has at least seven colonies on shady granite rocks in woods and ravines, and in block screes, at low altitudes. The Tunbridge fern appears more sensitive to frost than the other, and is absent from the central valleys, where winter is evidently too cold, however suitable they may be otherwise. Accompanying it in a very few woods is the hay-scented fern, another Lakes rarity, though formerly known elsewhere from the Windermere woods and Furness gills. Its pale green, crinkly fronds are smaller and more delicate than those of the ordinary buckler fern which luxuriate in most oak woods. Two constant associates of Tunbridge filmy and hay-scented ferns are the moss *Dicranum scottianum* and lichen *Sphaerophorus melanocarpus*. All four occur together in Eskdale as in many other British localities, including the Wealden Sandstone outcrops in Sussex.

These last two ferns have their British Isles headquarters in the rocky wooded hills and glens of south-west Ireland, as does the third and largest of our filmy ferns, the famous Killarney fern. This plant was discovered in the Lake District in 1863, supposedly in the Rydal area. Herbarium specimens still exist, but no knowledge of the find remains and, despite much searching, it has not been re-found and may have disappeared. So it was with much pleasure that I found a second colony of this fern when searching likely habitat in a different area. There were about 25 fronds, up to 23 centimetres long, in a deep, wet rock cave. This was in 1960, and in 1998 there were still the same number of fronds, occupying the same part of the cave. It is undoubtedly native here, and is the most distinctive member of the vascular Atlantic flora in the Lakes, where suitable wet habitats are legion, but the climate is probably not warm enough to have allowed a more abundant growth of the Killarney fern.

The Killarney fern story has been complicated in recent years by the discovery that its quite different sexual generation stage (the gametophyte) is more widespread in Lakeland and in Britain generally than the mature fern plant or sporophyte. The gametophyte is a dense weft of fine threads forming a dark-green felt more resembling a filamentous green alga than a fern. This growth was first found in 1989 at Lodore and Dalegarth Force by a United States fern expert, Don Farrar, who was familiar with the gametophyte stage of North American filmy ferns. The search was taken up by Fred Rumsey and Clive Jermy, who found the *Trichomanes* gametophyte in many damp ravines and rocky woods in western Britain and Ireland, but mostly in places with no trace of sporophytes. Experimental work has so far failed to induce gametophytes to produce mature fern plants, and they appear to live – at least, under present conditions – in an independent state of indefinitely suspended development, almost as though they had become a different species.

The mixed broadleaved woodlands on basic soils show variable development of the herbaceous communities of limestone ash woods, with dog's mercury, wild garlic and other herbs such as primrose, herb robert, bugle, self-heal, enchanter's nightshade, water avens, herb bennet, sanicle, wild strawberry, barren strawberry, wall lettuce and heath violet. Grazing reduces these and gives advantage to grasses, such as tufted hair, false brome and wood melick. Brambles are rampant in many ungrazed woods on richer soils, but are kept in check by sheep and deer. The wild daffodil (Fig. 8.10) grows in rather open woodland on fairly basic soils. It is probably less abundant than when Wordsworth saw it in his famous locality at Glencoyne on Ullswater side, but is still common in the southern and south-western valleys, and around Bassenthwaite. Its more spectacular flow-

Fig. 8.10 Wild daffodil in Wordsworth's original locality at Glencoyne, Ullswater.

ering displays are in thinned or coppiced woods, and it flourishes in grassland on the site of former woodland.

Alpine enchanter's nightshade, wild columbine, tutsan and narrow-leaved bitter-cress are rarer plants of the basic woods, and the grasses wood fescue and mountain melick grow on cliffs or ravine sides. The prickly shield-fern is frequent on the basic rock faces, but the more southern soft shield-fern much more local. Lily-of-the-valley grows in some basic woods, but is sometimes on fairly acid soils. A nationally rare herb of the base-rich woods is the yellow balsam, which forms dense patches in woods and tree-lined glens mainly in the southern half of the Lakes – Ambleside and Windermere, Coniston Water, Dunnerdale and Eskdale. It is native in Britain only in the Lake District and North Wales. A large patch may be seen near the shore of Derwentwater, just below the Great Wood car park (Fig. 8.11).

Alder woods occur in patches on the wet base-rich soils of lower hillsides, as in Martindale, but are heavily grazed and almost devoid of botanical interest. Beside some lakes there are also small areas of alder wood of the 'carr' type, usually with abundant willows and fenced against domestic stock. Good though small examples of alder–willow carr (W 5 & 6, Rodwell, 1991a) occur at Esthwaite North Fen and The Ings on the east side of Derwentwater. The carr communities have meadowsweet, valerian, angelica, yellow flag, kingcup, woody nightshade, hemlock water dropwort, large bitter-cress and skullcap, while the two localities above have the rare elongated sedge and Scandinavian small-reed.

Fig. 8.11 Yellow balsam, a local woodland herb that is the food-plant of the rare netted carpet moth: Great Wood, Derwentwater.

The ground layer: mosses, liverworts and lichens

The most distinctive feature of the Lake woodlands is the profusion of mosses and liverworts, and the luxuriance of the communities they form, especially on rocky terrain (types belonging to W 17). The block-strewn floors of many hill woods are smothered with carpets of golden-green moss (Fig. 8.12), and even where rocks are few, the grazed sward beneath the trees typically has a high cover of these plants. The bulk of this abundant growth is of common species that occur in woods all through the western lowlands and are listed on p. 115 (Fig. 8.13). Less profuse, though still locally abundant, are other species restricted to the upland woods, and these tend to increase in variety and quantity with rainfall. The Borrowdale Woods are the richest in mosses and liverworts of oceanic distribution, and those at the dale head, at Longthwaite and Seatoller, are the best of all. In a recent survey, Ben Averis found 30 species of oceanic bryophyte in the wood between Seatoller and Seathwaite (Plate 30), and noted that it is the richest wood in Britain for these plants, south of the Scottish Highlands. In a survey of 448 west Highland woods, he had found only 16 with 30 or more oceanic bryophyte species.

The beautiful feather moss *Ptilium crista-castrensis* (Plate 41) is abundant in many Lake woods, but is a Boreal more than an oceanic species. It reach-

Fig. 8.12 Moss-covered blocks in rocky hill woodland at Johnny's Wood, near Rosthwaite, Borrowdale: a National Trust property.

es extreme profusion in the open, rocky woods under the Benn north of Thirlmere. The moss *Rhytidiadelphus loreus* is more constant than in lowland woods and often dominant in the cushions growing over rocks. *Thuidium delicatulum* and *Hylocomium umbratum* and the liverwort *Bazzania*

Fig. 8.13 The moss *Thuidium tamariscinum*, common in woods throughout Lakeland.

trilobata are plentiful in the moss carpets, but it is the sides of the more open blocks and outcrops that produce the greatest variety of species. *Scapania gracilis* and *Plagiochila spinulosa* are abundant here, often with Wilson's filmy fern, and *Saccogyna viticulosa* is plentiful where water seeps. In a few woods the rare moss *Sematophyllum micans* forms golden-green flakes on inclined slabs, and probably grows more finely here than anywhere else in Britain. An equally rare liverwort *Radula voluta* forms pale green patches on stones and slabs in rills, and in crannies of cascading streams. Both these last two species have no other English localities, and are only in Cumberland. The liverwort *Adelanthus decipiens*, almost as rare, grows on blocks and outcrops in several woods; and this is one of only two English localities for *Plagiochila atlantica*.

Some oceanic bryophytes, especially small liverworts of the Lejeuneaceae, grow especially on the dry but shady sides of large blocks and flanking walls in waterfall ravines, where the atmosphere is constantly moist. The conspicuous large moss *Isothecium holtii* covers rocks within the flood zone of some streams, and the liverwort *Jubula hutchinsiae* forms dark green patches where water drips among shady crevices and overhangs, but neither is as widespread as in North Wales. The Lodore Falls (Fig. 8.14) are the best of these wooded gorge habitats, with a wide variety of species resulting from the presence of both basic and acidic rocks. Other good localities are Dalegarth Force, Launchy Gill, Rydal Falls and Brown Gill. Tree trunks are an important bryophyte habitat, though the prevailing green cover is mainly of the common mosses *Isothecium myosuroides* and *Hypnum mamillatum*. Liverworts of the genus *Frullania* favour trees, and the oaks in some damp woods have a dark red tint from the sheets of *F. tamarisci*. Rotting fallen trees and branches are an important habitat, especially for liverworts, and the dull red patches of *Nowellia curvifolia* are quite frequent.

On the whole, the best woods and ravines for these plants have shady aspects, facing between north-west and east, but the richest wood of all, on the steep slopes between Seatoller and Seathwaite, mostly faces south-east (Plate 30). Its richness can be ascribed to the tremendous rainfall, but also to the probable chance that it was never completely clear-felled, and retained patches at least of scrub which gave refuge to these sensitive bryophytes until a tree cover grew again. Their need for a constantly moist atmosphere is such that they are rapidly scorched out when exposed to the summer sun by removal of the overhead canopy. Richer pockets for them in woods elsewhere are mostly in rocky places which discouraged total clearance of woody cover, and their most sensitive species survived by this ecological chance. Many apparently suitable woods are poor in these oceanic bryophytes, though they have an abundance of widespread species. They were probably all completely cleared or coppiced at some stage, and stayed treeless long enough to lose all their sensitive species, before being replanted or regrowing. When trees grew up again and re-created canopy shade, only the more common species were able to recolonise; the rarer kinds, with more limited powers of spread, have been

Fig. 8.14 Wooded waterfall ravine of Lodore Falls in Borrowdale: a notable locality for Atlantic mosses and liverworts.

unable to return, though present conditions would suit them as well as before.

The same explanation applies to the shade-demanding ferns – notably hay-scented and Tunbridge filmy – which were probably once much more widespread in the Lake woods, but are at present unable to spread, and survive by chance in a few rocky places that were never completely cleared. The more resilient Wilson's filmy fern *is* able to spread, as shown by its occasional occurrence on walls in shady north-facing woods. The Killarney fern is a different case: there are thousands of dank, dripping holes in shady glens or cliffs where it could grow in Lakeland, and its presence in so few is a mystery. Perhaps it was once more widespread during the warmer Atlantic period and then unfavourable climate caused its chance restriction to these few places, none more special than the rest. The more widespread presence of the gametophyte adds to the puzzle, but if recent lack of warmth is its problem, this could be a plant to benefit from global warming.

Lichens are another important component of the rocky woods. Some grow on the ground, rocks, or steep mossy banks, such as *Peltigera horizontalis* and *P. leucophlebia*. Trees are, however, the major lichen habitat within the woods. Unlike the moisture-sensitive bryophytes, they do not need a closed canopy, and some species grow perfectly well on isolated trees in full sunlight. When I first knew Great Wood in 1956, the tree lungwort *Lobaria pulmonaria* was abundant on many of the larger oaks, but it looked poor and unhealthy and patches were peeling off. It was also confined to the larger and older trees. This was in such contrast to the west Highlands, where it seemed in some woods to grow on almost every tree, and quite often on small rowans and hazels, or even on the twigs of willows, in large luxuriant masses. In the other Borrowdale woods it was surprisingly rare.

There were fine patches of the rarer *L. amplissima* on oaks beside the road at Barrow House and nearer Keswick, but they later disappeared completely. *L. virens* is in a few woods, but *L. scrobiculata* evidently extinct, though it was recorded in Castlehead, Wallow Crag and Lodore Woods in the early 1800s by Nathanial Winch, who also noted that *L. pulmonaria* was 'in every wood near Keswick'. Other lichens of this Lobarion community in Lakeland include *Sticta sylvatica*, *S. fuliginosa*, *S. limbata*, *Nephroma laevigatum*, *Leptogium burgessii* and *Parmeliella plumbea*, though all are now uncommon. The outpouring of sulphur dioxide that began with the Industrial Revolution was the death knell for these plants. Their present restriction to the largest trees is readily explained, for these tend to be the oldest, which arboreal lichens colonised before conditions became so unfavourable through the build-up of acid deposition. As acidification grew, establishment on new trees became increasingly difficult, and in recent years there appears to have been no new colonisation at all. North Wales is slightly more productive for these Lobarion communities than Lakeland, suggesting that it is marginally less polluted.

Ash and elm trunks are the best for these large foliose lichens since, reflecting the more basic soils on which they grow, their bark is less acidic than that of oak. In Borrowdale some of best lichen communities were on large wych elms that died from Dutch Elm disease and were felled. Trees are also important for many mosses and liverworts, especially species with more basic bark such as ash, elm, hazel and elder, but they too have lost ground through pollution, especially species of *Ulota* and *Orthotrichum*.

The field edge trees of the fell farmlands typically include 'cropping ashes' which have been pollarded to encourage new growths of branches for use as poles and posts (Plate 27, left–centre). They have some value as lichen and moss habitat, as their bark often remains less acidified than on full-canopied trees with a larger foliage area for collecting acid deposition. *Sticta canariensis* is a notable lichen of such trees (see Gilbert, 2000 for a full list), and one near Watendlath was the last recorded locality for the moss *Pterygynandrum filiforme*. Old sycamores scattered around farms and in parkland were once the British headquarters for the rare Mediterranean moss *Habrodon perpusillus,* but this has not been seen for many years and appears to be a victim of acidification. It seems that, while acidification from sulphur has declined during the last ten years, there is a concurrent increase in low levels of overall eutrophication (through outfall of nitrogen and phosphorus), which does not favour the Lobarion or acid bark lichens (Peter James). Nitrogen can also be converted to nitric acid, leading to more acidification.

The poverty of conifer plantations in botanical interest is only too obvious. Go into any one and you will find very little species variety, whether of vascular plants or bryophytes and lichens, and seldom if ever any of the more local and sensitive species. Where are the glorious sheets of bluebells that add such distinction to many semi-natural woods? Often there is no more than a patchy growth of common herbs and ferns. The conifers are especially lacking in the important oceanic bryophytes and lichens, though fungi may be plentiful. In the more open stands there may be an abundance of the common woodland species, but *Rhytidiadelphus loreus* is about the only one of markedly western type. As tree stocking density increases, so the ground becomes covered with needle litter, steadily excluding all green plants. The conifers themselves are almost devoid of epiphytes, apart from lichens, which Gilbert (2000) notes as distinctive.

Mammals

Roe deer are in many Lake woods, especially those not grazed by sheep, where feeding is better, in the form of shrubs such as bramble. There are two main populations of red deer in Lakeland, one of them a woodland-dwelling group based on Grizedale Forest, Furness Fells and Claife Heights; and the second an upland herd centred on the High Street Fells (Mitchell & Delap, 1974). Red deer are also emparked at Lowther and Holker. The wild forest red deer hybridise with introduced sika deer that have escaped from parks and become largely woodland dwellers. The stags are mostly solitary and secretive except in the autumnal rutting season, and they range widely, with odd animals turning up in more distant Lakes forests. The more sociable hinds stay in groups with their immature followers and are more often seen. The woodland stags are much larger animals with more impressive heads of 14 or even 16 points than those of the bare, high fells, and commonly weigh 160 kilograms. Yew and juniper are eaten a good deal by these animals, which are also prone to garden marauding in the south.

The most famous mammal of the fell woods is the pine marten (Fig. 8.15), though it is much scarcer than before 1900 and is now rarely seen. The reasons for its decline are unclear. Persecution may have played a part, but probably a minor one, and it seems more likely that the habitat has become less suitable, perhaps through a decline in food supply. There was a local saying that, 'When foxes is rank, marts is scarce', implying competition between the two. Possibly the fox has been favoured by the great increase in sheep (and sheep carrion) on the fells. Fred Jackson told me that in the 1920s pine martens were often to be seen in the rocky woods of Rosthwaite and Stonethwaite, close by his home, but that they disappeared after World War II. In the nineteenth century they were deliberately hunted with dogs in winter (Mitchell & Delap, 1974), and some were undoubtedly killed later by foxhounds, but this agile animal could escape pursuit, by climbing trees or taking to wall-tops, and this seems not to have been a main cause of decline. Specimens were in demand by collectors, and a good many were trapped in earlier years. The dens were mainly in deep crevices among block litters and outcrops, or on crag ledges, though tree

Fig. 8.15 Pine marten, once frequent but now rare and elusive in Cumbria. (Dick Balharry.)

holes and magpie nests or squirrel dreys in trees were said also to be used. In Scotland large tree nests of buzzards are sometimes occupied.

The marten was not wholly a woodland dweller, and some lived among the rock-strewn open fells. Indeed, Francis Nicholson said in 1884 that it was found on all the hills around Keswick, and lived for the greater part of the year among the screes and higher ground, only descending to the woods to breed. He also noted that a few bred in rocks high on the fells. In 1924, writing to Arthur Astley, W. Nuttall of Langdale named numerous places in Borrowdale where he had seen pine martens, from Lodore and Catbells to Blea Tarn and Angle Tarn on the treeless fells. Jim Birkett watched a pair on heathery crags at the head of the Buttermere valley, and the name Mart Crag appears in several places on fells long treeless. Evidently, the animal is, or has become, largely nocturnal, and this may account for the scarcity of sightings.

Birks & Messenger (2000) conclude that while the marten is clearly rare in Cumbria, there is too much evidence of its occurrence in the late 1990s to regard it as extinct. They show a distribution map with records received during 1990–99. Of 51 reported sightings in Cumbria, 41 are regarded as high confidence reports following observer interviews. Fifteen per cent of Cumbrian gamekeepers also reported knowledge of martens. Sightings tend to be clustered, with Ennerdale, the area between Coniston and Milnthorpe, and higher, more rugged ground in the Westmorland sector particularly mentioned. Despite statements to the contrary, it seems certain that martens have hung on in small numbers in the less trodden parts of the fell country. Reports from outside the Lakes include the Penrith and Spadeadam areas. Birks and Messenger question the reliability of earlier surveys based especially on records of marten droppings (scats), because of the difficulty of finding these when the animal is at low density. They also point out that the focus on survey only of wooded country is misguided, given the marten's long history of living on the higher, unwooded Lake fells. The reasons for the animal's continuing scarcity remain puzzling, nevertheless.

The Lake woods are a remaining stronghold of the red squirrel (Fig. 8.16) south of the Scottish Border. It is still a common animal here, in the broadleaved woods as well as conifer plantations, which are increasingly their last refuge in some other districts of England. They are often to be seen about the Borrowdale woods and tall oaks are favoured for their dreys. Macpherson noted that the animal was partial to fungi in its autumnal diet. Until recently, the Lakes had remained free of grey squirrels, but they are now advancing through southern Lakeland as far as Ambleside–Grasmere–Langdale, and have colonised the Keswick–Threlkeld area to the north. It appears to be an unfortunate fact that, in the presence of greys, the red squirrel can only survive in the coniferous woods, which are unattractive to the other species. The Red Alert Scheme to promote the protection of this animal is considering several areas with mainly coniferous forest as red squirrel reserves, including Thirlmere, Whinlatter–Wythop, Blengdale and outside the Lakes, the Eden Valley and Bewcastle–

Fig. 8.16 Red squirrel: the Lakeland woods are a remaining England stronghold. (Keith Temple.)

Spadeadam (Friends of the Lake District, 2000). Rigorous control of grey squirrels is needed, but this is easier said than done.

Macpherson (1892) recorded the dormouse in the southern Lake valleys from Rusland to Kendal, and at the outlying Cumberland localities of Millom, Watermillock and Dalston. Recent surveys have shown that the species still occurs in some of the southern Lake woods and Hewitt (1999a) records its presence in five ten-kilometre squares, but there are no northern occurrences. The dormouse needs woods with a vigorous unshaded shrub layer producing berries and nuts, and is being helped by the provision of nest boxes (Webster, 1996). The wood mouse is common everywhere, in both woods and a variety of other habitats, and is an important prey species for many predators.

Birds

The woodland bird fauna overlaps that of the lowland woods. Although originally more widespread as a tree-nester, the raven is not to any extent a woodland bird in the Lakes nowadays. Where crags afford abundant nesting places, the ravens will always use them in preference to trees, evidently for their higher security through usually greater distance from human presence. It is mostly in areas where crags are few or absent that the bird nests in trees, though one pair alternated between a rock and a tree. There was a regular nesting place in the open trees on Great Mell Fell until afforestation of the adjoining area appreciably reduced its food supply. Raven tree nests have been reported recently from Greystoke Park, Thornthwaite, Muncaster Fell and the Skiddaw fells, and I suspect there will be more in the less rugged Silurian formation of southern Lakeland, with abundant woodland but few good crags.

Although commonly breeding on crags, the buzzard is the largest widespread woodland bird, with a tree-nesting population extending over the whole Lake District, from which it has increasingly radiated outwards into the low country beyond. Scattered clumps of trees and small shelter belts suit them as well as the larger woods and plantations, for the birds hunt mainly over open ground. Buzzards prefer big and difficult trees for their nest sites, often choosing a lofty larch or massive oak, whereas rock nests are frequently in simple places. In both situations they have the habit of adorning their nests with green leafy sprays of foliage, usually plucked from a tree, and from before eggs are laid until there are large young. Fryer (1986) explains the trait as a kind of territorial marking.

Sparrowhawks are widespread in the Lake woods, though perhaps at lower density than formerly in the lowland woods. They are often in plantations and prefer conifers for their nests but will use broadleaves when no others are available. They evidently take a higher proportion of woodland birds as prey than do the sparrowhawks nesting in a more agricultural setting. Several pairs of goshawks are now established as breeders in the wooded Lake valleys, and honey buzzards were reported to nest in a southern dale in 2001. Within the limits of their territorial demands, tawny owls are common, but recent information on status of the long-eared owl is lacking. Carrion crows are numerous, nesting from the lower woods and field-edge trees to the last scattered thorns, birches and pines high up the fellsides. Jays are widespread, especially in the denser woods, but magpies have only recently expanded into the remoter dales. Woodcock nest widely but sparsely through the woods and are often to be seen roding in the dusk. The other birds of lowland woods are mostly represented, though some that depend on abundant undergrowth of brambles or tall herbs are scarce or lacking in the grazed woods, for example, blackcap, garden warbler and whitethroat. The willow warbler, chiffchaff, robin, chaffinch, wren, blue tit, great tit, coal tit, long-tailed tit, dunnock, blackbird, song thrush, mistle thrush, great spotted woodpecker and wood pigeon are widespread.

The three most noteworthy passerines of the fell woods are the wood warbler, redstart and pied flycatcher. The first is a ground-nester and particularly a bird of the bare, grazed hanging oak woods such as those in Borrowdale. The other two are mainly tree-hole nesters, though the redstart will occasionally nest on the ground among bracken or rock crannies, and both will use crevices in buildings. Sometimes they compete for the same nest sites. The pied flycatcher was most numerous in places that supplied an abundance of natural tree-holes, such as parkland with aged trees or lakeside alder fringes, but the population has been boosted in recent years by the provision of nest boxes in plantation woods, to which they readily adapt.

The northwards spread of the green woodpecker took in central Lakeland, and by the early 1950s its ringing call was to be heard across all but the most tree-less dales. In more recent years it is heard much less, and has evidently thinned out, but remains widespread across the district. Another mainly southern bird, the nuthatch, has an intriguing history. Though locally common in the region during the early nineteenth century, it had gone from northern England by 1900. After only occasional records it began to appear more regularly again from around 1950, and by 1985 was a well-established breeder, while recent survey (1997–2001) has shown it to be widespread in the dales woods (Atkins, in Stott et al., in press). An uncommon and elusive but constant inhabitant is the hawfinch. Although inhabiting some broadleaved woods, it is particularly attracted by the large gardens with abundant ornamental trees and shrubs, and orchards, which grace the properties established by the retired Victorian and Edwardian affluent. It is especially in the south from Kendal to Windermere, Hawkshead and Coniston, but the Keswick area is another of its haunts. The woody cover provides food especially from fruit trees, as well as ideal undisturbed nesting sites.

Insects

The woodland butterflies are rather limited in variety. Purple hairstreaks are widespread in the oak woods, and probably under-recorded; the green hairstreak is frequent in open woodland with birch and bilberry, while the holly blue is abundant in good years in some of the dales woods and on open hillsides with plentiful holly bushes. Where recently felled woodland has allowed the abundant growth of herbaceous vegetation and brambles, the small pearl-bordered fritillary is often found, but it occurs also around damp lake-edge woodland where marsh violet is the larval foodplant. The pearl-bordered fritillary has been noticed in recent years only on the adjoining limestone ground of the Kendal and Silverdale areas, but once had scattered occurrences in the southern Lakes and around Keswick. The dark-green fritillary is only occasionally seen about open woodlands and plantation rides, and mainly in the south. The marsh fritillary still has at least one Lakes locality, in open woodland amongst marshy grassland.

Moths are not favoured by high rainfall, and some species of the lowland woods are missing. Uncommon species include the scarce prominent and saxon. There is one speciality in the netted carpet (Fig. 8.17), whose larva feeds on the yellow balsam, and is found only in the Lakes and North Wales, where the plant is native. It has colonies in many of the foodplant localities, and Hatcher & Alexander (1994) give an account of it. A still rarer micro-moth *Argyroploce penthinana* was recorded on a Windermere balsam colony in 1872 and 1911, but was evidently extinct by 1915 (Nurse, 1936). The green tortrix is sometimes so abundant as to cause serious defoliation of oaks, and the birch weevil sometimes defoliates that tree.

The northern wood ant occurs in some upland woods, from Borrowdale to Dunnerdale, making large and conspicuous domed nests that bustle with activity. Key (1996) notes that several scarce beetles inhabit the damp fell woods, of which the brown weevil *Procas granulicollis*, discovered near Bassenthwaite by John Read in 1989, is unknown outside Britain and

Fig. 8.17 Netted carpet moth: found only in Cumbria and North Wales. (Rob Petley-Jones.)

Ireland. Read also found another weevil *Furcipus rectirostris* new to Britain near Gosforth in 1979. The large ground beetle *Calosoma inquisitor*, which climbs trees to feed on green tortrix caterpillars, is another Cumbrian woodland speciality. The dung beetle *Aphodius nemoralis* of shady woods around Coniston is otherwise mainly Scottish. Birkett (1970) also notes the longicorn *Rhagium inquisitor* from Finsthwaite, Tilberthwaite and Glencoyne Woods, and the cardinal-red beetle *Pyrochroa coccinea* from some southern woods as local. Key says that the beetle fauna of dead wood is not particularly rich, but mentions the black-headed cardinal beetle, false click beetle, and two wood-boring weevils, *Trachodes hispidus* and *Mesites tardyii* as noteworthy. Of the uncommon Orthoptera, the dark, speckled and oak bush-crickets are in the woods and scrub of southern Lakeland.

Lakes and streams

The lakes from which the district takes its name are its most distinctive feature, and probably its most important scientific asset. Nowhere else south of the Highlands has such a cluster of large lakes, and in both their configuration and variety they are unique in Britain. Pearsall & Pennington (1973), whose special interest they were, have given an excellent account of the ecology of the English Lakes. For many years they have been the prime study areas for the Freshwater Biological Association, based at the Ferry House on Windermere, which Pearsall helped to set up and where both authors worked. The science of limnology has developed in Britain especially through research conducted here, and Pearsall's early account (1921) was a classic. Geoffrey Fryer, who also worked at Ferry House, has more recently (1991) written a fuller yet simple and readable account of *A Natural History of the Lakes, Tarns and Streams of the English Lake District*. Readers wishing for more information on the freshwater bodies of the district would do well to obtain this admirable book. I shall attempt only a brief outline of the main ecological features and wildlife.

Physical and chemical aspects

The standing open waters range in size from the dozen or so larger lakes (Table 3), to a large number of smaller tarns, and uncountable ponds and pools. The deeper main lakes occupy rock basins gouged by glaciers along the floors of the main valleys which were established through the ancient radial drainage pattern of the central district. The depth of a few has been variably enhanced by the damming effect of superficial glacial deposits at their outflows, and the depth and size of the corrie tarns depends even more on augmentation of their rock basins by surrounding moraines. Blea Water under High Street (Fig. 1.2) attains the astonishing depth of 63.1 metres (207 feet) with a surface area of only 0.173 square kilometres, and owes this largely to ice-excavation. Wastwater, surface area 2.91 square kilometres, is the deepest lake at 76 metres (249 feet), unsurprisingly from the steepness of the Screes descending into it (Plate 25).

Table 3 Physical features of the Lakes.

Lake	Area km^2	Maximum depth m	Volume m^3 x 10^6	% shoreline rocky	% drainage area cultivable
Windermere	14.76	64.0	314.6	30	30
Ullswater	8.94	62.4	223.0	28	16
Derwentwater	5.35	22.0	29.0	32	10
Bassenthwaite Lake	5.28	19.0	27.9	30	30
Coniston Water	4.91	56.1	113.3	27	22
Haweswater (dammed)	3.91	57.0	56.6	–	–
Thirlmere (dammed)	3.27	46.0	52.5	–	–
Ennerdale Water	3.00	42.0	53.3	67	5
Wastwater	2.91	76.0	115.6	73	5
Crummock Water	2.52	43.9	66.4	48	8
Esthwaite Water	1.00	15.5	6.4	12	46
Buttermere	0.94	28.6	15.2	50	5
Grasmere	0.64	21.5	5.0	25	–
Loweswater	0.64	16.0	5.4	–	–

Data from Fryer (1991).

The biological nature of the lakes and tarns depends on surrounding geology, both in the topography moulded by interaction of erosion processes and rock hardness, and in the chemistry of these rocks, especially their capacity to yield the elements essential to nutrition of plants and animals. These factors determine also land-use history of the lake catchments, which has impinged secondarily on the nutrient qualities of their waters, through runoff over the thousands of years that humans have occupied the surrounding land. Taken as a whole, the lakes lie within a district formed of hard, base-poor rocks that weather slowly to release only a meagre supply of nutrients, especially calcium carbonate, to the drainage water. This, combined with a terrain and soils frequently marginal for agriculture, has caused some lakes (for example, Wastwater, Ennerdale Water) to have very little adjoining farmland, while others (Windermere, Esthwaite Water) have a good deal, but at a low level of production.

The resulting lake waters range from deficient in dissolved compounds, especially of calcium, potassium, nitrogen and phosphorus (oligotrophic) to only moderately enriched (mesotrophic): trophic level is measured by concentrations of these dissolved nutrients. Few Cumbrian lakes approach the highest (eutrophic) level found, for example, in the Norfolk Broads, so that they lack the capacity of many lowland waters for supporting aquatic plant and animal production. The artificial enrichment of fresh waters by inputs of nitrogen and phosphorus from fertilisers and sewage has become known as 'eutrophication' (see below). Sutcliffe & Carrick (1988) found that the high Lakes tarns are generally acid, except in the eastern fells, where veins of calcite and other basic materials occur more frequently among the Borrowdale Volcanic catchment rocks, and raise alkalinity levels. The base-poor Skiddaw Slate, Ennerdale granophyre and Eskdale granite tend to give the most acidic waters.

The fell streams originate as springs and rills where cold water emerges on slopes and in hollows beneath the high watersheds, to run rapidly downhill and join together in forming larger watercourses. On level, peaty ground the becks may meander slowly and sinuously about, or even show stretches of stagnant 'dead' water, but mostly they course cheerfully over stony beds in a rapid descent to the valleys below. Some streams pour downhill from high hanging valleys in a continuous series of cascades (Sour Milk Gills), and many have cut deep ravines with notable waterfalls to which the designation Force is given (from the Norse Foss) (Fig. 8.18). The rivers of the main valleys are mostly also fast-flowing clear waters with rocky beds, but in times of flood they carry sediment loads that have built up deltas where they enter lakes, or have even filled up and obliterated earlier lakes. Derwentwater and Bassenthwaite Lake were once a single lake, but became separated by the wide alluvial flat formed by the River Greta and Newlands Beck. The ancient lakes in upper Borrowdale, Kentmere and Longsleddale disappeared long ago through varying combinations of siltation, internal accumulation of sediments and downwards cutting by their emergent streams.

While animal manures were always a component of the nutrients derived from farming down the ages, during the last 50 years the routine addition of inorganic fertilisers containing nitrogen and phosphorus to farmland has seen an associated enrichment of streams, lakes and peatlands receiving runoff water from the treated ground. This eutrophication greatly boosts the capacity of many aquatic organisms for growth and multiplica-

Fig. 8.18 Looking down the shady, wooded ravine of Dalegarth Force (Stanley Gill), Eskdale.

tion. Latterly, this enrichment has been exacerbated by the amounts of human sewage containing high levels of these nutrients in drainage effluent entering some lakes, especially from adjoining towns and sewage works. Derwentwater and Bassenthwaite Lake receive sewage from Keswick and adjoining villages; Windermere from Ambleside, Bowness and Windermere town; Coniston Water from Coniston village; and Esthwaite Water from Hawkshead. Esthwaite also receives enrichment from a fish farm on the lake.

The FBA has studied the enrichment process intensively at Blelham Tarn near Hawkshead, though sewage is not involved here. Its familiar effects are algal blooms and deoxygenation of the water, causing loss of larger aquatic plants (macrophytes), fish kills and general impoverishment in biological diversity. Most of the Lakeland lakes and tarns have shown less severe effects, but there is concern that some rare and sensitive species of plant and animal are becoming threatened. Bennion et al. (2000) found

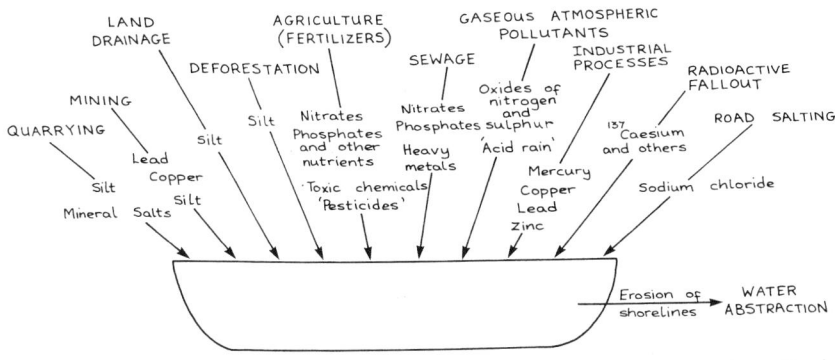

Fig. 8.19 Modern human influence on lake chemistry (from Fryer, 1991, p. 46)

indications of increasing trophic levels in Bassenthwaite Lake and Esthwaite Water from the mid-1800s, but a more marked gain in nutrient inputs after 1960. Whereas Esthwaite has suffered eutrophy which is causing loss of its notable flora (p. 199), Bassenthwaite has not yet been affected to this extent. The water of the most affected lakes has a greenness and turbidity that contrast with the clear blue of the least enriched such as Wastwater.

Further human influence on stream and lake chemistry includes pollution from mining, quarrying and industrial activities; siltation from land drainage and deforestation; human and farm sewage; road salt; and radioactive fall-out (see Fig. 8.19). Some lakes have shown a marked increase in heavy metals such as lead, zinc, copper and mercury, deriving partly from mine waste, but also from sewage.

Yet another change in water chemistry has resulted from pollution of the atmosphere by acidifying gases, mainly sulphur dioxide and nitrogen oxides, leading to the phenomenon of acid rain or, strictly, acid deposition, since some of this outfall is of solid particles. This became significant with the Industrial Revolution, dating from around 1850. Areas such as the Lake District with base-deficient rocks, soils and waters, and already low pH values, have little capacity to resist further acidification from atmospheric sources. The evidence for enhanced acidity of lake waters here is, however, variable, and less clear-cut than in the Galloway hills. Scoat, Greendale and Low Tarns on acidic, unbuffered substrates in the Wasdale catchment and Devoke Water above Eskdale show clear evidence of water acidification since 1850–1900, but Burnmoor Tarn under Scafell shows only slight loss of alkalinity and no change in pH (Battarbee et al., 1988; Whitehead, et al., 1997). Wastwater, as the most nutrient-poor of the larger lakes, might seem the most susceptible to recent acidification, but shows no evidence of this trend (Bennion et al., 2000). Sutcliffe (1983) stated that there was no evidence of an increase in acidity of water bodies in the Lake District over the last 50 years, so that the effect had evidently stabilised in the places where it had occurred.

The picture is complicated by the evidence that, while sulphur deposition peaked in the 1970s and has since decreased, atmospheric nitrogen is increasing. The tarn of Devoke Water, not subject to direct nutrient inputs from either farming or sewage, has shown recovery in pH and alkalinity since 1974 to estimated values for before 1850 (Tipping et al., 1998). Ennerdale Water has shown an increase in mean pH from 6.1–6.3 in the late 1970s to a current mean of 6.8, along with a notable increase in alkalinity (Tipping & Sutcliffe, unpubl.).

The unravelling of the history of changes in water chemistry and biological character of the lakes down the millennia has been greatly assisted by the abundant presence of diatoms, minute photosynthetic algae of the plankton that have the important characteristic of possessing an outer coat impregnated with silica, and sculpted into a pattern peculiar to each species. So, like pollen grains, they do not decay after death, but accumulate on lake beds, where they are individually identifiable to their species by their distinctive skeletons. Since some species are known, from their present-day ecology, to be faithful indicators of particular conditions of water acidity or nutrient status, changes in their presence or abundance in the lake sediments point to corresponding shifts in these conditions in earlier times (see Pearsall & Pennington, 1973; Fryer, 1991). In a few places, diatoms have been so abundant as to build up deep deposits on lake floors, and on the bed of a former ancient lake in Kentmere, this diatomite has been excavated for commercial uses.

The chemistry of stream waters naturally reflects that of the rocks and soils from which they flow, and surrounding human activity (especially farming). No streams are as calcareous as those of the Pennines, and the hill becks are mostly deficient in lime and other dissolved nutrients – 'soft' in ordinary parlance. Sutcliffe (1983) showed the tendency for water acidity to decrease between the headstreams and lower course of the River Duddon. Kernan et al. (2001) also showed that while most of the Duddon catchment has a medium to low sensitivity to surface water acidification, the upper parts are the most sensitive. It seems likely that the post-1850 surge in acid deposition would have increased the acidity of many headstreams, but Tipping et al. (2000) showed a reversal of acidification in the upper tributaries of the Duddon, attributable to decline in pollutant sulphur, since the 1970s. Tipping et al. (in press) have also found a recent increase in macroinvertebrate diversity in some streams, especially in the appearance of three acid-sensitive stoneflies. In three of six lakes, diatoms of circumneutral waters increased, while acidophilous species decreased.

The lakes long ago drew the engineers to raid them for urban and industrial water supply. First was Thirlmere, dammed to raise its level by 50 feet, and supplying water to Manchester by 1894. Then Haweswater was dammed in 1938 and raised by 95 feet, drowning Mardale village with its church and adjoining farmland, and Manchester was also receiving its water by 1941. As if that were not enough, Ullswater has been pumped, a new reservoir built in Wet Sleddale, and the valleys of Heltondale, Swindale and Naddle tapped, all to feed more water into Haweswater. Even

Windermere is required, when necessary, to add its tribute to this thirsty part of Lancashire. It was not long before British Nuclear Fuels were eyeing the clean water of Wastwater (Plate 25), and it is now pumped to supply the Sellafield complex. Whitehaven and its surrounds draw upon Ennerdale Water, and the Workington–Cockermouth–Aspatria area taps Crummock Water. Seathwaite Tarn supplies Barrow-in-Furness via the Duddon, and Hayeswater provides for Penrith.

Vegetation

The richness of the aquatic flora increases with the trophic status of the lake waters. Beginning with the most nutrient-poor lakes – Wastwater, Ennerdale Water and Buttermere – the shore-line of boulders, stones, gravel and sand has an open growth of rosette plants: quillwort, shoreweed, with water lobelia present more locally and awlwort rare. They are submerged in the shallow water, though the attractive pale blue flowers of the lobelia emerge in summer (Fig. 8.20). Floating but rooted plants include alternate water-milfoil, common and intermediate water-starwort, floating bur-reed and the charophyte *Nitella opaca*. Within the zone of fluctuating water level are the moss *Fontinalis antipyretica* and liverwort *Jungermannia exsertifolia* ssp. *cordifolia*, while bulbous rush, lesser spearwort and bog pondweed are often exposed in a shore community. Communities A 22–24 (Rodwell, 1995) refer to these types.

Among the first indicators of slightly richer water are the white and yellow water lilies, which occur widely in the lakes and tarns, especially in sheltered bays. The variety of pondweeds increases, with perfoliate, blunt-

Fig. 8.20 Water lobelia, an aquatic plant of shallow and stony lake edges.

leaved, small and red. Rooted in the shallow water but emerging from it is the bottle sedge, which forms a marginal open water swamp in places. The common reed also forms an emergent zone, but usually in slightly richer water and, while it grows sparsely in a few upland bogs, the higher the water nutrient status, the denser and more luxuriant the growth. Reed beds occur in sheltered places alongside some richer lakes and tarns (Plate 28), but seldom as densely as in many lowland wetlands. In many places the reed-grass is abundant. Other emergent plants of the richer waters are common club-rush, bulrush, branched bur-reed, tufted sedge, bladder sedge and lesser pond sedge, while submerged plants include broad-leaved and curled pondweeds, and the introduced Canadian and American pondweeds. The open water communities A 7, 9, 13, 14 & 15 and swamp types S 4, 8, 9 & 10 (Rodwell, 1995) are represented.

Organic muds accumulate beneath these swamp communities of open water, and then peat as the vegetation closes and consolidates in hydroseral development towards fen and carr at the margins of the more mesotrophic lakes. Bottle sedge is the principal species in a sedge fen, though other Carices may be present. Herbs such as purple loosestrife, yellow loosestrife, meadowsweet, great hairy willowherb, skullcap, water mint, water forget-me-not, marsh marigold, marsh cinquefoil, gypsywort and marsh bedstraw form fen meadow communities, notably S 27 & 28 (Rodwell, 1995). Invasion by willows and alders is the final stage of the succession. Esthwaite Water is celebrated as the richest (most mesotrophic) of the larger lakes, but has probably suffered more from recent nutrient enrichment than almost any other lake. It also has the best examples of marginal fen and carr, on which Pearsall's studies of 1914 and 1929 established a baseline for monitoring of succession. Further study of the North Fen in 1967–69 by Pigott & Wilson (1978) confirmed this as a true hydrosere, with reed-swamp advancing into open water and being replaced along its landward edge by fen dominated by bottle sedge: the boundary had moved up to 47 metres south since 1848. Still more prominently, the alder–willow carr had extended south on the alluvial part of the fen, birch and ash had spread, and alder was invading the sedge-fen. A few saplings of oak had established beneath dying birch in the oldest carr.

Some lake and tarn plants are decidedly local, such as water sedge, slender tufted sedge, lesser bulrush, rigid hornwort, various-leaved pondweed, ivy-leaved duckweed, greater and intermediate bladderworts, common water-crowfoot, purple small-reed and least bur-reed. Other local species favour the shallow water and muddy, sandy or stony margins of some lakes and tarns, such as thread rush which has its British headquarters here, six-stamened waterwort, small water-pepper, lesser marshwort, water purslane, and the hybrid between lesser and creeping spearworts, which grows along the length of the Ullswater shore. Pillwort, a fern-relative of unlikely appearance, occurs by Derwentwater and a few southern tarns, but has lost some former localities. There are also several rare species, though most are more widespread in other parts of Britain. Ralph Stokoe discovered spring quillwort in three localities, including Derwentwater, and the Scottish hybrid yellow water lily in two tarns on the Watendlath fells. The floating water plantain was long known from Derwentwater and has recently been found also in Bassenthwaite Lake: it is an Annex II species under the European Union Habitats and Species Directive. The most outstanding rarity is, or was, the Esthwaite waterweed discovered in 1914 in that lake by the two W. H. Pearsalls, father and son. It has not been seen since 1941, and is regarded as a victim of eutrophication. The species has never been found elsewhere in Britain, but still grows in Galway. In 1914, the Pearsalls also discovered in Esthwaite Water the slender naiad, a plant otherwise known in Britain only in scattered Scottish localities. It too has declined, for the same reasons, and was last seen in 1981.

Rocky lake margins are an important bryophyte and lichen habitat. Both groups show variations in their communities according to water alkalinity, as well as a zonation of species in relation to water level. Gilbert (2000) has described the Cumbrian Lakes lichen flora according to these controlling factors, and interested readers should consult his book.

While some aquatics occur over a narrow range of water nutrient content and pH, and thus have indicator value, others have too wide a tolerance to be used in this way. The bottle sedge is a good example of the second group, but the water lilies and some pondweeds also occur over a fairly wide range of conditions. The oligotrophic shore-line growths of quillwort and shoreweed are mostly found around the more exposed margins of the mesotrophic lakes as well. A most surprising recent find is a luxuriant colony of reed sweet-grass in the high-lying, oligotrophic waters of Sprinkling Tarn (Halliday, 1997), for this plant flourishes in the highly eutrophic Norfolk Broads. Possibly different physiological races have evolved in some of these species of wide tolerances.

The invasive alien New Zealand pygmyweed has appeared on the shores of Derwentwater, Bassenthwaite Lake and Coniston Water. It is a vigorously competitive plant that forms dominant carpets on the bare margins of standing water bodies, eliminating most of the existing plant community, and its arrival in the Lakes is a matter for serious concern.

Some lake margins have shown increased erosion in recent years, with cutting back into the glacial drift and exposure of tree roots. Up to 1960, an extensive though rather thin reed bed occurred around the outflow of the Lodore stream into Derwentwater (Plate 28), but it has since entirely disappeared. Salt from the adjoining road and the frequent wash from passing launches and other boats could have been harmful. Marjory Garnett noted even in 1946 that reed beds on Windermere were much less dense than in earlier years. Some of the fell streams have suffered the scouring effects of torrential 'cloudburst' rainfall, which has stripped the bryophyte growths from their rocks and even physically moved some of the stream-bed material: Hause Gill above Seatoller is an example. The artificial Keppelcove Tarn on Helvellyn was drained away when its flimsy dam breached in 1927 and nearly caused catastrophe in Glenridding village downstream. The major reservoirs of Thirlmere and Haweswater have broad draw-down zones during times of heavy water abstraction (Fig. 12.4), which are both unsightly

Fig. 8.21 Derwentwater and Skiddaw from High Lodore.

and have mostly negligible vegetational interest, though the former lake has retained a population of the uncommon thread rush.

The erratic appearance of a small floating island up to 0.2 hectare in extent in the shallow south-east sector of Derwentwater has excited intermittent interest, and was first investigated by Jonathan Otley in 1819. It was

Fig. 8.22 Waterworn rocks of stream bed in Deepdale, under Fairfield.

described as a surface clayey layer in which the common plants of lake margins were rooted, underlain by nearly two metres of decaying vegetable matter, and its emergence, between June and September, was thought to be caused by the gases of decomposition periodically buoying up the submerged mass. It was seen during the long, hot summer of 1976, but I have not come across more recent reports.

I have dealt with the bryophyte communities of stream ravines under Woodlands (p. 182), and those of the high springs, rills and flushes under Uplands (pp. 211–12). The fast-running, stony becks and bigger streams have little special vegetation, other than semi-aquatic mosses, liverworts and lichens, but where they slow down and take on the character of sluggish lowland rivers, their fringing vegetation tends to be composed of the lake margin species.

Mammals

The otter was once so numerous in the Lakes as to be the subject of bounty payments for its destruction, the quarry of otter hunts, and the source of pelts for hat-making (Macpherson, 1892). It suffered the general decline of the late 1950s (believed to result from pesticides such as dieldrin), and is now slowly recovering. Most recent reports are from the northern Lakes – the River Derwent, Bassenthwaite Lake, Derwentwater, the Glenderamakin and Thirlmere – but there are a few from the south (Hewitt, 1999a). Alien mink are more widespread but rather sparse in some areas. The water shrew remains widespread, but the once common water vole has recently been recorded only from the extreme south of the district. Daubenton's bat occurs in places around the lake edges and along the main rivers.

Birds

Among the breeding birds, the common sandpiper is widely distributed around the lakes, tarns and streams. Pairs are closer together where waters are richest in nutrients and there are good feeding places in alluvial margins and exposed shingle beds. Numbers are highest at lower altitudes, for example, 16 pairs on Bassenthwaite Lake in 1997 and 12 pairs on Derwentwater in 1998, but the sandpiper frequents the higher tarns and a pair usually nests by the Red Tarn on Helvellyn at 713 metres. Dippers nest along most larger streams, but grey wagtails are less numerous than in earlier years.

The gulls are well represented, with a few colonies of black-headed nesting in swamp by lake and tarn edges, and on islands, though they are prone to fluctuations or even desertions for no obvious reasons. The Bassenthwaite Marshes were once a regular haunt with at least 50 pairs, and Wastwater had 142 pairs in 1987, while hill tarns and marshes had from one to 230 pairs (Potter Fell) in 2000. A small colony of great blackbacks bred beside Devoke Water until the late 1800s, but only the odd nest at unfrequented hill tarns has been reported since. During recent years, both lesser black-backs and herring gulls have established a nesting station on the island near Wood How at the head of Haweswater, with 125 and 97 pairs in 1998 (Crowle, 1999). A single pair of common gulls bred on a rock in Easedale Tarn for some years (Fryer, 1991), but only black-headed gulls have occupied this tarn recently.

The great crested grebe first began nesting in Lakeland on Esthwaite Water in 1908 and four pairs were established by 1922. It spread to Grasmere, Blelham Tarn and Little Langdale Tarn, and then to some of the larger lakes. Bassenthwaite Lake had seven pairs in 1998. While remaining a sparse breeder, it has recently colonised oligotrophic tarns (G. Fryer). Little grebes breed sparingly on some larger lakes and tarns with fringing swamp and floating vegetation. The lakes are not, however, notable breeding haunts of waterfowl. Among the ducks are modest numbers of mallard and teal, nesting away from the water, but wigeon, pintail and shoveler have bred only at rare intervals, and the diving ducks are even less in evidence in summer. Nest boxes at Bassenthwaite have so far failed to tempt wintering goldeneye to stay to breed. Shelduck colonised the southern shores of Windermere from around 1920 (Garnett, 1946), but disappeared again after myxomatosis in 1954–55 removed the rabbits and their burrows which were the favourite nesting sites. The important recent additions are the two sawbill ducks, goosander and red-breasted merganser, which have spread south from Scotland over the last 50 years, and now nest widely but thinly around the larger lakes. In 1968, 14 merganser broods were counted on Windermere, but numbers are usually less in more recent years.

Mute swans nest widely, with up to seven pairs on Windermere, while smaller lakes and tarns have only a single pair. Until recently, the life of swans reaching Ullswater was extremely short, the result, it was surmised, of long-continued pollution from the Glenridding lead-mines. Both the Canada goose and greylag goose were introduced by wildfowlers in the late 1950s to establish feral populations, and they now breed regularly on several of the larger lakes. In 1998, 71 greylag goslings were counted on Derwentwater and 52 nests of Canada goose at Killington Reservoir. Coots are numerous on the lakes and tarns with fringing swamp, especially Windermere, moorhens nest widely on lower level standing water bodies of all sizes, and water rails are rare in a few marginal fens. Sedge warblers and reed buntings are widespread around some fen and carr edges, but the reed warbler is rare and breeds irregularly, and only where reed beds are sufficiently dense.

Macpherson (1892) could only chronicle an uncertain history of the osprey breeding in Lakeland, with probable nesting places on the crags above Ullswater and in the trees of Whinfell Forest during the late eighteenth century. The 1800s produced only a melancholy list of birds shot or trapped, and only occasional visiting ospreys were seen up to 1950. Then, in the ensuing decades, following the recolonisation of the Highlands by the species, ospreys were seen increasingly in Cumbria and their return as breeders became a keenly anticipated event. Encouragement was given by the construction of tree-top platforms in likely locations near known feeding grounds. It can accordingly be reckoned the ornithological event of the new millennium that ospreys have finally returned to nest in the Lakes. The first successful breeding was in 2000, but the news was kept quiet. In 2001 a pair took over a platform in a pine tree in Thornthwaite Forest above Bassenthwaite Lake and reared a single youngster. With viewing facilities across the lake, the birds became a tourist attraction of the district. A second pair reared three young in 2001 in an undisclosed locality (M. Stott).

The Lakes are also less important for their wintering populations of waterfowl than might be supposed. The low nutrient content of the water, and general lack of marginal cover and shelter, make some of them distinctly unattractive to these birds. Windermere, Bassenthwaite Lake and Derwentwater consistently hold the largest variety and numbers. The birds of Windermere were recorded by Marjory Garnett over the period 1912–33 (Garnett, 1946). This lake was notable for the diving ducks: tufted duck in dispersed groups each of up to 50 birds, goldeneye also scattered in barely half those numbers and pochard in parties mostly of less than ten. Common and velvet scoters, and scaup were occasionally seen, while long-tailed duck and smew were rare visitors, and goosander and red-breasted merganser infrequent before 1933. Dabbling ducks on Windermere were mainly mallard and teal, in modest numbers, with occasional shovelers and wigeon. Mute swans were widely present, with usually a few whoopers, though these became more numerous on Elterwater and other nearby tarns. Of the other winter waterfowl, coots were numerous (100–200), cormorants, great crested and little grebes present in small numbers and Slavonian, black-necked and red-necked grebes rare visitors. The three divers, great northern, black-throated and red-throated, were fairly regular visitors. Mixed flocks of gulls, mainly herring with varying proportions of black-headed and common, roosted on the open water all winter.

The wintering birds were not evenly distributed about Windermere, and the ducks especially favoured sheltered bays with fringing reed beds and other shallow water vegetation. Numbers of some species fluctuated between autumn and spring, with peaks mostly in midwinter; and they also varied between years, tending to be highest during hard winters. Bird records for all the larger lakes have become more systematic in recent years, with counts of numbers for most species (Crowle, 2000). Coots numbered nearly 1,000 on Windermere in early January 1969, while mallard peaked at almost 700 during the previous month (K. M. Atkinson & K. Shepherd in Pearsall & Pennington, 1973). Bassenthwaite is now an equally important winter wildfowl site, with a record 898 mallard in October 1999, and Derwentwater had 464 the following month. Most of the Windermere waterfowl mentioned above appear at times on one or more other lakes. Mixed gull roosts, mainly of common gulls, but with usually smaller numbers of the other four breeding species, have been known on Ullswater for many years: a total of 40,450 birds of five species were counted in February, 2000. Haweswater has also become an important roost site with nearly 20,000 birds in March 1999, and 18,000 in March 2000.

Fish

The Lake District has a somewhat low diversity in fish species (Fryer, 1991). Most of the main rivers have runs of the migratory Atlantic salmon and sea trout, heading for their spawning grounds in the upper streams, some of which lie beyond the intervening lakes, though the Thirlmere and Haweswater dams deny higher access in those catchments. The sedentary brown trout is the most widespread of the Lakes fishes, occurring in virtually all the lakes, tarns and streams, though varying greatly in size and growth rate according to conditions. Trout grow fastest and reach the largest size in the nutrient-rich and alkaline large lakes at low levels, especially Windermere, where fish of around 4.5 kilograms (10 lbs) have been recorded, compared with a common weight of 57–85 grams (2–3 oz) in the high fell becks with poor, acid waters.

Most of the richer lakes also have pike, perch and eel, and a few of these have introduced roach and rudd as well (Windermere and Esthwaite Water). The char is an arctic–alpine salmonid that favours the larger and deeper lakes and also occurs in poor waters, such as those of Wastwater, Ennerdale Water and Buttermere, but is now mysteriously absent from Ullswater, perhaps from the toxic effects of the Greenside lead mine washings that polluted the lake for many years. The rare species are the two whitefish, of which the schelly occurs only in Ullswater, Brotherswater, Haweswater and Red Tarn on Helvellyn, while the vendace (Fig. 8.23) is confined to Derwentwater and Bassenthwaite Lake. The schelly is found also in Snowdonia where it is known as the gwyniad, and quite widely in Scottish Highland lochs; but the vendace became confined to these two Lake District lakes after losing its only other known locations at Lochmaben and Mill Lochs in Dumfriesshire, through pollution. It is an endangered species in Britain, though not in continental Europe.

Readers interested in fish should consult Fryer (1991), who has also given an account of the earlier history of the Lakes fisheries, of which that

Fig. 8.23 Vendace: found only in Derwentwater and Bassnthwaite Lake in Britain. (J. P. Harding.)

on Windermere was the most important, and referred to as early as 1223. By the sixteenth century this lake was divided into 12 fisheries which were worked by seine (or draw) nets. Catch details are lacking, but Fryer suggests that a steady yield of about five tons of perch, three tons of char, two tons each of pike and eel, and one ton of trout could have been removed each year. Even in those times there were signs that overfishing was depleting stocks of some species, and in 1768 the capture of char spawning in the River Brathay was banned for seven years and a minimum mesh size of nets imposed, as an early conservation measure.

Of the smaller fish, the stone loach is in southern rivers and streams, the bullhead is also in southern streams, but frequents some stony lake margins as well, while the three-spined stickleback and minnow, both shoaling species, are widespread in the lakes and watercourses. Brook and river lampreys are in some of the streams, but their distribution is imperfectly known.

Aquatic invertebrates

The dragonflies are the largest insects and the Lakes have a wide range of good quality habitats, which give a greater richness in 'specialist' species than adjoining counties. Despite the northerly location, species diversity is quite good and increasing. The maximum Cumbrian count of 15 species per ten-kilometre square is achieved in seven squares of the southern Lake District centred on the Windermere area (Clarke, 1996). The common hawker (Plate 34) is probably the most numerous large dragonfly, breeding from the largest lakes down to small bog pools, and from low levels up to 610 metres. The golden-ringed dragonfly is widespread, but rather sparse, breeding in streams, but evidently much less numerously in those of the Lakes than in Galloway to the north. The four-spotted chaser is fairly common and the black darter widespread, but mainly at acid sites. Among the damselflies, the large red, common blue and blue-tailed are ubiquitous and abundant, sometimes occurring in large numbers around lake edges where these are shallow and well vegetated. The common darter, emerald and azure damselflies are widespread and fairly common. The local species are the beautiful demoiselle (streams), variable damselfly, downy emerald in the south-central Lakes, white-faced dragonfly in the Claife Heights and Skelwith areas, and the keeled skimmer mainly on southern moorland where it breeds in seepages and flushes in acid bogs.

For interested readers, Fryer (1991) has given a readable account of all the main groups of aquatic invertebrates in the English Lakes, from which I have drawn a few examples. He stresses the uniqueness of the Ennerdale Water fauna, with three crustaceans absent from the other Cumbrian lakes and regarded as ice age or marine-glacial relicts: *Mysis relicta* (also in Ireland), *Limnocalanus macrurus* (unknown elsewhere in Britain or Ireland) and *Salmincola edwardsii* parasitic on char (known in four Scottish lochs). The reasons for this puzzling restriction to one lake involve the basic assumption that the late- and post-glacial history of Ennerdale Water differed in some important way from that of the other main lakes.

There is, in general, a great variety of snails, stoneflies, caddis flies, beetles, water bugs and midges, besides myriad forms of microscopic life, which add up to a rich and diverse aquatic fauna. For instance, about half of the 220+ completely aquatic beetles reported in Britain are known in the Lakes. They include the large and fiercely predatory great diving beetle which can take small fishes larger than itself. Seven of the nine British species of 'moss animalcules' or Bryozoa occur in the Lakes: colonial animals, they have a remarkable appearance and a fascinating life history. Also of particular note are the now rare medicinal leech, still present in at least one south Cumbrian locality, the endangered native crayfish in streams in the Windermere area, and the glacial relict flatworms *Crenobia alpina* and *Polycelis felina* which need cool water. The freshwater pearl mussel has its largest remaining English population in the River Ehen, which emerges from Ennerdale Water, but flows mainly through the west Cumbrian lowland (see p. 144).

9

The Lake Fells

The Lake country massifs are modest hills compared with the great mountain ranges of continental Europe, and their original character has been profoundly modified by human hand. Yet they remain for many naturalists the best and most alluring part of Lakeland, with the most glamorous fauna and a flora fascinating in the story of the past that it tells. I shall not deal one by one with the different fell groups, but try instead to convey a picture of the interest across their wide range of variation.

Vegetation

Heaths and grasslands

Discerning visitors will notice that some hills are dark and heathery whereas others are green and grassy, and may wonder what causes the difference. The heather moorland that so generally replaced forest long ago was soon attacked by the sheep, goats and cattle of the earlier farmers. Where the land sustained heavy grazing, *Calluna* began to retreat, and was replaced by acidic grassland, of fescue and bents, or bracken on dry slopes and mat grass and heath rush on wetter ground. The sequence of communities H 10 and U 4 or 20 or 5 or 6 (Rodwell, 1991b, 1992) represent the biotic succession. Fire assisted the change and also the spread of bracken into the drier grasslands on the lower slopes. Bilberry heath (H 18) often became extensive and persistent as an intermediate stage in the conversion of heather moor to grassland, though it too is changed to fescue–bent grassland under continued heavy grazing.

By the mid-twentieth century, the Lake District hills were mainly grass-covered sheepwalks (and much bracken on lower slopes), with heather communities local and on the most acidic rocks – Skiddaw Slates, Ennerdale granophyre and Eskdale granite. The crucial influence of hill management is nowhere better seen than in Skiddaw Forest, where the River Caldew divides grouse moor to the north and west from sheepwalk to south and east. Grouse management aims to conserve heather, and sheep numbers are controlled; but elsewhere sheep stocks are usually allowed to rise to whatever level the ground will support, and grasses are more highly regarded as their fodder. The Caldew is too big a river for sheep to cross easily and thus neatly divides the dark heather slopes from Carrock Fell to Skiddaw from the pale grasslands of the Bowscale Fell–Blencathra range (Fig. 12.2).

Since 1952, when management of Skiddaw Forest for grouse ceased, sheep numbers have built up and less well-regulated burning has taken place. The heather moorland now shows replacement by bilberry and grasses in places, and spread of bracken, though a good deal of *Calluna* ground still remains (Plate 24). On the former grouse moor of Fauld's Brow above Caldbeck, heather has given way to mat grass extensively, with many moribund and dissected plants thickly grown with lichens (Fig. 12.1). Many areas of heather that survived in the Howgill Fells until 1940 have since disappeared, and the area is now covered mainly with dull *Nardus* grasslands. On the coastal slopes of Black Combe, where ling was mixed with western gorse, both these low shrubs are now in poor shape.

Heather is still more restricted on the Borrowdale Volcanic fells, and often confined to cliff faces or boggy ground as on Armboth Fells. Here and there, huge blocks with heathery crowns that sheep cannot reach, amidst miles of grasslands with hardly a vestige of heather, tell their own story of these land-use effects. On these hills the conversion of dwarf shrub heath to a range of acidic grassland has proceeded almost to completion. Possibly there is a subtle chemical difference in the soils from these igneous rocks which, even though they are generally base-deficient and acidic, has allowed a higher sheep stocking rate – and thus a more complete suppression of heather – than on the Skiddaw Slate. The continuing retreat of heather moorland in the British uplands generally is of great concern to nature conservation, and Lakeland is a worrying case, because few remaining areas are entirely healthy.

The heather moors have other dwarf shrubs besides the dominant ling: bilberry, cowberry, crowberry and bell heather, the last often abundant after fire. While floral variety is limited, there are the wonderful colours, of pink-red bell heather in July and mauve-purple ling in August, the latter setting whole hillsides aglow in its best areas, such as Skiddaw Forest (Plate 24). The botanical dullness of the acidic grasslands is enlivened only by the yellow of tormentil, white of heath bedstraw and blue to purple of milkwort, all tiny flowers with limited visual effect; though rocky places often have a profusion of the handsome foxglove (Plate 11). Very locally, where grassland is intermittently flushed from basic rocks, are patches of a richer turf, with red fescue, thyme, heath violet, fairy flax, eyebrights and, occasionally, carline thistle.

Montane heaths and grasslands

These dry heaths and grasslands that have replaced forest and scrub extend upwards beyond the potential tree line to merge imperceptibly into higher-level types. The loss of dwarf shrub heath becomes even more complete at higher elevations. In the Highlands, heather reaches its natural climatic limit over an upper zone 150–200 metres in vertical width, as an increasingly dense mat flattened to the ground, with accompanying prostrate patches of crowberry, bearberry, dwarf juniper, dwarf azalea and least willow (H 13, Rodwell, 1991b). This impoverished growth is especially vulnerable to grazing and fire, and often fails to regenerate where these are heavy. In Lakeland the natural upper limit of *Calluna* has been depressed by at least 100 metres and probably more. Stunted growths of ling, approaching the true prostrate carpets, occur up to 670 metres on the spurs of Skiddaw at Bakestall, Ullock Pike and Lonscale Fell.

Fig. 9.1 Reindeer moss lichens, mainly *Cladonia arbuscula*, now much reduced by sheep grazing: Great Calva, Skiddaw Forest.

The dwarf heather has mostly been replaced by short bilberry on the upper slopes of the Skiddaw Slate hills, often with abundant crowberry and cowberry, forming a kind of montane heath at 700–825 metres. In places the remnants of high-level heather and bilberry heaths were rich in lichens of the 'reindeer moss' type, especially *Cladonia arbuscula* and *C. uncialis*, but with some *Cetraria islandica* and *C. aculeatum*. *Cladonia rangiferina* is rare, decreasing and mainly on the Skiddaw Slate. The lichens were locally dominant and on Robinson and Great Calva reached 50–75 per cent cover (Fig. 9.1), approaching H 19 (Rodwell, 1991b). On the Borrowdale Volcanic hills the short bilberry often became partly replaced by viviparous fescue and bents to form a montane grass-heath. Brandreth had patches of a distinctive high-level community with alpine lady's mantle, least willow, crowberry, thyme, alpine clubmoss and fir clubmoss, besides the *Vaccinia*, grasses, fringe moss and lichens – close to a type frequent at high levels in the west Highlands (community H 20, Rodwell, 1991b).

On the highest plateaux and spurs above 760 metres are extensive fell-fields in which woolly fringe moss once formed dominant carpets, instead of the short fescue–bilberry grass–heath. The mountain sedge and least willow were usually present, as the true alpines of the Lakeland tops, with the montane lichens *Alectoria nigricans*, *Thamnolia vermicularis*, *Baeomyces placophyllus* and *Ochrolechia frigida*. The community closely resembled the fringe moss heaths so extensive on Highland summits such as those of Drumochter and Ben Wyvis (U 10, Rodwell, 1992). There were excellent examples on Grasmoor, the Broad End spur of Skiddaw and the Scafell range, with fringe moss cover of over 75 per cent in the mid-1950s. Elsewhere they had evidently lost ground and were patchy on Blencathra, Helvellyn, High Street and the Pillar group.

Since then, fringe moss heath has almost entirely disappeared from the Lake fells – the result of the relentless treading, manuring and grazing of sheep, which do not eat the moss, but pull it up by plucking at small plants growing through the carpet. This cause is confirmed by the continued presence of dense growths of fringe moss on stable block screes and old wall tops that sheep cannot reach, and by formation of a grassy sheep track through the Broad End moss carpets as the first sign of deterioration. On this site in 1975 *Racomitrium* was still good in places, but in 1978 I had difficulty finding a 2 x 2 metre plot with 33 per cent cover, and by 1981 found it almost gone. This loss of the high-level *Racomitrium* heaths is the most complete and conspicuous vegetational change on the Lake fells in my lifetime.

The Lake fells have little vegetation dependent on the influence of prolonged snow cover. In north to east-facing hollows of the Helvellyn Dodds, Dr R. W. M. Corner has noted dense patches of *Nardus* grassland of the type widespread in late snow beds of the Scottish Highlands (U 7, Rodwell, 1992), but the bilberry communities associated with moderate snow cover in that region are not recognisably different from the kinds in Lakeland derived widely from *Calluna* heath. Two mosses abundant in areas of latest snow cover in the Highlands, *Kiaeria starkei* and *K. falcata*, occur sparingly in gullies of the Scafell range and Helvellyn where snow lies late, and there are a few patches of *Pohlia ludwigii* and *P. wahlenbergii* var. *glacialis* in cold high springs.

Bogs, marshes and flushes

Within the natural forest zone, tree growth was limited by high ground water, producing varying extent of bog and marsh. Although the Lake fell topography is mostly not conducive to peat formation, the rounded tops and broad watersheds of some of the Skiddaw fells, Matterdale Common, Armboth Fells, the northern parts of High Street, and the lower Eskdale–Duddon moors have modest areas of blanket bog. Hare's-tail cotton-grass is the usual dominant, though common cotton-grass is usually present, with much deer sedge and flying bent on the south-western moors, and mat grass and heath rush on the higher fells. Heather is abundant on some of the Skiddaw and Armboth bogs, but has generally lost ground on the blanket bogs as it has on the drier slopes. The cross-leaved heath seems better able to survive the effects of fire and sheep on wet ground. *Sphagnum* cover is variable but locally high, and some bog areas have numerous pools and wet hollows: the dominant species are mostly those of the lowland raised bogs, but *S. affine* is abundant in the Eskdale area. Communities M 1–3 & 15–19 (Rodwell, 1991b) are all represented.

The blanket bog flora is limited. Common sundew, cranberry and bog asphodel are widespread, but cloudberry, so typical of the Pennine and Border moors, is sparse and only in the Skiddaw group and a few eastern Lake fells. Bog rosemary is in a few lower bogs such as Tarn Moss at

Troutbeck and around Mungrisdale, but reaches 455 metres on the Armboth Fells and in Skiddaw Forest. The northern few-flowered sedge is locally abundant, as on the Armboth and Eskdale moors, but hardly flowers in some years and then passes unnoticed. It is near its southern British limits here, and perhaps the Lakes climate is marginal for it.

The much more widespread type of peatland is flush bog associated with lateral water seepage at the ground surface. Wherever steep slopes flatten out and water hits impermeable drift, these ground-water marshes occur. They are typically dominated by soft and sharp-flowered rushes which, as Pearsall (1950) declared, are a sign of serious human disturbance. Hair moss is often in quantity and bog mosses, especially *S. recurvum*, may carpet the ground. Community M 6 describes the acidic types, and M 23 (Rodwell, 1991b) the kinds with richer water. Originally, these sites probably had variable growths of alder wood and willow scrub, and sedges rather than rushes. Extensive areas occur on the north slope of Carrock Fell, Bannerdale bottom, Matterdale Common and Mosedale behind Loweswater. They will test the waterproofing of the best boots when hikers leave the drier paths to cross the marshy fell bottoms. Some of these flush bog systems once had interesting plants, including uncommon mosses, but I suspect they have been treated with fertiliser: their scarcer plants have gone and the two moss indicators of eutrophication, *Rhytidiadelphus squarrosus* and *Acrocladium cuspidatum*, are now dominant.

In places are still spongier patches of 'poor fen' with marsh cinquefoil, bogbean, lesser spearwort, cranberry, marsh willowherb, creeping forget-me-not, bog pondweed, lesser and intermediate bladderworts, star sedge, bottle sedge and white sedge. *Sphagnum* lawns are often present, and include species associated with slight nutrient enrichment: *S. squarrosum*, *S. teres*, *S. contortum* and *S. warnstorfii*, and mosses such as *Acrocladium stramineum*, *A. cuspidatum*, *A. sarmentosum* and *Drepanocladus exannulatus*. Mire communities M 5 & 6 (Rodwell, 1991b) best represent this type. This is the habitat of a rarer moss *Drepanocladus (Hamatocaulis) vernicosus* – listed in Annex II of the European Union Habitats and Species Directive, and requiring special conservation measures by Member States. It is – or was – quite widespread in Lakeland, but has lost some of its localities through the eutrophication effects noted above. In some larger spongy bogs of this type are slender, bog and tall-bog sedges, the last having its British headquarters in the Lake fell bogs, where it has some large colonies. The bog orchid, oblong-leaved sundew and great sundew are rare plants of these habitats.

Some swamps among the hills are intermediate between blanket bog and poor fen, or represent a mixture of the two; Tarn Moss at Troutbeck, Great Moss in upper Eskdale, The Bog in Wythburn, and some of the Armboth bogs, for instance. Greenburn Bottom near Grasmere is a completely acidic valley mire. On more base-rich parent materials, the drainage water has a higher content of calcium or, sometimes, iron, and there is a different marsh vegetation, with the 'brown mosses' conspicuous in patches or carpets: *Scorpidium scorpioides*, *Drepanocladus revolvens*, *D. cossonii*, *Campylium stellatum*, *Cratoneuron commutatum*, *C. filicinum* and *Bryum pseudotriquetrum*.

Some of the sedges of the poorer marshes are present – bottle sedge, common sedge – but others appear: flea, dioecious, carnation, glaucous, yellow and tawny sedges, with jointed rush, bristle club-rush, marsh arrowgrass, butterwort and lesser clubmoss. The cream-flowered grass of Parnassus is sometimes present and locally in eastern areas there is bird's-eye primrose. *Drepanocladus vernicosus* also grows in some of these richer habitats, where it is easily confused with *D. cossonii*. These mires approach M 9 of the limestone (Rodwell, 1991b).

Highly localised springs and flushes with emergent water correspond to these different chemical conditions, the nutrient-poor types having bryophyte carpets with *Dicranella squarrosa, Philonotis fontana, Drepanocladus exannulatus, Sphagnum auriculatum, Scapania undulata, Solenostoma cordifolia*, with golden saxifrage, starry saxifrage, blinks, bog stitchwort, ivy-leaved crowfoot and bog violet (Community M 32, Rodwell, 1991b). Examples in the Eskdale area often have white beak-sedge, many-stalked spike-rush and the moss *Campylopus atrovirens*. High-level springs with the liverworts *Anthelia julacea* and *Marsupella emarginata* belong to community M 31. Calcareous sites have brown moss carpets and especially cushions of *Cratoneuron commutatum*, and open gravelly flushes with other plants of basic marsh, often yellow saxifrage (Plate 19) and occasionally the moss *Meesia uliginosa* (M 11 & 37).

The alpine flora

Many of the now strictly mountain plants of Lakeland were present in vegetation of a tundra or steppe type in full-glacial conditions of the last Ice Age in Britain, and so are survivors from those inhospitable times. After the end of the Ice Age, this tundra/steppe became late-glacial and then was increasingly restricted to high levels through the advance of forest across and up the hills under a warming climate (Pearsall & Pennington, 1973). The montane and northern flora of open ground became ever more limited to high altitudes and situations where closed woodland could not develop – cliffs, screes, unstable slopes and rocky summits. Many species were doubtless lost completely from this flora at the climatic optimum, when forest reached its maximum extent. Dwarf birch was widespread over the lowlands in late-glacial times and pollen of Iceland purslane was found at Windermere (Pennington, 1997); but as living plants, the only Cumbrian record of the first is on the Border moors and the second is confined to the Hebrides.

When early humans first reduced the woodland cover and created more open ground, there were opportunities for some species to expand again. But then increasing numbers of domestic animals grazing the hills began to suppress the more sensitive plants and restrict them even more to rocky ground. The steady leaching and acidification of soils during the millennia of the wet Atlantic/Sub-Atlantic periods also steadily reduced habitats for the more base-demanding alpines. Geological erosion with rock falls helped to deplete the survivors, while some languished under a marginal climate evidently too warm to suit them. Over the centuries, even the survivors in this relict flora declined, though variably, some remaining at least locally abundant while a few came to the verge of extinction.

The Victorian plant-hunters made a reasonably full record of the mountain flora, but also helped appreciably to deplete it still further, in their thoughtless quest for trophies, to grow in gardens and nurseries, and to stick on sheets of paper for their herbaria. Energetic and enterprising, in days when transport was so limited and access such an undertaking, they flocked to the district for its botanical promise, especially in rarities and the chance of new discoveries. The ferns drew them like a magnet, and regions such as this became especially places of pilgrimage. Doubtless the scenic attractions of their hunting grounds gave special zest to their explorations. I often wonder about the gear, and especially footwear, of these pioneers, for it was well before the invention of climbing nails: probably hobnails had to serve. Some of them clearly ventured into quite sticky places on the crags, but seemed to bear charmed lives. Chapter 2 mentions some individual contributions.

Distribution and ecology

The real mountain plants are anything but uniformly distributed over the Lake fells. Some hills have few species: Blencathra is especially poor, and the great climbing cliffs have few alpines on their hard, acidic rock. The key to botanical richness is lime availability in the substrate, since most British alpines need moderate to high levels of calcium. Geological chance has determined that the Lake mountains are composed predominantly of acidic rocks deficient in calcium carbonate. The Skiddaw Slate, Ennerdale

Fig. 9.2 A lime-rich Borrowdale Volcanic cliff at Iron Crag, Shoulthwaite Gill, Naddle Vale.

granophyre and Eskdale granite are uniformly poor, and only the Borrowdale Volcanic and Silurian formations have calcareous materials. Even on the Borrowdales, 'good' rocks are highly localised, and the prevailing rhyolites, tuffs and andesites are unproductive. Just here and there, dolerite, richer andesite, calcite veins or fault breccias give abundant lime. There is nothing to match the massive exposures of calcareous pumice tuff of Snowdonia and, even on the more productive cliffs, richer beds change to infertile rocks within a short distance.

Since number of alpines increases with altitude, the fells where calcareous rocks occur at the highest elevations are the most productive. Some of the most strongly calcareous Borrowdale rocks occur in St John's Vale and Naddle Fells, at Wanthwaite, Iron, Wallow and Falcon Crags, but at only 150–455 metres, far too low for the high-level alpines (Fig. 9.2). Honister Crag and Yew Crag opposite are good for the lower and middle level species, but lack those that come in above 600 metres. The quite strongly basic Silurian rocks at Black Force (Fig. 9.3) and Cautley Spout and Crags in the Howgill Fells are also too low-lying, and perhaps too isolated, to hold much more than a few of the more widespread alpines and an assortment of hawkweeds.

Fig. 9.3 Stream gorge cut in Silurian rocks at Black Force, Howgill Fells, near Tebay.

Fig. 9.4 The east-facing coves of Helvellyn and Fairfield: best Lakeland locality for alpine plants.

The best places for alpines are the north to east-facing coves of the Helvellyn, Fairfield and High Street ranges (Figs 9.4 & 9.5), where calcareous rocks are exposed most extensively, though patchily, above 600 metres. On the Scafell range the best spots are where fault lines have led to the carving of great chasms, as in Skew Gill, Piers Gill and Wasdale

Fig. 9.5 The east face of Helvellyn showing Nethermost, Red Tarn and Brown Coves from the air, with light snow cover. The low, boggy and heathery ridge of Armboth Fells is behind. (Ronald Mitchell.)

Screes (Plate 25). The north to east aspects of most good localities suggest that alpines benefit also from the shadier and cooler conditions on these sunless faces. It is, however, another geological accident that has caused ice-carving and corrie formation to occur especially on the shady aspects of the fells, and the apparent preference may be misleading.

The restriction of many alpines to higher levels suggests they are cold-adapted plants inhibited by the higher temperatures of lower elevations. Conolly & Dahl (1970) have developed this general thesis by correlating both the distribution patterns and the lower limits of occurrence for British alpines, to define limiting high temperatures for each species. The idea has general validity, but there are complications. Some species that appear restricted naturally to moderate elevations will grow successfully in lowland gardens, for example, roseroot, mossy saxifrage, green spleenwort and holly fern. The existence of different physiological genotypes will also upset the neatness of temperature correlations.

Probably many species now confined to high levels were unable to find lower survival niches at the time of maximum woodland expansion, and have since failed to descend again. A present inability to reproduce by seed and spread, other than vegetatively, could explain the very restricted distributions of some Lake mountain plants. Lack of dispersal capacity may be a climatic effect, but not necessarily a simple relationship with temperature. Some rare species with an apparent incapacity for spread are not at the highest levels, for example, pyramidal bugle, oblong woodsia, mountain avens, alpine catchfly, bearberry and forked spleenwort. Plants of wet habitats have been able to follow rills downwards to low levels, for example, yellow and starry saxifrages and chickweed willowherb. Others have spread downwards onto suitable open ground, as have alpine lady's mantle and purple saxifrage. A few have critically small populations for reproduction, notably the downy willow on Helvellyn, whose few surviving bushes are all female.

Some of the rarest alpines bring home forcibly the idea of a relict species, once widespread but reduced by historical factors to a tiny remnant, unable to spread and facing extinction. The alpine saxifrage may be declining naturally, perhaps through unfavourable climate, but has also been over-collected. Even though massive rock falls are rare on the human timescale, a few plants of alpine mouse-ear, purple saxifrage and oblong woodsia have been swept away in my time. Other species have hung on with little change since I first saw them, nearly half a century ago. Species truly limited to high altitudes by unfavourable warmth will be in serious trouble if climatic warming becomes more marked.

Calcifuge or acid-tolerant plants

The most celebrated Lakeland mountain plant is another full-glacial survivor, the alpine catchfly, known only in two steep gullies of Hobcarton Crag. Botanists have presumed special substrate conditions to explain its presence here (Raven & Walters, 1956). Soil analyses showed pH 4.0–5.2 and a higher concentration of manganese than usual, but otherwise nothing peculiar among the common elements examined. The Skiddaw Slate here is almost wholly acidic and its associates are common calcifuges. In its only other British locality, in the Angus Mountains, alpine catchfly grows on summit serpentine debris. In Scandinavia it is often on serpentine, but also various other parent rocks, and flourishes on roadside verges – as do many of our rarest alpines. Growing with it at Hobcarton is *Grimmia atrata*, regarded in Scandinavia as a 'copper moss' indicating high levels of this metal. Yet the copper level in a Hobcarton soil sample was quite low. Perhaps there are no special conditions at Hobcarton, and this is just the chance survival of a plant at the very end of its postglacial history in Britain. An intriguing old record for Coniston Old Man provoked numerous unsuccessful searches, but was later said to be a mistake. Yet, just to help keep speculation alive, I found its Hobcarton associate, *Grimmia atrata*, on these fells.

The Hobcarton catchfly is distinctive genetically. James Backhouse junior remarked that it resembled a 'pink' from Labrador, and it is a lankier, paler-flowered plant than the Clova one (Plate 22). The flowers are pink, though several pure white patches were seen in 1958, whereas the Clova flowers incline to the typical carmine of Scandinavian plants. The many pilgrims to Hobcarton have certainly taken a toll of this special Lakes plant, and perhaps more material lies stuck on sheets of paper than now exists in the wild. One Lakes nurseryman admitted replenishing his stock there periodically. Presumably there is now decidedly less than when first discovered. In 1958 I counted 133 plants, but Halliday (1997) ominously reports only 60 plants, and it must be regarded as endangered. National Trust ownership safeguards the site from the grosser forms of disturbance, but is unlikely to prevent further collecting, even though it is now a Schedule 5 species protected by special penalties.

Perhaps the most abundant of all Lakeland mountain plants is the parsley fern. It is northern rather than montane, but becomes scarce away from the fells. A scree plant *par excellence*, its pioneering ability as a colonist of bare talus was first described in the Lakes (Leach, 1930). In places the succession has proceeded to patches of fescue–bent grassland with dwindling fern tufts (community U 21); but often the scattered clumps of parsley fern represent an arrested stage that goes no further and may break down again. Parsley fern also grows in quite stable block scree (Fig. 10.17) and on rock faces up to the highest levels. The Lakes climate is sufficiently damp and mild for it to flourish widely, but in the colder Highlands it is mainly a late snow-bed plant.

Rigid sedge is the most widespread of the high-level Lakes alpines, common on all the high summits above 550 metres and marking the lower limit of the montane zone. It grows in short fescue–bent, fescue–bilberry and fringe moss heaths of exposed high watersheds, on skeletal ranker soils and bare debris, and in shallow peat bog. It is grazing resistant and persists abundantly as mostly non-flowering rosettes in fell-fields from which *Racomitrium* has been lost. The least willow is less ubiquitous on exposed summits and spurs and has a lower limit at 650 metres. It prefers rocky and bare soily places with open plant cover, where its wiry stems cling closely to the ground, and is especially abundant on the frost-heaved ground of Broad End on Skiddaw. Least willow is also more grazing sensitive and has declined along with the fringe moss carpets, as on the Helvellyn range. On steep rocks protected from sheep, both species grow much larger, the sedge with vigorous inflorescences up to 25 centimetres high, and the willow with leaves two centimetres across. The leaves of least willow are often galled by a sawfly *Pontania*. Colonies of this tiny shrub on Grasmoor and Crag Hill are associated with a rich and possibly unique arctic–alpine fungal flora, including *Amanita nivalis* in its only known British station outside Scotland (Taylor, 2001).

Three alpine dwarf shrubs have declined through land use effects: the montane form of the widespread crowberry, now relegated to a subspecies *hermaphroditum*; dwarf juniper, also reduced to a subspecies *nana* of the common juniper; and bearberry. The largest hermaphrodite crowberry population was in Riggindale, where in 1954 it grew abundantly on grass and bilberry slopes and in block screes down to 350 metres, but had become much reduced by 1977, evidently through grazing, which there includes fell ponies and red deer. Another four localities had only scattered patches on block screes or cliffs above 600 metres. Lakeland juniper shows confusingly continuous variation, from tall and prickly-leaved bushes to prostrate patches with smaller but still prickly leaves, and finally to similar prostrate forms with curved, soft needles – the true *nana*. It is mostly on cliffs, protected from grazing and fire, in ten well-scattered localities around 600 metres. In 1956 it still 'clothed the top ridge of Whiteside mountain [Lorton] like a carpet' (Hodgson, 1898), giving an approach to community H 15. Bearberry now has only four known occurrences, three on steep cliffs, but the largest colony is on Grasmoor. Here, good patches trail amongst heather on a network of open scree that has insulated it from the fires that have swept nearly all the upland dwarf shrub heaths, giving a fragment of community H 16. In the Lakes it regenerates with difficulty after fire, yet in the colder and drier eastern Highlands, bearberry often establishes dominance more rapidly than heather after muirburn.

The higher acidic grasslands are good habitat for the clubmosses. The stag's-horn and fir clubmoss are northern plants also on lowland heaths and bogs, and even the alpine clubmoss descends to low levels. The first two have declined in recent years, for the attractive stag's-horn is often taken away by visitors, and the fir clubmoss is pulled up by sheep. The western slopes of Scafell used to have great abundance of all three. A fourth species, the interrupted clubmoss, is more distinctly montane, growing in subalpine woods and late snow areas in the Highlands, though in its only Lake stations, in upper Langdale, it grows in ordinary *Nardus* and fescue–bent grassland at no great altitude.

Most of the saxifrages are calcicole, but the starry, as the most widespread of its genus in Lakeland (Fig. 9.6), grows in base-poor habitats over a wide range of altitude in all the fell groups. It is also the only calcifuge with a marked preference for moist places – rills, flushes, springs and wet rocks.

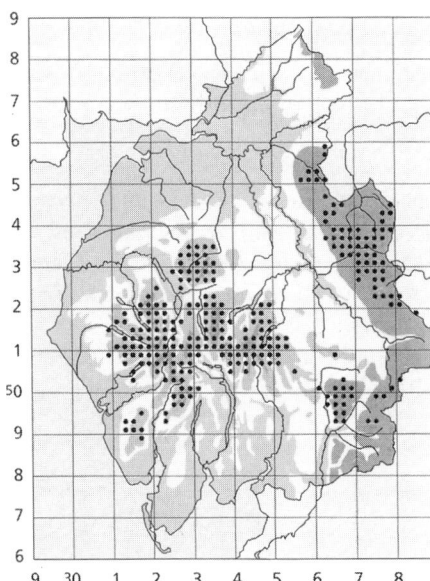

Fig. 9.6 Distribution of starry saxifrage, a widespread Lakeland mountain plant of fairly acidic habitats. (Halliday, 1997, Map 364.)

The fern that really whetted the appetites of Victorian pteridomaniacs was the oblong woodsia. While an attractive plant (Fig. 9.7), its special fascination was *rarity*. They proceeded to make it still rarer, and local shepherds scoured the crags for specimens to sell. Nine localities were reported between 1846 and 1866, mostly on the Helvellyn, Fairfield and High Street ranges, but one was in the Scafell massif. Only in 1954 was one of these colonies re-found. Extensive search suggests that the others have gone, collected out long ago, though it could yet linger in unseen corners.

Oblong woodsia appears calcifuge, but is a mysterious plant in Britain. Though our rarest fern, its remaining Lakeland habitat is unremarkable – dry, broken and rather acidic rocks at no great altitude. A Moffatdale colony is in closely similar habitat, but in Snowdonia and Clova it is on basic rocks. In Scandinavia and North America it is often on acidic rocks and sometimes luxuriates on stable block screes. The Lakes colony, with 90 tufts in 1954 and 71 in 1999, is probably the finest remaining in Britain. The largest tuft was 25 centimetres across, with over 100 fronds, many of them 18 centimetres long, in the very wet summer of 1954. My 1958 photograph shows it slightly less, and growth evidently fluctuates over the years. Although there is plenty of similar habitat nearby, and the fronds are densely fertile, it does not spread naturally. Since Edinburgh University botanists have successfully grown mature plants from this colony in cultivation (Dyer et al. 2001), the present Lakeland climate is perhaps unfavourable to its spread. In Norway, where it colonises drystone walls and roadworks rubble, it lives in a more continental climate than ours and grows to a larger size.

The forked spleenwort was another much sought-after fern, on dry and highly acidic rocks at only modest elevations. Its scattered colonies also

Fig. 9.7 Oblong woodsia in Lakeland: Britain's rarest fern.

became depleted, but it survives in at least eight localities. A small new-found colony in Mardale in 1958 had dwindled almost to nothing by 1994, even though most of it was out of reach. This fern hybridises with both maidenhair spleenwort and wall-rue. The first hybrid *Asplenium* x *alternifolium* was formerly regarded as a distinct species. It had two well-known localities and was reported from four others, but has not been seen recently. The second, *A.* x *murbeckii*, was rediscovered by Borrowdale fern enthusiast Fred Jackson, but has not been seen since 1961 (Halliday, 1997).

A few hawkweeds grow on acidic rocks, notably the handsome alpine hawkweed, but it is a rare plant here, in small quantity in its few localities, and has evidently declined. Confined to steep rocks in Lakeland, it grows also in stony fell-fields in the Highlands and is abundant in such habitats in the Norwegian mountains. Most other mountain hawkweeds show some need for lime in their rock or stream-side habitats, and a few are distinctly calcicole.

The bryophyte and lichen floras of acidic rocks are quite rich. Notable mosses include *Coscinodon cribrosus, Grimmia elongata, G. atrata, G. montana, G. incurva, Dicranoweissia crispula* and *Hedwigia integrifolia*. Among the lichens, *Umbilicaria crustulosa* (Fig. 9.8) is confined to Lakeland in Britain, while the conspicuous rock tripe is more widespread, and the map lichen ubiquitous. Lichens of the montane heaths are named on p. 209. Northern species are still being discovered, as in Dr Corner's recent finds of *Platysmatia norvegica* and *Lecanora achariana* on the Helvellyn range.

Fig. 9.8 Umbilicaria crustulosa on acidic rocks in Langdale; a lichen found nowhere else in Britain outside Lakeland.

Fig. 9.9 Alpine lady's mantle: one of the most widespread Lakes alpines.

Calcicoles

Alpine lady's mantle (Fig. 9.9) is one of the most interesting Cumbrian alpines. In profusion in many places here, it is completely absent from the Pennines (Fig. 9.10), Cheviots and Southern Uplands. This is its southernmost occurrence in Britain and it is missing from Snowdonia, which has most of the Lakes alpines. While many of its locations are on base-poor soils, it shows signs of need for a modest level of nutrients, and grows profusely on many of the good calcareous plant crags, so I include it with the calcicoles. *Alchemilla alpina* is mainly on the Borrowdale Volcanics, though sparse or even absent from some of the flintier types, as in Langdale, but is also on the Silurian Howgill Fells (Fig. 9.10). In Newlands Vale it grows on the Skiddaw Slate of Eel Crags only where this material receives water draining from Borrowdale Volcanics above. And while abundant on the Skiddaw Slates at Dove Crags, Grasmoor, it is completely absent from both this material and igneous rocks in the Skiddaw Group.

While mostly at over 300 metres, alpine lady's mantle descends to the shore of Wastwater at 60 metres. It is one of the herbs most resistant to grazing, for many abundant growths are on heavily grazed slopes. Perhaps it is unpalatable to sheep, and the silky-hairy undersides of the leaves may be discouraging. Locally it is profuse in fescue–bent swards, and where these are flushed intermittently, wild thyme and other slightly base-demanding plants are present, representing community CG 11 (Rodwell, 1992). The associated fescue is usually *Festuca vivipara*, now regarded as a distinct species of upland areas, though it too descends to low levels. Where grazed heavily it lacks flowers and the distinctive nodding spikes of bulbils mostly adorn steep rocks.

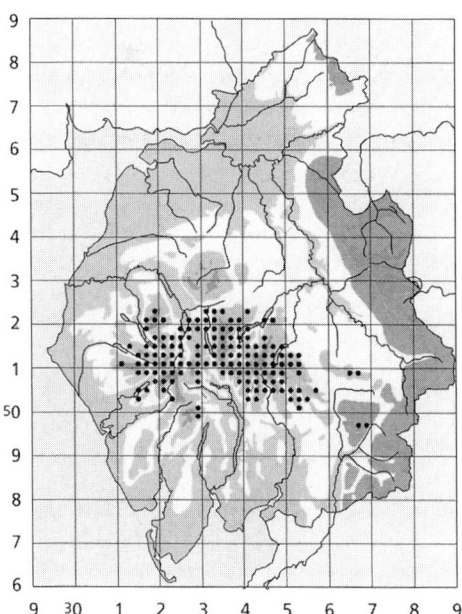

Fig. 9.10 Distribution of alpine lady's mantle, a mountain plant absent from the Pennines and Borders. (Halliday (1997), Map 434.)

On most outcrops of basic rock above 350 metres the roseroot sprouts its knobbly rhizomes from crevices and pockets of steep faces. It grows bigger on ledges where soil accumulates and its fleshy stems and leaves can make good clumps among the herbaceous vegetation of woodland or hay meadow type (Plate 26). Often with it are mountain sorrel and lesser meadow-rue, the first also a rather fleshy plant and the second a taller and more wiry herb of somewhat variable form. Northern bedstraw and stone bramble are frequent but patchy, and in wetter places alpine scurvy-grass forms luxuriant masses trailing down the rocks. On the steep rocks and soily banks of the cliffs, mossy and yellow saxifrages form either tight tufts or laxer patches, depending on amount of moisture. Alpine lady's mantle is usually abundant and mountain everlasting is patchy on exposed dry rocks. Shady crevices have brittle bladder fern and green spleenwort (Community OV 40).

These are the constants of the more calcareous mountain crags. Though not recommended for those nervous at heights or unprepared for modest scrambling, the great north-east face of Honister Crag is a good place to see them, with their typical lowland associates. An old quarry tramway runs obliquely up the face to emerge near Fleetwith summit (Fig. 9.11), and above this are perhaps the best 'hanging gardens' in Lakeland. Fine ledges with wood cranesbill, globeflower, water avens, marsh hawksbeard, angelica, hogweed, meadowsweet, common lady's mantle, red campion, devil's bit scabious and rosebay willowherb have all the upland calcicoles I have mentioned: a fragmentary community MG 3. The trackway, which was breached towards its lower end by a rock fall, has retaining walls that have

Fig. 9.11 The old greenslate workings, showing line of former railway track, on Honister Crag, Buttermere.

endured as a minor architectural feat and are festooned with growths of some alpines, showing their capacity for spread. Yellow and mossy saxifrages have also colonised the finer quarry waste below the cliffs. The rarer alpines are missing from Honister Crag, for its highest rocks are at only 600 metres, but Fred Jackson once found two plants of the rigid buckler fern – a species otherwise confined to the Carboniferous limestone.

The other lime-loving alpines are more scattered. Purple saxifrage is very local, though quite abundant on some rocks, where its flowers make a colourful display in early April, when other plants are only just stirring into leaf. High on Helvellyn it has colonised old mine spoil, proving its ability to spread by seed. Alpine meadow-rue is plentiful on moist slopes and ledges in many places, three-flowered rush is scattered in similar habitats and stony flushes, and pale forget-me-not and chickweed willowherb grow in many springs and rills down to low levels. Both moss campion and spring sandwort have good colonies in dry rocky habitats, mainly on Helvellyn and Fairfield. Alpine cinquefoil and hoary whitlow-grass each have several stations on dry rocks, while alpine saw-wort is scattered and mostly on damper ledges, especially on Helvellyn. Holly fern once had several sites in the Westmorland fells, but was reduced by those Victorian fern-hunters, especially in Mardale and on Helvellyn. It is still vulnerable: two plants on Helvellyn in 1953 had gone a few years later,, but a more hidden plant may have survived. Jim Birkett saw 30 plants in a less well-known place in 1960, and there were still at least eight in another old locality in 1977. These high-level rock face communities are an impoverished version of CG 14 (Rodwell, 1992).

All the remaining calcicole alpines are rarities, with tiny populations, in a very few places, mostly above 600 metres. The shrubby cinquefoil grows sparingly on crag ledges and in steep rock crevices of Wasdale Screes, the Pillar and Fairfield, contrasting with its large masses on the banks of the upper Tees (Plate 26). Its original station in Keppelcove ('one large mass at 760 m', as Backhouse noted on his herbarium specimen) appears long lost: perhaps a sheep became stuck on the ledge. Alpine mouse-ear, alpine saxifrage, viviparous bistort, alpine penny-cress, black sedge, alpine and glaucous meadow-grasses, and hairy stonecrop have from one to three extant small colonies each. About ten small bushes of downy willow on three Helvellyn crags (Fig. 9.12), six patches of mountain avens on Helvellyn and Wasdale Screes, and a few rosettes of pyramidal bugle on a ledge in Kentmere, are all that are known to survive. Mountain bladder fern and alpine timothy grass have evidently disappeared from their Helvellyn localities, though herbarium material exists as proof of their former presence.

'Critical' taxa are well represented in the fell flora. The eyebrights number several upland species, all needing fairly base-rich soils, and varying

Fig. 9.12 Botanically rich cliffs in Nethermost Cove, Helvellyn: the base of the near buttress has a bush of the rare downy willow.

Fig. 9.13 Great Gable behind Black Beck Tarn above Buttermere.

from widespread to rare: *Euphrasia nemorosa and E. confusa* are widespread in grazed grassland, while *E. scottica* is frequent in damper places and *E. arctica* is more local and in dry situations. The rarer species of rocky and often wet habitats at higher levels are *E. rivularis, E. frigida* and *E. ostenfeldii*. Several of the species of common lady's mantle now recognised are northern or upland, but of these, only *Alchemilla wichurae* and *A. filicaulis* occur in the Lake fells, where the first grows on many basic cliffs at higher levels, but the second is much rarer in the same habitats. The mountain form of yellow-rattle *Rhinanthus minor* ssp. *monticola* grows on at least ten basic cliffs. Halliday (1997) lists 62 species of *Hieracium* for Cumbria, mostly upland types found on open rock faces or stream sides. Among the more notable hawkweeds of basic rocks on the Lake fells are *H. subgracilentipes, H. clovense, H. ampliatum, H. anglicum, H. saxorum, H. leyi, H. lasiophyllum, H. stenopholidium, H. orimeles, H. sommerfeltii, H. caledonicum, H. subcrassum, H.strictiforme, H. vagense* and *H. prenanthoides*.

Noteworthy mosses of base-rich habitats are *Meesia uliginosa, Barbula icmadophila, Oncophorus virens, Hypnum hamulosum, Tomentypnum nitens, Orthothecium rufescens* and *Leptodontium recurvifolium*. Basiphilous lichens include *Dermatocarpon intestiniforme, D. miniatum, Belonia russula, Collema glebulentum, Gyalidea lecideopsis, Porpidia superba, Gyalideopsis scotica* and *Lecidea hypnorum*.

Animals

Mammals

The hill country is hardly notable mammal habitat, and all its species belong mainly to the dales and low ground, with their farmland and woods. Even the most striking Lakeland mammal, the red deer, was originally mainly a forest dweller, and the herds now centred on Martindale are merely the open country survivors of the once continuous forest deer populations that were spread over much of the Cumbrian lowlands as well as the hills. Macpherson (1892) gave a detailed historical review of this animal over the whole of the Lakeland area, and Pearsall & Pennington (1973) brought this up to date. The core population of Martindale numbers around 300 animals, but an increase has spilled over into the east side of the High Street fells in Mardale (Fig. 9.14) and south into Kentmere. Their eastwards roamings were shown by a Shap Fells raven nest containing several small antlers in its outerwork. Westwards, red deer have made their way to the Thirlmere slopes of Helvellyn and thence to the Armboth fells where a substantial herd has built up (Hewitt, 1999a). Stags are much lighter beasts with smaller 'heads' (12-pointers are rare) than the woodland deer. The separate herd of the Furness fells is part of the population that also inhabits Grizedale Forest.

Feral goats were once well known in the Coniston fells, and up to the 1920s a few roamed over Carrock Fell, but these have disappeared and the animal is presently represented by small herds in Wasdale and Kentmere.

The fox is perhaps the most celebrated fell-going mammal (Fig. 9.15), since it sustains a major preoccupation of the local populace in hunting it, with the five famous foot-packs of hounds, the Blencathra, Mellbreak, Eskdale and Ennerdale, Coniston and Ullswater. The place of the packs in the Lakeland social scene has been described by various authors, such as Singleton (1954). Even though each pack may kill up to 80–90 foxes in a

Fig. 9.14 Red deer hinds on the Haweswater Fells. (Dave Walker.)

Fig. 9.15 A young Lakeland fox aged 3–4 months. (Marjory Garnett.)

season, and the Blencathra as many as 120, (giving a total of 400–500), and an unknown additional number is shot, snared or poisoned, there is little evidence of any fluctuation in fox population, and none of long-term decline.

It is questionable whether any of these methods is effective in controlling numbers. The animal remains as numerous as ever and is probably – like the birds of prey – limited mainly by its territorial demands. Yet, despite the huge focus of attention – and passion – on this animal, the published information on its local natural history is derisory. The breeding places are well scattered over all the fells, in borrans (block litters) wherever these are available, or in deep and labyrinthine holes excavated in the earth where they are not. Foxes compete with ravens and other carrion-feeders for the carcases of sheep and lambs but, although they will forever be accused of lamb-killing, nobody knows just what scale of loss they cause to lambs that would otherwise have lived. It is almost certainly smaller than many prefer to believe. Rabbits are an important prey, and small rodents freely taken, especially the short-tailed vole in times of abundance, while large insects such as dor beetles are not despised.

Badgers have increasingly taken to living on the open fell, where the mounds of earth at the entrance to their setts are often conspicuous at a distance. As nocturnal animals they are seldom seen about the fellsides, but their increase in numbers since Macpherson's time is one of the more spectacular changes in mammal status. I have treated the pine marten mainly as a creature of the hill woods (p. 186), while noting its ability to live also on the open fells. Its population has shown a marked contrast to the badger's, in falling away to low numbers. Stoats follow the fells to some altitude, and may be seen up to at least 600 metres, though their food supply must there be somewhat limited in variety.

These are among the predators with which the short-tailed field vole has to contend. This little rodent is an important prey item for foxes, badgers, stoats, weasels, ravens, buzzards, kestrels and owls. As in many upland areas, it undergoes cycles of abundance, with a span usually of four years, but on the heavily grazed hillsides, where cover is rather sparse, its peaks are seldom spectacular. When its numbers are low, most predators turn to other prey, and only the kestrel shows fluctuations in parallel.

Birds

In national significance, birds are the most important wildlife group of the Lake fells. At the height of the game-preserving persecutions, the hill country provided an enduring refuge for ravens, peregrines and buzzards among its craggy fastnesses farthest from human presence. Even here they were far from secure, as Macpherson's diligent searches of old parish registers for bounty payments on ravens and his records of peregrine destruction reveal. Only when Eric Dunlop compiled records during 1900–14 did a detailed picture of raven and peregrine numbers and distribution begin to emerge. This was steadily built up by other observers, so that by the 1950s a quite full record was available, and this has been maintained with still greater completeness in later decades.

These two birds always drew adventurous young men to try their skill on the crags, and the difficulty of reaching many eyries only added to the challenge. They were widely but thinly spread, breeding in all the main fell groups, and usually choosing the loftiest and steepest crags, though few pairs nested in the cold montane zone above 600 metres. Although ravens outnumbered peregrines by more than two to one, they typically shared the same cliffs, often occupying each other's vacant nests, for both normally used a selection of different sites over a period of years. Occupied eyries of falcon and raven were often within 100 metres, occasionally much less, despite the constant mock warfare between them. Ravens mostly had full clutches by mid-March, when the higher crags were frequently icebound and surmounted by gleaming snow cornices. Early pairs had even hatched by then, and their young needed the warmth of the wool-lined nests in coping with their wintry world. Nesting about a month later, Peregrines too could face inclement weather, with heavy rain or late snow and frost causing many nest failures.

Much of the early information came from egg collectors, who seriously reduced the breeding performance of these birds. Ravens probably managed to rear a modest number of broods each year, but the peregrines were hammered relentlessly, and many pairs lost both first and repeat clutches every year. The Lakeland ravens were famous for producing more frequently than those elsewhere the rare erythristic or pink type of egg instead of the usual blue-green of the Crow tribe. Although intrinsically little more exciting than average eggs of moorhen (which were sometimes substituted, to make sure of incomplete sets while the rest were laid!), these 'red' eggs were irresistible to eggers, causing great competition and a continual search for new producers. In one Langdale locality they were known for over 30 years (Blezard et al., 1943), and in Cumberland three different pink egg birds were known during 1920–74.

Egging declined after 1960, but has far from died out and every year some ravens and peregrines lose their eggs to collectors said to come mainly from north-east England. But it has probably ceased to be significant to these birds, for both rear large numbers of young in most years. Even in the peak collecting years, it had remarkably little effect on population, since virtually the same number of pairs attempted to breed year after year. Yet depressed breeding probably led to desertion of certain time-honoured peregrine haunts during 1920–50, through lack of new birds to fill all the inevitable gaps among the breeders each year.

This led to minor fluctuations in numbers, but on the whole the populations of ravens and peregrines remained remarkably stable during 1900–60, a feature that struck me most after I began watching these birds in 1945. Something mysteriously held them to the same level, year after year. The nesting places were nearly all traditional, though with movement between alternative cliffs where there was a choice. Each haunt was occupied faithfully over a long period, except for a few used only occasionally or irregularly. Yet there were far more crags than were ever tenanted in any year, and each species appeared to have reached a different ceiling, at 69 pairs of ravens and 29 of peregrines (Ratcliffe, 1993, 1997).

For ravens, there was no shortage of birds to prevent an increase in breeders, since Lakeland had conspicuous non-breeding flocks at all times of year, but especially autumn and winter (Blezard et al., 1943; Coombes, 1948). Something resisted entry of new birds to the breeding population. A surplus of potential breeding peregrines was less obvious. Third, adult, birds occasionally joined pairs demonstrating around their eyries (Fig. 9.16). From 1946–52, the Skiddaw Forest keeper annually destroyed one or both of a nearby peregrine pair, yet a pair was always in occupation again the following spring, so that *some* new birds were available.

The other striking feature, common to both species, was that adjacent nesting pairs were regularly spaced out wherever they had plenty of crags to choose from. The average distance between each pair and its nearest neighbour was 2.7 kilometres for raven and 4.6 kilometres for peregrine. This even spacing pointed to a repulsion between neighbours, suggesting territorialism, though mutual hostility was seldom obvious. The birds were evidently giving and responding to subtle signals of possession, such as aerial display above the nesting cliffs, which kept them apart and avoided overt aggression. This spacing behaviour evidently balanced population against overall food supply, by limiting the capacity for increase and so escaping any marked oscillations in either food supply or predator. The

Fig. 9.16 Two female peregrines in confrontation at the eyrie of the left-hand bird. (W. C. Lawrie)

same mechanism apparently operated for both species, despite wide differences in diet, but food supply was evidently better for raven than peregrine. Ravens fed largely on sheep carrion, but peregrines, taking only live bird prey, were limited by scarcity of wild species in the Lakes and sustained especially by domestic pigeons.

The fortunes of these two birds later diverged. The peregrine was hit by the countrywide crash in numbers after introduction of dieldrin and related insecticides to agriculture. The first signs of decline in the Lakes were in 1960 when three regular pairs were missing. In 1961, 23 territories were occupied, but only 12 pairs laid eggs and only five reared young. By 1963, only nine territories remained occupied, with four clutches laid and two broods reared.

Many adults evidently died through acute secondary poisoning from a heavy load of toxic residues, but breeding failure of survivors was a conspicuous symptom of the crash. Remains of broken eggs in eyries were frequent, and appeared linked to a curious incident I witnessed as far back as 1951. Re-visiting a Thirlmere eyrie that had held three eggs, I watched the female peregrine eating one and found a second egg had been demolished earlier. In 1966 I decided to look at eggshells and had access to collections containing numerous Lakeland clutches. Specimens taken before 1947 had distinctly heavier shells than those taken later. Since the range of egg size had not changed, eggshell thickness must have decreased and this was confirmed by microscopic examination of shell structure. I connected the change with the widespread veterinary use of DDT on homing pigeons from 1946 onwards and, within another year or two, in agriculture (Ratcliffe, 1970). The role of DDT as the cause of eggshell thinning was confirmed experimentally by other scientists. Widespread breeding failure through eggshell thinning and breaking was clearly a contributory factor in peregrine population decline. Merlins, sparrowhawks, kestrels, golden eagles, herons and other birds also showed eggshell thinning, though their population response varied.

Fig. 9.17 Decline and recovery in peregrine population and breeding performance in Lakeland. (Data mainly from G. Horne, P. Stott, P. Marsden, T. Pickford, R. J. Birkett, F. Parr & D. A. Ratcliffe.)

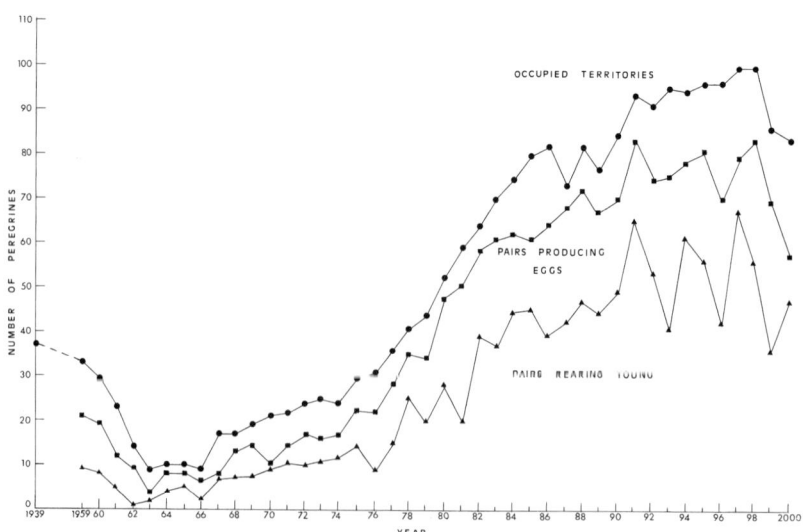

After a campaign against the organochlorine insecticides greatly reduced their use, peregrines began to recover, and the Lakes population was one of the first to show reoccupation of deserted territories. By 1977, numbers were back to normal here, but then surged on to new heights. Eggshell thickness and breeding success also recovered in parallel with the population recovery. Geoff Horne and his colleagues have monitored the Lake peregrines for many years and recorded this huge increase, involving the splitting of many territories into two or even three, and also many new nesting locations in low cliffs and quarries, and even on man-made structures (Horne & Fielding, in press). Numbers peaked in 1997 and 1998 with 100 Cumbrian territories occupied (a 270 per cent increase on 1930–39), but had declined by 2000 (Fig. 9.17). Such super-recovery can only be explained through increased protection, allowing a large annual output of young, and increased food supply (pigeons), leading to relaxation of spacing behaviour and territory contraction. Peregrine density in parts of the Lakes is now one of the highest in the world, with up to eight pairs per 100 square kilometres. It is a conservation success story, but there may now be a downturn.

The raven did not suffer this reversal of fortunes (Fig. 9.18). Although its sheep carrion food supply was widely contaminated by the same organochlorine pesticides from sheep-dips, it was evidently more resistant to their effects. There was no decline and no eggshell thinning. Its numbers remained more or less constant, but after 1970 increased locally to give a new average breeding population of at least 87 pairs by the 1990s. The increase has involved the splitting of several territories into two, as well as occupation of new areas and cliffs. The obvious cause is the increase in sheep numbers on the fells, boosting carrion supply. Breeding density is moderately high at up to nine pairs per 100 square kilometres and this is the only large raven population in England outside the West Country and the Welsh Borders. There has not been the spectacular increase reported from Snowdonia, where sheep numbers have risen still more sharply. The raven will continue to grace the Lake fells while sheep remain, but its fortunes will depend on the way these uplands are managed in future.

The buzzard probably increased as game preserving declined and grouse moors fell into disuse. Most likely it always had a large tree-nesting population, and it is content with much more modest crags than ravens and peregrines require. The densest population was in the adjoining limestone foothills of Greystoke Park (12 pairs in 25 square kilometres), where it nested in scattered woods. Numbers declined when these woods were mostly felled and the ground planted with conifers by the Forestry Commission in 1940, but there were still four pairs in 1949. The main setback for buzzards came with myxomatosis in 1954. Favoured haunts such as Greystoke and Glencoyne Parks swarmed with rabbits, and this part of the food supply collapsed. Some fell buzzards had always taken sheep carrion, and perhaps more birds turned to it, and to voles and birds (and their young). Buzzards appeared to adapt to the loss of rabbits and numbers did not change noticeably. The organochlorine sheep-dip episode also passed

Fig. 9.18 Raven nest with eggs in a typically overhung Lakeland site.

with no more than warning signs: there was no eggshell thinning, though one addled clutch had high dieldrin levels, and several pairs in 1963–64 built nests, but failed to complete them or lay eggs.

In some areas buzzard numbers thinned out among the fells, but increased markedly on the wooded fringes of Lakeland and have spread

Fig. 9.19 Raven at nest with large young. (Bobby Smith.)

through much of the lowlands, nesting in trees. The Skiddaw group lost several once regular crag-nesting pairs between 1950 and 2000. Densities nowhere approach those in central Wales, where food supply is exceptionally good, but the Cumbrian population is now quite large, at an estimated 1,000–1,200 pairs (G. Horne), and this is still the only part of northern England with significant numbers of buzzards.

Kestrels breed all through the fell country up to about 455 metres, mostly in the smaller crags, well away from ravens and peregrines. Their staple

Fig. 9.20 The bleak conditions at raven nesting time: the eyrie is under the middle of the three upper overhangs.

food is the short-tailed field vole, but other small rodents are taken, along with beetles, earthworms and other small fry. Numbers fluctuate according to the cycles of vole abundance, and can reach quite high density during their peaks. In Swindale, three pairs nested in a distance of 300 metres in 1957, and elsewhere that year near-colonial breeding and large clutches were reported.

All the previous four predators are opportunist hill birds, with southern, lowland and coastal haunts where conditions allow. The merlin is a real northern and upland raptor, adapted to the open fells, where it feeds on their small birds, especially meadow pipit, skylark and wheatear. The heather moors are its favourite habitat, in the Lakes as elsewhere, and it is sparse on the grass and bracken-clad hills. Merlins take many large day-flying moths, emperor, fox and northern eggar, that depend on dwarf shrubs, and this may be a factor in their preference for heather ground. The Skiddaw fells were a good area, with up to ten pairs in the 1940s and 1950s. Of 26 nests I saw here, 17 were in heather and nine in old crow nests in trees. Of another 12 nests seen by Geoffrey Fryer, eight were in heather and four in trees. Occasional pairs bred on rock ledges, and one Martindale crag has been favoured over many years. Nests have also been found in heather on top of huge detached blocks.

Up to 1960, merlins bred among all the more heathery fells throughout the Lakes: Whinlatter, Grasmoor, Melbreak, Watendlath and Castlerigg Fells, lower Ennerdale, Eskdale and Shap Fells. From 1924–55, Marjory Garnett followed three pairs in lower Kentmere, then managed as grouse moor. Sadly, the merlin is greatly reduced in numbers now. There were signs of a setback during the organochlorine episode, with the occasional deserted territory and unmated bird in the mid-1960s. But, unlike the peregrine, pairs continued to drop out after this menace passed. A survey of merlins in the National Park by D. Shackleton in 1994 showed the bird in only 12 of 58 known territories visited, with breeding confirmed in only eight. Ingram Cleasby gave me a list of 13 localities in the Howgill–Sedbergh Fells where he knew merlins breeding in the late 1930s to 1940s. Nearly all are deserted and that district now has very few pairs (Cleasby, 1999).

Deterioration and loss of heather moorland under increasing sheep stocking is the most obvious cause of merlin decline, and has been especially dramatic in the Sedbergh area. Yet the bird has also gone from many territories where plenty of heather ground remains. Merlins winter in the lowlands and may face problems there, but the breeding population of the Bowland Fells not far to the south is still in good shape (P. Stott). Bowland is managed largely as grouse moor and sheep numbers are presumably not allowed to rise too high. Much will depend on merlin food supply, and possibly this has deteriorated in the Lake fells, even where heather ground remains.

The earlier history of the golden eagle in Lakeland is obscure. Undoubtedly, the bird bred here during the 1700s, but the recorded nesting places of eagles, at Wallow Crag, Haweswater, Buck Crag, Martindale; Eagle Crag, Langstrath; and Birkness Combe, Buttermere, were all held by sea eagles. The more frequent name of Erne (or the derived Iron or Heron) Crag – ten, against five Eagle Crags – also suggests that this species was the more numerous. Its eyries were raided annually by shepherds who kept long ropes for this purpose, to reduce supposed depredations on their lambs. All breeding eagles had disappeared from the district by 1800, and for 150 years they (mainly goldens) were only occasional visitors (Blezard et al., 1943).

It was thus the major event in recent Lakeland ornithology when golden eagles returned to breed among these fells. The more frequent sighting of birds from Scotland during the early 1950s had given rise to anticipation. On 27 March 1957, I spotted a large nest on the crags of Harter Fell, Mardale, and an adult golden eagle launched itself from the rocks at my approach, to drift away in leisurely fashion. What excitement! From a higher ledge, I was disappointed to find the huge structure only partly lined. And so it remained on 7 April, when the owner was absent and only the plucking of a rook marked its recent presence. On 22 April I watched a single golden eagle chivvied by a raven over the Harter front.

Jim Birkett then found a second unused eagle nest on a crag in Eskdale. It was the same story at both nests each spring, year after year. The nests were usually repaired but not fully lined, and evidently held by single eagles, except in September 1959, when two adults were together over Harter. Something was preventing the birds from breeding, as should have happened after a year or so of residence. My guess was that the organochlorine sheep-dips were the problem, as they were causing numerous breeding failures among west Highland golden eagles. Sure enough, after these dips were withdrawn in 1966, the happy event took place. On 29 March 1969, Geoff Horne and Rob Brown found the sitting eagle on the Harter Fell eyrie with a single egg. Six days later there were two – the first eggs laid by eagles in the Lakes for about 170 years. Sadly they were then deserted. The crag overlooked the Mardale head car park, and disturbance over an early Easter was perhaps too much for the birds. By 1970, they sought quieter quarters in Riggindale and have stayed there ever since, guarded in nesting time by the RSPB, whose watchers have compiled a full record of their breeding performance and habits. Eggs were laid in most years up to 2000, and young reared in 16 seasons, but since 1996 breeding has failed (Table 4).

The Eskdale nest crag was deserted by 1973, probably through climbing disturbance, and breeding was never proved there. But in 1976 a second occupied eyrie was found in a quiet and unsuspected spot in the western fells. This pair attempted to breed up to 1982, but were successful in only three years and had disappeared by 1983. Despite hopes and rumours, no other eagles are known to have colonised the Lake fells, and the Mardale pair represents their tenuous foothold in the region. Recent breeding failure in Mardale has been attributed by some to ageing birds, but they are not ringed or marked, and identifying individuals by other features is always unreliable. Only a single youngster in a brood has ever been reared by these Lakeland eagles, suggesting a chronic food shortage. Dave Walker (2001), who has observed the Mardale eagles and their food supply over many years, concludes that availability of carrion, especially of red deer, during the pre-laying period is now critically low for this pair. Live wild prey is generally scarce in the Lakes and, in the west, sheep carrion is the main food source. The king of birds thus faces an uncertain future in a district now probably marginal to its needs.

The high mountain birds of the Highlands are poorly represented. Snow buntings are only winter visitors to the fells. The former occurrence of ptarmigan rests on the evidence of a single specimen in Hutton's museum

Table 4 Breeding performance of Lakeland golden eagles. Compiled by G. Horne.

Pair 1 Mardale	
1957–68	Territory established and nest repaired annually on Harter Fell, but no eggs laid.
1969	First clutch laid, two eggs, but deserted.
Pair moved to Riggindale thereafter, using three different nest sites.	
1970	One young reared.
1971	Failed: chick died.
1972	One young reared.
1973	Failed, eggs deserted.
1974	One young reared.
1975	Failed, nest deserted.
1976	Male died, female deserted.
1977	One young reared.
1978	One young reared.
1979	Failed, both eggs infertile.
1980	One young reared.
1981	Failed, the one young disappeared.
1982	One young reared (deformed bill).
1983	One young reared.
1984	One young reared.
1985	Failed, both eggs infertile.
1986	One young reared.
1987	Failed, chick died at ten days.
1988	One young reared.
1989	One young reared.
1990	Failed, both eggs infertile.
1991	One young reared.
1992	One young reared.
1993	Failed, both eggs infertile.
1994	Failed, both eggs infertile.
1995	Failed, both eggs infertile.
1996	One young reared.
1997	Failed, both eggs infertile.
1998	Failed, one infertile egg.
1999	Nest repaired, but no eggs laid.
2000	Failed, neither egg hatched.
2001	Nest repaired, but no eggs laid.
Pair 2. Western Fells	
1957–72	Territory established in Eskdale and nest repaired annually, but no eggs laid.
1976	Pair found nesting c.10 km away. One young reared.
1977	Failed: robbed of eggs.
1978	Failed: eggs deserted.
1979	One young reared.
1980	Failed: eggs snowed out.
1981	Failed: eggs snowed out in high-lying new site.
1982	One young reared (deformed bill).
1983	Territory deserted: female believed to have been shot during the previous winter.
No further evidence of nesting attempts: territory deserted.	

in Keswick in 1803, though Pennant had in 1776 spoken of their presence on the high fells near Keswick. An albino red grouse in Skiddaw Forest in the late 1800s could have been taken for a ptarmigan in winter plumage, but for its unmistakeable voice (Rawnsley, 1899). Probably ptarmigan once occurred, but faded out through the loss of high-level dwarf shrub heaths (pp. 208–9). The dotterel has, however, long been known as a breeder on the higher fells. Indeed, its history here is longer than in the Highlands, and given ten pages by Macpherson (1892). The first known nest was on Skiddaw in 1785, as recorded by Dr John Heysham, whose son, T.C. Heysham, took a special interest in dotterel and collated early accounts of its occurrence and breeding.

This was a bird that enthused certain people to search the tops for nests. But when the 'trips' were passing through the fells in May, it also drew the local anglers with their guns, for the small feathers of a dotterel's wing were highly prized for tying trout flies. And so these beautiful little birds were slaughtered for a minute part of their plumage. This could have reduced the breeding strength, but the birds shot may have been mostly on their way to more northerly breeding grounds. Even in the late 1800s nesting dotterel were elusive, and Francis Nicholson said in 1885 that he saw only three pairs during several days visiting all the most likely ground. In 1887 he again found three pairs, while H. E. Rawson found three pairs nesting in the Westmorland portion in each of the three years 1889–91. Every year a sprinkling of dotterel spread themselves thinly over the higher fells, in both the Lakes and the adjoining Pennines, though Watson (1888) said that five or six pairs frequently bred at no great distance from each other. In good years there could have been up to 50 pairs in the whole of northern England.

Numbers were said to be fewer by 1900, but between 1905 and 1924 J. F. Peters, a Manchester businessman, acquired an unsurpassed knowledge of the dotterel as a Lakes breeding bird. He found eggs or chicks or saw adults in most years, and even suggested that the bird had increased during this time, but said the number that stayed to nest was variable. In 1911, he and two other searchers independently found three nests on a 30-hectare plateau. Numbers then dropped away and 1927 appeared to mark the end of regular nesting. Further nests were reported in 1932, 1934, 1937 and 1942–44. Blezard et al. summarised breeding status in 1943: 'In part, the elusiveness of the dotterel is accounted for by the fact that any given haunt is not necessarily resorted to annually, and may not be occupied for several seasons. It is sufficient to add that, in one haunt or another, the dotterel continues as a nesting species, although a scarce one.'

Despite numerous visits to old nesting haunts from 1945 onwards, I did not see a single dotterel until 1954 and it was not nesting. This dearth of breeding records corresponded with the disappearance of passage trips in May, as though the migration stream had shifted northwards. A nest was reported in 1956 and from around 1960 there was a slight recovery. Strowger (1998) reported that during 1972–95, dotterel bred in northern England (this included the Pennines) in 18 of the 24 years, and he and

John Callion knew of 41 nestings. Never more than three fells were used in any one year, and that only twice. This may have been only a temporary recovery, for there were no nesting records in 1997 or 1998, and during a national census of breeding dotterel in 1999 only a single pair was reported in northern England.

Breeding records refer to all the main fell groups, except the Coniston range. Most nests were above 760 metres, but a favoured locality was at 730 metres, and Rob Brown found a nest at only 670 metres. If earlier records are true, they nested as low as 395 metres on the limestone Shap Fells. Probably the nature of the ground is more important than altitude per se, and stony flats with abundant moss or lichen are attractive to dotterel (Fig. 9.21). A curious early comment was that 'they do not lay their eggs where the fringe moss grows but in a depression upon short dense grass, a little below the summit' (Macpherson & Duckworth, 1886). Many 1900s nests were certainly among fringe moss, and the retreat of dotterel from the Lake fells has coincided with the general disappearance of the *Racomitrium* heaths, and increase of the 'short dense grass'. Des Thompson believes that fringe moss heath has important feeding value for dotterel in its crane-fly populations, and this food source declines as the moss is reduced. Increase in fell-walkers has been blamed for dotterel decline, but it seems to tolerate casual disturbance and nests can be close to footpaths – perhaps

Fig. 9.21 Dotterel about to incubate on a windswept Lakeland fell-top. This northern bird barely hangs on in the region.

because foxes and other predators avoid these. The high numbers of sheep threaten nests by trampling, and at least one was spoiled this way. Perhaps, through awareness of this risk, a certain density of sheep discourages prospecting birds and they move on north.

Global warming could be the most fateful factor for the dotterel in Lakeland, which is its southern breeding limit, perhaps already with a marginal climate. The recovery from around 1960 matched a run of cold, backward springs, and the return of passage trips to the region. The more significant recent trend to a gradual increase in mean spring and summer temperatures may cause a more permanent northwards shift in climatic limits and the dotterel will be – perhaps already is – an early casualty of the all-pervading influence of profligate human energy demands.

So often, the high tops produce nothing more exciting than wheatears, meadow pipits and skylarks, but the unexpected can happen. On 2 June 1970 Ian Prestt and I were crossing peat haggs at 640 metres below a higher top when there flew away a small wader that we concluded was a purple sandpiper. My wife Jeannette and I were crossing the same place on 26 May 1975 when we came upon an undoubted purple sandpiper that let us approach to 20 metres. It fed a little and then just stood watching us. A search of the surrounding ground produced no mate, but the bird was evidently attached to the place. A fortnight later it had gone, leaving a primary beside a pool. I searched higher fell-fields but saw nothing. During visits in several subsequent years I never saw another. Could there have been a nest? Quite possibly, for the 1975 bird behaved just like the off-duty purple sandpipers that we later watched amidst the vast, snowy fell-fields and stony tarns of the Norwegian mountains. The incubating bird sits until almost trodden upon, but its mate feeding or resting elsewhere gives no clue to its whereabouts, and they change over only at long intervals. The species was found breeding in the Cairngorms a few years later, in high montane habitat closer to the Norwegian kind. Our two birds remain a tantalising mystery, and they appear to be the only records from the northern England fells.

Golden plover were never numerous in these hills as the terrain is mostly unsuitable. They were absent from the steeper and more rugged massifs and confined to gently contoured moorlands and higher watersheds where peaty ground is best developed. I saw my very first on the grouse moor of Fauld's Brow in the Caldbeck foothills, and found a nest in burned heather ground, in 1944. A pair or two bred there up to 1970, but they have long gone. In the 1940s and 1950s some 15–20 pairs nested at around 600 metres in the Skiddaw group. Elsewhere, Matterdale Common, the Helvellyn Dodds, the Ullscarf–Armboth Fells, the High Street range, Shap Fells, and the low moorlands of Eskdale–Duddon around Devoke Water and Birker Fell had a scattering of pairs. In most of these areas they have declined to low numbers, and in the Skiddaw group seemingly gone from the Bowscale Fell–Blencathra section, though four pairs were reported from the Caldbeck Fells in 1992. On Askham Fell, south of Pooley Bridge, 20 pairs were reported as recently as 1990.

The plover's frequent Pennine associate, the dunlin, is still scarcer in the Lake fells. Rob Brown saw a pair probably nesting on the Helvellyn Dodds and I once saw a single bird in bogs under Carrock Fell, but the only proven breeding is on the blanket bogs of Shap Fells, above Wet Sleddale, where the best habitat occurs. Lapwings, curlews and redshanks are all scarce among the higher fells and mainly on the lower moors or in the dale bottoms. Canon Rawnsley mentioned wheeling lapwings over the intakes of Latrigg under Skiddaw, but they have long gone from such places. Fauld's Brow was once good curlew ground, but they are now reduced to an odd pair or two. Snipe probably nest widely but sparingly, and frequently rise from their feeding places among the rushy hill marshes. Common sandpipers belong to lake and stream sides (p. 201).

The red grouse has declined greatly as a Lakes bird. There were, up to World War II, managed moors at Fauld's Brow, Skiddaw Forest, Castlerigg and Armboth Fells, Birker Fell and Devoke Water, Kirkby Moor, lower Kentmere, Askham Fell and Shap Fells. These were presided over by resident keepers, who took their toll of the bird predators. Rawnsley noted in 1899 that the Skiddaw Forest keepering included the use of strychnine as well as gun and trap. Percy Parminter found a brood of peregrines dead in the nest after the female parent had been shot, when the Castlerigg moor was active, in 1912. Even merlins were killed in places. Moderate grouse bags were made, though none of these moors was famous.

Moor management ceased in 1940 and when I first knew Skiddaw Forest, in 1944, the front of Great Calva was an unbroken sweep of long heather from base to summit. Moor burning in patchwork fashion was resumed here after 1945, but when this Leconfield estate was sold in 1952, regular keepering ceased and management became desultory. Sheep numbers built up in succeeding decades, and heather retreated (p. 207). On Great Cockup and at Askham Fell, lines of old shooting butts stand now amidst *Nardus* grassland. Grouse numbers gradually dwindled away, on some moors almost to nothing. Even in Skiddaw Forest you can now walk far before seeing a single bird. Probably the best grouse ground now is on steep heather slopes where the plant was never systematically managed, such as Blencathra front, and the bird still occurs widely in small numbers on heathery fells. In 1872, red grouse were sent from Binsey, north of Skiddaw, to New Zealand, in an attempt to establish the bird on the heather ground that had been created there, but they died out.

The story of the black grouse is even more dismal. Blezard et al. (1943) describe it as widespread around the more peripheral dales and fells, though largely absent from the central area. Greystoke, Troutbeck, Kentmere and Longsleddale were favoured areas, but the Lakes population collapsed in the 1940s, for reasons that were unclear. It has never recovered and blackgame are now rarely seen in the district. In other regions, the increase in sheep and their adverse effects on dwarf shrub heaths are blamed for the crash in black grouse numbers, and this could be an explanation here. Nightjars bred on some of the heathery fells and Marjory Garnett found them nesting regularly in lower Kentmere up to the early 1940s, but they too seem to have gone.

Of the small birds, the meadow pipit is the most ubiquitous, nesting all over the fells, from the lowest levels to the highest. Its nest is usually concealed under a grass tussock, or amongst bilberry or heather, but they also build on steep ground and rocky banks, or even crag faces. Possibly annual variations in their strength may account for the more obvious fluctuations in numbers of the cuckoo, the most insistent of the bird voices of the fell country. Despite their dependence on meadow pipits as principal host, I never saw a single cuckoo egg or chick in 50 Lakeland pipit nests found at random, and the only parasitised nest was when I chanced to see the cuckoo, scolded by the parent pipits, go in to lay. Skylarks range widely over the fells, breeding up to 790 metres or so, but avoiding steep and rocky ground. On still, summery days, parties of swifts, of up to 300, often appear over the high tops, skimming low to the ground in pursuit of insects, and then fade out again as mysteriously as they came.

Wheatears vary in numbers from year to year, but are sometimes numerous, nesting in rock crannies on fell slopes, drystone walls and rabbit burrows. They breed up to the highest rocky tops of the Scafell range at 915 metres or over. Their perky, bobbing stance and cheerful bursts of song endear them to hill-goers, and their appearance in late March is the first sign that spring migration is under way in the uplands. The whinchat is more local and arrives later, breeding only up to 455 metres, on the lower slopes and fell bottom land. The stonechat is the rarest of the three chats and prefers the lower, heathery hillsides, such as those of Skiddaw Slate. Although it tends to leave the hill ground in autumn, it suffers badly during hard winters and numbers may be decimated by prolonged frosts, taking several years to recover.

In Skiddaw Forest, whinchats appear to replace stonechats entirely after a severe winter, but gradually reduce again as the latter recover. John Callion has found that when both are present, the stonechats occupy a higher and drier zone above whinchats, which prefer damper ground, though both share bracken beds. Along an eight-kilometre section of the upper Caldew in Skiddaw Forest, he found an average 19 pairs of stonechats and 16 pairs of whinchats from 1989–2000. Callion finds that inland stonechats lay about ten days earlier than those on the coast, many beginning before the end of March; and early nesters often attempt three broods. Ringing has shown that all juveniles leave high inland sites for the coast, and that some Cumbrian stonechats are partial migrants.

The ring ouzel arrives with the wheatear or just after, and the triple piping of the territorial males sounds from many a crag or rocky slope across all the fells. Their favourite nesting site is the rocky side of a heathery gill, where the nest can be concealed amongst the vegetation of a broken face or bank. Nests are also built in block screes, old mine buildings and juniper bushes. The blackbird-like structures are solidly built, of stout grasses, and lined with finer material over a mud casing, so that they can endure for years. Breeding occurs probably up to almost 900 metres. The Skiddaw fells were as good as anywhere for them, with pairs about 400–800 metres apart on suitable ground. They are, like blackbirds, fond of earthworms and seek these on the more fertile grass swards, but take a variety of invertebrate food and from late summer eat berries where these are available.

Wrens range high into the fells and few crag haunts of ravens and peregrines are without these little birds, which build their nests in the rocks. They work old, lanky growths of heather and crevices of block screes and drystone walls for small insects and spiders. Dippers were once on all the hill streams up to moderate elevations, finding nest sites on their rocky sides or amongst overhanging shaggy heather. They seem to be fewer nowadays, and the cascade on Carrock Beck where I saw my first nest no longer has them. Grey wagtails were often in their company, to the point of building in or on top of an old dipper nest, but they too appear fewer in the places where I knew them.

The fell bird populations become much depleted after the breeding season, and most of the waders have departed by the end of July. Meadow pipits flock and move around the hills in August, heading for the lowlands by September, and are followed by the merlins. The migrant passerines leave in September. Of the invertebrate feeders, only the dipper and wren stick it out through the depths of winter, and suffer heavy losses during hard and prolonged frost. Flocks of fieldfares and redwings arrive in October and follow the fells when there are good crops of bilberries, crowberries, haws and rowan berries, but move away later. Bullfinches sometimes seek high heather slopes to feed on the seeds, and parties of snow buntings from the north work the rushes (especially heath rush) for seeds. There is an autumnal influx of snipe to lower marshy hillsides, such as the extensive rushy flush bogs on the north side of Carrock Fell, where I flushed dozens on a recent November day. During February and March a scattering of woodcock on heather and bracken-covered hillsides is evidently a movement of immigrant birds soon to leave for other shores. Only the larger predators and the vegetarians – now only the red grouse – endure winter on the fells, and even they may be driven to lower levels during heavy snow and prolonged frost. In some winters a few rough-legged buzzards from Fennoscandia are to be seen working the fellsides. The resident buzzards become more sociable in winter, when up to 18 birds may be seen circling together (G. Horne).

Amphibians and reptiles

Frogs occur commonly over the Lake fells, up to at least 600 metres, spawning in pools and temporary flooded tractor ruts along hill tracks, where the tadpoles often become dried out. They are often taken by hill-going herons, and provide ravens and crows with a variation in diet. Natterjacks have an inland station on the low moorlands of the south-west. The common lizard is widespread and frequent on all the more heathery fells, but is less common where grassland prevails, perhaps because of the lesser shelter. Adders are curiously local and absent from many apparently suitable areas. In many years of roaming Skiddaw Forest I never saw a single one, nor heard of any, but they are quite common on the lower south-western moorlands of Eskdale and Dunnerdale, and around Hawkshead, and have a surprising outpost at Mardale head, in a secluded spot where few people tread.

Insects

Taking butterflies first, the mountain ringlet is the most famous insect of the Lake fells (Fig. 9.22). Known since 1809, it was found in widely scattered localities and some traditional haunts retain strong colonies to this day, as on Fleetwith and around Sprinkling Tarn. It has a short season, in late June and early July, and flies only in the sun; as soon as cloud casts a shadow, the little blackish flitting forms drop into the grass. Distribution is odd, for the larva feeds on mat grass, one of the most abundant fell plants, yet the butterfly's occurrence is very patchy. It is, I believe, completely absent from the Skiddaw Slate hills, despite their extensive *Nardus* grasslands, and only on the Borrowdale Volcanics, but occurs erratically even there. In good years it spreads out from the main colonies at 455–760 metres, descending to lower levels (120 metres in Wasdale), but does not colonise new ground permanently. In 1977 I found a single female at 215 metres behind Patterdale, presumably from St Sunday Crag above, yet over miles of *Nardus* grasslands on Helvellyn that day, I saw no more. Most of these grasslands are derived from dwarf shrub heath, and the mountain ringlet may be restricted to places where mat grass was originally present in the natural vegetation – as it often is in the Highlands – on flushed ground and late snow beds. Yet its failure to reach a more continuous distribution is still puzzling.

Fig. 9.22 Mountain ringlet: confined in England to the Lake fells, and otherwise only in the Scottish Highlands. (David Clarke.)

The small heath is the most abundant hill butterfly, occurring freely over all the dry grasslands up to 900 metres. Its bigger relative, the large heath, is decidedly local and confined to boggy ground up to 455 metres. In 1977 I found four separate colonies on the bogs of Skiddaw Forest, where many specimens approached the typical Scottish form with obsolete eye-spots. It occurs also on the Armboth Fells and some of the wet Eskdale moorlands, but is probably under-recorded still. The green hairstreak is widespread but patchy, and found especially where its favourite combination of birch and bilberry occurs. Dark green fritillaries are sometimes seen on lower bracken-clad slopes, but this powerful flier may come up from lower breeding places where the violets needed by the larva are more numerous. Immigrant butterflies reach the fells in variable numbers. The three common whites sometimes cross high ground continuously during fine summer days, and flowering heather in August draws peacocks, small tortoiseshells, red admirals and painted ladies to feed.

The moths include many day-flying species. The large emperor, fox and northern eggar are common on heather ground, though in varying abundance from year to year. Males career over the fells in search of females and their conspicuous larvae feed among the dwarf shrubs later, while the flask-shaped cocoons of emperor and the more cylindrical types of the other two are spun among the twigs. Mature larvae of northern eggar pupate in autumn, but the similar (though darker) caterpillars of the fox overwinter and emerge in March before pupating. Dry heather slopes also have silver-Y (often immigrant), scarce silver-Y, golden-Y, true lover's knot, pale eggar, wood tiger, ruby tiger, beautiful yellow underwing, heath rustic and neglected rustic. Geometrid moths galore flit among the heather: mainly the common and latticed heaths, but also the red, galium, beech-green, yellow-ringed and grey mountain carpets. Skiddaw Forest is a good place to see all these day-fliers. The antler moth feeds on grasses and swarms in certain years, to the detriment of the sheep grazings; and a small grass-moth *Crambus furcatellus* is frequent. The micro-moth *Coleophora caespititiella*, whose larva feeds on the fruits of rushes, was found by Pearsall (1950) to decline in frequency with altitude.

Most of the upland moths are fairly small, but once, when I looked over the abrupt edge of Force Crag, a hummingbird hawk-moth hovered at heather flowers just below, as an unusual fell item. The greatest moth rarity was a northern dart taken under a stone high on Skiddaw. It is an arctic–alpine species with crowberry as larval foodplant, and has been found also on the Cross Fell range and the Cheviot, but is otherwise confined to the Highlands.

I have dealt with the upland dragonflies under the open waters in which they breed (Chapter 8). The beetle fauna of the uplands is quite large, and I refer specialists to the accounts by Day (1909, 1912, 1923) and Key (1996). The most conspicuous species are the large dor beetles *Geotrupes stercorosus* and the rarer *G. vernalis*, and violet ground beetles *Carabus violaceus* and *C. problematicus*, which often figure in the castings of ravens and kestrels. Among the other carabids, the coppery-coloured *C. arvensis* is frequent, the blue-black *C. glabratus* uncommon, and the metallic green *C. nitens* rare, while the dung beetle *Aphodius lapponum* is common. The metallic green and brown bracken-clock and the metallic purple or dull orange click beetle sometimes swarm on the fell pastures, where their larvae feed on grass roots and can cause much damage. They also are then an important food source for some of the hill birds. The green tiger beetle is less numerous but widespread.

Several distinctly montane beetles occur on the high fells, notably *Leistus montanus* and *Elaphrus lapponicus* on Skiddaw and *Nebria nivalis* on Scafell Pike, all Red Data Book species. Of two montane weevils, *Otiorhynchus nodosus* is widespread, but *O. arcticus* is known only from Wasdale Screes. Of the grasshoppers, only the common green is widespread on the fells, and then mainly at lower levels.

Calcareous rocks on the fells produce molluscs such as the copse, two-toothed door, cellar, rounded and garden snails, but the commonest species is the shell-less large black slug, widespread in acidic habitats and evidently relished as food by ravens.

10

The Pennines

From their southern border with the Craven district of Yorkshire to their northern extremity at the Tyne Gap, the Lakeland Pennines form the finest sweep of high moorland in England. Though contrasting with the steep, rugged and often precipitous fell country of the Lakes proper, the Pennines have some abrupt and rocky sections also. The deep trench of the Mallerstang valley is flanked by steep slopes with numerous outcrops of gritstone and shale, while behind Brough and Warcop the Eden valley scarp rises in tier upon tier of gleaming white limestone scars. The gentle moorlands drained by the Lune, Tees, South Tyne, Croglin Water, Gelt and Black Burn are more hidden from view, and in their lonely recesses the wanderer can feel remote from civilisation. They have the best claim to the description of wilderness south of the Scottish Border. Parts of them are still incompletely explored for wildlife, and offer a challenge to curious naturalists.

Tourism has come to some parts of the Pennines, and they are not as untrodden as when I first knew them. In particular, the Pennine Way has become an extremely popular long-distance footpath for hill walkers. First declared open in 1965, it enters our area at Cauldron Snout waterfall on the upper Tees and follows the Maize Beck across to High Cup Nick and thence over the fell to Dufton village. It then reascends the long slopes to the summit of Knock Fell and traverses the main watershed over the Duns to Cross Fell, dropping over the north edge of the plateau to pass the old Screes mine (now Greg's Hut) and along the Cashwells mine track down to Garrigill and Alston. In places where there was previously no track, there is now a conspicuous one, often worn deep into the ground and widening out into a messy slough through peaty stretches. Its impact is mainly visual, for most people keep faithfully to the path, and there is little effect on either plants or animals. Just south of the Hartside road the renewal of an old track to a shooting box has made an unsightly scar on the grouse moors of the Black Burn, and four-wheel drives sometimes make unauthorised access to Cross Fell summit from old tracks above Alston. The fells north of Hartside remain little trodden, except by shepherds and gamekeepers, though they, too, have suffered recent incursions from bulldozed tracks for vehicles.

The boundary changes involved in creation of the new county of Cumbria in 1974 added substantially to the area of the Pennines in the south, doubtless to the chagrin of Yorkshire naturalists, whose county was depleted accordingly. The main additions were the whole of the catchments of the Rawthey, Garsdale and Dentdale, with the hills from Swarth and Baugh Fells to the northern half of Whernside and most of the Barbon

Fells. It included the whole of the Howgill Fells, which do not really belong either to the Pennines or the Lake District: they are closer to the first geographically, but have been treated with the second because of their geological affinities.

Vegetation and flora

Woodland

The Pennines have suffered even greater depletion of native woodland than the Lake District, and only scattered fragments remain in Cumbria. On acidic soils, oak woods were once no doubt extensive, but hardly any are left. On the calcareous substrates, ash–hazel is the indigenous type, and there is a fine example on the limestone slopes above Helbeck at Brough, which rivals the best of the Dales ash woods. Oak and birch are abundant also, as once was wych elm, and there are scattered trees of wild cherry, bird cherry and aspen. Spindle occurs sparingly, buckthorn is recorded, and the spineless midland hawthorn has an outlying northern locality here. Besides the usual communities of dog's mercury and wild garlic, there is a rich flora, with local plants such as columbine, Solomon's seal, wood forget-me-not, lily-of-the-valley, sword-leaved and broad-leaved helleborines, herb paris, giant bellflower, stone bramble, wood vetch and mountain melick. Nearby Swindale has an old record for meadow horsetail (unknown elsewhere in Cumbria), and the Dutch rush (another horsetail) is still present. These woodlands belong to community W 8 (Rodwell, 1991a). Alder wood is represented in the Pennines, at the foot of Rundale and in Geltsdale, and many streams have fringing growths of this tree.

Some of the streams draining from the Stainmore and Mallerstang catchments have cut deep, craggy limestone glens with fringing ash wood, and where ungrazed these are quite rich botanically. Swindale adjoining Helbeck (Fig. 10.1), Augill and Argill east of Brough, the Belah glen, Podgill behind Kirkby Stephen, Deep Gill and Ais Gill are the best examples. Some of the woodland here had abundant wych elm, and there were particularly fine trees at Hartley, but they are virtually all dead, and soon even the forlorn skeletons with peeling bark will have fallen to the ground. They were some of the best habitats for mosses, liverworts and lichens that need basic bark and these plants will be diminished accordingly. The narrow defile of Hell Gill near the source of the Eden is almost devoid of trees. The limestone ledges of these ravines have herbaceous patches, with wood cranesbill, globeflower, water avens and wood melick grass, and at least one colony of dark red helleborine. Fine and varied growths of brittle bladder fern sprout from bare rock crevices, and the prickly shield-fern grows luxuriantly. These gills are happy hunting grounds for the bryologist, and some have beautiful silky red tufts of the moss *Orthothecium rufescens* (Plate 40).

Other rocky glens with open wooded fringes and waterfalls occur farther north, on the Croglin Water above Scarrowmanwick, on the Black Burn in Tindale Fells, at Garrigill on the South Tyne, and at Ashgill on the Alston–Middleton road. Ashgill is interesting for the high-level plantation

Fig. 10.1 Ash woods on limestone, Swindale Beck, near Brough.

of conifers that was established on the slopes above the road, reaching a height of 600 metres, the greatest altitude now attained by trees in Cumbria. At this upper limit the growth of larches and firs is depauperate, with little more than gnarled and contorted bushes. Another high-level woodland was established near Moor House, on the sides of a sheltered gill, Green Hole, at 580 metres, in an attempt to reconstitute an example of the type of forest that once naturally occupied favourable sites on these bleak moorlands. Scots pine, birch, rowan, bird cherry and willows were planted, but the native species, especially, suffered frost damage. The experiment told more about the difficulty of re-establishing high-level woodland, once completely lost, than about the nature of earlier forest at these altitudes. In a reconstruction of former forest limits, Turner (1984) has conjectured that even the summit plateau of Cross Fell at 885 metres was covered with scrub at the postglacial climatic optimum. I have doubts about placing the upper scrub limit quite as high, and feel that 800 metres was a more probable level.

Farmland

The enclosed land of the hill farms reaches its greatest elevation in the Pennine part of the region. The old shooting box of Moor House has, as Wilson commented, a meadow of good grass at 565 metres, and fields reach a similar altitude around Nenthead. The relatively continental climate of this eastern district, with warm, sunny summers, as well as the favourable limestone soils, provide an explanation. The herb-rich meadows of the limestone foothills (MG 3, see p. 158) were once widespread here too, but have lost ground similarly. As well as the usual plants, they had the extremely local wood bitter-vetch, in many localities along the scarp fell-foot from Renwick to Dufton. This plant has lost ground greatly, but hangs on sparingly in two localities (Halliday, 1997). The lady's mantle *Alchemilla xanthochlora* is fairly common here, and the rare Teesdale species *A. monticola* and *A. glomerulans* have been found within our boundaries. Another rare plant of the hay meadows around Alston and Nenthead was the northern hawk's-beard, but its present status is uncertain.

A notable Pennine plant that has declined widely as the pastures of the marginal land and lower slopes were drained and fertilised is the bird's-eye primrose. It was always more abundant in the Westmorland section, but had scattered localities in Cumberland from Blencarn to Geltsdale, and also in upper South Tynedale. Although usually in moist or even marshy ground, it still grows plentifully on the steep shaded slopes and ledges of limestone in one rocky glen. Its typical associates, butterwort and marsh valerian, have declined with it. In the 1960s, and especially in 1967, many of the Pennine dales were a blaze of yellow from the abundance of flowering buttercups in their meadows (Plate 42). While striking as a visual spectacle, this actually represented a half-way stage in deterioration from the former herb-rich communities; it appears to be a form of grassland MG 6 (Rodwell, 1992). There were few other plants – besides the buttercups themselves – other than commoner herbs and grasses. Now even the buttercup displays are much less often to be seen. In wetter meadows, abundance of king-cup flowers also produces yellow displays at times (grassland MG 8).

Acidic grasslands and heaths

While the steeper ground of the Eden scarp slopes has been managed as sheepwalk, much of the gentler moorland of the eastward draining dip slopes to the Tees and Tyne, and the Geltsdale–Tindale fells, has been preserved for red grouse. The result has been to produce a contrast between the green, grassy slopes of the sheep ground, and the heathery heaths and blanket bogs of the grouse moors. On the leached and acidified soils where the influence of limestone has been lost or overridden, or over gritstone, shale or the Cross Fell Inlier, there is a range of communities virtually identical with those of comparable ground on the Lake fells. Fescue–bent grasslands with wavy hair grass (U 4) occupy the steep slopes with skeletal soils, *Nardus* grasslands (U 5) the moister, slightly gleyed podsols and heath rush swards (U 6) the deeper, wetter gleys. Bracken has invaded the drier types quite extensively, but is never so dense and luxuriant as in the Lakes – perhaps reflecting the colder winters. Lemon-scented mountain fern and scaly male fern are also abundant on some hillsides (U 19).

The acidic grasslands extend almost unchanged up to the highest tops. There is no alpine lady's mantle to enliven the dry fescue–bent turf, and the innumerable flowers of tormentil and heath bedstraw, with some milkwort, provide about the only colour. Even the clubmosses are scarce and not often seen. From 550 metres, rigid sedge becomes abundant in the high-level grasslands and is almost the only montane plant of these grazed poorer swards. In block screes of gritstone and Whin Sill parsley fern is abundant (Fig. 10.2), mountain male fern grows on acid rocks and there are records of northern buckler fern. Faces and ledges of acidic crags have a limited flora, with great woodrush, bilberry, golden rod, bitter-vetch, fir clubmoss and rigid sedge.

On the broad block-strewn ridge of Stony Rigg between Melmerby Fell and Green Fell, at 670 metres, there was formerly a short heath of bilberry, crowberry and near-prostrate heather with a great abundance of the lichens *Cladonia arbuscula* and *Cetraria islandica*, with *Pseudevernia furfuracea* plentiful on the rocks. Similar patches of montane heath occurred at around the same elevation on Lodge Haggs above Mallerstang, and short heather growth occurs up to the summit of Burnhope Seat at 747 metres, but the true prostrate *Calluna* heath of the Highlands (H 13) is no better represented in the Pennines than on the Lake fells. Fringe moss heath (U 10) was once in places along the higher tops at over 750 metres, such as Skirwith Fell and Knock Fell, and occurred extensively on the broad sum-

Fig. 10.2 Parsley fern on gritstone block scree, Cross Fell.

Fig. 10.3 The best remaining woolly fringe moss heath in Lakeland in 1985: north side of Cross Fell summit plateau.

mit plateau of Cross Fell at 850–900 metres (Fig. 10.3). On the soil hummocks of this plateau (pp. 29–30) the fringe moss formed a crown to each hummock, while the intervening hollows were grass-dominated, the contrast giving a repetitive pattern (Fig. 10.4). The fringe moss has been lost from the lower tops, and has declined greatly on Cross Fell itself (Fig.

Fig. 10.4 Soil hummocks and ridges on the summit plateau of Cross Fell: Cow Green Reservoir, Upper Teesdale, in the distance.

Fig. 10.5 Soil hummocks of limestone plateau of Tailbridge Hill, formerly with dense populations of lapwings and golden plovers.

10.3). Lichens of the reindeer moss type, including *Cladonia rangiferina*, capped the soil hummocks on Tailbridge Hill (Fig. 10.5) and, in combination with the grassy hollows, made a similar pattern. All the lichen heaths are much reduced by grazing.

Bogs, marshes and flushes

Extensive blanket bogs cover the gentle moorlands of Stainmore Common, Tees Head and the upper South Tyne catchment (Plate 36). The broad watershed of the Pennine ridge from Hartside to Tindale Fells is also clad with a continuous mantle of such peatland. The prevailing type has co-dominance of ling heather and hare's-tail cotton-grass, with varying amounts of bogmoss. Common cotton-grass is abundant, especially on bare peat, and other typical plants are cross-leaved heath, deer sedge, cowberry, crowberry, bog asphodel and round-leaved sundew (Community M 19). Cloudberry is one of the most characteristic plants of these Pennine blanket bogs (Fig. 11.7), but occurs more profusely along the eastern border, on the Burnhope Seat range, than farther west. In places it fruits well but, as a dioecious plant, has some populations that are entirely male and thus never fruit. Taylor (1971) found that when areas were protected from sheep grazing, cloudberry flowered and fruited more copiously than when grazed. Lesser twayblade occurs sparingly among the bogs, but the flora is quite limited. The bog bilberry was a much rarer plant of these bogs or drier heaths and none of its several old records has been verified in recent years. In 1965 a few sprigs of dwarf birch were found in the bogs of Widdybank Fell, lower down the Tees and on the Durham side but, despite the huge area of suitable habitat, it has never been found elsewhere in the Pennines. Much of the ground in our area is never trodden by a botanist's foot, though, and it is something to watch out for.

Actively growing areas of bog with a high cover of *Sphagnum* were formerly extensive on Alston Moor, but have been reduced in recent decades by burning and 'moor-gripping'. This last, involving mechanical cutting of parallel drains, has scarred and spoiled the pristine appearance of the wild moorlands at the back of Cross Fell, for negligible gain. The practice has been discontinued through withdrawal of Ministry of Agriculture grants on which it depended, but much damage has already been done. These peat drains take ages to heal, and sometimes deepen and erode. Good examples of wet, active bog still occur on the watershed of Yad Moss and near Moor House, with high cover of *Sphagnum papillosum, S. magellanicum, S. rubellum* and *S. cuspidatum*, and occasional hummocks of the rare *S. imbricatum* and *S. fuscum* (Bog community M 18). Spongy bog surfaces here have the uncommon bog sedge and tall bog sedge, and a large population of the second species in Westmorland, together with the rare bogmoss *S. riparium*, was drowned by the Cow Green Reservoir.

The blanket bogs mostly show some erosion by gullying of the peat and its removal by wind and water (Fig. 10.6). There is only slight erosion, with incipient channels, on Cold Fell, but farther south, on parts of Yad Moss, near Moor House and on Stainmore, it is severe, with networks of deep gullies ('brocks') exposing peat depths up to three metres or more, down to the underlying stones and drift (Fig. 10.7). In places there is sheet erosion, with bare expanses of almost black peat wasting away, and leaving areas

Fig. 10.6 Blanket bog on the Pennine watershed of Burnhope Seat, between South Tyne and Wear, showing early gully erosion.

Fig. 10.7 Blanket bog on Yad Moss, Alston Moor, showing deep gullying of the peat down to the mineral substrate.

denuded to the mineral substrate (Fig. 10.8). The most extreme erosion is on Lodge Haggs, along the Swaledale–Eden watershed, where scattered peat islands, still eroding, remain to suggest a once continuous peat mantle (Fig. 10.9). Here, various stages in recolonisation of the bared substrate

Fig. 10.8 Sheet erosion of blanket bog, but with recolonisation of underlying mineral substrate, Lodge Haggs, Mallerstang Fells.

Fig. 10.9 Sun after rain: steaming of heavily eroded blanket bog on Lodge Haggs, Mallerstang Fells.

may be seen. Where the ground remains wet, shallow peat-forming communities with mat grass and heath rush occur, but dry ground shows variable development of a mossy community with *Campylopus flexuosus* and *Polytrichum juniperinum*, remaining stone-littered and resembling montane fell-field heaths.

In places here a secondary cycle of erosion and recolonisation is visible. Elsewhere a short heath of crowberry and bilberry, with almost prostrate heather, has developed. Such erosion cycles are quite widespread on plateaux of the Irish mountains, and suggest that possibly some summit watersheds of the Lakeland hills, now with little or no bog, once had an extensive peat cover that has been lost. Blanket bog occurs up to 790 metres on Knock Fell and Cross Fell, but the peat at high levels is usually shallow, with little but cotton-grass. Bare, peaty pools are frequent and there are larger dystrophic tarns with peaty, acid water, on Dufton Fell at Seamore, Great and Little Rundale Tarns.

Flush bogs of the type described for the Lake fells are widespread, especially those with common rush, star sedge and white sedge, and varying amounts of bog moss, notably *S. recurvum*. In many places they occur along soakways amongst the blanket bogs, as well as along wet hillsides and valley floors. Springs and rills fed by nutrient-poor water have the moss carpets and small herbs described on p. 212, and are also the typical habitat of chickweed willowherb and pale forget-me-not. The last was first described by C. E. Salmon in 1926 from material collected on Cross Fell, and was once thought to be a British endemic, but has been found also on the mountains of northern Portugal and Spain. The small, pale flowers, short

Fig. 10.10 Late snow beds on the high north slopes of Cross Fell on 6 May 1988.

leaves and densely stoloniferous shoots are quite distinctive. Starry saxifrage is fairly common in this type of spring, but the largest plants are mostly on wet rocks.

These three plants all have a wide altitudinal range, but two alpines are confined to higher level springs and rills. Above 550 metres the little alpine willowherb is widespread – one of the Pennine plants unknown in the Lake District. In 1959, Alan Eddy and I quite independently found the alpine foxtail grass in high cold springs in late snow areas of the Dun Fells and Cross Fell, at around 825 metres (Fig. 10.10). This is strictly an arctic plant, and one of the very few species occurring in Britain but not Scandinavia: it is widespread in high mossy springs in the east of the Highlands, but then the nearest localities are in Greenland. I later found good colonies on Knock Fell and saw it as low as 670 metres above Ardale head. Some of these cold, montane springs have the distinctive red moss *Bryum weigelii* and the apple-green *Pohlia wahlenbergii* ssp. *glacialis*, while on Little Fell they have the rare *Splachnum vasculosum*.

Limestone communities

The limestone more than makes up for any floral deficiencies on the acid rocks and soils. This wonderful rock outcrops extensively in the Westmorland section, but becomes decreasingly less exposed northwards through Cumberland. At all levels, the limestone typically bears a grassland heavily grazed by sheep, for it is highly nutritious and selectively sought by these animals (Plate 36). On the lower slopes the sward is similar to that widespread in the limestone foothills, with blue moor-grass abundant in chewed-down, non-flowering form, and other grasses such as sheep's fescue, red fescue, cock's-foot, crested dog's-tail, crested hair, yellow oat, vernal and quaking grass. Nearly always wild thyme is creeping through the turf, which is fragrant with its scent as you walk and crush the plant. There are numerous small herbs – daisy, harebell, eyebright, fairy flax, limestone bedstraw, self-heal, ribwort plantain, yarrow, white clover, mouse-ear hawkweed, common mouse-ear, heath violet and carnation sedge. The small scabious is locally abundant and at low levels there is often salad burnet, while autumnal gentian and moonwort are widespread, and around Kirkby Stephen the southern horseshoe vetch grows in some limestone swards. Another southern plant, the musk thistle, has outposts in the limestone grasslands, mainly of the south-eastern Pennines.

Where grazing is less heavy and the ground rockier, as on the slopes above Helbeck, a profusion of rock-rose and biting stonecrop can colour the ground yellow in early summer. It was somewhere in this area that the younger James Backhouse found a mysterious field fleawort intermediate in size between the typical form and the large coastal subspecies that grows at the South Stack on Anglesey. His description (Backhouse, 1884) suggests that it occurred mainly as non-flowering rosettes in grazed turf, and so may be overlooked rather than extinct as some botanists have presumed. The scars, screes and rocky gills of limestone at moderate elevations in the Hilton–Brough–Kirkby Stephen area produce a crop of uncommon plants, in dark-red helleborine, alpine cinquefoil, hoary whitlow-grass, native wall whitlow-grass, bird's-foot sedge, rigid buckler fern and limestone fern. On the steep ungrazed faces, blue moor-grass grows in large tufts, flowering profusely, and is then a strongly competitive plant that may have reduced other less aggressive species. Small scabious, hairy

Fig. 10.11 Horseshoe vetch, a southern chalk plant near its northern limit on Carboniferous limestone in Dukedale, near Kirkby Stephen.

rock-cress and horseshoe vetch (Fig. 10.11) also flower copiously out of the reach of sheep.

The dry limestone scars (Fig. 10.12) and gill-sides are important habitats for hawkweeds, many of which are lime-loving plants, with *Hieracium anglicum* as the most widespread, and noteworthy species including *H. vulgatum*, *H. rubiginosum*, *H. glanduliceps*, *H. oistophyllum*, *H. maculosum*, *H. auratiflorum*, *H. cymbifolium*, *H. duriceps*, *H. pellucidum*, *H. decolor*, *H. dicella* and the Cumbrian endemic *H. itunense* known only from south Stainmore (Halliday, 1997). Some lowland and woodland plants reach their upper altitudinal limit on the highest limestone outcrops, which attain 750 metres at the head of Knock Ore Gill. Cowslips flourish here, while shady potholes on Knock Fell plateau have moschatel and alternate-leaved golden saxifrage. Limestone pavements are less extensive than on the Carboniferous foothills, but areas with typical grike communities (p. 151) occur at Fell End Clouds on the west side of Wild Boar Fell and from Helbeck towards Long Fell, while the Tailbridge plateau has examples with rather open grikes which are grazed.

On the shadier and more sheltered rock faces, woodland plants are well represented, and bigger ledges have fragments of herb-rich communities found in ungrazed woods. The limestone potholes on Tailbridge Hill have good examples (Fig. 10.13). Brittle bladder fern and green spleenwort flourish in the steep crevices, while ledges have wood cranesbill, cow parsley, meadowsweet, rosebay willowherb, wall lettuce, dog's mercury, wood anemone, herb robert, stone bramble, wild strawberry, barren strawberry, wood sorrel, moschatel, prickly shieldfern, broad buckler fern and polypody. A small pothole near Moor House once had an isolated patch of

Fig. 10.12 Moorland stream, limestone scars, grassland and blanket bogs, at Tees Head near Moor House, looking to Cross Fell.

Fig. 10.13 Limestone potholes with natural rock gardens, Tailbridge Hill, near Kirkby Stephen.

Jacob's ladder, far from its nearest stations, but this has gone, probably because sheep managed to gain access. The grikes in limestone pavements have some of these plants, plus an abundance of hart's tongue fern.

Above 450 metres alpines increasingly appear in the limestone swards and rock habitats. Mountain everlasting occurs down to 100 metres, but is mainly in the higher level sites, forming tight patches in the turf. Mossy saxifrage is one of the most widespread, and grows in tight, compact cushions in dry, grazed situations, but becomes more straggly on steep, moist banks and shady cliffs. Often in its company is spring sandwort, another white-flowered plant of rather similar habit. Alpine scurvy-grass grows in small-leaved, compact forms amongst the grazed turf and scree, but becomes luxuriant on steep, moist rocks (Fig. 10.14). Northern bedstraw, viviparous bistort and hoary whitlow-grass all occur in non-flowering, depauperate form in the grasslands, but reach their normal stature on the rock ledges.

The Lakeland Pennines lack any outcrops of the metamorphosed sugar limestone that accounts for so much of the botanical richness of Widdybank and Cronkley Fells, lower down the upper Tees in Durham. In

Fig. 10.14 Luxuriant plant growth with alpine scurvy-grass and roseroot along a wet seepage from limestone over acidic whin sill: Black Doors, Ardale, Cross Fell.

consequence, some of the most notable plants of that famous ground are either lacking or in only small quantity. Alpine rush, false sedge and variegated horsetail still grow in stony calcareous flushes near Birkdale farm, but an outlying patch of shrubby cinquefoil beside the Maize Beck has gone. The little hair sedge has scattered localities in limestone turf and spills over from Tees Head into the catchments of Tyne and Eden. The celebrated spring gentian does likewise and its vivid, deep blue flowers still spangle the short turf and rocky ledges in several localities. In Westmorland it is near Birkdale and on Little Fell, and possibly still on Meldon Hill. The Alston naturalist George Bolam found several patches on Alston Moor in Cumberland, at least four of which survive, but reports of spring gentian north of the Hartside road have not been confirmed. The remaining colonies are mostly small, even where the habitat is extensive, and the plant appears unable to spread. In one of the best populations, 110 flowers were counted in one recent year. Another Teesdale speciality, the rock violet, was first found in Westmorland by the younger Backhouse in stony turf along the crest of a limestone fell above Warcop. It is still there, scattered over a large area, but flowers only sparingly in the close-cropped sward (Halliday, 1997). A few plants have also been reported from Alston Moor, though not recently.

Pride of place in this montane limestone flora should go to the alpine forget-me-not (Plate 37). First discovered by the two Backhouses on the Yorkshire (now Durham) side of Mickle Fell in 1852, it was found still more abundantly by James junior on Little Fell in 1866. He later stated (Backhouse, 1884) that in 1880 he found a third colony, 'many miles distant' from the previous two. In the late 1950s, Ken Park found the plant growing very sparingly at the head of Knock Ore Gill; and this could have been Backhouse's third locality, though it is only eight miles from Little Fell. In July 1955 I saw alpine forget-me-not flowering in such profusion on Little Fell as to colour the turf blue in places, in one of the most memorable botanical displays I have ever seen. There could have been a million plants or more, mostly only 2.5–6 centimetres high, and with relatively large flowers. It was confined to the top band of limestone, which girdles the whole summit slopes at 700–730 metres and extends on to the plateau. The next and only other British stations are on the Ben Lawers range in Perthshire, where the forget-me-not grows mainly on cliff faces, as a much taller plant, of up to 15 centimetres. These high-level grasslands are a montane sub-community of CG 9.

Some alpines are only on steep rocks of limestone or basalt. Alpine cinquefoil has several colonies on the higher outcrops, and roseroot, lesser meadow-rue and a lady's mantle *Alchemilla wichurae* are scattered in these places. Several rare species are in only small quantity. Holly fern has four localities, in pavement grikes, block scree and potholes, and its total population is quite small. Alpine meadow-grass is still on the faces of Maize Beck Scars, and has been found on the basalt at High Cup. Alpine timothy grass grows in very small quantity on three high-lying limestone scars around Crowdundle, but is only recognisable when in flower and so would pass unnoticed in grazed situations. The boundary adjustments that placed part of Whernside, Garsdale and upper Dentdale in Cumbria added the endemic little lady's mantle *Alchemilla minima* to our flora, growing around springs and in short limestone turf (Halliday, 1997). The extreme rarity is the alpine saxifrage, another discovery of the Backhouses on the Whin Sill crags of High Cup Scars, where it grew in fair amount up vertical faces in two ravines. Just five small rosettes remained in 1984, but by 1995 one had disappeared. It has seldom flowered in recent years and seems to be slowly fading out. On the same rocks are scattered plants of alpine penny-cress.

The Whin Sill is itself an acidic rock, but the outcrop at High Cup is overlain by limestone (Fig. 10.15), and water draining from this down the basalt faces allows a calcicole flora to flourish. The same effect may be seen at the head of Ardale, where a water trickle gives a luxuriant cascade of base-loving plants, on an otherwise rather sterile range of Whin Sill crag (Fig. 10.14). A few species prefer intermediate soil conditions, notably the mountain pansy, which is in slightly leached limestone turf in places, but grows more luxuriantly on rock faces. Around Kirkby Stephen the yellow-flowered form occurs with the purple, but farther north dark flowers prevail. It is another declining species.

Where calcareous drainage water emerges at the ground surface, there are brown moss springs and little sedge-moss marshes similar to those described for the Lake District and the limestone foothills, but belonging to community M 38 (Rodwell, 1991b).

Sometimes these are amongst grasslands or on stony ground, but they also appear in places among the blanket bogs, making a sudden contrast in ground chemistry and vegetation. Their most notable plant is the yellow marsh saxifrage, a rarity of upland marshes and sufficiently uncommon in Europe to be listed in Annex II of the European Union Habitats and Species Directive as requiring special protection. The northern Pennines are its headquarters in Britain, and the majority of the scattered colonies

Fig. 10.15 The regular, sub-columnar cliffs of quartz–dolerite whin sill, with Carboniferous limestone above, at High Cup Scars.

lie within the Cumbrian sector. Though easily overlooked when not in flower, the marsh saxifrage has distinctive apical clusters of spear-shaped leaves on reddish stems that poke through the moss carpets at an angle. The yellow petals are peppered over their lower half with tiny orange-red spots, to distinguish them from the flowers of buttercups and lesser spearwort that are often in the same flushes. The plant occurs in at least 15 separate sites between Little Fell and Bullman Hills north of Cross Fell, and is also on Burnhope Seat straddling the catchment with Weardale. Some localities have hundreds of leaf clusters, but the flowers, usually one to a stem, are never dense and often become cropped by sheep.

The ordinary yellow saxifrage is uncommon here, in contrast to its abundance in the Lake fells, but also grows in calcareous flushes and beside rills. Marshy grasslands fed by limestone seepages have the alpine meadow-rue in several places, while stony flushes and wet rocks have scattered colonies of the little three-flowered rush, and the hairy stonecrop is quite widespread in the richer flushes. Sedge marshes with *Sphagnum warnstorfii* are outposts of the Highland community M 8 (Rodwell, 1991b).

The Pennines have many of the upland bryophytes and lichens of the Lake fells, but are poor in Atlantic species. The mosses *Drepanocladus vernicosus, Tomentypnum nitens, Oncophorus virens, Rhytidium rugosum* and *Entodon orthocarpus* are noteworthy species of both districts. *Orthothecium rufescens* and *Pseudoleskeella catenulata* are mainly in the Pennines, while *Haplodon wormskjoldii, Splachnum vasculosum, Encalypta rhabdocarpa* and the liverwort *Lophozia lycopodioides* are Pennines only. The liverwort *Scapania aspera* is common on the Pennine limestone but rare on calcareous igneous rocks in the Lakes. The lichens include the Lakes species *Cladonia rangiferina, Pseudevernia furfuracea, Cetraria hepatizon, Massalongia carnosa* and *Umbilicaria deusta. Cetraria commixta* and *Parmelia incurva* are commoner on the Pennines, and *Allantoparmelia alpicola* and *Umbilicaria hyperborea* confined to their highest rocks.

The lead-mining industry that flourished among these hills during the nineteenth century has left an interesting habitat in the weathered heaps of spoil that mark the site of the many long-abandoned workings. Some old mine tips have little of botanical interest, and acidic material is often sterile, but where the waste contains plentiful calcite a distinctive flora has developed. Alpine scurvy-grass and spring sandwort are also on many of the natural limestone exposures, but not the alpine pennycress which grows in profusion on many of these spoil heaps, especially on Alston Moor. The form here appears adapted to the heavy metal concentrations, and is possibly different physiologically from that occurring as a rarity of natural basic rocks.

In a few places, inland populations of thrift grow on the dumps, as at High Plains and near Shield Hilltop beside the Alston–Middleton road. These ungrazed locations have some of the largest and most vigorous populations of mountain pansy now remaining. In the Nent valley, most of these lead mine plants grow abundantly on the alluvial river banks, which have sediment washed down from the Nenthead mines. There is also a noteworthy amount of grass of Parnassus here. The narrow-lipped helleborine has a well-known colony on river gravels influenced by mine waste on the South Tyne in Northumberland, and in 1993 a few plants were found under birch trees above Alston (Halliday, 1997). The community OV 37 exactly fits this lead mine spoil vegetation (Rodwell, 2000).

On a limestone outcrop in Rough Sike near Moor House, the Nature Conservancy introduced various alpine plants, including purple saxifrage, alpine lady's mantle, moss campion and net-leaved willow, which were unknown in the Pennines in recent times; and mountain avens, alpine cinquefoil and viviparous bistort, which had other north Pennine localities. The idea was to re-create a high-level plant community containing species that were presumed to have been present before the sheep came, but this was not necessarily a legitimate assumption. Unless there is direct evidence, from subfossil pollen or macroscopic plant remains, of their former occurrence in the area, it is safer to assume that species not recently present did not reach the Pennines in postglacial times. Establishment of a rock garden does not prove anything about the natural processes of plant dispersal.

Increase in grazing

The build-up in sheep numbers has damaging effects beyond their relentless suppression of the dwarf shrubs. Many of the Pennine grasslands had small herbs that tolerated moderate grazing. Mountain pansy was locally plentiful while mountain everlasting, hoary whitlow-grass, viviparous bistort and northern bedstraw could all persist in grazed turf, albeit with few if any flowers. Spring gentian and alpine forget-me-not flourished and the latter was thought to have evolved a dwarf ecotype adapted to grazing (Elkington, 1964). The disappearance of marsh saxifrage within a fenced flush near Moor House was quoted as evidence that a certain level of grazing was essential to the survival of some uncommon plants.

It is clear that there is a limit to the grazing tolerance of these plants, and that it is now widely exceeded. Mountain pansy is no longer common, and the only good flowers are where sheep are excluded. Many former records of mountain everlasting appear lost, and alpine forget-me-not is much reduced, including on Little Fell. Around 1914 George Bolam was told by J. Markham of Skirwith Hall of 'a wide and flourishing patch' of mountain avens on the rocky rim of Melmerby Fell overlooking the village, and the Supplement to Lees' *West Yorkshire Flora*, gives a record of this plant for Tailbridge Hill. Bolam himself saw a single patch of *Dryas* near the summit of Mickle Fell, just outside our area, in 1912. None of these finds has been seen again, despite many visits to the places by botanists in recent years. If they were in sheep-grazed swards, it is a fair assumption that they have gone. Least willow was once on Cross Fell and Mickle Fell, but has never been seen in recent times. The once fine fringe moss heath of Cross Fell summit is much reduced, and even the good lichen heaths of Melmerby Fell, Burnhope Seat and Tynehead Fell are now in a poor state. The Pennine crags are far too few and small to be a sufficient plant refuge, and the district is suffering even greater botanical depletion than the Lake fells. Ken Park's caustic remarks to me in 1958, when he was in charge of Moor House, on 'the white maggots devouring the hillside' were apposite and justified.

Animals

Mammals

There are no red deer on the Pennines, nor any feral goats, though roe deer are widespread in woodland and rapidly colonise new plantations, up to 550 metres, as at Nenthead (Mitchell & Delap, 1974). The main wild grazer is the rabbit, which once swarmed on many lower limestone slopes, in numbers sufficient to keep local rabbit catchers in business. Some of them worked along quite narrow ledges of limestone scars, so that even on these steep outcrops, the plant life could be somewhat vulnerable to rabbit attentions. They crashed during the myxomatosis epidemic of 1954–55 and, while now widely distributed, are seldom abundant and have never recovered to former numbers. Brown hares are mainly in the enclosed fell-bottom lands, but range the hill slopes to moderate altitudes. Moles are especially favoured by the limestone soils with abundant earthworms, and many of the close-cropped 'greens' are thickly dotted with hillocks of the rich brown loam that they have thrown up. They occur on isolated patches of limestone surrounded by miles of sterile blanket bog, and follow this rock up to its highest occurrences at 750 metres. The small rodents – short-tailed vole, wood mouse and bank vole – are all widespread, but subject to marked fluctuation in numbers. The water vole is a noteworthy mammal, for it has gone from much of its once widespread Cumbrian range, and the main occurrences since 1990 are nine tetrads in the upper South Tyne catchment (Hewitt, 1999a).

The predators are those of the Lake fells, with the fox pre-eminent, still widespread and maintaining its numbers despite unrelenting persecution by shepherds and keepers, and hunting with hounds. Along the Cross Fell range, the numerous block screes and litters ('borrans') provide foxes with much scope for their dens, but a good many others excavate tunnels in the soft peat faces of the eroding blanket bogs. Foxes are serious predators of ground nesting birds, especially grouse and waders, and will have a go at any nests of raven or buzzard with young that they can reach.

The pine marten has a somewhat uncertain presence, though some claim that it still occurs and is simply elusive: they need to produce some more convincing evidence. The badger has become widespread on the open lower slopes and among woodland fragments in the Pennine glens. The grouse keepers do not welcome them, but on the sheepwalks they are mostly left alone. Stoats range over the fells up to 600 metres, but are less numerous than before myxomatosis arrived. Weasels do not go so high, and mostly keep to the bottom lands, where they are frequent.

Birds

From the much greater scarcity of high cliffs, the crag-nesting birds were always scarcer in the Pennines than the Lake fells. Yet this was not the sole reason for their low numbers. Blezard (1946) noted that seldom were more than two out of nine raven breeding places occupied in a season, and that 'the raven here fares badly in its nesting'. Mallerstang and Scordale or High Cup had regular pairs, but in other territories the record was of only irregular or occasional breeding. Raven fortunes then improved a little up to the 1960s. A pair usually attempted to nest at an old haunt in Tindale Fells from 1946, but seldom succeeded in rearing young. Cross Fell was irregularly used but had a pair from 1958–64, and separate pairs bred in High Cup and Scordale from 1962–73. A pair returned to Dukedale above Kirkby Stephen in 1960 and bred in the crags, but then turned to tree-nesting farther down the dale. Sometimes there was a separate pair on Mallerstang Edge. Six pairs was still a poor total for so large an area (c. 7,200 square kilometres), and numbers dropped again after 1970. During the last decade they have been at an uncertain one to three pairs, and although in 1997 a new pair reappeared at an old haunt not used since 1936, they had gone again the next year.

The explanation of this chequered history is quite simple: persecution by grouse preservers. All these raven territories were either on or close to keepered grouse moors. Sometimes broods were found dead in or below the nests, and keepers were known to come from their own ground in Swaledale to shoot ravens (and peregrines) in Dukedale and Mallerstang. Yet it was probably the more insidious use of poison on the grouse moors that claimed the breeders and mopped up new birds seeking territories. Birds in all the nine territories would be at risk, as they would inevitably forage onto keepered ground. With an increase of grouse shooting interest in recent years, the future of the raven here is not bright. The Pennines could hold quite a large population, for tree-nesting could make good any shortfall in suitable crags; but unless there is a more tolerant attitude among grouse preservers, and an end to the illegal use of poison, the bird is likely to maintain only its tenuous foothold in this district.

It may be significant that a former communal roost of non-breeding ravens on the Cross Fell range has been abandoned. First reported in 1909 by E. B. Dunlop and A. Mason, the location varied between Rundale, Knock Ore Gill, High Cup Dale and Scordale, and the flock between 17 and 57 birds. Numbers were greatest in midwinter and thinned out or even disappeared during the spring. The non-breeding flock was maintained up to 1964, but then disappeared. A second roost with up to 100 birds was reported on Wild Boar Fell around 1960, but also faded out later.

The peregrine was also scarce, and Blezard (1946) put its breeding strength at one to three pairs, though it seems likely that in some years a fourth pair bred. The old Cross Fell haunt became deserted from 1939 to 1958, and had only just been reoccupied when the countrywide peregrine crash included this pair. Two pairs bred in 1961, one in 1962 and none in 1963. Three pairs were back by 1967, two of them successful, and by 1969 there was again the previous full complement of four pairs. In 1973 a pair began to breed in a locality near the Tyne Gap where nesting had never been known before. This was the beginning of a remarkable upswing, which saw numbers rise to an incredible 11 pairs by 1987. A new pair in 1982–83 had dropped out by 1987. Most of the increase was through establishment of completely new territories, involving the use of very small crags or even broken banks. In earlier years when peregrines were fewer they were seldom if ever attracted by such third-rate nesting places, but with the pressure of large numbers of new recruits seeking to establish themselves, they had to use these or forgo breeding. Two quarry sites were used, one of them in a working excavation.

Some of this increase evidently involved the greater forbearance of game preservers than in earlier years. At least five haunts were amidst grouse moors where the keepers must have known of the peregrines, but decided to put up with them – perhaps from the publicity given to what was regarded for some years as an endangered species. It is equally clear that this tolerance has worn thin and keepers have once again decided peregrines are bad news on grouse moors, and to take the law into their own hands. Three keepered territories have been deserted and, although yet other new pairs have established elsewhere, some other localities have a dismal recent record of breeding failure and vanishing or dead falcons. The female at the old Cross Fell site was found shot on her eyrie in 1998, and another pair was poisoned in 1999. The Lakeland Pennines had ten pairs of peregrines in most years from 1990, but in 1997 and 1998 12 pairs attempted to breed.

Although domestic pigeons are again the staple food item, the Pennine peregrines undoubtedly take grouse, which are far more generally available here than in the Lake fells. They show a wider food spectrum than the Lakes falcons, with waders such as snipe, lapwing and golden plover more frequently represented. Studies of peregrine and hen harrier predation on the Langholm grouse moors, not far to the north, have shown they take red grouse there in numbers sufficient to reduce the shootable stock. Grouse preservers no doubt feel that this message justifies their illegal persecution.

Blezard (1946) suggested a Pennine buzzard population of a dozen pairs, noting a considerable increase from the two pairs for the Cumberland section given by Macpherson & Duckworth (1886). Numbers continued to build up along the Eden valley scarp and in Mallerstang, and by 1954 probably at least 25 pairs bred between Hartside and the Yorkshire border. Roughly half nested on the bare fell scars, up to 650 metres, while the rest were in scattered woods and clumps of trees along the fell-foot. The hill nests were often in very small rocks and a few were virtually on the ground. Distribution tailed off north of Hartside and into South Tynedale, and there was a conspicuous scarcity of nesting buzzards on the grouse moors. Ernest Blezard found a bird trapped on its nest at Croglin in 1928, and a pair attempting to breed in Geltsdale in 1934 had a large stone dropped on their eggs.

These Pennine buzzards fed especially on rabbits, which then swarmed on the limestone slopes and along the fell-foot. When myxomatosis struck in 1955 the food supply crashed, and for a few years small clutches or non-breeding were reported. For a time numbers appeared to hold up well, nevertheless, and most territories remained occupied. Yet something has gone wrong, and while buzzards have expanded across the low ground of the whole Eden valley and the Solway Plain, they have slowly declined along the fells. The higher sites on rocks have particularly shown this decrease, and most remaining pairs are in the fell-bottom woods. Possibly there is a food supply problem, for the rabbits are fewer than formerly. Buzzards take carrion, however, and would be as vulnerable as ravens to poisoned meat baits when they hunt moorlands where these are put out. Many of the fell-going pairs have hunting ranges that extend onto grouse moor and thus place them at risk. In contrast to the peregrine, which is less vulnerable to poison, the buzzard has remained largely absent from the Pennine grouse moors.

There is no history of eagles of either species nesting in the Cumbrian Pennines, but the golden eagle would surely establish breeding territories if left alone. Walter Thompson had a close view of one on north Stainmore in August 1956, and Ernest Blezard saw an immature bird in Tindale Fells in May 1957. On 11 July 1959, in Crossgill on the Alston Moor side of Cross Fell, a golden eagle swept down the valley, passing close to where I sat, and was soon joined by a second bird. Both were immature ring-tails, no doubt seeking a place to settle and drawn by the abundant grouse. The pluckings of two fresh grouse kills lay nearby and I found roosting places littered with eagle feathers. I did not rate their chances of survival highly, and no more was ever heard of them. A juvenile eagle was seen far away in the Westmorland Pennines at the end of that month, and a female approaching maturity was found dead in the adjoining Shap Fells in the winter of 1960.

So eagles were reaching the Pennines with some frequency, and food supply for them is better here than in the Lakes where they duly bred (p. 238). But the grouse men are unlikely to tolerate the drain on their precious birds for the sake of having even one pair of these magnificent raptors as established breeders. The Moor House NNR is almost big enough to support a pair, but has few suitable nesting places, and eagles would inevitably wander on to other ground where a hostile reception could be guaranteed. If the species is ever to make a home in the Pennines, a lot will have to change.

The merlin (Fig. 11.5) is more tolerated by grouse keepers nowadays, though still destroyed on certain moors. The Lake Pennines are a stronghold, though the bird seldom breeds away from the heather ground of the grouse moors. The Geltsdale-Tindale Fells regularly have six or seven pairs, and in 1927 Ritson Graham found two nests only 400 metres apart in Tindale Fells. Another four pairs breed between Croglin and Hartside, Moor House regularly has two pairs and Alston Moor probably has several more. South of Moor House merlins may be more scattered, but breeding occurs on the blanket bogs of south Stainmore. In the sector of the Pennines east of Sedbergh, from Dentdale to Baugh Fell, Ingram Cleasby knew nine merlin territories in the late 1930s. A few of these were still tenanted in the mid-1970s, but even by then some pairs had disappeared, and hardly any are now left. Loss of heather ground explains the decline, as it does on the adjoining Howgill Fells.

Kestrels are widespread, though varying in numbers according to vole populations. In good years the RSPB Geltsdale reserve has up to 23 pairs, but in poor ones only five pairs. Nesting is mainly in small crags and old quarries, but buildings are also used, such as the ruins of Pendragon Castle in Mallerstang. The short-eared owl breeds widely but thinly over the grouse moors from Tindale Fells south to Stainmore, and maintains a more constant population here than on the afforested moorlands of the Borders, its other main Cumbrian area. It appears to be just tolerated, but the hen harrier is everywhere unwelcome on the grouse moors. Macpherson mentioned nesting near Alston as the only Pennine record, but in earlier times the species probably bred quite widely on these eastern moors. Their recent attempts to recolonise the area make a sorry tale. Hen harriers were first recorded in the Pennines north of Hartside (including the Northumbrian sector) in 1978, with a pair or two on suitable nesting grounds each year. Yet because of interference, successful breeding was not confirmed until 1988, when four young were reared. Since then, the number of pairs has fluctuated between two and seven. In 2000, seven females held territory, but only two reared young, and in 2001, when foot-and-mouth disease prevented observation until late in the breeding season, none was seen (G. Horne).

The observers are in no doubt about the cause of this dismal record – gamekeepers. In 1989 a gamekeeper seen at a nest where the young were found dead was unsuccessfully prosecuted for wilful disturbance. The watchers have had to stand by impotently while the law is flagrantly broken, even when this persecution takes place on the RSPB's Geltsdale reserve. One grouse preserver is reported to have supplied his keepers with night-viewing equipment and encouraged nocturnal forays for destruction of this and other raptors. Two keepers wearing balaclavas were seen retreating across the estate boundary after shots were fired at harriers on supposedly protected ground.

The red grouse (Plate 38), whose management determines so much of the upland ecology here, and especially the fate of its predatory birds, occurs on heather ground along the length of the Pennines, though it is absent from the grassy Eden scarp slope. Breeding occurs up to 700 metres where the last poor growths of ling and crowberry provide its food. Numbers are only moderate these days, and there is the usual problem of increasing sheep numbers, with consequent deterioration of heather. Heather has gone from steeper hills such as Baugh and Wild Boar Fells, and is also in decline on Croglin Water on gentler ground. Black grouse were once widely distributed, from Geltsdale to Stainmore, Mallerstang and the Barbon fells, but they have declined greatly and are now scarce. Some wooded or scrub-grown gills draining the moors were favoured places, but a recent lek is on the open grassy fells above Renwick.

The Pennines are pre-eminent for the waders in nesting time. Nationally, their most important bird is the golden plover (Plate 39), which breeds on level and gently sloping ground all along the range, from 230 metres on Denton Fell to 900 metres on Cross Fell summit. Its largest numbers are on the heathery moors and blanket bogs managed for grouse, but it also breeds on the grassy sheep ground. Breeding density varies quite widely. On Tindale and Geltsdale Fells it was moderate during 1946–74, while on the Moor House NNR plover were patchy, and mainly along the high watershed of Eden–Tees. During 1962–75, on the moorlands of Yad Moss adjoining Moor House, I found nesting pairs regularly spaced, at about 400 metres apart, with an average density of five pairs per square kilometre: an area of four square kilometres had at least 20 pairs. They seemed to vary hardly at all from year to year, and even after the terrible winter of early 1963, numbers were normal here. The regular spacing of nests was a constant feature, suggesting marked territorialism.

During late April and early May, when most of the plovers were incubating, a walk over Yad Moss conveyed no idea of the numbers present. Most of the birds sat tight, their off-duty mates were clearly elsewhere, and only occasional subdued alarm piping came from a bird off its nest. Now and then there was the wonderful flight song, *tirr-pee-you, tirr-pee-you*, with slow wing beat, of a territorial male, perhaps indicating a pair not yet sitting, or one that had lost its eggs. Towards evening there was often a burst of activity, with birds flying over the moor, more song and alarm calling. The off-duty birds were returning to change over with their sitting mates, which then took their turn to go away and feed. These moorland plovers had favourite feeding places beyond the moor edge, on certain pasture fields of the upper farms, where improved and fertile soils had good quantities of earthworms and other invertebrate food.

But after hatching, both parents stayed with their chicks, alarming noisily and often coming to meet human intruders and following them across the moor. Sometimes adjoining pairs became mixed up in little parties of six or eight birds, so that keeping a count of numbers was difficult. The whole family now depended on the moorland for food and sometimes broods were moved quite rapidly from the nest site to more productive feeding places elsewhere on the fells. It seemed that, having served the earlier function of limiting the demands of the whole population on feeding capacity of its nesting grounds, territorial behaviour was no longer necessary and ceased.

The golden plover is a typical bird of the acid moorlands, but my friend Walter Thompson showed me a contrasting habitat on short limestone turf of Tailbridge Hill plateau near Kirkby Stephen. I visited this locality from 1963–76 and regularly found 18 pairs on an area slightly over one square kilometre, nesting with almost mathematical regularity at every 200 metres or so. Most nests were on the low but conspicuous hummocks of short limestone turf (Fig. 10.5), but a few were among fragmentary limestone pavements. Some were also in the ridges and islands of mat grass and heath rush grassland that occupied acidic drift soils remaining on parts of

Fig. 10.16 Golden plover nest and eggs in acidic grassland, Mallerstang Fells. An incubating bird is shown in Plate 39.

the plateau (Fig. 10.16). The plovers shared these nesting grounds with a still larger though more variable population of lapwings (see below).

In their book *Tundra Plovers*, Byrkjedal & Thompson (1998) concluded that this was the highest breeding density of golden plovers recorded anywhere in the world. It seemed that the extremely high feeding value of the breeding grounds, with fertile brown limestone soils, and abundant earthworms, supported families at more than twice the level normally found on the best heather moors and blanket bogs. And this was although the off-duty birds still preferred to feed mainly on other limestone pastures lower down the fells. On the surrounding acid moorlands, density fell rapidly, though it was still fairly high, with pairs at 400-metre intervals on the eroded gritstone plateau of Lodge Edge overlooking Tailbridge to the south (Fig. 10.9).

Not that the Tailbridge plovers had an altogether happy time. Nest losses were typically high and many pairs had repeat clutches in late May and June. The more numerous – but noisier and more aggressive – lapwings usually fared rather better in their hatching success. Golden plover numbers nevertheless remained steady until the late 1980s, but by 1988 hang-gliding enthusiasts had discovered Tailbridge, and thereafter the place became increasingly frequented by them. Plover numbers soon began to drop, and the bird retreated first from the launching area on the western edge of the plateau. Gliders increasingly landed anywhere on the plateau, so that disturbance became general, and para-gliders were presently added. By 1998 the golden plover was down to five territorial birds, and in 2000 to three pairs (Ron Baines). Other disturbance, including walkers with dogs running loose, has also increased on Tailbridge. Cleasby (1999) finds golden plovers much reduced on Wild Boar, Swarth and Baugh Fells, which once had good populations: 39 pairs on Baugh in 1939 had dwindled to six in 1993, and there were no longer any on the lower slopes of the fell. Up to 1980, probably at least 1,000 pairs of golden plover bred annually in the Cumbrian Pennines, but it is doubtful whether these numbers have been sustained in the new millennium.

Dunlin are the frequent companions of golden plover, and their 'plover's page' act is often to be seen, as the one faithfully follows the other about the moor. They breed all along the range from Baugh Fell to Cold Fell, but only on the uncultivated moor above 450 metres. Blanket bog with pools and wet hollows is their favourite ground, but they also nest in the high *Nardus* grasslands and sparse cotton-grass where good pools and small tarns are within commuting reach. There are always at least two pairs on the summit plateau of Cross Fell, and nests are sometimes close to the trig point at 885 metres. Density is mostly rather low, but pairs are about 400 metres apart in the better places, and almost colonial groups were reported in earlier years from Amber Hill and Cold Fell. Numbers in the Mallerstang area have been lower during dry springs, when the feeding pools dry out, and Cleasby (1999) points to a long-term decline in this area. The highest recent figure for Geltsdale was 11 pairs in 1990, but over about 25 square kilometres of suitable ground this may represent a decrease from earlier decades.

Lapwings were common along the Pennines, from the fell-foot farms and marginal land up into the fells wherever there were good limestone 'greens'. RSPB warden R. Squires counted 86 pairs on the Geltsdale reserve in 1975. Numbers were prone to fluctuations and on the Tailbridge plateau rose from a few pairs after the 1962–63 winter to at least 45 pairs in 1974, while in 1989 I estimated 60 pairs, in slightly over one square kilometre. Despite the hang-gliding disturbance here, the lapwings have hung on, in reduced numbers, and in 2000 there were still 34 pairs (R. Baines). While the fertile soils with earthworms and short turf were the preferred habitat, in places a few pairs bred on acid blanket bog, as on the Yad Moss, where nests were on spongy *Sphagnum* ground. Breeding was general up to 600 metres, and nesting along the highest Pennine tops not uncommon. From one to a few pairs often laid eggs on Knock Fell, the Duns and Cross Fell itself, where occasional nests were close to the summit cairn at 885 metres. The high nesters had poor success, and their attempts did not lead to permanent colonisation. While the Pennines remain a lapwing stronghold, numbers have declined rapidly even here in the last decade, and this is now another wader in trouble. In Cumbria as a whole breeding population declined by 60 per cent between 1987 and 1998, but the county still held 10 per cent of English lapwings (RSPB/BTO, 1999).

Redshanks ascended the fells from their favourite rush-grown fell-bottom lands, where they were in moderate numbers. At higher levels they were mostly in scattered pairs, preferring acidic grassland and patches of richer sward and marsh. They were mostly up to 535 metres, but a pair was at 730 metres on Green Fell. Snipe similarly were most numerous on the damp, rushy marginal land under the fells, but ranged high into the moorlands. The RSPB counted 41 breeding pairs on its Geltsdale reserve in 1975, mainly on the lower ground. Numbers appear to vary from year to year, rather more than those of the other waders, but are difficult to count on the higher ground. They are widely spread up to high levels, with a nest at 790 metres on Cross Fell. Curlews are widespread, nesting on almost every kind of moorland except steep ground and the shortest limestone swards. They, too, are probably most numerous on the rough bottom-lands, but breed widely over both drier moorland and blanket bog. The RSPB count on Geltsdale in 1975 was 128 pairs, though these were unevenly distributed over the 6,000 hectares. There were still 98 pairs in 1992. On blanket bog pairs are spaced at about 800-metre intervals or less. Nesting is general up to 600 metres, but a few went higher and a pair bred regularly on the summit plateau of Knock Fell at 790 metres.

All these last four waders have declined greatly through the 'improvement' of the marginal land, involving draining and herbicide treatments, which have dried the wet pastures with good feeding, and removed the rushes that provided nesting cover. David Baines' work (1988) in the northern Pennines has shown these effects very clearly. He found that the only wader to have increased in this district is the oystercatcher, which may have benefited from these changes. Walter Thompson watched this bird colonise the Mallerstang valley from about 1940, following the River Eden shingle beds upwards to near its source. More lately the oystercatcher has spread out over the pastures of the fell-foot and is now quite widespread there. The Ringed Plover appeared along the Eden much later, and has remained restricted to the riversides. Sandpipers are more numerous along the bigger streams than on the Lakes fell becks, and the Eden in Mallerstang is a favoured stretch. They breed up to 600 metres on the upper Tees.

Dotterel have long bred on the high Pennine tops, but the nesting haunt on Great Dun Fell described by Blezard (1926) was obliterated by an aircraft navigational radar station in 1952 (Fig. 10.17) Though most nests were at over 760 metres, some pairs were evidently attracted by the appearance of the ground rather than altitude per se, and the first recorded Pennine nest was at only 640 metres on the stony flats of Dun Edge, Melmerby Fell (Macpherson, 1892). Nests have been reported on the Mallerstang fells at 640–700 metres, and one was found not far outside our boundary on sugar limestone fell-field at a mere 540 metres. They were mostly on stony ground, in fringe moss or sparse fescue, but one was in mat grass and another among short cotton-grass, and birds nesting in these unexpected peatier habitats will tend to escape notice. In recent years trips of up to 30 birds have occurred regularly on the higher fells in early May, and a few birds appear on lower stretches of short limestone turf. Most of these dotterel do not stay to nest, but move on to more northern breeding grounds. A bird found plucked, evidently by a peregrine, on high ground was perhaps from one of these passage groups. A red knot, in breeding

Fig. 10.17 Large-scale stone nets on summit plateau of Cross Fell, looking to Dun Fells (radar station), Little Fell and Mickle Fell.

plumage, was once shot high on Cross Fell by a keeper, but was presumably passing over on migration, as these high Arctic waders occasionally fall victim to hill peregrines also.

Other waterfowl are limited by the lack of lakes and tarns, but include a few of the ducks. Mallard are widely though thinly distributed over the fells as nesting birds, but teal are scarce and breed mainly on moorland around the larger water bodies. Wigeon have bred around the Cow Green Reservoir, and possibly on the Cumbrian side. Goosanders colonised Geltsdale in the 1950s, breeding in the holes in old alders, and they have spread to Croglin Water and the South Tyne. Black-headed gulls have had small and mostly ephemeral colonies on some moorlands, either based on small tarns, such as Greencastle on Alston Moor, or on wet stretches of level flow amongst the blanket bogs. The large and long-established colony on Bowes Moor lies outside our area, and the scattered pairs of lesser black-backed gulls that breed on those flows are probably also mostly in Durham.

The Ring Ouzel bred widely through the Pennines, and every gill and rocky scar seemed to have a pair. In Tindale Fells, Blezard (1946) once found five nests in a day, and the RSPB recorded 36 pairs on its Geltsdale reserve in 1975. Old mine buildings provided some pairs with nest sites, and on Tailbridge Hill two pairs regularly nested below ground level on the ledges of limestone potholes, up to 1975, after which they disappeared. Declines are reported elsewhere (Geltsdale down to 14 pairs in 1998) but are puzzling, and suggest the problem may be in their winter quarters, far from our shores. The other passerine birds of the Lake fells are well represented. Meadow pipits, skylarks and wheatears are numerous up to the highest tops, though the last is absent from the blanket bogs. John Coulson (1956) studied the meadow pipits around Moor House and found that their laying date was retarded by one day for every 40-metre increase in altitude, while clutches were nearly all of four eggs above 305 metres compared with an equal frequency of fives in nests near sea level beyond the Pennines. Half the Pennine pairs he watched were double brooded. Whinchats and Stonechats are on the lower slopes: the Geltsdale reserve had 29 and 11 pairs, respectively, in 1975. Reed buntings are frequent in lower marshy ground. Wrens are widespread on the steeper and rockier ground, nesting up to 600 metres, and crag nests are sometimes lined with feathers collected from pluckings of peregrine prey. As on the Lake fells, parties of swifts hawking insects over the high summits are a familiar sight in good weather.

Dippers are probably on every stream of any size, and reach high density on the limestone. Mostly they are below 450 metres, but a high nest was at 670 metres on Crowdundle Beck. Grey wagtails are in many of the rocky gills lower down. Stock doves nest commonly in the lower scars, in tree holes, and in the stone barns ('field houses'), so characteristic of the Pennine fell-bottom lands. Jackdaws inhabit these places also, and old lime-kilns provide other nesting sites. The carrion crow is everywhere along the lower slopes, nesting in woods, clumps of trees, but just as often in the windswept thorn bushes of the fell-foot. Occasional high-level nests were in rocks and, once, on top of a stone shelter. Though systematically hounded by grouse keepers and kept down on their moors, the more desultory attentions of shepherds, mainly in destroying nests, make little impression on their numbers. In some places adjoining nests are only 200–400 metres apart on the sheepwalks of the western slopes of the Cross Fell range. They are largely vegetarian and invertebrate feeders, which do well on the improved pastures, and their penchant for the eggs and chicks of other birds provides only a small part of their diet. It is this, however, and their propensity for pecking out the eyes of sick or 'cast' sheep, which makes them outcasts everywhere.

The hay meadows of the fell farms were once the nesting place of four birds whose status in Britain now gives much concern. The corncrake was a familiar bird here, well known around Kirkby Stephen in 1920–40, but seldom heard even by 1970. Corn buntings had scattered loose colonies, all along the Eden valley to Brough and Kirkby Stephen, where they were common, and Alston was a fairly elevated haunt. They too have vanished. Yellow wagtails were numerous in the meadows and rougher pastures, nesting up to 300 metres at Alston; they are much reduced, but at least they survive. Grey partridges were locally frequent over the marginal land under the Pennines, but appear much less so in recent years.

The woods of the fell-foot and lower valleys are the last Pennine bird habitat. Where there were many old trees, especially alders, with abundant nestholes, redstarts, tree sparrows and pied flycatchers were notable species. Geltsdale was a particularly good area for them. All three also nested in the stonework of the numerous field houses and other buildings. Tree pipits were common in open woodland and scrub, especially around Kirkby Stephen. Barn owls and the occasional little owl similarly had this dual nesting habitat, but tawny owls were mainly in the woods or clumps of trees. Sparrowhawks were scattered all through the district, wherever there were woods, and often seen soaring high into the open fells. Woodcock are thinly but widely spread in the woods, and a few breed among bracken and heather on the open fells, but the birds often flushed from such hill ground during February and March are mostly immigrants on the move. Rooks have long had colonies in the fell-foot shelter-belts and clumps of trees (Fig. 5.6), often close to farmhouses, and new rookeries have been established in recent years, as in the alder wood below Rundale.

The birds of autumn and winter are those of the Lake fells, though with the red grouse much more numerous. Tindale Tarn and the Castle Carrock Reservoir (supplying Carlisle) have variable numbers of wintering waterfowl, including tufted duck, pochard, goldeneye, goosander, mallard, teal, mute and whooper swans, and coot. The peaks can number hundreds of fowl (up to 150 pochard) but are usually much less.

Amphibians, reptiles and fish

Frogs are in many parts of the fell country, breeding in the high pools and tarns up to 800 metres on Cross Fell. Lizards are probably widespread, especially on the heather moors, but under-recorded. Adders are in very few places and appear to be absent from large parts of the northern Pennines, such as the Cross Fell range and the hills south of Kirkby Stephen. I never saw any during my wanderings there, but am told that they occur on the Black Burn moors in Tindale. There are records for Stainmore eastwards of our boundary. No other reptiles are reported, but all three species of newt were found in an old quarry pond at Forest Head, Tindale (E. Blezard). The fish are mainly brown trout which flourish in most of the fell becks, particularly the limestone streams. With the recent clean-up of the Tyne, and reported runs of salmon, this fish probably makes its way up the headstreams of the South Tyne above Alston. In the Eden catchment it ascends the bigger streams into the fells until its path is blocked by waterfalls too high to leap.

Invertebrates

The area is rather poor for butterflies. The mountain ringlet of the Lake fells is absent, despite the large extent of *Nardus* grassland, and the large heath is limited to lower cotton-grass flows in the extreme north on Denton and Tindale Fells and perhaps the far south on Stainmore. Small heaths are widespread, and the fell meadows have meadow browns, ringlets and – earlier in the year – orange tips. The migrant butterflies described on p. 241 cross the fells and the vanessids seek heather and other flowers. Small tortoiseshells are often seen at golden-rod and devil's bit scabious on the higher scars in late summer. Among moths, the northern dart has been found high on the Moor House reserve, and the day-flying species typical of heather moorland (p. 247), such as the emperor (Fig. 11.6) are well represented. Other upland species include the grey mountain, yellow-ringed and red carpets, and the more widespread water carpet is frequent. A rare montane beetle of the Lakes, *Nebria nivalis*, occurs also on Cross Fell, and the rove beetle *Olophrum assimile* is known in Britain only from Dun Fells and a single site in Scotland (Key, 1996). The common hawker is frequent at bog pools and along the fell becks, but dragonfly variety is low on the Pennines.

The intensive studies at Moor House have revealed a number of uncommon insects unknown in the Lake fells, especially craneflies and other Diptera. Whether this is a real biogeographic feature or the result of concentrated expert attention in the high Pennines, only a similarly focused survey of the Lake fells can show.

The Pennine limestone is important habitat for molluscs, and among the more widespread species listed by Blezard (1967) are the slippery, chrysalis, large chrysalis, Craven door, copse, brown-lipped, hairy, wrinkled and cellar snails.

Moor House research

In 1951, the Nature Conservancy bought 3,894 hectares of high fell-land straddling the Eden–Tees watershed of the Dun Fells and Knock Fell, and containing the old shooting lodge of Moor House, where they developed a field research station for ecological studies of the moorland ecosystem. The facility was much used by both staff from the Conservancy's own Merlewood Research Station in southern Lakeland, and visiting scientists from universities. During the period 1952–79, a huge amount of work took place, making the Moor House National Nature Reserve one of the most closely studied upland areas in the world. I have already mentioned the attempts at restoration of woodland and alpine vegetation, and give below a brief summary of the main lines of research.

Verona Conway, the first Director of Merlewood, developed large-scale experiments to understand more fully the effects of land management practices on the carrying capacity and hydrology of the moorlands. Selected catchments were drained and burned, while possible ensuing changes in vegetation and stream runoff were monitored, and the nutrient budget of the ecosystem was measured. Sheep-grazing continued under the common grazing rights that held over the area, but a number of fenced plots excluding sheep were established to study the effects of grazing removal on different plant communities. Efforts were also made to promote the recolonisation by cotton-grass and other species of eroding blanket bog peat, under different nutrient treatments. A comprehensive vegetation survey of the Reserve, with community descriptions, permanent quadrats and detailed maps was begun by Ken Park, and continued by Alan Eddy, David Welch and Michael Rawes (Eddy et al., 1969). The second in the Nature Conservancy's series of scientific monographs was on the Geology of Moor House in 1963, by G. A. L. Johnson and K. C. Dunham of Durham University. This was a valuable account of hard rock structure and

Quaternary features, with periglacial forms, peat deposits and soils of the reserve, and contained detailed maps, pollen diagrams, treatment of vegetational history and archaeology – all aimed at providing background for ecological research.

When the International Biological Programme was launched in 1965, to study the productivity of different ecosystems around the world, Moor House was chosen as the location for the British contribution to the Tundra Biome project under the leadership of Bill Heal at Merlewood. Visiting university scientists, notably John Coulson from Durham and John Whittaker from Lancaster, with their colleagues, contributed to studies of nutrient-cycling and the decomposer process in the blanket bogs. The station was used by the University College, London, M.Sc. Conservation Course as a training site, and some of its staff engaged in research there, such as Ken Taylor's work on cloudberry. The resident scientists, under Michael Rawes, undertook long-term study of grazing effects on vegetation, especially by means of the fenced exclosures. The unshot red grouse population was monitored for natural changes in numbers.

Eventually, after the area had become world-famous as a centre for the study of moorland ecology, the programmes were wound down. Partly this was because of the increasingly parsimonious government attitudes towards the funding of basic research, but partly also because some aspects of the research potential of the reserve had largely been realised. The new Health and Safety regulations required that the resident warden be transferred to a more accessible location on the Eden valley side, and the house itself was later dismantled. The area remained a Biosphere reserve under the UNESCO programme for establishing benchmark sites around the world where environmental and biological features would be monitored for possible changes. It has lately seen a revival of research interest, with modest laboratory facilities, and a programme under the Environmental Change Network led from the Merlewood Research Station of CEH (the Centre for Ecology and Hydrology), involving further measurements of climate, pollutants and biological features.

The Moor House meteorological station provided a valuable series of high-level (565 metre) climate data from 1952 onwards. Earlier than this, from 1937–41, climatologist Gordon Manley had lived at times in a hut high on Great Dun Fell to make records of extreme weather conditions on the fell-tops at 835 metres. I remember a lecture in which he showed spectacular photographs of the snow and ice formations under the arctic conditions of winter.

11

The Borders

When I first visited this district, in 1944, its rather low and gently contoured moorlands contained the wildest and least known country in all England. While resembling the Lakeland Pennines in some respects, these Bewcastle and Irthinghead moorlands were much lower and still more tamely undulating. They formed the south-west end of the Cheviot range, which lies mostly in Northumberland and Roxburgh, and was vividly described by Abel Chapman (1907) as 'A region largely of peat as distinguished from soil, of flowe, moss, and crag; of tumbling burns and lonely moorland, glorious in all its primeval beauty'. Our part was known locally as the 'Waste of Cumberland', reflecting its unproductive nature – a land managed largely for sheep and red grouse. Yet in its main valleys of Liddel, Lyne and Irthing, the drift derived from Scottish Calciferous Sandstone rocks gave fertile soils that sustained scattered 'outbye' farms amidst the moors, and all around its edges. The enclosed pastures of the marginal lands and the hay meadows resembled those of the Pennines, as good breeding habitat for the waders, lapwing, snipe, curlew and redshank, and notable for the rich herbaceous communities described on p. 158. As in that region, both pastures and meadows have been extensively improved, to the detriment of their wildlife, both animal and plant.

Vegetation and flora

By sheer good luck, there has survived a classic old-style northern hay meadow system, on Butterburn farm in the Irthing headwaters. Named Gowk Bank, it begins on the level alluvial terrace of the river behind which fairly steep banks of glacial drift rise for up to 15 metres and then flatten out. The level river terrace and the flat strip between the bank crest and the road had been regularly cut for hay and have a different type of herb-rich grassland from the steep bank. This may have been cut by hand in places, but not mechanically. Fences isolated the meadow system from the surrounding acid moorland, and excluded sheep, though both they and cattle were allowed in during winter and early spring. The impression is of an oasis amidst the barren moorlands (and now conifer plantations) that have to be crossed for several miles to reach Gowk Bank.

Scattered alders and willows grow upon it, but the most distinctive vegetation is the tall herb community with wood cranesbill, melancholy thistle, meadowsweet, marsh hawksbeard, water avens, great burnet, knapweed and hedge woundwort. Globeflower, northern bedstraw, burnet saxifrage, lady's mantle, zig-zag clover, greater twayblade, frog orchid, common spotted orchid, field scabious and rough hawkbit are notable plants of this community (a good example of MG 3 (Rodwell, 1992). More open places on the unstable, clayey bank have other orchids in early purple, fragrant, northern and crimson marsh, with red rattle, grass of Parnassus, marsh valerian, knotted pearlwort, bristle club-rush and lesser clubmoss: a community approaching mire type M 10. The upper mown grassland has abundance of yellow-rattle and the large-flowered eyebright *Euphrasia officinalis* ssp. *monticola* (MG 5). Field gentian and kidney vetch grow sparingly within the site on sandy knolls.

Gowk Bank is now a National Nature Reserve, though doubtfully in as good condition as when I first saw it, in 1954. There were patches of similar vegetation along the Kirk Beck above Bewcastle, grading into a birch and alder fringe and showing the relationship with the field layer of subalpine woodland. Saw-wort is frequent on this side of the moorlands. Good herb-rich grasslands also occurred on roadside verges, such as those near Blackpool Gate. These communities have, however, become increasingly rare in recent decades.

Woodland is extremely fragmentary in this district and mostly along the rocky glens of the Rivers Irthing and Lyne, whose lowland sections are treated in Chapter 5. The Irthing has an especially picturesque wooded gorge extending over three kilometres above Gilsland, with the fine waterfall of Cramel Linn at its head (Plate 43). It is clothed in a mixture of trees – oak, ash, wych elm, birch, hazel and a native colony of yew. Grazing is light and the flora includes wood cranesbill, globeflower, wood vetch, stone bramble, wood fescue, mountain melick and prickly shield-fern. The Black Lyne gorge below Roadhead shows an interesting contrast between typical sessile oak wood (W 11) and the mixed broadleaved kind (W 9) (Rodwell, 1991a) on soils of higher base-status. It also has ungrazed alder wood with an unmodified community containing great horsetail, hemp agrimony, greater tussock-sedge and herb paris (W 5). Fringing growths of alder on alluvial stream banks are a characteristic feature of the Border hills generally. Near Bewcastle is a quite large alder wood, Mollen Wood, though, being open to sheep and cattle, it is rather poor botanically, with a dominance of grasses (close to W 7). A rare shrub, the downy currant *Ribes spicatum* has three localities in this district, though it may not be native here (Halliday, 1997).

The calcareous sandstone and shale crags of the Irthing gorge provide a refuge for a few subalpine plants, most notably the yellow saxifrage (Plate 19), which has an isolated outpost here, 42 kilometres from its nearest locality, in the Pennines, and is unknown anywhere else in the whole Cheviot range. It is abundant, along with green spleenwort and brittle bladder fern. Northern bedstraw is occasional, but variegated horsetail has been seen only on the Northumberland side of the river in recent years. Acidic rocks have bog bilberry in extremely small quantity, and it has evidently lost ground in the area. These are the biggest crags (up to 20 metres or so) in the whole of the Cumbrian Borders, which otherwise have rather little exposed rock. A lesser gorge of acid sandstone flanks the Moss Catherine waterfall at Sunday Burn Linns farther up the Irthing valley, but Paddaburn Crags beyond Churnsike are in Northumberland. On the rest

Fig. 11.1 Carboniferous sandstone tor of Christianbury Crags and blanket bogs, Bewcastle Fells.

of the Bewcastle Fells, the gritstone tor of Christianbury Crags forms a commanding skyline feature (Fig. 11.1), though the biggest face is only eight metres high. A line of small grit outcrops runs across the western slope of Sighty Crag, and some stream sides have minor scars.

The lower moorlands towards the southern edges have shallow blanket bog with abundant flying bent (contrasting with the Pennines), as a variant of M 25, and rushy ground of the marginal fields (MG 10) is widespread. Most of the area northwards from the middle section expressively known as Spadeadam Waste was covered by deeper peat with extensive Pennine type *Eriophorum–Calluna* blanket bog (M 19). *Sphagnum* cover varied according to burning and draining, and has evidently declined over the years, though it is still high in places. Butterburn Flow is the best *Sphagnum*-dominated blanket bog in England, an almost level five square kilometre expanse half-encircled by the bend of the Irthing north of Butterburn farm. The peat-forming species *S. papillosum*, *S. magellanicum* and *S. rubellum* are abundant, and there are scattered hummocks of the rare *S. fuscum* and *S. imbricatum*. Cross-leaved heath, bog asphodel and round-leaved sundew are abundant in the bog moss carpets, bog rosemary and cranberry frequent, great sundew and white beak sedge occasional, and tall bog sedge and few-flowered sedge rather rare. The tall bog sedge grew in scattered places in the spongier bogs of Spadeadam, and in the miry channel of Foul Bog on White Preston it was with the ordinary bog sedge. *Andromeda* was widely scattered over these moors and probably had its most extensive population in Lakeland here. The bog community is represented by M 18 (Rodwell, 1991b).

Fig. 11.2 Cloudberry, an abundant plant of the Border and Pennine moorlands.

Above 300 metres the cloudberry (Figs 11.2 & 11.3) becomes increasingly abundant, and on the high watersheds from Sighty Crag to Glendhu Hill forms dense carpets with its leaves. The white flowers in late May can appear like a thin fall of snow in some years, but even here there is not the abundance of fruit so typical of Fennoscandian bogs. This is the only abundant true mountain plant of the area, but an important recent find, by

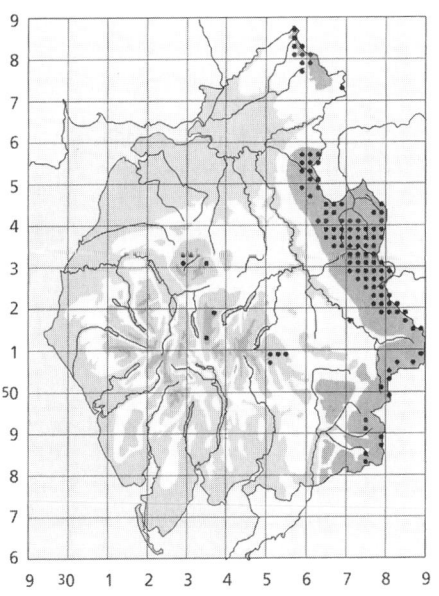

Fig. 11.3 Distribution of cloudberry, showing scarcity in central Lake fells. (Halliday, 1997, Map 380.)

forester William Burleton in company with Simon Webb of English Nature, was a quite large patch of dwarf birch at only 275 metres on the Spadeadam moors. This small arctic-alpine shrub, so profuse over most of Fennoscandia, was once thought to be confined to the Scottish Highlands in Britain, but had been found some years before on Emblehope Moor beyond Kielder in the North Tyne valley. The habitat, ordinary blanket bog, is extremely extensive in the Borders, but this plant is highly localised, for reasons that are mysterious, other than that it is a species at its southern limits of British distribution here. Of the northern, but only sub-montane plants, fir clubmoss occurs about some higher gritstone outcrops, lesser twayblade is in the heathery bogs, chickweed wintergreen grew in forest rides above Bewcastle, and parsley fern was in a sheepfold on the White Lyne. Crowberry, cowberry and bilberry are in great abundance in the blanket bogs and, with ling heather and cross-leaved heath, give these a dwarf shrub-rich facies.

The banks of the Irthing have calcareous drift in places, as around Butterburn farm, but with none of the botanical richness of the similar banks of the Tees near Langdon Beck. There are luxuriant moss communities and an abundance of common lowland calcicole flowering plants. On the moors, calcareous flushes and flush bogs of M 9 type appear in many places amongst the blanket bogs, and Caudbeck Flow on the west side of Spadeadam is an interesting complex of marsh with 'brown moss' and sedge communities. Broad-leaved cotton-grass and grass of Parnassus were widespread in these base-rich habitats, and a large flush system on The Beck under Christianbury Crags had a small patch of mossy saxifrage. Butterwort (Fig. 11.4) is abundant in the more basic flushes. Other than the few 'peat alpines' mentioned above, the vegetational history of the area has not been favourable to survival of high-level plants. Apart from the wetter bogs, the whole area was probably covered in forest at the Climatic Optimum, and any alpines became completely lost. There was no ground high enough to remain above the tree limits, and none of the open ground refuges associated with the special habitats, notably on sugar limestone, which in Upper Teesdale allowed small and uncompetitive species to keep a foothold until forest clearance enabled them to spread again.

There are a few other plants of note. The small white orchid was recorded long ago from the south-west edge of Spadeadam, and still has a healthy colony in the area. Wood club-rush grows in wet meadows, and both brown sedge and lesser pond sedge are locally plentiful here and on river banks. Along the sluggish course of the upper Irthing past Butterburn, a group of uncommon aquatic plants is present, with water sedge, slender tufted sedge, northern spike-rush and common club-rush. Although this is the driest upland part of Lakeland in rainfall, there is an tiny isolated patch of Wilson's filmy fern in a gritstone block crater among the Bewcastle Fells, accompanied by a few western bryophytes. The northernmost British locality for calamint was found at Gilsland in 1945 by G. A. K. Hervey, but it has not been seen again.

Fig. 11.4 Butterwort, a common moorland plant of damp places.

Animals

Mammals

Christianbury Crags and the surrounding moorland were long famous for their herd of feral goats, survivors from earlier times when they were run with sheep as domesticated animals, and subject to plunder by the Border reivers. Whatever their origin, Graham (1993) has said well that 'These ragged moss troopers are the living embodiment of all that is wild and pristine in the romantic Border country today'. They lived completely wild and unmanaged, claimed by no one. Numbers fluctuated mainly according to severity or otherwise of the winters, and 30 was regarded as a fair total, though Mitchell & Delap (1974) state that numbers were as high as 86 in 1965. The goats suffered considerably during the savage winters of 1946–47 and 1962–63, and each time several animals were smothered in deep snow. The herd usually kept together as a mixture of billies, nannies and kids. Old, patriarchal billies could develop an impressive head of horns and, with their long, shaggy coats, were a striking presence in country otherwise bereft of large wild animals. Mostly grey in colour, there were also a few dark brown and piebald goats. Their fecundity was rather low and six kids in a herd of 15 was regarded by Graham as a good total.

Two other separate herds of goats formerly roamed these moorlands. One at High Grain, closer to Bewcastle, ran to teens of animals, and was alleged to be of more recent origin from a domestic flock, but disappeared by 1910. The second, about 20-strong, frequented the King Water around Wileysike, but was said to have been killed off after raiding gardens during a severe winter, some time between 1910 and 1915. Unpopularity with foresters led to the demise of the Christianbury herd. With the advance of trees across the Bewcastle moorlands the goats declined, no doubt through 'control' against damage to young trees. Mitchell & Delap believe the last 20 or so animals were systematically shot out in the late 1970s, and that wild goats no longer grace the remaining open moorlands of Bewcastle.

The other notable mammal of these moors was the mountain hare, supposedly introduced to this part of the Borders from farther north in Scotland around 1900, or perhaps from earlier releases 50 years before that (Blezard, 1958). It is the only part of Lakeland where it is recorded, apart from an odd occurrence in the Coniston Fells, and was unknown when Macpherson wrote in 1892. Graham (1993) said that it was widespread on the higher moors of both the Bewcastle and Gilsland sectors, but seldom appeared on the lower ground of the southern fringes. Numbers in the earlier decades of the twentieth century were evidently moderate, but the hard, snowy winter of 1946–47 reduced them severely. From 1950 onwards they were evidently sparse, and may never have recovered, for there are no records of them since 1980. Many of the animals had full white coats in winter, but some showed only a partial change and appeared intermediate or pied. The brown hare occurs all over the farmland and marginal land of the district, and penetrates the lower moorlands to overlap with the previous species. Graham noted that numbers fluctuated according to severity of the winters, and that brown hares were also at a low ebb for some years after the great snows of early 1947. They are still widespread in the district.

While generally distributed over the lower farmlands, rabbits are irregularly scattered over the moors and found mainly in dry places with good soil, such as river banks, patches of improved ground, and some rock outcrops. Graham believed that some of the isolated moorland colonies escaped the myxomatosis that raged all over the low country. Black individuals were common in some groups on the upper Irthing. Rabbits have declined further through the planting of many of their regular haunts with conifers.

There is some evidence that the elusive pine marten occurs in this district. Forestry Commission Conservator J. Chard told me around 1970 that he had tracked them in the snow in the Bewcastle forests. The habitat would seem suitable enough, but there has been a dearth of more recent records, and while the recent pine marten distribution map published by Johnny Birks shows a cluster of dots in immediately adjoining areas of Northumberland, there are none for the Cumbrian Borders. It is evidently an overlooked animal that may be more widespread in northern England than is generally suspected. Still more puzzling was a large cat trapped near Bewcastle in 1963 and sent in to Tullie House Museum. Ernest Blezard, who made a cabinet skin of it, found that it resembled a true wild cat in all respects except the tail, which was rather indistinctly, instead of boldly, banded with dark rings. With a weight of almost four kilograms and length of 84 centimetres, it was probably big enough for the true wild species.

Foxes were not numerous on these uplands, perhaps from the scarcity of block litters and other rocky ground in which to make dens. They were hunted by the Bewcastle pack and a famous, because impregnable earth, was in huge blocks under Shot Scar in the Gilsland gorge. A completely white fox was seen during 1953–55. Badgers were still fewer on these mainly peaty moors, but quite numerous on the more productive marginal lands and river valleys lower down. Stoats and weasels were common and widespread, ranging high into the moorlands, but also more numerous within the farmland zone. Otters ranged the moorland rivers and becks quite widely, and in winter the shepherds often found their tracks crossing from one stream to another, up to six kilometres apart. Only a few instances of proved breeding were known, and mostly along the sluggish section of the Irthing between Churnsike and Paddaburn. The lower courses of the rivers draining from these moorlands, the Irthing, King Water, Lyne and Liddel, are now the Cumbrian stronghold of this animal (Hewitt, 1999a).

Graham found water voles more numerous on these upland streams than anywhere else in Cumbria, especially along the more sluggish sections, and in ditches around swampy ground. They were particularly common on the King Water and the Cramel Burn, but recent records of the animal in this area are lacking. The short-tailed vole increased spectacularly in many newly established conifer plantations, providing an abundant food supply for short-eared owls, kestrels and ground predators. As elsewhere it showed cyclical fluctuations with a periodicity of about four years, but has become generally less numerous during the maturing phase of forest growth. Moles occurred widely over the moorlands wherever there were 'greens' with fertile loam soils, but were absent from the peaty ground. They were numerous on the pastures of the marginal land.

Birds

Ritson Graham (1993) has given a detailed account of the birds, and I have drawn on this a good deal in compiling the following summary. The much earlier treatment by Abel Chapman in his *Bird-life of the Borders* (1907) also deals partly with our area, which he regarded as a western extremity of the Cheviot range. Even more than in the Pennines, scarcity of crags has always limited the scope for the big predators that thrive in the Lake fells. An ancient nesting place of ravens in the Irthing gorge above Gilsland was occupied up to at least 1911, but then deserted for many years through the 1920s to the 1940s. It became reoccupied again in 1954, though the site was on the Northumbrian side. The birds bred undisturbed until 1956 under a colossal overhanging sandstone slab, but disturbance from MoD rocket site activities, beginning in 1957, banished them. A weir and pumping house were made near the crag, and after this intrusion the birds never nested here again, though I suspect they found an alternative site in one of the shelter clumps of conifers scattered over these moors. After this absence of more than 40 years, it is welcome news that a pair returned to nest successfully in the Irthing gorge in 2000. Another small rock in a remote spot just outside our limits was occasionally used, but attempts by ravens to build at Christianbury Crags, indicated by a litter of fallen sticks, were thwarted by lack of suitable lodgement on the only sizeable face. A successful tree nest close to the Scottish Border was reported in 1999, and the district has the potential to support a good many more tree-nesting ravens.

Peregrines were recorded breeding in the Gilsland gorge in 1781, but were shot even then, by bird collector Dr John Heysham. Successors bred there up to at least 1840, but nesting records then lapsed. Graham was told of a probable nesting around 1914 at another Irthinghead locality, but knew of no other instances during 1925–60, though peregrines were frequently seen on the moors. During this period, the nearest nesting haunt was far down the North Tyne moors towards Kielder. New territories became established from the 1980s on the Northumbrian side of these moors and, finally, with the amazing increase of the species, nesting took place in 1996 in a completely new Cumbrian locality. It has so far been an unsuccessful attempt; the eggs were found addled, there were no birds the following year, and in 1998 the nest was apparently robbed.

Kestrels bred widely over the moors, for they were satisfied with little more than broken stream banks for their nests, and old crow nests in trees were also available. Many rock sites were regularly occupied over a long period. A nest was found two years running on the mantleshelf above a fireplace in a ruined cottage, in a remote spot on the Gilsland moors. A pad of castings on the bare wood sufficed as a nest. Here, as elsewhere, numbers fluctuated in parallel with those of their principal prey, the short-tailed vole. Graham (1993) noted that there was sometimes a late summer and early autumn influx of kestrels to the moorlands, and that this tended to be after planting of new areas with trees. Numbers usually declined through the winter, when the bird left the more barren areas and hunted mainly about the moor edges and marginal land. Nesting territories were reoccupied by late March.

Merlins (Fig. 11.5) return to the moors in April, with their meadow pipit prey. Graham found them better represented, with four to six pairs, on the more heathery Bewcastle side of the moors than on the grassier Gilsland sector, with two to four pairs. In his day nests were nearly always on the ground, in long heather. Some pairs occupied the same sites regularly, but others moved around over a period of years. A shepherd pointed out to me the nesting places of two pairs on heather ground of the White Lyne in 1947. Much of their habitat is now afforested and there is no recent information on status, though in adjoining Northumberland Brian Little has found merlins nesting widely around the extensive forest edges, where these abut unplanted ground over which the birds can hunt. Buzzards were only occasionally seen on these moors during most of the twentieth century, and the grouse keepers picked off any that tried to settle. As part of the general expansion of the species into the Cumbrian lowlands in the 1980s and 1990s, a few pairs eventually became established in woods around the outer fringes of the Borders district, and this nucleus has

Fig. 11.5 Merlin, male with prey. Raptor of the heather moors. (Bobby Smith.)

expanded along the Rivers Lyne and Irthing from Roadhead to Lanercost and thence to Gilsland. G. Horne suggests a present population of 15–25 pairs.

Macpherson found in old documents referring to 'Nichole forests in the Manor of Lydel' a statement that the small tenants 'must preserve the nests of sparrowhawks and eagles'. Nicholforest is in Cumbria north-west of Bewcastle, and the estate may have run up into the moors. In 1843, T. C. Heysham learned that an eagle had in 1824 frequented the vicinity of Christianbury Crags for several weeks before departing. Between 1833 and 1835, another eagle visited the same area and was shot by a keeper on the Northumberland side; from the description it was a golden eagle. The striking tor of Christianbury continued to attract golden eagles, and in 1950 another took up residence there and ranged the surrounding moors, receiving attention in both local and national press for alleged lamb-killing. It survived for several months, but was then shot by a grouse keeper from the North Tyne valley. In the 1970s, an eagle frequenting the Tarras valley among the Langholm hills some 18 kilometres to the west was said to move to Christianbury, but no more was heard of it. There is little doubt that golden eagles would be permanent residents on these moors if they were left in peace. Now, when interest in grouse here is virtually dead, there may be too little open moor left to support even one pair.

The hen harrier attempted a return to these moors in 1928, but the female was shot and the four eggs taken by the keeper at the Flatt, Bewcastle. The nest was in long heather on the moors of the Black Lyne to the north. Graham (1993), who chronicled this record, also listed sightings, mainly of male harriers, in 12 years between 1932 and 1962: all but two were in the spring and mainly on the Irthinghead moors. The planting of the adjoining Kielder Forest saw a return of the hen harrier there from around 1959. A group of at least six pairs built up, but then faded out again as the forest matured, and had gone by the early 1970s. This colonisation was not repeated when the plantations extended round into the Cumbrian side of these moors, though birds have been seen in suitable nesting habitat (M. Henry). Macpherson (1892) quoted evidence that both hen and marsh harriers nested on the wild moors of the Borders early in the nineteenth century, and described a bird in the Carlisle Museum, killed on Netherby ground some time before 1880, as possibly the last of the marsh harriers from north Cumberland.

These Border moorlands were long known as the stronghold of the short-eared owl in Lakeland. They bred widely though sparingly over the open moors of both Bewcastle and Gilsland sectors, and Graham (1993) gives many nesting records. With the coming of the forests, numbers increased on newly planted ground where field voles flourished, but then thinned out and finally disappeared as the forests matured. The bird is now much reduced, but odd pairs survive on unplanted ground. Barn owls nested in some of the deserted cottages scattered over the moors, and long-eared owls were reported from old shelter woods of conifers, but tawny owls were mainly in the lowland woods away from the fell country.

Black-headed gulls nested on wet flows on the Gilsland moors, though the individual colonies waxed and waned in the usual manner of this species. The longest established was at Butterburn Flow, known since 1870 and with hundreds of pairs up to about 1935, when it faded away. Colonies on the Northumberland side at the Wou (a long valley mire) and Blackaburn Lough may have absorbed most of the birds, which had suffered much egg-taking for food. A few black-headed gulls had long nested around Paddaburn higher up the Irthing from Butterburn, and by 1951 began increasing here, reaching 150 pairs in 1956 and around 500 pairs in 1959. The birds bred in roughly equal numbers on flows on both sides of the river. Graham in 1959 found a high mortality among the unfledged chicks, which he attributed to attacks by adults as the chicks wandered from their nests in the densely packed colony, and within a year or so the birds had all gone. A lesser colony, based on the small tarn on White Preston above Bewcastle, varied according to the amount of standing water: it was known from 1898, had 40 pairs in 1932, two in 1938 and at least 100 in 1950. Another ephemeral group at Blackshaws south of Paddaburn was said to be connected with movements from that colony.

Macpherson (1892) mentioned Butterburn Flow as the only inland nesting place of the lesser black-backed gull in Lakeland, but gave no details. Graham mentions that 40 pairs nested here up to 1926, a little apart from the more numerous black-headed gulls. A few years earlier, Abel Chapman noted that the long-established colony of some 150 pairs of lesser blackbacks nesting on Hindleysteel Moss, seven kilometres east-south-east of Butterburn and in Northumberland, were said to move westwards to the Bewcastle area. Although a few pairs were later reported breeding near Blackshaws, no such influx was known to shepherds in the area. Tullie House Museum has a clutch of eggs of the great black-backed gull taken on Wileysike Moss four kilometres north of Gilsland in 1909. This was evidently a one-off attempt, and though the species may have attempted to breed elsewhere on these wild moorlands in earlier years, it was still less welcome to grouse keepers than its smaller relative. Great black-backs were only occasionally seen on the moors in later years.

The waders were well represented in the Borders. Graham regarded the Gilsland sector of the moorlands as the best golden plover breeding ground in Lakeland, and in the early 1930s estimated their numbers as a pair to every quarter of a mile of moor and flow. A shepherd informant spoke of coming across up to 20 nests in a season. They were less numerous over the Bewcastle side, such as the more heathery ground of Black and White Lyne Commons, and on the high watersheds of Christianbury and Glendhu. My impression also, in 1944 and 1945, was that they were only sparingly present on this ground. Probably the number of farms with rich inbye pastures scattered over the Gilsland moors provided a better distribution of good feeding places close at hand for the birds after arrival and during incubation. Numbers held up until at least 1958, but a decline was reported on the Bewcastle side the next year, and after the severe winter of early 1963, Graham found the plover here at only one third of their previous level – contrasting with my Pennine experience.

The Irthinghead moors were also a stronghold of breeding dunlin, which nested especially on the wet flows, mostly singly but occasionally almost colonially in little groups. Many of them fed by the River Irthing and in adjoining enclosed pastures, the five-kilometre stretch from Whitehill to Redsike being especially favoured. Graham saw up to 20 birds in walking this section, but noted annual variations. Scattered pairs also bred along the blanket bogs of the high watershed from Sighty Crag to Glendhu Hill, mainly in wet areas with good pools. The common sandpiper was another wader that reached its best numbers in this district. In 1944 and 1945 pairs were distributed all the way up the Black Lyne from Hole of Lyne to beyond the foot of Robbie's Grain at intervals of no more than 400 metres. Each attentive pair handed me on to its next upstream neighbour. The course of the main Irthing stream from immediately above Gilsland held a large population, and the subsidiary headwaters added many more pairs. Although they drained from peaty catchments, probably the feeding value of these streams was boosted by the extensive occurrence of calcareous drift along their banks.

The curlew's undulating display flight, with liquid, bubbling calls, is one of the most evocative sights and sounds of early springtime on the moors. This was always great curlew country, with birds breeding up to the highest watersheds, though more numerously at lower levels. Philipson (1954) found their territories in this district were often as small as eight hectares, but he observed a serious decline in population, to about half, between 1920 and 1954. He also noted a surplus, non-breeding population in parties of five or six, all through the summer. Each pair of curlews appears to feed largely within its nesting territory, so that breeding density directly reflects feeding capacity of the nesting ground. Some adults and still more chicks fall victim to foxes, and crows often predate nests with eggs. Repeat nests extend the breeding season, and noisy parents with unfledged young scold intruders through June until the end of July.

Lapwings were once so numerous in this district as to supply a regular trade in their eggs to the London market. The main nesting grounds have always been on the richer soils of the improved farm pastures and the marginal lands. Graham found breeding groups around the scattered remote farms on the Irthinghead moors, with up to ten pairs on the Whitehill meadows. Even small patches of naturally richer ground amidst the moors would have a pair or two. An observant shepherd noted that they occurred on 'greens' with molehills, and made the connection with earthworms as the food of both. The harsh winter of early 1963 saw a great reduction in lapwing numbers, from which the bird never seemed fully to recover, and it is now sparse in the area.

The redshank was said to be unknown here before 1900, but by the 1930s had spread widely over the damp, rushy pastures of enclosed fields and marginal land. Its distribution followed that of the lapwing, but extended a little higher into the moorlands in places. Local shepherds noticed a decline by the 1960s. Snipe breed widely over all these moors, but are most numerous on the rushy lower ground favoured by redshanks. They are the only wader to be found in their upland haunts all the year round, but whether autumn and winter birds are the breeders or incomers is not known. Oystercatchers are a twentieth-century addition to the moorland streams, and appeared first on the upper Irthing in 1930 and on the Black Lyne in 1945. From 1960, Graham found from four to eight pairs nesting on the gravel beds of the first river, and a similar number on the streams of the Bewcastle side.

Among the moorland passerines, the ring ouzel was always rather uncommon and found mainly on the Bewcastle side, where its favourite habitats of rocky scars and steep-sided heathery gills are best represented. Meadow pipits were the most common bird of the uplands, everywhere from the marginal land to the highest tops, and they played host to cuckoos as usual. Skylarks came a good second in numbers, with a similarly wide distribution. Wheatears were much less common and found mainly in rocky places, including sheepfolds and drystone walls; and they preferred grassland to heather moor. On bracken and heathy ground of the main valleys, whinchats occurred sparingly but have disappeared from the hay meadows; and the stonechat was a rarity in the district. A few yellow wagtails bred in the upland meadows, but they were much less numerous than on the Pennine fell farms. Pied wagtails were associated mainly with farm buildings, walls and sheepfolds, and both swallows and house martins faithfully resorted to many of the remote upland farms for their nesting.

These were never particularly notable moors for red grouse, and only modest bags were made even in the heyday of grouse management, such as 350 brace on the 4,000 hectares of the Churnsike estate in 1930 (Graham, 1993). Although the winter of 1962–63 was followed by a good breeding season, Graham noted a decline in grouse numbers by the mid-1960s. He attributed this to the decreasing area of heather under long-continued and steadily increasing grazing by sheep, and to the reduction of gamekeeping through the spread of forests and declining interest in grouse. The forests themselves eventually eliminated most of the grouse. In 1943, the Border moorlands were regarded as the main stronghold of black grouse in Lakeland, and they were said to be on the increase in young forests there. Graham quoted Bewcastle game bag records for 1868–74 that suggested that this species far outnumbered the red grouse then, and Chapman (1907) regarded the North Tyne valley on the Northumbrian side as the best blackgame area he knew. The shepherd at the remote farm of Red Sike at Irthinghead saw up to 80 black grouse on his meadows in 1910–12, but 20 years later a decline was apparent. After some recovery in the mid-1930s, decrease set in around 1945, and blackgame lost ground on the open moor and in forest alike. Closed plantation forest does not suit them and they are now scarce.

The grey partridge was a distinctive resident of both the farmlands and the moorland edge, with a distribution similar to the lapwing, and extending to the improved ground around all the remoter moorland farms. Small numbers clung to these places for long after the farms were abandoned, but they gradually declined and are now only sparsely present. Other lowland birds found on the moors include the jackdaw and stock dove, nesting in the gritstone scars, often close to kestrels. A few pairs of moorhens bred by the more stagnant watercourses and ponds, and corncrakes were once familiar birds on the fell-foot farms of the Bewcastle side, though less so on those of the Gilsland moors.

Of the ducks, pairs of mallard nested thinly but widely over the moors, and teal were still scarcer. Goosanders colonised the Liddel, Lyne and Irthing first in 1950, and a few pairs gradually spread farther up these rivers into the moorlands. Dippers were on all the main streams, especially the rockier sections, up to 425 metres, but grey wagtails were restricted mainly to the river gorges, that above Gilsland being a noted haunt.

The winter bird populations of the Borders do not differ in any marked degree from those of the Lake fells and Pennines. Flocks of fieldfares and redwings work the fellside hawthorns and rowans for berries in autumn but then move on, and the depths of winter see few birds on the uplands.

Other animals

Graham (1993) found that the adder occurs widely over these Bewcastle and Gilsland moors, though they are not common and I have yet to see one. Lizards appear scarcer than might be expected, from the suitable nature of the ground, but the slow worm has occasionally been recorded. Graham also noted that toads were more numerous and widely distributed than frogs, especially where the water is peaty at the head of the moorland streams. Though he referred to the years before afforestation became extensive, Graham said that the Rivers Irthing and Lyne were good streams for salmon and sea trout, though both were unable to ascend the former beyond the Cramel Linn waterfall. On the Bewcastle side the sea trout ascend the upper tributaries of the Lyne higher than do salmon, and during spates will forge up quite small and narrow runners. Salmon caught on the Lyne were typically of 7–7.5 kilograms with occasional fish of up to 10 kilograms. Graham remarks on the variety of gaffs and leesters (tridents) hung up in farmhouses and barns in the area, as pointing to a tradition of illicit taking of these fish in this outbye district.

The brown trout was widespread and abundant in the hill streams all over these moorlands, almost up to their source. Many fish are small, but some large trout have been caught, especially in the deep waters of the more sluggish sections of the Irthing, where one of just under 2.5 kilograms was taken. Graham found that trout appeared fewer where streams ran through large forest sections. He also noted that where farms were fed from a spring, it was the custom to introduce a trout to the open pool, to keep down the other aquatic life, and that some of these fish grew to a great size and lived to a considerable age – 27 years in one case. The Irthing was a favoured river for loach, both below and above Cramel Linn, and it was plentiful in some of the small becks as well as the main stream. Graham commented that the domestic ducks of the moorland farms eagerly devoured them. Eels were widespread but not common in the upper streams of the Irthing and King Water, one of which is called Eels Sike. Some specimens reach 60 centimetres in length, though 45 centimetres is more usual.

Invertebrates

Of the Lepidoptera, the large heath butterfly is probably the most notable, and formerly occurred on all the wetter moorlands and flows, especially on the Irthing side. The large day-flying moths emperor (Fig. 11.6), fox and northern eggar were numerous, at least in favourable years, but the moths of the district have not been closely studied. The common and widespread insects of the Lake fells and Pennine moors are well represented here, and I shall not repeat the information on p. 247.

Afforestation and defence

I have tended to talk about the wildlife of these Border moorlands in the past tense, because, to a large extent, it no longer exists as described. The vast plantations of the Forestry Commission and, more recently, private

Fig. 11.6 Emperor moth, female, a common insect of the heather moors.

forestry companies, have obliterated the former open moorland habitats with their plants and animals on a huge scale. The scene has been transformed over the last 50 years, from treeless moor and flow to a dark blanket of conifers. My old Ordnance Survey one inch map of 1947 was little amended from the 1920 survey: it shows the beginnings of the Kielder Forest as a few modest blocks of forest on the North Tyne moors, but in Cumberland there is nothing beyond odd small shelter woods on the King Water and lower Irthing. Land around the Kershope Burn along the Cumbria-Scotland Border was acquired by the Forestry Commission in 1920, and the dark edge of the new forest was already visible on my first visit in 1944. The foresters concentrated first on the Northumberland side, and by 1956 almost 25,000 hectares of the Kielder and Wark moors had been planted. They then advanced south from Kershope and across the Black Lyne to the lower slopes of Christianbury Crags.

When I first visited the Irthinghead moors in 1954, they were virtually treeless, and the great expanse of Spadeadam Waste was an empty flowland. But in 1957, rocket engineers descended on this desolate country and began to build installations for testing the motors of the Blue Streak missile, on land acquired by the Government. They welcomed forestry as helping to give concealment to their works, and within a few years a large block of young trees had spread over the whole of the moorland surrounding their site, north of the farm of Moscow. The OS map of 1969 shows these developments. This was the writing on the wall. Afforestation then proceeded to advance over the remaining moorlands of both the Bewcastle and Gilsland sectors. The map of 1983 shows that in a total of some 141 square kilometres of moorland in the Cumbrian Borders, 89 square kilometres (63 per cent) had been converted to forest.

The plantations stopped only just below the summit of Christianbury Crags, and were taken to the very top of Glendhu Hill at 514 metres, on the south-west side. Elsewhere a considerable extent of the high watershed along the Cumbria–Northumberland border at over 400 metres has been left unplanted. Below this level only some of the wettest flows and the improved ground of some of the moorland farms have been left free of trees; with the exception of a belt along the western edge of the Bewcastle Fells from Caudbeck Flow and Side Fell to Greyfell Common and Sighty Crag summit. The SSSIs at Caudbeck Flow, Christianbury Crags and Butterburn Flow were respected, but the later National Nature Reserve at the last site was compromised by the planting of the sloping south edge of the bog.

So, the moorland ecosystem has largely been exchanged for forest. The sheep and grouse have gone from the planted areas, most of the moorland farms are abandoned and their houses ruinous or demolished, and dense, unthinned, unbrashed thickets of Sitka spruce, lodgepole pine and larch dominate the scene. The moorland fauna has been exchanged for one of woodland, but the flora has hardly managed even to do that. Let me look at the details.

Sheep are removed from ground to be planted and fences erected against their return. Deep ploughing then lowers the water table (Fig. 11.7), and nursery-grown tree seedlings are planted in the upturned furrows, with ground rock phosphate to boost growth. Herbicides are sometimes applied where 'weed' competition is foreseen, and insecticides may

Fig. 11.7 Blanket bog ploughed for afforestation, Spadeadam Waste, Irthinghead Moors.

Fig. 11.8 Newly established forest of Sitka spruce on Spadeadam Waste: habitat of short-eared owl until the trees close into thicket.

be used against specific insect pests, such as pine beauty moth on lodgepole pine. Within a few years the existing ground vegetation, freed from grazing and burning, grows up dense and luxuriant. Any shrubs, notably heather, become especially tall and rank, and seedlings of rowan and birch often begin to sprout. For a period of ten years or so, before the young trees close into thicket, there is a dense growth of grasses, cotton-grasses, dwarf shrubs and other plants, which forms excellent cover for some birds and other animals (Fig. 11.8).

Birds such as golden plover, dunlin, lapwing, raven, ring ouzel and wheatear disappear almost at once, but others such as curlew, red grouse and meadow pipit can linger for a few years. The whinchat, stonechat and black grouse benefit from the increased cover, and species such as willow warbler, grasshopper warbler, tree pipit and yellowhammer may colonise. Dippers on afforested catchment streams usually disappear because of increased water acidity (see below). The increased cover allows small rodents to flourish, especially the short-tailed vole, and this draws in predators – short-eared owl, kestrel and, sometimes, hen harrier. Vole numbers may rise so high as to induce a considerable increase in the first two species. Mammal predators such as weasel, stoat and fox also benefit from the boost to food supply.

There is quite often a thriving wildlife ground community during this early stage of forest growth. But this is merely a passing phase. When the young trees close into thicket, the open ground birds drop out, and are replaced by those of woodland or scrub: song thrush, blackbird, chaffinch, robin, dunnock, goldcrest, redpoll, jay, wood pigeon, woodcock, sparrowhawk and tawny owl. The numbers of some of these depend on forest management, particularly the amount of thinning and brashing. In thicket stands, breeding birds are limited to canopy-nesting species, and to those able to breed in rides and forest edges or places where tree growth has remained open. The colonising species are mostly woodland birds common in woods all over Cumbria. The bonus is the small group of birds formerly rare or unknown in the region. Crossbills and siskins have been attracted to breed in these new forests, but their numbers are greatly influenced by the size of the annual cone crops and show considerable fluctuations over a period. The most spectacular newcomer is the goshawk, which has become well established in the Border forests, with up to eight pairs nesting in the Cumbrian section (G. Horne). Its restoration to Britain was the result of deliberate introductions and falconers' escapes, but it has done well and expanded its range greatly.

Some of the mammals have also found benefit in the new forests. Roe deer, foxes and badgers gain from the increased cover, and reports of pine martens followed establishment of the plantations. The main effect, however, is to provide breeding refuges and shelter, which promote increase in these animals, but without a parallel provision of food. The mainly bare forest floor is almost devoid of food, either for vegetarians or predators, so that they have to forage on open ground outside – either the rides and roadsides, or unplanted moorland beyond. The foresters shot out the wild goats for alleged tree damage, and have the loss of this ornament to the Borders to answer for. Some insects flourish along the rides and roadsides, and butterflies are advantaged by the shelter of the trees from wind, but they live on a much reduced area of habitat.

The vegetation and flora suffer most of all through afforestation. The bogs and marshes are destroyed by ground treatment, and the ribbons of peat communities left along rides are irrevocably altered by draining and drying of the ground. Some of their species may remain, but in much reduced amount that gives only a token presence. Even wet patches of bog left unplanted have tended to dry out through the effects of surrounding forest, as happened to the NNR of Coom Rigg Moss two kilometres north of Butterburn Flow, in Northumberland. Some of the rare and local plants of these Border moors have suffered considerable reduction in their populations through tree planting; bog rosemary, cranberry, bog asphodel, broad-leaved cotton-grass, grass of Parnassus, great sundew, tall bog sedge and few-flowered sedge. The important find of dwarf birch (p. 284) was fortunately made before trees had been planted, and measures for its conservation are in hand, but there could have been other colonies that are now lost.

The new forests provide little botanical compensation to match those in the fauna. The intense shade and needle-fall of the conifers exclude almost all green plants, even in thinned compartments, and the floor of larch stands can be as bare as under Sitka spruce. In the most open growths of trees there are sparse growths of a few ferns and common mosses but, apart from some mosses and liverworts on the exposed mineral soils or drying peat along rides and roadsides, very few new colonists enter to add variety to the impoverished flora. The wall whitlow-grass, a garden weed, is one of them, now plentiful along forestry tracks. The moss *Campylopus introflexus*, an introduced species from North America, often grows profusely on the upturned peat ridges of ploughed ground.

After 30 to 50 years the fast-growing conifers are felled, and there is then another ten-year open phase before the replanted ground becomes closed thicket again. The original open ground communities are not usually re-established, and the ground tends to become mainly grassy, with patchy growth of heather. The brash from the felled trees is usually left in heaps and further limits the development of vegetation. Some of the open ground birds may reappear, but the true moorland species hardly do so, and it is mostly the birds of woodland edge or scrub that colonise. Blackgame have shown little tendency to recover on clear-fells, and predators such a short-eared owls appear only sparingly. In some districts nightjars have exploited such ground, but there is no information on them in the Border forests. Then it is back to closed forest of the second rotation. The foresters have declared their intention to diversify at this stage and subsequently, but there is a limit to the possibilities, and it will be mainly a matter of increasing the age-class diversity of compartments. Small areas and fringes of broadleaved trees are a gesture to amenity and wildlife interests, but on a scale that can only be cosmetic.

It will no doubt be argued that some ground has been left unplanted. Yet it is insufficient to retain more than a poor representation of the previous landscape and its wildlife. The enclaves of lower-lying flow are too small for some birds, and they are the focus for foraging crows and foxes that come from the surrounding forest. The much larger area of high-level blanket bog remaining is of very limited value, too; for, ungrazed and unburned, its vegetation has grown too rank for birds such as golden plover, dunlin and curlew. These birds have also largely lost the lower and richer feeding grounds on which they depended. Even grouse are now very few on these high watersheds.

In the end, it all depends on which you prefer: open moorland and its wildlife or that of mostly dense and uniform conifer plantation. This is without taking account of the profound physical and chemical effects of afforestation on the catchment. Hydrology is permanently altered, first by greatly increasing water runoff after ploughing, and then reducing it through the greater water uptake of the trees. While flash spates still occur, interception losses of 20 per cent of precipitation have been found in similar forests elsewhere. Soil and peat erosion are much increased by ploughing and then at the clear-felling stage. Acidification of both drainage water and substrate are increased by the 'scavenging' effect of tree foliage in collecting acidity from the atmosphere. Aerial applications of fertiliser to stimulate tree growth result in higher levels of phosphate in the drainage water, and this enrichment can cause local algal blooms. These changes have been shown to have adverse effects on trout and salmon fisheries within heavily afforested catchments.

Besides the forests, there is also the intrusive effect of the military presence on Spadeadam Waste. The Blue Streak rocket having proved yet another expensive but abortive technological project, a continuing use had to be found to justify the heavy investment in this site. It has become an electronic warfare testing and practice ground for the Ministry of Defence. What happens on the ground is concealed from prying eyes, but the roar of A10 'tank-buster' and Tornado planes diving low over the moors is all too obvious. The site perimeter is bounded by dire notices that forbid entry and warn against touching metallic objects. On the new maps, the words 'Danger Area' appear not only within the understood site but at various places up to a kilometre or more outside. People walking the open moor outside the perimeter notices have been accosted by MoD guards and brusquely ordered off.

So, besides the transformation in the moorland landscape, there is now a pervasive sense of entering even the area unenclosed by MoD on sufferance, as though it would be preferable if you did not go at all. You can at least drive along the road as far as Churnsike and see how it all looks, but beyond the MoD range you will have to enjoy walking forest rides to reach any open moorland. The thicket forests are impenetrable. Some features are much as they were. Probably from extensive draining of the catchment for forestry, after heavy rain the Irthing comes down in even more spectacular brown flood than before and thunders over the waterfalls of Moss Catherine and Cramel Linn (Plate 43). The Gilsland gorge is unchanged, save where conifers crowd its upper rim, and the nature reserves at Gowk Bank and Butterburn Flow try to maintain these important habitats, though I see deterioration at both. The farms of the Bewcastle fringe and the surviving few on the upper Irthing look superficially the same, but the emerald green of the NPK improvement gives an unnatural flush to the scene, and their old meadows are mostly destroyed. The skyline of the Christianbury ridge has been kept mercifully free of trees, and can still be enjoyed as a reminder of how the Waste of Cumberland used to be. Ritson Graham's book has gained in value as an evocative account of the area and its wildlife that have changed hugely and forever.

12

The Future: Conservation Problems and Approaches

The effects of agriculture, urbanisation and industrialisation have, increasingly over several millennia, widely transformed the Lakeland scene from a natural wilderness to a highly modified, 'cultural' landscape. The region has also had its share of recent intrusive developments with profound impacts on its environment and wildlife. I have dealt with both the earlier and the more recent human impacts, as seemed relevant, under the previous chapters, but now want to round these up with an assessment of their significance, and of the measures available to counter or compensate for their adverse effects.

The problems and impacts

Agriculture

The post-war farming revolution, encouraged by government policies for agriculture, has affected the whole region. I have described the wholesale loss of floral hay meadows and pastures, widespread removal of hedges, cleaning of weeds from cereal crops, and reclamation of rough grassland, heath, moorland and bog to permanent improved pasture and arable. In the uplands, burgeoning sheep numbers have accelerated the loss of surviving dwarf shrub heath (Fig. 12.1), and increase in grasses, rushes and bracken, while even the summit fringe-moss heaths have nearly all been eradicated. Certain plant species have declined seriously from this striving for maximum production. The destructive organochlorine insecticide episode passed away, but farming is now chemical-dependent and a galaxy of approved pesticides assaults all possible crop competitors, thereby reducing or removing the food supply of many animals, apart from any continuing direct effects on wildlife. Inorganic fertilisers are poured onto the land (and, I suspect, even sprayed from the air onto the hills), and run off into other habitats, so that eutrophication of open waters and wetlands is widespread. They even enter the atmosphere and fallout more widely, in solution and as solid particles. This relentless rain of nutrients from the sky has become an especially worrying and seemingly uncontrollable form of pollution. In terms of the extent and range of habitats and species affected, agricultural intensification since 1945 has probably been the most serious cause of damage and loss in Lakeland. Virtually all of it is subsidised by the taxpayer, through price support mechanisms, direct grant-aid and headage subsidies, and tax-deductible allowances.

Fig. 12.1 Retreat of heather moorland at Faulds Brow, Caldbeck, with moribund *Calluna* being replaced by acidic grassland under heavy sheep grazing.

Forestry

From more modest beginnings in the eighteenth and nineteenth centuries, coniferous afforestation hit the Lake District after 1900, and by the mid-1930s was sufficiently extensive and obtrusive to generate a huge row. Although the Forestry Commission agreed not to seek to acquire further land for planting within a defined central area of the Lakes, they continued to plant conifers within the peripheral areas where they had already established plantations, and to pick up woods and other habitats (such as limestone grasslands and raised bogs) that they could coniferise in the lowlands. As a result, important sites such as Wythop Wood at Bassenthwaite, Sowerby Wood near Carlisle, Walton Wood near Brampton, Coombs Wood at Armathwaite, Greystoke Park, Whitbarrow Scar and Foulshaw Moss, lost some or most of their previous wildlife interest. But the Commission reserved its real onslaught for the wild moorlands of the Borders, and proceeded to destroy a large part of the existing vegetation and animal communities of that district. Its undeviating policy on conifers and their relation to grant-aid also caused other bodies such as the National Trust and private landowners to follow suit in planting mostly non-native trees. While local in its impact and bringing some compensatory gains, commercial forestry since 1945 has, I believe, caused a substantial net loss of wildlife interest within the region.

Energy

The most controversial development within the whole region has been the nuclear complex at Windscale–Sellafield on the west Cumbrian coast, involving both a power station and plant for producing weapons-grade plutonium, dating from the early 1950s. Although the site itself covers only about two square kilometres, its influence is infinitely more pervasive. Apart from the serious fire accident in one of the atomic reactors in 1957, which spread radiation over a wide area locally, there has been continual discharge of radionuclides to the sea, resulting in pollution of marine sediments not only around the coast of Britain, but along those of Ireland and Norway as well. Search for a local site for the underground disposal of high-level nuclear waste seemed likely to cause further intrusion into the south-west edge of the National Park, until the proposed location was ruled out because of unsuitable geology. The two plutonium reactors are being decommissioned and the ominous chimneys slowly dismantled, but the development here of a nuclear re-processing facility causes continuing protest. The known effects on wildlife are perhaps slight, though little information about them is generally available.

The search for alternative, non-polluting sources of energy is not without problems. The harnessing of tidal power was briefly considered for the Solway, where it would have been extremely disruptive, but wave energy from the open sea has not so far been seriously entertained. The preferred method is from clusters of onshore windmills, which have spread around the periphery of the Lake District, as at Askam-in-Furness, Kirkby Moor above Ulverston and Lambrigg Fell near Kendal, where they are obtrusive. Other wind farms have been built on the Solway Plain near Great Orton and at Oldside, Workington. For Cumbria the Government has awarded 32 contracts under the Non Fossil Fuel Obligation, and applications have been made for 20, of which 13 have been approved, while those for Brocklebank near Wigton, Lowick Beacon near Greenodd and Wharrels Hill at Bothel were rejected (FLD, 2000, 2001). The effect of these structures is mainly on scenic values, and there have not so far been the adverse effects on birds reported from huge wind farms in the United States. Interest in offshore windpower has seen the placing of a 40-metre windpower mast to collect wind and wave data at Robin Rigg, a sandbank opposite Maryport in the Solway Firth, but will not necessarily be followed by commercial development there (FLD, 2000).

Recent enthusiasm for small-scale hydroelectric power schemes has worrying portents for the moisture regimes of stream ravines important for their ferns, mosses and liverworts. Despite efforts to minimise disturbance by the laying of gas pipelines, waterfowl were slow to recover from the effects of that across the north side of Morecambe Bay.

Water use

Water supply has long been a contentious issue in Lakeland, beginning with the demands of the Manchester Corporation for the tapping of Thirlmere in 1894 and then Haweswater in the 1930s (p. 196) (Figs 12.2 and 12.3). It was not long before the Windscale–Sellafield nuclear complex cast covetous eyes on adjoining lakes as a convenient source of necessary water and, after a public enquiry, was allowed limited extraction from Wastwater. The outflows of both this lake and Ennerdale Water (supplying Whitehaven and environs) now have large weirs and their water levels fluc-

Fig. 12.2 Thirlmere from near Launchy Gill. The hard edge of a reservoir, with moderate draw-down. Mixed coniferous and broadleaved woodland.

tuate unnaturally. The proposal, shortly after World War II, to dam the Caldew in Skiddaw Forest for a local water supply reservoir fortunately came to nothing. The Shap Borrowdale, with important hay meadows, was another candidate for damming, but was also reprieved. A new reservoir was, however, built in Wet Sleddale west of Shap, in 1967. The Cow Green Reservoir in Upper Teesdale, to supply additional water to industry on Tees-side, was

Fig. 12.3 Haweswater Reservoir full and draw-down zone hardly showing. First modern nesting place of golden eagles in 1969 on Harter Fell behind.

completed in 1970, but most of the considerable botanical damage it caused was on the Durham side of the boundary. The feasibility study for water impoundment in Morecambe Bay in 1972 did not come to anything, and similar proposals for the Solway failed to reach even that stage.

Mining

The demise in west Cumbria of the 'sunset' industries of coal and haematite mining has been remarked, and iron is no longer smelted in the region, though Workington still has a steel works that produces rails from ingots made elsewhere, and the Barrow-in-Furness shipyard survives on limited orders. The metalliferous mines of the Lake District are all abandoned, while in the Pennines the lead mines of Alston and Nenthead are also disused, and only the Silverband mine on Great Dun Fell continues, in extracting barytes. At Whitehaven anhydrite was mined until recently towards St Bees Head, and this mineral and gypsum are still extracted near Kirkby Thore, east of Penrith. Quarrying of Borrowdale greenslate continues on a small scale at Honister, but the main slate quarries now are on the Silurian formation at Kirkby Moor. Petts quarry on Red Screes and Shap Pink granite quarry produce igneous stone, while limestone is extracted at Hardendale, Shap; Hartley, Kirkby Stephen; Clawthorpe Fell, Burton-in-Kendal; Moota, Cockermouth; and Warnell Fell, Caldbeck.

The removal of surface-weathered material for rockery stone from the limestone pavements of the Arnside, Kendal and Orton areas was an extremely damaging activity that has more or less been stopped, except perhaps surreptitiously in places. Commercial peat extraction continues on the raised bogs at Wedholme Flow, Solway Moss (Fig. 12.4) and Bolton

Fig. 12.4 The ruin of a raised bog through peat extraction: Solway Moss in 2001, the surface a sea of bare peat, and a great perimeter trench dug deep into the underlying boulder clay.

Fell, and is seriously damaging to the interest of these sites, even though Fisons made over to English Nature their holdings on Bowness and Glasson Mosses. English Nature has just (February 2002) announced its intention to buy out the peat extraction rights of Scotts (the latest owners) on the cut-over part of Wedholme Flow, as the first step towards restoration of the bog surface. Sand and gravel mining has created new tarns in a few places (p. 142), and on balance its effects have been beneficial. The flooded Hodbarrow iron mine is also now an important bird site (p. 89).

Transportation

Rail communication in the region has declined considerably, with the post-1950 closure of the lines from Carlisle to Silloth, Carlisle to Riddings (for Edinburgh), Penrith to Keswick and Workington, Foxfield to Coniston, Ulverston to Haverthwaite, and Tebay to Bowes Moor (for Darlington). Mineral lines serving the coal and iron mines of west Cumberland were also all closed. The embankments and cuttings of railways are often an important botanical and invertebrate habitat, and some along both used and disused lines have remained so, but parts of some abandoned lines have been incorporated into adjoining farmland, or become scrubbed over, and lost their interest. Road verges too are locally important for plants and lowlier animals, especially on the limestone, but some have been modified by winter road-salt – to the point of gaining salt-marsh plants – and even deliberately reclaimed, with total loss of their interest (p. 161). Road construction, widening and realignment has caused some botanical losses. The M6 motorway destroyed a famous population of the rare spignel at Dillicar while, perversely, the isolation of a section of the Millom to Muncaster road led to the demise of a fine colony of lanceolate spleenwort, which became overgrown by brambles.

Carlisle was once linked to Port Carlisle by a canal, opened in 1823, but with the silting of the dock and the coming of the railway, Silloth became the northern Solway port and the canal was abandoned in 1853. It was later drained, but fenny sections survived and retained some wildlife interest. The more important man-made waterway was the Kendal to Preston Canal (known as the Lancaster Canal) which remained in use until the opening of the M6 motorway. The short section that lies in Cumbria has developed a particularly rich aquatic flora, and the current proposal to reopen the whole length of the canal for powered boats can only damage its botanical value (Halliday, 1997). The bizarre attempt to resuscitate the ancient idea of a canal from the Solway to the Tyne is mentioned below (p. 312): few more damaging developments to the nature conservation value of the district could be imagined.

Defence lands

Lakeland has suffered major intrusions by the Ministry of Defence. The Eskmeals gunnery proving range has for a long time disturbed this sand dune system south of the Irt estuary, though an interesting flora still persists. In the Pennines, the Warcop tank artillery range occupies an extensive sweep of fell country along the Eden valley scarp and extends far over the dip slope into the Upper Teesdale catchment. It has grown larger over the years, taking in the delightful valley of Scordale and extending over the Tees watershed to the Maize Beck and the vicinity of the Pennine Way, and onto Stainmore. To allow increased use of the range, including for infantry training, there is now a MOD proposal to buy out the commoners' grazing rights (FLD, 2001). The Border moorlands have the Spadeadam rocket motor and weapons testing range described in Chapter 11, which has helped to obliterate some of the upland habitats there. These defence lands may have helped to retain some of the wildlife interest, especially for plants, by restricting or preventing other damaging activities, and concerned personnel have formed conservation groups, as at Eskmeals. Yet on the ground there is a pervasive sense of their primary purpose, even when access is permitted.

Air-wave communications

The building of the civil aviation radar navigational centre on the summit of Great Dun Fell destroyed a former breeding site of dotterel, as well as creating a highly conspicuous blot on the Pennine landscape (Fig. 10.17). The multiplicity of tall wireless masts on the old Fleet Air Arm station at Anthorn is now part of the national Early Warning System of radar defence. The BBC World Service transmitting complex at Skelton creates another forest of masts within the ancient Inglewood Forest. On the foothills of the Caldbeck fells, two high television masts tower above the Solway Plain. The march of the mobile phone masts has also assaulted Cumbria: despite enormous pressure they have been kept at bay in sensitive landscapes in the Lakes by the National Park Authority, but along the Eden valley, Barrock Fell and Penrith Beacon are now crowned with these alien structures. Whinfell and Cockermouth have them disguised as trees. The effects are mainly on landscape quality, though access roads cause disturbance.

Recreation

The effects of hordes of trampling boots become ever more obvious in the more popular places, with older paths now worn feet deep into the fells and new ones conspicuous where once there was no sign of them. Most of the high fells are now scarred by these tracks. Human trampling also combines with sheep treading to damage soil and vegetation in sensitive places. On the low ground, the bare soil and exposed roots of trees around popular beauty spots, such as waterfall glens and lake-sides, show the results of this human pressure. Organised events, such as the 'Mallerstang Yomp' cause a sudden deluge of human traffic galumphing over once quiet tops.

Even the noisier and more disturbing forms of recreation have been allowed, though power-boating and waterskiing on Windermere are now to be stopped, through imposition of a 10 mph speed limit in 2005. Vehicle congestion in the Lakes during summer is becoming an increasing problem that is causing the authorities to experiment with traffic management schemes. Beyond this, the aggressive assertion – or even contravention – of their supposed rights by four-wheel drive and motorcycle owners causes growing damage and unacceptable disturbance to unmade tracks and lanes that are no longer green but a sea of mud. Mountain bikers career along fell paths and help to erode them still further.

Rock climbers have increasingly opened up the cliffs where peregrines and ravens nest, sometimes to the point of causing these birds to desert their nests, while some time-honoured haunts such as Dow Crags and Pavey Ark (Fig. 1.3) have largely been abandoned as breeding places. Climbers' 'gardening' of climbs has threatened rare plants on some cliffs and produced conspicuous scars where whole banks of vegetation have been stripped off. In an early test case, the Lake District Special Planning Board leased land and created a Local Nature Reserve at Whitbarrow Scar, and also passed bylaws to ban climbing during the bird breeding season. The bird problem has been reduced elsewhere by voluntary agreements through the British Mountaineering Council to avoid peregrine and raven crags at nesting time. Notices at the foot of the crags also warn climbers on the spot. The more recent sports of hang- and para-gliding have caused the virtual demise of the densest golden plover population in the world (p. 274), besides the loss of peregrine and raven broods.

Gardening, which has created the markets for weathered limestone and horticultural moss litter, should be included here. The gathering of living moss for related purposes and floral tributes has caused local damage. In certain National Trust woods it took place illegally, and recovery of the denuded blocks has been slow. But on Yad Moss SSSI, one of the best remaining areas of *Sphagnum*-dominated blanket bog, it took place with the agreement of English Nature, on the very dubious grounds of 'sustainable use'. Although a subsequent management agreement excluded this practice, its potentially damaging effects at the time were not monitored.

The geographical picture

The possibilities for development also have to be looked at geographically. The Lake District National Park is fairly well defended against major intrusions, and the North Pennines and other AONBs have some protection from further developments, but other parts of the wider Lakeland are vulnerable to damaging projects. The Borders have taken so much disruption, through blanket afforestation and defence works, that perhaps little more damage can be done; but the Cumbrian lowlands could face much more, and the coast is especially fragile. In some areas, the attrition is by a thousand cuts, but mega-proposals have a way of surfacing unexpectedly. The estuaries have fortunately escaped despoliation so far, but it is worth considering the threats they have faced, even quite recently.

The Solway has remained one of the least industrialised estuaries in Britain. It even lost an intrusion of the railway age when the Solway viaduct carrying the line from west Cumberland to Annan was declared unsafe from shifting sands and dismantled in 1935. Port Carlisle fell into decay as a port and the canal connecting it with Carlisle was superseded by the railway, but this in turn was removed. On Morecambe Bay, the Barrow-in-

Furness steelworks once disfigured the skyline, but they have gone (though the shipyards remain); and the conurbations of Morecambe and Blackpool are too far away to impinge on the Lakeland sector. On the Duddon estuary, too, the blast furnaces and chimneys of Millom were dismantled, and recreational growth has not been disruptive. Yet, there has been one new intrusion of a more sinister kind. The Chapelcross nuclear power station is five kilometres from the shore, beyond Annan, but its four cooling towers are a conspicuous feature of the Solway landscape from the Cumbrian side, and a constant reminder of the unwelcome presence of invisible pollution from the atomic age.

Engineers and industrialists now and then set ambitious eyes on the Solway and dream of how it could be developed for human benefit and as a personal monument to their imaginative enterprise. In 1964, nuclear physicist Dr R. L. Drew proposed a grandiose barrage scheme to impound the waters of the upper estuary for the purpose of water supply, linked with a national water grid, and to provide cooling water for another four nuclear power stations in the area. The line of the barrage was to approximate that of the old Solway viaduct, with a motorway crossing, and the development of the Solway region into a huge urban-industrial complex (*The Scotsman*, 12 August 1964). A second idea, mooted by Alcan Industries Ltd., was for another barrage 14 miles to seaward to generate electric power from tidal energy. A desk study of the reservoir proposal was soon made but, fortunately, the costs of the scheme, including that of transporting the water to more needy areas, became prohibitively large and it was dropped. The whole upper Solway would have been transformed into a vast freshwater lake with Burgh and Rockcliffe Marshes either submerged or fossilised into grasslands no longer subject to the dynamic processes of their formation. Energy generation and water supply are one thing, but unwanted urban sprawl is another. Dumfries was envisaged as a major growth centre: it is a quietly prosperous country town, which was not long ago voted the most desirable town in which to live anywhere in Britain, and it has no need for such gratuitous expansion.

Next in the firing line was Morecambe Bay, though a barrage here from Morecambe to Barrow had been suggested as long ago as the 1890s (Prater, 1981). In 1965 the Water Resources Board was asked to conduct a feasibility study of water impoundment in this complex estuary and this was done between 1967 and 1970. The report of 1972 considered four possible schemes, all in the northern, Lakeland, part of the Bay, and involving the damming of the Kent and Leven estuaries, either with a single barrage or twin barrages plus one or more pumped storage reservoirs in the shallow waters of the Bay beyond. Motorway crossings from the M6 motorway to Barrow-in-Furness were also included in three of the alternative schemes. Disruption to the Lakeland sector of Morecambe Bay would have been great and the effects on waterfowl populations considerable though unpredictable. Again this threat gradually faded away. Reservoirs on the Wash and the Cheshire Dee became a more favoured choice, but in the end the creation of the huge inland reservoirs at Kielder Water in the

Cheviots and Rutland Water in the east Midlands satisfied water demands for the time being.

But there is now a fragility to the estuarine scene, and the latest threat was provoked once more by the Solway. Way back in 1795, plans were drawn up to link the western and eastern seas by the cutting of a canal from the Solway to the Tyne. Fortunately, the scheme was eventually abandoned as uneconomic, even in an age of enthusiastic canal-making (Blake & Blake, 1958). In 1996 engineer Derek Russell resurrected the scheme for a Solway–Tyne canal, with all modern trimmings, to move twentieth-century shipping more easily between the east and west sides of the country. It would involve not only the canalisation work per se, but also barrages/crossings of the Solway, Duddon and Morecambe Bay. Either knowing or caring nothing of the incalculable damage this madcap project would do to the Lakeland estuaries and their internationally important habitats and wildlife, to other valuable nature conservation sites inland, and to the Roman Wall and other archaeological features, Russell proceeded to plug his grotesque idea with others.

There will always be a coterie of contractors and entrepreneurs who sniff rich pickings from this kind of idea, and local politicians are seduced by the persuasive jobs-creation bait (300,000!). In no time at all, a development company, the Western Waterway Highway Association, was being promoted to carry the Solway–Tyne canal forward. Maybe the burning of numerous investors' fingers over the Channel Tunnel sounded warning notes, or perhaps government quietly disapproved, having realised the almighty environmental battle that would most surely ensue. For whatever reason, the matter has gone quiet, and let us hope that it has faded away forever. The Solway and Morecambe Bay so far remain relatively untouched by developers' pipedreams, and the beauty of their dawns and sunsets can be enjoyed with a minimum of intrusive background clutter. Yet keeping the Philistines at bay will be a matter of eternal vigilance.

Available measures for conservation

The creation of the National Trust and the steady expansion of its property acquisitions in the Lake District was for several decades the only measure to help wildlife conservation, though its influence was incidental rather than deliberate. Manchester Corporation's control of the Thirlmere and Haweswater catchments carried certain environmental obligations, including bird protection. Force of public opinion became increasingly influential, and with the founding of the Friends of the Lake District in 1934, it began to bear upon the management practices of landholders, notably the Forestry Commission. It was not, however, until 1949 and the legislation that gave the National Parks and Access to the Countryside Act and set up the Nature Conservancy, that statutory measures for land management and wildlife conservation came into force. The declaration of the Lake District National Park in 1951 placed the whole area under a higher degree of landscape protection, but the recommendations on nature conservation *per se* were not followed through. The protection of wild nature became largely incidental, though later enhanced by the inclusion of flora and fauna, geological and physiographic features within the definition of 'natural beauty' in the Parks' statutory purpose. The Nature Conservancy's powers to establish National Nature Reserves and notify Sites of Special Scientific Interest were by far the strongest measures available for wildlife conservation, and applied throughout Cumbria, not just to the Lake District.

Protected areas

The most convincing means of protecting wildlife and habitats from further loss is by managing the most important areas primarily for nature conservation. The nature reserve had been a live concept ever since Charles Rothschild's report of 1916, though only a few Lakeland sites were proposed: Roudsea Wood and Mosses, Meathop Moss, Hutton Roof Crags and Hobcarton Crag. The Carlisle Corporation gave an early lead in setting up the Kingmoor Nature Reserve on the edge of the city in 1913. The 1949 legislation introduced National Nature Reserves, and the Nature Conservancy established one of the largest English NNRs of 3,894 hectares at Moor House in the Lakeland Pennines in 1952. Up to November 2001, 26 NNRs have been designated (see Appendix). The 1949 legislation also enabled local authorities to set up Local Nature Reserves and Cumberland County Council established the very first at Drigg Dunes. The Nature Conservancy (now English Nature) also had the duty to notify Sites of Special Scientific Interest (SSSIs), when of the opinion that these were sufficiently important for their flora, fauna, geological or physiographic features. A total of 281 SSSIs has been notified within Cumbria, though 75 of these are for physical features and 29 have both biological and geological interest (see Appendix).

The post-war period of growing voluntary effort for nature conservation has increasingly seen nature reserves created by non-governmental organisations, notably the RSPB, the Woodlands Trust, the Wildlife Trusts Partnership and, in this region, the Cumbria Wildlife Trust. The Countryside Agency does not manage land directly and its role is largely advisory, though it has considerable power, for example, through the preparation of definitive access maps under the new rights of way legislation. The Lake District National Park Authority owns and leases land (7,710 and 1,332 hectares). It has to balance other objectives, especially public enjoyment of the Park through appropriate recreation, against nature conservation within its overall remit but, in having regard to natural beauty, wildlife and cultural heritage (Environment Act, 1995), it can give priority to one of these. It owns land and water, including Bassenthwaite Lake, where its priority for nature conservation is emphasised in the management plan and reflected in the National Nature Reserve status agreed with English Nature. Development of recreational potential has taken second place.

The National Trust protects 55,645 hectares under freehold (c.81 per cent), leasehold and covenant, covering almost one quarter of the National Park, by far the largest area managed by a single body within the

Park. But it is a hybrid organisation, both in the sense of being controlled by statute yet dependent on private funding, and in caring for historic houses and gardens as well as the countryside. Its multiple objectives ensure that the needs of nature conservation are often in competition with other interests and subject to a balancing act over management.

Ideally, the surest protection is given by management as nature reserve under freehold ownership, with no strings attached. Even NNRs owned by English Nature do not always meet these conditions, as at Moor House NNR, where there are common grazings and the mineral rights are not within the freehold, while intrusions in the form of an aircraft navigational radar station, winter skiing activities and the long-distance walking route of the Pennine Way, were all accepted by the earlier Nature Conservancy. The reserves of the NGOs (Non-Governmental Organisations) have no statutory safeguard, except where notified as SSSIs, but may in practice be as safe as the official kind. National Trust land is inalienable, requiring an Act of Parliament for its disposal. The Heritage Lottery Fund has become a welcome source of money for the acquisition of important sites by the NGOs.

The SSSIs did not necessarily protect the designated areas, but were simply a means of consultation over proposed developments that required planning consent. Because farming and forestry were outside planning law, an increasing number of SSSIs was damaged or destroyed by these activities. To remedy this, the Wildlife and Countryside Act, 1981, required landholders to consult the Nature Conservancy Council over any of a specified list of damaging agricultural or forestry activities that they intended to carry out on an SSSI. While loopholes still remained, this allowed for management agreements to safeguard the interest of the sites, but with the unsatisfactory award of compensation for supposed loss of profit in foregoing development. The Countryside and Rights of Way Act, 2000 removed this right to compensation and should tighten the safeguards for SSSIs appreciably, as by promoting positive management agreements.

Most if not all important wildlife sites need active management, if their value is to be sustained, restored or enhanced. Achieving appropriate management is often difficult and costly, and has to be a long-term aim when present problems prevent satisfactory inputs. English Nature site manager Frank Mawby has put much effort into restoration of Glasson and Bowness Mosses, and Wedholme Flow, with good results; and RSPB management of Campfield Marsh with adjoining moss and farmland has increased wader numbers. Yet the desirable management of reserves and SSSIs as a whole is severely limited by shortage of necessary resources.

Protection of the best wildlife sites has been greatly strengthened by designation under international conservation treaties (Ramsar Convention on Wetlands, Berne Convention on European Wildlife and Natural Habitats, Bonn Convention on Migratory species of Wild Animals), and especially under the European Union's Directives on the Conservation of Wild Birds and the Conservation of Wild Habitats and Fauna and Flora. These last two Directives oblige member states to contribute to a European network of outstanding sites (Natura 2000) and to maintain them at 'favourable conservation status'. At least 85 Lakeland sites are proposed for Natura 2000 (see Appendix).

English Nature is the Government's wildlife agency, administering the site protection measures and dispensing advice on conservation. While diligent in extending the NNR series, notifying SSSIs and seeking management agreements, its stance in the face of direct threats to sites is at times overly timid. It has, for instance, known about the hang-gliding disturbance on Tailbridge Hill SSSI for over ten years, but still dithers over tackling the problem. It has also weakly capitulated to potentially damaging proposals on other SSSIs, such as the *Sphagnum* gathering on Yad Moss.

For all their shortcomings, I believe that the various categories of protected area have done most to guarantee the survival of important wildlife areas in Lakeland. Sites such as Rockcliffe Marsh, Glasson Moss, Bowness Moss, Wedholme Flow, Finglandrigg Woods, Gowk Bank, Butterburn Flow, Caudbeck Flow, Great Asby Scar, Hutton Roof Crag, Drigg Dunes, Sandscale Haws, Borrowdale Woods, Roudsea Wood and Mosses, Whitbarrow Scar, Scout Scar, Smardale, Clints Quarry (Egremont), Newton Reigny Moss and Tarn Moss would all have been highly vulnerable to further damage and deterioration, or even total loss, had such safeguards not been in place. The lists of the various categories of nature reserve and the SSSIs in the Appendix cover the most highly concentrated nature interest within Lakeland. While SSSIs countrywide have a notorious record of vulnerability to damage, without them the loss of important sites would have been far worse.

Sympathetic management policies

After safeguard of the important sites and enforcement of the law on protected species of plant and animal, few powers are available to promote nature conservation in any active way, especially in the wider countryside. Other approaches have to rely essentially on persuasion of the many bodies and interests that control or influence use of land and natural resources within the region. If other parties are unsympathetic or play at 'smiling non-co-operation', little can be done to shift their position, other than the kind of gentle pressure that the Friends of the Lake District have exerted over many years. Inputs to the planning process are important in claiming recognition of conservation needs, but cannot apply to farming and forestry, which are still outside planning law. Within the National Park, the Park Authority has used its planning powers to stop developments damaging to nature conservation interests. It has co-ordinated management plans for all the major lakes, and has also helped to fund relevant surveys and other projects. In various ways the Authority has become a force for nature conservation, and has ecologists supportive of this interest. The Environment Agency also has considerable powers to enforce good environmental practice, especially in regard to aquatic habitats. It is, for instance, helping to promote recovery of the otter.

Beyond this, here has been a steady and beneficial increase in the persuasion approach to those who control the use and management of land, not only landholders but also planners, local authority ecologists, statutory agencies and private concerns. On farming, it is heavy going. Despite all the talk of the opportunities for landscape and wildlife gain offered by the downturn in farming, improvements are slow to appear. All the hopes of Common Agricultural Policy reform under Agenda 2000 for environment needs were severely dashed in the event, with virtually nothing in benefits to wildlife management. Paying farmers to manage their land for other purposes, in the face of uneconomic production of plant and animal crops, sounds fine in theory. Yet, so long as the agricultural lobby has a stranglehold on actual practice, and determinedly shores up the 'traditional' activities dependent on public money, it will remain pie in the sky. In particular, continuing payment of headage subsidies on hill sheep promotes relentless overstocking of the fells (Fig. 12.5), and the steady loss of remaining heather and bilberry heath to grassland and bracken. Some observers believe that the Environmentally Sensitive Area mechanism is achieving good results with meadows, wetlands and hedges, but it is limited by the difficulties of agreement over common land. The various 'environmentally friendly' official but voluntary schemes available to farmers should be supported, but so much of the damage has already been done, and it will take a long, long time to reverse on any meaningful scale.

The best solution is for conservation interests to acquire farmland and take it out of cultivation or intensive grazing. Where this can be done on land adjoining existing reserves, the results will be especially beneficial. The RSPB has given a lead at Campfield Marsh, and groups of individuals are also pursuing this initiative.

Fig. 12.5 Too many sheep on the fells: Swaledales on Tailbridge Hill, Cumbrian Pennines.

National Trust ownership of an increasing part of the Lake District has been a bulwark against the more intrusive kinds of development, and over the last 20 years the Trust's management has become more sympathetic to maintenance of wildlife values per se, as distinct from scenic beauty. This is especially so in the ancient semi-natural woodlands, through avoidance of clear-felling, replanting with native broadleaves, and removal of non-native trees – especially conifers. It has set up a Biological Advisers and Survey team and management of its properties is now guided by them wherever possible into practices sympathetic to nature conservation. Yet the Trust is still constrained by the dictates and economics of farming on its estate, and has often been party to the modern methods of increased agricultural production so damaging to wildlife and its habitats. Until recently, it has been unable or unwilling to do anything about the over-grazing of its upland properties. In 1987 an agreement was reached between the National Trust and the Nature Conservancy Council to compensate the Trust's tenant farmer on Armboth Fells, above Thirlmere, for reducing his sheep flock to allow heather regeneration. Similar reductions have been arranged under an Environmentally Sensitive Area scheme covering the Trust's Buttermere Fells property, and on other smaller farms. The National Park Authority has more recently taken initiative over this kind of arrangement to reduce grazing on parts of the Helvellyn range and the Skiddaw fells.

Informed opinion is that these measures have so far achieved little if anything, and that on Armboth Fells the heather continues to deteriorate because the sheep reductions are insufficient. On Helvellyn the dwarf shrubs have largely disappeared and it will be ages before any beneficial results show from reduction in grazing, but in Skiddaw Forest there is much more prospect of restoring heather communities to a desirable state, given a sufficiently forceful approach (Plate 24 and Fig. 12.6).

The foot-and-mouth disease epidemic that raged over Cumbria in 2001 has seen a misguided clamour to maintain sheep stocks supposedly to preserve the scenic beauty of the fell country. There are agonised assertions that without these wretched animals chewing away for evermore the hills will become a dreadful wilderness of scrub, a term always used with pejorative connotations. Those of this view seem oblivious to the charms of anything but farm buildings, stone walls and billiard table greenswards or bracken thickets marching uphill and downdale. Insistence on the importance of keeping 'hefted' flocks seems to me an irrelevant sidetrack from the point that there are simply far too many sheep. Cutting their numbers by half would still maintain the kind of scenery that many people desire. Others concerned with wildlife believe the best thing that could happen to the Lake fells is for the sheep to disappear from at least some of them.

There will never be a better chance to reduce or remove the 'white maggots', and welcome the return of scrub and woodland to parts of the fells, and the recovery of the battered and fast-retreating dwarf shrub heaths. These lost or dwindling habitats support a much greater diversity of plants and animals than the dull and uniform grasslands produced by the sheep,

Fig. 12.6 Land-use effects in Skiddaw Forest: heather moorland managed for grouse on the near side of the River Caldew, acidic grassland sheepwalks on the far side.

and need to be restored on a large scale. Ravens and other carrion feeders would suffer, but this would be an acceptable loss in return for a much richer fauna on the sheep-less ground. Where sheep grazing is deemed necessary to retain valuable wildlife interest, as on areas important for breeding waders, it could continue, albeit at a lower level than hitherto.

Not that rapid change could be expected on most hill ground even if the sheep were completely removed. Exclosure plots at Moor House and elsewhere, and fenced forestry plantations in many places, show that where dwarf shrubs have been eliminated, the resulting grassland has a considerable stability in the absence of grazing. The grasses grow taller and the relative abundance of different species changes, while a dense layer of litter builds up below. But a grassland is what it remains, and other species, including woody types, have difficulty in invading the dense mat. Only very slowly and patchily will it revert to scrub and woodland, especially at higher levels, unless given a helping hand. Rowan and birch would be the first trees to appear, with gorse and hawthorn, but colonisation by other species would depend on proximity of seed sources. Juniper scrub, an important community, would have a chance of regenerating. Where dwarf shrubs had survived in grassland, they would recover and grow rank, with bilberry spreading rapidly, but heather more slowly, to replace the grasses eventually. The speed of this reverse succession would depend on how much the dwarf shrubs had receded before being freed from grazing. The National Trust has made a commendable start to the recreation of broadleaved woodland on the south side of Ennerdale Water, with support from English Nature, National Park Authority and Forestry Commission.

While the Forestry Commission (or the part now Forest Enterprise) has over the last 20 years shown much greater concern to manage its estate in the interests of flora and fauna, putting forestry under meaningful control has been a long and uphill struggle. Perhaps the most helpful shift in government policy was the declaration in 1997, that there would be no more large monoculture plantations of conifers in England. The agreement of 1936 helped to save the central Lake District from further intrusive plantations, but coniferisation of important broadleaved woods in other parts of Cumbria proceeded greatly to reduce the extent of ancient semi-natural woodland in the region. The foresters' failure to penetrate appreciably into the Pennines and Shap Fells results from the extent of commons, and this position must remain. No such constraints applied in the Borders, hence a virtual free-for-all in the wholesale expansion of coniferous afforestation over the moorlands.

Much of the scenic and wildlife damage from this blanket afforestation is irreversible, at least on a timescale that we can contemplate. Belated efforts are being made during felling operations to introduce irregularities into the hard, straight edges of plantations that caused so much offence, but the artificial look to most of them will be difficult to remove. The almost complete lack of ground vegetation in most of these plantations gives them an irredeemably unnatural appearance, compared with the Boreal forests of Fennoscandia, which nearly everywhere have a dwarf shrub heath beneath the trees. Grizedale Forest is held up as a showpiece of what sympathetic commercial forestry can achieve, in mixed species-composition and age-class, and woodland structure, but it is almost a lowland site where good soils and climate allow more opportunities for diversification than in the uplands.

The coniferised ground on Whitbarrow is being cleared by the Commission and is not to be replanted, and this gives real hope of regaining some of the earlier limestone communities, though it will take time and some species may need help to spread. The coniferised Foulshaw Moss has also been sold to the Cumbria Wildlife Trust, who intend to restore it as raised bog, and have begun removing the trees. But the blanket forests of the Borders seem a lost cause. Already the oldest stands have been felled and replanted in much the same way as previously, except that Norway spruce is now replaced by Sitka spruce, to give even darker and denser thickets of trees. The red squirrel is at least a beneficiary, along with goshawks, crossbills and siskins, so we should be thankful for small mercies. I do not see the remedy to blanket afforestation as trying to increase diversity of the established forests in succeeding rotations, so much as preventing the further extension of such planting, and not replacing existing plantations after felling. The coniferisation of existing broadleaved woodland has almost stopped under the Forestry Commission's post-1985 Policy for Broadleaves, and there are significant reconversions back to broadleaves (and also in the private sector). Yet, as with farming, once the damage is done, it cannot easily be rectified.

Species protection

The legislation that prohibits the killing and taking of listed species of animal has undoubtedly reduced the wastage of uncommon and vulnerable species, especially birds. Wildfowling has become more regulated than in earlier years and the list of species that may be shot is now quite limited. Egg collecting persists despite being outlawed and outdated, and continues to focus on birds such as peregrine and raven, though no longer on the seriously damaging scale of earlier years. The listing of rare species, and the embargo on disturbing them at the nest, with special penalties for contravention, still does not deter some gamekeepers and their employers from destroying the rarer birds of prey. The Pennine situation (p. 272) shows a continuing fraught relationship between birds of prey and game preservers. The fateful question is whether these 'sportsmen' can forgo the maximising of their bags by allowing fellow hunters of grace and beauty to share their domain. If they persist in flouting the law, there must be a will to seek legal redress. Whenever action is urged upon those who could take it, the response is that obtaining evidence valid in a court of law is terribly difficult. It would seem to require that someone else is prepared to adopt SAS tactics and lie out in the heather to obtain the necessary photographic evidence. Is it beyond the wit of humankind in Britain of the twenty-first century to stop this kind of lawlessness?

Apart from the hen harrier, golden eagle and merlin, the status of the birds of prey in Lakeland is, nevertheless, mostly a success story. The internationally important estuarine wildfowl and wader populations in autumn and winter, and many coastal breeders, also hold their numbers well or are even increasing. It is the birds of farmland that are in trouble, including species that may winter outside the region or breed in non-agricultural habitats. The species-protection laws are almost wholly irrelevant to this problem.

Bats have benefited from the legal protection measures introduced in 1981, which include their roosts and breeding places, but it is more doubtful whether reptiles, amphibians and various invertebrates have gained appreciable advantage from inclusion. Similarly, the law on safeguard of wild plants from picking and uprooting, and the listing of specially protected species, is unlikely to have achieved much. Identifying some of the obscurer species is a problem, and it is unlikely that the average constable would recognise the high brown fritillary or the moss *Drepanocladus vernicosus* when confronted with their illegal taking! For most of these creatures and plants generally much depends on the integrity and good sense of the knowledgeable naturalists themselves, and there is little to stop the irresponsible few from causing further damage. Knowledge of the risks often leads to the view that secrecy on location of rare species is the only solution.

The Biodiversity Action Plan endorsed by government adopts especially a species-based approach, with management prescriptions and numerical targets for restoring the populations of numerous plants and animals that have declined to levels causing conservation concern. These will apply both on protected areas and beyond, depending on the precise distribu-

Fig. 12.7 Regenerating surface of raised bog, ten years after the disastrous fire of 1976. Glasson Moss National Nature Reserve.

tion of the species involved. The often one-at-a-time, compartmentalised approach tends to be extravagant of resources, and whenever possible, these action plans should use habitat restoration that can deal with groups of species simultaneously. For many plant species known to have been depleted through human action, especially collecting, there is a strong case for propagating material in cultivation, by means of seed or cuttings from surviving plants, and using it to re-stock the wild populations. This has been done successfully for some rarities elsewhere, such as lady's slipper orchid in Yorkshire, tufted saxifrage in Snowdonia and oblong woodsia in the Moffat Hills and Upper Teesdale. It should be applied to depleted Lakeland rarities such as alpine catchfly, shrubby cinquefoil, oblong woodsia and holly fern.

Pervasive environmental change

These are the insidious effects of pollution, especially of the atmosphere. Acid deposition has been a significant problem in Lakeland, especially in high rainfall areas. Even if the acidification of some tarn and stream waters is being reversed through decrease in sulphur pollution, the increased fall-out of atmospheric nitrogen (mainly from vehicle emissions and agricultural fertilisers) may cause both eutrophication and further increase in acidity. If the failure of affected lichens and bryophytes to recover is any indication, there are still serious problems to address over this rain of chemicals from the sky. The presumably parallel effects on soils and peats are not known, except in theory, and should be studied more closely. The pesticides of agriculture also have an atmospheric fallout, with unknown effects.

Probably the most serious threat facing Lakeland wildlife is global warming and sea-level rise, the result of excessive 'greenhouse gas' emissions, regarded by a scientific consensus as a reality, here and now. There are already biological indications of the trend to warmer summers in the spread northwards of mobile insects from more southern and continental districts. Among butterflies, the comma now appears regularly as far north as the Carlisle area, the silver-washed fritillary and speckled wood have returned to the far south of Cumbria, and the arrival of the small skipper and white-letter hairstreak is anticipated, from their northward spread in adjoining counties. The handsome red underwing moth has arrived at Roudsea, while southern dragonflies, in emperor, migrant hawker, ruddy darter and broad-bodied chaser have reached Cumbria (David Clarke). The orthopteran slender groundhopper, discovered in Cumbria in 1997 at Hale Moss by Jennifer Newton, is another southerner moving north. The northwards spread of the nuthatch through the district may well be a response to warmer conditions. Warmth-loving plants may appear or increase, and perhaps the riddle of the Killarney fern will be solved if the various colonies of inconspicuous gametophyte produce mature fern plants.

These are gains, but a downside may be predicted in the northwards retreat of species adapted to the cool conditions of the higher hills. The recent fade-out of the dotterel as a breeding bird, after its recovery from around 1960, may be a case in point. Northern invertebrates may well be even more sensitive to adverse temperature shift. Plants may show a greater inertia in responding to climatic change, but the tiny populations of relict mountain species must be increasingly disadvantaged as conditions become warmer. Some plants may be able to ascend to higher levels, or to lose only the lower-level part of their populations, and thus survive; but for the species already confined to the highest altitudes, there is nowhere else to go. In the lowlands, species of both plant and animal adapted to the cool northern conditions have just as many problems in migrating, since so many exist now in islands or pockets of favourable habitat surrounded by large areas of inhospitable farmland or conifer forest.

Beyond this, climatic warming could see shifts in land use that would be detrimental, as farming and forestry climb up to higher elevations, excluding still more of the semi-natural habitats they have so extensively destroyed in the lowlands. Some invasive aliens from warmer climates, such as New Zealand pygmyweed, Japanese knotweed and the New Zealand flatworm, would be still more favoured in their spread and competitive power.

Sea level rise would begin to submerge or erode the coastal saltings, and alter the extent of intertidal flats, so important for their wintering and passage bird populations. Sand dune systems and shingle beaches would hardly escape change either. Tidal effects at the mouths of rivers would tend to move farther inland. In the face of this irresistible force, the notion of 'managed retreat' seems to be a pretentious expression for letting nature take its course.

The future

I am not going to attempt to foresee the shape of the Lakeland of even 50 years hence. It will depend on various uncertain factors, and especially the precise nature of climatic change. The state of agriculture will be all-important and, in particular, whether the fell country continues to be run as one vast sheepwalk, at taxpayers' expense; or whether there will be some retraction from this now uneconomic and damaging practice. There may be at least local restoration of upland dwarf shrub heath and native woodland, and possibly some recovery of the woolly fringe moss community of the windswept tops. Yet it will be hard work to bring back the retreating or vanished habitats of the fells on any significant scale, and there can hardly be anything but further increase in the effects of human feet and the other pressures that visitors create in the Lake District. Maybe the Pennines will still be the last refuge of the seeker after solitude, but what will be the state of the Borders and their vast tree-farms?

The future of some birds, such as the raven, and other animals will be closely tied to land use (pp. 317–18). If the racing of homing pigeons loses popularity, or ways of reducing their vulnerability are found, then the present high density of breeding peregrines will not last. Even if global warming does not tip the scales against their survival, the tiny populations of relict alpine plants may fade away, perhaps to extinction in some cases, through natural events such as rock falls, unfavourable weather episodes, plant disease and lack of reproduction by seed. It is not too much to hope that, if grouse moors still survive as sporting preserves – which itself must be in doubt – the killing of protected predators will be a thing of the past. Some of these moorlands offer the best chance of restoring a diverse upland ecosystem akin to that of bygone days, and nature conservationists should aim to acquire some of them for this purpose.

In the lowlands, much will also depend on future trends in farming. It remains to be seen whether some of the heavily fertilised grasslands and arable will have been planted with broadleaved trees, as currently proposed in solution of the problem of over-producing agricultural land. Possibilities for other habitat restoration exist, but depend on how far farming continues to be accepted as a public good in its own right or is pressurised into broadening its objectives, or even abandoned in places. The status of many birds and other animals adversely affected by modern agriculture will also be determined by its future trends. The control or, preferably, reduction of eutrophication and acidification, emanating especially from farming and vehicles, will be necessary if botanical losses are to be reversed. Urban sprawl may be rather limited here, as it has been over the last half-century.

As regards the less welcome intrusions on the Cumbrian scene, who would dare to predict whether Sellafield will still be in operation in 50 years time? Will the military presence still exist, at Warcop, Spadeadam and Eskmeals? No doubt the National Park will continue to be protected from disfiguring development by strict planning control, and its matchless beauty will survive, but the part of Cumbria beyond its boundaries will be at risk.

Whether energy generation and telecommunications will eventually produce a skyline bristling with masts in every direction is an unknown but daunting possibility.

The knowledge necessary for management and restoration should at least be freely available. In another half-century, every major group of plants and animals should have been recorded fully, mapped and perhaps remapped, monitored and studied in depth. Ecological research will have advanced our insight into the processes of nature much further still, and new techniques – especially in the computer world – will no doubt evolve. How far the politics of nature conservation will allow the application of all this science is the fateful question. One thing only is certain: that the quality of landscape, the health of natural and semi-natural habitats, and the diversity and abundance of wildlife, will depend very largely on the determination of concerned people to preserve them.

Appendices

APPENDIX 1: Cryptogams

Cumbria has the richest cryptogamic flora of any English county. While many of its species are widespread in Britain, this account notices two groups in particular: those depending mainly on the high rainfall and atmospheric humidity of the Lake District, and those associated with the cool conditions conferred by northern latitude and/or high elevation. A few bryophytes are both oceanic and montane. Another small but distinctive group of calcicoles occurs especially on the limestone hills around Arnside and Kendal.

The oceanic ferns and bryophytes of Lakeland

These include all species with a markedly 'Atlantic' tendency of distribution in mainland Europe and in Britain. Some show a northern bias (N) whilst others are mainly southern (S), and a few are also Mediterranean (M). In addition the list includes a selection of species, well represented in Lakeland, which have a western or sub-Atlantic occurrence in Europe.

Ferns

Killarney fern *Trichomanes speciosum* *
Tunbridge filmy fern *Hymenophyllum tunbrigense* *
Wilson's filmy fern *H. wilsonii*
Hay-scented buckler fern *Dryopteris aemula*
Lanceolate spleenwort *Asplenium obovatum* M
Maidenhair fern *Adiantum capillus-veneris* M
Soft shield-fern *Polystichum setiferum* *
Rustyback fern *Ceterach officinarum* M

Mosses

Breutelia chrysocoma *
Campylopus atrovirens
C. setifolius
C. schwarzii
Dicranum scottianum *
Eurhynchium alopecuroides
F. curnowii
Grimmia hartmanii *
Glyphomitrium daviesii N
Hedwigia integrifolia
Hygrohypnum eugyrium
Hylocomium umbratum N
Isothecium holtii
Leptodon smithii M
Orthodontium gracile *

Bryum riparium
C. brevipilus
C. flexuosus *
C. subulatus
Dicranodontium uncinatum
Fissidens celticus
Fontinalis squamosa
G. retracta
Habrodon perpusillus M
Heterocladium heteropterum *
Hyocomium armoricum *
Hypnum callichroum N
I. striatulum S
Leptodontium recurvifolium N
Orthotrichum rivulare

O. sprucei
Rhynchostegium lusitanicum
Sphagnum strictum

Rhabdoweissia crenulata
Sematophyllum micans
Ulota hutchinsiae N

Liverworts

Adelanthus decipiens S
Anastrophyllum hellerianum
Bazzania tricrenata N
Cololejeunea rossettiana
Colura calyptrifolia
Drepanolejeunea hamatifolia
F. teneriffae
Gymnomitrion crenulatum
Harpanthus scutatus *
H. stramineus N
Jubula hutchinsiae S
Lepidozia cupressina
Lophocolea fragrans *
Metzgeria conjugata *
Mylia taylorii *
Plagiochila atlantica
P. killarniensis
P. spinulosa *
Radula aquilegia
Riccardia chamedryfolia
Saccogyna viticulosa *
S. ornithopodioides N
Targionia hypophylla * M

Anastrepta orcadensis N
Aphanolejeunea microscopica
B. trilobata *
C. calcarea
Douinia ovata
Frullania microphylla
F. fragilifolia *
Harpalejeunea ovata
Herbertus aduncus N
Jamesoniella autumnalis
Lejeunea lamacerina *
L. pearsonii
Marchesinia mackaii M
M. leptoneura
Nowellia curvifolia *
P. exigua
P. punctata *
Porella pinnata S
R. voluta S
R. palmata
Scapania gracilis *
Sphenolobopsis pearsonii
Tritomaria exsecta *

* Present in the sandstone glens of the Carlisle basin.

Northern and montane ferns and bryophytes of Lakeland

These include species which in Britain occur especially in the hilly districts of the north and west and mostly reach their greatest abundance in the Scottish Highlands: some are only sub-montane, but others occur up to high elevations. The rest are montane plants confined to high altitudes and also with their headquarters in the Highlands. Some occur only in the Lake District (L) or in the Pennines (P).

Ferns

Forked spleenwort *Asplenium septentrionale* L
Green spleenwort *A. viride*
Holly fern *Polystichum lonchitis*
Mountain bladder fern *Cystopteris montana* (extinct) L
Mountain male-fern *Dryopteris oreades*
Northern buckler-fern *D. expansa*
Oblong woodsia *Woodsia ilvensis* L
Parsley fern *Cryptogramma crispa*
Rigid buckler-fern *Dryopteris submontana* F

Mosses

Amphidium lapponicum
Andreaea alpina
Anoectangium aestivum
Aplodon wormskjoldii P
Barbula icmadophila L
Blindia acuta
Bryum cyclophyllum L
B. weigelii
Cinclidium stygium
Coscinodon cribrosus L
Dicranella palustris
Dicranum undulatum
Drepanocladus vernicosus
Encalypta rhaptocarpa P
Grimmia affinis
G. doniana
G. funalis
G. montana L
Gymnostomum recurvirostrum
Hygrohypnum dilatatum L
Hypnum hamulosum L
Kiaeria blyttii
K. starkei L
Mnium thomsonii
Oedipodium griffithianum
Orthothecium intricatum
Plagiobryum zierii
Pohlia cruda
P. ludwigii L
Polytrichum alpinum
Pseudoleskeella catenulata P
Ptilium crista-castrensis
R. fugax L
Rhytidium rugosum
S. imbricatum
Splachnum sphaericum
Tomentypnum nitens

A. mougeotii
A. frigida L
Anomobryum filiforme
Arctoa fulvella
Bartramia hallerana
Bryoerythrophyllum ferruginascens
B. mildeanum L
Calliergon sarmentosum
Conostomum tetragonum L
Cynodontium polycarpon L
Dicranoweissia crispula L
Ditrichum zonatum L
Dryptodon patens
Fissidens osmundoides
G. atrata L
G. elongata L
G. incurva L
G. torquata
Homomallium incurvatum (F)
H. ochraceum
Isopterygium pulchellum
K. falcata L
Meesia uliginosa
Oncophorus virens
Oligotrichum hercynicum
O. rufescens
Plagiopus oederi
P. elongata L
P. wahlenbergii var glacialis
Pseudobryum cinclidioides L
Pterygynandrum filiforme L
Rhabdoweisia crispata L
Racomitrium ellipticum L
Sphagnum fuscum
S. warnstorfii
S. vasculosum P

Liverworts

Anthelia julacea L
Barbilophozia hatcheri
Eremonotus myriocarpus L
G. obtusum
Jungermannia exsertifolia ssp. cordifolia
J. obovata

Apometzgeria pubescens
B. lycopodioides P
Gymnomitrion concinnatum L
Hygrobiella laxifolia

J. paroica L

J. subelliptica L
L. bantriensis
Lophozia longidens L
L. sudetica
Marsupella adusta L
M. boeckii var. *stableri* L
M. sprucei
Scapania aequiloba
S. degenii
S. subalpina
Tritomaria quinquedentata

Leiocolea alpestris
L. rutheana F
L. opacifolia L
L. wenzelii L
M. alpina L
M. sphacelata
Nardia compressa
S. cuspiduligera P
S. paludosa L
S. uliginosa

Mosses of southern limestone in Lakeland

Bryum elegans
Funaria muhlenbergii
Homomallium incurvatum
Pleurochaete squarrosa
Tortella nitida

Campylium calcareum
Grimmia orbicularis
Isothecium striatulum
Thuidium recognitum

Reference

Ratcliffe, D.A. (1968). An ecological account of Atlantic bryophytes in the British Isles. *New Phytologist*, **55**, 365–439.

Fungi in Lakeland
by Peter Marren

Cumbrian fungi are poorly recorded, compared with adjoining Yorkshire and Lancashire, probably because few resident mycologists lived in the county. Many incomplete lists exist (for example, in *The Carlisle Naturalist*), but they consist of mostly widespread species, and reveal little about the special nature of the Cumbrian fungus flora. Many fungi may fruit less often in Cumbria than farther south, for it is often remarked that fungi are relatively sparse in north-western woods, and have to be carefully sought. Yet some Cumbrian sites are rich in scarce or seldom-recorded species. Most information on these comes from forays based at the Blencathra Field Studies Council centre near Keswick, and reported in British Mycological Society newsletters, or from the few local specialists. Silverdale fungi were well recorded by Pat Livermore from the 1970s, and, since 1996, forays by the North West Fungus Group are reported in the group's newsletter (also website www.abfg.org with link to all Fungus Group websites). Active resident mycologists include John Taylor, Geoff Naylor, John Nelson, and John and Sheila Weir (website Johnweir@which-net).

Because many fungi fruit only briefly and intermittently, repeated visits are necessary to build up a reasonably complete site list. Well-recorded sites elsewhere suggest that mature woodland of 50 hectares or more should support some 400 species of macro-fungi, and a comparable area of semi-natural grassland perhaps 100 species. Only the Gait Barrows NNR, just over the border in Lancashire Silverdale, has been systematically recorded, producing a list exceeding 1,000 species over 25 years. This extraordinary richness is no doubt shared by other woods on the nearby Cumbrian limestone, such as Roudsea Wood, which has a large proportion of rare fungi, including one of our most massive agarics *Cortinarius praestans*, a species of warm limestone areas. This species belongs to the *Cortinarius* section *Phlegmacium*, characteristic of limestone woods in places where there is little root competition, and well represented in this corner of Cumbria. Another notable species is the recently discovered *Russula fuliginosa*, a robust, dusky-grey species, first found at Witherslack Wood in 1999. Other relatively well-recorded sites with interesting fungi include the dunes at Sandscale Haws and North Walney; and the mixture of woodland, grassland and mire at Blencathra, Tarn Hows, Harrop Tarn (Thirlmere), White Moss Common and Blind Tarn Moss (both near Grasmere).

Among the most exciting recent discoveries is the remarkable arctic–alpine fungus flora associated with fell-fields where least willow forms dense mats. Those on Grasmoor and Crag Hill have produced a range of little-known species, including *Amanita nivalis*, *Laccaria proximella*, *Cortinarius subtorvus*, *Inocybe humilis*, and the waxcap *Hygrocybe salicis-herbaceae*. There is also a mystery milkcap, provisionally identified as *Lactarius nanus*. Two red-capped *Russula* species *R. norvegica* and *R. persicina* var. *intactior* are associated with willow mats in contrasting habitats: the summit fell-field of Crag Hill and the dune-slacks of Sandscale Haws. Very probably these are all mycorrhizal species that have colonised willow roots. Another feature of least willow beds are upland races of more widespread fungi, such as the fly agaric *Amanita muscaria* and the cep *Boletus edulis*.

A snow patch species recently recorded from Helvellyn and Skiddaw is the myxomycete *Diderma niveum*, which forms clusters of yellowish or iridescent sporocarps on bilberry, clubmosses and other vegetation irrigated by melting snow. Such fungi may become early victims of climate change if our winters become milder. Forming tiny, trumpet-shaped fruit bodies on open peaty ground, the genus *Omphalina* is characteristic of the higher fells. The egg-yellow *O. alpina* and the ochre *O. hudsoniana* are rare examples of lichenised agaric fungi, whose fruit bodies arise from a scum of green algae on bare, moist peat. Moorland dung is another fungal microhabitat. Sheep and cattle droppings often support clusters of tiny orange speckles, the granular fruit bodies of an ascomycete, *Coprobia granulata*.

Cumbrian grassland is poorly recorded, but, as in other parts of Britain, unimproved pasture can be rich in fungi, especially waxcaps *Hygrocybe* spp., fairy clubs and earth tongues, as well as other toadstool genera like *Entoloma* and *Stropharia*. A foray in 1999 at The Greens, a 300-metre plateau on the Geltsdale limestone, produced 13 species of waxcap, including the well-known pink waxcap *Hygrocybe calyptriformis* (it also occurs on lawns), five fairy clubs and an earth tongue. Some 16 waxcap species have been recorded from the RSPB's Geltsdale reserve. A field near Blencathra is even richer, with more than 20 waxcaps, the attractive lilac fairy club *Clavaria zollingeri* and a rare black or olive-green earth tongue *Microglossum olivaceum*. The diversity of these 'waxcap grasslands' plunges steeply, and probably permanently, when the pasture is 'improved' with fertiliser. Under-draining also compromises the future of species dependent on marshy ground and flushes, like the pretty little bog beacon *Mitrula paludosa* and the pale yellow tongues of *Clavaria argyllacea*. One wetland site, Sunbiggin Tarn, is the main British locality for the marsh honey fungus *Armillaria ectypa*, a species being investigated under the Biodiversity Action Plan.

Woodland is the habitat richest in macro-fungi. A survey in the 1960s by Merlewood Research Station showed that a 100 square metre plot can produce over 50 kinds of fungal fruit bodies in autumn. While most species encountered casually will be widespread, some Cumbrian woods also support species characteristic of rather open oceanic woodland, among them the beautiful blue *Entoloma nitidum*, one of several *Entolomas* found in wet woodland near Tarn Hows, and a newly discovered species *E. sphagnorum*. Another local speciality is the yellowish, funnel-shaped bolete *Pulveroboletus lignicola*, usually found associated with a bracket fungus *Phaeolus schweinitzii* on rotting conifer stumps. In 1999, a BMS foray at Aira Force near Ullswater uncovered a new British species of *Amanita, A. olivaceogrisea*, fruiting under hazel. It is related to *A. friabilis*, another recently discovered species, which grows under alder at Gait Barrows and is likely also to occur in Cumbria. One interesting woodland fungus that sometimes turns up on Cumbrian forays is the club-shaped fruit body of *Cordyceps ophioglossoides*, a parasite of the false truffle *Elaphomyces muricatus*, which can usually be found by digging underneath.

Sand dunes are an important habitat for fungi, in both the fixed 'grey' dunes and the mobile 'yellow' dunes. The Duddon sandhills have specialists characteristic of Atlantic dunes, rarely found on the east coast, such as stalked puffball *Tulostoma melanocyclum* and the tiny puffball *Bovista limosa*. Among the coastal fungus flora are apparently fragile species that can grow through pure sand, such as *Psathyrella ammophila* and *Coprinus ammophilae*, as well as the remarkable mule-dung fungus *Pisolithus arhizus*, a puffball-relative with bright yellow mycelia. The large, ringed, purple-grey toadstool *Stropharia rugosoannulata* was found at Sandscale Haws in 1999, confirming it as a British species. Dune grasslands are perhaps the habitat in which fruiting fungi occur most abundantly in Cumbria.

The many exciting discoveries from Cumbria in recent years will undoubtedly bring more field mycologists to the area, especially to the coast and high fells. The region seems to be at a biogeographic crossroads, where arctic, Atlantic and southern species all occur within close proximity. We have probably only begun to uncover the Lakeland's elusive mycological riches.

APPENDIX 2: Arachnids
by John R. Parker

Cumbria has a rich Arachnid fauna, with 326 out of 645 British species of spider, 16 out of 25 harvestmen and eight out of 25 pseudoscorpions. This richness owes much to the diversity of habitats, at various altitudes, though some species occur over a wide range of conditions, from sea level to mountain tops, and appear unspecialised. Quite a number inhabit occupied buildings. Some species are very rare and when discovered in Cumbria were new to Britain or even to science, and in this generally under-worked district new discoveries continue to be made. Others reach their northern or southern distribution limits here. There is space to mention only some more noteworthy species, but the references below give fuller information. The main published sources for this group are Britten (1912) and Parker (1996). Spiders marked with an asterisk are included as Red Data Book species by Bratton (1991).

Spiders: Araneae

The majority of the spiders are very small animals less than three millimetres in length, especially those associated with mountains, bogs and woodland.

Coastal habitats

Under tidal debris of drift-line zones on sand or shingle beaches, submerged at Ordinary High Tides or High Water Spring Tides: *Argenna patula*, *Erigone longipalpis* and *Halorates reprobus*.
In shingle or maritime plants above High Water Mark: *Silometopus ambiguus*, *Erigone arctica*, *Drassodes lapidosus* and *Drassyllus lutetianus*.
On sand dunes: *Philodromus fallax*, *Arctosa perita*, *Sitticus saltator*, *Tibellus oblongus* and *T. maritimus*.
In leaf litter at the edges of tidal estuaries: *Arctosa leopardus* and *Satilatlas britteni*.

Woodland and scrub

Hyptiotes paradoxus* (conifers), *Lepthyphantes expunctus* (juniper), *Drapetisca socialis* and *Moebelia penicillata* (on bark of trees).

Limestone

Below outcrops: *Atypus affinis*
Bottom of pavement grikes: *Peponocranium ludicrum*, *Pocadicnemis pumila*, *Metopobactrus prominulus*.
Lacustrine marshes
Tetragnatha striata, *Trochosa spinipalpis*, *Rugathodes instabilis* (at northern limit).

Ponds

Argyroneta aquatica.

Rivers

Arctosa cinerea, in burrows under large stones of shingle beds often inundated by winter torrent water. *Larinioides sclopetarius* in large radiate webs on buildings, boathouses and bridges (near its northern limit).

Raised bogs, kettlehole bogs and valley bogs

Dolomedes fimbriatus, Glyphesis cottonae (at northern limit), *Maro lepidus*, M. sublestus, Bathyphantes setiger* and *Centromerus levitarsis**: all in *Sphagnum*.

Blanket bogs

Clubiona norvegica, Erigone welchi, Macrargus carpenteri, Meioneta mossica and *Walckenaera clavicornis* (a high Arctic species).

Summit areas of highest mountains

Entelecara errata, Hilaira nubigena, H. pervicax, Lepthyphantes pinicola, Rugathodes bellicosus, Euophrys petrensis, Semljicola calignosus (the only British endemic): all found under stones. *Pardosa trailli* (scree shoots).

Buildings

Interiors – synanthropic spiders: *Pholcus phalangioides, Psilochorus simoni*. In cellars: *Meta manardi, Theridion mystaceum, Oonops domesticus, Tegenaria saeva, T. atrica* and *T. gigantea*.
Roof exteriors: *Pseudeuophrys lanigera*
Drystone walls: *Textrix denticulata* and *Theridion melanurum*.
Old eroded brick and ashlar walls, and mortar crevices: *Segestria florentina* (recently discovered at Bowness-on-Solway, its northern limit and only locality north of the Bristol area).

Widespread species

Perhaps the most ubiquitous Lakeland spiders are *Amaurobius similis*, which spins a grey, lacey and untidy web out of almost any crevice in a wall, fence, door or gate; and *Zygiella X-notata*, which spins a radiate web out of the underside of any cornice or window soffit. In early summer *Neriene peltata* and in late summer *L. triangularis* make horizontal sheet webs everywhere on gorse and other shrubs. All but one of the species on the British list also occur on mainland Europe. The exception is the unique *Semljicola caliginosus*, first described as a British species in 1910 and known only from England and Scotland.

Harvestmen: Opiliones

These are found in shady situations such as old walls and low damp herbage where they prey on small insects and their larvae, dead or alive.

Pseudoscorpions: Pseudoscorpionidae

These live in moss and decaying vegetable matter, where they prey on *Collembola*, tiny insect larvae and very immature spiders.

References

Bratton, J. H. (Ed.) (1991). *British Red Data Books. 3. Invertebrates other than insects.* Joint Nature Conservation Committee, Peterborough.

Britten, H. (1912). The arachnids (spiders etc.) of Cumberland. *Trans. Carlisle Nat. Hist. Soc.*, **II**, 30–65.

Harvey, P. R., Nellist, D. R., and Telfer, M. G. (2002). *Provisional Atlas of British Spiders* (Arachnida, Araneae). Joint Nature Conservation Committee.

Parker, J. R. (1996). The study of Cumbrian spiders. *The Carlisle Naturalist*, **4**, 45–52.

Roberts, M. J. (1985–87). *The Spiders of Great Britain and Ireland.* 3 Vols. Harley Books, Colchester.

APPENDIX 3: Protected areas in Cumbria

* also notified as Site of Special Scientific Interest (SSSI)
+ suffered significant damage since first surveyed
SAC Special Area of Conservation (proposed or accepted)
SPA Special Protection Area (proposed or accepted)
R Ramsar Convention on Wetlands site
NT National Trust property
GCR Geological Conservation Review site
CWT Reserve of Cumbria Wildlife Trust
LDNP Owned by Lake District National Park Authority
P Plantlife Reserve
Bracketed area figures are the SSSI areas where these are appreciably larger than the nature reserves.

National Nature Reserves	**Area (ha)**	**Grid reference**
Bassenthwaite Lake * + SAC LDNP	673	NY 218290
Blelham Bog *	2	NY 365005
Butterburn Flow * + SAC R	416	NY 672760
Clawthorpe Fell * SAC	14	SD 540788
Cliburn Moss, Whinfell * +	37	NY 576256
Drumburgh Moss * + SAC CWT	187	NY 255584
Duddon Mosses * SAC	55	SD 219862
Finglandrigg Woods * +	65 (97)	NY 278570
Glasson Moss * + SAC	97 (226)	NY 235605
Gowk Bank * SAC	15	NY 680737
Great Asby Scar * SAC GCR	166 (350)	NY 650097
Hallsenna Moor *	24 (30)	NY 064006
High Leys *	9	NY 062181
Moor House * + SAC SPA	3,894	NY 758328
North Fen *	2	SD 358977
North Walney &		SD 172725
Sandscale Haws * + CWT NT		SD 185750
Park Wood * SAC	15	SD 565777
Roudsea Woods and Mosses * SAC	423 (481)	SD 335825
Rusland Moss *	24 (94)	SD 334886
South Solway Mosses * SAC see SSSIs		
Smardale Gill * + CWT	40 (118)	NY 730077
Tarn Moss *	17	NY 400275
Thornhill Moss and Meadow *	12 (25)	NY 174486
Walton Moss * SAC	286	NY 500665
Whitbarrow * + SAC	? (1177)	SD 445885

Local Nature Reserves		
Chapel Head Scar		SD 442861
Cowraik Quarry *	5	NY 541309
Drigg Dunes * SAC	383 (1,398)	SD 070958
Siddick Pond *	22	NY 002302

Reserves of the Royal Society for the Protection of Birds

Campfield Marsh * SAC	310	NY 207620
Geltsdale * + SAC SPA	5,083 (5,886)	NY 616593
Haweswater * (part)	9,503	NY 470108
Hodbarrow	105	SD 174791
St Bees Head * GCR	22 (172)	NX 962118

Reserves of the Cumbria Wildlife Trust

Allan Wilson	1.8	NY 457526
Argill Woods *	7.4	NY 844141
Ash Landing	2.3	SD 386952
Barkbooth	12.0	SD 415906
Beachwood	0.8	SD 452786
Biglands Bog * +	2.8 (12)	NY 260536
Blawith & Brown Robin	26.9	SD 415787
Boathouse Field	0.7	NY 253231
Bowness-on-Solway gravel pits	7.3	NY 207618
Bucknills Field * (Orton Moss)	0.6	NY 338543
Causewayend Heronry	0.4	SD 341849
Christcliff	0.4	NY 185007
Clints Quarry, Egremont *	9.2 (14)	NY 009124
Dorothy Farrer's	1.0	SD 480983
Dubbs Moss	7.7	NY 104288
Ellonby Waste	2.4	NY 423359
Enid Maples	2.8	SD 526897
Eskmeals * (Drigg Coast)	67.0	SD 087944
Foulney * (Morecambe Bay) SPA	11.2	SD 243655
Goldrill 1.1	NY	394165
Grubbins Wood	7.2	SD 445780
Hale Moss & Wood *	2.9	SD 510776
Hervey * (Whitbarrow)	100.0	SD 442871
Humphrey Head * GCR	29.1	SD 393740
Ivy Crag Wood	1.6	NY 245265
Juniper Scar	0.4	NY 475012
Lancelot Clark Storth * SAC	57.2	SD 541777
Latterbarrow	4.0	SD 440828
Meathop Moss *	64.0 (68)	SD 445820
Newton Reigny Moss *	0.3 (13)	NY 477312
Next Ness	1.0	SD 302787
Rockcliffe Marsh * SPA SAC	1,120.0	NY 340637
South Walney *	92.0	SD 215620
Tarn Sike *	2.6	NY 665076
Waitby Greenriggs	4.4	NY 757086
Willow Pond	0.2	NY 346082
Wreay Woods	17.7	NY 444500

Properties of the Woodland Trust

Arrowthwaite Wood, Whitehaven	8.4	NX 971174
Beckmickle Ing Wood, Staveley	3.6	SD 489980
Beech Hill Wood, Storrs	4.5	SD 390923
Blackbank Wood, Longtown	7.1	NY 350677
Brothybeck Wood, Welton	5.7	NY 334433
Church Plantation, Bassenthwaite	1.2	NY 227292
Crag Wood, Meathop *	3.7	SD 457807
Croglinhurst Wood, Broughton	4.0	SD 208897
Crossfield, Arnside	0.1	SD 453784
Crow Park, Whitehaven	11.1	NX 979178
Dobshall Wood, Arnside	4.0	SD 451779
Dufton Ghyll Wood, Appleby	10.5	NY 687250
Garth Wood, Keswick	0.5	NY 281238
Harras Moor, Whitehaven	1.5	NX 978186
Hawcoat Youth Fields, Barrow	6.4	SD 203717
Hawkeswood, Low Moresby	1.8	NX 993208
Hebblethwaite Hall Wood, Sedbergh	5.0	SD 688930
Knipe Fold Coppice, Hawkshead	1.5	NY 342002
Low Wood, Ulpha *	11.0	SD 205944
Midgey Gill, Whitehaven	3.6	NX 982177
Miltonrigg Wood, Brampton	62.3	NY 560615
Moss & Height Spring Wood, Bouth	19.8	SD 325864
Old Hutton, Kendal	5.4	SD 564878
Ridgewood, Brampton	9.8	NY 540618
Round Hill Wood, Kendal	0.6	SD 531929
Scroggs Wood, Kendal	1.2	SD 512906
Sea Wood, Bardsea *	23.6	SD 294735
Shank Wood, River Lyne *	8.1	NY 465704
Spooner Vale, Windermere	0.2	SD 407990
Stevney Spinney, Hawkshead	0.2	SD 356999
Swarthmoor Hall Wood, Ulverston	1.4	SD 284774
Tarn Wadling, High Hesket	0.6	NY 486440
The Glen, Heads Nook	0.9	NY 493551
Warriners Wood, Kendal	3.5	SD 498904

Sites of Special Scientific Interest – Biological

(Additional to those indicated above)
Data supplied by English Nature, as at 1 October 2001

Alston Shingle Banks SAC GCR	17 N	Y 716448
Annaside	17	SD 081875
Annaside & Gutterby Banks	23	SD 096849
Appleby Fells SAC SPA	10,689	NY 750260
Argill Woods and Pastures	29	NY 844139
Armboth Fells NT (part) SAC	2,346	NY 290150
Arnside Knott NT (part)	168	SD 455773

Ash Fell	550	NY 743053
Augill Valley Pasture P	3	NY 816146
Barf and Thornthwaite	23	NY 216265
Barker Scar GCR	17	SD 335778
Baysbrown Wood	49	NY 315046
Beech Hill Wood, Longsleddale	31	NY 500020
Belah Woods and Pastures	52	NY 828114
Birk Fell SAC	265	NY 402182
Birkett Hill & High Out Wood	58	NY 792072
Black Moss, Egremont	16	NY 030107
Black Snib, Lontown	30	NY 423676
Blackdike Bog, Matterdale	9	NY 407233
Blea Tarn	4	NY 293043
Blea Water, High Street	104	NY 448107
Bleacham Tarn and Bog NT GCR	51	NY 365004
Bolton Fell Moss	379	NY 490690
Borrow Beck Meadows SAC	7	NY 546040
Bowber Head & Piper Hole Meadows SAC	20	NY 732033
Bowness Common (Moss) SAC	807	NY 200600
Braithwaite Moss SAC	38	NY 237249
Brantrake Moss & Devoke Water	20	SD 151974
Bretherdale Meadows SAC	11	NY 587043
Broad Dales, Gamelsby	16	NY 253525
Brothers Water NT	34	NY 403127
Burns Beck Moss, Killington	21	SD 594880
Buttermere NT SAC	93	NY 183157
Buttermere Fells NT SAC GCR	6,142	NY 200200
Butterwick Meadows	10	NY 508193
Castlehead Wood, Keswick NT	8	NY 270227
Caudbeck Flow, Spadeadam SAC	456	NY 580725
Cautley Thwaite Meadows & Ecker Secker Beck SAC GCR	47	SD 699954
Chapel Bridge Meadows	3	NY 231192
Claife Tarns and Mires	148	SD 375980
Clints Crags, Blindcrake	5	NY 163354
Clints Quarry, Egremont GCR	14	NY 007122
Clints Quarry, Moota SAC	12	NY 158365
Cotehill Pastures & Ponds	10	NY 465517
Cropple How Mire	9	SD 131975
Crosby Gill, Orton SAC	123	NY 615114
Crosby Ravensworth Fell SAC	1,537	NY 592093
Cumwhitton Moss	44	NY 515520
Deepdale Meadows, Dent SAC	14	SD 716861
Dodgson Wood, High Nibthwaite	127	SD 303924
Drigg Coast SAC	1,398	SD 074934
Drigg Holme	9	SD 075988

Duddon estuary SAC SPA R GCR	6,791	SD 184772
Duddon Valley Woodlands	361	SD 222966
Dungeon Gill	10	NY 284069
Eden Gorge, Armathwaite	142	NY 525430
Elterwater	36	NY 333042
Ennerdale Water & Side Woods	429	NY 110147
Esthwaite Water R	156	SD 360963
Ewefell Mire SAC	32	NY 696067
Eycott Hill, Greystoke GCR	124	NY 387302
Far Arnside	2	SD 450760
Farleton Knott SAC GCR	291	SD 545797
Foulshaw Moss SAC	347	SD 457826
Gelt Woods, Brampton	29	NY 525588
Glencoyne Wood NT SAC	30	NY 384182
Gowbarrow Park NT	53	NY 410210
Great Blencow Meadows & Fen	8	NY 459326
Great Wood, Keswick NT SAC	48	NY 275217
Greendale Mires, Wasdale	84	NY 143050
Gribbs Meadows	4	NY 221557
Haggs Bank SAC	2	NY 767451
Haile Great Wood, Egremont	31	NY 037097
Hallinhag Wood, Ullswater SAC	16	NY 430202
Helbeck Wood SAC	91	NY 785165
Helvellyn & Fairfield SAC GCR	2,488	NY 340150
High Lickbarrow Mires & Pastures	19	SD 425970
Hollin Hill	5	NY 592050
Honister Crag SAC	302	NY 216140
Hutton Roof Crags SAC GCR	396	SD 555780
Irthing Gorge, Gilsland	44	NY 633686
Jenny Dam	1	SD 462954
Johnny Wood, Rosthwaite NT SAC	36	NY 252143
Kielder Mires SAC	1,813	NY 603810
Kirkby Moor	781	SD 254824
Knipe Tarn, Winster	6	SD 427943
Lamonby Verges & Fields	13	NY 400352
Lazonby Fell	331	NY 520395
Leck Beck Head Catchment GCR	267	SD 676813
Little Asby Inrakes & Outrakes SAC	12	NY 699102
Little Langdale Tarn	37	NY 305032
Lodore-Troutdale Woods NT (part) SAC	370	NY 260172
Longsleddale Woods	21	NY 507025
Loughrigg Fell Flushes	14	NY 365042
Low Beckside Meadow	3	NY 365292
Low Church Moss, Beckermet	5	NY 016057
Low Wood, Hartsop NT SAC	77	NY 400130
Ludderburn & Candlestick Mires	142	SD 403927

Lyne Woods	142	NY 477722
Mallerstang & Swaledale Head SAC SPA	942	NY 800020
Marble Quarry & Hale Fell SAC	44	SD 498783
Maryport Harbour	4	NY 029363
Meathop Woods & Quarry GCR	39	SD 435799
Middlebarrow, Arnside SAC	19	SD 463764
Middlesceugh Woods & Pastures SAC	46	NY 400409
Milkingstead Wood	14	SD 153996
Millfield Verges	2	NY 375357
Miterdale Head Wood	5	NY 164027
Mollen Woods, Bewcastle	30	NY 561708
Moor House & Cross Fell SAC SPA GCR	13,435	NY 711355
Moorthwaite Moss, Cumwhitton	12	NY 512510
Morecambe Bay SAC SPA R	22,831	SD 383701
Mungrisdale Mires	108	NY 372302
Murthwaite Park, Rawthey	20	SD 709981
Nichols Moss, Witherslack SAC	93	SD 431826
Oakshaw Ford	6	NY 510760
Orton Moss (Woods), Carlisle +	64	NY 340545
Orton Pastures, Tebay	16	NY 626093
Oulton Moss, Wigton	24	NY 254513
Outley Mosses	34	SD 362818
Over Water, Uldale	30	NY 251350
Penton Linns GCR	8	NY 432774
Pillar & Ennerdale Fells SAC	1,498	NY 137119
Raisbeck Meadows, Tebay SAC	14	NY 635068
River Derwent & Tributaries SAC	1,250	NY 261207
River Eden & Tributaries SAC GCR	2,486	NY 462237
River Ehen SAC	24	NY 055160
River Kent & Tributaries SAC	109	SD 508952
River Nent at Blagill SAC GCR	9	NY 743467
Rusland Valley Mosses	94	SD 335882
Salta Moss, Allonby	45	NY 085454
Sandybeck Meadow, Cockermouth SAC	1	NY 134268
Scafell Pikes NT SAC	1,117	NY 215072
Scaleby Moss	69	NY 430635
Scales Wood, Buttermere SAC	54	NY 165165
Scout & Cunswick Scars SAC	375	SD 488909
Sea Wood, Ulverston	26	SD 294734
Seatoller Wood, Sourmilk Gill & Seathwaite Graphite Mine NT SAC GCR	137	NY 241132
Shap Fells SAC GCR	2,144	NY 536094
Shaw Meadow & Sea Pasture	9	SD 122810

Silloth Dunes & Mawbray Bank	189	NY 101518
Silver Tarn, Hollas & Harnsey Mosses, Nethertown	5	NX 998068
Skelsmergh Tarn, Kendal	4	SD 533967
Skelton Pasture SAC	12	NY 437378
Skiddaw Group SAC GCR	10,385	NY 300300
South Walney & Piel Channel Flats SAC SPA R GCR	2,333	SD 216634
Spadeadam Mires SAC	1,133	NY 619726
Stagmire Moss	7	NY 737121
Stanley Gill (Dalegarth Force)	8	SD 173999
Stonethwaite Woods NT SAC	99	NY 265140
Subberthwaite, Blawith & Torver Low Commons SAC	1,865	SD 269896
Sunbiggin Tarn & Moors & Little Asby Scar SAC GCR	997	NY 677077
Swindale Meadows, Shap SAC	8	NY 509125
Swindale Wood SAC	45	NY 805164
Tarn Hows, Hawkshead	190	NY 330000
Temple Sowerby Moss	6	NY 616270
The Clouds SAC GCR	108	NY 738000
The Ings, Derwentwater NT SAC	6	NY 268221
Thirlmere Woods	47	NY 310156
Thurstonfield Lough	18	NY 320563
Tilberthwaite Gill, Yewdale	7	NY 303007
Town End Meadows, Little Asby SAC	11	NY 705101
Troutbeck	784	NY 420090
Udford Low Moss	17	NY 582300
Underlaid Wood, Beetham SAC	106	SD 485795
Unity Bog, Brampton	10	NY 528590
Upper Solway Flats & Marshes SAC SPA R GCR	9,706	NY 200630
Wan Fell, Plumpton	309	NY 520360
Wart Barrow, Grange-over-Sands	26	SD 393768
Wasdale Screes NT SAC GCR	345	NY 160058
Wastwater NT SAC GCR	298	NY 163061
Wedholme Flow SAC	780	NY 215520
Wet Sleddale Meadows SAC	4	NY 553119
Whernside GCR	1,239	SD 730800
Whitbarrow SAC	1,177	SD 440870
White Moss, Crosby Moor	38	NY 462606
Whitesike Mine & Flinty Fell SAC	8	NY 763423
Wilson Place Meadows SAC	9	NY 316031
Winster Wetlands 40 S	D	422937
Yewbarrow Woods SAC	113	SD 348874

Sites of Special Scientific Interest (Geological)
Included in the Geological Conservation Review (GCR)

Ash Fell Edge, Ravenstonedale	8	NY 734049
Ashgill Quarry, Torver	160	SD 269954
Backside Beck & Spen Gill	2	SD 694985
Barf and Thornthwaite	23	NY 216265
Beckfoot Quarry, Eskdale	2	NY 160003
Birk Fell Hause Mine	2	NY 292015
Birky Cleugh	3	NY 591753
Blagill Mine	1	NY 741472
Blea Tarn	4	NY 293043
Bothelcrags Quarry, Bothel	1	NY 187371
Bowness Knott, Ennerdale	40	NY 112156
Bramcrag Quarry & Wanthwaite Mine	44	NY 320220
Brathay Quarries	25	NY 360016
Browgill & Stockdale Becks	27	NY 495058
Buckbarrow Beck	2	SD 136909
Burrell's Quarry, Appleby	1	NY 676179
Cairnbridge Sandpit, Heads Nook	2	NY 507541
Comb Beck	1	NY 182149
Coniston Mines & Quarries	128	SD 297984
Cumpston Hill	4	SD 784977
Ellery Sike	4	NY 545759
Elliscales Quarry	1	SD 224747
Florence Mine	27	NY 021104
Force Crag Mine	53	NY 197215
George Gill	6	NY 718188
Gill Beck	3	NY 149343
Hale Moss Caves, Yealand	22	SD 498774
Hell Gill, Mallerstang	1	SD 787969
Hollows Farm Section	2	NY 248170
Iron Pit Spring Quarry	1	SD 310784
Janny Wood Section, Mallerstang	1	NY 783037
Jockie's Syke	3	NY 423756
Jumb Quarry	1	NY 448073
Keisley Quarry	8	NY 142238
Kershope Bridge	6	NY 500834
King Water, Spadeadam	1	NY 608698
Langdale Pikes	473	NY 286073
Langdale, Bowderdale & Carlin Gill	1,772	SD 673997
Little Mell Fell Quarry	1	NY 429239
Low Wray Bay	4	NY 376012
Melmerby Road Section	1	NY 623384
Mousegill Beck, Brough	8	NY 830126
Nab Gill Mine	5	NY 173014
Oakshaw Ford	6	NY 510760
Pets Quarry	1	NY 389070

Pinskey Gill	1	NY 697040
Pooley Bridge Section	1	NY 465243
Pus Gill	3	NY 700259
Ray and Crinkle Crags 147	NY 249046	
River Calder Section	1	NY 068117
River Rawthey, Wandale Beck and Sally Beck	45	SD 710979
River South Tyne & Tyne Bottom Mine	17	NY 738420
Rosthwaite Fell NT (part)	230	NY 257123
Scandale Beck & Stone Gill	12	NY 719048
Scandale Beck, Brunt Hill	1	NY 742024
Scaw Gill & Blaze Beck	14	NY 179253
Seathwaite Copper Mines	1	SD 265994
Shap Fell Road Cuttings	17	NY 556053
Short Gill Cave System	35	SD 669845
Side Pike	10	NY 290052
Skelghyll Beck NT	4	NY 396032
Skelwith Hill	3	SD 332807
Smallcleugh Mine	5	NY 787429
Stile End, Kentmere	6	NY 473050
Swindale Beck		NY 688276
Tebay Road Cuttings	10	NY 609018
Thornsgill Beck, Mosedale Beck & Wolf Crags	98	NY 355238
Throstle Shaw & Sandbeds Fan	3	NY 234291
Upper Dentdale Cave System	61	SD 739864
Waberthwaite Quarry, Ravenglass	4	SD 112944
Water Crag	4	SD 152973
Whitberry Burn	1	NY 521740
Yeathouse Quarry	5	NY 043168
Yewdale Beck	1	SD 307985

Further information on SSSIs may be obtained from the English Nature website: www.english-nature.org.uk

Areas of Outstanding Natural Beauty (AONB)

North Pennines
Solway Coast
Arnside and Silverdale

Priority habitats of the European Union Habitats Directive

Those especially well represented in Cumbria are active raised and blanket bogs, and limestone pavements.

APPENDIX 4: Organisations concerned with Lakeland nature and its conservation

English Nature
Lake District National Park Authority
National Trust
Forest Enterprise
Friends of the Lake District
Cumbria Wildlife Trust
Royal Society for the Protection of Birds
Woodlands Trust
The Wildlife Trusts Partnership
Cumbria Regionally Important Geological Sites Group
Environment Agency
Countryside Agency
Butterfly Conservation
Tullie House Museum, Carlisle
Kendal Museum
Keswick Museum
Cumbria Naturalists' Union: Member Societies
  Ambleside Field Society
  Arnside Natural History Society
  Carlisle Natural History Society
  Carlisle RSPB Members Group
  Cumbria Bird Club
  Eden Field Club
  Grange Natural History Society
  Kendal Natural History Society
  Keswick Natural History Society
  Maryport and District Natural History Society
  Walney Bird Observatory
  West Cumbria RSPB Members Group
Cumberland Geological Society
Westmorland Geological Society

Small groups deal with specialist interests, such as bats.

Numerous other bodies are involved in or have some responsibility for nature conservation, and are listed in the Cumbrian Biodiversity Partnership (Biodiversity Action Plan); but the above list is of those with a major concern.

There are also natural history displays in information centres, such as Brockhole, Windermere; and Grizedale Forest.

References and Further Reading

Abraham, G. D. (1919). *On Alpine Heights and British Crags*. Methuen, London.

Aitken, I. (1968). Vegetation survey of the Skiddaw group of fells. Unpublished BSc thesis, University of Bristol.

Atty, D. (1999). Some noteworthy beetle records for Cumbria. *The Carlisle Naturalist*, **7**, 6–7.

Backhouse, J. (1856). *Monograph of the British Hieracia*. York.

Backhouse, J. (1884). Teesdale Botany: historical and personal recollections. *The Naturalist*, 10–13.

Baines, D. (1988). The effects of improvement of upland, marginal grasslands on the distribution and density of breeding waders (Charadriiformes) in northern England. *Biological Conservation*, **45**, 221–36.

Banks, B. (1997). Cumbria – Stronghold of the British Natterjack. *British Wildlife*, **9**, 1–6.

Barrow, G., Jacobs, A. & Binks, G. (1985). *Interpreting the heritage of the Carlisle–Settle railway line*. CCP 192. Countryside Commission, Cheltenham.

Battarbee, R. W. & 15 co-authors (1988). *Lake Acidification in the United Kingdom*. Report to the Department of the Environment, HMSO.

Bennion, H., Monteith, D. & Appleby, P. (2000). Temporal and geographical variation in lake trophic status in the English Lake District: evidence from (sub) fossil diatoms and aquatic macrophytes. *Freshwater Biology*, **45**, 394–412.

Binstead, C. H. (1922). Mosses of the English Lake District. *The Vasculum*, 65–83.

Birkett, N. L. (1970). Insects, in Hervey, G. A. K. & Barnes, J. A. G. *Natural History of the Lake District*. Warne, London.

Birks, J. (2000). Pine Martens in England and Wales. *The Bulletin of the British Ecological Society*, **31**, 42–43.

Birks, J. D. S. & Messenger, J. E. (2000). The Pine Marten (*Martes martes*) in Cumbria in the late twentieth century. *The Carlisle Naturalist*, **8**, 6–10.

Blake, J. & Blake, B. (1958). *The Story of Carlisle*. City of Carlisle Education Committee, Carlisle.

Blezard, E. (1926). Breeding of the Dotterel in the Pennines in 1925. *British Birds*, **20**, 17–19.

Blezard, E. (1928). On the Raven. *Trans. Carlisle Nat. Hist. Soc.*, **IV**, 16–22.

Blezard, E. (1933). On the Buzzard. *Trans. Carlisle Nat. Hist. Soc.*, **V**, 61–66.

Blezard, E. (1946). The Lakeland Pennines and their birds. *Trans. Carlisle Nat. Hist. Soc.*, **VII**, 100–115.

Blezard, E. (1958). The Wild Animal Life of the Border Forests. Pp. 55–61 of *The Border*, National Forest Park Guides, HMSO, London.

Blezard, E. (1967). Non-marine Mollusca of Lakeland. *Trans. Carlisle Nat. Hist. Soc.*, **XI**, 48–68.

Blezard, E. (1920–1970). Unpublished journals. Cumbria County Archive Office, Carlisle.

Blezard, E., (ed.), Garnett, M., Graham, R. & Johnston, T. L. (1943). The Birds of Lakeland.

Trans. Carlisle Nat. Hist. Soc., **VI**. p. 163.
Branston, J. W. (1912). The minerals of Cumberland. *Trans. Carlisle Nat. Hist. Soc.*, **II**, 14–29.
Britten, H. (1909). Mammals of the Eden Valley. *Trans. Carlisle Nat. Hist. Soc.*, **I**, 24–30.
Britten, H. (1912). The Arachnids (Spiders, etc.) of Cumberland. *Trans. Carlisle Nat. Hist. Soc.*, **II**, 30–65.
Brown, A. E., Burn, A. J., Hopkins, J. J. & Way, S. F. (eds) (1997). *The Habitats Directive: selection of Special Areas of Conservation in the UK*. JNCC Report No. 270. Joint Nature Conservation Committee, Peterborough.
Brown, R. H. (1974). *Lakeland Birdlife*. Thurnam, Carlisle.
Byrkjedal, I. & Thompson, D. B. A. (1998). *Tundra Plovers*. Poyser, London.
Chapman, A. (1907). *Bird-life of the Borders*. Second edition. Gurney & Jackson, London.
Clapham, A. R. (ed.) (1978). *Upper Teesdale. The Area and its Natural History*. Collins, London.
Clarke, D. J. (1996). Dragonflies in Cumbria – a centenary review. Cumbrian Wildlife. *Trans. Carlisle Nat. Hist. Soc.*, **XII**, 27–38.
Clarke, D. J & Hewitt, S. M. (eds) (1996). Cumbrian Wildlife in the Twentieth Century. *Trans. Carlisle Nat. Hist. Soc.*, **XII** (Centenary Volume), 1–134.
Cleasby, I. (1999). *Birds and Boys at Sedbergh*. Privately published, Sedbergh.
Collingwood, W. G. (1932). *The Lake Counties*. Warne, London.
Connor, D. W., Hill, T. O., Little, M. C. & Northen, K. O. (1995). *Marine Nature Conservation Review: Intertidal biotope manual. Version 6.95*. Joint Nature Conservation Committee Report No. 249, Peterborough.
Conolly, A. P. & Dahl, E. (1970). Maximum summer temperature in relation to modern and Quaternary distributions of certain arctic-montane species in the British Isles. In **Walker, D. & West, R. G.** (eds): *Studies in the vegetational history of the British Isles*. pp. 159–223. Cambridge University Press, Cambridge.
Coombes, R. A. H. (1948). The flocking of the Raven. *British Birds*, **41**, 290–295.
Cooper, M. P. & Stanley, C. J. (1990). *Minerals of the English Lake District: Caldbeck Fells*. British Museum (Natural History), London.
Countryside Commission (1986). *The Lake District: A sort of national property*. Countryside Commission & Victoria & Albert Museum, Cheltenham and London.
Crowle, A. (1999). Bird Report 1998. In *Birds and Wildlife in Cumbria*, pp. 3–63. Cumbria Naturalists' Union.
Crowle, A. (2000). Bird Report 1999. In *Birds and Wildlife in Cumbria*, pp. 2–61. Cumbria Naturalists' Union.
Crowle, A. (2001). Bird Report 2000. In *Birds and Wildlife in Cumbria*, pp. 2–65. Cumbria Naturalists' Union.
Cumbria Wildlife Trust (1989). *Reserves Handbook*, CWT, Ambleside.
Day, F. H. (1909). The Coleoptera of Cumberland. Part I. *Trans. Carlisle Nat. Hist. Soc.*, **I**, 122–150.
Day, F. H. (1912). The Coleoptera of Cumberland. Part II. *Trans. Carlisle Nat. Hist. Soc.*, **II**, 201–256.
Day, F. H. (1923). The Coleoptera of Cumberland. Part III. Conclusion. *Trans. Carlisle Nat. Hist. Soc.*, **III**, 70–107.
Day, F. H. (1933). Further addenda

to the Coleoptera of Cumberland. *Trans. Carlisle Nat. Hist. Soc.*, V, 117–125.

Day, F. H. (1943). The present status of Cumberland butterflies. *The North Western Naturalist*, **18**, 284–289.

Day, F. H. (junr) (1928). Some notes on the minerals of Caldbeck Fells. *Trans. Carlisle Nat. Hist. Soc.*, **IV**, 66–79.

Dunlop, E. B. (1912). The Natural History of the Peregrine Falcon. *Trans. Carlisle Nat. Hist. Soc.*, **II**, 89–93.

Dunlop, E. B. (1902–1914). Unpublished MS Diaries in the Alexander Library, Edward Grey Institute, University of Oxford.

Dyer, A., Lindsay, S. & Lusby, P. (2001). The fall and rise of Oblong Woodsia in Britain. *Bot. J. Scotl.*, **53**, 107–120.

Eddy, A., Welch, D. & Rawes, M. (1969). The vegetation of the Moor House National Nature Reserve in the Northern Pennines, England. *Vegetatio*, **16**, 239–284.

Elkington, T. T. (1963). Biological Flora of the British Isles: Gentiana verna L. *J. Ecol.*, 51, 755–767.

Elkington, T. T. (1964). Biological flora of the British Isles: *Myosotis alpestris* F W Schmidt. *J. Ecol.*, **52**, 709–722.

Ford, E. B. (1945). *Butterflies.* New Naturalist. Collins, London.

Friends of the Lake District (FLD) (2000). Report and Newsletter, Spring 2000, Kendal.

Friends of the Lake District (2001). Report and Newsletter, Spring 2001, Kendal.

Fryer, G. (1986). Notes on the breeding biology of the Buzzard. *British Birds*, **79**, 18–28.

Fryer, G. (1991). *A Natural History of the Lakes, Tarns and Streams of the English Lake District.* The Freshwater Biological Association, Ambleside.

Fryer, G. (2001). Conservation, meddling and realism. *Cumbrian Wildlife*, **59**, 30–31.

Fuller, R. J. (1995). *Bird life of woodland and forest.* Cambridge University Press, Cambridge.

Garnett, M. (1946). Winter Birds on Windermere. *Trans. Carlisle Nat. Hist. Soc.*, **7**, 49–70.

Garnett, M. (1907–1972). Unpublished diaries and records. Tullie House Museum, Carlisle.

Garnett, M. & Milne, M. M. (1967). A preliminary list of the marine Mollusca of Lakeland. *Trans. Carlisle Nat. Hist. Soc.*, **XI**, 7–47.

Gibbons, D. W., Reid, J. B. & Chapman, R. A. (1993). *The New Atlas of Breeding Birds in Britain and Ireland.* Poyser, London.

Gibbons, R. (1997). Reserve Focus. Roudsea Wood and Mosses NNR, Cumbria. *British Wildlife*, **8**, 245–247.

Gilbert, O. (2000). *Lichens.* New Naturalist, 86. HarperCollins, London.

Godwin, H. & Clapham, A. R. (1951). Peat Deposits on Cross Fell, Cumberland. *New Phytol.*, **50**, 167.

Godwin, H., Walker, D. & Willis, E. H. (1957). Radiocarbon dating and post-glacial vegetational history: Scaleby Moss. *Proc. Roy. Soc., B*, 352–366.

Graham, R. (1928). Local Wildfowl (Ducks and Geese). *Trans. Carlisle Nat. Hist. Soc.*, **IV**, 80–104.

Graham, R. (1933). The Roe Deer in Cumberland. *Trans. Carlisle Nat. Hist. Soc.*, **V**, 104–116.

Graham, R. (1946). The Badger in Cumberland. *Trans. Carlisle Nat. Hist. Soc.*, **VII**, 88–99.

Graham, R. (1993). *A Border*

Naturalist. Bookcase, Carlisle.
Halliday, G. (1997). *A Flora of Cumbria.* University of Lancaster, Lancaster.
Hatcher, P. E. *The Netted Carpet.* Leaflet. University of Reading, Reading.
Hatcher, P. E. & Alexander, K. N. A. (1994). The status and conservation of the netted carpet *Eustroma reticulatum* (Denis & Schiffermüller, 1775) (Lepidoptera: Geometridae), a threatened moth species in Britain. *Biol. Cons.,* **67**, 41–47.
Heaton Cooper, W. (1938). *The Hills of Lakeland.* Warne, London.
Heaton Cooper, W. (1960). *The Tarns of Lakeland.* Warne, London.
Heaton Cooper, W. (1966). *The Lakes.* Warne, London.
Hervey, G. A. K. & Barnes, J. A. G. (1970). *Natural History of the Lake District.* Warne, London.
Hewitt, S. (ed.) (1993–2001). *The Carlisle Naturalist,* Vols 1–8. Carlisle Natural History Society.
Hewitt, S. (1993). Grasshoppers and Crickets in Cumbria. Provisional Distribution Maps. Tullie House, Carlisle.
Hewitt, S. (1996). Carlisle Natural History Society – the first hundred years. *Trans Carlisle Nat. Hist. Soc.,* **XII**, 107–125.
Hewitt, S. (1999a). Putting Cumbria's mammals on the map. Provisional Atlas. Tullie House, Carlisle.
Hewitt, S. (1999b). Butterflies in Cumbria. Provisional Atlas. Tullie House, Carlisle.
Hirons, G. (1980). The significance of roding by Woodcock *Scolopax rusticola*: an alternative explanation based on observations of marked birds. *Ibis,* **122**, 350–354.
Hodgson, W. (1898). *Flora of Cumberland.* Meals & Co, Carlisle.
Holdgate, M. W. (1955a). The vegetation of some springs and wet flushes on Tarn Moor near Orton, Westmorland. *Journal of Ecology,* **43**, 80–89.
Holdgate, M. W. (1955b). The vegetation of some British upland fens. *Journal of Ecology,* **43**, 389–403.
Hollingworth, S. E. (1934). Some solifluction phenomena in the northern part of the Lake District. *Proc. Geol. Assoc.,* **45**, 167.
Hope, L. E. (1909). Gulls and Diving Birds of the Solway. *Trans. Carlisle Nat. Hist. Soc.,* **I**, 75–97.
Hope, L. E. (1912). The Ducks and Geese (Anseres) of the Solway. *Trans. Carlisle Nat. Hist. Soc.,* **II**, 184–200.
Horne, G. (1996). Birds of Prey in Cumbria. Cumbrian Wildlife. *Trans. Carlisle Nat. Hist. Soc.,* **XII**, 51–75.
Horne, G. & Fielding, A. H. (in press). The recovery of the Peregrine Falcon *Falco peregrinus* in Cumbria, 1966–1999. *Bird Study.*
Jenkinson, H. I. (1885). *Practical Guide to the English Lake District.* 8th edition. Edward Stanford, London.
Johnson, G. A. L. & Dunham, K. C. (1963). The Geology of Moor House: a National Nature Reserve in North-east Westmorland. *Monographs of the Nature Conservancy,* No. 2, HMSO, London.
Johnston, T. L. (1909). The Wading Birds of the Solway. *Trans Carlisle Nat. Hist. Soc.,* **I**, 49–62.
Johnston, T. L. (1933). The Barnacle Goose on the English Solway. *Trans. Carlisle Nat. Hist. Soc.,* **V**, 67–82.
Johnston, T. L. (1936). Nesting habits of the Willow Tit in

Cumberland. *British Birds*, **29**, 378–80.

Johnston, T. L. (1946). The Grey Lag goose in Cumberland. Lakeland Natural History, *Trans. Carlisle Nat. Hist. Soc.*, **VII**, 75–87.

Johnston, T. L. (1954). The Greater Black-backed Gull on the Cumberland Solway. Lakeland Ornithology, *Trans. Carlisle Nat. Hist. Soc.*, **VIII**, 8–13.

Kernan, M., Hall, J., Ullyet, J. & Allott, T. (2001). Variation in freshwater critical loads across two upland catchments in the UK: implications for catchment scale management. *Water, Air and Soil Pollution*, **130**, 1169–1174.

Key, R. (1996). Beetles and beetle recording in Cumbria. Cumbrian Wildlife. *Trans. Carlisle Nat. Hist. Soc.*, **XII**, 39–50.

Kydd, W. & Hewitt, S. (eds) (2000). *A Checklist of the Butterflies and larger Moths of Cumbria*. Carlisle City Council, Carlisle.

Leach, W. (1925). Two relict upland oakwoods in Cumberland. *J. Ecol.*, **13**, 289–300.

Leach, W. (1930). A preliminary account of the vegetation of some non-calcareous screes. *J. Ecol.*, **18**, 321–32.

Lewis, F. J. (1904). Geographical distribution of the vegetation of the basins of the rivers Eden, Tees, Wear and Tyne. Parts I & II. *Geogr. J.*, **23**, p. 313; **24**, p. 267.

Littlewood, N. (2000). Breeding Eiders *Somateria mollissima* in Cumbria, 1949–2000. In *Birds and Wildlife in Cumbria*, pp. 62–65. Cumbria Naturalists' Union.

Lumb, C. (2000). Biodiversity beneath the waves: Cumbria's marine wildlife heritage. *Cumbrian Wildlife*, **58**, 11–17.

Macpherson, H. A. (1892). *A Vertebrate Fauna of Lakeland*. David Douglas, Edinburgh.

Macpherson, H. A. (1902). Mammals, in the *Victoria County History of Cumberland*, Archibald Constable, London.

Macpherson, H. A. & Duckworth, W. (1886). *The Birds of Cumberland*. Thurnam, Carlisle.

Manley, G. (1945). The Helm Wind of Cross Fell, 1937–39. *Quart. Journ. Roy. Met. Soc.*, **71**, 197–219.

Manley, G. (1952). *Climate and the British Scene*. New Naturalist. Collins, London.

Manley, G. (1973). Climate, in **Pearsall, W. H. & Pennington, W.**, *The Lake District*. pp 106–120, Collins, London.

Marr, J. E. (1916). *The Geology of the Lake District*. Cambridge University Press, Cambridge.

Marren, P. (1994). *England's National Nature Reserves*. Poyser, London.

Mawby, F. J. & Armstrong, R. (1995). *Breeding waders in Lowland Wet Grasslands in Cumbria*. Cumbria Bird Club.

McAlone, D., Carrier, M., Makin, B. & Milligan, K. (1997). Cumbria Bird Club Rookery Survey: April 1996. *Birds and Wildlife in Cumbria*, 1996, 71–76.

Meteorological Office (1952). *Climatological Atlas of the British Isles*. HMSO, London.

Milligan, K. (2001). Reserve focus – Drumburgh Moss National Nature Reserve. *Cumbrian Wildlife*, **59**, 8–10.

Mitchell, W. R. & Delap, P. (1974). *Lakeland Mammals – a visitors' handbook*. Dalesman, Clapham.

Morecambe Bay Partnership (1996). *Morecambe Bay Strategy: draft topic papers for fisheries, pollution and wildlife working group.*

Moseley, F. (1978). *The geology of the Lake District*. Yorkshire Geological

Society Occasional Publication No. 3.

Murray, J. (1909). A Byegone Cumberland Naturalist. A Memoir of T C Heysham. *Trans. Carlisle Nat. Hist. Soc.*, **I**, 1–12.

Murray, J. (1909). The Land and Freshwater Shells of Cumberland. *Trans. Carlisle Nat. Hist. Soc.*, **I**, 114–121.

Murray, J. (1926). Cumberland Sphagna. *The North Western Naturalist*, **I**, 83–84.

Murray, J. (1926–1934). Cumberland Mosses. *The North Western Naturalist*, **I**, 215–216; II, 101, 258–259; III, 42–43, 91–92, 141; IV, 24–25, 73, 137, 194–195; V, 41–42, 113–114, 186–187, 254; VI, 31, 100–101, 166–167, 231–232; VIII, 53–54, 141–142, 49–250, 331: XI, 58–59, 161, 281–282, 386–388.

Murray, J. (1928). William Hodgson, ALS, Botanist. *Trans. Carlisle Nat. Hist. Soc.*, **IV**, 1–15.

Murray, J. (1935–1937). Cumberland Hepaticae. *The North Western Naturalist*, **X**, 49–50, 144, 267, 363; XI, 56, 165, 276, 365–366; XII, 62–63.

Nature Conservancy Council (1986). *Nature conservation and afforestation in Britain*. NCC, Peterborough.

Naylor, G. (1996). Cumbrian Butterflies since 1893. Cumbrian Wildlife. *Trans. Carlisle Nat. Hist. Soc.*, **XII**, 15–26.

Nethersole-Thompson, D. (1973). *The Dotterel*. Collins, London.

Nurse, E. J. (1936). The moth *Argyroploce penthinana* Guen. on *Impatiens noli-tangere*. *North Western Naturalist*, 11, 339–40.

Patterson, A. H. (1929). *Wildfowlers and Poachers*. Methuen, London.

Pearsall, W. H. (1918). The aquatic and marsh vegetation of Esthwaite Water. *J. Ecol.*, **6**, 53–74.

Pearsall, W. H. (1921). The Development of Vegetation in the English Lakes, considered in relation to the general evolution of glacial lakes and rock basins. *Proc. Roy. Soc. B*, **92**, 259–284.

Pearsall, W. H. (1950). *Mountains and Moorlands*. New Naturalist, Collins, London.

Pearsall, W. H. & Pennington, W. (1947). Ecological history of the English Lake District. *J. Ecol.*, **34**, 137–148.

Pearsall, W. H. & Pennington, W. (1973). *The Lake District*. New Naturalist. Collins, London.

Pennington, W. (1991). Palaeolimnology in the English Lakes – some questions and answers over fifty years. *Hydrobiologia*, **214**, 9–24.

Pennington, W. (1997). Vegetational History. In **Halliday, G.** *A Flora of Cumbria*, pp. 42–50. University of Lancaster, Lancaster.

Perring, F. H. & Walters, S. M. (1962). *Atlas of the British Flora*. Nelson, London and Edinburgh.

Peterken, G. F. (1996). **Natural Woodland**. Cambridge University Press, Cambridge.

Philipson, M. (1954). North-eastern bird studies: the Curlew and the Black Grouse. *Trans. Carlisle Nat. Hist. Soc.*, **VIII**, 14–22.

Pigott, C. D. (2001). Living History. *Conserving Lakeland. The magazine of the Friends of the Lake District*. No 37, 14–17.

Pigott, C. D. & Wilson, J. F. (1978). The vegetation of North Fen at Esthwaite in 1967–9. *Proc. Roy. Soc. Lond. A*, **200**, 331–351.

Pigott, C. D. & Huntley, J. P. (1978). Factors controlling the distribution of *Tilia cordata* at the northern limits of its geographical range. I Distribution in Northwest England. *New Phytologist*, **81**,

429–441.
Prater, A. J. (1981). *Estuary Birds of Britain and Ireland*. Poyser, Calton.
Pritchard, D. E., Housden, S. D., Mudge, G. P., Galbraith, C. A. & Pienkowski, M. W. (1992). *Important Bird Areas in the United Kingdom, including the Channel Islands and Isle of Man*. RSPB, Sandy.
Pullen, O. J. (1942). A Dumfriesshire gullery. *Trans. & Proc. Dumfr. & Gall. Nat. Hist. & Ant. Soc.*, **22**, 1938–40.
Ratcliffe, D. A. (1960). The Mountain Flora of Lakeland. *Proc. Bot. Soc. Brit. Isles*, **4**, 1–25.
Ratcliffe, D. A. (1962). Breeding density in the Peregrine *Falco peregrinus* and Raven *Corvus corax*. *Ibis*, **104**, 13–39.
Ratcliffe, D. A. (1970). Changes attributable to pesticides in egg breakage frequency and eggshell thickness in some British birds. *J. Appl. Ecol.*, **7**, 67–115.
Ratcliffe, D. A. (1976). Observations on the breeding of the Golden Plover in Great Britain. *Bird Study*, **23**, 63–116.
Ratcliffe, D. A. (ed.) (1977). *A Nature Conservation Review*. Cambridge University Press, Cambridge.
Ratcliffe, D. A. (1993). *The Peregrine Falcon*. Second edition. Poyser, London.
Ratcliffe, D. A. (1996). Ernest Blezard (1902–1970). Lakeland Wildlife. *Trans. Carlisle Nat. Hist. Soc.*, **XII**, 127–132.
Ratcliffe, D. A. (1997). *The Raven*. Poyser, London.
Ratcliffe, D. A. (2000). *In Search of Nature*. Peregrine Books, Leeds.
Ratcliffe, D. A. & Eddy, A. (1960). *Alopecurus alpinus* Sm. in Britain. *Proc. Bot. Soc. Brit. Isles*, **3**, 389–91.
Raven, J. & Walters, M. (1956). *Mountain Flowers*. New Naturalist, No. 33. Collins, London.
Rawnsley, H. D. (1899). *Life and Nature at the English Lakes*. James MacLehose, Glasgow.
Ritchie, J. (1920). *The influence of Man on animal life in Scotland*. Cambridge University Press, Cambridge.
Robinson, N. A. (2000). Status of the Red Wood Ant (*Formica rufa* L.) in Cumbria. *The Carlisle Naturalist*, **8**, 24–28.
Robinson, N. A. (2000). A survey of bees at Heathwaite (National Trust), Arnside, in 1998. *The Carlisle Naturalist*, **8**, 40–48.
Rodwell, J. (1991–2000). *British Plant Communities*.
Vol 1 (1991a). *Woodlands and scrub*.
Vol 2 (1991b). *Mires and heaths*.
Vol 3 (1992). *Grasslands and montane communities*.
Vol 4 (1995). *Aquatic communities, swamps and tall-herb fens*.
Vol 5 (2000). *Maritime communities and vegetation of open habitats*.
Cambridge University Press, Cambridge.
Routledge, G. B. (1909). The Butterflies of Cumberland. *Trans. Carlisle Nat. Hist. Soc.*, **I**, 98–113.
Routledge, G. B. (1912). The Lepidoptera of Cumberland (Part II, Moths). *Trans Carlisle Nat. Hist. Soc.*, **II**, 94–183.
Routledge, G. B. (1923). The Lepidoptera of Cumberland (Part III, Geometrae). *Trans. Carlisle Nat. Hist. Soc.*, **III**, 40–69.
Routledge, G. B. (1933). The Lepidoptera of Cumberland. Additional Species and Further Records. *Trans. Carlisle Nat. Hist. Soc.*, **V**, 126–143.
RSPB/BTO (1999). Lapwing numbers fall across England and Wales. RSPB/BTO News Release, 17 February 1999.
**Rumsey, F. J., Jermy, A. C. &

Sheffield, E. (1998). The independent gametophytic stage of *Trichomanes speciosum* Willd. (Hymenophyllaceae), the Killarney Fern and its distribution in the British Isles. *Watsonia*, **22**, 1–19.

Shackleton, E. H. (1966). *Lakeland Geology*. Dalesman Publishing Co., Clapham.

Sharrock, J. T. R. (1976). *The Atlas of Breeding Birds in Britain and Ireland*. British Trust for Ornithology, Tring.

Simpson, D. (2001). Whatever happened to the Ravenglass gullery? *British Wildlife*, **12**, 153–162.

Singleton, F. (1954). *The English Lakes*. Batsford, London.

Smith, A. G. (1959). The mires of south-western Westmorland: stratigraphy and pollen analysis. *New Phytol.*, **58**, 105.

Smith, R. A. (2000). Jonathan Otley: A pioneer of Lakeland geology. *Geology Today*, **16**, 31–34.

Solway Firth Partnership (1996). *Solway Firth Review*.

Steers, J. A. (1946). *The Coastline of England and Wales*. Cambridge University Press, Cambridge.

Stokoe, R. (1952). Siddick Pond and its Birds. *Trans. Carlisle Nat. Hist. Soc.*, **VIII**, 33–74.

Stokoe, R. (1962). Birds of the Lake Counties. *Trans. Carlisle Nat. Hist. Soc.*, **X**, 7–112.

Stokoe, R. (1983). *Aquatic macrophytes in the tarns and lakes of Cumbria*. Freshwater Biological Association. Occasional Publication No. 18.

Stott, M., Callion, J. C. et al. (2002). *Cumbria Atlas of Breeding Birds*. Cumbria Bird Club, Harrington.

Strachan, R. & Jefferies, D. J. (1996). *Otter Survey of England 1991–1994*. Vincent Wildlife Trust, London.

Strowger, J. (1998). The status and breeding biology of the Dotterel *Charadrius morinellus* in northern England during 1972–95. *Bird Study*, **45**, 85–91.

Sutcliffe, D. W. (1983). Acid precipitation and its effects on aquatic systems in the English Lake District (Cumbria). *Freshwater Biological Association Annual Report*, **51**, 30–62.

Sutcliffe, D. W. & Carrick, T. R. (1988). Alkalinity and pH of tarns and streams in the English Lake District (Cumbria). *Freshwater Biology*, **19**, 179–189.

Symonds, H. H. (1936). *Afforestation in the Lake District*. Dent, London.

Tansley, A. G. (1939). *The British Islands and their Vegetation*. Cambridge University Press, Cambridge.

Taylor, K. (1971). *Rubus chamaemorus*. Biological Flora of the British Isles. *Journal of Ecology*, **59**, 293–306.

Tipping, E. & eight other authors (1998). Reversal of acidification in upland waters of the English Lake District. *Environmental Pollution*, **103**, 143–151.

Tipping, E. & ten other authors (2000). Reversal of acidification in tributaries of the River Duddon (English Lake District) between 1970 and 1998. *Environmental Pollution*, **109**, 183–191.

Tipping, E. & five other authors (in press). Biological responses to the reversal of acidification in surface waters of the English Lake District.

Tubbs, C. R. (1996). Estuary Birds – before the counting began. *British Wildlife*, **7**, 226–235.

Turner, J. (1984). Pollen diagrams from Cross Fell and their implications for former tree-lines. In

Haworth E. Y. & Lund J. G.(eds) *Lake Sediments and Environmental History*, pp. 317–357. Leicester University Press, Leicester.

Uttley, D. (1998). *The Anatomy of the Helm Wind*. Bookcase, Carlisle.

Walker, D. (1966). The late Quaternary history of the Cumberland Lowland. *Philosoph. Trans. Roy. Soc., B*, **251**, 1–210.

Walker, D. (2001). Food Supply and Breeding Performance of the Haweswater Golden Eagles. In *Birds and Wildlife in Cumbria*, January–December 2000, pp. 65–68.

Ward, S. D. & Evans, D. F. (1976). Conservation assessment of British limestone pavements based on floristic criteria. *Biological Conservation*, **9**, 217–233.

Watson, J. (1888). The Ornithology of Skiddaw, Scafell and Helvellyn. *The Naturalist*.

Watson, J. (1888–1889). The Northern Distribution of the Dotterel. *Westmorland Nat. Hist. Record*, **6**, 162–64, 176–79.

Webb, S. (1995). Conservation of limestone pavement. *Cave and Karst Science*, **21**, 97–100.

Webster, J. (1996). Mammals in Cumbria. In **Clarke, D. J. & Hewitt, S. M.** Cumbrian Wildlife in the Twentieth Century. *Trans. Carlisle Nat. Hist. Soc.*, **XII**, 77–88.

Whitehead, P. G., Barlow, J., Haworth, E. J. & Adamson, J. K. (1997). Acidification in Three Lake District Tarns: Historical long-term trends and modelled future behaviour under changing sulphate and nitrate deposition. *Hydrology and Earth System Sciences*, **1**, 197–204.

Wilson, A. (1938). *The Flora of Westmorland*. Privately published, Conway.

Yapp, W. B. (1962). *Birds and Woods*. Oxford University Press, Oxford.

Young, B. (1987). *Glossary of the Minerals of the Lake District and Adjoining Areas*. British Geological Survey, Newcastle-upon-Tyne.

Nomenclature
Scientific and English names

Flowering plants and ferns

Stace, C. (1997). *New Flora of the British Isles. Second edition.* Cambridge University Press, Cambridge.

Mosses and liverworts

Blockeel, T. L. & Long, D. G. (1998). *A Check-list and Census Catalogue of British and Irish Bryophytes*. British Bryological Society, Cardiff.

Lichens

Purvis, O. W., Coppins, B. J., Hawksworth, D. L., James, P. & Moore, D. M. (1992). *The Lichen Flora of Great Britain and Ireland.* The British Lichen Society and Natural History Museum Publications, London

Fungi

Courtecuisse, R. & Duhem, B. (1995). *Mushrooms and Toadstools of Britain and Europe.* Collins Field Guide. HarperCollins, London.

Mammals

Mitchell-Jones, A. J. and nine others. (1999). *The Atlas of European Mammals.* Academic Press, London.

Birds

Cramp, S., Simmons, K. E. L. & Perrins, C. M. (1977–1994). *Handbook of the Birds of Europe, the Middle East and North Africa. The*

Birds of the Western Palaearctic. Oxford University Press, Oxford.

Amphibians and reptiles

Beebee, T. J. C. & Griffiths, R. A. (2000). *Amphibians and Reptiles* New Naturalist 87. HarperCollins, London.

Marine fish

Hayward, P. J. & Ryland, J. S. (eds) (1998). *Handbook of the Marine Fauna of North-West Europe.* Oxford University Press, Oxford.

Freshwater fish

Maitland, P. S. (2000). *Hamlyn guide to freshwater fish of Britain and Europe.* Hamlyn, London.

Butterflies

Asher, J. and five others (2001). *The Millennium Atlas of Butterflies in Britain and Ireland.* Oxford University Press, Oxford.

Moths

Skinner, B. (1984). *Moths of the British Isles.* Penguin Books, Harmondsworth.

Dragonflies

Hammond, C. (1977). *The Dragonflies of Great Britain and Ireland.* Curwen Press, London.

Beetles

Kloet, G. S. & Hinks, W. D. (1977). *A Check List of British Insects (ed. 2) 3. Coleoptera and Strepsiptera.* Royal Entomological Society, London.

Arachnids

Merrett, P. & Murphy, J. A. (2001). A Revised Check-list of British Spiders. *Bulletin of the British Arachnological Society*, 11, 345–358.

Molluscs

Kerney, M. P. (1999). *Atlas of land and freshwater molluscs of Britain and Ireland.* Harley Books, Colchester.

Crustacea

Gledhill, T., Sutcliffe, D. W. & Williams, W. D. (1993). British Freshwater Crustacea Malacostraca: a key with ecological notes. *Scientific publication no. 52.* Freshwater Biological Association, Windermere.

Gazeteer

Two, four or six figure references of the Ordnance Survey National Grid are given, as appropriate. Where the area is extensive, a nearly central one kilometre square is given and the term '& adj.' indicates additional adjoining squares. For a few very extensive areas, the 10 kilometre square is given. Place names shown on the map in Plate 1 are mostly omitted.

Aisgill 34 (SD) 771975
Alston Moor 35 (NY) 73, 74
Anthorn 35 (NY) 200585
Ardale 35 (NY) 6534,6835
Armathwaite 35 (NY) 505460
Armboth Fells 35 (NY) 2915 & adj.
Arnside 34 (SD) 4578
Knott 34 (SD) 456775
Ashgill 35 (NY) 758405
Askam-in-Furness 34 (NY) 2177
Askham Fell 35 (NY) 4922 & adj.

Bampton 35 (NY) 514182
Bannerdale (Mungrisdale) 35 (NY) 3329
Barbon Fells 34 (SD) 6883 & adj.
Baron Wood 35 (NY) 5144
Bassenthwaite 35 (NY) 230322
Baugh Fell 34 (SD) 7492 & adj.
Bewcastle 35 (NY) 565747
Fells 35 (NY) 58
Biglands Bog 35 (NY) 259537
Binsey 35 (NY) 225355
Birk Fell 35 (NY) 4018
Birkdale 35 (NY) 804278
Birkrigg Oaks 35 (NY) 214205
Black Burn (Tindale) 35 (NY) 6155-6358
Black Burn (Cross Fell) 35 (NY) 6935-7143
Black Combe 34 (SD) 1385 & adj.
Black Force 34 (SD) 643991
Blackmoss Pool 35 (NY) 485478

Blaze Fell 35 (NY) 496433
Blea Water 35 (NY) 448107
Blelham Tarn 35 (NY) 365004
Blencathra 35 (NY) 3227
Blindcrake 35 (NY) 148348
Clints 35 (NY) 163353
Bolton Fell 35 (NY) 4968
Borrowdale 35 (NY) 2312-2619
Bowfell 35 (NY) 245065
Bowness Moss (Common) 35 (NY) 2160 & adj.
Bowscale 35 (NY) 359317
Fell 35 (NY) 333306
Tarn 35 (NY) 337313
Brandreth 35 (NY) 215120
Brandygill 35 (NY) 322332
Braystones Tarn 35 (NY) 003060
Brigsteer 34 (SD) 481895
Wood 34 (SD) 487883
Brotherswater 35 (NY) 402127
Brown Cove 35 (NY) 342157
Brown Gill 35 (NY) 264048
Bullman Hills 35 (NY) 706374
Burgh Marsh 35 (NY) 3060 & adj.
Burnhope Seat 35 (NY) 7837
Burnmoor Tarn 35 (NY) 184044
Burns Beck Moss 34 (SD) 594878
Butterburn 35 (NY) 676744
Flow 35 (NY) 6776

Caerlaverock 35 (NY) 0364 & adj.
Caldbeck Fells 35 (NY) 3135 & adj.

Caldew, River 35 (NY) 2929-3956
Calf 34 (SD) 667971
Campfield Marsh 35 (NY) 185610
Cardew Mires 35 (NY) 345507
Cardurnock 35 (NY) 172588
Carrock Fell 35 (NY) 342337
Castle Carrock Reservoir 35 (NY) 543546
Cash Force 35 (NY) 701837
Catstye Cam 35 (NY) 348158
Caudbeck Flow 35 (NY) 5872
Cauldron Snout 35 (NY) 814286
Cautley Spout 34 (SD) 682975
Cavendish Dock 34 (SD) 213683
Chapelcross power station 35 (NY) 216697
Christianbury Crags 35 (NY) 598823
Claife Heights 34 (SD) 3797 & adj.
Clawthorpe Fell 34 (SD) 540788
Cliburn Moss 35 (NY) 577256
Clints Quarry (Egremont) 35 (NY) 008124
Clints Quarry (Moota) 35 (NY) 158364
Cold Fell 35 (NY) 606556
Combe Crag (Irthing) 35 (NY) 591649
Coniston Fells 34 (SD) 2999 & adj.
Old Man 34 (SD) 272978

Water 34 (SD) 3094 & adj.
Coombs Wood 35 (NY) 5144
Crag Hill (Pennines) 34 (SD) 692833
Cramel Linn 35 (NY) 640697
Croglin Water 35 (NY) 5342-6346
Cross Fell 35 (NY) 687343
Crowdundle Beck 35 (NY) 6531-6933
Cumwhitton Moss 35 (NY) 515520
Cunswick Scar 34 (SD) 491940
Tarn 34 (SD) 490938

Dalegarth Force (Stanley Gill) 34 (SD) 173996
Dentdale 34 (SD) 7286 & adj.
Denton Fell 35 (NY) 6262 & adj.
Derwent, River 35 (NY) 0029-2515
Devoke Water 34 (SD) 158970
Dove Crags (Grasmoor) 35 (NY) 177205
Dove Crag (Hartsop) 35 (NY) 376110
Drigg Dunes 34 (SD) 0696 & adj.
Drumburgh 35 (NY) 263599
Moss 35 (NY) 2558
Dubmill Point 35 (NY) 076458
Duddon
   River 34 (SD) 2087-35 (NY) 2602
   Estuary 34 (SD) 2081 & adj.
   Valley (Dunnerdale) 34 (SD) 1988-35 (NY) 2401
Dufton 35 (NY) 690251
   Fell 35 (NY) 7428 & adj.
Dukedale 35 (NY) 812053
Dykesfield 35 (NY) 308592

Easedale Tarn 35 (NY) 307087
Ease Gill 34 (NY) 6680 & adj.
Eden
   Gorge 35 (NY) 5044-5341
   River 35 (NY) 3561-34 (SD) 7998
   Valley 35 (NY) 4654-34 (SD) 7796
Ehen, River 35 (NY) 0203-0815
Ellen, River 35 (NY) 0336-2535
Ennerdale 35 (NY) 1413 & adj.
Eskdale 34 (SD) 1095-35 (NY) 2206
Esk, River (Lakes) 34 (SD) 1095-35 (NY) 2307
Esk, River (Border) 35 (NY) 3464-3873
Eskmeals 34 (SD) 0893 & adj.
Esthwaite Water 34 (SD) 3596
Eycott Hill 35 (NY) 3829

Fairfield 35 (NY) 359118
Farleton Knott 34 (SD) 5480
Faulds Brow 35 (NY) 2940
Fell End Clouds 34 (SD) 7399
Fingland 35 (NY) 256571
Finglandrigg Woods 35 (NY) 2756-2857
Fleetwith 35 (NY) 2113
Flookburgh Marsh 34 (SD) 3573 & adj.
Force Crag 35 (NY) 197215
Foul Bog 35 (NY) 596775
Foulney Island 34 (SD) 2464
Foulshaw Moss 34 (SD) 4582

Gaitbarrows 34 (SD) 482774
Garrigill 35 (NY) 745416
Garsdale 34 (SD) 7489 & adj.
Gelt
   River 35 (NY) 4758-6250
   Woods 35 (NY) 5258
Geltsdale 35 (NY) 5456-6250
Glasson Moss 35 (NY) 2360
Glencoyne 35 (NY) 387190
   Park 35 (NY) 3819
   Wood 35 (NY) 383183
Glenridding 35 (NY) 387170
Gowbarrow 35 (NY) 410210
Gowk Bank 35 (NY) 680737
Grasmoor 35 (NY) 175204
Great Asby Scar 35 (NY) 6509 & adj.
Great Gable 35 (NY) 211103
Great Calva 35 (NY) 291312
Great Dodd 35 (NY) 342205
Great Dun Fell 35 (NY) 710322
Great End 35 (NY) 227084
Great Mell Fell 35 (NY) 397254
Great Orton 35 (NY) 328541
Great Wood 35 (NY) 2721
Greendale Tarn 35 (NY) 147075
Greta, River 35 (NY) 2523-2924
Greystoke Park 35 (NY) 4032 & adj.
Grizedale Forest 34 (SD) 3394 & adj.
Grune Point 35 (NY) 1356

Hale Moss 34 (SD) 505775
Hallsenna Moor 35 (NY) 063005
Hartside 35 (NY) 647418
Harter Fell (Mardale) 35 (NY) 460093
Haverigg 34 (SD) 1478
Hayeswater 35 (NY) 431122
Helbeck Woods 35 (NY) 7816
Hell Gill (Eden) 34 (SD) 787969
Helvellyn 35 (NY) 341151
High Cup
   Dale 35 (NY) 7325
   Nick 35 (NY) 747263
   Scars 35 (NY) 7425
High Pike 35 (NY) 319350
High Street Fells 35 (NY) 4411
Hobcarton Crag 35 (NY) 215142
Hodbarrow 34 (SD) 182782
Honister 35 (NY) 225136
   Crag 35 (NY) 215142
Howgill Fells 34 (SD) 6797 & adj.

Humphrey Head 34 (SD) 3973, 3974
Hutton Roof Crags 34 (SD) 5577 & adj.

Inglewood Forest 35 (NY) 4539 & adj.
Ings, The 35 (NY) 268221
Irthing, R 35 (NY) 4959-6178
  Gorge 35 (NY) 6368, 6369
Irthinghead 35 (NY) 629784
Irongill Wood 35 (NY) 343453

Johnby Moor 35 (NY) 410343
Johnny's Wood 35 (NY) 253143

Kent
  Estuary 34 (SD) 4680 & adj.
  River 34 (SD) 4884-35 (NY) 4408
Kentmere 35 (NY) 456041
Keppelcove 35 (NY) 3416
Kershope Burn 35 (NY) 4782-5689
Keskadale Oakwood 35 (NY) 207196
Kielder 35 (NY) 627935
Killington Reservoir 34 (SD) 590910
King Harry 35 (NY) 5349 & adj.
King Water 35 (NY) 5263-6072
Kingmoor Nature Reserve 35 (NY) 388585
Kirkby Moor 34 (SD) 2583 & adj.
Kirkland 35 (NY) 646325
Knock Fell 35 (NY) 722303
Knock Ore Gill 35 (NY) 7030, 7130

Lamonby 35 (NY) 409359
Lancaster Canal 34 (SD) 5276-5285
Langdale
  Great 35 (NY) 2806 & adj.
  Little 35 (NY) 3103
  Pikes 35 (NY) 273073, 282074

Langstrath 35 (NY) 2712 & adj.
Launchy Gill 35 (NY) 307157
Lazonby Fell 35 (NY) 5139 & adj.
Leven
  Estuary 34 (SD) 3379 & adj.
  River 34 (SD) 3283-3786
Liddel, River 35 (NY) 4074-5998
Little Dun Fell 35 (NY) 704330
Little Fell 35 (NY) 7821, 7822
Lodge Haggs 35 (NY) 8002
Lodore
  Falls 35 (NY) 264185
  Woods 35 (NY) 2618
Longsleddale 35 (NY) 4708-5100
Low Tarn 35 (NY) 162093
Loweswater 35 (NY) 1221
Low Wood (Hartsop) 35 (NY) 3912
Lune, River 34 (SD) 6178-7005
Lyne, River 35 (NY) 3665-4972
  Black 35 (NY) 4973-5685
  White 35 (NY) 5578-5881
Lyth Valley 34 (SD) 4688 & adj.

Maize Beck 35 (NY) 7427-8128
Mallerstang 35 (NY) 7705-34 (SD) 7796
Mardale 35 (NY) 4610 & adj.
Martindale 35 (NY) 4316 & adj.
Martin Tarn 35 (NY) 258516
Matterdale Common 35 (NY) 3522 & adj.
Mawbray 35 (NY) 080470
Meathop Moss 34 (SD) 4481
Melbreak 35 (NY) 1419
Melmerby Fell 35 (NY) 652380
Mickle Fell 35 (NY) 803243
Middlebarrow 34 (SD) 463767

Middleton Fells 34 (SD) 6586 & adj.
Midgeholme 35 (NY) 637588
Monkhill Lough 35 (NY) 338583
Moorthwaite Moss 35 (NY) 512510
Moorthwaite Tarn 35 (NY) 292485
Moor House National Nature Reserve 35 (NY) 758328 & adj.
Moss Catherine waterfall 35 (NY) 685731
Muncaster Fell 34 (SD) 1198

Naddle Forest 35 (NY) 5015 & adj.
Newlands Vale 35 (NY) 2320 & adj.
Newton Marsh 35 (NY) 1855-2057
Newton Reigny Moss 35 (NY) 478308
Newtown Common 35 (NY) 3735
Nunnery Walks 35 (NY) 5342

Orton Woods (Carlisle) 35 (NY) 340545
Oulton Moss 35 (NY) 253514

Pavey Ark 35 (NY) 284079
Penrith Beacon 35 (NY) 5231
Penton Linns 35 (NY) 430773
Petteril, R 35 (NY) 4156-4429
Pillar 35 (NY) 171121
Port Carlisle 35 (NY) 240622

Raven Crag (Thirlmere) 35 (NY) 304188
Red Tarn 35 (NY) 348152
Riggindale 35 (NY) 4411-4611
Robinson 35 (NY) 203170
Rockcliffe 35 (NY) 359617
  Marsh 35 (NY) 3263 & adj.

Moss 35 (NY) 374626
Roudsea Mosses 34 (SD) 3382, 3481
  Wood 34 (SD) 330820
Roughtengill 35 (NY) 3034-3036
Rundale 35 (NY) 6927-7127
Rusland Moss 34 (SD) 335886
Rydal 35 (NY) 364062

Salta Moss 35 (NY) 085450
Sandford Mire 35 (NY) 720170
Sandscale Haws (Roanhead) 34 (SD) 1875 & adj.
Scafell 35 (NY) 207065
Scafell Pike 35 (NY) 215072
Scaleby Moss 35 (NY) 433635
Scales Tarn 35 (NY) 329081
Scales Wood 35 (NY) 165165
Scoat Tarn 35 (NY) 159103
Scordale 35 (NY) 7521-7623
Scout Scar 34 (SD) 486913
Seathwaite (Borrowdale) 35 (NY) 235121
Seathwaite Tarn 34 (SD) 253987
Seatoller Woods 35 (NY) 242134
Sedbergh 34 (SD) 6592
Shap Fells 35 (NY) 5208 & adj.
Siddick Pond 35 (NY) 001302
Sighty Crag 35 (NY) 601809
Silverdale 34 (SD) 4675
Skiddaw 35 (NY) 260291
  Forest 35 (NY) 2930 & adj.
Skinburness 35 (NY) 127559
  Marsh 35 (NY) 1455
Skirwith Fell 35 (NY) 679354
Smardale 35 (NY) 728073
Solway Moss 35 (NY) 3469 & adj.

Viaduct 35 (NY) 212627
Spadeadam Waste 35 (NY) 67
Sprinkling Tarn 35 (NY) 228091
St John's Vale 35 (NY) 3120-3123
Stainmore 35 (NY) 8516 & adj.
Sunbiggin Tarn 35 (NY) 677077
  Moor 35 (NY) 665076
Sunday Burn Linns 35 (NY) 687733
Swarth Fell 34 (SD) 756967
Swindale (Brough) 35 (NY) 8016
Swindale (Shap) 35 (NY) 4911-5214

Tailbridge Hill 35 (NY) 803055
Talkin Tarn 35 (NY) 546587
Tarn Moss 35 (NY) 400275
Tarn Wadling 35 (NY) 485445
Tees, River 35 (NY) 7034-8128
Temple Sowerby Moss 35 (NY) 617270
Terrybank Tarn 34 (SD) 592825
Thornthwaite 35 (NY) 2225 & adj.
Thurstonfield 35 (NY) 316567
  Lough 35 (NY) 320563
Tindale 35 (NY) 617593
  Fells 35 (NY) 65
  Tarn 35 (NY) 605587

Underlaid Wood 34 (SD) 485795
Unity Bog 35 (NY) 528590
Upper Teesdale 35 (NY) 73
Urswick Tarn 34 (SD) 270745

Walney North 34 (SD) 1773 & adj.
Walney South 34 (SD) 2362 & adj.

Walby Moor (White Moss) 35 (NY) 460608
Walton Moss 35 (NY) 5066 & adj.
Walton Wood 35 (NY) 550653
Wampool, River 35 (NY) 2157-3242
Wan Fell 35 (NY) 5136 & adj.
Warcop Fell 35 (NY) 7820 & adj.
Wasdale Screes 35 (NY) 1504 & adj.
Watendlath 35 (NY) 276163
Watermillock 35 (NY) 446225
Waver, River 35 (NY) 1753-2941
Wedholme Flow 35 (NY) 2152 & adj.
Wet Sleddale 35 (NY) 5109-5511
Whernside 34 (SD) 738814
Whinfell 35 (NY) 5727
Whinlatter 35 (NY) 1924 & adj.
Whins Pond 35 (NY) 555307
Whitbarrow Scar 34 (SD) 4486 & adj.
Whitbeck Moss 34 (SD) 112842
Whiteside (Helvellyn) 35 (NY) 338167
Whiteside (Lorton) 35 (NY) 170220
Wild Boar Fell 34 (SD) 758987
Winster, River 34 (SD) 4290-4279
Witherslack 34 (SD) 433837
  Moss 34 (SD) 433822
Wragmire Moss 35 (NY) 456493
Wythop Woods 35 (NY) 2128 & adj.

Yad Moss 35 (NY) 7735 & adj.
Yewbarrow 34 (SD) 432850

General Index

Abraham, G.D. 47
acidification 115, 184, 185, 195, 196, 212, 301, 321, 323
afforestation 13, 33, 109, 130, 133, 153, 154, 160, 169–71, 272, 288, 290, 292, 295, 296–302, 304
agriculture 12, 14, 31–3, 92, 100, 105, 109, 125, 132, 165, 252, 303
Aisgill 23, 250
alderwood 65, 179, 211, 279, 283
algal blooms 194, 301
Allonby 45, 80, 84, 98, 104, 136,
alpine flora 221–6, 262–7
Alston 12, 14, 28, 32, 37, 48, 143, 249, 250, 252, 267, 279, 307
  Block 23, 25
  Moor 34, 256, 264, 266, 270, 277
altitude effects 14–19, 20, 32, 214, 216, 272, 278
Ambleside 19, 179, 187, 194,
amphibians 78, 98, 99, 163, 245, 279, 296,
Anthorn 47, 309
Appleby 15, 100, 112, 143
  Fells 40
aquatic plants 41, 194, 198
arachnids 46, 56, 164, 331–3
Ardale 24, 259, 265
Areas Of Outstanding Natural Beauty (AONBs) 310
Armathwaite 26, 111, 112, 118, 123
Armboth Fells 40, 208, 210, 211, 227, 242, 243, 247, 317
Arnside 117, 148, 149, 164, 309
  Knott 23, 148, 149, 163, 164
Ashgill 250
Askham Fell 242, 243
Askrigg Block 23
Aspatria 27, 197

aspect effects 19, 182, 184, 216
Atlantic flora 178, 180–4
Atlas of the British Flora 41
Atlas of Breeding Birds in Britain and Ireland 70
(*New*) *Atlas of Breeding Birds in Britain and Ireland* 69, 70, 89

Backhouse, J. jnr. 35, 36, 217, 225, 260, 264
Backhouse, J. snr. 35, 36, 264
Baker, J.G. 36
Bampton 20, 23, 159
Bannerdale (Mungrisdale) 20, 211
Barbon Fells 21–3, 249, 272
Barnes, J.A.G. 40, 54
Baron Wood 47, 107, 109, 112, 120, 123, 143
barrage-scheme proposals 311, 312
Barrow-in-Furness 14, 15, 27, 79, 81, 100, 197, 307, 311
Bassenthwaite 104
  Lake 142, 167, 170, 178, 193, 195, 199, 201–3, 313
  Marshes 167, 201
bats 56, 103, 104, 166, 201, 320
Baugh Fell 23, 249, 271, 272, 275
beetles 46, 56, 124, 164, 206, 247, 248
Ben Nevis 16, 17
Bewcastle (Fells) 25, 26, 52, 116, 127–9, 132, 139, 282–8, 290–3, 296, 297, 302
Biglands Bog 137, 138
Binsey 20, 243
birch woods 111, 112, 121, 128, 136, 138
bird-ringing 51, 54, 56, 96
birds 42–5, 47–57, 66–78, 86–91, 93–7, 104–7, 110, 111, 119–23, 132–4, 137–43, 162, 163, 166, 167, 188–90, 201–3, 229–45, 268–79, 289–95,

299–301, 314, 319–20, 322
Birds of Cumberland 43, 44
Birds of Lakeland 47, 49, 50, 53, 71
Birk Fell 174
Birkdale 263, 264
Birkett, R.J. 41, 49, 187, 224, 138
Birkrigg Oaks 38, 112, 176
Black Burn (Cross Fell) 24, 249
Black Burn (Tindale) 24, 249, 250, 279
Black Combe 20, 22, 208
Black Force 22, 214
Blackmoss Pool 139, 140
blanket bog 26, 210, 252, 255, 256, 265, 268, 273–8, 292, 297, 310
Blaze Fell 120, 140
Blea Water 21, 192
Blelham Tarn 194, 202
Blencathra 20, 28, 207, 210, 212, 242, 243
Blezard, D. 39, 40, 42, 49–51, 104, 105, 271, 276, 280, 288
Blezard, E. 39, 40, 42, 49–51, 104, 105
Blindcrake
  Clints, 23, 159, 162
bog
  burst 136
  formation 127, 210
bog mosses (see *Sphagnum* in Species Index)
Bog, The 211
Bolam, G. 38, 48, 264, 267
Bolton Fell 125, 133, 136, 307
Borders 12–15, 25, 52, 67, 68, 118, 142, 145, 167, 171, 210, 212, 272, 282–302, 310, 319, 323
boreal forest 168, 176, 319
Borrowdale 21, 36, 40, 165, 168, 174, 186, 187, 189, 190, 193
  Volcanic Series 20–2, 28, 29, 32, 193, 208, 222, 246, 307
  Woods 168, 169, 180, 184, 315

Botanical Society of the British Isles 40, 41, 57
boulder (mussel) scars 65, 79, 82
Bowfell 14
Bowland Fells 237
Bowness Moss (Common) 69, 112, 125, 127, 128, 133–6, 308, 314, 315
Bowness-on-Solway 60, 96, 97
Bowscale
  Fell 207, 242
  Tarn 20
brackish habitats 63, 65
Brampton 111, 112
Brandygill, 28
Brandreth 209
Braystones Tarn 141
Brigsteer 152, 153
  Wood 153
Britten, H. 38, 46, 164
British Trust for Ornithology 56, 57, 71, 105
broad-leaved woodlands 114, 168, 169, 171, 172, 190, 318
  mixed 111, 147, 153, 155, 283
  policy for 171, 319
Brotherswater 204
Brough 18, 23, 249, 250, 260, 278
Brown, R.H. 53, 70, 238, 241, 243
Brown Cove 17
brown earth soils 146, 172, 176, 268, 274
Brown Gill 182
bryophyte communities 115, 127, 128, 137, 138, 180–3, 211, 212, 256, 284, 286
Bullman Hills 266
Burgh-by-Sands 14, 47
Burgh Marsh 59, 60, 62, 63, 66–71, 74, 77, 78, 311
Burnhope Seat 253, 255, 266, 267
Burnmoor Tarn 195
Burns Beck Moss 139
Butterburn 282, 284, 286
  Flow 26, 284, 292, 293, 298, 300, 302, 315
butterflies 46, 53, 54, 56, 99, 107–9, 123, 124, 134, 163, 164, 246, 247, 279, 300

Buttermere 49, 169, 171, 187, 197, 237, 317

Caerlaverock 59, 74, 75, 77
Cairngorms 17, 242
calcite 32, 193, 214, 266
Caldbeck 23, 112, 159, 244, 307
  Fells 27, 28, 242, 309
Caldew, River 27, 118, 142, 144, 159, 207, 244, 306
Calf 22
Callion, J. 56, 241, 244
Campfield Marsh 60, 63, 67, 314, 316
Carboniferous formation 19, 22–8, 32, 100, 112, 113, 145, 224, 249, 282
Cardew Mires 136, 142
Cardurnock 60, 62
Carlisle 12, 14, 19, 26, 28, 34, 40, 43–7, 100, 104–7, 112, 116–23, 125, 128, 130, 135, 137, 144, 308, 310, 313, 322
  Basin 100, 112
  Natural History Society 34, 45, 46, 48, 49, 52
carrion, as food 18, 186, 228, 231, 238, 271, 318
Carrock Fell 22, 27, 174, 207, 211, 227, 243–5
carrying capacity 31, 32, 132, 238, 273, 274, 280, 294
Cartmel 23
Cash Force 24
Castle Carrock 18, 23, 45, 112
  Reservoir 279
Caudbeck Flow 286, 298, 315
Cauldron Snout 249
Cautley Spout 22, 214
Cavendish Dock 79, 83, 97
Centre for Ecology and Hydrology 58, 281
Chapelcross power station 59, 311
Chapman, A. 49, 68, 77, 282, 289, 293
Cheviots 12, 247, 282, 283, 312
Christianbury Crags 25, 284, 286–8, 290, 291, 293, 297, 298, 302
Claife Heights 185, 205
Clarke, D. 56

Clawthorpe Fell 307
Cleasby, T.W.I. 54, 237, 271, 275
Cliburn Moss 138
Climatic Optimum (Postglacial) 168, 212, 251, 286
climatic (global) warming 184, 212, 216, 242, 322
climate 14–19, 168, 212, 281
Clints Quarry (Egremont) 162, 315
Clints Quarry (Moota) 163
cloud cover 18
Coal Measures 24, 27, 91, 100
coast 79–99
Cockermouth 23, 41, 100, 163, 197, 307, 309
Cold Fell 24, 256, 275
collecting
  birds 43, 45, 53
  eggs 47, 53, 70, 67, 70, 90, 133, 229, 230, 320
  insects 44, 46, 47, 53, 107
  plants 37, 213, 216, 217, 219, 224, 310, 314, 320
Combe Crag (Irthing) 112
conifer plantations 117, 123, 153, 185, 187, 251, 282, 288, 292, 295, 303
coniferisation 111, 123, 153, 170, 171, 304, 319
Coniston 28, 187, 190, 191, 194, 227, 308
  Limestone 21
  Old Man (Fells) 20, 217, 227, 241, 288
  Water 22, 169, 179, 194, 199
Conway, V.M. 280
Coombs Wood 111, 112, 304
copper-mining 28
coppicing 172, 179, 182
Corner, R.W.M. 42, 210, 221
corrie-formation 20, 216
Council for the Protection of Rural England 170
Countryside Agency 313
Countryside and Rights of Way Act, 2001 314
Cow Green Reservoir 256, 277, 306
Crag Hill (Pennines) 23
Cramel Linn 26, 283, 296, 302
craneflies 241, 280

Croglin Water 112, 249, 250, 270–2, 217
Cross Fell 14, 17, 18, 23–5, 29, 37, 38, 40, 247, 249, 251, 254, 256, 258, 266, 267, 269–71, 273, 275–80, Inlier 24, 252
cropping ashes 185
Crowdundle Beck 264, 278
Crummock Water 197
cultivation 31, 32, 100, 102, 165, 166, 252, 282, 303
Cumbria Bird Club 56, 57
Breeding Bird Atlas 57
Cumbria Naturalists' Union 57, 71
Cumbria Wildlife Trust 57, 60, 141, 142, 156, 313, 319
Cumwhitton Moss 117, 125, 135, 137, 138
Cunswick
Scar 23, 153, 155
Tarn 155

Dalegarth
Force 178, 182, 194
Woods 171
data collection 57
Davidson, W.F. 53, 58
Day, F.H. jnr. 58
Day, F.H. snr. 46, 123
Dentdale 12, 249, 264, 271
Denton Fell 273
Derwent, River 81, 140, 201
Derwentwater 167, 179, 193, 194, 199, 201–4
development threats 311, 312, 323
Devensian glaciation 168
Devoke Water 195, 196, 201, 242
Devonian Period 22
diatoms 196
disturbance, effects on birds 86, 89, 241, 274, 275, 309, 310, 313, 315
Dove Crag (Hartsop) 20, 49
Dove Crags (Grasmoor) 20, 222
draining, of wetlands 31, 125, 128, 161, 256, 276, 284, 298
dragonflies 46, 54, 56, 135, 142, 144, 205, 247, 322
drawdown, in reservoirs 199
Drigg 139
Dunes 85, 88, 99, 313, 315

drought 15, 115
drowned forest 62
Drumburgh 64, 80
Moss 125, 127, 133, 135
drumlins 26
Dubmill Point 82, 86, 88
duck-rearing, at Netherby 133, 138
Duddon, River/Valley 18, 22, 27, 59, 61, 142, 196, 197, 242, 312
Estuary 65, 71, 73–5, 85, 88, 99, 311
Dufton 249, 252
Fell 256
Pike 24
Dukedale 23, 269
Dumfries 311
Dunlop, E.B. 48, 51, 229, 269
Dunnerdale 169, 170, 179, 190, 246
Dutch elm disease 172, 185
dwarf shrubs, loss of 33, 168, 207, 208, 243, 246, 272, 295, 303, 316–18, 323
Dykesfield 59, 64, 105

earthworms 106, 245, 273–5, 294
Easedale Tarn 202
Ease Gill 23
ecological variety, in Cumbria 12
Eden
Gorge 26, 112, 115, 123
River 23, 64, 81, 142–4, 216
Valley 14, 15, 23, 26, 28, 37, 38, 46, 100–2, 104, 117, 118, 137, 187, 249, 257, 264, 270, 271, 273, 278, 309
Eddy, A. 259, 280
egg-breaking 119, 232
eggshell-thinning 119, 232–4
Egremont 23, 27, 159, 162, 199, 256
Ehen, River 142, 144, 206
Ellen, River 142, 144
Elterwater 203
energy demands 305, 311
English Nature 57, 135, 146, 308, 310, 313–15, 318
Ennerdale 22, 142, 187, 237
granophyre 22, 32, 193, 207, 214

Water 169, 170, 193, 196, 197, 204–6, 305, 318
enrichment, of nutrients by gulls 69, 133, 157
Environment Agency 315
Environmentally Sensitive Areas 316
epiphytes 176, 182, 184, 185
erosion 19–21, 145, 212, 301
peat 25, 256–8
salt marsh 63, 64
Eskdale 18, 21, 22, 165, 170, 171, 177–9, 195, 210–12, 237, 238, 242, 246, 247
granite 22, 32, 193, 207, 214
Esk, River (Border) 59, 60, 98, 136, 142
Esk, River (Lakes) 59, 85, 142
Eskmeals 41, 85, 308, 309, 323
Esthwaite Water 37, 41, 193, 195, 199, 202, 204
North Fen 179, 198
European Union Birds and Habitats/Species Directives 81, 144, 164, 199, 211, 265, 314
eutrophication 86, 100, 102, 138, 157, 193–5, 303, 321, 323
Eycott Hill Lavas 20, 24

Fairfield 20, 215, 219, 224, 225
Farleton Knott 23, 149, 150, 152, 153
farming 'improvement' 12, 33, 92, 95, 96, 100, 104–6, 109, 160–2, 165, 252, 273, 276, 282
farming reform, need for 316, 323
Faulds Brow 142, 159, 208, 242, 243
Fauna of Lakeland 12, 43, 45
fell-fields 29, 209, 217, 221, 276
fell-walking 13, 241, 249, 309
Fell End Clouds 23, 261
fen 127, 136–9, 152
oligotrophic (poor) 136, 138, 139, 211
mesotrophic (intermedi-

ate) 138, 140, 167, 179, 198, 211, 212
eutrophic (rich) 137, 138, 148, 155, 157, 161, 162, 198
Fennoscandia 31, 111, 131, 134, 217, 219, 221, 242, 245, 285, 286, 305
fern-craze, Victorian 36, 213, 219, 224
ferns 115, 176–8, 219–21, 223, 224, 253, 283, 300, 305
fertiliser 32, 100, 165, 193, 252, 298, 301, 302, 321
Fingland 104
Finglandrigg Woods 108, 110, 116, 117, 120, 315
fire, effects of 33, 110, 128, 207, 208, 218, 243, 280, 284, 299
fish
 freshwater 144, 204, 205, 279, 296
 marine 66, 80
fisheries 80, 144, 204, 205
Fleetwith 223, 246
floating island, Derwentwater 200, 201
Flimby 95, 111
Flookburgh Marsh 72, 73, 81
Flora of Cumberland 37
Flora of Cumbria 42, 57
Flora of Westmorland 38, 39
flush bogs 211, 245, 258, 265, 266, 286
flushes 157, 212, 218, 286
flushing 32, 265
footpath erosion, 13, 309
Force Crag 20, 28, 247
Ford, E.B. 53, 107
forest
 clearance and loss 31, 111, 112, 168, 172, 182, 207, 286
 drowned 62
 history 168, 212, 286
 limits, upper climatic 31, 33, 168, 172, 251, 318
 zone 33, 168
Forestry Commission 169–71, 233, 296, 297, 304, 312, 318, 319
Foulney Island 75, 80, 82, 83, 87–9, 91, 97
Foulshaw Moss 126, 130, 132, 133, 304

foxhounds 186, 227, 268, 289
freezing, of lakes 16, 18
Freshwater Biological Association 38, 56, 58, 191, 194
Friends of the Lake District 170, 312, 315
fringe-moss heaths 209, 217, 241, 253, 267, 323
frost 15, 16, 18, 28, 29, 115, 134, 244, 245, 251
Fryer, G. 56, 58, 191, 204, 205, 237
fungi 36, 42, 185, 218, 328–30
Furness 23, 26, 34, 36, 177, 185, 227

Gaitbarrows 148, 163
Galloway 65, 80, 81, 86, 93–5, 99, 163, 195, 205
gamekeepers 67, 104, 105, 120, 187, 268–272, 278, 290–2, 320
Garnett, M. 49, 53, 199, 203, 237, 243
Garrigill 249, 250
Garsdale 12, 249, 264
Gelt
 River 144, 249
 Woods 112, 118
Geltsdale 34, 40, 51, 250, 252, 270–3, 275–8
geology 19–32, 35, 58, 192, 280
Gilpin, River 61, 88
Gilsland 25, 26, 37, 42, 44, 52, 112, 283, 288–93, 296, 297, 302
glacial features 19, 26, 127, 137, 192
glaciation 19–26, 145, 192
Glasson Moss 125, 128, 130, 132, 133, 135, 136, 307, 314, 315
Glencoyne 178, 179
 Park 175, 233
 Wood 161, 191
Glenridding 28, 174, 199, 202, 204
gley soils 252
goose damage 75
Gosforth 191
Gowk Bank 282, 283, 302, 315
Graham, R. 49, 52, 118, 287–96, 302

Grange-over-Sands 104
graphite mining 28
Grasmere 187, 202
Grasmoor 20, 209, 216, 218, 237
grassland
 base-rich (greens) 208, 259, 268, 274, 275, 289, 294
 fescue-bent 175, 207–9, 217, 218, 241, 252, 253
 flying bent 130, 284
 mat grass 157, 208, 210, 218, 246, 252, 258
 neutral 63, 101, 158, 160, 161, 165, 282, 283
 limestone 146–9, 151, 153, 155–7, 161, 162–4, 259–62, 264, 273, 275
grazing, effects on vegetation 33, 63, 67, 157, 165, 172, 174–6, 207–10, 237, 243, 252, 255, 267, 268, 272, 280–3, 298, 303, 317
Great Asby Scar 156–8, 315
Great Calva 209, 243
Great Dodd 17
Great Dun Fell 15, 18, 19, 25, 28, 249, 259, 275, 276, 280, 309
Great End 17
Great Gable 14
Great Mell Fell 166, 188
Great Orton 53, 305
Great Salkeld 34, 38, 46, 102
Great Wood 168, 169, 171, 172, 179, 184
Greendale Tarn 195
Greta, River 167, 193
Greystoke Park 23, 108, 118, 120, 159–61, 188, 233, 243, 304
Grizedale Forest 170, 171, 185, 227, 319
grouse moors 33, 207, 237, 243, 252, 269–78, 281, 295
Grune Point 54, 59, 79, 81, 83, 84, 96
gulls
 breeding colonies 69, 70, 89–91, 138, 139, 141, 157, 201, 202, 277, 292, 293
 roosts 75, 203
gypsum mining 28, 142, 307

Haaf-netting 80
haematite mining 27, 79, 307

General Index

Hale Moss 149
Halliday, G. 34, 42, 158
Hallsenna Moor 109
hang-gliding 274, 310
hanging valleys 21, 193
Harter Fell (Mardale) 238, 306
Hartside 24, 241, 255, 270–2
Haverigg 85, 88, 99
Haweswater 169, 196, 199, 202–4, 237, 305, 312
Hawkshead 190, 194, 246
hawkweeds 36, 42, 214, 221, 261
Hayeswater 197
heath
 acidic 109–11
 limestone 149, 152, 157, 160
hedges 100, 102, 105, 119, 303
Helbeck Woods 24, 36, 250, 260, 261
Hell Gill (Eden) 23, 250
Helm Wind 18
Helvellyn 17, 20, 36, 41, 199, 201, 215, 216, 218, 219, 224, 225, 227, 242, 243, 246, 317
herbaria 37
Hervey, G.A.K. 40, 54, 286
Hewitt, S. 34, 56
Heysham, J. 42, 109, 240
Heysham, T.C. 43, 104, 240
Highlands, Scottish 14, 15, 68, 117, 180, 191, 204, 208, 209, 217–19, 221, 240, 246, 247, 253, 259, 264, 286
High Cup 24
 Nick 249
 Scars 24, 36, 264, 265, 269
High Pike 20, 27
High Street Fells 14, 17, 20, 36, 41, 185, 192, 210, 215, 219, 227, 242
Hobcarton Crag 216, 217, 313
Hodbarrow 23, 27, 79, 88, 89, 95, 97, 99, 308
Hodgson, W. 34, 37, 45
Honister
 Crag 21, 40, 214, 223, 224, 307
Hope, L.E. 48, 49
Horne, G. 53, 55, 96, 120, 233, 238, 291
Howgill Fells 12, 21–3, 208, 214, 222, 250, 272

human impact 13, 31–3
Humphrey Head 23, 93, 148, 164
Hutton Roof Crags 23, 146, 149, 150, 153, 313, 315
hydroelectric power 305
hydrology 280, 301
hydrosere 198

ice action 19–21, 216
Ice Age 212
industry 13, 27, 95, 168, 184, 195, 306, 307, 310, 311
Inglewood Forest 37, 52, 100, 105, 107, 118, 121, 142, 309
Ings, The 179
Institute of Terrestrial Ecology 58
International Biological Programme 281
inversions, temperature 15, 16
iron-smelting 27,
Irongill Wood 117
Irthing, River 26, 44, 112, 118, 142, 144, 282–4, 286, 289, 290, 293, 295–7, 302
 Gorge 25, 283, 289, 290, 295, 302
Irthinghead 282, 294, 295, 297
Isle of Man 93, 95
isostatic rise, in sea level 62, 64, 127

Jackson, F. 40, 186, 221, 224
Johnby Moor 160, 161
Johnston, T.L. 49, 67–9, 104
Johnny's Wood 169, 180, 181
Jurassic formation 26

Kendal 23, 35, 39, 43, 118, 145, 147, 152, 162, 188, 190, 305, 307, 308
Kent, Estuary/River 23, 27, 61, 81, 98, 126, 142, 143, 148, 311
Kentmere 165, 193, 196, 225, 227, 297, 243
Keppelcove 199, 225
Kershope Burn 297
Keskadale Oakwood 38, 172, 176
Keswick 14, 15, 35, 36, 184, 187, 190, 194, 240, 308

Kielder 286, 290, 292, 297, 311
Killington Reservoir 139, 202
King Harry 26, 109
King Water 26, 287, 289, 296
Kingmoor Nature Reserve 43, 48, 110, 313
Kirkbride 106, 137
Kirkby Moor 243, 305, 307
Kirkby Stephen 23, 26, 54, 104, 137, 144, 155, 163, 250, 260, 269, 273, 278, 307
Knock Fell 249, 253, 258, 259, 275, 280
Knock Ore Gill 24, 261, 264, 269

Laidler, R. 54, 55, 117
lakes – listed under individual names
lake formation 19, 192, 193
Lake District National Park Authority 309, 310, 313, 315, 317, 318
Lakeland, definition 12
Lamonby 160, 161
land management 12, 193, 280, 312–17, 322, 323
Lancaster Canal 308
Langdale 21, 36, 187, 218, 222, 230
 Little 41, 49, 174, 202
 Pikes 20
Langstrath 237
Langwathby 104
Late-glacial Period 37, 93, 127, 168, 205, 212
Launchy Gill 182
Lazonby 26, 112
 Fell 26, 109, 110, 120, 140
Leach, W. 38
lead-mining 27, 28, 266, 307
Leven, River 27, 61, 65, 98, 142, 148, 311
Lewis, F.J., 37
lichens 36, 39, 42, 128, 184, 185, 199, 201, 208, 221, 253, 266, 267, 321
Liddel, River, 26, 112, 118, 142, 144, 282, 289, 295
lime, importance of, 31, 32, 145–64, 193, 213, 221–6
limestone 25, 27, 31, 100, 102, 145–64, 250, 251, 259–67, 280

General Index

pavement 19, 22, 23, 145–56, 159, 273
potholes 261, 262, 277
removal 146, 151, 156, 307
scars 22, 23, 145, 153, 249, 260, 268
screes 22, 23, 145, 148, 152, 153, 260
Limestone Pavement Orders 146
limnology 38, 191
Little Dun Fell 25, 249, 259, 275, 280
Little Fell 24, 36, 264, 266, 267
liverworts 17, 36, 38–40, 42, 46, 115, 180–2, 185, 199, 201, 221, 266, 305, 321
Lobarion community 184, 185
Local Nature Reserve 310, 313
Loch Lomond Re-advance 168
Lodge Haggs 40, 253, 257, 274
Lodore
  Falls 15, 21, 178, 182, 183
  Woods 169, 184, 187
loess 145, 152
Longsleddale 169, 193, 243
Low Tarn 195
Loweswater 211
Low Wood (Hartsop) 169
Lune, River (Morecambe Bay) 143
Lyne, River 26, 144, 172, 282, 289, 291, 295, 296
  Black 112, 283, 293, 294, 297
  White 112, 290, 293
Lyth Valley 27, 152

Macpherson, H.A. 12, 34, 44, 45, 51, 68, 71, 73, 74, 81, 89, 90, 93, 94, 105, 118, 123, 132, 134, 187, 228, 229, 240, 270, 272, 292
Maize Beck 249, 263, 264, 309
Mallerstang 23, 54, 249, 250, 253, 269, 270, 272, 275, 276, 309
mammals 46, 56, 78, 90, 97, 98, 162, 185–8, 201, 226–9, 268, 287–9

Manley, G. 17, 18, 281
Mardale 221, 224, 227, 238, 246
marginal land 167, 276, 282–4, 288–90, 294
marl lake 157
Martindale 179, 227, 237
Martin Tarn 140
Maryport 15, 26, 27, 79–81, 88, 95, 99, 100, 111, 305
masts 309, 323
Matterdale Common 20, 210, 211, 242
Mawby, F. 57, 67, 120, 314
meadows, floral 39, 101, 107, 158, 160, 165, 223, 252, 278, 282, 283, 303, 306
Meathop Moss 126, 128, 313
Melbreak 237
Melmerby 38
  Fell 253, 267, 276
Merlewood Research Station 39, 280, 281
Mickle Fell 23, 264, 267
Middlebarrow 22, 148
Middleton Fells 21
migration, bird 70, 71, 96, 97, 141, 245
Millom 15, 18, 20, 26, 27, 73, 79, 100, 188, 311
minerals 13, 27, 28, 53, 58
mine-spoil 224, 266, 267
mining 13, 27, 28, 195, 202, 266, 307
Ministry of Defence 289, 297, 302, 308, 309
Moffat Hills 219, 321
molluscs 44, 46, 65, 66, 79–82, 164, 248, 279
Monkhill Lough 138, 140
montane zone 17, 208–10, 212, 216, 217, 242, 253, 322
Moorthwaite Moss 125, 127, 128, 135, 137
Moorthwaite Tarn 138
Moor House National Nature Reserve 15, 17, 19, 39, 57, 251, 252, 256, 267, 271, 273, 278–81, 313, 314, 318
moor-gripping 256
Morecambe Bay 12, 14, 27, 38, 59, 60, 65, 66, 68–70, 73–75, 79–81, 98, 102, 126, 134, 147–9, 162, 163, 305, 307, 310–312

Moricambe Bay 59–61, 73, 74, 78, 94, 98, 142
mosses 15, 36, 38–40, 42, 46, 115, 180–182, 185, 199, 201, 221, 266, 305, 321
moss-litter 136, 307, 308
Moss Catherine waterfall 26, 302
moths 46, 54, 56, 99, 109, 123, 124, 135, 164, 279, 280
Muirhead, C.W. 40, 42
Muncaster Fell 169, 188
Mungrisdale 211
Murray, J. 38, 46
myxomatosis 90, 103, 233, 268, 270

Naddle Forest 38, 169
National Nature Reserves 41, 108, 128, 148, 156, 271, 280, 281, 283, 302, 313–15
National Park, Lake District 12, 13, 100, 144, 171, 237, 305, 310, 312–15, 323
National Trust 57, 153, 171, 174, 217, 304, 310, 312–14, 317, 318
Natura 2000 315, 334–40
Nature Conservancy 39–41, 57, 267, 280, 281, 312, 313
Nature Conservancy Council 41, 314, 317
Nenthead 28, 252, 266, 268, 307
New Red Sandstone 19, 26
Newlands Vale 193
Newton Marsh 61, 62, 64, 69, 74, 77
Newton Reigny Moss 136, 161, 162, 164, 315
Newtown Common 42, 43, 109
Nichol, W. 47, 76, 77
Nicholson, F. 44, 187, 240
North Tyne, River 286, 290, 295, 297
nuclear industry 13, 304
Nunnery Walks 112

oak woods 38, 65, 111, 147, 172, 174–6, 178, 190, 198
oceanic conditions 14–19
Ordovician formation 19, 20, 21, 28

organochlorine pesticides 119, 120, 201, 232–4, 238, 303
Orton (Shap) 23, 154, 156–8, 163, 164, 307
Orton Woods (Carlisle) 47, 107, 116–21, 123
Otley, J. 35, 200
Oulton Moss 125, 130, 135
overgrazing 207, 208, 316, 317

Park, K. 264, 268
park woodland 175, 185, 189
Parker, J.R. 56
Parminter, P.W. 47, 243
patterned ground 28–31, 254, 255, 277
Pavey Ark 20, 22, 310
Pearsall, W.H. jnr. 37–9, 41, 58, 191, 198, 199
Pearsall, W.H. snr. 37, 199
peat
 erosion 25, 256–8
 extraction 116, 128, 135–8, 307
 formation 19, 25, 26, 32, 125–7, 137, 138, 258, 284
 mosses 53, 70, 109, 111, 112, 119, 121, 125–39, 148
Pennines 12, 14–19, 21, 23–9, 32,33, 36–8, 49, 52, 54, 67, 104, 105, 118, 120, 155, 175, 196, 210, 222, 240, 249–81, 319, 320, 323
Pennine Way 161, 249, 309, 314
Pennington, W. 41, 58, 191
Penrith 23, 104, 109, 111, 117, 121, 161, 187, 197, 307, 308
 Beacon 110, 309
Penton Linns 113, 114
periglacial features 30, 281
Permian formations 19, 26, 32, 61, 91, 100, 101, 109, 112
Peters, J.F. 47, 240
Petteril, River 112, 142, 144
Philipson, M. 49, 294
Pigott, C.D. 11, 172, 173
Pillar 20, 26, 210, 225
pine woods 111–13, 117, 121, 128, 137, 138
podsols 32, 109, 252
poisons, illegal use 243, 269, 271

pollen analysis 112, 126, 167
pollution 13, 33, 137, 138, 184, 185, 193–6, 301, 303, 305, 321–3
polychlorinated biphenyls 93
ponds 140–2
Port Carlisle 308, 310
Postglacial Period 112, 127, 148, 167, 205, 212, 216
Potter, B. 36, 37
precipitation 14, 15, 127, 165, 180, 182, 286
predation, on bird eggs and young 66–8, 89–91, 105, 294
predators, destruction of 33, 118, 132, 229, 243, 268–72, 278, 290–2, 320, 323
propagation, as conservation measure 320
punt-gunning 76, 77

quarries & quarrying 13, 21, 22, 26, 91, 102, 118, 146, 159, 163, 223, 270, 307
Quaternary Period 19, 281

radiocarbon dating 126, 127
rainfall (see precipitation)
raised beaches 19, 63, 127
raised bogs 27, 125–39
Ramsar Convention on Wetlands 314
Raven Crag (Thirlmere) 20, 169
Ravenglass 59, 61, 65, 69, 88–91, 99
Rawes, M. 280, 281
Rawnsley, C.H. 240, 243
Ray, J. 34
reclamation, for farming 100, 125, 126, 161, 303
Red Tarn (Helvellyn) 201, 204
reedswamp 65, 140, 199, 202, 203
regeneration, of trees 174
relict
 fauna 205, 206
 flora 212, 213, 216–26, 262–6, 286, 323
reptiles 99, 111, 134, 163, 245, 246, 279, 296, 320
research, analytical 38, 41, 56–8, 90, 91, 126, 167, 168, 172, 173, 191, 193–6,

232, 280, 281, 323
reservoirs 196, 305, 311
Riggindale 218, 238
rivers 142–4
Robinson 29, 209
Robson, R.W. 54
rock-band 28
rock climbing 13, 20, 48, 310
rock falls 216
Rockcliffe 59, 112, 125, 144
 Marsh 60, 62, 64, 67–70, 73, 74, 77, 133, 311, 315
 Moss 42, 125
rocky shores 80, 82, 92, 97
Rodwell, J. 41
Roudsea
 Mosses 126, 133, 313, 315
 Wood 65, 147, 148, 153, 162, 164, 313, 315
Roughtengill 20, 27
Routledge, G.B. 45
Royal Society for the Protection of Birds 27, 60, 67, 89, 93, 95, 238, 272, 276, 313, 314, 316
Rundale 250, 269, 279
Rusland Moss 126, 128, 188
Rydal 178, 182

Salta Moss 109, 133, 139
salt marsh 26, 59–65, 311
 accretion 61–4
 erosion 59, 63, 64
 grazing 63
 turf-cutting 63
saltpans 62
sand and gravel extraction 79, 308
sand dunes 19, 26, 65, 83, 84–91, 110
sands, intertidal 59, 61, 65, 66, 73, 79, 82
Sandford Mire 138
Sandscale Haws (Roanhead) 85, 86, 88, 99, 110, 315
Scafell (Range) 14, 17–19, 36, 209, 210, 215, 218, 219, 244
Scafell Pike 20, 248
Scaleby Moss 125–8, 131, 133, 136
Scales Tarn 20
Scales Wood 169
Scoat Tarn 195
Scordale 24, 269, 309
Scout Scar 23, 153, 315

screes 20, 21, 25, 38, 186, 217–19, 228, 244, 253, 268
scrub 31, 33, 84, 92, 110, 128, 148, 151, 152, 167, 168, 251, 317, 318
seacliffs 91–5
sea-level change 62, 64, 126, 322
Seascale 83, 93
Seathwaite 14, 28, 168, 174, 180, 182
Seathwaite Tarn (Duddon) 197
Seatoller Woods 172, 180, 182, 199
seawalls 59, 63
Sebergham 27, 112, 159, 161
Sedbergh 54, 237
Sedbergh School, ornithology 54, 141
sedimentation 142, 193
Sellafield 13, 15, 19, 79, 90, 197, 304, 305, 323
shade, importance of 115, 146, 182
Shap 15, 22, 34, 38, 155, 163, 306, 307
  Fells 22, 23, 155, 159, 162, 227, 237, 241–3, 270, 306, 319
sheep 12, 33, 63, 109, 157, 172, 174, 176, 178, 207, 208, 210, 218, 222, 228, 233, 238, 252, 259, 266–8, 282, 283, 298, 303, 314, 316–18, 323
sheepwalks 12, 33, 157, 207, 208, 252, 259, 282, 323
shingle beaches 19, 26, 65, 83, 87
Siddick Pond 88, 140, 141
Sighty Crag 25, 284, 285, 293, 298
Silecroft 83, 91
Silloth 18, 19, 37, 59, 81, 82, 84, 86, 96, 98, 104, 308
Silurian formation 19, 21–3, 32, 65, 100, 139, 141, 147, 173, 189, 214, 222, 307
Silverdale 23, 148, 149, 164
Sites of Special Scientific Interest 40, 298, 310, 313–15, 334–42
Skiddaw (Fells) 14, 20, 29, 40, 43, 52, 188, 208–10, 218, 222, 235, 237, 240, 242–4, 246–8, 317

Forest 142, 207, 208, 211, 230, 240, 243–5, 247, 306, 317
Slates 20, 22, 24, 28, 29, 32, 193, 208, 209, 213, 217, 222, 244, 246
skiing 314
Skinburness 47, 106
  Marsh 60, 64
Skirwith Fell 25, 253
slacks, dune 84, 85
slag-banks 27, 91, 95
Smardale 155, 163, 164, 315
smelting, iron 27, 91
snow 16–18, 210, 229, 245, 287
  beds 210, 246, 259
Snowdonia 12–14, 175, 179, 182, 184, 190, 204, 214, 219, 222, 233, 321
soils 31–3, 63, 111, 113, 121, 146
soil-hummocks 29, 254, 255
solifluction 28, 29, 254, 255
Solway
  Firth 12, 14, 37, 52, 59–81, 96, 98, 144, 305, 307, 308, 311, 312
  Moss 125, 132–4, 138, 307
  Plain 14, 26, 100, 102, 104, 105, 107, 112, 120, 271, 305, 309
  Viaduct 63, 310, 311
South Tyne, River 12, 23, 37, 143, 249, 252, 255, 264, 267, 270, 277, 279
Sowerby Wood (Newby Cross) 119, 120, 123, 304
Spadeadam Waste 26, 42, 52, 187, 188, 284–6, 297, 302, 309, 323
springs 157, 161, 193, 201, 212, 218, 258, 259, 265
Sprinkling Tarn 14, 199, 246
St Bees 15, 83, 93, 99, 141
  Head 12, 26, 79–83, 91–5, 97–9, 307
St John's Vale 214
Stainmore 23, 37, 54, 250, 255, 271, 272, 309
Steward, E.S. 47, 53, 67
Stokoe, R. 42, 53, 54, 93, 96140, 198
stone axes 20, 21
stone nets and stripes 30
Storey, J. 47, 76, 77
streams 193, 201, 289, 293,

295, 296
Strowger, J. 56, 240
subtidal zone 79, 82
succession 37, 41, 61–3, 127, 128, 198, 207, 208, 217, 318
Sunbiggin
  Tarn 141, 156, 157, 162, 164
  Moor 157
Sunday Burn Linns 25, 283
sunshine 18, 19
Swaledale 23, 257, 269
Swarth Fell 23, 249, 275
Swindale (Brough) 36, 250, 251
Swindale (Shap) 196, 236
Symonds, H.H. 170

Tailbridge Hill 29, 40, 54, 255, 261, 267, 273–5, 315
Talkin Tarn 140
tarns 140–2, 192–6
Tarn Moss 210, 211, 315
Tarn Wadling 138
Tebay 155, 308
Tees, River 12, 23, 37, 249, 255, 264, 273
temperature 15, 16, 172, 216
Temple Sowerby Moss 139
tern colonies 70, 87–9
Terrybank Tarn 141
territory, in birds 228, 230, 233, 270, 273, 294
Tertiary Period 19
Thirlmere 169, 171, 174, 181, 187, 196, 199, 201, 227, 232, 305, 312
Thompson, W. 54, 271, 273, 276
Thornhill Moss 171
Thornthwaite 28, 170, 188, 203
Thurstonfield 118
  Lough 138, 140
tides 59, 64, 69, 70, 76, 92
Tinbergen, N. 90, 91
Tindale
  Fells 24, 252, 255, 270, 272, 273, 277
  Tarn 279
tourism 13, 249, 309, 310, 323
trampling, effects 242, 309
trees, as plant habitats 182, 184, 185
tree line 168, 251, 286

Triassic formations 26, 27, 32, 100
Troutbeck (Westmorland) 48, 243
Tullie House Museum 28, 40, 45, 46, 48–51, 53, 57, 288, 292, 293
Tyne Gap 23, 24, 145, 249, 269

Ullswater 20, 48, 169, 174, 178, 196, 202–4
Ulverston 141, 148, 305, 308
Underlaid Wood 23, 148
Unity Bog 125, 130
Upper Teesdale 15, 36, 148, 149, 158, 252, 262, 276, 286, 306, 309, 320
Urswick Tarn 148

valley mires 136–9, 210, 211
vegetation
 classification (plant communities) 41, 61–3, 65, 83–5, 92, 110, 113–15, 128, 130, 136, 140, 142, 152, 156, 157, 160, 162, 165, 172–4, 176, 179, 197, 198, 207–12, 224, 250, 252, 253, 256, 265–7, 280, 282–4, 286
 history 37, 41, 126, 127, 167, 168, 172, 173, 281, 286
vehicles, effects of 309, 310, 323
verges
 railway 101, 104, 108, 158
 road 100–2, 104, 108, 158, 161, 283, 308
Victoria County History, Cumberland 38, 45, 46

waders 66, 71, 72, 73, 76, 140, 167, 201, 273–6, 282, 293, 294, 314, 320
Walby Moor (White Moss) 110, 135
Walker, D. 126, 136
Walney Island 14, 26, 27, 65, 75, 79, 81–3, 88–90, 97, 110
 North 61, 85, 86, 110
 South 61, 79–81, 83, 86, 90, 91
walls, as plant habitat 167
Walton Moss 125
Walton Wood 111, 304
Wampool, River 60, 142, 144
Wan Fell 109, 110, 139
Warcop 249, 308, 323
 Fell 36, 264
Wasdale 18, 21, 22, 227, 246
 Screes 20, 40, 192, 216, 225
Wastwater 192, 193, 195–7, 201, 204, 222, 305
Watendlath 21, 165, 185, 199, 237
water
 dystrophic 258
 oligotrophic 193, 197, 199, 204, 258
 mesotrophic 137, 140, 193, 197, 199, 204
 eutrophic 142, 157, 193–5, 265
 use 196, 197, 305, 311
waterfalls 112, 177, 178, 182, 183, 193
Watermillock 37, 188
Waver, River 60, 142, 144
Weardale 37, 266
Wedholme Flow 125, 128, 130, 132, 133, 136, 307, 308, 314, 315
weeds 86, 95, 102
wet-days (meteorological) 14, 15
Wet Sleddale 196, 243, 306
Whernside 23, 24, 264
Whinfell 26, 109, 117, 202, 309
Whinlatter 170, 187, 237
Whin Sill 24, 263–5
Whins Pond 140
Whitbarrow Scar 23, 95, 145, 152–4, 304, 310, 315
Whitbeck Moss 109, 139

Whitehaven 26, 27, 79, 81, 83, 197, 305, 307
Whiteside (Helvellyn) 43
Whiteside (Lorton) 218
Wigton 104, 106, 111, 305
Wild Boar Fell 23, 261, 269, 272, 275
wildfowl 66, 71, 72–7, 140, 141, 202, 203, 277, 279, 295, 320
Wildfowl and Wetlands Trust 56, 71
wildfowlers 47, 76, 77, 202
wildfowling 76–8, 320
Wildlife Trusts Partnership 313
willow carr 116, 127, 128, 137–40, 162, 179, 198, 211
Wilson, A. 34, 38, 39, 158
Winch, N.J. 35, 184
wind 18
wind farms 305
wind-shaping of trees 18, 96
Windermere 36, 53, 177, 179, 194
 Lake 16, 22, 38, 41, 169, 171, 190–3, 194, 197
Winster, R. 27, 61
winters, severe 17, 18, 229, 242, 245, 287, 288, 293, 294
Witherslack 134, 152, 153
 Moss 126, 134
woodlands 31, 65, 111–24, 128, 146–8, 152, 153, 155, 156, 162–4, 167–91, 250, 251, 283, 296–302, 304, 317, 319
Woodlands Trust 313
Wordsworth, W. 12, 13, 174, 178
Workington 27, 81, 82, 91, 95, 97, 197, 305, 307, 308
Wragmire Moss 104, 105
Wythop Woods 170, 187, 304

Yad Moss 256, 273, 275, 310, 315
Yewbarrow 152, 153

Species Index

Flowering Plants
alder *Alnus glutinosa* 111, 153, 168, 172, 175, 179, 189, 198, 250, 278, 282, 283
alder buckthorn *Frangula alnus* 116, 137
allseed *Radiola linoides* 86
alpine bartsia *Bartsia alpina* 34, 138, 157
alpine catchfly *Lychnis alpina* 216, 217, 321
alpine foxtail *Alopecurus borealis* 259
alpine lady's mantle *Alchemilla alpina* 34, 209, 222, 223, 253, 267
alpine penny-cress *Thlaspi caerulescens* 225, 265, 266
alpine saw-wort *Saussurea alpina* 224
alternate water-milfoil *Myriophyllum alterniflorum* 197
angelica *Angelica sylvestris* 92, 179, 223
annual knawel *Scleranthus annuus* 102
arrowgrass *Triglochin*
　marsh *T. palustre* 212
　sea *T. maritimum* 62
ash *Fraxinus excelsior* 33, 111, 147, 148, 151, 153, 155, 156, 172, 173, 175, 178, 184, 185, 198, 250, 283
aspen *Populus tremula* 111, 123, 155, 250
aster *Aster*
　goldilocks *A. linosyris* 148
　sea *A. tripolium* 63
autumn lady's tresses *Spiranthes spiralis* 149
awlwort *Subularia aquatica* 197
balsam *Impatiens*
　Indian *I. glandulifera* 143
　touch-me-not *I. noli-tangere* 34, 179, 190
baneberry *Actaea spicata* 149, 157, 162
barren strawberry *Potentilla sterilis* 114, 178, 261
beaked tasselweed *Ruppia maritima* 83
bearberry *Arctostaphylos uva-ursi* 208, 216, 218
bedstraw *Galium*
　heath 175, 208, 253
　hedge *G. mollugo* 101, 160
　lady's *G. verum* 84, 101, 157, 158
　limestone *G. pumilum* 153, 160, 260
　marsh *G. palustre* 198
　northern *G. boreale* 34, 114, 157, 223, 262, 267, 282, 283
beech *Fagus sylvatica* 111, 153
bellflower *Campanula*
　clustered *C. glomerata* 142, 158, 161
　giant *C. latifolia* 148, 161, 250
bent *Agrostis* 152, 165, 175, 207, 252
　common *A. capillaris* 63
　creeping *A. stolonifera* 62
betony *Stachys officinalis* 101, 158, 160, 165
bilberry *Vaccinium myrtillus* 33, 110, 113, 116, 152, 175, 187, 190, 207, 209, 210, 217, 218, 244, 245, 253, 258, 286, 316, 318
　bog *V. uliginosum* 36, 130, 255, 283
birch *Betula* 111, 112, 117, 123, 128, 138, 147, 148, 153, 155, 167, 168, 172, 189, 190, 198, 247, 250, 251, 267, 283, 299, 318
　downy *B. pubescens* 33, 112, 172–4
　dwarf *B. nana* 31, 42, 212, 255, 286, 300
　silver *B. pendula* 33, 112
bird cherry *Prunus padus* 156
bird's-foot *Ornithopus perpusillus* 84, 102
bird's-foot trefoil *Lotus corniculatus* 63, 84, 101, 157, 160, 161
bistort *Persicaria*
　alpine *P. vivipara* 158, 225, 262, 267
　amphibious *P. amphibia* 140, 142
　common *P. bistorta* 101
bitter-cress *Cardamine*
　large *C. amara* 114
　narrow-leaved *C. impatiens* 179
black bog-rush *Schoenus nigricans* 93, 149, 157, 162
blackthorn *Prunus spinosa* 33, 84, 92, 96, 102, 147, 151, 153, 156
bladderwort *Utricularia*
　greater *U. australis* 161, 198
　intermediate *U. intermedia* 198, 211
　lesser *U. minor* 211
blinks *Montia fontana* 212
bluebell *Hyacinthoides non-scripta* 33, 113, 176, 185
blue fleabane *Erigeron acer* 85
blue moor-grass *Sesleria caerulea* 148, 151, 153, 156, 161, 163, 259, 260
bog asphodel *Narthecium ossifragum* 127, 137, 210, 255, 284, 300
bog myrtle *Myrica gale* 116, 129
bog pimpernel *Anagallis tenella* 85, 139
bog rosemary *Andromeda polifolia* 116, 127, 129, 137, 210, 211, 284, 300
bogbean *Menyanthes trifoliata* 136, 157, 162, 211
brambles *Rubus fruticosus* agg. 42, 84, 96, 109, 113, 115, 118, 153, 178, 185, 189, 190, 300
briars *Rosa* spp. (see rose)
brooklime *Veronica beccabunga* 63, 140
broom *Cytisus scoparius* 84
broomrape *Orobanche*
　common *O. minor* 95
　purple *O. purpurea* 95
bryony
　black *Tamus communis* 102
　white *Bryonia dioica* 103

buckthorn *Rhamnus catharticus* 147, 148, 153, 164, 250
bugle *Ajuga reptans* 114, 178
  pyramidal *A. pyramidalis* 36, 216, 225
bugloss *Anchus arvensis* 102
  viper's *Echium vulgare* 102
bulrush *Typha latifolia* 138, 198
  lesser *T. angustifolia* 148
bur-marigold *Bidens*
  nodding *B. cernua* 141, 148
  three-lobed *B. tripartita* 141, 148
burnet *Sanguisorba*
  great *S. officinalis* 101, 158, 160, 165, 282
  salad *S. minor* 153, 157, 158
burnet saxifrage *Pimpinella saxifraga* 161, 282
bur-reed *Sparganium*
  branched *S. erectum* 198
  floating *S. angustifolium* 197
  least *S. natans* 198
buttercup *Ranunculus* 252
  celery-leaved *R. sceleratus* 63
  creeping *R. repens* 114
  goldilocks *R. auricomus* 114
  meadow *R. acris* 63
butterwort *Pinguicula vulgaris* 137, 157, 212, 252, 286
calamint *Clinopodium ascendens* 286
campion *Silene*
  moss *S. acaulis* 224, 267
  red *S. dioica* 92, 101, 113, 176, 223
  sea *S. maritima* 83, 92
Canadian waterweed (pondweed) *Elodea canadensis* 142, 198
cat's-ear *Hypochaeris radicata* 101
  smooth *H. glabra* 83
  spotted *H. maculata* 148
celandine *Ranunculus ficaria* 114
centaury *Centaurium*
  common *C. erythraea* 85
  lesser *C. pulchellum* 63
  seaside *C. littorale* 63
chaffweed *Anagallis minima* 86

cherry *Prunus*
  bird *P. padus* 33, 172, 173, 175, 250, 251
  wild *P. avium* 147, 250
chickweed wintergreen *Trientalis europaea* 286
chives *Allium schoenoprasum* 154
cinquefoil *Potentilla*
  alpine *P. crantzii* 224, 260, 264, 267
  marsh *P. palustris* 136, 157, 162, 198, 211
  shrubby *P. fruticosa* 36, 225, 263, 321
  spring *P. neumanniana* 149, 152, 157
climbing fumitory *Corydalis claviculata* 176
cloudberry *Rubus chamaemorus* 210, 255, 281, 285
clover *Trifolium* 161
  red *T. pratense* 165
  strawberry *T. fragiferum* 65
  white *T. repens* 63, 260
  zigzag *T. medium* 160, 282
club-rush
  bristle *Isolepis setacea* 212, 283
  common *Schoenoplectus lacustris* 198, 286
  floating *Eleogiton fluitans* 140, 141
  sea *Bolboschoenus maritimus* 63
  slender *Isolepis cernua* 83
  wood *Scirpus sylvaticus* 143, 286
cock's-foot grass *Dactylis glomerata* 165, 260
columbine *Aquilegia vulgaris* 148, 179, 250
common saltmarsh-grass *Puccinellia maritima* 61
cordgrass *Spartina anglica* 61, 65
corncockle *Agrostemma githago* 102
cornflower *Centaurea cyanus* 102
corn marigold
  Chrysanthemum segetum 102
cotton-grass *Eriophorum* 127, 134, 137, 299
  broad-leaved *E. latifolium* 138, 157, 286, 300
  common *E. angustifolium*

116, 136, 210, 255
  hare's-tail *E. vaginatum* 116, 210, 255, 258, 275, 279, 280, 284
cowberry *Vaccinium vitis-idaea* 33, 110, 117, 208, 209, 255, 286
cow parsley *Anthriscus sylvestris* 261
cowslip *Primula veris* 164, 261
cranberry *Vaccinium oxycoccus* 127, 137, 138, 210, 211, 284, 300
cranesbill *Geranium*
  bloody *G. sanguineum* 84, 85, 93, 152, 156, 158
  meadow *G. pratense* 101, 158, 161
  wood *G. sylvaticum* 101, 156, 158, 165, 223, 250, 261, 282, 283
creeping lady's tresses *Goodyera repens* 40, 117
creeping soft-grass *Holcus mollis* 92, 113, 175
crested dog's-tail *Cynosurus cristatus* 260
crested hair-grass *Koeleria micrantha* 153, 260
cross-leaved heath *Erica tetralix* 110, 127, 160, 210, 255, 284, 286
crosswort *Cruciata laevipes* 101
crowberry *Empetrum nigrum*
  ssp. *nigrum* 33, 110, 117, 208, 209, 245, 247, 253, 255, 258, 272, 286
  northern ssp. *hermaphroditum* 40, 218
cuckoo-pint *Arum maculatum* 114
cudweed
  common *Filago vulgaris* 102
  heath *Gnaphalium sylvaticum* 102, 114
  small *Filago minima* 85, 102
currant *Ribes*
  black *R. nigrum* 102
  downy *R. spicatum* 283
  mountain *R. alpinum* 153
  red *rubrum* 102
daffodil *Narcissus pseudonarcissus* 153, 178
dandelions *Taraxacum offici-*

INDEX

nalis agg. 42
daisy *Bellis perennis* 260
deer sedge *Trichophorum cespitosum* 127, 134, 210, 255
dewberry *Rubus caesius* 101
dock *Rumex*
    water *R. hydrolapathum* 148
dog's mercury *Mercurialis perennis* 114, 148, 151, 178, 150, 261
dogwood *Cornus sanguinea* 102
dropwort *Filipendula vulgaris* 149, 152
dwarf azalea *Loiseleuria procumbens* 208
eelgrass *Zostera marina* 61
    narrow-leaved *Z. angustifolia* 61, 65
elder *Sambucus nigra* 84, 92, 96, 102, 185
elm *Ulmus*
    English *U. procera* 172
    wych *U. glabra* 33, 111, 151, 153, 155, 168, 172, 184, 185, 250, 283
enchanter's nightshade
    Circaea lutetiana 114, 178
    alpine *C. alpina* 179
Esthwaite waterweed *Hydrilla verticillata* 199
eyebright *Euphrasia* 42, 165, 208, 225, 226, 260
    E. officinalis ssp. *monticola* 283
false brome *Brachypodium sylvaticum* 114, 148, 153, 178
False sedge *Kobresia simpliciuscula* 263
fescue *Festuca*
    giant *F. gigantea* 114
    red *F. rubra* 62, 92, 165, 208, 260
    sheep's *F. ovina* 175, 207, 259
    viviparous *F. vivipara* 209, 222
    wood *F. altissima* 114, 179, 283
field fleawort *Senecio integrifolius* 36, 260
field maple *Acer campestre* 111, 147
figwort *Scrophularia*
    common *S. nodosa* 114

green *S. umbrosa* I 142
flat sedge *Blysmus compressus* 63, 157, 158
    saltmarsh *B. rufus* 63
flax *Linum*
    fairy *L. catharticum* 153, 208, 260
    perennial *L. perenne* ssp. *anglicum* 34, 158
flowering rush *Butomus umbellatus* 142
flying bent *Molinia caerulea* 130, 134, 160, 163, 210, 284
fool's water-cress *Apium nodiflorum* 140
forget-me-not *Myosotis*
    alpine *M. alpestris* 36, 264, 267
    creeping *M. secunda* 211
    early *M. ramosissima* 85
    pale *M. stolonifera* 224, 258
    water *M. scorpioides* 140, 198
    wood *M. sylvatica* 114, 250
foxglove *Digitalis purpurea* 34, 101, 167, 208
gentian
    autumn *Gentianella amarella* 260
    field *G. campestris* 85, 283
    marsh *Gentiana pneumonanthe* 110, 130
    spring *G. verna* 34, 38, 264, 267
glasswort *Salicornia* 61
globeflower *Trollius europaeus* 101, 158, 160, 165, 223, 250, 282, 283
golden samphire *Inula crithmoides* 93
goldenrod *Solidago virgaurea* 253
gooseberry *Ribes uva-crispa* 102
gorse *Ulex*
    common *U. europaeus* 63, 70, 84, 96, 102, 109, 110, 151, 318
    dwarf *U. minor* 110
    western *U. gallii* 110
grass of Parnassus *Parnassia palustris* 85, 157, 212, 267, 283, 286, 300
great mullein *Verbascum thapsus* 153
green hellebore *Helleborus*

viridis 149
gromwell *Lithospermum officinale* 148, 149
ground ivy *Glechoma hederacea* 114
guelder rose *Viburnum opulus* 147, 151, 153
gypsywort *Lycopus europaeus* 198
hair-grass *Deschampsia*
    tufted *D. cespitosa* 178
    wavy *D. flexuosa* 152, 175
hairy brome *Bromopsis ramosa* 114
hairy rock-cress *Arabis hirsuta* 152, 261
hard grass *Parapholis strigosa* 63
harebell *Campanula rotundifolia* 84, 101, 153, 165, 260
hawkbit *Leontodon*
    autumn *L. autumnalis* 63
    rough *L. hispidus* 158, 282
hawksbeard *Crepis*
    leafless *C. praemorsa* 158
    marsh *C. paludosa* 223, 282
    northern *C. mollis* 252
    smooth *C. capillaris* 63, 101
    rough *C. biennis* 83
hawkweed *Hieracium* 36, 42, 226, 261
    alpine *H. holosericeum* 36, 221
    (lists of scientific names on pp. 226 & 261)
hawthorn *Crataegus monogyna* 33, 96, 102, 147, 151, 155, 156, 172, 175, 245, 295, 318
    Midland *C. laevigata* 250
hazel *Corylus avellana* 33, 111, 147, 148, 151, 153, 155, 156, 168, 172, 173, 175, 185, 250, 283
heather
    ling *Calluna vulgaris* 26, 33, 85, 91, 92, 109, 110, 127, 128, 136, 149, 152, 157, 159, 160, 176, 187, 207–10, 236, 237, 243–7, 253, 271, 272, 273, 284, 286, 294, 316, 318
    bell *Erica cinerea* 110, 149, 160, 208
hedge woundwort *Stachys sylvatica* 282

helleborine *Epipactis*
  broad-leaved *E. helleborine* 114, 156, 250
  dark red *E. atrorubens* 149, 152, 250, 260
  dune *E. leptochila* var. *dunensis* 85
  green-flowered *E. phyllanthes* 85
  marsh *E. palustris* 85, 155, 162
  narrow-lipped *E. leptochila* 267
  sword-leaved *Cephalanthera longifolia* 114, 155, 250
hemp agrimony *Eupatorium cannabinum* 91, 92, 114, 142, 283
henbane *Hyoscyamus niger* 83
herb bennet *Geum urbanum* 114, 178
herb paris *Paris quadrifolia* 114, 250, 283
herb robert *Geranium robertianum* I 92, 114, 151, 178, 261
hoary mugwort *Artemisai stelleriana* 83
hogweed *Heracleum sphondylium* 92, 223
holly *Ilex aquifolium* 33, 102, 116, 117, 147, 151, 172, 173, 190
honeysuckle *Lonicera periclymenum* 116
hornbeam *Carpinus betulus* 111
horned pondweed *Zannichellia palustris* 142
hound's tongue *Cynoglossum officinale* 86, 153
hutchinsia *Hornungia petraea* 157
Iceland purslane *Koenigia islandica* 212
Isle of Man cabbage *Coincya monensis* 83
ivy *Hedera helix* 176
ivy-leaved crowfoot *Ranunculus hederaceus* 212
ivy-leaved duckweed *Lemna trisulca* 198
Jacob's-ladder *Polemonium caeruleum* 35, 262
jack-by-the-hedge *Alliaria petiolata* 108

Japanese knotweed *Fallopia japonica* 322
juniper *Juniperus communis*
  ssp. *communis* 31, 33, 148, 151, 153, 167, 168, 174, 186 218, 244,
  dwarf ssp. *nana* 208, 218
knapweed *Centaurea*
  common *C. nigra* 101, 158, 160, 282
  greater *C. scabiosa* 101, 158, 161
kidney vetch *Anthyllis vulneraria* 108, 109, 158, 161, 283
Labrador tea *Ledum groenlandicum* 131
lady's mantle *Alchemilla* 42, 223, 226, 252
  A. filicaulis 226
  A. glabra 223, 282
  A. glomerulans 252
  A. minima 264
  A. monticola 252
  A. wichurae 226, 264
  A. xanthochlora 252
lady's smock *Cardamine pratensis* 108
larch *Larix decidua, L. kaempferi* and hybrids 119, 148, 153, 169–71, 189, 251, 298, 300
lesser chickweed *Stellaria pallida* 86
lesser marshwort *Apium inundatum* 198
lily of the valley *Convallaria majalis* 148, 152, 153, 161, 179, 250
lousewort *Pedicularis palustris* 109
lyme grass *Leymus arenarius* 83
maiden pink *Dianthus deltoides* 86
mare's-tail *Hippuris vulgaris* 148
marjoram *Origanum vulgare* 156, 158
marram *Ammophila arenaria* 84, 85, 87, 89
marsh marigold (kingcup) *Caltha palustris* 136, 157, 160, 179, 198, 252
marsh pennywort *Hydrocotyle vulgaris* 84
mat grass *Nardus stricta* 157, 208, 210, 218, 246, 252,

258, 273, 275, 279
meadowsweet *Filipendula ulmaria* 92, 140, 179, 198, 223, 261, 282
meadow grass *Poa*
  alpine *P. alpina* 225, 264
  glaucous *P. glauca* 36, 41, 225
  smooth *P. pratensis* 165
  wood *P. nemoralis* 114
meadow oat-grass *Helictotrichon pratense* 152
meadow-rue *Thalictrum*
  alpine *T. alpinum* 224, 266
  common *T. flavum* 65, 148
  lesser *T. minus* 152, 223, 264
meadow vetchling *Lathyrus pratensis* 101
melick grass *Melica*
  mountain *M. nutans* 152, 156, 179, 250, 283
  wood *M. uniflora* 114, 178, 250
mezereon *Daphne mezereum* 147, 153
milkwort *Polygala*
  dwarf *P. amarella* 157
  heath *P. serpyllifolia* 208, 253
moschatel *Adoxa moschatellina* 114, 253
mountain avens *Dryas octopetala* 36, 216, 225, 267
mountain everlasting *Antennaria dioica* 223, 262, 267
mountain sorrel *Oxyria digyna* 34, 223
mouse-ear *Cerastium*
  alpine *C. alpinum* 216, 225
  common *C. fontanum* 260
  field *C. arvense* 102
  little *C. semidecandrum* 84
mouse-ear hawkweed *Pilosella officinarum* 260
musk mallow *Malva moschata* 101
navelwort *Umbilicus rupestris* 167
New Zealand pygmyweed *Crassula helmsii* 199, 250, 322
nightshade
  deadly *Atropa belladonna* 35, 148, 149
  woody *Solanum dulcamara* 179

oak *Quercus* 111, 116, 118, 148, 153, 155, 168, 169, 174, 187, 189, 190
  pedunculate *Q. robur* 33, 147
  sessile *Q. petraea* 33, 147, 153, 172, 283
orache *Atriplex*
  Babington's *A. glabriuscula* 83
  frosted *A. laciniata* 83
  grass-leaved *A. littoralis* 65
  spear-leaved *A. prostrata* 83
orchid
  bee *Ophrys apifera* 85, 95, 162
  bird's nest *Neottia nidus-avis* 114, 156
  bog *Hammarbya paludosa* 211
  burnt *O. ustulata* 101, 149, 160, 162
  common spotted *Dactylorhiza fuchsii* 95, 101, 156, 160, 282
  coralroot *Corallorrhiza trifida* 41, 85
  early (crimson) marsh *D. incarnata* 85, 157, 160, 283
  early purple *Orchis mascula* 92, 101, 114, 156, 160, 283
  fly *Ophrys insectifera* 148, 152, 156
  fragrant *Gymnadenia conopsea* 101, 158, 160, 283
  frog *Coeloglossum viride* 101, 156, 160, 282
  greater butterfly *Platanthera chlorantha* 101, 156, 160
  green-winged *O. morio* 149
  heath spotted *D. ericetorum* 130, 160
  lady's slipper *Cypripedium calceolus* 154, 321
  lesser butterfly *P. bifolia* 101, 130, 160
  northern marsh *D. purpurella* 91, 95, 149, 157, 160, 283
  pyramidal *Anacamptis pyramidalis* 85, 95, 162
  small white *Pseudorchis albida* 286
orpine *Sedum telephium* 101

oxeye daisy *Leucanthemum vulgare* 101, 158, 160, 165
oysterplant *Mertensia maritima* 83
pansy *Viola*
  mountain *V. lutea* 161, 265–7
  wild *V. tricolor* 84
pea *Lathyrus*
  narrow-leaved everlasting *L. sylvestris* 91
  sea *L. japonicus* 83
pearlwort *Sagina*
  alpine *S. saginoides* 36
  knotted *S. nodosa* 283
pepper saxifrage *Silaum silaus* 160, 161
pettywhin *Genista anglica* 110, 116, 160
pine *Pinus*
  lodgepole *P. contorta* 298
  Scots *P. sylvestris* 110, 111, 112, 116, 117, 119, 123, 148, 168, 169, 189, 251
pitcher-plant *Sarracenia purpurea* 132
plantain *Plantago*
  buck's-horn *P. coronopus* 62, 63, 84
  hoary *P. media* 153, 158
  ribwort *P. lanceolata* 260
  sea *P. maritima* 62, 92
ploughman's spikenard *Inula conyza* 85, 148, 152
pondweed *Potamogeton* 140
  American *P. epihydrus* 198
  bog *P. polygonifolius* 197, 211
  blunt-leaved *P. obtusifolius* 197
  broad-leaved *P. natans* 198
  curled *P. crispus* 142, 157, 198
  perfoliate *P. perfoliatus* 197
  red *P. alpinus* 198
  small *P. berchtoldii* 198
  various-leaved *P. gramineus* 198
prickly saltwort *Salsola kali* 83
primrose *Primula vulgaris* 92, 114, 164
  bird's-eye *P. farinosa* 34, 101, 149, 157, 160–2, 212, 252
privet *Ligustrum vulgare* 102, 153
purple loosestrife *Lythrum salicaria* 198
purple milk-vetch *Astragalus danicus* 86, 93
quaking grass *Briza media* 153, 260
ragwort *Senecio*
  broad-leaved *S. fluviatilis* 143
  common *S. jacobaea* 84
  marsh *S. aquaticus* 140
Rannoch rush *Scheuchzeria palustris* 37
raspberry *Rubus idaeus* 118
Ray's knotweed *Polygonum oxyspermum* 83
red rattle *Pedicularis palustris* 136, 138, 157, 160, 283
reed *Phragmites australis* 65, 138, 140, 157, 198
reed-grass *Phalaris arundinacea* 137, 198
restharrow *Ononis repens* 84, 102, 158
  spiny *O. spinosa* 63
rigid hornwort *Ceratophyllum demersum* 140, 198
rock-rose *Helianthemum*
  common *H. nummularium* 93, 148, 152, 153, 156, 159, 164, 260
  hoary *H. oelandicum* 148, 153
rock samphire *Crithmum maritimum* 92, 148
rose (briar) *Rosa* 102
  burnet *R. pimpinellifolia* 84, 149, 152
  dog *R. canina* 102
  Japanese *R. rugosa* 84
  soft downy *R. mollis* 102
roseroot *Sedum rosea* 34, 216, 223, 264
rowan *Sorbus aucuparia* 33, 151, 172, 245, 251, 295, 299, 318
rush *Juncus*
  alpine *J. alpinoarticulatus* 263
  blunt-flowered *J. subnodulosus* 148
  bulbous *J. bulbosus* 197
  heath *J. squarrosus* 110, 210, 245, 252, 258, 273
  jointed *J. articulatus* 63, 157, 212
  round-fruited *J. compressus* 114
  saltmarsh *J. gerardii* 62

sea *J. maritimus* 63
sharp-flowered *J. acutiflorus* 211
soft *J. effusus* 63, 68, 70, 141, 211, 258
thread *J. filiformis* 198, 200
three-flowered *J. triglumis* 224, 266
sand cat's-tail *Phleum arenarium* 85
sand couch-grass *Elytrigia juncea* 83
sand leek *Allium scorodoprasum* 91, 114, 143, 148
sand spurrey *Spergularia rubra* 102
sandwort
  spring *Minuartia verna* 152, 224, 262, 266
  thyme-leaved *Arenaria serpyllifolia* 102
  three-nerved *Moehringia trinervia* 113
sanicle *Sanicula europaea* 114, 178
saw-wort *Serratula tinctoria*
saxifrage *Saxifraga*
  alpine *S. nivalis* 36, 216, 225, 264
  alternate-leaved *Chrysosplenium alternifolium* 114, 261
  golden *C. oppositifolium* 114, 212
  mossy *S. hypnoides* 34, 216, 223, 224, 262, 286
  purple *S. oppositifolia* 216, 224, 267
  starry *S. stellaris* 212, 218, 259
  tufted *S. cespitosa* 321
  yellow *S. aizoides* 34, 157, 212, 223, 224, 266, 283
  yellow marsh *S. hirculus* 36, 265–7
scabious
  devil's-bit *Succisa pratensis* 207, 108, 160, 163, 223, 279
  field *Knautia arvensis* 101, 161, 282
  small *Scabiosa columbaria* 153, 158, 159, 260
scurvygrass *Cochlearia*
  alpine *C. pyrenaica* 223, 262, 266
  common *C. officinalis* 63, 92

sea beet *Beta vulgaris* ssp. *maritima* 83
sea bindweed *Calystegia soldanella* 83
sea-blite *Suaeda maritima* 62
sea buckthorn *Hippophae rhamnoides* 85
sea cabbage *Crambe maritima* 83
sea holly *Eryngium maritimum* 83
sea lavender *Limonium* 65
  rock *L. binervosum* 92
sea-milkwort *Glaux maritima* 62
sea-purslane *Atriplex portulacoides* 65
sea radish *Raphanus raphanistrum* ssp. *maritimus* 83
sea rocket *Cakile maritima* 83
sea sandwort *Honckenya peploides* 83
sea-spurrey *Spergularia*
  greater *S. media* 62
  lesser *S. marina* 62
  rock *S. rupicola* 92
sea wormwood *Seriphidium maritimum* 65
sedge *Carex*
  bird's-foot *C. ornithopoda* 114, 152, 156, 260
  black alpine *C. atrata* 36, 41, 225
  bladder *C. vesicaria* 148, 198
  bottle *C. rostrata* 116, 136, 157, 162, 198, 199, 211, 212
  bog *C. limosa* 137, 162, 211, 256, 284
  brown *C. disticha* 137, 148, 162, 286
  carnation *C. panicea* 63, 157, 212, 260
  common *C. nigra* 63, 84, 136, 212
  cyperus *C. pseudocyperus* 148
  dioecious *C. dioica* 157, 212
  distant *C. distans* 63
  elongated *C. elongata* 148, 179
  false fox *C. otrubae* 63
  few-flowered *C. pauciflora* 211, 284, 300
  fingered *C. digitata* 148,

149, 153
  flea *C. pulicaris* 212
  glaucous *C. flacca* 63, 153, 160, 212
  great fen *Cladium mariscus* 154, 157, 162
  greater tussock *C. paniculata* 114, 137, 138, 148, 157, 283
  hair *C. capillaris* 157, 158, 263
  large yellow *C. flava* 148
  lesser pond *C. acutiformis* 140, 198, 286
  lesser tussock *C. diandra* 137, 138, 148, 157, 162
  long-bracted *C. extensa* 63
  pendulous *C. pendula* 92, 114
  rare spring *C. ericetorum* 149, 157
  remote *C. remota* 114
  rigid *C. bigelowii* 209, 217, 253
  sand *C. arenaria* 84
  slender tufted *C. acuta* 137, 143, 157, 162, 198, 286
  smooth *C. laevigata* 114
  spring *C. caryophyllea* 153
  star *C. echinata* 211, 258
  tall bog *C. magellanica* 139, 211, 256, 284, 300
  tawny *C. hostiana* 157, 212
  tufted *C. elata* 157, 198
  water *C. aquatilis* 198, 286
  white *C. curta* 211, 258
  wood *C. sylvatica* 114
  yellow *C. viridula*
    ssp. *Ioedocarpa* 212
    ssp. *Ibrachyrrhyncha* 157
    ssp. *Iviridula* 140
selfheal *Prunella vulgaris* 114, 178, 260
service tree *Sorbus domestica* 147
sheep's-bit *Jasione montana* 92, 96, 101
shoreweed *Littorella uniflora* 197, 199
silverweed *Potentilla anserina* 84
six-stamened waterwort *Elatine hexandra* 41, 198
skullcap *Scutellaria galericulata* 179, 198
  lesser *S. minor* 139
slender naiad *Najas flexilis* 199

small-leaved lime *Tilia cordata* 33, 41, 147, 153, 172, 173
small-reed *Calamagrostis*
  Scandinavian *C. purpurea* 179
  purple *C. canescens* 148, 198
  wood *C. epigejos* 116, 148
smooth rupturewort *Herniaria glabra* 38, 102
Solomon's seal *Polygonatum multiflorum* 250
  angular *P. odoratum* 152
spearwort
  lesser *Ranunculus flammula* 197, 198, 211, 266
  greater *R. lingua* 138, 148, 162
speedwell *Veronica*
  blue water *V. anagallis-aquatica* 142
  germander *V. chamaedrys* 101
  spiked *V. spicata* 148, 149
  wood *V. montana* 114
spignel *Meum athamanticum* 34, 308
spike-rush *Eleocharis*
  common *E. palustris* 63, 84, 140
  few-flowered *E. quinqueflora* 157
  many-stalked *E. multicaulis* 212
  needle *E. acicularis* 140
  northern *E. austriaca* 286
spindle *Euonymus europaeus* 102, 147, 161, 250
spring squill *Scilla verna* 93
spruce *Picea*
  Norway *P. abies* 169, 319
  Sitka *P. sitchensis* 298, 300, 319
spurge *Euphorbia*
  Portland *E. portlandica* 85
  sea *E. paralias* 85
spurge laurel *Daphne laureola* 153
squinancywort *Asperula cynanchica* 149, 152
St John's wort *Hypericum*
  marsh *H. elodes* 139
  pale *H. montanum* 148, 152
  slender *H. pulchrum* 101
star-of-Bethlehem
  Ornithogalum angustifolium 148

stitchwort *Stellaria*
  bog *S. palustris* 212
  greater *S. holostea* 113, 176
  wood *S. nemorum* 114
stone-bramble *Rubus saxatilis* 148, 151, 156, 223, 250, 261, 283
stonecrop *Sedum*
  biting *S. acre* 84, 260
  English *S. anglicum* 83, 92, 96
  hairy *S. villosum* 225, 266
storksbill *Erodium*
  common *E. cicutarium* 84
  sticky *E. lebelii* 85
sundew *Drosera*
  great *D. anglica* 127, 137, 211, 284, 300
  oblong-leaved *D. intermedia* 130, 211
  round-leaved *D. rotundifolia* 110, 127, 210, 255, 284
sweet cicely *Myrrhis odorata* 167
sweet-grass *Glyceria*
  floating *G. fluitans* 140
  reed *G. maxima* 138, 199
sweet woodruff *Galium odoratum* 114
sycamore *Acer pseudoplatanus* 111, 148, 151, 153, 166, 185
tansy *Tanacetum vulgare* 142
thistle
  carline *Carlina vulgaris* 85, 152, 156, 208
  melancholy *Cirsium heterophyllum* 101, 156, 158, 165, 282
  musk *Carduus nutans* 260
  slender *Carduus tenuiflorus* 86, 92
thrift *Armeria maritima* 62, 266
timothy grass *Phleum pratense* 165
  alpine *P. alpinum* 40, 225, 264
toothwort *Lathraea squamaria* 148
tormentil *Potentilla erecta* 152, 175, 208, 253
traveller's joy *Clematis vitalba* 102
tree lupin *Lupinus arboreus* 84
tree-mallow *Lavatera arborea* 41

tutsan *Hypericum androsaemum* 148, 179
twayblade *Listera ovata* 101, 156, 158, 160, 282
  lesser *L. cordata* 117, 160, 255, 286
valerian *Valeriana officinalis* 179
  marsh *V. dioica* 157, 160, 252, 283
vernal grass *Anthoxanthum odoratum* 152, 165, 260
vetch *Vicia*, *Lathyrus*
  bitter *L. linifolius* 116, 157, 160, 253
  bush *V. sepium* 92, 101, 160
  horseshoe *Hippocrepis comosa* 34, 152, 156, 260, 261
  spring *V. lathyroides* 84
  tufted *V. cracca* 101, 160, 161
  wood *V. sylvatica* 34, 92, 250, 283
  wood bitter V. orobus 34, 165, 252
  yellow *V. lutea* 86
violet *Viola*
  hairy *V. hirta* 152, 153
  heath *V. riviniana* 113, 176, 178, 208, 260
  marsh *V. palustris* 190, 212
  rock *V. rupestris* 36, 149, 264
wall lettuce *Mycelis muralis* 178, 261
water avens *Geum rivale* 101, 114, 160, 161, 178, 223, 250, 282
water-cress *Rorippa nasturtium-aquaticum* 140
water-crowfoot
  brackish *Ranunculus baudotii* 63
  common *R. aquatilis* 198
  pond *R. peltatus* 140
  river *R. fluitans* 142
water-dropwort *Oenanthe*
  hemlock *O. crocata* 63, 179
  parsley *O. lachenalii* 63
water lobelia *Lobelia dortmanna* 34, 138, 197
water mint *Mentha aquatica* 198
water pepper *Persicaria hydropiper* 140
  small *P. minor* 198

water plantain *Alisma plantago-aquatica* 140, 148
floating *Luronium natans* 199
lesser *Baldellia ranunculoides* 141, 148
water purslane *Lythrum portula* 198
water-starwort *Callitriche*
common *C. stagnalis* 140, 197
intermediate *C. hamulata* 197
Welsh poppy *Meconopsis cambrica* 167
white beak-sedge *Rhynchospora alba* 127, 134, 212, 284
white water lily *Nymphaea alba* 197
whitebeam *Sorbus*
Swedish *S. intermedia* 112
Lancastrian *S. lancastriensis* 148, 151, 153
rock *S. rupicola* 153
whitlow-grass *Draba*
hoary *D. incana* 224, 260, 262, 267
wall *D. muralis* 260, 301
whorled caraway *Carum verticillatum* 43, 110
wild basil *Clinopodium vulgare* 148
wild carrot *Daucus carota* 92, 161
wild celery *Apium graveolens* 63
wild garlic *Allium ursinum* 114, 178, 250
wild onion *Allium vineale* 114
wild strawberry *Fragaria vesca* 114, 178, 261
wild thyme *Thymus polytrichus* 84, 153, 208, 209, 222, 260
willow *Salix* 31, 111, 123, 138, 139, 168, 251, 282
almond *S. triandra* 140
bay *S. pentandra* 137, 162
creeping *S. repens* 85
dark-leaved *S. myrsinifolia* 162
downy *S. lapponum* 36, 216, 225
goat (sallow) *S. caprea* 33
grey *S. cinerea* 136, 137
least *S. herbacea* 208, 209, 217, 218, 267
net-leaved *S. reticulata* 267
tea-leaved *S. phylicifolia* 162
willowherb *Epilobium*
alpine *E. anagallidifolium* 259
chickweed *E. alsinifolium* 224, 259
great hairy *E. hirsutum* 140, 198
marsh *E. palustre* 211
rosebay *Chamerion angustifolium* 92, 109, 223, 261
short-fruited *E. obscurum* 140
wintergreen *Pyrola*
lesser *P. minor* 116, 117, 160
round-leaved *P. rotundifolia* 41, 85
serrated *Orthilia secunda* 176
wood anemone *Anemone nemorosa* 113, 157, 160, 176, 261
wood millet *Milium effusum* 114
wood sage *Teucrium scorodonia* 101, 113, 175
wood sorrel *Oxalis acetosella* 113, 175, 176, 261
woodrush *Luzula*
great *L. sylvatica* 33, 113, 175, 253
hairy *L. pilosa* 113
yarrow *Achillea millefolium* 101, 260
yellow bartsia *Parentucellia viscosa* 86
yellow bird's-nest *Monotropa hypopitys* 85, 148, 154
yellow-cress *Rorippa*
creeping *R. sylvestris* 142
marsh *R. palustris* 140
yellow flag *Iris pseudacorus* 63, 140, 179
yellow horned poppy *Glaucium flavum* 83
yellow loosestrife *Lysimachia vulgaris* 198
yellow oat-grass *Trisetum flavescens* 153, 260
yellow-rattle *Rhinanthus minor* 160, 165, 226, 283
yellow star of Bethlehem *Gagea lutea* 114, 161
yellow water lily *Nuphar lutea* 197
hybrid *N. spenneriana* 199
yew *Taxus baccata* 33, 147, 148, 153, 173, 174, 186, 283
Yorkshire fog *Holcus lanatus* 92

Ferns and allies
adder's tongue *Ophioglossum vulgatum* 85
small *O. azoricum* 86
beech fern *Phegopteris connectilis* 177
bladder fern *Cystopteris*
brittle *C. fragilis* 151, 156, 223, 250, 261, 283
mountain *C. montana* 40, 225
bracken *Pteridium aquilinum* 33, 85, 109, 110, 113, 115, 152, 176, 207, 245, 252, 294, 316
buckler fern *Dryopteris*
broad *D. dilatata* 92, 113, 114, 116, 176, 261
hay-scented *D. aemula* 41, 92, 115, 177, 184
narrow *D. carthusiana* 116
northern *D. expansa* 36, 253
rigid *D. submontana* 40, 151, 153, 156, 224, 260
filmy fern *Hymenophyllum*
Tunbridge *H. tunbrigense* 115, 177, 178, 184
Wilson's *H. wilsonii* 43, 177, 184, 286
hard fern *Blechnum spicant* 115, 176
hart's tongue fern *Phyllitis scolopendrium* 92, 115, 151, 153, 156, 262
holly fern *Polystichum lonchitis* 36, 147, 216, 224, 264, 321
Killarney fern *Trichomanes speciosum* 36, 115, 178, 184, 322
lady fern *Athyrium filix-femina* 92, 115, 176
lemon-scented fern *Oreopteris limbosperma* 176, 253
limestone fern *Gymnocarpium robertiana* 151, 153, 156, 260
maidenhair *Adiantum capil-*

lus-veneris 148, 149
male fern *Dryopteris filix-mas* 115, 156, 176
  mountain *D. oreades* 253
  scaly *D. affinis* 176, 253
marsh fern *Thelypteris palustris* 138, 148
moonwort *Botrychium lunaria* 85, 260
oak fern *Gymnocarpium dryopteris* 151, 177
oblong woodsia *Woodsia ilvensis* 36, 216, 219, 321
parsley fern *Cryptogramma crispa* 167, 217, 253, 286
pillwort *Pilularia globulifera* 41, 198
polypody *Polypodium vulgare* 101, 176, 261
  limestone *P. cambricum* 149
royal fern *Osmunda regalis* 116, 139, 141
rustyback *Ceterach officinarum* 153, 167
shield fern *Polystichum*
  prickly *P. aculeatum* 115, 151, 156, 179, 250, 261, 283
  soft *P. setiferum* 92, 115, 179
spleenwort *Asplenium*
  black *A. adiantum-nigrum* 96, 167
  forked *A. septentrionale* 36, 40, 216, 219–21
  green *A. viride* 151, 156, 216, 223, 261, 283
  lanceolate *A. obovatum* 41, 96, 308
  maidenhair *A. trichomanes* 36, 151, 153, 167, 221
  sea *A. marinum* 92
wall rue *Asplenium ruta-muraria* 151, 153, 167, 221

alpine clubmoss *Diphasiastrum alpinum* 43, 209, 218
fir clubmoss *Huperzia selago* 130, 209, 218, 253, 286
interrupted clubmoss *Lycopodium annotinum* 218
lesser clubmoss *Selaginella selaginoides* 212, 283
marsh clubmoss *Lycopodiella inundata* 41, 110
stag's-horn clubmoss

Lycopodium clavatum 130, 218

quillwort *Isoetes lacustris* 197, 199
  spring *I. echinospora* 41, 198

Dutch rush *Equisetum hyemale* 250
giant horsetail *E. telmateia* 91, 92, 114, 283
marsh horsetail *E. palustre* 157
shady horsetail *E. pratense* 250
variegated horsetail *E. variegatum* 114, 263, 283
water horsetail *E. fluviatile* 157

Mosses
Acrocladium cuspidatum 138, 211
A. giganteum 137
A. sarmentosum 211
A. stramineum 211
Aulacomnium palustre 138
Barbula icmadophila 226
Bryum pseudotriquetrum 211
B. weigelii 259
Campylium calcareum 155
C. stellatum 137, 211
Campylopus atrovirens 212
C. flexuosus 258
C. introflexus 301
Coscinodon cribrosus 221
Cratoneuron commutatum 157, 211, 212
C. filicinum 211
Dicranella squarrosa 212
Dicranoweissia crispula 221
Dicranum bergeri 128
D. majus 115
D. polysetum 117
D. scoparium 110, 115
D. scottianum 178
Drepanocladus cossonii 157, 211, 212
D. exannulatus 211, 212
D. revolvens 137, 211
Encalypta rhabdocarpa 266
Entodon orthocarpus 266
Fontinalis antipyretica 197
Grimmia atrata 217, 221
G. elongata 221
G. incurva 221
G. montana 221

Habrodon perpusillus 185
Hamatocaulis (Drepanocladus) vernicosus 211,212, 266, 320
Haplodon wormskjoldii 266
Hedwigia integrifolia 221
Homomallium incurvatum 155
Hylocomium splendens 115
H. umbratum 181
Hypnum cupressiforme 115
H. hamulosum 226
H. imponens 110
H. jutlandicum 110
H. mamillatum 182
Isothecium holtii 182
I. myosuroides 182
I. striatulum 155
Kiaeria falcata 210
K. starkei 210
Leptodontium recurvifolium 226
Leucobryum glaucum 115
Meesia uliginosa 212, 226
Mnium hornum 115
Oncophorus virens 226, 266
Orthothecium rufescens 226, 250, 266
Orthotrichum spp. 115
Philonotis fontana 212
Plagiothecium undulatum 115
Pleurochaete squarrosa 155
Pleurozium schreberi 110, 115
Pohlia ludwigii 210
P. wahlenbergii var. *glacialis* 210, 259
hair moss *Polytrichum commune* 116
P. formosum 115
P. juniperinum 258
Pseudoleskiella catenulata 266
Pterygynandrum filiforme 185
feather moss *Ptilium crista-castrensis* 117, 180, 181
woolly fringe moss *Racomitrium lanuginosum* 209, 210, 240, 253, 254, 267
Rhytidiadelphus loreus 181, 185
R. squarrosus 138, 211
Rhytidium rugosum 155, 266
Scorpidium scorpioides 137, 211
Sematophyllum micans 182
bogmoss *Sphagnum* 117, 127, 128, 136, 137, 284, 310, 314

S. affine 210
S. auriculatum 212
S. compactum 127
S. contortum 136, 211
S. cuspidatum 127, 256
S. fimbriatum 128
S. fuscum 128, 256, 284
S. imbricatum 128, 256, 284
S. magellanicum 127, 256, 284
S. molle 127
S. palustre 128
S. papillosum 127, 256, 284
S. pulchrum 128
S. recurvum 128, 138, 211, 258
S. riparium 256
S. rubellum 127, 256, 284
S. squarrosum 136, 211
S. subnitens 127
S. subsecundum 136
S. tenellum 127
S. teres 136, 211
S. warnstorfii 211, 266
Splachnum vasculosum 259, 266
Thuidium delicatulum 181
T. tamariscinum 115, 181
Tomentypnum nitens 138, 226, 266
Tortella nitida 155
Tortula ruraliformis 84
Ulota spp. 115, 185

Liverworts
Adelanthus decipiens 182
Anthelia julacea 212
Bazzania trilobata 181
Frullania tamarisci 182
Jubula hutchinsiae 182
Jungermannia exsertifolia ssp. *cordifolia* 197
Lophocolea bidentata 115
Lophozia lycopodioides 266
Marsupella emarginata 212
Nowellia curvifolia 182
Pellia epiphylla 115
Plagiochila atlantica 182
P. spinulosa 182
Radula voluta 182
Saccogyna viticulosa 182
Scapania aspera 266
S. gracilis 182
S. undulata 212
Solenostoma cordifolia 212

Lichens
Alectoria nigricans 209
Allantoparmelia alpicola 266
Baeomyces placophyllus 209
B. roseus 110
Belonia russula 226
Bryoria fuscescens 115
Caloplaca marina 82
Cetraria aculeatum 110, 209
C. chlorophylla 115
C. commixta 266
C. hepatizon 266
Iceland moss *C. islandica* 209, 253
reindeer moss *Cladonia arbuscula* 209, 253
reindeer moss *C. portentosa* 110, 128
reindeer moss *C. rangiferina* 209, 255, 266
reindeer moss *C. uncialis* 128, 209
Cladonia coccifera 110
C. floerkiana 110
C. furcata 110
C. gracilis 110
C. macilenta 110
C. pyxidata 110
C. rangiformis 110
Collema glebulentum 226
Dermatocarpon intestiniforme 226
D. miniatum 226
Evernia prunastri 115
Gyalidea lecideopsis 226
Gyalideopsis scotica 226
Hypogymnia physodes 110
rock tripe *Lasallia pustulata* 221
Lecanora achariana 221
L. atra 82
Lecidea hypnorum 226
Leptogium burgessii 184
Lobaria amplissima 184
tree lungwort *L. pulmonaria* 115, 184
L. scrobiculata 184
L. virens 184
Massalongia carnosa 266
Nephroma laevigatum 184
Ochrolechia frigida 209
O. tartarea 115
Parmelia caperata 115
P. incurva 266
P. saxatilis 115
P. sulcata 115
Parmeliella plumbea 184
Peltigera horizontalis 115, 184
P. leucophlebia 184
P. praetextata 115

Platysmatia glauca 115
P. norvegica 221
Porpidia superba 226
Pseudevernia furfuracea 253, 266
Ramalina farinacea 115
Rhizocarpon geographicum 221
Sphaerophorus globosus 115
S. melanocarpus 178
Sticta canariensis 185
S. fuliginosa 184
S. limbata 184
S. sylvatica 184
Thamnolia vermicularis 209
Umbilicaria crustulosa 221
U. deusta 266
U. hyperborea 266
Witches' beard *Usnea* spp. 128
U. subfloridana 115
Verrucaria maura 82
Xanthoria parietina 82
Marine algae
Alaria esculenta 83
Ceramium rubrum 82
Chondrus crispus 82
Corallina officinalis 82
Enteromorpha spp. 61, 65, 82
kelp *Laminaria digitata* 80
L. hyperborea 80
Lomentaria articulata 82
Mastocarpus stellatus 82
Palmaria palmata 82
Porphyra spp. 82
Ulva lactuca 65, 82
wrack
 bladder *Fucus vesiculosus* 82
 channelled *Pelvetia caniculata* 82
 knotted *Ascophyllum nodosum* 82
 serrated *Fucus serratus* 82
 spiral *F. spiralis* 82

ANIMALS
Mammals
badger *Meles meles* 45, 52, 111, 117–19, 228, 229, 268, 289, 300
bat
 barbastelle *Barbastella barbastellus* 104
 Brandt's *Myotis brandtii* 103, 166
 brown long-eared *Plecotus auritus* 103, 166
 Daubenton's *Myotis*

daubentonii 103, 201
Natterer's *Myotis nattereri* 103, 166
noctule *Nyctalus noctula* 103, 166
pipistrelle *Pipistrellus pipistrellus* 103, 166
whiskered *Myotis mystacinus* 103, 166
deer
  muntjac *Muntiacus reevesi* 162
  red *Cervus elaphus* 132, 162, 185, 186, 227, 238, 268
  roe *Capreolus capreolus* 52, 111, 117, 118, 132, 162, 178, 300
  sika *Cervus nippon* 185
dolphin
  bottle-nosed *Tursiops truncatus* 80
  common *Delphinus delphis* 80
dormouse *Muscardinus avellanarius* 162, 188
fox *Vulpes vulpes* 75, 78, 90, 91, 103, 111, 132, 186, 227–9, 268, 289, 299, 300, 301
goat, feral *Capra hircus* 227, 268, 287, 288, 300
harbour porpoise *Phocaena phocaena* 80
hare
  brown *Lepus europaeus* 78, 103, 268, 288
  mountain *L. timidus* 288
hedgehog *Erinaceus europaeus* 111
mink *Mustela vison* 78, 98, 144, 201
mole *Talpa europaea* 268, 289, 294
otter *Lutra lutra* 78, 97, 98, 144, 201, 289
pine marten *Martes martes* 45, 186, 187, 229, 268, 288, 300
polecat *Mustela putorius* 45, 105, 132
rabbit *Oryctolagus cuniculus* 78, 86, 90, 98, 103, 111, 120, 162, 202, 228, 233, 268, 270, 288
seal
  common *Phoca vitulina* 80
  grey *Halichoerus grypus* 80

shrew
  common *Sorex araneus* 104
  pygmy *S. minutus* 104
  water *Neomys fodiens* 201
squirrel
  grey *Sciurus carolinensis* 117, 187, 188
  red *S. vulgaris* 117, 187, 188, 319
stoat *Mustela erminea* 104, 111, 229, 268, 289, 299
vole
  bank *Clethrionomys glareolus* 104, 162, 268
  field *Microtus agrestis* 104, 111, 162, 228, 229, 233, 236, 268, 289, 290, 292, 299
  water *Arvicola terrestris* 137, 201, 268, 289
weasel *Mustela nivalis* 104, 111, 229, 268, 289, 299
wildcat *Felis silvestris* 288
wood mouse *Apodemus sylvaticus* 104, 162, 188, 268

Birds
avocet *Recurvirostra avosetta* 73
bittern *Botaurus stellaris* 136
blackbird *Turdus merula* 96, 107, 123, 189, 299
blackcap *Sylvia atricapilla* 122, 189
bullfinch *Pyrrhula pyrrhula* 122, 245
bunting
  corn *Miliaria calandra* 104, 278
  reed *Emberiza schoeniclus* 96, 132, 202, 278
  snow *Plectrophenax nivalis* 238, 245
buzzard *Buteo buteo* 47, 49, 56, 103, 120, 189, 229, 233–5, 245, 268, 270, 271, 290, 291
  honey *Pernis apivorus* 189
  rough-legged *Buteo lagopus* 245
carrion crow *Corvus corone* 66, 105, 121, 166, 189, 245, 278, 301
chaffinch *Fringilla coelebs* 96, 107, 123, 166, 189, 299
chiffchaff *Phylloscopus collybita* 122, 189
chough *Pyrrhocorax pyrrhoco-*

rax 95
coot *Fulica atra* 140, 202, 203, 279
cormorant *Phalacrocorax carbo* 76, 94, 140, 143, 203
corncrake *Crex crex* 104, 278, 295
crossbill *Loxia curvirostra* 110, 300, 319
cuckoo *Cuculus canorus* 107, 244
curlew *Numenius arquata* 49, 68, 69, 71, 104, 105, 110, 132, 140, 163, 167, 243, 276, 282, 294, 299, 301
dipper *Cinclus cinclus* 18, 201, 245, 278, 295, 299
diver
  black-throated *Gavia arctica* 76, 97, 203
  great northern *G. immer* 76, 97, 203
  red-throated *G. stellata* 76, 97, 203
domestic pigeon *Columba livia* 94, 95, 231–3, 270, 323
dotterel *Eudromias morinellus* 43–5, 47, 56, 69, 240–2, 276, 322
dove
  collared *Streptopelia decaocto* 107
  rock *Columba livia* 95
  stock *C. oenas* 94, 95, 122, 278, 295
  turtle *Streptopelia turtur* 122
duck
  long-tailed *Clangula hyemalis* 75, 97, 203
  ruddy *Oxyura jamaicensis* 141
  tufted *Aythya fuligula* 75, 133, 140, 142, 162, 203, 279
dunlin *Calidris alpina* 54, 66–8, 71, 73, 76, 132, 243, 275, 293, 299, 301
dunnock *Prunella modularis* 96, 107, 189, 299
eagle
  golden *Aquila chrysaetos* 45, 51, 232, 237–9, 271, 291, 292, 320
  white-tailed (sea) *Haliaeetus albicilla* 45
eider *Somateria mollissima* 75,

91, 97, 237
fieldfare *Turdus pilaris* 96, 175, 245, 295
flycatcher
    pied *Ficedula hypoleuca* 45, 122, 189, 278
    spotted *Muscicapa striata* 122
fulmar *Fulmarus glacialis* 94, 97
gadwall *Anas strepera* 75, 133, 162
gannet *Sula bassana* 93, 97
garganey *Anas querquedula* 75, 133, 137
godwit
    bar-tailed *Limosa lapponica* 73
    black-tailed *L. limosa* 69, 73, 140
goldcrest *Regulus regulus* 96, 122, 299
goldfinch *Carduelis carduelis* 107
goldeneye *Bucephala clangula* 75, 76, 202, 203, 279
goosander *Mergus merganser* 141, 143, 202, 203, 277, 279, 295
goose
    barnacle *Branta leucopsis* 51, 74, 76, 77
    bean *Anser fabalis* 73
    brent *Branta bernicla* 74, 75
    Canada *B. canadensis* 141, 202
    greylag *Anser anser* 51, 73, 74, 77, 202
    pink-footed *A. brachyrhynchus* 73, 77
    white-fronted *A. albifrons* 74
goshawk *Accipiter gentilis* 120, 189, 300, 319
grebe
    black-necked *Podiceps nigricollis* 76, 97, 140, 162, 203
    great crested *P. cristatus* 76, 97, 141, 202, 203
    little *Tachybaptus ruficollis* 76, 97, 140, 142, 202, 203
    red-necked *Podiceps grisegena* 76, 97, 203
    Slavonian *P. auritus* 76, 203
greenfinch *Carduelis chloris* 96, 107

Greenland falcon *Falco rusticolus* 96
greenshank *Tringa nebularia* 73
grey partridge *Perdix perdix* 104, 105, 278, 295
grouse
    black *Tetrao tetrix* 49, 243, 272, 295, 299, 301
    red *Lagopus lagopus scoticus* 33, 132, 207, 240, 243, 245, 270–2, 279, 281, 295, 299, 301
guillemot
    black *Cepphus grylle* I 94
    common *Uria aalge* 93, 97
gull
    black-headed *Larus ridibundus* 48, 69, 75, 89–91, 97, 133, 134, 138, 140, 141, 157, 161–3, 167, 201–3, 277, 292
    common *L. canus* 70, 75, 91, 97, 202, 203
    glaucous *L. hyperboreus* 97
    great black-backed *L. marinus* 51, 69, 75, 91, 94, 97, 133, 201, 203, 293
    herring *L. argentatus* 69, 75, 90, 91, 94, 97, 133, 201, 203
    Iceland *L. glaucoides* 97
    lesser black-backed *L. fuscus* 69, 75, 90, 91, 97, 133, 201, 203, 277, 293
    little *L. minutus* 97
    Mediterranean *L. melanocephalus* 97
harrier
    hen *Circus cyaneus* 42, 132, 272, 292, 299, 320
    marsh *C. aeruginosus* 292
hawfinch *Coccothraustes coccothraustes* 123, 162, 190
heron *Ardea cinerea* 18, 76, 122, 163, 232
jackdaw *Corvus monedula* 106, 121, 165, 278, 295
jay *Garrulus glendarius* 121, 189, 299
kestrel *Falco tinnunculus* 59, 76, 106, 107, 120, 229, 232, 235–6, 247, 272, 289, 290, 295, 299
kingfisher *Alcedo atthis* 18, 143
kittiwake *Rissa tridactyla* 94, 97

knot *Calidris canutus* 73, 76, 276
lapwing *Vanellus vanellus* 18, 54, 66, 71–3, 104, 105, 162, 166, 243, 270, 274, 275, 282, 294, 299
linnet *Carduelis cannabina* 70, 96, 107, 111
magpie *Pica pica* 105, 121, 187, 189
mallard *Anas platyrhynchos* 70, 75, 76, 133, 140, 141, 202, 203, 277, 279, 295
Manx shearwater *Puffinus puffinus* 97
martin
    house *Delichon urbica* 107, 166, 295
    sand *Riparia riparia* 70, 107, 143
merlin *Falco columbarius* 42, 43, 56, 76, 87, 132, 232, 236, 245, 271, 272, 290, 320
moorhen *Gallinula chloropus* 70, 104, 105, 142, 202, 295
nightjar *Caprimulgus europaeus* 110, 122, 133, 243, 301
nuthatch *Sitta europaea* 190, 322
osprey *Pandion haliaetus* 140, 202, 203
owl
    barn *Tyto alba* 107, 279, 292
    little *Athene noctua* 107
    long-eared *Asio otis* 121, 189, 292
    short-eared *A. flammeus* 76, 96, 272, 289, 292, 299, 301
    tawny *Stryx aluco* 121, 189, 279, 292, 300
oystercatcher *Haematopus ostralegus* 68, 71, 82, 86, 90, 132, 276, 294
Pallas's sandgrouse *Syrrhaptes paradoxus* 44
peregrine *Falco peregrinus* 42, 47–9, 55, 56, 76, 94, 163, 229–34, 243, 269, 270, 276, 278, 290, 310, 320, 323
petrel
    Leach's *Oceanodroma leucorhoa* 97

storm *Hydrobates pelagicus* 97
phalarope
  grey *Phalaropus fulicarius* 73
  red-necked *P. lobatus* 73
pintail *Anas acuta* 75, 133, 202
pipit
  meadow *Anthus pratensis* 70, 87, 110, 132, 237, 242, 244, 245, 294, 299
  Richard's *A. novaeseelandiae* 96
  rock *A. spinoletta* 95
  tree *A. trivialis* 104, 105, 111, 279, 299
plover
  golden *Pluvialis apricaria* 54, 72, 73, 132, 163, 242, 270, 273–5, 293, 299, 301, 310
  grey *P. squatarola* 73
  ringed *Charadrius hiaticula* 69, 71, 86, 90, 276
pochard *Aythya ferina* 75, 133, 138, 140, 141, 203, 279
ptarmigan *Lagopus mutus* 238, 239, 240
puffin *Fratercula arctica* 94
raven *Corvus corax* 47–9, 55, 56, 94, 163, 188, 189, 229–34, 245, 247, 248, 268, 269, 289, 290, 299, 310, 318, 320, 323
razorbill *Alca torda* 93, 94, 97
red-backed shrike *Lanius collurio* 105
red-breasted merganser *Mergus serrator* 70, 75, 143, 202, 203
red kite *Milvus milvus* 43
redpoll *Carduelis flammea* 107, 111, 299
redshank *Tringa totanus* 66, 71, 104, 105, 132, 163, 167, 242, 275, 282, 294
  spotted *T. erythropus* 73
redstart *Phoenicurus phoenicurus* 122, 189, 278
redwing *Turdus iliacus* 96, 175, 245, 295
ring ouzel *Turdus torquatus* 43, 54, 244, 277, 294, 299
robin *Erithacus rubecula* 96, 123, 189, 299

rook *Corvus frugilegus* 66, 105, 106, 121, 166, 238, 279
ruff *Philomachus pugnax* 69, 140
sanderling *Calidris alba* 73
sandpiper
  common *Actitis hypoleucos* 201, 243, 276, 293
  curlew *Calidris ferruginea* 73
  green *Tringa ochropus* 73
  purple *Calidris maritima* 97, 242
  wood *Tringa glareola* 73
scaup *Aythya marila* 75, 97, 203
scoter
  common *Melanitta nigra* 75, 97, 203
  velvet *M. fusca* 75, 97, 203
shag *Phalacrocorax aristotelis* 94, 97
shelduck *Tadorna tadorna* 70, 75, 87, 90, 133, 202
shoveler *Spatula clypeata* 70, 75, 133, 140, 162, 202, 203
siskin *Carduelis spinus* 110, 123, 300, 319
skua
  arctic *Stercorarius parasiticus* 97
  great *S. skua* 97
  pomarine *S. pomarinus* 97
skylark *Alauda arvensis* 70, 87, 96, 107, 110, 132, 237, 242, 244, 294
smew *Mergus albellus* 75, 203
snipe
  common *Gallinago gallinago* 68, 73, 104, 105, 132, 163, 166, 167, 243, 245, 270, 276, 282, 294
  jack *Lymnocryptes minimus* 73
sparrow
  house *Passer domesticus* 107, 166
  tree *P. montanus* 96, 104, 105, 278
sparrowhawk *Accipiter nisus* 119, 120, 189, 232, 279, 300
spotted crake *Porzana porzana* 137
starling *Sturnus vulgaris* 106, 107, 140, 166

stint
  little *Calidris minuta* 73
  Temminck's *C. temminckii* 73
stonechat *Saxicola torquata* 18, 56, 95, 110, 244, 278, 295, 299
swallow *Hirundo rustica* 70, 107, 166, 295
swan
  Bewick's *Cygnus columbianus* 75, 140
  mute *C. olor* 75, 140, 202, 203, 279
  whooper *C. cygnus* 75, 203, 279
swift *Apus apus* 107, 244, 278
teal *Anas crecca* 70, 75, 133, 140, 202, 203, 277, 279, 295
tern
  arctic *Sterna paradisea* 70, 89, 97
  black *Chlidonias niger* 97, 134, 140
  common *S. hirundo* 70, 89, 97, 134
  little *S. albifrons* 87, 88, 97
  roseate *S. dougallii* 89
  Sandwich *S. sandvicensis* 70, 88, 89, 97
thrush
  mistle *Turdus viscivorus* 107, 123, 166, 189
  song *T. philomelos* 107, 123, 189, 299
tit
  blue *Parus caeruleus* 96, 123, 189
  coal *P. ater* 123, 189
  great *P. major* 123, 189
  long-tailed *Aegithalos caudatus* 107, 123, 189
  marsh *Parus palustris* 123
  willow *P. montanus* 51, 122
tree creeper *Certhia familiaris* 123
turnstone *Arenaria interpres* 73
twite *Carduelis flavirostris* 44, 132, 162
wagtail
  grey *Motacilla cinerea* 201, 245, 278, 295
  pied *M. alba* 70, 107, 295
  yellow *M. flava* 70, 104, 105, 166, 278, 295

warbler
  barred *Sylvia nisoria* 96
  garden *S. borin* 122, 189
  grasshopper *Locustella naevia* 133, 299
  reed *Acrocephalus scirpaceus* 141, 202
  sedge *A. schoenobaenus* 140, 202
  willow *Phylloscopus trochilus* 96, 107, 122, 189, 299
  wood *P. sibilatrix* 122, 189
  yellow-browed *P. inornatus* 96
water rail *Rallus aquaticus* 140, 202
waxwing *Bombycilla garrulus* 43
wheatear *Oenanthe oenanthe* 87, 237, 242, 244, 294, 299
whimbrel *Numenius phaeopus* 73
whinchat *Saxicola rubetra* 56, 110, 244, 278, 294
whitethroat *Sylvia communis* 96, 107, 122, 189
  lesser *S. curruca* 122
wigeon *Anas penelope* 75, 76, 133, 140, 141, 162, 202, 203, 277
woodcock *Scolopax rusticola* 121, 189, 245, 279, 299
woodlark *Lullula arborea* 105
woodpecker
  great spotted *Dendrocopus major* 122, 189
  green *Picus viridis* 122, 189, 190
  lesser-spotted *Dendrocopus minor* 122
woodpigeon *Columba palumbus* 189, 299
wren *Troglodytes troglodytes* 18, 107, 123, 189, 245, 278
wryneck *Jynx torquilla* 105
yellowhammer *Emberiza citrinella* 70, 96, 107, 111, 299

Amphibia
common frog *Rana temporaria* 99, 110, 245, 279, 296
newt
  great crested *Triturus cristatus* 78, 99, 163. 279
  palmate *T. helveticus* 99, 279
  smooth *T. vulgaris* 279
toad
  common *Bufo bufo* 99, 110, 296
  natterjack *Bufo calamita* 78, 98, 99, 245

Reptiles
adder *Vipera berus* 99, 110, 134, 163, 245, 246, 279, 296
common lizard *Lacerta vivipara* 99, 110, 134, 245, 279, 296
grass snake *Natrix natrix* 99, 163
slow worm *Anguis fragilis* 99, 163

Freshwater fish
Atlantic salmon *Salmo salar* 45, 81, 144, 204, 279, 296, 301
bullhead *Cottus gobio* 144, 205
char *Salvelinus alpinus* 204, 205
chubb *Leuciscus cephalus* 144
dace *Leuciscus leuciscus* 144
eel *Anguilla anguilla* 81, 144, 204, 205, 296
lamprey
  brook *Lampetra planeri* 144, 205
  river *L. fluviatilis* 81, 144, 205
  sea *Petromyzon marinus* 81, 144
minnow *Phoxinus phoxinus* 144, 205
perch *Perca fluviatilis* 204, 205
pike *Esox lucius* 204, 205
roach *Rutilus rutilus* 204
rudd *Scardinius erythrophthalmus* 204
schelly *Coregonus lavaretus* 204
shad
  allis *Alosa alosa* 81
  twaite *A. fallax* 81
smelt (sparling) *Osmerus eperlanus* 81
stone loach *Noemacheilus barbatulus* 144, 205, 296
three-spined stickleback *Gasterosteus aculeatus* 144, 205
trout
  brown *Salmo trutta* 204, 205, 279, 296, 301
  sea *S. trutta* 81, 204, 296
vendace *Coregonus albula* 204

Marine fish
bass *Dicentrarchus labrax* 81
butterfish *Pholis gunnellus* 81
cod *Gadus morhua* 81
common goby *Gobius minutus* 81
dab *Limanda limanda* 81
dogfish *Scyliorhinus canicula* 81
flounder *Platichthys flesus* 79, 81
grey mullet *Chelon labrosus* 81
herring *Clupea harengus* 81
mackerel *Scomber scombrus* 81
monkfish *Squattina squattina* 81
plaice *Pleuronectes platessa* 81
sandeel *Ammodytes tobianus* 81
shark
  basking *Cetorhinus maximus* 81
  porbeagle *Lamna nasus* 81
sole *Solea solea* 81
sprat *Sprattus sprattus* 81
sturgeon *Acipenser sturio* 81
swordfish *Xiphias gladius* 81
thornback ray *Raja clavata* 81
turbot *Scophthalmus maximus* 81
whitebait (juvenile herring & sprat) 81
whiting *Merlangius merlangus* 81

Lepidoptera
Butterflies *Rhopalocera*
blue
  common *Polyommatus icarus* 99, 108, 164
  holly *Celastrina argiolus* 123, 190
  silver-studded *Plebejus argus* 134, 135
  small *Cupido minimus* 99, 108, 109

brimstone *Gonepteryx rhamni* 164
Camberwell beauty *Nymphalis antiopa* 108
clouded yellow *Colias croceus* 108
comma *Polygonia c-album* 124, 322
Duke of Burgundy *Hamearis lucina* 124, 163
fritillary
  dark-green *Argynnis aglaja* 99, 108, 123, 163, 190
  high brown *A. adippe* 163, 320
  marsh *Euphydryas aurinia* 107, 108, 163, 190
  pearl-bordered *Boloria euphrosyne* 108, 124, 163, 190
  silver-washed *Argynnis paphia* 163, 322
  small pearl-bordered *Boloria selene* 108, 123, 190
gatekeeper *Pyronia tithonus* 99
grayling *Hipparchia semele* 99, 111
hairstreak
  brown *Thecla betulae* 124, 164
  green *Callophrys rubi* 13, 134, 190, 247
  purple *Quercusia quercus* 123, 190
  white-letter *Satyrium w-album* 322
heath
  large *Coenonympha tullia* 134, 247, 279, 296
  small *C. pamphilus* 108, 247, 279
marbled white *Melanargia galathea* 164
meadow brown *Maniola jurtina* 108, 279
mountain ringlet *Erebia epiphron* 246, 279
northern brown argus *Aricia artaxerxes* 164
orange tip *Anthocaris cardamines* 108, 279
painted lady *Vanessa cardui* 108, 247
peacock *Inachis io* 108, 247
red admiral *Vanessa atalanta* 108, 247
ringlet *Aphantopus hyperantus* 108, 279
Scotch argus *Erebia aethiops* 163
skipper
  dingy *Erynnis tages* 108, 164
  grizzled *Pyrgus malvae* 164
  large *Ochlodes venata* 108, 164
  small *Thymelicus sylvestris* 164, 322
small copper *Lycaena phlaeas* 108
small tortoiseshell *Aglais urticae* 108, 247, 279
speckled wood *Pararge aegeria* 164, 322
wall brown *Lasiommata megera* 108
white
  green-veined *Pieris napi* 108, 247
  large *P. brassicae* 108, 247
  small *P. rapae* 108, 247
  wood *Leptidea sinapis* 124, 164

Moths *Heterocera*
alder moth *Acronicta alni* 123
angle shades *Phlogophora meticulosa* 109
angle-striped sallow *Enargia paleacea* 124
antler *Cerapteryx graminis* 247
arches
  buff *Habrosyne pyritoides* 164
  dark *Apamea monoglypha* 109
  green *Anaplectoides prasina* 124
Argyroploce penthinana 190
buff-tip *Phalera bucephala* 123
burnished brass *Diachrysia chrysitis* 109
cabbage moth *Mamestra brassicae* 109
carpet
  beech-green *Colostygia olivata* 247
  galium *Epirrhoe galiata* 99, 247
  grey mountain *Entephria caesiata* 247, 280
  netted *Eustroma reticulatum* 190
  red *Xanthorhoe munitata* 247, 280
  yellow-ringed *Entephria flavicinctata* 247, 280
  water *Lampropteryx suffumata* 280
chimney sweeper *Odezia atrata* 109
cinnabar *Tyria jacobaeae* 99
clay triple-lines *Cyclophora linearia* 164
clouded buff *Diacrisia sannio* 135
Coleophora caespiticiella 247
C. tripoliella 78
common heath *Ematurga atomaria* 135, 247
dart
  Archer's *Agrotis vestigialis* 99
  coast *Euxoa cursoria* 99
  northern *Xestia alpicola* 247, 279
  sand *Agrotis ripae* 99
  square-spot *Euxoa obelisca* 135
  white-line *E. tritici* 99
December moth *Poecilocampa populi* 123
drinker *Philudoria potatoria* 107
emperor *Pavonia pavonia* 135, 247, 280, 296, 297
footman
  common *Eilema lurideola* 164
  four-spotted *Lithosia quadra* 164
  northern *Eilema sericea* 164
forester *Adscita statices* 135
fox moth *Macrothylacia rubi* 135, 247, 296
frosted green *Polyploca ridens* 123
goat moth *Cossus cossus* 123
ghost swift *Hepialis humuli* 109
golden-Y *Autographa jota* 247
  beautiful *A. pulchrina* 109
grass moth *Crambus furcatellus* 247
grass wave *Perconia strigillaria* 135
green oak tortrix *Tortrix viridana* 190
hawk moth

bedstraw *Hyles gallii* 109
convolvulus *Agrius convolvuli* 109
death's-head *Acherontia atropos* 109
eyed *Smerinthus ocellata* 123
humming bird *Macroglossum stellatarum* 247
large elephant *Deilephila elpenor* 109
narrow-bordered bee *Hemaris tityus* 109, 124
poplar *Laothoe populi* 123
small elephant *Deilephila porcellus* 164
striped *Hyles lineata* 109
herald *Scoliopterix libatrix* 123
hook-tip
  oak *Drepana binaria* 164
  pebble *D. falcataria* 123
  scalloped *Falcaria lacertinaria* 123
lackey *Malacosoma neustria* 123
latticed heath *Semiothisa clathrata* 247
large emerald *Geometra papilionaria* 123
light knot-grass *Acronicta menyanthidis* 135
lutestring
  oak *Cymatophorima diluta* 123
  poplar *Tethea or* 123
  satin *Tetheella fluctuosa* 164
magpie *Abraxas grossulariata* 109
Manchester treble-bar *Carsia sororiata* 135
marbled brown *Drymonia dodonaea* 164
marsh moth *Athetis pallustris* 123
marsh oblique-barred *Hypenodes humidalis* 135
minor
  Haworth's *Celaena haworthii* 135
  least *Photedes captiuncula* 164
northern eggar *Lasiocampa quercus callunae* 135, 247, 296
oblique-striped *Phibalapteryx virgata* 99

old lady *Mormo maura* 123
orange underwing *Archiearis parthenias* 123
light *A. notha* 124
pale eggar *Trichiura crataegi* 247
peach blossom *Thyatira batis* 123
pod lover *Hadena perplexa* 99
Portland moth *Ochropleura praecox* 99
prominent
  coxcomb *Ptilodon capucina* 123
  great *Peridea anceps* 164
  iron *Notodonta dromedarius* 123
  lesser swallow *Pheosia gnoma* 123
  pebble *Eligmodonta ziczac* 123
  scarce *Odontosia carmelita* 164, 190
purple-bordered gold *Idaea muricata* 135
puss moth *Cerura vinula* 123
red underwing *Catocala nupta* 322
rustic
  heath *Xestia agathina* 247
  neglected *X. castanea* 247
sallow kitten *Furcula furcula* 123
satin moth *Leucoma salicis* 99
saxon *Hyppa rectilinea* 190
shore wainscot *Mythimna litoralis* 99
short-cloaked moth *Nola cucullatella* 164
silver-Y *Autographa gamma* 109, 247
scarce *Syngrapha interrogationis* 124,247
six-spot burnet *Zygaena filipendulae* 99
slender brindle *Apamea scolopacina* 124
square spot *Paradarisa consonaria* 164
Svensson's copper underwing *Amphipyra berbera svenssoni* 123
thrift clearwing *Bembecia muscaeformis* 99
tiger
  garden *Arctia caja* 109
  ruby *Phragmatobia fuliginosa* 247
  wood *Parasemia plantaginis* 247
true lover's knot *Lycophotia porphyrea* 247
tussock
  dark *Dicallomera fascelina* 99
  pale *Calliteara pudibunda* 164
vapourer *Orgyia antiqua* 109
white colon *Sideridis albicolon* 99
white ermine *Spilosoma lubricipeda* 109
white-marked *Cerastis leucographa* 164
yellow horned *Achlya flavicornis* 123
yellow underwing
  beautiful *Anarta myrtilli* 247
  large *Noctua pronuba* 109

Dragonflies
chaser
  broad-bodied *Libellula depressa* 322
  four-spotted *L. quadrimaculata* 135, 205
damselfly
  azure *Coenagrion puella* 205
  blue-tailed *Ischnura elegans* 205
  common blue *Enallagma cyathigerum* 205
  emerald *Lestes sponsa* 135, 205
  large red *Pyrrhosoma nymphula* 135, 205
  variable *Coenagrion pulchellum* 205
darter
  black *Sympetrum danae* 135, 205
  common *S. striolatum* 205
  ruddy *S. sanguineum* 322
  yellow-winged *S. flaveolum* 144
demoiselle
  banded *Agrion splendens* 144
  beautiful *A. virgo* 144, 205
downy emerald *Cordulia aenea* 205
emperor dragonfly *Anax imperator* 322

golden-ringed dragonfly
  Cordulegaster boltonii 205
hawker
  brown *Aeshna grandis* 142
  common *A. juncea* 135,
    205, 280
  migrant *A. mixta* 322
  southern *A. cyanea* 142
keeled skimmer *Orthetrum coerulescens* 205
white-faced dragonfly
  Leucorrhinia dubia 135, 205

Grasshoppers & crickets – Orthoptera
cricket
  bog bush *Metrioptera brachyptera* 135
  dark bush *Pholidoptera griseoaptera* 99, 191
  oak bush *Meconema thalassinum* 191
  speckled bush *Leptophyes punctatissima* 99, 191
grasshopper
  common field *Chorthippus brunneus* 109
  common green *Omocestus viridulus* 109, 135, 248
  mottled *Myrmeleotettix maculatus* 111
groundhopper
  common *Tetrix undulata* 109, 135
  meadow *Chorthippus parallelus* 109, 135
  slender *Tetrix subulata* 322

Beetles – Coleoptera
black-headed cardinal beetle *Pyrochroa coccinea* 191
brackenclock *Phyllopertha horticolor* 248
click beetles
  Agriotes lineatus 248
  Ctenicera cuprea 248
dor beetles
  Geotrupes stercorarius 247
  G. vernalis 247
dung beetles *Aphodius lapponum* 248
  A. nemoralis 191
false click beetle *Dirrhagus pygmaeus* 191
flower beetles
  Oedemera lurida 164
  Psilothrix viridocaeruleus 164
great diving beetle *Dytiscus marginalis* 206
ground beetles
  Calosoma inquisitor 191
  Carabus arvensis 247
  C. glabratus 248
  C. nitens 248
  C. problematicus 247
  C. violaceus 247
  Elaphrus lapponicus 248
  Leistus montanus 248
  Nebria nivalis 248, 280
heather beetle *Lochmaea suturalis* 111
longhorn beetles
  Rhagium inquisitor 191
malachite beetle *Malachius bipustulatus* 123
rove beetle *Olophrum assimile* 280
sulphur beetle *Cteniopus sulphureus* 164
tiger beetles
  green *Cicindela campestris* 248
  C. hybrida 99
waterpenny beetle *Psephenus palustris* 164
weevils
  bird cherry *Furcipus rectirostris* 191
  brown *Procas granulicollis* 190
  marram *Philopedon plagiatus* 99
  Otiorhynchus arcticus 248
  O. atroapterus 99
  O. nodosus 248
  wood-boring *Mesites tardyii* 191
  Trachodes hispidus 191

Other insects
horseflies
  cleg *Haematopota pluvialis* 109
  Chrysops caecutiens 109
  Tabanus sudeticu 109
  T. bisignatus 109

sawfly *Pontania* sp 218

giant lacewing *Osmylus fulvicephalus* 144

ants
  red wood *Formica rufa* 164
  northern wood *F. lugubris* 190

Freshwater Crustacea
Atlantic stream crayfish
  Austropotamobius pallipes 144
Mysis relicta 205
Limnocalanus macrurus 205
Salminicola edwardsii 205

Marine Crustacea
barnacles
  Australian *Elminius modestus* 82
  common acorn *Semibalanus balanoides* 82
  star acorn *Chthamalus montagui* 82
brown shrimp *Crangon vulgaris* 79, 81
crabs
  edible *Cancer pagurus* 81
  hermit *Eupagurus bernhardus* 79
  shore *Carcinus maenas* 80
  spider *Macropodia rostrata*, *Hyas araneus* 79
  swimming *Portunus depurator*, *P. holsatus* 79
lobster *Homarus gammarus* 81
sandhoppers
  burrowing *Corophium volutator* 65, 66
  Talitrus saltator 66
  Eurydice pulchra 65
scampi prawn *Nephrops norvegicus* 81

Freshwater bivalves
pearl mussel *Margaritifera margaritifera* 144, 206

Marine bivalves
banded wedge-shell *Donax vittatus* 79
cockle *Cerastoderma edule* 65, 81
Fabula tenuis 79
furrow shell *Scrobicularia plana* 65
white *Abra alba* 79
mussel *Mytilus edulis* 81
  horse mussel *Modiolus modiolus* 80
Nucula sulcata 79
oysters *Crassostrea gigas* 81
  Ostrea edulis 81
rayed trough-shell *Mactra corallina* 79

razor shells *Ensis* spp. 65
scallops *Pecten maximus* 81
  queen scallops *Aequipecten opercularis* 81
tellin *Tellina fabula* 65
  Baltic tellin *Macoma balthica* 65, 66
  thin tellin *Angulus tenuis* 65
trough-shell *Spisula solida* 79

Land snails
apple *Pomatias elegans* 164
black slug *Ario ater* 248
brown-lipped *Cepaea nemoralis* 280
cellar *Oxychilus cellarius* 248, 280
copse *Arianta arbustorum* 248, 280
Craven door *Clausilia dubia* 280
chrysalis *Lauria cylindracea* 164
crystal *Vitrea subrinata* 164
garden *Cepaea hortensis* 248
Geyer's whorl *Vertigo geyeri* 164
hairy *Hygromia hispida* 280
large chrysalis *Abida secale* 164, 280
milky crystal *Vitrea contracta* 164
narrow-mouthed whorl *Vertigo angustior* 164
rounded *Discus rotundatus* 248
slippery *Cochlicopa lubrica* 280
two-toothed door *Clausilia bidentata* 248
wrinkled *Helicella caperata* 280

Marine single-shells
dog whelk *Nucella lapillus* 82
grey topshell *Gibbula cineraria* 82
limpet *Patella vulgata* 82
mud snail *Hydrobia ulvae* 65, 66
periwinkle *Littorina littorea* 81, 82
whelk *Buccinum undatum* 81

Marine worms
catworm *Nephthys hombergi* 65
  N. cirrosa 79
honeycomb worm *Sabellaria alveolata* 80, 82
  S. spinulosa 82
lugworm *Arenicola marina* 65, 80
Pygospio elegans 65
ragworm *Hediste diversicolor* 65, 80
Scolelepis squamata 65
seamouse *Aphrodite aculeata* 79

Echinoderms
brittlestar *Ophiura texturata* 79
common sunstar *Solaster papposus* 79
sand star *Astropecten irregularis* 79
heart urchin *Echinocardium cordatum* 65

Cephalopods
little cuttlefish *Heterosepiola atlantica* 79

Other marine invertebrates
beadlet anemone *Actinia equina* 82
breadcrumb sponge *Halichondria panicea* 82
hairy seamat *Electra pilosa* 80
hornwrack *Flustra foliacea* 80
moss animals *Bryozoa* 80
Alcyonidium hirsutum 79, 80
red sea squirt *Dendrodoa grossularia* 79
sea anemone *Actinothoe sphyrodata* 80

Other freshwater invertebrates
flatworms
  Crenobia alpina 206
  Polycelis felina 206
medicinal leech *Hirudo medicinalis* 206
moss animals *Bryozoa* 206